The Making of American Liberal Theology: Imagining Progressive Religion

THE MAKING
OF AMERICAN
LIBERAL THEOLOGY:
IMAGINING PROGRESSIVE
RELIGION

1805–1900

Gary Dorrien

Westminster John Knox Press
LOUISVILLE • LONDON

Book design by Sharon Adams
Cover design by Night & Day Design

First edition
Published by Westminster John Knox Press
Louisville, Kentucky

This book is printed on acid-free paper that meets the American National Standards Institute Z39.48 standard. ♾

PRINTED IN THE UNITED STATES OF AMERICA

02 03 04 05 06 07 08 09 10—10 9 8 7 6 5 4 3 2

Library of Congress Cataloging-in-Publication Data is on file at the Library of Congress, Washington, D.C.

ISBN 0-664-22354-0

In memory of Brenda

Brave, wisecracking, radiant spirit
Cherished wife, mother, friend, and pastor
Beloved companion and soulmate

THE MAKING OF AMERICAN LIBERAL THEOLOGY:
IMAGINING PROGRESSIVE RELIGION
1805–1900
Gary Dorrien

Contents

Acknowledgments

For the rights of access to and permission to quote from the unpublished letters and papers of Henry Ward Beecher, Charles A. Briggs, William Ellery Channing, and Washington Gladden, grateful acknowledgment is made respectively to the Yale University Library Manuscript and Archives Division in New Haven, Connecticut; to the Burke Library of Union Theological Seminary in New York, New York; to the Massachusetts Historical Society in Boston, Massachusetts; and to the Archives/Library Division of the Ohio Historical Society in Columbus, Ohio. Special thanks go to Mr. Tom Hyry, Archivist at Yale University Library; to Ms. Clare McCurdy, Special Collections Director at Burke Library of Union Theological Seminary; to Mr. Nicholas Graham, Reference Librarian at the Massachusetts Historical Society; and to Mr. Gary Arnold, Chief Bibliographer at the Ohio Historical Society. For permission to quote from *The Works of William E. Channing,* grateful acknowledgment is made to the American Unitarian Association of Boston, Massachusetts. For permission to use photographs of Henry Ward Beecher, Borden Parker Bowne, Charles Briggs, Elizabeth Cady Stanton, Washington Gladden, Newman Smyth and Theodore Parker, and the photographs of Arlington Street Church, Boston and the William Ellery Channing statue, grateful acknowledgment is made respectively to the Manuscripts and Archives Division of Yale University Library, New Haven, CT; Boston University Photo Services in Boston, MA; the Burke Library of Union Theological Seminary in New York, NY; Rhoda Jenkins and Coline Jenkins-Sahlin of the Elizabeth Cady Stanton Family Collection in Greenwich, CT; the Ohio Historical Society in Columbus, OH; the First Church of Christ of New Haven, CT, with thanks to Doris B. Townshend, archivist for the First Church of Christ; the Boston Athenaeum in Boston, MA, and Rev. Carol E. Strecker of Arlington Street Church, Boston. The back cover photograph was taken by Keith Mumma and the photographs of Horace Bushnell, William Ellery Channing, Ralph Waldo Emerson, and Theodore Munger are in the Public Domain.

For their important roles in preparing this book for publication, I am grateful to my editor Stephanie Egnotovich, copyeditor Hermann Weinlick, project editor Daniel Braden, and indexer Diana Witt. My personal debts are deep and numerous at the splendid liberal arts college at which I teach. Foremost among the many colleagues whose friendship makes it a joy for me to teach at Kalamazoo College are chapel assistants Becca Kutz-Marks and Pam Sotherland, president James F. Jones Jr., provost Gregory Mahler, administrators Alison Geist, Vaughn Maatman, and Lisa Palchick, anthropologist Marigene Arnold, artist and administrator Bernard Palchick, Education and Music professor emeritus Romeo Phillips, English professors Ellen Caldwell, Gail Griffin, Conrad Hilberry (emeritus), Bruce Mills, and Diane Seuss, French scholars Kathleen Smith and Janet Solberg, German professors Joe Fugate and Margo Light, historian David Barclay, musicians Paula Pugh Romanaux and Barry Ross, philosophers David Scarrow (emeritus) and Christopher Latiolais, physicist Tom Askew, psychologists Gary Gregg and Robert Grossman, religion scholars Carol Anderson and Waldemar Schmeichel, sociologists C. Kim Cummings and Robert Stauffer, and theatre professors Ed Menta and Lanny Potts. Jan Maatman and Laura Packard Latiolais are less directly tied to Kalamazoo College, but my friendships with them are especially cherished. To all of these colleagues and many others, I am grateful for the gift of friendship at the teaching and learning community of Kalamazoo College.

Introduction:
The Liberal Idea in American Religion

The idea of liberal theology is nearly three centuries old. In essence, it is the idea that Christian theology can be genuinely Christian without being based upon external authority. Since the eighteenth century, liberal Christian thinkers have argued that religion should be modern and progressive and that the meaning of Christianity should be interpreted from the standpoint of modern knowledge and experience. The intellectual giants of nineteenth-century theological liberalism were German theologians and philosophers, but the questions that gave rise to this tradition were not unique to German academics: Is it possible to be a faithful Christian without believing that God willed the annihilation of nearly the entire human race in a great flood, or that God commanded the genocidal extermination of the ancient enemies of Israel, or that God demanded the literal sacrifice of his Son as a substitutionary legal payment for sin? Is it a good or true form of Christianity that teaches the doctrines of double predestination and biblical inerrancy? Can Christianity claim to be religiously true if the Bible contains myths and historical errors? Is there a progressive Christian "third way" between the authority-based orthodoxies of traditional Christianity and the spiritless materialism of modern atheism or deism?

Liberal theology arose in Germany as a creative intellectual response to these questions, but well before it acquired movement status there, similar religious stirrings began to appear in England, France, and the United States. The gods of the liberal tradition are German academics, but throughout the nineteenth century American Protestantism produced its own vital tradition of liberal religious thinking and piety. The American tradition of theological liberalism is nearly as old as its storied German counterpart and is stocked with figures rich in religious insights honed through pastoral experience.

In this book I argue that American theological progressivism in the nineteenth century shared the same animating impulse as the German "mediating theology" tradition with which it eventually became linked: to create a modernist Christian third way between a regnant orthodoxy and an ascending "infidelism." Culturally and religiously, I argue, the American pastors and academics who pioneered the liberal tradition in American theology were earnest Victorians. All of them conceived of religion as a civilizing—and thus personally and socially saving—power of spirit over the bestial forces of nature. As modernists of a distinctive kind, the founders of American theological liberalism were always concerned to find a progressive Christian way between the religious conservatism that they discarded and the rationalistic radicalism they dreaded. This book interprets the making of American liberal Christianity through the writings and preaching of these nineteenth-century founders and is the first volume of a projected three-volume interpretation of the entire history of American theological liberalism.

Theological liberalism in America has indigenous roots, though its forerunners and founders were open to European trends accessible to them. In the early decades of the American tradition, the foreign influences were mostly English and Scottish. A distinctively modern tradition of liberal Protestantism had already germinated in the United States when German theologian Friedrich Schleiermacher launched the modern epoch of theology with his book *Speeches on Religion* (1799). By the time Schleiermacher published his dogmatics in 1820, the liberal stream of American Congregationalism was a separate party led by a galvanizing spiritual seer, William Ellery Channing. It proclaimed itself to be liberal, modern, Arminian, experiential, and rationalist; fatefully, it also accepted the label "Unitarian." A generation later, American Congregationalism produced another wellspring of liberal Protestant thinking in the imaginative theorizing of Hartford pastor Horace Bushnell. Liberal theology gained entry to American academe in the later nineteenth century in conjunction with an ascending social gospel movement. By then it had expanded considerably beyond its early constituency of Unitarian and Congregationalist pastors; by then it was also a movement closely attuned to trends in German theology.

This book tells the story of the making of American liberal Christianity from the beginning of the Unitarian revolt to the beginning of its enfranchisement in many of America's elite universities and seminaries.

LIBERAL THEOLOGY AS IDEA AND TRADITION

The distinctively liberal tradition of Christian theology is often taken for dead. The word "liberal" became an epithet in American theology during the 1930s and 1940s for some of the same reasons that it later became a disparaging term in American politics. For most of the twentieth century, only a minority of American religious thinkers persisted in calling themselves liberals. With the ascendancy of a liberal-castigating "neo-orthodoxy" in the 1930s, most religious historians consigned theological liberalism to the nineteenth century. This trend was reinforced in the 1960s by the emergence of liberation theology movements that denounced both the liberal and neo-orthodox traditions of modern theology. There are two serious problems, however, with the tendency to relegate theological liberalism to its hegemonic period. First, it slights the creativity and persistence of an ongoing and still-important tradition of religious reflection. Second, it has the effect of obscuring the liberal origins of ideas that are now taken for granted by most theologians. Most of my argument on this theme occurs in the third volume of this series, but the argument begins in the present work. For all of the critical pounding that it took in the twentieth century, often deservedly, I believe that liberal theology has been and remains the most creative and influential tradition of theological reflection since the Reformation.

Before the modern period, all Christian theologies were constructed within a house of authority. All premodern Christian theologies made claims to authority-based orthodoxy. Even the mystical and mythopoetic theologies produced by premodern Christianity took for granted the view of scripture as an infallible revelation and the view of theology as an explication of propositional revelation. Adopting the scholastic methods of their Catholic adversaries, Protestant theologians formalized these assumptions with scholastic precision during the seventeenth century. Not coincidentally, the age of religious wars that preceded the Enlightenment is also remembered as the age of orthodoxy.

Reformed and Lutheran orthodoxy heightened the Reformation principle that scripture is the sole and infallibly sufficient rule of faith, teaching that scripture is also strictly inerrant in all that it asserts.[1] Roman Catholic doctrine placed the Bible within a tripartite structure of authority that included ongoing church tradition and the (later declared infallible) teaching office of the papal magisterium. The Orthodox churches of Eastern Christianity based their teaching on the Bible and an authoritative and long-closed ecclesiastical tradition. Following Richard Hooker (1554–1600), the Anglican tradition during the Elizabethan age implicitly opened the Protestant house of authority by appealing to the Bible, ongoing church tradition, and individual reason as authorities of faith, but Anglican Scholasticism subsequently built up its own fortress of authority-supported proofs of the verbal inspiration and infallibility of scripture.[2]

The liberal tradition of theology that flowed out of the Enlightenment established the methods and laid the enduring conceptual foundations of modern critical theological scholarship by appealing to the authority of critical rationality and religious experience. Theological liberalism derives historically from eighteenth-century Continental rationalism, but during its nineteenth- and early twentieth-century heyday it was also fueled by romanticist, pietist, critical and absolute idealist, social ethical, and historical critical influences. As a pathbreaking intellectual tradition, it was decidedly Teutonic. The founding giants of liberal theology were German philosophers and theologians: Immanuel Kant (1724–1804), Friedrich Schleiermacher (1768–1834), and G. W. F. Hegel (1770–1831). Rationalist-influenced German scholars laid most of the groundwork of modern biblical criticism, notably Johann Gottfried Eichhorn (1752–1827), Johann Jakob Griesbach (1745–1812), and Wilhelm Martin Leberecht de Wette (1780–1849).[3]

For more than a century after Schleiermacher proposed that the proper subject of theology is religious consciousness, German scholars dominated the fields of modern theology and historical criticism. Major figures included Ferdinand Christian Baur (1792–1860), David Friedrich Strauss (1808–1874), Isaak August Dorner (1809–84), Albrecht Ritschl (1822–89), Julius Wellhausen (1844–1918), Adolf von Harnack (1851–1930), and Ernst Troeltsch (1865–1923). As early as 1815, aspiring American theologians began to acquire their academic training in German universities. For nearly two generations a steady trickle of Americans studied in Germany to be trained in modern critical methods. They favored the University of Berlin, where Schleiermacher and Hegel established competing approaches to religion and philosophy. Cofounded by Schleiermacher in 1810 in the wake of the dismemberment of Prussia by Napoleon, the University of Berlin was congenial to Americans for its spirit of intellectual freedom. After Schleiermacher's death, a small but influential stream of American students was trained in the Schleiermacher-school "mediating theology" of Isaak Dorner; prominent among these Americans were Newman Smyth and Charles A. Briggs. A generation later, a larger number of Americans was trained at Berlin in the Ritschlian historicism of Adolf von Harnack.

The founders of American academic theological liberalism acknowledged the superiority of German universities and theological scholarship. In the later nineteenth century, under their leadership, American liberal theology became a genuine movement. While they tacked in a German direction, the best American thinkers did not merely recycle German ideas, but appropriated modern German trends for an existing American liberal Protestant tradition.[4]

The German influence over American liberal religious thinking was important, but came relatively late. Lacking the language, very few of the early American liberals were directly schooled in German philosophy or biblical scholarship. Among the few who were—Theodore Parker, Joseph Stevens

Buckminster, and Andrews Norton—Buckminster died young, and Norton disapproved of trends in German scholarship. William Ellery Channing relied mostly on English Unitarians; Ralph Waldo Emerson got his Kant and Schleiermacher mostly secondhand. The Channing Unitarians and Emerson transcendentalists looked mostly to England for inspiration, as did Horace Bushnell and his later disciples Theodore Munger and Washington Gladden. For much of the nineteenth century, the most important intellectual influence over American liberal religious thinking was not Schleiermacher, but the English poet and religious philosopher Samuel Taylor Coleridge.

The key work was Coleridge's *Aids to Reflection,* which convinced a host of American transcendentalists and Bushnellians that religion belongs to the faculty of imagination. Emerson and Bushnell were predisposed to the view of religion that Coleridge described; both of them deeply absorbed Coleridge's argument and distinctions. For Emerson, however, *Aids to Reflection* was an antidote to theology; for Bushnell, it was an inspiring call to reinvent theology. Bushnell embraced Coleridge's focus on religious experience as the subject of theology, his rejection of apologetic appeals to miracles, and his crucial distinction between reason and understanding. Coleridge's ideas on these subjects were developed under the influence of Kant and Schleiermacher; thus the early German influence in American liberal theology was mostly indirect. American thinking was also shaped by Scottish common-sense epistemology and moral intuitionism, and by English Anglican and Unitarian thinkers. The latter group included the luminaries of English Unitarianism: John Locke, Samuel Clarke, and Richard Price. Aided by these religious thinkers, a small assortment of nineteenth-century American pastors imagined the possibility of a progressive Christianity.

Theodore Parker, the single major figure among them who knew the German tradition firsthand, advocated an "Absolute Religion" that founded Christian truth on the moral influence of Jesus. I argue that Parker's transcendental Kantianism, like Coleridge's, took a sizable leap beyond Kant's epistemological boundaries and that Parker did not grasp the dialectical character of Schleiermacher's theory of religion. At the same time, I argue for the reconsideration of Parker as an important figure in the history of American religious thought. He was the first American to approach theology from a standpoint deeply informed by German theology, philosophy, and historiocritical scholarship. He was the first American to present a nearly full-orbed *liberal* view of Christianity in the nineteenth-century sense of the term; and he is the pivotal figure of the Unitarian tradition, the one from whom its neo-Christian and humanistic traditions both derive.

I argue that Bushnell is the major theologian of nineteenth-century American liberal Christianity and the key figure to its history as a whole. With less grounding than Parker in German thought, Bushnell established much of the conceptual groundwork of subsequent theological liberalism, especially its critique of traditional supernaturalist dualism, its commitment to philosophical idealism, its espousal of moral influence atonement theory, its emphasis on imagination and the metaphorical nature of religious language, and its stress on divine immanence. In the mid-nineteenth century and Gilded Age these ideas were popularized by legendary preacher Henry Ward Beecher; in the years following Bushnell's death, they were also taken up by the first wave of a liberal theology movement. By the time a significant movement existed, however, liberal theology had acquired additional commitments. Vexing new questions had arisen that required the Bushnellians to move beyond Bushnell.

Three issues were crucial: How was Christianity to deal with the increasing scientific acceptance of Darwinian evolutionary theory, the recent developments in German biblical criticism, and the problems of a rapidly industrializing social order? These questions fundamentally shaped what came to be called American theological liberalism. On the strength of their creative revision of Bushnellian "progressive orthodoxy," the Bushnellians and Ritschlian liberals conquered the field of American theology and gained ecclesiastical acceptance in the closing years of the nineteenth century. Henry Ward Beecher preached liberal theology to a mass audience, conceived true religion as the flourishing of personality, and played a key role in legitimizing evolutionary theory within American Christianity. Theodore Munger preached an aesthetically stylish update of Bushnell's theology that endorsed evolution and a panentheistic religious worldview. Washington Gladden accented Bushnell's moral theology and pioneered the American social gospel movement. Newman Smyth appropriated German mediation theology to the American scene and argued for the compatibility of Christianity and modern science. Charles A. Briggs defended modern biblical criticism and advocated denominational reunion. Borden Parker Bowne criticized the popular mechanistic Darwinism of Herbert Spencer and developed a new religious philosophy called "personalism."

American liberal Christianity in the later nineteenth century emphasized the convergence between Christianity and evolution, the constructive value of modern historical criticism, the spiritual union between God and humanity, and the kingdom-building social mission of the church. Virtually all of its leading advocates assumed that American Christianity could become modern and appropriately critical only by facing up to Darwinian theory, the implications of biblical criticism, and the social upheavals of capitalist civilization. They also took for granted that theological progressivism was not a Unitarian or Congregationalist project only; American liberal theology crossed denominational lines in the 1880s and 1890s.

On all these counts, the late-nineteenth-century leaders of American Protestantism ventured into new territory. Some of the early Protestant liberals thematized evolution as an important theological concept, but Darwin made the theory of evolutionary natural selection unavoidable and, arguably, totalizing. Developments in mid-nineteenth-century German biblical scholarship were slow to cross the Atlantic, but Briggs and his cohorts modernized American scripture scholarship. Most of the early liberals had a social conscience, and some of them were passionate reformers, but only in the later nineteenth century did the problems of economic inequality and entitlement become core concerns of an ascending social gospel movement. I argue that virtually all of the leading nineteenth-century American liberal Christian thinkers were Victorians in sensibility and conviction. As good Victorians, they conceived true Christianity as a third way between orthodoxy and "infidelism." They conceived true religion as the triumph of spirit over nature. They took for granted that true religion is concerned with the cultivation of spiritual character and a good society and were greatly concerned to save and inculcate the civilizing virtues of Western Christian gentility. And most of them, I emphasize, accepted and purveyed the Anglo-Saxon cultural racism that pervaded nineteenth-century American society.

DEFINING LIBERAL THEOLOGY

The *Oxford Encyclopedic English Dictionary* defines "liberal" as "giving freely, generous, not sparing; open-minded, not prejudiced; not literal (of interpetation); for general broadening of the mind"; and, most pertinently for the present work, "regarding many traditional beliefs as dispensable, invalidated by modern thought, or liable to change." The great nineteenth-century apologist of orthodox Catholicism, John Henry Newman, bore the latter attributes in mind when he explained that the consuming battle of his life was fought against liberalism, by which he meant "the anti-dogmatic principle and its development." American liberal theology was fed by the wellsprings of eighteenth-century and early-nineteenth-century rationalism and romanticism, both of which developed the antidogmatic principle. It flowered, however, as a form of late-nineteenth-century social Progressivism. One of the most influential definitions of theological liberalism was offered in 1949 by an able latter-day proponent, Daniel Day Williams: "By 'liberal theology' I mean the movement in modern Protestantism which during the nineteenth century tried to bring Christian thought into organic unity with the evolutionary world view, the movements for social reconstruction, and the expectations of 'a better world' which dominated the general mind. It is that form of Christian faith in which a prophetic-progressive philosophy of history culminates in the expectation of the coming of the Kingdom of God on earth."[5]

This description appropriately emphasized the evolutionist orientation, the social gospel ethos, and the cultural optimism that distinguished liberal Protestant theology during its late-nineteenth- and early-twentieth-century heyday. With ample warrant, Williams identified Walter Rauschenbusch's *A Theology for the Social Gospel* as the classic expression of American theological liberalism. Like much of the secondary literature on liberal Protestantism, however, Williams overidentified the liberal tradition with factors that were peculiar to its period of dominance. His definition excluded the pre-Darwinian founders of theological liberalism, notably Kant and Schleiermacher, and identified liberal theology with long-outmoded beliefs about the "Christianizing" moral progress of Western civilization. The entire tradition of Schleiermacher-school experientialism that created and developed liberal theology in the first half of the nineteenth century thus dropped out of this understanding of theological liberalism.

I believe that something is wrong with a definition of theological liberalism that excludes Schleiermacher, Hegel, Theodore Parker, and Horace Bushnell. Though all these thinkers incorporated evolutionary ideas into their religious thinking in some way, the absorbing concern with evolution that marked later theological liberalism did not arise in Germany or the United States until Darwin's *Origin of Species* (1859) gained scientific acceptance. Moreover, Williams's definition made no reference to other kinds of intellectual inquiry (such as historical criticism) or to the values and authority of individual reason and experience, although these factors have been central in virtually all forms of liberal theology.

On the basis of Williams's definitional criteria, Lloyd Averill argues in *American Theology in the Liberal Tradition* that liberal theology began in Europe in the 1860s and was dethroned in 1918. By this reckoning, the American liberal tradition did not begin until 1879, when Newman Smyth's *Old Faiths in New Light* set forth the first programmatic statement of a rising proevolutionist "New Theology" movement. Averill's description of this part of the American liberal theological tradition is well argued, but as an account of the whole tradition, it reproduces all the problems of Williams's definition at both ends. A more inclusive and promising approach is advanced independently by Donald E. Miller and James Richmond, who push its founding point back to the closing years of the eighteenth century. Miller distinguishes between Liberal Protestantism and the liberal perspective in Christian theology. He argues that the category "Liberal Protestantism" should be reserved for the Schleiermacher-to-Harnack tradition of the nineteenth and early twentieth centuries and that all subsequent Protestant liberals should be assigned to the broader category of Christian liberalism.[6]

I welcome the spirit of Miller's distinctions and take a similar approach to liberal theology in this work, with the important caveat discussed below. Theological liberalism today is an ecumenical project, as Miller's definition recognizes. In England, France, and Italy, Catholic forms of liberal theology have existed since the late nineteenth century. American Catholicism was comparatively slow to develop a liberal theological tradition—the papal condemnation of "Americanism" in 1905 was a key inhibiting factor—but since Vatican Council II, American theological liberalism has been a broadly ecumenical project in the sense that Miller defines. American Catholic theologians such as David Tracy and Daniel Maguire have made important contributions to an ongoing liberal theological tradition. Today the liberal perspective in theology encompasses a wide spectrum of Christian and, arguably, post-Christian and interreligious positions.

The caveat is that "liberal Protestantism" did not end with Harnack or Rauschenbusch. Miller's distinction treats the First World War as the end of "liberal Protestantism," but taken literally, this is almost as exclusive and unrealistic as leaving out Schleiermacher and the pre-Darwinian Unitarians from the category of theological liberalism. For decades after the First World War, American liberal Protestantism continued to produce theological leaders whose identification with Protestantism was emphatic and exclusive. *Christian Century* editor Charles Clayton Morrison epitomized the type of ecumenical leader who stridently opposed ecumenical relations with Catholics. It would be bizarre not to describe such mid-century religious thinkers as Morrison, Justin Wroe Nixon, or Henry Van Dusen as liberal Protestants.

More important, the tradition of liberal Protestantism did not end after it became genuinely ecumenical. Liberal Protestant theology is an ongoing project that began with Kant and Schleiermacher and that stretches back, in the United States, to the theologies of Channing, Parker, and Bushnell. American liberal Protestant theology was reduced to modest dimensions in the generation after Rauschenbusch, at least in name, but it remained a vital and creative religious tradition that continues to produce important theological work. Moreover, most of what was called "neo-orthodoxy" in the liberal-bashing 1930s and afterward was actually a form of liberal theology that was often deeply Protestant. Therefore I do not strictly confine the term "liberal Protestantism" to the nineteenth century, though my definition of theological liberalism includes progressive Catholic theologies and though, for the most part, I speak of "liberal Christianity" rather than "liberal Protestantism."

IMAGINING THE THIRD WAY

My account accents the mediationist character of liberal theology. The "third way" rhetoric of early American liberal Christianity was not merely a rhetorical posture. The early American liberal theologians abhorred the tradition-smashing terror and "infidelism" of the French Revolution. Though often accused of infidelism themselves, they were appalled by the real thing. The anti-Christian sections of Edward Gibbon's *Decline and Fall of the Roman Empire* offended them deeply, as did the aggressively deist writings of Thomas Paine. Channing, Parker, and Bushnell believed that orthodoxy and infidelism were closely related, often as cause and effect. The outrages of orthodoxy bred infidels. They reasoned that the problem was not the Enlightenment, but rather the ecclesiastical power of a discredited orthodoxy that refused to reform. American liberal Christians believed that infidelism would wither away after America's churches embraced the best parts of the Enlightenment legacy, especially its ethical humanism and its emphasis on the liberating value of reason.

In this faith they shared the spirit, though not the scholarly infrastructure, of a contemporaneous phenomenon in Germany. The school of Schleiermacher founded its first journal, *Theologische Studien und Kritiken,* in 1827, late in Schleiermacher's career. Organized by G. C. F. Lücke, Johann Karl Ludwig Gieseler, Carl Immanuel Nitzsch, Carl Ullmann, and F. W. C. Umbreit, this journal described itself as the vehicle of the movement for "Mediating Theology." Lücke declared that modern theology needed a movement that steered a faithful, but critical path between the literalistic dogmatism of Christian orthodoxy and the antireligious dogmatism of modern rationalism. He explained that the new journal would seek "true mediations" with modern science, while holding fast to the religious authority of the Word. This conception of theological mediation was systematized by Bonn/Berlin theologian Carl Immanuel Nitzsch (1787–1868) and later epitomized by Heidelberg theologian Richard Rothe (1799–1867), whose theological system effected a creative synthesis of Schleiermacher's experientialism, idealist philosophy, and supernaturalist theism. A number of mediationists followed Rothe in negotiating between Schleiermacher and traditional orthodoxy; others departed from Rothe's orthodox-leaning notion of scripture as authoritative revelation.[7]

American liberal theology was considerably less scholarly and systematic. German theological liberalism had its home in modernity-embracing universities, was tied intellectually to German philosophical idealism, and retained much of the formal structure of classical dogmatics. For better and for worse, none of these factors obtained in the American situation. Aside from Unitarian Harvard, academe was off-limits to American theological progressives for most of the nineteenth century. Even at Harvard it was a conservative version of Unitarianism that prevailed, as Emerson famously protested.

American liberal Christianity was a product of the pulpit. It was imagined and defended by preachers who rebelled against their training in New England Theology orthodoxy. Rhetorically it was a more interesting, colorful, and spiritually moving tradition than its academic German counterpart on that account. Bushnell pined for a Harvard professorship, but American theology might have been deprived of some of its rhetorical jewels, had he won an academic perch. More important to Bushnell than his office was his audience. Throughout his career he waited for a theological following that emerged only in his twilight years.

By then, the German mediating movement was a highly developed intellectual and institutional tradition. By 1860 it boasted three journals and was led by such influential religious thinkers as Nitzsch, Ullmann (1796–1865), Carl Theodor Albert Liebner (1806–71), Julius Müller (1801–78), August Twesten (1789–1876), Willibald Beyschlag (1823–1900), and, most importantly, Isaak August Dorner (1809–84).[8] The influence of Dorner on Newman Smyth, Charles C. Briggs, and other American mediationists was immense. Non-Germans affiliated with the mediationist movement included the Swiss theologians Karl Rudolph Hagenbach (1801–74) and Alexander Schweizer (1808–88), as well as Søren Kierkegaard's nemesis, Danish bishop Hans Lassen Martensen (1808–84).[9] In England, a Coleridge-quoting tradition of theological progressivism was pioneered by Anglican clerics Frederick Denison Maurice and Frederick Robertson, whose "Broad Church" preaching and theologizing had a profound impact on Theodore Munger, Washington Gladden, and other American liberals. English traditions of liberal theology were subsequently developed in the Anglican, Protestant, and Catholic churches, while sophisticated forms of French theological liberalism were developed by Protestants Auguste Sabatier (1839–1901) and Jean Réville (1854–1907) and Catholic modernist Alfred Loisy (1857–1940).[10]

The liberal theologians were so successful that by the early twentieth century many of them dropped the language of mediation. As an approach to the understanding of Christianity and, more broadly, the phenomenon of religion, their movement became not a mere third way, but the first way. It became the language of a new academic orthodoxy, which set up the liberal tradition for a precipitous fall after the First World War. The tremendous impact of Karl Barth's polemic against liberal theology in the 1920s was made possible by the exalted position of a liberal establishment that he turned against. Having conquered the field of theology, theological liberalism had much to lose after the Great War, and it lost much.

In accord with my concept of it as a movement that began in the late eighteenth century, I define liberal theology primarily by its original character as a mediating Christian movement. Liberal Christian theology is a tradition that derives from the late-eighteenth- and early-nineteenth-century Protestant attempt to reconceptualize the meaning of traditional Christian teaching in the light of modern knowledge and modern ethical values. It is not revolutionary but reformist in spirit and substance. Fundamentally it is the idea of a genuine Christianity not based on external authority. Liberal thelogy seeks to reinterpret the symbols of traditional Christianity in a way that creates a progressive religious alternative to atheistic rationalism and to theologies based on external authority.

Specifically, liberal theology is defined by its openness to the verdicts of modern intellectual inquiry, especially the natural and social sciences; its commitment to the authority of individual reason and experience; its conception of Christianity as an ethical way of life; its favoring of moral concepts of atonement; and its commitment to make Christianity credible and socially relevant to modern people.

THEOLOGY AS BIOGRAPHY

In agreement with religious historian William Hutchison, my interpretation emphasizes that the founders of American liberal Protestantism were propelled by their concern to adapt the witness of Christianity to the democratic and scientific culture of modernity. The "modernist impulse" was strong in the social gospel Bushnellians and Ritschlians who rose to prominence at the end of the nineteenth century, and it was only slightly less pronounced in their progressive forerunners. Hutchison's excellent history of American liberal Protestantism is limited to this theme, however. His single-minded focus on modernism screens out a host of other important issues, such as Parker's role in challenging and redirecting American Unitarianism, the fact of Bushnell's racism and sexism, the significance of the Beecher scandal, the rise of the women's movement, the social gospel debate with social Darwinism, and the metaphysics of personalism.

Hutchison's work splendidly shows the relation of a wide range of thinkers to the modernist issue, but his approach affords little sense of the total thinking, contexts, or personalities of these figures. It also underplays the mediationist character of liberal theology.

His account ends with the liberal-fundamentalist conflict of the 1920s and an epilogue on Niebuhrian realism, while my account extends to the present day. In Volume 1 I interpret the nineteenth-century founders of American theological liberalism, presenting liberal theology as a form of theologically mediationist Victorianism. Volume 2 describes the movement's social gospel, modernist, and Niebuhrian heyday, treating Niebuhr's "antiliberal neo-orthodoxy" as a chastened species of liberal theology. Volume 3 offers an account of American theological liberalism since Niebuhr, emphasizing the pluralization of liberal theology and the crisis of liberal Christianity.[11]

This project is distinctive in examining the entire history of American theological liberalism and in taking a narrative approach with a strong biographical dimension that allows each thinker to speak in his or her own voice. The biographical aspect of my interpretation is accented throughout the three volumes and is especially prominent in this first book. The founders of American liberal Christianity were every-week preachers, civic and political activists, and men of letters, fully absorbed in the affairs of their society. They are much too interesting not to be treated biographically in the contexts of their time, with close interrogations of their writings and ample attention to their wide-ranging pursuits. They also deserve to be heard in their own words. I am more interested in making sense of these thinkers on their own terms and in their own rhetorical styles than in construing their significance exclusively in contemporary analytic categories. With one exception, I have focused in this volume on the major figures of nineteenth-century American theological liberalism—those whose distinctive thinking had the greatest influence on the development of American liberal Christianity. My account also contains detailed descriptions of Andrews Norton, Nathaniel Taylor, Octavius Brooks Frothingham, David Swing, Josiah Strong, Lyman Abbott, and other figures like them who do not rank with the likes of Bushnell or Bowne as major religious thinkers, but who were influential in the shaping of progressive Christianity as an intellectual tradition and popular movement.

The exception is Elizabeth Cady Stanton, who had very little impact on the liberal Protestantism of her time, mainly because her feminist criticism of Christianity was ahead of its and her time. Religiously, Cady Stanton advocated a feminist version of the Parkerite "Free Religion" theology of Octavius Brooks Frothingham. She has a place in this account as a forerunner of twentieth-century feminist theology and as a judgment on the mostly unspoken patriarchal bias of the liberal Victorians who dominate the narrative. Nineteenth-century liberal Christianity had a conscience about the subjection of women; most of its theological leaders supported the women's rights movement of their time, especially Beecher, Bowne, Emerson, and Parker. At the same time, none of its leading thinkers gave more than a passing consideration to the reinterpretation of theological issues from a feminist standpoint. Beecher came closest to feminist rethinking, but my chapter on Beecher and Cady Stanton recounts why both were seriously flawed advocates for their causes. The evidence of Beecher's personal hypocrisy and the light cast on his self-indulgent expressionism at a sensational public trial set back the cause of liberal Christian feminism, as did Cady Stanton's volatile blend of feminist radicalism and racist class snobbery. Moreover, the greatest theologian in the group—Bushnell—was straightforwardly reactionary on women's rights, adhering fervently to the "cult of true womanhood."

Bushnell is the central figure of this story and the symbol of its ironies. In my view, he is the most profound and spiritually uplifting American religious thinker of the nineteenth century. He is also the person in this narrative that I find most repugnant on issues pertaining to ethnicity, gender, and cultural politics. Bushnell proudly shared the prejudices of the dominant culture of his time. He folded them into his theology and used them to win the hearts and minds of audiences predisposed to reject his religious arguments. In his time he was bitterly attacked for his theology, but not for his prejudices, a fact that was not lost on his social gospel successors. Even the most admirable figures in this history, such as Channing and Gladden, were flawed in ways that diminished the causes they adopted; Bushnell's flaws loom especially large because they were widely shared.

The subjects of this narrative belong to the nineteenth century, though five of them lived into the twentieth century. The generation that made liberal Christianity a significant American movement lived to see the triumph of their movement in the mainline Protestant churches and divinity schools. This volume crosses into the world of the liberal social-gospel heyday, but only to account for the later careers of the movement builders, not to account for the religion of the youthful social gospelers and modernists who called their age "the Christian century." That story belongs to a succeeding volume.

1.

Unitarian Beginnings:
William Ellery Channing and the Divine Likeness

The idea of liberal Christianity was not novel to the nineteenth-century founders of American liberal theology. Before the founding of the United States, the seeds of what came to be called American theological liberalism were sown by an assortment of Boston-area pastors and religious thinkers in the 1740s and 1750s.

Against the emotionalism of the Great Awakening, Congregationalist pastors Charles Chauncy (1705–87), Jonathan Mayhew (1720–66), and Ebenezer Gay (1696–1787) called for a "supernatural rationalism" that correlated reason and revelation. They urged that New England Christianity needed, not a revival of Calvinist piety, but a modern, rational, freedom-affirming religion that caught up with the spirit of a burgeoning European Enlightenment. Against the aggressively asserted Calvinism of Jonathan Edwards, George Whitefield, and other preachers of the Great Awakening, the forerunners of American liberal theology rejected the Calvinist doctrines of total depravity and election to grace. They laid the groundwork for a liberal alternative to orthodox Calvinism and the various "New Light" Calvinisms of their generation by effecting a blend of Arminian and Enlightenment themes. Boston pastors Chauncy and Mayhew led the first-generation resistance to the revival of Calvinist thinking and piety in New England, often with a polemical edge. With the success that these figures attained in lengthy pastoral careers, it became much safer to contend in New England that the regnant orthodoxy was religiously misguided.

REASON AND FREE WILL:
EIGHTEENTH-CENTURY LIBERAL ARMINIANISM

The New England Arminians took their concept of reasonable religion from the leading English rationalists of the previous half-century, philosophers John Locke (1632–1704) and Samuel Clarke (1675–1729), as well as from an assortment of rationalist-leaning moral philosophers and Anglican divines, notably Francis Hutcheson, Joseph Butler, and John Tillotson. Without obscuring the differences between Locke's empiricism and Clarke's speculative rationalism, they appealed to a common core of Enlightenment assumptions in criticizing the inadequacy of traditional Christian supernaturalism. The first generation of rationalistic New England Arminians assumed the universality of reason, the orderly world picture of Newtonian physics, and the capacity of reason to decipher what they called "the Divine Book of Nature." Many of them also followed Locke and Clarke in asserting a Unitarian view of divine personality.[1]

A great-grandson and namesake of the second president of Harvard College, Charles Chauncy graduated from Harvard in 1721 and began his long pastoral career at First Church, Boston in 1727. His first blast against the "religious Phrenzy" of his time, published in 1742, was titled *Enthusiasm Described and Caution'd Against.* Chauncy called for rational interpretation of the Bible and criticized Awakening revivalists for a host of "bad Things" that included, most importantly, disregard for "the Dictates of reason." Later he denounced Whitefield's presumption in going about "from one Province and Parish to another" as though New England had never heard the gospel. He took incredulous note of the effects of revival preaching, especially the "bitter Shriekings and Screamings; Convulsion-like Tremblings and Agitations, Strugglings and Tumblings, which, in some Instances, have been attended with Indecencies I shan't mention."

Chauncy allowed that Whitefield was a spellbinding performer who made people want to do nothing but listen to sermons. He noted that Whitefield won such affection from the multitudes "that it became dangerous to mention his Name, without saying something in commendation of him." Chauncy dared to say nothing in commendation of prominent Awakening preachers like Gilbert Tennent, however: "A man of no great Parts or Learning; his preaching was in the *extemporaneous* Way, with much Noise and little Connection. If he had taken suitable Care to prepare his Sermons, and followed Nature in the Delivery of them, he might have acquitted himself as a *middling* Preacher; but as he preached, he was an *awkward Imitator* of Mr. *Whitefield,* and too often turned off his Hearers with *mere Stuff,* which he uttered with a Spirit more bitter and uncharitable than you can easily imagine; all were *Pharisees, Hypocrites, carnal unregenerate Wretches,* both Ministers and People, who did not think just as he did, particularly as to the Doctrines of *Calvinism;* and those who opposed him, and the Word of God he was sure he was carrying on, would have opposed *Christ Jesus himself* and *his Apostles,* had they lived in their Day."[2]

Opposed to the doctrine of total depravity, Chauncy insisted that the "natural powers" of human beings can be cultivated to attain "an actual likeness to God in knowledge, righteousness, and true holiness." He argued that human beings are meant by God to employ and improve their God-given natural powers "from one degree of attainment to another; and hereupon, from one degree of happiness to another, without end." This controlling conception of divine benevolence led him to reject outright the doctrine of eternal punishment. In his later career, Chauncy published an anonymous defense of universal salvation that featured nearly four hundred pages of biblical support for the view that God wills and effects the salvation of all human souls. *The Mystery hid from Ages and Generations* maintained that if God wills, as scripture attests, that all people should attain virtue, it cannot be that God sends any soul to eternal punishment. The God of love worshiped by Christians is devoted to the reformation of souls, not vengeance, Chauncy argued: "God has so loved us as to project a scheme, which in the final result of its prosecution, will inflate us *all* in *heavenly* and *immortal glory.*" He judged that the scriptural references to hell refer to a cleansing purgatory after death for those who do not attain virtue in this life, not to a state of everlasting torment.[3]

Chauncy's friend Jonathan Mayhew, pastor of West Church in Boston and a powerful orator, was an extraordinarily outspoken advocate of Arminian liberalism. Mayhew's independence from the Boston Association of Congregational Ministers gave him unusual latitude to criticize the prevailing orthodoxy. He rejected the very idea of an orthodox or creedal test of correct belief. "Let us despise the frowns and censures of those vain conceited men who set themselves up for the oracles of truth and the standard of orthodoxy; and then call their neighbors hard names," he exhorted. He urged, against the doctrine of total depravity, that human beings retain a potential for goodness after the Fall. Moral guilt is a personal matter, he contended; the notion that God holds any individual morally responsible for sins committed by another person is an offense against morality and the goodness of God. Against the Calvinist picture of God as impassible and inscrutable, Mayhew countered that God is perfect "in all those moral qualities and excellencies which we esteem amiable in mankind." Mayhew's Arminianism was unequivocal. He argued that human beings "resemble God himself" by virtue of their reason, and that by virtue of this divinely endowed power, they also possess the capacity to distinguish right from wrong and to choose the right. "Let us take pains to find out the truth, and after we are settled in our judgment concerning any religious tenet or practice, adhere to it with constancy of mind, till convinced of our error in a rational way," he declared. "We have not only a right to think for ourselves in matters of religion,

Episcopalians, Jews, Moravians, Quakers, and assorted others. A different kind of accounting would include sailors, prostitutes, retired sea captains, French and British army officers, rum merchants, slave traders, and slaves. In the 1770s, Newport was sufficiently bustling that New York City was commonly identified as "New York, near Newport." Much of Newport's prosperity derived from its slave and rum trading, and Channing's paternal grandfather was a businessman who imported slaves from Africa. His mother's poor health determined that Channing was placed in school at a tender age and was often carried to school by a family servant.

He thus acquired an intimate acquaintance with the early American coupling of devotion to liberty and acceptance of slavery. Though his father liberated the family servants after the Revolutionary War, Channing later recalled, with sorrow, that "my father had no sensibility to the evil."[7] Channing's parents were pious and morally high-minded, as was his renowned maternal grandfather, with whom he enjoyed a close and affectionate relationship; but no word was spoken in the Channing home about the evil of slavery, the moral contradictions of their prosperity, or the conflict between their devotion to freedom and their minimal regard for the lower classes. On all these issues, especially slavery, William Ellery Channing eventually became a prominent critic of his country's institutionalized hypocrisy and tyranny. Yet he also retained his acute awareness that it was possible for good people to accept terrible social evils in the name of self-preservation and even Christian morality. This empathic sense of the moral complexities of life, gained from personal experience, made Channing an effective pastor and Christian leader, even as it sometimes tempered his prophetic spirit.[8]

As a child, he accompanied his parents to the war-torn First Congregational Church in Newport, pastored by Samuel Hopkins, which his family attended after their own Second Church lost its pastor at the outbreak of the war. Hopkins was a disciple of Jonathan Edwards and the foremost proponent of "New Light" Calvinism of his generation. He also lived next door to the Channings. His creative revision of Edwards affirmed the doctrine of double predestination but rejected the doctrines of election to grace, imputed total depravity, and imputed righteousness. Hopkins taught that Christ's redeeming death was suffered for all sinners, not merely the elect, and that all people stand condemned before God on account of their own sin, not the imputation of Adam's sin. He believed that the practice of disinterested benevolence is the heart of Christian morality—a notion that Channing later embraced—but he insisted that Christians should therefore be willing to be damned to hell for eternity if God's will so destined them.

After liberal theology became a divisive force in New England Congregationalism, many conservatives took their stand on what came to be called "the New Divinity," or often, "Hopkinsianism." Traditional Calvinists forged an uneasy alliance with Hopkins's moderating "New Light" followers against a liberal tide. As a youth, however, like most church people, Channing had no concept of the differences between contending orthodoxies. Hopkins was a learned, elderly scholar; a rigorous theological thinker; a highly conscientious pastor; and a figure of immense moral integrity. He repeatedly condemned slavery from the pulpit, took part in abolitionist causes, and raised money to free slaves. His dreary preaching aside, he thus earned the ostracizing enmity of Newporters who resented his moralizing on this topic. Channing's family treated him with outward courtesy, but they returned to the Second Congregational Church as soon as it reopened in 1786.[9]

To Channing, the elderly pastor next door seemed a strange, oddly mannered, forbidding figure, whose appearance "was that of a man who had nothing to do with the world." Hopkins rode around town on horseback in a plaid gown, wearing a girdle around his waist and a study cap instead of a wig. "Add to all this, that his manners had a bluntness, partly natural, partly the result of long seclusion in the country," he later recalled. "We cannot wonder that such a man should be set down as hard and severe." Channing acknowledged that Hopkins was reviled in Newport mostly because he condemned slavery, but he strongly suggested that Hopkins's sermons on other topics didn't help: "I can distinctly recollect, that the prevalence of terror in his preaching was a very common subject of remark, and gave rise to ludicrous stories among the boys." Hopkins's preaching style was equally unfortunate. His speech was drawling and monotonous, his few gestures were awkward, and he spoke persistently in grave abstractions: "His delivery in the pulpit was the worst I ever met with. Such tones never came from any human voice within my hearing. He was the very ideal of bad delivery. Then I must say, the matter was often as uninviting as the manner."[10]

This evaluation of Hopkins reflected, to some degree, Channing's later judgment. It is believable that Channing's subjection to depravity-and-hellfire preaching heightened his emotional misery as a youth, as he claimed in later years. His misery was surely also aggravated, however, by his prolonged struggle with the question whether the theology of divine judgment preached in Newport pulpits by Hopkins, Ezra Stiles, and William Patten was true. Channing was thirty years old before he definitely resolved that it was not true. As a youngster and even as a young man, he regarded his former pastors as models of faithfulness. He questioned whether he would have the same courage to live faithfully by his principles. He later remarked of Hopkins that, "believing, as he did, in total depravity, believing that there was nothing good or generous in human nature to which he could make an appeal, believing that he could benefit men only by setting before them their utterly lost and helpless condition, he came to the point without any circumlocution, and dealt out terrors with an unsparing liberality."[11]

Channing dealt out terrors of his own during his early ministry, however. As a youngster, he may have complained or even snickered with his friends about the prevalence of terror in Hopkins's preaching, but this did not stop him, during his own early ministry, from occasionally dangling sinners above the fires of hell in a Hopkinsian tone. Channing's early sermons were filled with evangelical (if not Hopkinsian) warnings about the guilt of human sin, the depravity of human nature, and the threat of divine retribution. On his first Thanksgiving sermon, in 1803, he declared that "there is nothing in us to recommend us to God. Sinners as we are, we are vile in his sight. Our sins cry to God for unmingled vengeance." Several years later, at an ordination service, he preached that a good pastor cannot read in the New Testament "of that fire which is never quenched, of that worm which never dies, and yet see without emotion fellow beings . . . hastening forward to this indescribable ruin."[12]

These pronouncements, decidedly unlike Channing, have puzzled readers for decades. Some interpreters have cited them as evidence that Channing began his preaching career as an advocate of Hopkinsian Calvinism.[13] Though most of the evidence weighs against this reading of his development, Channing did, on one occasion, confess to "the deep impression which this system made on my youthful mind."[14] He shared certain philosophical commitments with Hopkins throughout his career and greatly respected his eminent neighbor's intellectual rigor and moral integrity. More importantly, the very emphasis that Channing later placed on the loving and compassionate nature of God is explicable as the outcome of his protracted personal struggle with the question whether God condemns people to suffer eternal torment in hell. Channing struggled with this question well into his pastoral career. Though he was never a good Calvinist, it took him years to resolve that he did not believe in a damnation-preaching evangelical religion, either. The struggle of the religion of fear with the religion of love in his spiritual development showed through in nearly every story that he told about it. The story of his encounter with revivalist apocalypticism, in the company of his father, is perhaps the most telling example.

Channing's father was engaging and friendly with most people, "the delight of the circle in which he moved," as his son recalled, but distant with his children. Channing explained of his father that "his early marriage and the rapid increase of his family obliged him to confine himself rigidly to his profession." On one occasion, however, having decided that some personal time with his son was in order, he took young William in his chaise to an evangelistic meeting that featured a noted revival preacher. Impressed that his father had given up an entire afternoon to take him to this service, Channing listened intently to the preacher's words. The theme was familiar from his church experience, but not the grandiloquent manner in which it was delivered and pressed home. Young Channing was transfixed by the evangelist's lurid picture of "the lost condition of the human race rushing into hell." It seemed to him that the entire world was being swallowed by the darkness and horror of hell. With dramatic flourishes, the evangelist warned that salvation from the endless torment of hell was available only in the arms of Jesus, "who was described as wounded and bleeding at the hand of an inexorable God, who exacted from him the uttermost penalty due to a world of sinners."

Channing was stunned. He felt the terror of his condition as a condemned being, but also a twinge of skepticism about the entire performance. After the meeting his father greeted an acquaintance with the pronouncement: "Sound doctrine, sir." The words struck Channing hard, because they seemed to answer the question whether the preacher spoke the truth. Neither of them spoke as they began their journey home, but on the way, incongruously, the elder Channing began to whistle. Nothing was said about how the family should attempt to flee the wrath to come. When they reached home, instead of speaking some word to his family about their apparently terrible plight, Channing's father pulled off his boots, propped his feet before the fireplace, and calmly relaxed with his newspaper. The scene was a revelation to Channing: His father didn't believe it! As this realization first washed over him, Channing felt relieved, but then, on further reflection, he began to feel violated. He felt angry at being manipulated and imposed upon. Why did the church preach that God is so vindictive? If people believed it, why did they praise God for his goodness and love? If people like his father didn't believe it, why did they pretend otherwise? Although he always told this story through the lens of his later theology, in each telling, to his best recollection, this was the event that caused him to resolve never again to be swept away by florid rhetoric.[15]

Years later, when he returned to Newport on a distinctly sentimental and triumphant occasion, to preach at the dedication of a Unitarian church, Channing pointedly recalled that the Newport of his youth was not a religiously healthy place in which to grow up. He reflected that his Newport pastors were models of religious integrity to him, and Ezra Stiles, who later became president of Yale College, was a saintly figure, but in his telling the preaching that he heard as a youth disseminated the same "stern and appalling theology" that cast a pall over New England religious life as a whole. Channing recalled that he lacked a religious guide or teacher to help him survive his childhood spiritual misery. Moreover, the social climate of Newport had a distinct tendency to corrupt its youth. On these counts, Newport had been a bad place to grow up, but for two things that made up for everything else. In Newport he was able to spend entire days studying in the town library without interruption; more important, he had access to the ocean.

Channing was highly reflective and introspective throughout his life. He shared some key family traits and values—especially his mother's intense moral sincerity, which he admired greatly—but his thinking and sensibility were shaped primarily by solitary reflection, reading, and communion with nature, rather than companionship. He spent many days of his youth alone at the ocean, out of sight of parents who taught him to know his place; in later life, he traced his core spiritual sensibility to his prolonged beach walking. "Seldom do I visit it now without thinking of the work which there, in the sight of that beauty, in the sound of those waves, was carried on in my soul," he recalled. "No spot on earth has helped to form me so much as that beach. There I lifted up my voice in praise amidst the tempest. There, softened by beauty, I poured out my thanksgiving and contrite confessions. There, in reverential sympathy with the mighty power around me, I became conscious of power within."[16] Against Calvinist orthodoxy and, later, the cold rationalism of his Unitarian friends, Channing held fast to the vaguely mystical apprehension of spiritual "power within" that sustained his early life.

His voracious reading habits prepared him for college, and at the age of twelve, Channing moved to New London, Connecticut, to prepare for Harvard under the tutelage of his uncle Henry Channing, a liberal Congregationalist pastor. Henry Channing had been a tutor at Yale but withdrew from the college over religious differences. He supported the evangelical movements of his time but openly expressed his disbelief in the divinity of Christ. His combination of liberal-leaning openness and evangelical enthusiasm were attractive to his young nephew, who would date his interest in the ministry to the year that he spent in New London. In 1794, at the age of fourteen, barely a year after the unexpected death of his father, Channing went off to Harvard College, where his grandfather William Ellery had gone. His grandfather assured him that his Greek and Latin were already strong enough for college study. "You must enter College this year by all means, and hasten to obtain a liberal education," William Ellery exhorted, adding that he pledged himself to "your honorable reception into the bosom of my Alma mater."[17]

HARVARD AT THE CROSSROADS:
MORAL PHILOSOPHY BEYOND LOCKE

In 1794, Harvard was Federalist and Puritan-rooted, like the Channings. It consisted of four professors, three tutors, and 173 students, of whom Channing was the second youngest. He may have exaggerated slightly in later years when he judged that Harvard "was never in a worse state than when I entered," but by all accounts, it was a low period.[18] The College was basically demoralized and confused about its future; his professors were elderly, defensive about the erosion of their worldview and manners, and repelled by the French Revolution. They clung to the vestiges of a classical curriculum, alarmed at the ascent of aggressive forms of deism and antireligious rationalism in the United States. During Channing's junior year, they felt threatened enough by Tom Paine's *The Age of Reason* to issue a copy of Bishop Richard Watson's rejoinder, *Apology for the Bible*, to every student.[19] As a committed Federalist with a decidedly moralistic bent, Channing sympathized with his teachers' bristling resistance to ill-mannered students, anti-Christian propaganda, and all things French, but he also smelled surrender in their edgy defensiveness. His disappointment with Harvard compelled William Ellery to remind him to read his Greek Testament, keep a respectful spirit, and stay on his best behavior. Channing later recalled that the French Revolution "diseased the imagination" of his peers and unsettled his teachers: "The old foundations of social order, loyalty, tradition, habit, reverence for antiquity, were everywhere shaken, if not subverted. The authority of the past was gone. The old forms were outgrown, and new ones had not taken their place. The tone of books and conversation was presumptuous and daring. The tendency of all classes was to scepticism. At such a moment, the difficulties of education were necessarily multiplied."[20]

In this environment, Channing's introspective learning style proved a distinct advantage. Puritan-rooted Harvard did not teach Calvin, or the classic texts of seventeenth-century Reformed orthodoxy, or even the writings of Jonathan Edwards.[21] As early as 1740, George Whitefield had complained that Harvard did not deserve its reputation as an excellent training school for ministers. "Bad books are becoming fashionable among the tutors and students," he reported, referring to books with rationalist or Arminian tendencies.[22] By the end of the century, Harvard was supplementing its watered-down classical curriculum of a little Latin and less Greek with a patchwork of courses in the humanities and natural sciences, featuring mostly secondary textbooks. Locke's *Essay Concerning Human Understanding* was a pillar of the curriculum, while the Hollis Professor of Divinity, David Tappan, gave gentle guidance to students who sought to read beyond Locke in philosophy.

Channing was one of them. He sailed through Harvard at the top of his class while imploring his teachers to guide his studies beyond the official curriculum. The canonical status of Locke was a sharp goad to his intellectual pilgrimage. Though he later joined a religious movement that treated Locke's empiricism as the final word in philosophy, Channing was repulsed by Locke's epistemological sensationalism. He felt deeply the spiritual wrongness of Locke's denial of innate ideas and resisted, without knowing how to refute, the Lockean doctrine that all ideas are products of sensory experience or reflection on experience. Lockean philosophy had Christian supporters, as Channing knew, but he was sensitive to its implicitly materialist character. The conflict between his spiritual sensibility and his sense of the antispiritual implications of Locke's empiricism drove him to search for a suitable philosophical alternative. Under the informal guidance of Tappan and Harvard logician Levi Hedge, he studied works by George Berkeley and the Unitarian philosophers Thomas Belsham and Joseph Priestley; probably for the sake of confronting the enemy, he read David Hume; most important, under Hedge's guidance in particular, he sought an alternative to Locke and Hume in the Scottish Enlightenment philosophies of Francis Hutcheson (1694–1747), Adam Ferguson (1723–1816), Thomas Reid (1710–96), and Welsh intuitionist Richard Price (1723–91).[23]

Channing was attracted to the nonnaturalistic accounts of morality put forth by Price and the Scottish moralists because they fit his spiritual predispositions. He began with Hutcheson's idea of disinterested benevolence, which affirmed the innate reality and determinative character of moral altruism. Hutcheson emphasized feeling as the crucial source of moral knowledge; following

Shaftesbury, he argued that rational agents possess an objective "moral sense" that perceives the moral right, as feeling, in much the same way that individuals see a physical object. His version of moral-sense theory contended that virtue consists essentially of the sacrifice of private interest and bearing of private evils for the public good. Because all individuals possess an innate moral sense, he contended, it is morally possible for all individual subjects to act for the good of others.[24]

This claim of innate altruism resonated deeply with Channing and confirmed his own sense of the intrinsically other-regarding moral nature of humankind. On one occasion, while reflecting on Hutcheson's account of moral psychology, Channing had one of the central mystical visions of his life. Walking in a favorite meadow near his uncle's home, with Hutcheson's text in hand, he experienced a convicting realization of "the glory of the Divine disinterestedness, the privilege of existing in a universe of progressive order and beauty, the possibilities of spiritual destiny, the sublimity of devotedness to the will of Infinite Love." For Channing it was a transforming moment, which he described as a "new spiritual birth" and a soul-penetrating experience of joy. "I longed to die, and felt as if heaven alone could give room for the exercise of such emotions," he later recounted. "But when I found I must live, I cast about to do something worthy of these great thoughts."[25]

His first impulse was to send a love letter to a young woman, his cousin Ruth Gibbs—whom he later married—but Channing shied away from sending the letter. He kept it for the rest of his life as a momento of his first ecstatic religious experience. His awakening to the soul's capacity for altruism deepened his interrelated spiritual and intellectual pursuits. From Hutcheson he caught his first glimpse of the infinite possibilities that human beings possess by virtue of their spiritual nature. From Adam Ferguson's socially oriented moral philosophy he embraced the view that the pursuit of virtue is a gradual social process that must include a struggle for social progress. Ferguson taught that a person becomes good, and therefore happy, in the process of becoming an other-regarding member of a community, "for whose general good his heart may glow with an ardent zeal."[26]

Because it affirmed the reality of an external world independent of consciousness, the current of the Scottish Enlightenment tradition to which Hutcheson, Ferguson, and Thomas Reid belonged, and to which Price was closely related, is appropriately categorized as a type of epistemological realism. It sought to provide a credible alternative to the blend of skepticism and naturalism propounded by David Hume, the greatest of the Scottish Enlightenment philosophers. The Hutcheson/Reid school of Scottish philosophy effected a distinctive kind of realism, however, inasmuch as it protected and affirmed the idea of the spiritual nature of consciousness. This idea was the heart of Channing's faith. Channing's basic philosophical undergirding came from Price, but the major theorist of Scottish "common sense" philosophy was Thomas Reid. A professor of moral philosophy at Glasgow, where he succeeded Adam Smith,

Reid argued that all the main schools of modern philosophy led to skepticism because all of them, from Descartes to Locke to Berkeley to Hume, consisted essentially of variations on the faulty idea of an ideal system.

Despite his famous denial of innate ideas, Locke conceded the reality of one intuitive belief: self-consciousness of one's existence. This exception was crucial to Reid's concept of the self as a mind that contains the powers of perception. Every ideal system eventually comes into conflict with the innate principles of conception and belief by which the mind actually works, he contended. Thus, with each successive critical turn in the history of philosophy since Descartes, modern philosophers became successively less able to secure intellectual certainty about anything, including finally, as with Hume, the existence of a continuous self.

Reid countered that the way forward in philosophy was to affirm the realistic verdict of "common sense" that sensation automatically causes belief in external objects. When I feel a pain in my toe, he reasoned, I am given not only a notion of pain, but also a belief in its existence, as well as the belief that something is wrong with my toe. These beliefs are not produced by comparing ideas; they are caused by the occurrence of the sensation and are included in the very nature of the sensation. Reid reasoned that the principles of self-consciousness thus exist in the constitution of the mind. Though he never developed a systematic account or even a complete list of these principles, he urged that a return to reality in philosophy necessitated the recognition that self-consciousness contains various fundamental principles prior to and independent of experience. These natural judgments are "a part of that furniture which Nature hath given to the human understanding," he wrote. "They are the inspiration of the Almighty, no less than our notions or simple apprehensions. They serve to direct us in the common affairs of life, where our reasoning faculty would leave us in the dark. They are a part of our constitution; and all the discoveries of our reason are grounded upon them. They make up what is called *the common sense of mankind;* and, what is manifestly contrary to any of those first principles, is what we call *absurd*."[27]

Modern philosophy was driven to absurdity by its resolve to begin the process of thinking by doubting everything. By a slight logical turn in one direction or other, philosophers found themselves denying the existence of mind or matter or both. Reid and Price worried especially about the implications of modern philosophical skepticism for morality. Against a variously argued relativistic tide in moral philosophy, especially utilitarian theory, the Scottish moralists reasoned that if the fundamental principles of self-consciousness are not products of experience, the fundamental principles of morals must be self-evident intuitions.

Reid and Price built upon Hutcheson's moral philosophy while significantly departing from it. Hutcheson claimed that the existence of a universal moral sense in human beings was "one of the strongest evidences" of the goodness of God. Having argued for the self-evident status of such intuitive concepts as "cause" and "existence," Reid and Price similarly contended that moral ideas of right and wrong are inherent in the very process of reasoning. At the same time, they protested that Hutcheson's ethical sentimentalism was too subjective. Price made the case against Hutcheson's theory of moral knowledge. Hutcheson conceptualized morality as the function of an innate moral sensibility, but Price argued that this view undercut the power of human understanding to determine right from wrong. Invoking Locke's distinction between "primary" and "secondary" qualities, he noted that Hutcheson's account relegated moral qualities to the status of subjective realities like taste or color. Price countered that moral qualities must not be regarded as existing merely in the mind of the perceiver. Moral qualities possess the same primary status as the concepts of substance, extension, and mass, he argued. They are fundamental synthetic propositions that assert objective facts. Against Hutcheson's emphasis on the determinative power of moral sense, Price emphasized the effective agency of the self in making moral choices.[28]

His signature distinction between understanding and reason framed his account of the moral agency of the self. It also prefigured Kant's distinction between theoretical and practical reason. Price argued that reason consists "in investigating certain relations between objects, ideas of which must have been previously in the mind." That is, reason necessarily presupposes the existence of the ideas that it seeks to trace. The faculty of reason is calculating and empirical, without the capacity to create new ideas: "It is undeniable that many of our ideas are derived from the *intuition* of the truth, or the discernment of the natures of things by the understanding of our moral ideas." Happiness and misery belong to the world of effects, Price reasoned, but virtue and vice belong to the nature of things. Their relation is one of cause and effect. Against the utilitarian claim that happiness is a product of the moral utility of an act, Price contended that virtue derives from the recognition that virtue and vice are the primary causes of happiness and misery. Like Reid, he reconceptualized the moral sense as an aspect of innate human reason; more important to Channing in his later debates with Transcendentalists, Price and Reid also agreed that the moral sense is educable. Rudimentary moral reason is innate, they explained, but moral refinement requires education and training. Moreover, just as an individual always has the possibility of intellectual improvement, an individual always has the possibility of further moral growth.[29]

To Channing, these were inspiriting, life-founding ideas. Much of his childhood religion was troubling to him, but the philosophers of Scottish intuitionism provided a constellation of concepts that confirmed his intuitions about the spiritual nature and infinite moral value of humanity. These concepts undergirded Channing's thinking for the rest of his life. In the half-century that followed Tappan's death, they also provided the basis of a dominant tradition of Unitarian moral philosophy at Harvard. Near the end of his life, Channing expressed his gratitude to Price for providing his essential philosophical grounding. Unlike the posture that he adopted toward Joseph Priestley, Channing overlooked Price's radical politics. He took great pleasure in observing that Price's work, though little noticed in England, may have been a formative influence on Kant and other early German idealists. "He gave me the doctrine of ideas, and during my life I have written the words Love, Right, etc., with a capital," Channing later recalled. "That book probably moulded my philosophy into the form it has always retained."[30]

In his senior year, spurred by "the prevalence of infidelity, imported from France," Channing studied Christian apologetics, which helped him decide between medicine and the ministry. After college, he returned to Newport and the ocean, where, as he related to a friend, "my soul ascends to the God of nature, and in such a temple I cannot but be devout." Channing resolved to seek ordination, in the expectation that as a pastor he could become "a shepherd of the flock of Jesus, a reformer of a vicious, and an instructor of an ignorant world." Explaining to a former classmate that he wanted to help make America a better country, he remarked, "In my view, religion is another name for happiness, and I am most cheerful when I am most religious."[31]

THE WILDERNESS WITHIN

The question of how he might prepare for the ministry while earning a living was resolved when a prosperous Virginia visitor to Newport, U.S. marshal David Meade Randolph, offered him employment as a tutor. "I am resolved to prosecute divinity," Channing told his mother, who was struggling to maintain a large family on her own. For eighteen months, Channing lived with the Randolphs in Richmond, getting his first taste of the world outside New England. The experience cast a lengthy shadow over the rest of his life. The Randolphs epitomized the values and manners of the Old Dominion aristocracy, and at first Channing was charmed by their elegance, urbanity, and hospitality. He took delight in the warmth and color of upper-class Southern culture, by which New England, even Newport, seemed staid and repressed by comparison. Though the Randolphs were Federalists, in Richmond Channing made his first contact with apparently respectable people who were Democrats; for the first time he also encountered the reality of slavery as an institutionalized social system. His first stab of alienating disaffection from his hosts, or at least from their civilization, occurred while contemplating the fate of their slaves. "There is one object here which always depresses me," he wrote home. "It is *slavery.* This alone would prevent me from ever settling in Virginia. Language cannot express my detestation of it. Master and slave! Nature never made such a distinction, or established such a relation." In a statement that prefigured the basis of his later abolitionism, Channing reflected that what he hated above all about slavery was its evil in stripping human beings of their capacity to live as moral agents: "No right is so inseparable from humanity, and so necessary to the improvement of our species, as the right of exerting the powers which nature has

uncle Henry was dismissed by his New London congregation, after twenty years of service, for insufficient orthodoxy. That same year, Henry Ware's appointment to the Hollis chair at Harvard sparked a conservative protest that heightened the pressure on pastors to choose sides. The conservative backlash eventually produced a strategic alliance between "Old Light" Calvinists and Hopkinsians that led to the founding of Andover Theological Seminary in 1808 as an antidote to liberal-turning Harvard.

Both sets of events stirred Channing's repressed liberal feelings. As early as 1806, in letters to his beloved grandfather William Ellery, he began to take the liberal side in church debates that had become unavoidable. Channing exhorted his orthodox grandfather that the "great point by which a Christian is to be judged" is one's heart and affections, not dogma, and that the distinguishing feature of Congregationalism was its liberality, not its orthodoxy. It is true that scripture denounces those who do not believe in Christ, he allowed, but the failing that scripture condemns is always corruption of the heart, not lack of orthodoxy in doctrine.[40]

A year later, after Ellery insisted that the church was obliged to uphold "just ideas" concerning the divine attributes, human depravity, and the atonement of Christ, Channing conceded the general point while cautioning against a rigid standard of orthodoxy. Human perception of the attributes of God is surely fallible, he noted, and even strict Calvinists were divided over the nature of Christ's atonement. Channing assured his grandfather that he still believed in the doctrine of total depravity; he even believed that all Christians should believe it. What he didn't believe was that a Christian had to believe it. "A man may doubt on that subject, yet hate sin," he reasoned.[41]

This was a small step, but a crucial one, because Channing was describing himself. His sense of cognitive dissonance was deeply unsettling. He loved Richard Price's moral philosophy, but as a carefully vague cleric, he adhered to a moral religion that was barely to the left of Hopkins. He preached a gospel of warm-hearted devotion to Christ and ecumenical inclusivity, but was forced to deal with the fact that many conservatives didn't share his devotion to ecumenical fellowship. At a time when conservatives increasingly refused to exchange pulpits with liberals, Channing continued to exchange pulpits freely with both sides. He gained a large popular following in the process, but found it very difficult to sustain a mediating posture when friends were attacked for heresy.

The crucial issue for him was always, as he would later put it, "the shock given to my moral nature" by orthodox teaching.[42] In the years leading up to "the Unitarian controversy," Channing became increasingly clear that he embraced a different kind of religion. He taught that the Infinite Mind wills and effects the perfection of human minds in knowledge, love, and action.[43] The events of 1812 moved him to become not only a public movement liberal, but a liberal movement leader.

As a near-pacifist and ardent foe of government overreach, Channing opposed the War of 1812 as a grotesque and unnecessary government plunge into carnage. A friend of England and bitter opponent of French military despotism, he pleaded that it was perverse for America to favor France over England, much less "select England as our enemy." America was linked to England by history, language, culture, Christianity, and all other marks of civilization, while France was the enemy of civilization, an infidel power driven by its lust for conquest. "When I view my country taking part with the oppressor against that nation which has alone arrested his proud career of victory,—which is now spreading her shield over desolated Portugal and Spain,—which is the chief hope of the civilized world,—I blush,—I mourn," Channing declared on the Commonwealth's Day of the Public Fast. "We are linking ourselves with the acknowledged enemy of mankind,—with a government . . . which has left not a vestige of liberty where it has extended its blasting sway,—which is at this moment ravaging nations that are chargeable with no crime but hatred of a foreign yoke."[44]

In later years, repulsed by his party's antidemocratic spirit and its loathing of the French Revolution, Channing disavowed the abstract Francophobia of his antiwar statements. He repudiated the boilerplate conservative ploy of invoking the Revolution to prevent democratic reforms in American politics and society. He held fast to his hatred of military aggression and tyranny, however, and thus continued to condemn Napoleon as a monstrous tyrant.[45] In 1812, Channing's prophetic judgments on this theme raised his profile as a public figure at the very moment when the liberal movement needed a galvanizing new voice.

His blistering sermon against the War of 1812 was preached on July 23, a month after the liberal Congregationalists lost their greatest voice, Joseph Stevens Buckminster (1784–1812) who had pastored the socially exclusive Brattle Street Church in Boston and also served as the first Dexter Lecturer on Biblical Criticism at Harvard. A brilliant scholar and preacher, Buckminster gave eloquent, aesthetically refined sermons that made him the undisputed leader of New England liberal Christianity while he was still in his mid-twenties. His many admirers called him "the seraph of the pulpit." As the chief founder of the Boston Athenaeum and a founder and regular contributor to *The Monthly Anthology and Boston Review,* he epitomized the early-nineteenth-century liberal ideal of the pastor as a cultured man of letters. Buckminster was the first American to acquire scholarly proficiency in the writings of Johann Gottfried Eichhorn, Johann David Michaelis, and other founders of modern German biblical scholarship. His articles in *The Monthly Anthology* introduced to cultured American readers developments in German biblical criticism, especially textual criticism, which he expounded from the pulpit. An American pioneer of textual criticism and the study of canon formation, Buckminster was principally responsible for the first American edition of Johann Jacob Griesbach's manual edition of the New Testament.[46]

Buckminster's preaching blended moral and aesthetic concerns, appealing to conscience and imagination as the keys to spiritual development. In this respect Channing resembled him, though Channing was no match for him as a cutting-edge scholar. In 1812, Buckminster's early death from epilepsy was a devastating blow to the liberal movement. His massive library was auctioned off to a grief-stricken gathering of budding scholars that included Edward Everett, Moses Stuart, and Andrews Norton. Tributes to his saintliness and intellect poured in immediately from churches across New England, and that was only the beginning. The eulogizing for the brightest hope of American liberal Protestantism continued until the Civil War.[47]

ENGLISH UNITARIANISM
AND THE AMERICAN UNITARIAN CONTROVERSY

Amidst these circumstances, Channing reluctantly became a liberal leader. With Samuel C. Thacher, he edited Buckminster's sermons for publication. For a year, pressing his frail health to the limit, he took Buckminster's place as Dexter Lecturer at Harvard. At the same time, under increasingly strident attacks from conservatives who threatened to start heresy trials against them, Channing and a handful of friends launched a magazine, *The Christian Disciple,* edited by Noah Worcester, that proposed to speak for a good-spirited, inclusive understanding of the Christian faith.[48] The liberals, Channing especially, vowed not to go on the offensive. They were not out to attack or exclude anyone, they insisted. Neither were they selling out the faith, as the conservatives insinuated. They vowed to continue to speak for Christian love, the unity of the church, and the primacy of the religion of Jesus. This strategy held conservative-liberal conflict at a tolerable level until 1815, when two conservatives, Jedediah Morse, a famed geographer, leader of the conservative protest against Henry Ware's appointment to the Hollis chair at Harvard, and founder of Andover Theological Seminary, and Jeremiah Evarts, who edited the conservative *Panoplist and Missionary Magazine,* provoked the liberals by attacking their faith and integrity.

The conservatives charged, first, that the liberal Christian movement in New England was not Christian at all, but a form of imported Unitarianism. Second, they claimed that in the Boston area, most Congregational churches were pastored by Unitarians who retained their ministerial credentials and positions by hypocritically concealing their true beliefs. Their true beliefs were spelled out in a recent biography of the English Unitarian Theophilus Lindsey, written by fellow English Unitarian Thomas Belsham, in which Belsham disavowed the doctrines of the divine Trinity and the deity of Christ. In point of doctrine, Evarts remarked, Belsham was rotten "to the very core," but as a moral figure, he was "purity itself" in comparison to the American liberals, who perverted the faith of their churches while pretending to be Christians. Morse and Evarts buried the

American liberals in a heap of invective, accusing them of heresy, infidelity, cowardice, "hypocritical concealment," and "cunning and dishonesty."[49] These accusations built up to a fateful climax: Because the so-called liberal Christians were actually deceitful Unitarians plotting to overthrow the Christian religion, Evarts urged, third, the time had come for genuine Christian believers to break fellowship with them. The real Christians remaining in the churches were obliged to "come out and be separate" from the heathens in charge. Some of Evarts' most bitter derision was reserved for orthodox pastors who refused to draw this conclusion.[50]

In the form of a public letter addressed to Thacher, Channing responded to Morse and Evarts and thus entered the lists as a defender of liberal Christianity. The first charge was mistaken, if only by half, in Channing's reckoning; the second was wholly wrong and deeply offensive; the third was alarming, and, in the single sense that mattered to him, heretical. Since Morse and Evarts identified Unitarian thinking with Belsham's rationalistic Socinianism, Channing was able, for the moment, to deflect the first charge. His label-splitting evasiveness in 1815 set into motion the historical dynamic by which the name "Unitarian" was fervently embraced barely four years later.

In the early nineteenth century, Unitarianism was a revisionist form of Protestant Christianity that replaced the traditional doctrines of the divine Trinity and the full deity of Christ with the idea of divine unipersonality. Historically, the Unitarian tradition derives from the anti-trinitarian teaching of Spanish martyr Michael Servetus (1511–53), who was burned as a heretic at Champel (near Geneva), and the transcendentalist-like theology of German religious leader Caspar Schwenckfeld (1489–1561). A major figure of the succeeding generation was the Italian exile Faustus Socinus (1539–1604), founder of "Socinian"-school Christology and pioneer of Polish Unitarianism, who rejected the doctrines of the Trinity, the deity of Christ, and the substitutionary atonement of Christ while emphasizing Christ's humanity and exemplary moral influence.[51]

In England, the Unitarian tradition stretches back to the anti-trinitarian tracts of John Biddle (1615–62) and includes its naming by Unitarian tractarian Stephen Nye in 1687. As a theological perspective, the English Unitarian tradition claims such thinkers as Hugo Grotius (1583–1645), Isaac Newton (1642–1727), Isaac Watts (1674–1748), Nathaniel Lardner (1684–1768), William Paley (1743–1805), John Locke, Samuel Clarke, and Richard Price. As an organized denominational movement, English Unitarianism is a descendent of the dissenting English Puritan and Separatist movements, and founded its first congregation in 1773 under the leadership of dissident Anglican cleric Theophilus Lindsey (1723–1808). Lindsey's chief collaborator in making Unitarianism a denominational tradition in England was Joseph Priestley (1733–1804), an epic figure in Unitarian history, who represented everything that Morse and Evarts tried to pin on the New England liberals, however implausibly.[52]

Priestley was a descendent of English Puritans, a political and religious radical, dissenting pastor, philosophical materialist, brilliant scientist (he discovered oxygen in 1774, and also wrote on electricity) and prolific historical theologian. His friends and religious sympathizers included Benjamin Franklin, Thomas Jefferson, and Richard Price. Under his energetic theological influence, the Unitarian movement founded numerous chapels in England. In 1780, after serving as an increasingly notorious pastor to several dissenting congregations, he assumed the pastorate of the New Meeting in Birmingham, probably the largest dissenting congregation in England.

An ardent Socinian, Priestley specialized in condemning the errors of traditional Christianity. In 1782, he assembled dozens of earlier tracts and books into a two-volume polemic, *An History of the Corruptions of Christianity,* which converted Jefferson to Unitarianism and ignited a controversy in English Christendom. Priestley argued that the orthodox doctrines of Christ and the Trinity were products of the early church's infection by Gnostic religious movements, Platonist philosophy, and other corrupting influences. His debate with conservative church leaders raged on for years, until the French Revolution gave his clerical enemies cause to heighten their attacks upon him. Priestley vigorously defended the Revolution while carrying on his scientific experiments. In 1791, on Bastille Day, a church-incited mob took its revenge, burning his home, laboratory, and library, as well as the Unitarian chapels of Birmingham. Anxious to continue his scientific work and vulnerable to charges of treason for supporting the Revolution, Priestley fled to the United States in 1794, settling in Northumberland, Pennsylvania. He founded a short-lived Unitarian congregation there, and in 1796, established in Philadelphia the first enduring American church to call itself Unitarian.[53]

This was not quite the same thing as *being* the first American Unitarian church, a designation that properly belongs to the formerly Anglican King's Chapel in Boston, which converted to Unitarianism in the late 1780s under the leadership of James Freeman. In both cases, however, what is pertinent about the beginning of Unitarian denominationalism in the United States is the kind of liberal Christianity that it espoused. In both of the places where it established an independent beachhead in the late eighteenth century, American Unitarianism was theologically a descendant of the radical wing of its English forerunner. Priestley's Christ-centered piety made him more explicitly Christian than his good friend Benjamin Franklin or his friendly admirer Thomas Jefferson, but his radical politics, philosophical materialism, and theological Socinianism made him a poor model, in the eyes of the leaders of New England liberal Christianity.[54]

Under the influence of Priestley and his associate William Hazlitt, an English Unitarian who moved to Boston in 1784, James Freeman adopted a Socinian Christology in the process of converting his orphaned Anglican congregation to Unitarianism. The American Unitarians emphasized what they called "the simple humanity of Christ," in opposition to the high Christologies of the Arian and orthodox Athanasian traditions. Priestley argued that first-century Christianity viewed Jesus as a mere man who was aided by the power of God. He found "no trace" in the New Testament that the apostles regarded Jesus as a supernatural being. Though he conceded that the prologue of the fourth Gospel contained the seed of the church's mythologization of Jesus, Priestley argued that in John's gospel, the idea of Logos or Word was conceived as an *attribute* of the divine mind. The notion of the Word as an intelligent *being* was a later Christian invention, he taught. No Christian writer before Justin Martyr ascribed anything like divinity to Christ. It was the corrupting identification of Christ with Logos that gave rise to the christological corruptions of the fourth-century church, in which the dominant debate pitted high-Christology Athanasians against slightly lower-Christology Arians. Having opted to personify the wisdom of God the Father, he explained, it was inevitable that "the philosophizing Christians" later deduced "that Christ was, in power and glory, equal to God the Father himself."[55]

Priestley insisted that Christian teaching was thoroughly corrupted by the time the church's consuming debate featured a struggle over the precise nature of Christ's divinity. Jewish religion was this-worldly and materialistic in its ethos, worldview, and spiritual sensibility, he explained, but under the influence of hellenistic dualism, Christianity enshrined a separate world of "spirit" as the true object of religious language and devotion. The hellenization of Christianity engendered bad scriptural exegesis and replaced the religion of Christ with a paganized neo-Platonist concoction that Jesus would not have recognized. "The causes of corruptions were almost wholly contained in the established opinions of the heathen world, and especially the philosophical part of it; so that when those heathens embraced christianity they mixed their former tenets and prejudices with it," he contended. Having split material reality from the world of spirit, the Platonizing church fathers "were enabled to give to the soul of Christ what rank they pleased in the heavenly regions before his incarnation." The same spiritual dualism serviced a host of new beliefs and rituals, including the practice of praying for the dead, and later to the dead, "with a long train of other absurd opinions and superstitious practices."

Priestley-style Unitarianism was thus distinctively radical and radically restorationist. For all of its plainly modern and rationalistic features, it amounted, at root, like much liberal theology after him, to a call for a recovery of the "pure Christianity" of Jesus and the early church. Early Christianity had nothing to do with a divinized man, a Triune God, or a substitionary atonement, he argued. What early Christianity did assert was that "the universal parent of mankind commissioned Jesus Christ, to invite men to the practice of virtue, by the assurance of his mercy to the penitent, and of his purpose to raise to immortal life and happiness all the virtuous and the good, but to inflict an adequate punishment on the wicked." As proof of this commission, Priestley asserted, Jesus wrought many miracles, "and after a public execution he rose again from the dead." He also instituted the practices of baptism and a commemorative Lord's Supper. By God's grace and providential will, the man Jesus lived an exemplary life, instituted an ethical religion, and gave us the promise of resurrected life (not immortality) by being raised from the dead. That is the sum of genuine Christianity, Priestley taught.[56]

DEFENDING NEW ENGLAND LIBERAL CHRISTIANITY

This was the crucial background to Channing's early attempt to evade the Unitarian label. Supported by statements made by Freeman and William Wells, Morse and Evarts described American Unitarianism as an offshoot of English Unitarianism in the style of Priestley and Belsham. They surely comprehended, though they gave no hint of it, why this designation was offensive to the New England liberals. Priestley-style Unitarianism was hard-edged, politically radical, philosophically materialist, and theologically Socinian, but New England liberal Christianity was mildly rationalist, sentimental, and enfranchised. Virtually all the liberal Christian leaders were Federalists who staunchly opposed the French Revolution, the Jeffersonians, and the plague of deists. They identified with the establishment no less than their orthodox opponents. Priestley's attack on the Platonist corruption of early Christianity was too radical for them, since they were spiritualizing neo-Platonists.

The liberal Christians were appalled by Priestley's materialism and his sweeping rejection of traditional Christianity. Though he was respectful toward the tradition of Socinian Unitarianism that Priestley's follower, Thomas Belsham, represented, Channing distinguished between good liberal Christianity and a dubious Unitarian tradition. Leaving the politics in the background, Channing believed that the crucial difference between American liberal Christianity and English-rooted Unitarianism was that American liberal Christians believed in the deity of Christ, albeit not in the way prescribed by the victorious party of the fourth- and fifth-century church councils.

In a word, most of the American liberals were Arians. They held that Jesus was divine, but subordinate to God the Father. They turned aside the Socinian protest that gods do not die. Channing was conflicted about how to speak for his movement on this matter. On the one hand, he was ambivalent about defending something called "liberal Christianity." He disliked party-line thinking of all kinds, and in this case, the notion of a "liberal party" had oxymoronic qualities. Liberality is about freedom, liberty, "enlargement of the views and affections," he noted. A truly liberal theology cannot secure established positions. Moreover, Channing had no desire to involve "liberal Christianity" in well-forgotten early church debates about the natures of God and Christ. This sentiment spoke to the conservative charge that liberals hypocritically concealed their true beliefs about the nature of divine reality. Channing allowed that "we seldom or never introduce the Trinitarian controversy into our pulpits." But this was not because they were out to trick anyone with evasive tactics or cunning wordplay. Liberals like himself tended to avoid the subject in their sermons, he explained, for the same reason that they made no reference to Sabellianism, Eutychianism, or Nestorianism.[57]

With this argument, Channing's other hand prevailed. Sabellius was excommunicated as a heretic in the third century for his modalist theory of the radical unity of the Godhead. Eutyches was excommunicated as a heretic in the fifth century for teaching that Christ had a divine nature only. The fifth-century theologian Nestorius of Constantinople taught that because two natures adhered in Christ, the title "Mother of God" could not be used for Mary, since she was the mother only of Christ's human nature. This doctrine was condemned as a heresy at the Council of Ephesus in 431. Channing's point was remarkably dismissive. By implication, he placed the doctrine of the Trinity in a class with other misguided theologies best confined to museums of ecclesiastical history. Channing noted that while he never preached against any of these views, he also never hid from anyone that he believed in the unipersonality of God and the "peculiar union" between the Father and Son. To his understanding, this was the usual liberal approach: "As to my brethren in general, never have I imagined for a moment, from their preaching or conversation, that they had the least desire to be considered as Trinitarians; nor have I ever heard from them any view of God or of Jesus Christ, but Unitarian in the proper meaning of that word." In the proper sense of the term, conservatives Morse and Evarts were right; the Boston liberal Protestants were all Unitarians. Channing spelled out what this meant: "We are accustomed to speak of the Father as the only living and true God, and of Jesus Christ as his son, as a distinct being from him, as dependent on him, subordinate to him, and deriving all from him. This phraseology pervades all our prayers, and all our preaching."[58]

He professed not to see anything problematic or strange in this state of affairs. Why should Congregationalists be bound by Athanasian Christology? Why should any good-spirited person question the motives of a Christian pastor who quietly disregarded the Trinity? "In following this course, we are not conscious of having contracted, in the least degree, the guilt of insincerity," Channing asserted. "We have aimed at making no false impression." Liberal Christian pastors generally kept this subject out of the pulpit because they cared deeply about Christian unity, he explained: "We have only followed a general system, which we are persuaded to be best for our people and for the cause of christianity; the system of excluding controversy as much as possible from our pulpits." By avoiding controversy and striving to hold the church together, he noted, "we have thought that we deserved, not reproach, but some degree of praise for our self denial."[59]

He insinuated that it was second nature for conservatives and radicals alike to proselytize unbelievers, fill the air with controversy, and blast their opponents. Liberal Christianity was a more peaceable, if less exciting faith, he reflected, "because we are not governed by a proselyting temper." Liberal Christians had no interest in relighting the flames of persecution that disgraced "the professed disciples of the meek and lowly Jesus" in centuries past. Warming to this theme, Channing delivered a sizable boast: "I will venture to assert, that there is not on earth a body of men who possess less of the spirit of proselytism, than the ministers of this town and vicinity." Liberal Christians were open to genuine piety in all corners of the church, he declared, and they did not press for conversions to their own opinions: "I could smile at the idea of a *Unitarian plot*, were not this fiction intended to answer so unworthy an end."[60]

The end in question was a schism between conservatives and liberals. Channing noted that there was nothing new in the current conservative back-lash, "but I believe that this is the first instance, in which christians have been deliberately called to deny us the christian name and privileges." As the first such call, he admonished, "let it be remembered; and let the consequences of it lie on its authors." Drawing on scripture scholar George Campbell's study of the root meaning of *heresy* in the Bible, he observed that heresy does not consist in the adoption of mistaken opinions, but "in a *spirit of division, of dissension, of party, in a factious and turbulent temper.*" Christ commanded us to love each other, Channing noted, and Paul exhorted us to bear each other's burdens, but the *Panoplist* implored Christians to "cast out your brethren, and treat them as heathens." As for the liberal party that was, in the ordinary sense, no party at all, he concluded, it would go on treating its enemies with good will, despite being subjected by them to "deep rooted prejudices, false views of religion, unsuspected biasses to censoriousness, and disordered imagination."[61]

Channing's heart was in this claim to liberal openness and ecumenicity. He did not wish to belong to a party-line liberal movement, much less assume its leadership. If he belonged to a liberal party nonetheless, this was only because he and his friends were subjected to gratuitous attacks fueled by false views of religion and disordered imagination. Having protested that his group did not deserve the Unitarian label, he allowed that, of course, in the proper sense of the word, they were all Unitarians. Channing mentioned that this viewpoint had distinguished company that included Locke, Newton, Grotius, Clarke, Lardner, Price, and Paley.[62]

In essence, his defensive but seething response to Morse and Evarts pleaded for others to see his group as they saw themselves. They were progressive post-Calvinists who deserved to inherit the churches built by their orthodox Calvinist forebears. They understood that the Unitarian label was a threat to this expectation. Channing and his friends soon perceived that the controversy over Unitarianism raised the question of the Trinity to a level of importance that distorted their primary concerns. The liberal pastors were concerned chiefly about the spiritual nature of humanity, the moral likeness of God and humankind, and the correlation of revelation and reason. Their congregations were no longer interested in the doctrines or scholastic language of Protestant orthodoxy and did not wish to hear sermons about them, even in criticism. Near the end of his life, Buckminster assured that "sincere" believers did not bother with "fruitless inquiries" into the precise relation between Jesus and the Father. In the same vein, Channing repeatedly exhorted that what mattered in Christianity was the "great principle" that "our eternal happiness depends on the character we form." In religious terms, this meant that "we must have Christ's *spirit,* which means his temper; or in other words, we must have an habitual state of the soul answering to our Lord's."[63] This was the theme on which the liberal Protestants wanted to take their stand. They were willing to argue about good and bad views of Christ's atonement, but they did not want to be defined by their anti-Trinitarianism or fight a schism-threatening battle over it. In the heated aftermath of his reply to Morse and Evarts, however, Channing recognized that this was exactly what was happening.

Channing noted that Trinitarians and Unitarians both believed in one God who is one infinite and self-existent mind. Trinitarians believed that this one God is three persons, while Unitarians believed that God is one person. Differences about Christ followed from this difference, "which relates to the obscurest of all subjects, to the essence and metaphysical nature of God, and which common Christians cannot understand." Trinitarians taught that Jesus is a derived being who is *personally* united with the self-existent God, while Unitarians taught that Jesus is a derived being who is *intimately* united with the self-existent God. The differences between these theologies were mostly verbal and not worth a schism, Channing pleaded. He implored conservatives to recognize that Unitarians did not disbelieve in the Father, Son, and Holy Spirit: "We all believe in these; we all believe that the *Father* sent the *Son,* and gives, to those that ask, the *Holy Spirit.*" All faithful Christians would be Trinitarians if this were all that Trinitarianism meant, he asserted.[64]

But liberal Christians were obliged to take seriously that Christian orthodoxy defined the divine triunity more precisely and divisively than this. Orthodox Trinitarianism taught that the one God is three distinct persons as Father, Son, and Holy Spirit, Channing observed; moreover, it claimed "that each of these persons is equal to the other two in every perfection, that each is the only true God, and yet that the three are only one God." Though he emphasized that liberal Christians did not believe that this obscure matter provided a warrant for excluding either side from Christian fellowship, Channing did not pretend to believe that Trinitarian doctrine was plausible as an interpretation of scripture or as a rational idea. "The Unitarian believes that there is but one person possessing supreme Divinity, even the Father," he wrote. "This is the great distinction; let it be kept steadily in view."[65]

He insisted that this distinction had nothing to do with differences between high and low views of Christ. Some Unitarians ascribed divine titles to Christ; some believed that as the Son of God, Jesus is not a creature; others taught that he is literally the firstborn of creation. Like Samuel Clarke, who judged that scripture sheds no light on the subject, Channing believed that it was presumptuous to take any position on whether the Son was created. He complained that, in any case, the root problem for the church was that Trinitarians clouded the question of the divine nature with a great "mist of obscure phraseology."

Confused and misled by their own language, he lamented, Trinitarian Christians supposed that they were separated from Unitarians by an immeasurable gulf: "Were this mist dispersed, I believe that they would be surprised at discovering their proximity to the Unitarians, and would learn that they had been wasting their hostility on a band of friends and brothers."[66]

ACCEPTING A DIVIDED HOUSE:
THE UNITARIAN MANIFESTO

The liberal Christians tried to say that the Trinitarian issue was not of major importance, but then vigorously defended their anti-Trinitarianism. They tried to evade the Unitarian label, but found themselves defending Unitarian teaching more insistently and publicly than before they were provoked. The label stuck to them, and in 1819, Channing resolved that they should wear it proudly. The ordination of Jared Sparks to the ministry in Baltimore provided the occasion for him to call for a self-affirming Unitarian movement. Having drawn the accusation of cunning concealment while trying to protect the unity of the church, Channing told the liberals to accept and celebrate their existence as a distinct religious movement. His Baltimore sermon owed much of its electrifying effect to his personal reputation for opposing party spirit.[67]

The occasion was carefully selected for maximum impact. The First Independent Church of Baltimore was the first offshoot of Boston-type Unitarianism to take root outside the Boston area. In 1816, James Freeman had journeyed to Baltimore to conduct three Sunday services in a hired hall; by the following year, the city had its first Unitarian congregation and the beginnings of a church building. One of its regular supply preachers in the period before the church secured a regular pastor was Harvard president John Thornton Kirkland. On May 5, 1819, the church ordained its first pastor, Jared Sparks, a youthful Unitarian graduate of Harvard who later became a distinguished historian and Harvard president. To a congregation of parishioners and ministers that included a significant Harvard contingent, Channing proclaimed the need for an unapologizing liberal movement to lift up and carry forward the true teaching of scripture.[68]

With remarkably little prolegomena for a nineteenth-century address of its kind, he moved directly to his biblical claim. Channing placed his scriptual warrant first, because he was anxious to refute the conservative charge that liberals exalted reason over revelation: "We regard the Scriptures as the records of God's successive revelations to mankind, and particularly of the last and most perfect revelation of his will by Jesus Christ. Whatever doctrines seem to us to be clearly taught in the Scriptures, we receive without reserve or exception." Channing said nothing about the implications of distinguishing between scripture as inspired revelation and scripture as the record of God's revelation. This was not the occasion to take up the slippery question of the nature of biblical inspiration. He rushed to the assurance that liberal Christianity respected the divine authority of the Bible without attaching equal importance to all of its books. Unitarians believed that scripture is God's unique revelatory record and that all essential Christian truths are authoritatively taught within it, he explained, but they did not read the Bible as a single, flat text. They regarded much of the Old Testament as "a preparation for a nobler system." Channing explained that because Unitarians regarded Jesus Christ as their only master, their religion—the religion of Christ—"lies chiefly in the New Testament." It followed for him that the canon within the canon of scriptural religion was the teaching of Jesus and the apostles: "Whatever he taught, either during his personal ministry or by his inspired Apostles, we regard as of divine authority, and profess to make the rule of our lives."[69]

American Christianity was not strong on critical biblical scholarship, as Channing knew. For him, as for Buckminster, the crucial promise of the liberal movement was to create a genuinely biblical Christianity that was not polluted by external creeds and dogmatic systems. Buckminster had lamented that while America had no biblical scholars worth mentioning, the villages and hamlets of New England were filled with "scholastic theologues, hair splitting metaphysicians, longbreathed controversialists, pamphleteers, and publishers of single sermons." Channing shared the sentiment behind this complaint, while lacking Buckminster's critically trained vision of the remedy to America's religious immaturity. His model of good biblical scholarship was Samuel Clarke's *Scripture Doctrine of the Trinity* (1712), which used a mildly rationalist, taxonomical method of analysis to determine the content of scriptural teaching on doctrinal issues. Channing was fond of saying that while Christ was his only master, if he had to choose a human authority, he would choose Clarke, whose blend of Enlightenment rationalism and biblically grounded Unitarian piety prefigured his own. In opposition to proof-texting orthodoxies that appealed to isolated scripture verses often quoted out of context, Clarke and other eighteenth-century liberals contended that the only responsible way to interpret scripture was to collect and compare all the Bible's passages on a given subject. This was the method that Charles Chauncy used in challenging traditional Christian teaching on salvation and eternal punishment and that Channing associated with enlightened Christian use of reason during the formative period of his own theological training.[70]

Channing had learned enough from Buckminster and the newly established Dexter Lecturer at Harvard, Andrews Norton, however, to know that the kind of biblical scholarship he associated with enlightenment was already passé in Germany. German scholars such as Johann G. Eichhorn, Johann Jakob Griesbach, Johann David Michaelis, and Johann Georg Rosenmüller were revolutionizing the field of biblical studies. The methods of taxonomical analysis and naturalistic interpretation developed by rationalist scholars were giving way to early forms of textual and source criticism in which the reconstruction of a text's historical background was held to be crucial to understanding it.

Channing criticized the flat-text fundamentalism of his conservative opponents, but rationalist biblical criticism contained flat-text assumptions of its own. Clarke and his followers harmonized discrepant accounts, approached interpretation as taxonomy, and provided naturalistic explanations for miraculous events. The new historical criticism dismantled this approach to scripture by exploring the history of the text itself. Historically oriented critics such as Eichhorn and Michaelis sought to decipher scriptural meaning by reconstructing the historical circumstances that produced the scriptural text.[71]

Channing recognized that this was where theology was going. Like Norton, he was not prepared to go very far in this direction, but he recognized the futility of opposing the current historical turn outright. While assuring them that all the old barricades against historical refutation were still in place, he therefore told the assembled liberals that they were obliged to analyze scriptural history and teaching critically in the manner of any other book: "Our leading principle in interpreting Scripture is this, that the Bible is a book written for men, in the language of men, and that its meaning is to be sought in the same manner as that of other books." The Bible is a complicated and demanding work, he cautioned: "It has infinite connections and dependences. Every proposition is linked with others, and is to be compared with others, that its full and precise import may be understood. Nothing stands alone."[72]

The latter was a Clarkeian theme, but Channing moved beyond the eighteenth century, if only with one foot: "We find, too, that the different portions of this book, instead of being confined to general truths, refer perpetually to the times when they were written, to states of society, to modes of thinking, to controversies in the church, to feelings and usages which have passed away, and without the knowledge of which we are constantly in danger of extending to all times and places what was of temporary and local application." With an assuring tone he suggested that modern biblical criticism could be a friend to Christianity. It promised to illuminate the meaning of scriptural teaching and solve long-standing interpretive problems: "With these views of the Bible, we feel it our bounden duty to exercise our reason upon it perpetually, to compare, to infer, to look beyond the letter to the spirit, to seek in the nature of the subject and the aim of the writer his true meaning; and, in general, to make use of what is known for explaining what is difficult, and for discovering new truths."[73]

A faithful church had no fear of any truth derived from reason. Reason disclosed the richness and hidden depths of biblical revelation to a forward-moving church. Channing assured that reason would never prove any contradiction in the Bible's teaching: "We believe that God never contradicts in one part of Scripture what He teaches in another; and never contradicts in revelation what He teaches in his works and providence." Nothing can be lost to Christianity by casting the searchlight of reason upon the books of revelation and nature, he insisted, for both are authored by the same rational divine Mind. This was why Unitarians had no qualms about rejecting interpretations of the Bible that violated the laws of nature or other truths established by reason. In dealing with the issue of variable interpretation, Channing explained, Unitarians selected the interpretation "which accords with the nature of the subject and the state of the writer, with the connection of the passage, with the general strain of Scripture, with the known character and will of God, and with the obvious and acknowledged laws of nature." Reason is the means that God has given us to understand the revelation of God's mind and will in scripture, history, and nature. Without reason, he warned, we are condemned to either universal skepticism or orthodox Calvinism. To Channing, these seeming opposites were, in effect, the same thing.[74]

He regarded both skepticism and Calvinism as forms of perverted intellectualism that used reason to annihilate the redemptive, God-given, truth-finding power of reason. "We object strongly to the contemptuous manner in which human reason is often spoken of by our adversaries," he declared, referring to Calvinists. "It is astonishing what a fabric they rear from a few slight hints about the fall of our first parents; and how ingeniously they extract from detached passages mysterious doctrines about the divine nature." Channing charged that Calvinists made use of reason in a manner that violated the fundamental rules of reasoning. Calvinist theology sacrificed the "general strain of Scripture" to a handful of proof texts, it privileged the obscure over the plain, and it taught that reason is depraved. "It is worthy of remark, how nearly the bigot and the sceptic approach," he mused, casually tagging Calvinists as bigots. "Both would annihilate our confidence in our faculties, and both throw doubt and confusion over every truth. We honor revelation too highly to make it the antagonist of reason, or to believe that it calls us to renounce our highest powers."[75]

In effect, Channing assured his audience that the old Christian rationalist arguments would suffice for a new generation. Liberal Christianity viewed itself as standing on the side of enlightenment, progress, moral sensitivity, and faithfulness. Its eighteenth-century rationalist forerunners had been required to establish that reason is the friend, not the enemy of faith. Clarke and Chauncy were sure that reason always confirms true faith because all truth comes from God. There is no conflict between reason and revelation because God does not contradict himself. Channing knew enough about the ongoing transformation of biblical criticism in Germany to realize that a new age in modern Christian self-understanding was beginning. He emphasized the problems of historical distance and relative context in scriptural interpretation to signal that American liberal Christianity was up to date. It was not long, however, before his structure of certainties appeared quaint at best to the movement he called into being. Liberal Christianity did not assure itself for long that it possessed a perfectly coherent and historically infallible revelation.

Channing genuinely believed that the divided house of American Protestant Christendom could be reunited if the church straightened out the irregularities of scripture. He had no concept of a Unitarian movement that did not assume and respect the Bible's revelational authority. His doctrine of scripture prescribed an apologetic agenda that repelled a succeeding generation of transcendentalists and that did not stand up to historical-critical scrutiny. A half-century after his death, American liberal Christianity as a whole was defined, in part, by its recognition that scriptural narrative and teaching contain contradictions. Channing's doctrine of scripture had a short life in the progressive Christian movement for which he spoke, but the doctrines that he derived from scripture epitomized the spirit of this movement in his time and defined much of American liberal theology for a century afterward. He proclaimed at Baltimore that, as a movement that recovered the authority and transforming spiritual power of the full biblical witness, liberal Christianity professed the unity of God, the unity of Christ, the moral perfection of God, the mediation of Christ, and the possibility of true holiness.

Channing's second major theme concerned the Trinity: "The proposition that there is one God seems to us exceedingly plain." It meant that God is one being with one mind. Trinitarians claimed to agree that God has only one mind, he noted, but they also spoke of God as "three intelligent agents, possessed of different consciousnesses, different wills, and different perceptions, performing different acts, and sustaining different relations." This language does not appear in the Bible or make any sense on its own, Channing admonished. Jesus worshiped the Father as the only living God and repeatedly spoke of the Father as superior to himself. "We challenge our opponents to adduce one passage in the New Testament where the word God means three persons," Channing declared. "From the many passages which treat of God, we ask for one, one only, in which we are told that He is a threefold being, or that He is three persons, or that He is Father, Son, and Holy Ghost." The doctrine of the Trinity is a later church deviation from the teaching of Jesus and the early church, he judged. The church of the apostles was too Jewish to come up with such a notion, and in the epistles "we see not a trace of controversy called forth by the Trinity."

Trinitarian doctrine was irrational and it distorted scripture; it also distorted Christian piety. Channing argued that the practical effect of the Trinitarian idea in Christian history was that it took from the Father "the supreme affection which is his due," and transferred it to Christ. In the course of church history, the exaltation of Christ into the Godhead turned Christ into the more interesting, and then more attractive, figure. Channing judged that Christian piety was grievously distorted by the later Christian fixation on "a bleeding, suffering God." He suggested that the same idolatrous impulse later gave rise to the cult of the Virgin Mary. "Men want an object of worship like themselves, and the great secret of idolatry lies in this propensity," he argued. "A God, clothed in our form, and feeling our wants and sorrows, speaks to our weak nature more strongly than a Father in heaven, a pure spirit, invisible and unapproachable, save by the reflecting and purified mind."[76]

Liberal Christianity was obliged to call Christians back to this more refined spiritual discipline. Channing exhorted that the purpose of true religion was to "spiritualize the mind," not create gods in our image. The Unitarian movement that was needed would therefore cultivate "deep veneration of the moral perfections of God." Channing's other planks spelled out the belief system of this spiritual vision. Against orthodox Christology, which distinguished between Christ's human and divine natures, he asserted that Jesus Christ "is one mind, one soul, one being, as truly one as we are, and equally distinct from the one God." The latter phrase smacked of Socinianism, but Channing bypassed the Arian/Socinian issue. This was the moment for Unitarian unity. He merely repeated that the assumption of Christ's subordination to the Father "pervades the New Testament" and argued that the speculative dualism of orthodox Christology turned Jesus into a figure "composed of incongruous and infinitely differing minds." For example, orthodox Christology imagined an infinite disjunction between the human and divine minds of Christ during his death on the cross, but liberal Christianity assumed with the New Testament that Jesus was a unified being who died in Godforsaken agony on the cross.

Channing's third major theme was the crucial one; it defined his liberalism: "We consider no part of theology so important as that which treats of God's moral character; and we value our views of Christianity chiefly as they assert his amiable and venerable attributes." Virtually all Christians attribute infinite justice, goodness, and holiness to God, he observed, but these ascriptions tell us very little, since people in all ages "have hoped to soothe the Deity by adulation." Christian history amply documents that it "is very possible to speak of God magnificently, and to think of him meanly; to apply to his person high-sounding epithets, and to his government principles which make him odious." Channing instructed that the views of God that people actually hold are disclosed not in the attributes they assign to God, but in the ways they conceive God's purposes, the principles by which God administrates the world, and, most importantly, "his disposition towards his creatures."

Here especially, liberal Christianity was a corrective to bad religion, which "tends strongly to pervert the moral faculty, to form a gloomy, forbidding, and servile religion, and to lead men to substitute censoriousness, bitterness, and persecution, for a tender and impartial charity." Genuine Christianity praises God not because God is overpowering, Channing declared, but because God is the perfection of virtue: "We cannot bow before a being, however great and powerful, who governs tyrannically. We respect nothing but excellence, whether on earth or in heaven. We venerate not the loftiness of God's throne, but the equity and goodness in which it is established." He took only a glancing swipe at Calvinist soteriology before turning to a favorite subject, the fatherhood of God. Think of how a good father loves his children, Channing exhorted. Think of how a father looks out for his children, cares for them, takes joy in their progress, hands out punishment for their misdeeds, and readily accepts their penitence. This picture has nothing to do with the vengeful, predestining deity pictured in orthodox theology, he insisted: "We look upon this world as a place of education, in which He is training men by prosperity and adversity, by aids and obstructions, . . . by a various discipline suited to free and moral beings, for union with himself, and for a sublime and ever-growing virtue in heaven."[77]

He conceded that the doctrine of atonement was more perplexing to liberals. Liberal Christians did not agree on the nature of Christ's mediating work, but Channing ventured that they surely agreed that the traditional view was horrible. In his reckoning, all liberal Christians believed that Christ was sent by the Father "to effect a moral or spiritual deliverance of mankind; that is, to rescue men from sin and its consequences, and to bring them to a state of everlasting purity and happiness." They also agreed that Christ accomplished this purpose by various means that included his compassionate moral example, his religious teaching, his promise of pardon to the penitent, his sacrificial suffering and death, and his resurrection to new life. Channing allowed that liberals disagreed on the precise influence of Christ's death on the reality of forgiveness. Some believed that Christ's death on the cross made the forgiveness of sin possible in some way, or contributed to the possibility of forgiveness, and thus contributed to our pardon. Others, himself included, believed that pertinent scriptural texts on the remission of sins were too peculiar and unclear to provide a biblical warrant for any version of the claim that Christ had to die to obtain or make possible the forgiveness of sins.

In either case, Channing assured, liberals surely agreed that the traditional doctrine of Christ's substitutionary atonement was "pernicious . . . unscriptural, and absurd." The notion that Christ had to die to appease the wrath of God for sin and pay off the debt of sinners was simply horrible, he asserted. It turned God into a monster. It communicated "very degrading views of God's character" and turned the mission of Christ on its head. Christ came to bring people to holiness, not to change God's mind, Channing protested: "How dishonorable to him is the supposition, that his justice is now so severe as to exact infinite punishment for the sins of frail and feeble men, and now so easy and yielding as to accept the limited pains of Christ's human soul as a full equivalent for the endless woes due from the world?" In place of the God of the Bible, he lamented, who was plenteous in forgiving sin, orthodox soteriology presented a god who refused to forgive anything apart from the sacrifice of a divine substitute: "A scheme more fitted to obscure the brightness of Christianity and the mercy of God, or less suited to give comfort to a guilty and troubled mind, could not, we think, be easily framed."[78]

Channing's favorite riposte claimed the simple gospel for liberal Christianity: "For ourselves, we have not so learned Jesus." He gave no quarter to the patripassionist position, whether conservatively or liberally interpreted, that God *himself* took on the suffering of the world in order to redeem it through his self-sacrificing love. This was an absurd fiction of theologians: "What can be plainer than that God cannot, in any sense, be a sufferer, or bear a penalty in the room of his creatures?" To his understanding, the gospel testimony to Christ as savior referred to Christ's saving moral example as "guide of the dark, diseased, and wandering mind." Christ was the model in whose image all are meant to be changed. Channing retold the gospel story from the standpoint of this theme, citing "the greatness of the work of Jesus, the spirit with which he executed it, and the sufferings which he bore for our salvation." The religion of Christ is the way to true holiness, he emphasized, not a doctrine about the abstract debt payment of a God-man. The way of Christ cultivates and is marked by the virtues of "the spirit of love, charity, meekness, forgiveness, liberality, and beneficence." Channing closed with the petition "that He will overturn, and overturn, and overturn the strongholds of usurpation, until He shall come whose right it is to rule the minds of men."[79]

CREATING AND DEFENDING
A LIBERAL DENOMINATION

The Baltimore sermon ignited a firestorm of controversy and made Channing famous. Published immediately as a pamphlet, his manifesto for Unitarian Christianity gained an enormous readership. It inspired a critical mass of pastors to stop equivocating about their liberalism. It simultaneously horrified and gratified conservatives, who at least were finally given the satisfaction of confronting an openly declared enemy. The pamphlet wars that it sparked raged throughout the 1820s and well into the 1830s. The spectacle of an ascending, openly Unitarian movement appalled orthodox conservatives such as Moses Stuart and Leonard Woods, both of Andover Seminary, who wrote detailed polemics against Channing's position.

A brilliant philologist and grammarian, later an eminent scripture scholar, Stuart was Andover Seminary's answer to Buckminster. He was also a chief beneficiary of the Buckminster library auction. Channing was no match for him on scholarly details or trends, though Stuart failed to catch Channing's implied distinction between scripture as revelation and scripture as the record of revelation. Stuart later admitted that if he had comprehended that Channing rejected the doctrine of scripture as verbally inspired revelation, he would have criticized Channing more sharply. As it was, he nearly read Channing out of the Christian church. For several years Stuart had worried that liberal Protestantism was producing a different religion in New England. His critique of Channing's manifesto allowed that Channing-style Unitarianism was still a form of Christianity, but only barely so. He protested that Channing allowed reason to function not merely as the interpreter of scriptural revelation, but also as its legislator. Even if Channing did not take the next logical step, he warned, it was inevitable that many of his followers would conclude "that the Bible is not of divine origin, and does not oblige us to belief or obedience." In Stuart's reading, Channing's appeal to the authority of scripture was fatally undermined by his attribution of authority to the laws of nature and other extrabiblical ideas.[80]

Woods, the other Andover polemicist, contended that one extrabiblical idea in particular made Channing's Unitarian Christianity an impossible mess of contradictions: his sentimental conception of God. Channing based his critique of Calvinism on his account of the "known character and will of God," and he vested this account with scripture-judging authority, but Woods observed that the Bible often presents a quite different picture of divine fatherhood. He played up the contrast:

> What human father, possessing even a common degree of paternal kindness and compassion, would ever treat his children, as God treated his rational offspring, when he destroyed the world by a deluge, or Sodom by fire, or when he caused the earth to open and swallow up the company of Korah? Would a compassionate father drown his children, or consume them by fire, or bury them alive in the earth?

Channing claimed to believe in the Bible, but, Woods charged, he ignored much of what the Bible says about God. Woods therefore turned Channing's charge of proof-texting against him, noting that, for all the points that Channing scored against traditional Christianity on this ground, he fashioned his position with isolated fragments of scripture. Channing's polemic against the moral repugnance of Calvinism was fueled by his appeal to the analogy of divine and human fatherhood, but from the standpoint of the entire biblical witness, Woods admonished, this analogy was grossly exaggerated. Human fatherhood belongs to the sphere of worldly domesticity, but the God of the Bible is infinite, transcendent, inscrutable, and righteous.[81]

Thus did the pamphlet wars of the 1820s begin. With occasional exceptions, Channing stayed out of the crossfire. He spelled out his commitment to Arian Christology in an essay titled "Objections to Unitarian Christianity Considered," but on most counts he lacked the requisite temperament and training to defend his position from detailed scholarly criticism. The task of defending Unitarianism from its chief critics thus fell mainly to Harvard professors Andrews Norton and Henry Ware, not without irony in Norton's case. In 1818 Channing had opposed Norton's appointment to the Dexter chair at Harvard on account of his polemical divisiveness. The following year he found himself encouraging Norton to defend Unitarianism from its polemical opponents.

Norton's opening defense took a pass at criticizing Stuart's hermeneutical procedure, contending that Stuart failed to establish clear rules of interpretation for scriptural study. His second offering made a stronger argument on a more sensitive issue. *A Statement of Reasons for Not Believing the Doctrines of Trinitarians* pronounced that classical Trinitarian theology was "essentially incredible." Though he allowed that pre-Nicene Trinitarianism was not *essentially* incredible inasmuch as it conceived the Son and Spirit as distinct beings derived from the Father, Norton judged that, by the early fifth century, Christian orthodoxy was hopelessly nonsensical by virtue of its attribution of divine personality to the Holy Spirit. "Three persons, each equally possessing divine attributes, are three Gods," he admonished. "A person is a being. No one who has any correct notion of the meaning of words will deny this." Norton assured that no discerning thinker "ever did, or ever could believe" that

Trinitarian teaching was true. On the side he noted his astonishment that Stuart bothered to read modern German scholars, since they really *were* heretics.[82]

Many others joined this factional war of words in the decade following Channing's call to freedom, most notably "Wood'n Ware," whose famously verbose rhetoric reached its climax with Ware's question about the orthodox portrayal of children. Did the orthodox doctrine of total depravity accurately describe the character of young children? Are children inclined to evil, and evil only? Ware emphatically answered no, claiming that "innocence, and simplicity, and purity are the characteristics of early life." He exhorted that it was unbiblical and ungodly to view little children exclusively as "objects of the divine displeasure and wrath, beings wholly averse to God and all that is good."[83]

These debates inflamed a deeper schism when church property became the issue. In the early 1820s, the essential structure of the colonial Puritan theocracy still existed in New England: the system of tax support for centers of public worship. In the Congregationalist churches, the Puritan-rooted distinction between the *parish* and the *church* made the politics of Unitarianism especially dicey. In New England Congregationalism the *parish*, generally defined as a town's entire group of male voters, was required to maintain, and was taxed to support, a system of public worship. In Boston, Salem, and Newburyport, it was also necessary to buy or rent a pew to be counted as a member of the parish. Boston Congregationalism was not elitist by accident. The *church* consisted of the religiously observant members of a parish who assented to a covenant, or made a confession of faith, or took part in the Lord's Supper. Many Massachusetts churches consisted largely of women. Thus the parish memberships were large and entirely male, while the church memberships were smaller and often mostly female. The distinction between the parish and church became critical during the Unitarian controversy. To whom did the church property belong when a schism over doctrine created a conflict between the parish and the church?

In 1820, the conservative majority of a congregation in Dedham, Massachusetts, pressed this question after its liberal parish appointed a liberal minister to the church's vacant pastorate. After two ecclesiastical councils came down on opposite sides of the conflict, the majority of the church withdrew from the parish and kept their church's property. The remaining church members sued for return of the property. The case rose to the Massachusetts Supreme Court, which ruled in 1820 that the protesting conservatives had no right to the building, communion silver, or anything else belonging to the church. It reasoned that "the only circumstance which gives a church any legal character is its connection with some regularly constituted society." In effect, the court ruled that the church belonged to the parish and that the parish had power over all civil matters pertaining to the church.[84]

Since most of the parishes in eastern Massachusetts were liberal and it was usually the conservatives who seceded from the churches, the Dedham decision was a devastating blow to orthodox and Hopkinsian Congregationalists. Many of them bitterly alleged that the judge in the Dedham case, a Unitarian, was corrupted by his sectarian interest. During the same year, Channing organized an association of liberal pastors called the Berry Street Conference. At the urging of younger Unitarians such as Henry Ware Jr., James Walker, and Ezra Stiles Gannett, who did not share Channing's reservations about starting a new denomination, the Berry Street Conference developed into a predenominational caucus. In 1825, the American Unitarian Association (AUA) was formed, more or less with Channing's approval, though he declined to serve as its president. The AUA had few resources and no authority over Unitarian churches. Less than half of the liberal congregations joined it, a dozen congregations split in a conservative direction, and for years nothing changed in appearances. The Unitarian congregations did not display any distinguishing or official designation.

The founding of the AUA was, nonetheless, an historic event. It formalized the separation between Congregationalism and a growing Unitarian movement. By the late 1820s, there were approximately 135 Unitarian churches in Massachusetts, nearly a hundred of which came off the Congregational rolls. Many of Congregationalism's largest and most prestigious churches and twenty of the twenty-five original churches in Massachusetts became Unitarian; in Boston, only the Old South Church remained Congregationalist. Conservatives consoled themselves with resentment-tinged slogans such as "They kept the furniture, but we kept the faith." Conservative leader Lyman Beecher offered a more pungent image: "They sowed tares while men slept and grafted heretical churches on orthodox stumps." His daughter, Harriet Beecher Stowe, recalled with slight hyperbole that when her father moved to Boston in 1825 to fight the Unitarian insurgency, orthodox Christians roamed the streets like wandering mendicants in a city they once ruled: "All the literary men of Massachusetts were Unitarian. All the trustees and professors of Harvard College were Unitarians. All the elite of wealth and fashion crowded Unitarian churches. The judges on the bench were Unitarian, giving decisions by which the peculiar features of church organization, so carefully ordained by the Pilgrim fathers, had been nullified." Upon taking over the old churches and foundations, she bitterly reflected, the liberals turned the reason for the existence of these institutions on its head: "A fund given for preaching an annual lecture on the Trinity was employed for preaching an annual attack upon it, and the Hollis professorship of divinity at Cambridge was employed for the furnishing of a class of ministers whose sole distinctive idea was declared warfare with the ideas and intentions of the donor."[85]

CHANNING AS LIBERAL LEADER AND APOLOGIST

Though he avoided organizational responsibilities, which were assumed chiefly by Gannett and Aaron Bancroft, and though he left the task of defending Unitarian theology chiefly to Norton and the elder Ware, Channing was the liberal movement's unrivaled spiritual leader throughout the 1820s and 1830s. His eloquence as a preacher, his increasing fame as a religious leader, and, within the Unitarian movement, his mediating posture as a religious thinker made him singularly valuable to the movement. Congregants packed his Federal Street Church in Boston with an admiring intensity that bordered on idolatry. At the same time, Channing's influence radiated well beyond the liberal movement. Ralph Waldo Emerson would later recall that "Dr. Channing, whilst he lived, was the star of the American Church, and we then thought, if we do not still think, that he left no successor in the pulpit." Though he allowed that Channing's coldly introspective temperament "made him the most unprofitable private companion," Emerson enthused that Channing was made for the public: "All America would have been impoverished in wanting him."[86] Upon Channing's death in 1842, Theodore Parker observed, "It is speaking with moderation to say, that no man, of our century, who writes the English tongue, had so much weight with the wise and pious men who speak it."[87]

A quarter-century after his death, memorialists were still struggling to account for the power of Channing's influence. Frederick Henry Hedge, a younger colleague of Channing's who was a minister and Harvard professor, a friend of Emerson, and the son of Harvard logician Levi Hedge, reflected in 1867 that it remained a curiosity "how this man—without learning, without research, not a scholar, not a critic, without imagination or fancy, not a poet, not a word-painter, without humor or wit, without profundity of thought, without grace of elocution—could, from the spiritual height on which he stood, by mere dint of gravity (coming from such an elevation), send his word into the soul with more searching force than all the orators of his time." As a privileged and intellectually gifted man of learning who never quite lived up to his own promise, Hedge exaggerated Channing's limitations, but he rightly pointed to Channing's riveting moral and spiritual sincerity as the source of his singular power. He explained that Channing "differed from the rest of us, not so much in severity of practice, as in spirituality of mind." He lived continually "in the contemplation and pursuit of the highest; the habit of viewing all things in reference to the supreme good."[88]

This quality made Channing a formidable liberal icon. Though he left the finer points to others, he promoted Unitarianism as a recovery of "pure Christianity." His movement polemic, "The Moral Argument against Calvinism," written in 1820, essentially pronounced "good-bye to all that." Orthodox Calvinism was almost unbelievably repugnant, Channing judged, and the idea of a moderate Calvinism would have struck Calvin himself "as a solecism, a contradiction in terms." Fortunately, he observed, the "progress of the human mind" and the "progress of the spirit of the gospel" were over-taking the power of Calvinism to terrify and depress people: "We think the decline of Calvinism one of the most encouraging facts in our passing history; for this system, by outraging conscience and reason tends to array these high faculties against revelation. Its errors are peculiarly mournful, because they relate to the character of God. It darkens and stains his pure nature, spoils his character of its sacredness, loveliness, glory, and thus quenches the central light of the universe, makes existence a curse, and the extinction of it a consummation devoutly to be wished."[89]

The following year, in his Dudleian Lecture at Harvard, Channing pressed a vigorous case for the intelligibility of Unitarian supernaturalist rationalism, especially its use of reason to provide "evidences" of revealed religion. He defended the historicity and necessity of the miracle events recorded in scripture, taking special aim at David Hume's contention that all testimonies to miracles conflict with the laws of nature known to human experience. Channing countered that it was contradictory to speak of human experience as an absolute authority if it was true, as Hume attested, that the senses sometimes give false reports. Hume's dismissal of miracles on the basis of knowledge given to the senses subverted the very order of nature on which his argument rested, Channing argued, "for this order of nature is learned only by the exercise of my senses and judgment, and if these fail me in the most unexceptionable circumstances, then their testimony to nature is of little worth." Since God is the author of the order of nature, the serious question for theology was not whether God could cause a miracle, but why God would do so. Channing answered that God's purpose is always "to form and advance the mind." The order of nature is not an end in itself, but merely the chief means by which God brought about his overriding purpose. It followed that the divine miracles described in scripture were enacted to advance the progress of mind in instances where a departure from the regular order of nature was required.[90]

While asserting that Christian faith does not require external proofs, Channing rushed to provide them. He observed that "the worst abuses of our religion have sprung from this cowardly want of confidence in its power. Its friends have feared that it could not stand without a variety of artificial buttresses." At the same time he excused his own evidentialist proofs from the category of artificial buttresses.[91] If he had to choose between reason and revelation, he explained, he would choose reason, since it would be wrong "to sacrifice to any religion that reason which lifts me above the brute and constitutes me a man." In fact, however, Channing found the idea of such a conflict almost impossible to conceive, because he viewed Christianity as rationality itself expressed in religious terms. The truth of Christianity is "founded in our nature," he reasoned: "It meets our deepest wants. Its proofs as well as principles are adapted to the common understandings of men, and need not be aided by appeals to fear or any other passion." Though it needed no external proofs, Christianity thus abounded in them, among which Channing counted various historical facts reported in the Gospels, the brief historical interval between the death of Jesus and the writing of the Gospels, the "native frankness" of the Gospel narratives, and the marks of their apostolic authorship.[92]

This blend of liberal spirituality, biblicism, and rationalistic proofs served liberal Christianity well during its movement-making early years. Much of Channing's immense value to the Unitarian church derived from the mediating role that he played in holding together its conflicting theological tendencies.

American Unitarianism broke apart in the 1830s with the rise of Emersonian transcendentalism, but the seeds of this generational schism existed a decade earlier. On one side, old-style supernaturalist rationalists like Norton, Henry Ware, and Nathaniel L. Frothingham upheld Channing's claims about the authority of scripture, the historicity of the biblical miracle stories, the historical reliability of biblical narrative in general, and the rational nature of divine revelation. The older Unitarians were liberal, to be sure, but barely so in comparison to a rapidly historicizing liberal movement in Germany. They loathed the impious spirit of German theology and its deconstruction of the biblical text. They recycled with alarm the reports of a young Harvard student, George Bancroft, that his theology courses at Göttingen were so "vulgar and indecent" that they "would have disgraced a jail-yard or a fishmarket." Bancroft claimed that in Eichhorn's classroom, "the bible is treated with very little respect, and the narratives laughed at as an old wive's tale, fit to be believed in the nursery." The old Unitarians took such reports very seriously, with Norton taking personal responsibility for making sure that American Unitarian liberalism stopped short of German radical liberalism. He fervently opposed Eichhorn's higher critical deconstruction of the scriptural text into a multiplicity of authorial traditions and later rejected Eichhorn's "original gospel" theory of Gospel origins and the entire German critical focus on the literary interdependence of the Gospels. Norton saw clearly that Eichhorn-style criticism threatened to dismantle the historical basis of his apologetic. Though he did not fit the picture of the unfeeling "corpse-cold" empiricist that Emerson later pinned on the Unitarian establishment, Norton did believe that all would be lost if Unitarianism did not hold fast to the historicity and rationality of the New Testament.[93]

Most of the Unitarian establishment agreed with him. They took offense at the German critical tendency to sweep away the Gospel miracles. Some of the old-guard Unitarians followed Norton in giving ample leeway to Old Testament criticism, but virtually all of them insisted, like him, that the Gospels were independently written accounts authored by apostolic witnesses or companions of the apostles. They believed that the Gospel narratives were nearly always reliable as history and that Unitarian doctrine was rationally provable. They also had a pietistic side that later interpreters either overlooked or, under Emerson's influence, unfairly denied. Even the frostiest New England Unitarian congregations warmed to the gentle emotional hymnody of English dissenters Isaac Watts (1674–1748) and Philip Doddridge (1702–51). The old-school Unitarians blasted their opponents with appeals to logic, historical evidence, and John Locke, but many of them shared Channing's tender piety. Norton, for example, was extremely sentimental in his personal relations, especially with women and children. He loved romanticist poetry, wrote a good deal of it himself, and was easily wounded by criticism.[94]

The differences between the old-school Unitarian rationalists and the generation of Unitarian pietists who succeeded them are therefore easily

exaggerated, and often are. Many of the old-school Unitarians were temperamentally warmer than Emerson, and the middle-generation pietistic Unitarians
who preceded Emerson were good Unitarians, not transcendentalists. Viewed
historically, however, it is not incorrect to view such figures as Buckminster,
Henry Ware Jr., and John Emery Abbot as forerunners of the transcendentalist
reaction. During the period that liberal Christianity became a movement and
embraced the Unitarian label, these liberal pietists and others like them established a form of Unitarian religion that reversed Norton's priorities. Without
opposing the apologetic dogmas of Norton, Channing, and the elder Ware, they
emphasized what they called "the religion of the heart." Unwittingly, they paved
the way, in New England Unitarianism, for the transcendentalist movement.
To the extent that he was viewed, rightly, as the father of them all, so did
Channing.

Henry Ware Jr. was pastor of Second Church, Boston; before his untimely
death in 1817, John Emery Abbot pastored North Church, Salem. Together
with Buckminster, Charlestown pastor (and later Harvard president) James
Walker, and others, they established a form of New England Unitarianism that
valued spiritual living more than correct doctrine. Like Buckminster at Brattle
Street Church, though without his elitist aestheticism, Abbot devoted his ministry to the cultivation of emotional refinement, preaching sermons of tender
pathos and affectionate, personal warmth that made piety the central concern of
religion. In his services, the sermon blended easily with the gentle hymnody
of Watts and Doddridge. The younger Ware maintained a more balanced integration of rationalist and pietist commitments than his colleagues, but all the
"heart-religion" Unitarians devoted their ministries and scholarly work to
the cultivation of the affections. They gave respectful assent to Channing's
apologetic proofs, but what moved them more profoundly and fired their own
sermonizing was the impression of more deeply rooted spiritual truth that his
preaching conveyed. Ware was a leading advocate of personal, extemporaneous preaching. His sermons and writings radiated a persistent concern with the
spiritual life, especially character formation and the cultivation of love for God.

His ministry also became the means by which Ralph Waldo Emerson became
an ordained Unitarian pastor. Through pastoral skill and frenetic overwork, Ware
rebuilt Second Church into a thriving parish in the 1820s. In 1828,
after Ware fell gravely ill, Emerson substituted for him. The following year,
Ware's congregation hired Emerson as an assistant pastor, with the understanding that Emerson would soon succeed Ware. In the misguided pursuit of a less
stressful vocation, Ware had accepted a faculty position at what was then called
The Theological School (of Cambridge). Emerson was ordained in March 1829,
believing that stirring utterance on spiritual themes was the heart of the ministerial vocation. Ware, by then, had misgivings about Emerson's capacity and
desire to sustain his beloved congregation. Although he at first believed that his
own biblically oriented piety and Emerson's inward-looking poetic spirituality
were similar, within a few months, Ware realized, to his disappointment, that

Emerson's religion, whatever it was, was qualitatively different from his own. Emerson became a pastor with the thought of inspiring others in the way that Channing, Edward Everett, and, to a lesser extent, the younger Ware had inspired him. Fatefully for Unitarianism, Emerson soon reconsidered his judgment that the church was a good venue for prophetic utterance.[95]

BEYOND LIBERAL RATIONALISM: EMERSON AND THE POETIC SPIRIT

As a child and later as a minister, Ralph Waldo Emerson was a product of Boston Unitarianism. He cherished this inheritance long after he renounced Unitarianism. Like Channing, Emerson lost his father at a young age; even more than Channing, he retained mostly negative memories of his father while acquiring the religious strain in his personality from his mother.

His father, William Emerson, was the pastor of First Church in Boston and a pillar of Boston-area liberal Congregationalism. Channing was a friend and Buckminster a close colleague and rival. William Emerson was a Federalist in politics, a well-read, rationalistic Unitarian in theology, and a stern father, though perhaps not as cold or severe as Emerson biographers, following their subject's lead, later claimed. One of his sons and both of his daughters died in early childhood, leaving five surviving sons whose ages were separated by a range of only seven years. Ralph was the second oldest of this group. His father's hero was Charles Chauncy, whose portrait hung in the dining room and after whom one of the Emerson boys was named.

William Emerson wrote nothing of note, but he gave much attention to literary concerns, serving for a brief time as editor of *The Monthly Anthology.* His bland, high-minded sermons were tinged with a suggestion of deism. His private Christology was Socinian, though his sermons were carefully vague on the subject; Emerson later recalled that his father showed "a studied reserve on the subject of the nature and offices of Jesus." He thus epitomized everything that Emerson later condemned in the cold rationalism of the Unitarian establishment, except its defensiveness about the miracles of Jesus. Emerson's mother, Ruth, more pious than her husband, who died when Emerson was eight, consumed devotional literature and, like Channing's mother, maintained a disciplined individual prayer life while holding her family together. She raised her sons in the company of highly literate and religiously intense women like herself, especially Emerson's brilliant aunt, Mary Moody Emerson, who influenced him profoundly for many years.[96]

Emerson's Aunt Mary, his father's sister, gave him a model of artful, shimmering writing. Emerson loved her rhetorical inventiveness, especially her distinctive wordplays and parades of images, and savored her letters for decades. Mary Emerson prized her literary freedom and unmarried independence. She mentored all the Emerson boys after her brother died, and for many years,

Ralph Waldo gave no sign of being the one who would repay her years of religious and literary instruction. He became one of her favorites only after he chose to enter the ministry under the influence of the contemporary religious figure she admired most, although in a short time, he would fall to the bottom of her list.

Mary Moody Emerson is usually identified in the Emerson literature as a Calvinist, but in fact she was a deeply conflicted Unitarian. She revered Channing most of the time, but she also accused Unitarianism of ruining the Congregational church. On most days, her religious worldview closely resembled Channing's blend of liberal Unitarian, rationalist, romanticist, and orthodox elements. Theologically, she ascribed to the same Arian Unitarian tradition to which her brother belonged, but, like Channing, she clung to a cluster of spiritually rooted orthodox and romantic convictions that were foreign to her brother; unlike Channing, she also worried that even Unitarianism at its best was too Arminian. Mary Emerson described herself variously as a Paulinist, an "old Unitarian," a "bible theist," and, most tellingly, a "deistical pietist." Her favorite religious writers were Samuel Clarke and Richard Price. With her brother's example closely in mind, she passionately opposed the secularizing deism that she judged was overtaking the liberal churches and claimed to prefer old-style Calvinism to it. At least Calvinism took seriously the realities of the soul, death, and eternal life, she explained. Moreover, New England Calvinism produced Jonathan Edwards, whose nature-aestheticism and deep piety she respected greatly. Mary Emerson's opinions on these themes acquired a harshly judgmental tone after her nephew made a public display of his heresy. She attacked what she viewed as the heretical drift of the Unitarian movement so bitterly that many Emerson interpreters have tagged her as some kind of Calvinist. His patronizing tone aside, Emerson gave a more discerning account of her religious conservatism. In the early 1830s, upon hearing that she sharply disapproved of his heathen syncretism and apparent disbelief in a personal God, Emerson remarked that his aunt was not a Calvinist but wished everybody else to be one.[97]

These were the decisive influences that shaped Emerson's early life and worldview. He was raised by a circle of highly expressive women who cultivated his literary and religious interests and who admired Channing above all other contemporary religious figures, because they judged that his eloquence proceeded from "an acquaintance with his own heart." As a youth, Ralph Waldo Emerson disappointed them. He seemed less suited for intellectual endeavor, or success of any kind, than his achievement-oriented brothers, and his early performance as a student at Harvard was mediocre. In the year that Edward Everett returned to Harvard to assume his chair as Eliot Professor of Greek Literature, Emerson was a depressed and underachieving junior. On the whole, he had found the college's prescribed course of study deflating, mechanical, and unsuited to his strengths. His Aunt Mary had taught him to love literary inventiveness, but, in his reckoning, Harvard seemed mostly concerned to correct his grammar and drill facts into him. He later remarked that even though people knew that the university was hostile to genius, they sent their children anyway and hoped for the best. In September 1819, his new teacher's arrival was keenly anticipated. Everett had graduated with highest honors from Harvard in 1811, earned a master's degree, and served briefly as a pastor at Brattle Street Church before being named to the Eliot chair in 1815. He was the first American to earn a Ph.D., completing his doctorate at Göttingen in 1817 in preparation for assuming the Eliot chair. Finally, after four years of study in Europe, he was ready to begin his teaching career. It took him only a few weeks to rouse Emerson from his depression and give Andrews Norton chastening exposure to the future of historical criticism.[98]

Everett introduced students and colleagues to the higher criticism of German scholarship. He spelled out the implications of Eichhorn-style biblical criticism. He taught that a similar analysis by F. A. Wolf made a strong case for the multiple authorship of the *Iliad* and the *Odyssey.* He explained that a new approach to the study of religion, pioneered by Christian Gottlob Heyne, showed that all religions began as mythology. Most importantly, in word and by the power of his example, Everett convinced his students that rhetorical eloquence is one of the highest manifestations of art. In his later career he became a congressman, governor of Massachusetts, minister to England, president of Harvard, secretary of state, and U.S. senator, but Everett attained much of his early fame as the figure who inspired the American transcendentalists.

Emerson later would compare Everett's impact on the transcendentalist generation to that of Pericles in Athens: "Germany had created criticism in vain for us until 1820, when Edward Everett returned from his five years in Europe, and brought to Cambridge his rich results, which no one was so fitted by natural grace and the splendor of his rhetoric to introduce and recommend." Everett possessed a gift of inspiration "which did not go beyond his head, but which made him the master of elegance." His "special learning" had an electrifying effect on students, Emerson remembered, "and all his learning was available for purposes of the hour. It was all new learning, that wonderfully took and stimulated the young men." Emerson was enthralled by his teacher's flowing array of allusions, daring images, stunning wordplays, parables, and quotations: "All his speech was music, and with such variety and invention that the ear was never tired."[99]

Intellectually, emotionally, even physically, Emerson came alive. Though he never completely shook off the effects of poor health or his feelings of being "vagrant" and "hollow," Everett showed him that the life of the mind could be exciting. Emerson read avidly in history and literature, especially imaginative literature, and started calling himself Waldo. Under the influence of Everett's dazzling intellectual performances, giving thought to his future only a few months before graduation, he dutifully attended Channing's Dudleian Lecture on Christian evidences. The college laws, forty pages in length, required his attendance. Emerson respected the Channings. His mother had joined Channing's church after the death of her husband, and at Harvard, his rhetoric professor was Edward Tyrell Channing, a younger brother. Yet he would not have faced a lecture on Christian apologetics with great enthusiasm, for even during his early ministerial career, Emerson took minimal interest in evidentialist arguments for Christian belief. Nonetheless, he was unexpectedly converted by Channing's poetic spirit, impressed not by the evidences, but by the spiritual art that he sensed in Channing's presentation. A lifetime of misgivings about the pulpit, Unitarianism, and his father's world fell away; he was moved by his Aunt Mary's favorite religious figure to enter the ministry. For the rest of his life he cited this experience as a crucial turning point.[100]

Upon beginning his studies in theology, Emerson reflected that imagination was the driving force in his life and produced in him "a keen relish for the beauties of poetry." He had no hope of writing a book like Butler's *Analogy of Religion*: "Nor is it strange that with this confession I should choose theology, which is from everlasting to everlasting 'debateable Ground.'" Emerson judged that "Reasoning Machines" did not produce good theology, whether the machine was like John Locke, Samuel Clarke, or David Hume. What did make theology worthwhile, even beautiful, he reasoned, was imagination, like the moral imagination that Channing possessed. To pursue theology as a form of imaginative reflection was "akin to the higher flights of the fancy," and such flights, he believed, were his strong suit. In the study and practice of divinity, he reflected, "I hope to thrive. I inherit from my sire a formality of manner and speech, but I derive from him or his patriotic parent a passionate love for the strains of eloquence."[101]

Like many Harvard divinity students of his generation, Emerson undertook some of his theological studies with Channing on an independent basis, "for the sake of saying I am studying divinity."[102] During the same period, he wrote to his Aunt Mary that Channing's preaching was gloriously inspiring to him: "Dr. Channing is preaching sublime sermons every Sunday morning in Federal Street one of which I heard last Sunday, and which infinitely surpassed Everett's eloquence. It was a full view of the subject of the light of Revelation compared with Nature and to shew the insufficiency of the latter alone. Revelation was as much a part of the order of things as any other event in the Universe."[103] Though Channing's prose style was too unadorned for some, like Frederic Hedge, to hear the creative spiritual art it contained, Emerson and many others found it profoundly inspiring. In the mid-1820s, at the height of his creative power and influence as a preacher, Channing began to develop a related literary style that prefigured the Emersonian essay.

CULTURAL CRITICISM:
CHANNING'S LITERARY TURN

Channing was a keen judge of the poetry and literature that reflected his own spiritual sensibility. He especially loved the poetry of Samuel Taylor Coleridge and William Wordsworth, both of whom he knew personally; with Mary Emerson, he was among the first Americans to herald Wordsworth's poetic genius. In the mid-1820s, while younger followers like Ezra Stiles Gannett and Henry Ware Jr. struggled to build an institutionalized Unitarian movement, Channing branched out to literary and cultural criticism, starting with a perceptive essay on Milton. Channing argued that Milton's poetry exemplified his own ideal of poetry as a mode of inspiration and claimed that Milton, because of his greater capacity for aspiration, was a greater prose artist than Samuel Johnson. Milton and Johnson both had a genius for showing the condition of a fallen humanity, he explained, but Milton possessed, in unique measure, an unbounded quality of mind that allowed him to imagine a higher state of mind within all humanity. Channing allowed himself the partisan aside that Milton also opposed the doctrine of the Trinity.[104]

His literary criticism included essays on Napoleon Bonaparte, Francois de Salignac de La Moth Fénelon, and the lack of a worthy American national literature. Channing reserved a special loathing for Napoleon, but he analyzed the seductive attraction and pathos of Napoleon's "blinding egotism" with an empathic understanding that disclosed his own often-obscured realism about human nature. Napoleon's attainment of power did not make him free, he cautioned; for lack of an inner moral life, Napoleon was a slave. He had no experience whatever of the freedom that derives from virtuous self-disregard: "Though clothed with the power of a god, the thought of consecrating himself to the introduction of a new and higher era, to the exaltation of the character and condition of his race, seems never to have dawned on his mind. The spirit of disinterestedness and self-sacrifice seems not to have waged a moment's war with self-will and ambition."[105]

Emerson later praised Channing's essays on Milton and Napoleon as the first American examples of what he called *Edinburgh Review*–style "large criticism." In an essay on the problem of American literature, Channing keenly prefigured a central Emersonian theme:[106] With the same concern that he applied to Milton and Napoleon, he analyzed the problem of American cultural development in terms of its expansive capacity and relative moral growth. Channing loved the American experiment and celebrated American liberty and democracy. He cherished the hope that his country would become not merely prosperous, but great in character. A half-century after the United States gained its political independence, he yearned for signs that America was becoming a genuinely independent country where it mattered most, but sadly judged that his country showed barely any sign of cultural refinement. In terms of cultural self-definition and accomplishment, America barely existed, with no literature, very little research, and no intellectual culture to speak of. "We know it will be said that we cannot afford these. But it is not so. We are rich enough for ostentation, for intemperance, for luxury. We can lavish millions on fashion, on furniture, on dress, on our palaces, on our pleasures; but we have nothing to spend for the mind. Where lies our poverty? In the purse, or in the soul?"[107]

He cautioned that rightly believing in the divine capacities of human nature has nothing to do with ignoring the predatory evils of human beings. Though he reverenced human nature, Channing knew its history of crimes. He understood why so many people believed that humans are beasts, safe only in chains, and needing of masters. "But injured, trampled on, and scorned as our nature is, I still turn to it with intense sympathy and strong hope. . . . "The signatures of its origin and its end are impressed too deeply to be ever wholly effaced. I bless it for its kind affections, for its strong and tender love. I honor it for its struggles against oppression, for its growth and progress under the weight of so many chains and prejudices, for its achievements in science and art, and still more for its examples of heroic and saintly virtue. These are marks of a divine origin and the pledges of a celestial inheritance; and I thank God that my own lot is bound up with that of the human race."[115]

SPIRITUAL IDEALISM
AS RELUCTANT RADICALISM

American liberal Christianity in its first cycle of moral optimism got its bearings and took its distinctive path by emphasizing humanity's divinely endowed capacity for good. Channing, who gave classic utterance to this theme, epitomized the difference that it made for theology and personal religion. In crucial respects, his thinking was decidedly preliberal, but his spellbinding preaching of the theme that American liberal Protestantism first claimed for itself made him a revered figure in liberal Christian circles long after his fustier Unitarian contemporaries were forgotten. Aside from his venerable status, Channing's sublime exposition of the divine likeness in humanity spared him from most transcendentalist attacks after the transcendentalists rebelled against their Unitarian fathers. Near the end of his life, while the transcendentalist controversy was at its height, he capsulized the controlling concern of his life's writings by remarking that "a respect for the human soul breathes through them."[116]

Channing exemplified the meaning of this faith for personal religion throughout his ministry. In mid-career, he became its champion in the spheres of theology and church politics, taking on the burden of factional leadership responsibilities that went against his predispositional caution and ecumenism. In the last twelve years of his life, his respect for the human soul drove him into wilder territory. Channing is the rare figure who became more progressive and outspoken with age. This gradual transformation is all the more remarkable because he possessed a decidedly aristocratic temperament and spent most of his life serving the religious needs of privileged-class Bostonians.

In his early career, he was so cautious that colleagues were unable to discern if he stood for anything on divisive issues. By mid-career, he was a heretical liberal who convinced a critical mass of status-anxious Congregationalist pastors to wear the Unitarian label as a badge of honor. In his last years, he committed himself to various social causes that outraged many of his congregants, some of his relatives, and most of his polite society friends. Channing was selectively naïve about politics for most of his life, but he increasingly perceived the class limitations of his idealism. He moved to the religious and democratic left throughout his later career, steadily though always methodically, hesitantly, and with the appearance of genuine reluctance. As a preacher on moral progress who sought with utmost sincerity to practice what he preached, he took it to heart in the 1830s when less-privileged social reformers, especially abolitionists, told him that he stood in the way of progress.

Channing's hatred of tyranny was the animating core of his politics. His sermons and lectures against militarism, standing armies, imperialism, and government interference flowed from his abhorrence of domination. He felt deeply the horror and depravity of war, as well as its occasional unavoidability.[117] His support of democracy flowed mainly from his feelings about tyranny. Channing cherished democracy to the extent, and on the condition, that it strengthened the rights of individuals. Though it took him many years to recognize that most of his office-holding Federalist friends did not share his love of American democracy, he viewed civilization, democracy, and true religion as an interconnected way of life that stood in opposition to aristocracy and tyranny.

"I know no wisdom but that which reveals man to himself, and which teaches him to regard all social institutions, and his whole life, as the means of unfolding and exalting the spirit within him. All policy which does not recognize this truth seems to me shallow."[118] This programmatic statement, written early in Channing's progressive-activist closing years, expressed the order of values that fueled his social activism. Social institutions are good to the extent that they contribute to the flourishing of individuals, he argued. They are harmful whenever they are given equal or higher value than individual development. In like manner, he reasoned, civil and political liberty are valuable in themselves and as means to freedom of spirit, but they are less intrinsically valuable than spiritual freedom. "A man is not created for political relations as his highest end, but for indefinite spiritual progress," Channing explained. "The human soul is greater, more sacred, than the state, and must never be sacrificed to it." He therefore opposed his office-holding friends who asserted the priority of their notion of a national interest: "To me, the progress of society consists in nothing more than in bringing out the individual, in giving him a consciousness of his own being, and in quickening him to strengthen and elevate his own mind."[119]

SOCIAL JUSTICE
AND THE ABOLITIONIST QUESTION

In 1830, Channing knew where this argument needed to take him. On a health-seeking trip to St. Croix in the West Indies he was forced to face the enslavement of human beings. "This infinite wrong cannot endure for ever in

He spoke and wrote repeatedly against slavery in the United States and West Indies, which drew him into contact with movement abolitionists. In 1836 he told English social activist Harriet Martineau, "I am more and more willing to accept the enthusiasm of men in a glorious cause, with all its errors." The same year, in an open letter to antislavery journalist James G. Birney, he defended the abolitionists with ringing praise—"They have rendered to freedom a more essential service than any body of men among us. . . . I look on them with unmixed respect"—before mixing in his usual complaints that the movement was too condemnatory and self-righteous.[128] The following year he enlisted against the annexation of Texas, writing an inflamed protest to Henry Clay, and took a leading role in organizing a Faneuil Hall protest meeting against the murder of Elijah Lovejoy by a proslavery mob in Alton, Illinois.[129] By 1840 it was second nature to Channing, though still remarkable to Emerson, to take part in something like the Garrison-organized Convention of Friends of Universal Reform, which Emerson described as a gathering of "Madmen, madwomen, men with beards, Dunkers, Muggletonians, Come-outers, Groaners, Agrarians, Seventh-Day Baptists, Quakers, Abolitionists, Calvinists, Unitarians and Philosophers."[130]

This activism cut against Channing's temperament and preferences. He preferred abstractions to specific commitments, and if his conscience had allowed, he would have ended his career preaching word paintings of religious ideals. As it was, his conscience did not allow him merely to preach the good without struggling for it, but he did not convince his congregation. Channing was chastened in later life by the realization that his congregation had little tolerance for social justice politics. Most of his later activism was repugnant to the wealthy church officers at Federal Street Church who paid his salary. In the mid-1830s, his involvement in the antislavery movement turned the church into a zone of hostility for him, as members of his once-adoring congregation took to insulting him in the street. Channing usually claimed that he was unfazed by the frontal attacks, cutting remarks, and criticism that he endured. On one occasion he assured Elizabeth Peabody, "I care little for opinion, because it does not run in my channel." In truth, however, Channing was deeply hurt by the loss of his affectionate religious home. He arranged a partial retirement to his farm in Rhode Island to avoid having to deal with disapproving church members. In 1840, his congregation delivered its crowning response to his activism by refusing to permit a memorial service for his cherished friend, antislavery activist Charles Follen. Channing admitted afterward that he wondered whether anything was left of his ministry. Though he remained the church's nominal pastor, he severed his financial connection to it and only rarely preached there again.[131]

Channing's abolitionism cost him his Federal Street home, but he did not find a home among abolitionists. He and Garrison both hated slavery, but otherwise they were opposites. Garrison burned with righteous impatience, his language was harsh and self-dramatizing, and he condemned his enemies as a class. Channing avoided conflict as much as conscience allowed, he examined all sides of every issue before making a decision, and he judged that most slaveholders were probably no less moral than other persons. Though he defended the abolitionists repeatedly and heightened the public respectability of their cause, especially among ministers, he also criticized abolitionist leaders in ways that ensured their enmity. Three factors alienated him from Garrison: Channing claimed that the only good way to abolish slavery was by gradual change through moral persuasion, he refused to condemn all the slaveholders, and he charged that the abolitionists were consumed with self-righteousness.[132]

He was capable of willful nonsense on this subject. Channing contended that the duty of "settling and employing the best methods of liberation" belonged solely to the slaveholders. "We have no right of interference, nor do we desire it," he assured. He assigned "the highest importance" to the attainment of a "friendly relation" between master and slave during and after the disestablishment of slavery. To this end, he reasoned, "the latter must see in the former his benefactor and deliverer." Channing and Garrison agreed that moral persuasion, not politics, was the key to abolition, but they disagreed about gradualism and the slaveholders. Channing opposed immediate emancipation on the ground that the abolition sought by Garrison would be disastrous for the slaves. He countered that an emancipation worthy of the name was within reach if enlightenment and moral progress continued on both sides. Channing claimed to believe that the convicting power of moral truth would be enough to make the slaveholders voluntarily abolish the entire system of slavery. "Breathe into men a fervent purpose, and you awaken powers before unknown," he exhorted. "How soon would slavery disappear were the obligation to remove it thoroughly understood and deeply felt!"[133]

Channing and Garrison both naïvely believed that slavery could be abolished by moral persuasion alone, yet Channing's naïveté on this point was linked to his deep moral seriousness on the issue of abolitionist self-righteousness. Channing conceded to the Garrisonites that many of the slaveholders deserved "the severest reprobation" for their hateful love of tyranny: "They perpetuate this odious system not reluctantly, but from choice; not because the public safety compels them, as they think, to act the part of despots, but because they love despotism, and count money their supreme good." Such people cared nothing about the bodies that they mutilated and the souls that they crushed, he recognized; for them "no rebuke can be too severe."[134]

He refused to believe, however, that the majority of slaveowners belonged to this category. More importantly he clung to the illusion that most slaveholders would set their slaves free if they were morally persuaded of the righteousness of this action. Channing imagined that many of them believed it was their moral duty to maintain the system of slavery out of concern for their presumedly incompetent slaves. "I believe that the majority, could they be persuaded of the consistency of emancipation with the well-being of the colored race and with social order, would relinquish their hold on the slave, and sacrifice their imagined property in him to the claims of justice and humanity,"

2.

Subversive Intuitions:

Ralph Waldo Emerson, Theodore Parker,
and the Transcendentalist Revolt

American Unitarianism in Channing's generation was a form of liberal
Christianity, although not in the full-orbed sense that "liberal" would acquire
later in the nineteenth century. One could say that liberal Christianity stepped
into the nineteenth century with one foot. Channing-style theology was liberal
in its religious humanism and individualism, but its defining belief in the
enlightening universality of reason curtailed its acceptance of historical criticism. Channing had little historical consciousness at all, and the rather stodgy
group of Unitarian rationalists for which he spoke possessed even less. They
applied historical criticism to certain postbiblical developments that they
rejected, but eschewed its application to the ground on which they stood. Their
mid-century successors took historical criticism further, but, with one exception, only modestly so by the standard of the generation that succeeded them.
The exception is the main subject of this chapter.

One of the ironies of American theological liberalism is that the first
American attempt to appropriate for theology the verdicts of modern historical
criticism was led by transcendentalist Unitarians who sought to minimize the
importance of history. The story of the transcendentalist revolt is familiar to
American readers by virtue of Emerson's canonical status in American literature.

As an episode in the history of American theological liberalism, however, the transcendentalist revolt is significant chiefly for producing Theodore Parker. Both Emerson and Parker advised liberal Christians to employ historical criticism to demote the importance of history for religious belief.

EMERSON'S ROAD TO TRANSCENDENTALISM

Ralph Waldo Emerson, the American apostle of self-religion, acquired secondhand most of his scholarly acquaintance with the topic of transcendentialism. As a college student, he was enthralled by Edward Everett's descriptions of contemporary Göttingen-style historical criticism, especially Johann Gottfried Eichhorn's biblical criticism and the early history of religions' mythography of Christian Gottlob Heyne. In the mid-1820s, his older brother William began to play a similar educational role for him. Against Channing's advice that modern German criticism was destructive, William enrolled at Göttingen during the same year (1824) that Waldo began his study in theology at Harvard Divinity School. William listened to Eichhorn lecture on biblical criticism; Waldo worked independently with Channing and struggled with the Bible concordances, lexicons, atlases, harmonies, commentaries, and language aids that Channing assigned to him. The brothers judged, at first, that William had the better deal. Repeatedly William exhorted Waldo to learn German and join him in Göttingen. In the meantime he urged his younger brother to read Schleiermacher and Johann Gottfried Herder and get started on Hebrew. Emerson took his advice on Schleiermacher and Herder, to the extent that he could read them in English; but he balked at learning Hebrew and German and sailing to Germany.[1]

He tried to will himself through Channing's thirty-four-page syllabus of scripture studies while consoling himself with Schleiermacher and Rousseau on the side. In February 1825 he became a full-time divinity student, but within a month of moving into Divinity Hall, Emerson lost his sight. Half the adults in Boston had tuberculosis; he was undoubtedly one of them. His eyes and limbs suffered from painful rheumatic inflammation, and his eyes worsened with the strain of doing tedious academic work, so that for several months he was unable even to write in his journal. As he gradually regained his sight over the succeeding months, Emerson resolved that he would use it to read Plato, Plutarch, and Montaigne, not Bible atlases.

Then in October 1825 came the shocker: William Emerson returned from Germany and told his brother that he could not, in good conscience, continue to study for the ministry. The historical critical approach to religion that had excited him at first had over time drained away the faith that inspired him to study divinity in the first place. William had arranged a private meeting with Johann Wolfgang Goethe to ask what he should do, and Goethe told him not to worry about it: there was no reason a minister should not be able to keep his true beliefs and doubts to himself. On the trip home from Germany, however, a terrible storm nearly capsized the ship on which William was sailing, and in this crisis, he realized that he could neither live nor die with the kind of insincerity that Goethe recommended. Upon reaching home, he told his younger brothers, beginning with Waldo, that he would, instead, study law.[2]

This was chastening to Waldo and alarming to Mary Moody Emerson, whose ambition for all of her Emerson nephews was that they become itinerant old-guard Unitarian preachers. She questioned, at first, whether William's virtue had slipped more than his faith. Was he switching to law because he wanted the prestige and pleasures that came with worldly success? She warned that it was impossible to be a lover of virtue and "choose a less degree of virtue."[3] Upon recognizing that William's exposure to the deconstructionism of modern biblical criticism had truly weakened his faith, she demanded to know on what authority Eichhorn substituted his "mutilated gospel" for the Christian gospel of the miracle-working and resurrected Christ.[4]

Mary Moody Emerson was no fundamentalist. She allowed that the infancy narrative in Matthew was problematic and that the New Testament resurrection stories contained discrepancies. She told Waldo that she would not tremble for Christianity "if they should take away every written gospel"; "if they left one epistle of Paul genuine I should find that *Jesus had risen,*" she explained.[5] This was the core of the genuine gospel faith, a faith that was worthy of one's life and voice. Though she worried about his health, she urged Waldo not to delay entering the ministry. Prolonging his studies was fraught with peril, as William's defection had shown. As usual, Mary had a strong influence over Waldo, though not exactly in the way that she desired. He prepared for ministerial candidacy while cautioning her, on William's authority, that German criticism appeared to be sundering the traditional historical foundation of Christianity. His own starting point was a blend of Descartes, Schleiermacher, and Channing: "I know that I exist, and that a part of me, as essential as memory or reason, is a desire that another being exist." Though his early sermons were cautiously vague on this point, the task of preaching every week strengthened Emerson's conviction that spiritual experience comprised a better foundation for religious belief than any historically based creed.[6]

This conviction was deepened by his study of Samuel Taylor Coleridge's *Aids to Reflection* (1825). Upon reading the 1829 American edition of Coleridge's book, which contained an influential fifty-eight-page introduction by James Marsh, Emerson copied into his journal Coleridge's maxim "Quantum scimus sumus" (we are what we know). Coleridge's next sentence was equally important to him: "That which we find within ourselves, which is more than ourselves, and yet the ground of whatever is good and permanent therein, is the substance and life of all other knowledge." Aided by Marsh's introductory exposition, Emerson agreed with Coleridge's claim that the self possesses an active power of self-determination. He had long struggled with David Hume's skeptical naturalism, feeling uncertain that a credible alternative existed. In

Coleridge's Kantian-like distinction between Reason and Understanding, Emerson found the theory of truth that contained, for him, the convincing ring of truth.[7]

Like Kant, Coleridge insisted that the ultimate ground of morality (and therefore, religion) must be intuitive if the very notion of moral truth is to be secured. Just as Kant distinguished between the sense-bound knowledge of "pure reason" and the intuitive, constitutively human knowledge of "practical reason," Coleridge distinguished between the sense-bound faculty that he called "the Understanding" and the sense-transcendent power of "Reason." The Understanding processes knowledge derived wholly from experience, he proposed, while Reason gives birth to thought and all life-enhancing action. The Understanding is discursive, but Reason is fixed. The Understanding is a reflective faculty that abstracts, names, and compares; it brings no immediate truths; because of its dependence on sense experience, it always refers to another faculty as the authority behind its judgments. By contrast, Coleridge proposed, Reason is contemplative; it is the realm of conscience and insight. The truths of Reason are immediate, for Reason is self-referential in all its judgments with respect to the ground and substance of its truth claims. It followed for Coleridge that the wellspring of religion is a human source of ideas that is distinct from the sense-bound knowledge of the Understanding. The Understanding produces theologies, but it has no knowledge of spiritual experience. Coleridge pressed this claim into a defense of Christian truth: "Christianity is not a theory, or a speculation; but a life. Not a philosophy of life, but a life and a living process." The life that one seeks in religion is a mystery, he affirmed, "but so both in itself and in its origin is the life we have."[8]

The Coleridgean notion that religion is about being, not knowledge, was confirming and liberating to Emerson, immediately making his sermons clearer, bolder, and more personal. He declared in 1830 that "every man makes his own religion, his own God, his own charity." The root of religion is first-hand, he asserted emphatically; for the truly religious person, religion is not derived "from the Bible or his neighbour." Emerson cautioned that this claim should not be construed as diminishing or undermining religion, for at its best, the notion of God is "the most elevated conception of character that can be formed in the mind. It is the individual's own soul carried out to perfection."[9]

From here it was a short step to rethinking "salvation" as friendship, a notion Emerson developed in a series of sermons, and then in the journal assertion of the following year that "God in us worships God." It is irrational to fear reason for religious reasons, he reflected. To think is to receive; so, to fear reason for religious reasons is to fear that "the faculties which God made can outsee God." In a Coleridgean twist on the old rationalist apologetics, he assured his congregation that God would never bring a report to Reason that contradicted Godself: "To reflect is to receive truth immediately from God without any medium. That is living faith." On the other hand, he judged, to base one's faith on claims of the Understanding is to kill it. Faith is not about trusting in the veracity of particular bits of knowledge. "A trust in yourself is the height not of pride but of piety, an unwillingness to learn of any but God himself," he explained. "It is by yourself without ambassador that God speaks to you."[10]

Emerson thus developed the ego-theism of the American literature anthologies while he was still a pastor. "God in us worships God" gave rise to Emerson's famous neo-Platonist assertion in "The Over-Soul" that "the simplest person, who in his integrity worships God, becomes God." Emerson's spiritual resolve to project God out of the self was vividly expressed from the pulpit in the closing months of his pastoral career. Though he delivered his share of conventional Unitarian sermons, replete with appeals to rationalistic evidence, by the end of his ministry he no longer believed that sense knowledge had any bearing on genuine religion. In 1833 he took a nine-month tour of Europe and proclaimed that he felt himself pledged, if health and opportunity allowed, "to demonstrate that all necessary truth is its own evidence; that no doctrine of God need appeal to a book; that Christianity is wrongly received by all such as take it for a system of doctrines." Christianity is true as a life of moral truth, he judged: "It is a rule of life, not a rule of faith."[11]

Emerson could be arrogant in esteeming his superior grasp of this insight. After visiting with William Wordsworth, Thomas Carlyle, and Coleridge, he pronounced that all of them fell woefully short of his own perceptiveness: "They have no idea of that species of moral truth which I call the first philosophy."[12] He complained that the fatal deficiency of contemporary religious thinkers was their uncomprehending blindness to "the extent or the harmony or the depth of their moral nature." When European intellectuals asked him to expound his new teaching on this theme, he reflected, he had to explain that his teaching was actually very old: "It is the old revelation, that perfect beauty is perfect goodness, it is the development of the wonderful congruities of the moral law of human nature." Every man is a law unto himself, Emerson insisted: "He is not to live to the future as described to him, but to live to the real future by living to the real present. The highest revelation is that God is in every man."[13]

By then, except for his links to a close-knit family circle, he was on his own. Emerson was a widower and a former pastor in 1833 and thus had the leisure to visit European intellectuals. His unemployed status was connected to his bereavement in 1831, after his nineteen-year-old wife, Ellen Tucker, had died of tuberculosis. Ellen Tucker was a gifted poet, long of frail health, and Emerson loved her deeply. Her death was devastating to him; it also turned him back upon himself. Out of respect for his sorrow, Emerson's congregation treated him gingerly, but Ellen's death eliminated his main reason for staying in parish ministry. She had anchored him to the church, and with her loss, Emerson's negative feelings about organized religion began to take over. His remaining family ties to the church were not strong enough to overcome his growing personal conviction that "institutionalized religion" was an oxymoron. Four months after Ellen died, Emerson wrote that because religion is the relation of the soul to God, "the progress of Sectarianism marks the decline of religion." Four months after that, he bitterly criticized the "sham" of organized religion, confiding to his journal that "these great religious shows" concealed an inner lack of love. The Calvinist churches were fueled by pride and ignorance, Emerson judged, while Unitarianism merely lived off its opposition to Calvinism: "It is cold and cheerless, the mere creature of the understanding, until controversy makes it warm with fire got from below."[14]

As it happened, the ostensible cause of his resignation from Second Church in 1832, the year after Ellen's death, was his refusal to administer the rite of the Lord's Supper. The rite of communion, he believed, violated the antiformalistic spirit of Jesus and true religion. This conviction did not reflect a recent change of heart, however. Emerson had inherited his opposition to communion from his brother William, who criticized the institutionalization of the Lord's Supper before Emerson was ordained, but only after he began to talk about leaving the ministry, causing several months of emotional turmoil for his Aunt Mary, did Emerson raise his objections to the church's sacramental practices. In effect, the communion issue was his exit strategy. Had he not settled on this controversy, he would have found another. The church officers tried to negotiate a compromise, but Emerson held to his position. He was sensitive to the irony of his principled anti-formalism: "The most desperate scoundrels have been the over-refiners. Without accomodation society is impracticable." His position was that forms should not be important, but at Second Church, it was only his protest against the Lord's Supper that made the issue of forms controversial or important. Emerson conceded the obvious while holding fast to his distaste for "an institution which they esteem holiest."

In October 1832, Emerson left Second Church, still on reasonably good terms with the congregation, and set out on his literary career. He was relieved to be a pastor no longer, but in his own way he still considered himself a follower of the "minister of pure Reason," Jesus Christ.[15]

PROJECTING GOD OUT OF THE SELF:
THE TRANSCENDENTALIST CLUB

A host of aspiring Unitarian intellectuals, most of them recent Harvard students, shared Emerson's excitement at the prospect of making a new religious beginning along the lines of Coleridge's critical idealism and romanticism. They included Amos Bronson Alcott, James Freeman Clarke, Margaret Fuller, Frederic Henry Hedge, George Ripley, and Sophia Ripley. Others who joined the early transcendentalist movement included Orestes Brownson, William Henry Channing, Charles Follen, William Henry Furness, Theodore Parker, Elizabeth Palmer Peabody, Sampson Reed, and Caleb Stetson.

Various thinkers in both groups were influenced as much by Carlyle, French transcendentalist Victor Cousin, and the Swedish mystic Emanuel Swedenborg as by Coleridge. Reed was essentially a Swedenborgian mystic; Emerson's closest friend, Furness, was largely concerned with the quest of the historical Jesus; most of the transcendentalists were influenced by Cousin's emphasis on the immediacy of intuited truth. In a variation of Coleridge's schematism, Cousin distinguished between "spontaneous reason," which he described as intuitive, involuntary, and nonreflective, and "reflective reason," which he conceived as deliberative and dependent upon the antecedent action of spontaneous reason. The American transcendentalists were attracted to Cousin's emphasis on the direct immediacy of the intuitive truths known by spontaneous reason. Following Cousin and Coleridge, many of Emerson's spiritual kin took this to be a Kantian argument and thus regarded themselves as Kantians.[16]

"Transcendentalism" acquired an unwieldy array of meanings in the course of its American adoption. Some Emersonians emphasized its egalitarian implications as a philosophy of democratic politics. Parker advocated a host of radical political causes; Emerson more quietly supported several reformist causes; Brownson, against the movement's effete image, vigorously claimed that transcendentalism made sense only as a politics that supported union organizing and other working-class interests. Closer to the center of the movement, in the 1840s Alcott, Fuller, and the Ripleys made an ill-fated attempt to establish an ideal communal society in West Roxbury, Massachusetts. Emerson supported the Brook Farm experiment, as it was known, financially and morally, even while harboring private doubts about it.

Its tangents and various intellectual sources, disagreements over politics, and often-eccentric proponents aside, however, the transcendentalist reaction did have a defining center: its subversive intuitionist challenge to the ethos and philosophy of a dominant Lockeanism. Both sides of the liberal/conservative debates of the past generation had been dominated by Lockeans. Some advocates on both sides had softened Locke's empiricism by fitting aspects of Scottish commonsense realism to it, but neither side questioned the verificationist apologetic agenda that Lockean philosophy bequeathed to theology. American transcendentalism challenged the shared fundamental premises of traditional and Unitarian Protestantism, insisting that modern Continental transcendentalism and romanticism offered a better way. At first, few Emersonians had much direct acquaintance with Kant or Schleiermacher, but all of them read and seized upon *Aids to Reflection*.

The American transcendentalist attraction to Coleridge was loaded with irony. In his early career Coleridge had been a liberal Unitarian, but *Aids to Reflection* was a product of his more orthodox later life. His creative appropriation of Kant and Schleiermacher was offered as a novel way to defend ecumenical Anglican orthodoxy, not as a manifesto for radical religious individualism. Moreover, the American edition of *Aids to Reflection* was produced by an orthodox Calvinist, University of Vermont philosopher James Marsh, who judged that the time had come for religious conservatives to give up their attachment to Lockean philosophy. Marsh explained that it was the "peculiar misfortune" of American orthodoxy that it had received the Christian gospel and Lockean epistemology so intimately bound together "that by most persons they are considered as necessary parts of the same system." He criticized the orthodox tendency to exalt a received dogmatic system over spiritual experience. He proposed that the "deep-toned and sublime eloquence of Coleridge" deserved to be heard as a credible and, perhaps, more compelling philosophical support system for orthodox religious beliefs.[17]

The transcendentalists brushed all of this aside in claiming Coleridge as their spiritual trailblazer. They looked past his orthodox intentions, especially his insistence that the will is essentially corrupt. To the Romantic sensibility of Emerson and his friends, Coleridge was the prophet of liberated self-authenticating Spirit. Margaret Fuller proclaimed that "to the unprepared he is nothing, to the prepared, everything." Even on his own terms, Coleridge's orthodoxy was qualified by his ethical interpretation of Christianity, his "broad church" ecumenism, and the lingering pantheist affinities that fired his romanticism.[18] On all these counts, especially his ethical romanticist exaltation of spiritual Reason over the mere sense-knowledge of the Understanding, Coleridge spoke to the hearts of Emerson's generation of Unitarians.

In 1833, Frederic Henry Hedge boldly proclaimed that in America, the genuine Kantians and Coleridgeans were younger-generation liberals. He called for an end to all apologies for the obscurity of Coleridge and the German transcendentalists. "We believe it impossible to understand fully the design of Kant and his followers, without being endowed to a certain extent with the same powers of abstraction and synthetic generalization which they possess in so eminent a degree," he pronounced. In other words, the Lockean establishment was too simplistic to understand transcendental thinking: "In order to become fully master of their meaning, one must be able to find it in himself. Not all are born to be philosophers, or are capable of becoming philosophers, any more than all are capable of becoming poets or musicians. The works of the transcendental philosophers may be translated word for word, but still it will be impossible to get a clear idea of their philosophy, unless we raise ourselves at once to a transcendental point of view. Unless we take our station with the philosopher and proceed from his ground as our starting-point, the whole system will appear to us an inextricable puzzle."[19]

The Harvard establishment, Hedge believed, was too simple and unimaginative to comprehend transcendental thinking, but Hedge knew his German idealism firsthand. His father was the reknowned Harvard logician Levi Hedge. As a youth the young Hedge had studied for four years in a German gymnasium before entering Harvard as a junior, in 1822, where he was called Germanicus Hedge. In 1829, before entering the Unitarian ministry, he had taken a degree from Harvard Divinity School. He was thus uniquely qualified to give voice to a younger generation's sense of superiority over what it viewed as a doddering Unitarian establishment. More than any figure in his Unitarian circle, with the arguable exception of Theodore Parker, Hedge was schooled in the transcendental idealisms of Kant, J. G. Fichte, and F. W. J. Schelling. Lamenting that

Coleridge had never given a precise account of the fundamental claims of transcendental philosophy or its various schools of thought, Hedge sought to provide one.

He observed that the object of transcendental thinking was "to discover in every form of finite existence, an infinite and unconditioned as the ground of its existence, or rather as the ground of our knowledge of its existence." Transcendental thinking referred all phenomena to given "noumena" or laws of cognition, he explained. Following Kant, it assumed that the external world depends on the existence of innate human intuitions. Hedge cautioned that this doctrine could be taken too far, into purely subjective idealism, as in Fichte's *Wissenschaftslehre*. Like Coleridge, Hedge believed that the spiritual implications of Kantian idealism were developed in a more balanced and compelling manner by Schelling, in whose system of transcendental idealism, he explained, "there are two elements or poles, subject and object, or intelligence and nature, and corresponding to these two poles then are two fundamental sciences, the one beginning with nature and proceeding to intelligence, the other beginning with intelligence and ending in nature." Schelling respected the field-specific integrity of each of these sciences, calling the first natural philosophy, and the second transcendental philosophy. Schelling's system thus gave a spiritualized Kantian answer to the question of how the mind intuits objects of sense data without falling into the subjectivist abyss of epistemological solipsism.[20]

Hedge's sweeping dismissal of his American elders in the Unitarian *Christian Examiner* was a provocation to a Unitarian establishment that regarded itself as forward-looking and enlightened. His bold proclamation of the superiority of transcendental thinking exhilarated a scattered vanguard of youthful Unitarian pastors and independent intellectuals. Emerson enthused that Hedge was "an unfolding man" whose article was "a living leaping Logos" and hoped that Hedge would help him find his way. A few months later Emerson exhorted his brother Edward to pay heed to the difference between reason and understanding:

> Reason is the highest faculty of the soul—what we mean often by the soul itself. . . . It never *reasons*, never proves, it simply perceives, it is vision. The Understanding toils all the time, compares, contrives, adds, argues, near sighted but strong-sighted, dwelling in the present the expedient the customary.

Religion, poetry, and honor all belong to the Reason, he proclaimed, and Christ was its true prophet.[21]

To Emerson and many others, Hedge's argument marked the turn at which a younger generation of independent romantics took the offensive. Hedge dared to dismiss completely Lockeanism, including the modified Lockeanism of the Scottish commonsense realists. His superior tone epitomized his group's subsequent offending polemics against the old-guard Unitarians. Hedge realized that his transcendentalized religion was closer to Schelling than to Kant or even

Coleridge; he may have realized that Coleridge spiritualized Kant's philosophy beyond the point that Kant would have accepted, but the differences between his European lodestars were erased in the manifestos of American transcendentalism.

In 1835, Hedge moved from Cambridge to a Unitarian church in Bangor, Maine. The following year, he organized what came to be called the Transcendental Club. Emerson usually called it "Hedge's Club," because it met whenever Hedge made a trip to Boston. The original membership included education reformer Bronson Alcott, Canton pastor and labor-movement journalist Orestes Brownson, Watertown pastor and later Harvard homiletics professor Convers Francis, Boston Purchase Street pastor and later Brook Farm Community founder George Ripley, and a handful of divinity students including John Weiss, later an advocate of post-Christian Free Religion. Approximately twenty others attended many of the group's thirty meetings over the next four years, including Boston West Church pastor Cyrus A. Bartol, historian George Bancroft, Harvard German professor Charles Follen, feminist writer and Goethe enthusiast Margaret Fuller, West Roxbury pastor Theodore Parker, education reformer and Channing associate Elizabeth Peabody, Boston Second Church pastor Chandler Robbins, writer Henry David Thoreau, and poet Jones Very. From his ministerial outpost in Louisville, Kentucky, James Freeman Clarke kept in touch with his friends Hedge and Fuller and established the first transcendentalist periodical, *The Western Messenger*. Brownson was invited only once or twice, for Hedge found him unbearable. William Ellery Channing, averse to socializing, came only once, but Emerson, also leery of socializing, nearly always attended.

The Transcendental Club was Hedge's ploy to remain in contact with like-minded Boston-area friends and acquaintances. The group acquired a movement consciousness quickly, however. Hedge's informal circle of aesthetes and activists shared a visceral disdain for what they regarded as the backward-looking mediocrity of Unitarian culture, exemplified by the long-awaited first volume of Norton's massive New Testament apologetics, published in 1837. Norton piled up rationalistic arguments in defense of the biblical miracles and the apostolic authorship of the Gospels; he took barely a glance at the past half-century of historical critical scholarship; he declared that the object of his work was "to prove the genuineness of the Gospels." With Norton foremost in mind, Hedge acidly complained that there was "a rigid, cautious, circumspect, conservative *tang* in the very air of Cambridge which no one, who has resided there for any considerable time, can escape."[22]

The transcendentalists created a literary counterculture that had a flair for stylish intellectual expression that was new in America. They translated Kant, Schleiermacher, and Goethe into American idioms and created their own rhetorical tropes. Under Margaret Fuller's editorship, they launched a literary journal, *The Dial*, that proved a gold mine for later anthologists of American literature. Under Ripley's leadership, they published several volumes of translated new European literature under the title *Specimens of Foreign Standard Literature*.

Most of them were too effete in their individualism to support Jacksonian democracy, and some were outright snobs, but they took up a variety of progressive social causes. Alcott founded educational and communal experiments that failed disastrously; Brownson launched the *Boston Quarterly Review* as a forum for transcendental philosophy and labor movement politics; Fuller advocated women's rights and later supported the Italian revolution; Peabody was a pioneer in the kindergarten movement and also advocated Native American rights; Ripley poured himself into the communal Brook Farm experiment and its periodical, *The Harbinger;* Parker took up numerous social causes and later committed himself passionately to the radical wing of the antislavery movement.

Emerson began as a typical Whig opponent of the Jacksonian Democrats, calling them "the bad party," but by the late 1830s—to the extent that he felt compelled to think about such things—his political thinking was decidedly democratic and reformist. Parker thought for a time that Emerson was headed toward the radical democratic politics of the "Loco-foco" movement, which split to the Workingmen's Party in 1831 and joined the reform wing of the Democratic Party in 1834. Though not a political activist, Emerson later spoke out for abolition and other reformist causes, as did his anarchist individualist friend, Thoreau. Philosophically, the American transcendentalists were intuitionists and romantics. They called for a Coleridgean rethinking of philosophy and religion, insisting that the mind contains more than sense data. As they conceived it, this was the germ of transcendentalism. Opposing empiricist philosophy, secondhand religion, and ultimately, the spiritual shackles of sense imprisonment, transcendentalism proclaimed that religious and moral truth is founded not upon sense-derived knowledge, but on immediate intuitions of the divine.[23]

THE TRANSCENDENTALIST REVOLT

By 1838 there were two Unitarianisms. The first, the old guard of philosophical realists who controlled Harvard and most of the churches, believed in a miracle-working personal God and the epistemological primacy of sense perception. To them, the authority of Jesus as the unique channel of divine revelation was established by the miracles described in the New Testament. The second group, the Emersonian spiritualists, countered that Christianity is true only to the degree that its assertions are grounded in direct intuitions of absolute truth. With movement fervor, they unfolded the implications of this criterion of religious truth. Boston pastor George Ripley and Philadelphia pastor William Henry Furness pressed the issue of miracles, gently at first, arguing that the standard liberal appeal to the necessity and factuality of biblical miracles was illogical. Later they claimed that it was also irreligious.

Conventional Unitarianism had rejected Calvinist orthodoxy mainly because it eviscerated the divine image in humanity. Channing had famously proclaimed that Calvinism, because it negated the image of God in humanity, was a perverted religion that maligned the character of God and humanity. The transcendentalists charged that the conventional Unitarian appeal to miracles had the same effect: The liberal belief in God's indwelling immanence is not strengthened by appeals to confirming miracles, they argued. Rather, all apologetic appeals to the factuality or necessity of miracles detract from the claim that the soul's intimate union with God provides a sufficient basis of religious knowledge. In the age of modern science and biblical criticism, the transcendentalists warned, appeals to miracles have the effect of jeopardizing the credibility of Christian belief.

Ripley's early writings on this theme made it the flashpoint issue between the two Unitarianisms. He did not deny that Jesus performed miracles, but he did deny the legitimacy of basing religious claims about Jesus upon appeals to his miracles. Ripley noted that Jesus usually performed miracles in "the sphere of action," that is, to heal people, not in the sphere of thought, to prove anything. Moreover, since miracles are impossible to prove, he argued, it is wrong to make belief in them an essential foundation of Christian faith.[24] Ripley proposed that the way forward in American theology was to take Schleiermacher's path. American theology was mired in the problems of two competing and deeply flawed approaches to Christian truth, he contended: Conservatives clung to a supernaturalist orthodoxy, while Unitarians countered with a rationalist revision of supernatural Christianity. What was needed was a transcendental alternative that founded Christian truth on the revelation given to every human soul. Schleiermacher's grounding of theology in innate precognitive religious "feeling" (*Gefühl*) was Ripley's model:[25] "Let the study of theology commence with the study of human consciousness. Let us ascertain what is meant by the expression, often used, but little pondered,—the Image of God in the Soul of Man. Let us determine whether our nature has any revelation of the Deity within itself; and, if so, analyze and describe it. If we there discover, as we firmly believe we shall, a criterion of truth, by which we can pass judgment on the Spiritual and Infinite, we shall then be prepared to examine the claims of a Divine Revelation in history."[26]

Norton's reply affected a superior tone, though he shocked well-mannered New England by publishing it in a daily newspaper. As a rule, he admonished his detractors, commentators should acquire scholarly competence in theology before they dispute doctrines long cherished by wise and faithful believers. Worthwhile theology is rarely written by people who lack the ability or training to seriously discuss Christian doctrine. He doubted that the Emersonians had sufficient regard for the interests of truth and goodness. In the 1820s, when Ripley, Emerson, Clarke, Furness, and Hedge were students at Harvard Divinity School, Norton was the dominant figure on the faculty. He was accustomed to deferential treatment, but Ripley's reply set him straight about his standing among the new generation. "You are a disciple of the school which was founded by Locke—the successor of Hobbes and the precursor of Condillac and Voltaire," Ripley observed, nastily linking Norton and Locke to unwelcome company. "For that philosophy I have no respect. I believe it to be superficial, irreligious and false in its primary elements. The evils it has brought upon humanity, by denying to the mind the power of perceiving spiritual truth, are great and lamentable. They have crept over Theology, Literature, Art, and Society. This age has no higher mission than to labor for their cure."[27]

This was the factional fight that Channing tried to mediate in his later career. His emphasis on the spiritual likeness of the divine indwelling had opened the door to transcendentalism, and he maintained friendly relations with the Emersonians, sympathizing with their hostility to the increasingly dogmatic spirit of the Unitarian establishment. But Channing remained an old schooler on these issues. He loved Coleridge but did not read him as an incipient religious radical. He held firmly to personal supernaturalist theism, the apologetic necessity of the biblical miracles, and the revelational authority of scripture. In 1837, Emerson therefore dismissed him: "Once Dr. Channing filled our sky. Now we become so conscious of his limits and of the difficulty attending any effort to show him our point of view, that we doubt if it be worth while. Best amputate."[28]

Emerson was now a country gentleman of Concord, New Hampshire, remarried and the ringleader of an upstart religious and literary movement, the author of a brief, little-noticed book on nature, and a reasonably successful professional lecturer. He was also near the end of his career as a preacher. He had continued to serve as a stated-supply preacher in the mid-1830s, but his feeling of alienation from the church deepened throughout this experience. In the spirit of "best amputate," he noted that he had recently shuddered with disdain at the sight of a young minister's library (the minister happened to be young Barzillai Frost): "Priestley; Noyes; Rosenmüller; Joseph Allen, and other Sunday School books; Schleusner; Norton, and the Saturday Night of Taylor; the dirty comfort of the farmer could easily seem preferable to the elegant poverty of the young clergyman." George Rapall Noyes, then a pastor at Petersham, Massachusetts, was the liberal movement's most competent Old Testament scholar; a protégé of Norton's, he was soon to become an eminent Harvard professor of Hebrew and Sacred Literature. Johann Georg Rosenmüller and Johann Friedrich Schleusner were prominent German theological scholars; Joseph Priestley was the dean of radical eighteenth-century Unitarianism.[29] Emerson's sense of disaffected superiority to them made sense only as a sign of his complete alienation from formal theology. He was breaking entirely from the New England preoccupation with logic-chopping theological correctness. At least, that was what he told himself while making a dogma of the difference between Reason and Understanding. "The world needs a missionary to denounce its conventions," he mused. "Why should each new soul that is launched out of

God into Nature be wrecked at the beginning of the voyage by following the charts of its mates instead the compass, the stars, and the continents?"[30]

A few months before he relinquished his ecclesiastical charge, Emerson quoted his wife Lidian as remarking, "It is wicked to go to church Sundays." Several weeks later he rephrased the sentiment: "Let the clergy beware when the well disposed scholar begins to say, 'I cannot go to Church, time is too precious.'"[31] The previous year, while Hedge gave him a break from his clerical duties at East Lexington, Emerson had sampled the preaching of Concord's new assistant pastor, Barzillai Frost, and was appalled. Emerson judged that Frost meant well but knew nothing about converting life into truth: "Not one single fact in all his experience has he yet imported into his doctrine. And there he stands pitiable and magisterial, and without nausea reads page after page of mouthfilling words and seems to himself to be doing a deed."[32] The following year, after Emerson resigned from the ministry, he found Frost's sermonizing had not improved: "He had lived in vain. He had no one word intimating that ever he had laughed or wept, was married or enamoured, had been cheated, or voted for, or chagrined." Emerson found it depressing to consider that Concord churchgoers apparently preferred "this thoughtless clamorous young person" to their own houses. Having severed his last tie to his clerical vocation and inheritance, Emerson resolved to explain why clericalism inevitably distorted Christianity: "I ought to sit and think and then write a discourse to the American clergy showing them the ugliness and unprofitableness of theology and churches at this day and the glory and sweetness of the Moral Nature out of whose pale they are almost wholly shut."[33]

A few days later, he received a serendipitous invitation to address this subject, if not its ugliness and unprofitableness. The graduating class of Harvard Divinity School, seven members strong, invited him to deliver "the customary discourse" at the annual Divinity School ceremony that marked the entrance of its graduates into active Christian ministry.[34] Emerson knew most of these students personally. He knew they were interested in the upcoming trial in Massachusetts for blasphemy and atheism of Abner Kneeland, a Voltairean gadfly and former Universalist minister, who had been under indictment since 1833. Though they apparently did not expect a bombshell, the students surely knew that Emerson could be counted on to give a tweak-the-establishment graduation address. Both sides got far more controversy than they bargained for. Two days after he preached his last obligatory sermon at East Lexington, Emerson accepted the students' invitation. He was not the speaker that the Divinity School faculty would have chosen, but, as he expected, the faculty, including Norton, Henry Ware Sr., Henry Ware Jr., Dean John G. Palfrey, and perhaps William Ellery Channing, attended. Emerson's rooting section of personal friends was at least equally formidable: James Freeman Clarke, Frederic Hedge, Theodore Parker, Elizabeth Peabody, and George Ripley, and two observers who soon became close friends, William Henry Channing and Jones Very. Other attendees included recent Divinity School graduates Cyrus

Bartol, John Sullivan Dwight, Convers Francis, and Caleb Stetson. These Unitarian notables witnessed an historic occasion; some of them helped make it one.[35]

DIVINITY SCHOOL NEGATIONS

Emerson's Divinity School address began on an appreciative, nature-mystical note: "In this refulgent summer, it has been a luxury to draw the breath of life. The grass grows, the buds burst, the meadow is spotted with fire and gold in the tint of flowers." In actuality, this was his essential point, not a prefatory warm-up. Divinity indwells all that lives. Emerson quickly added, however, that the most profound reflection of divinity in the natural world is contained in human nature. For all of the power and sweetness of the color-spotted meadow, there is an even more glorious beauty that appears whenever a person's heart and mind open to the sentiment of virtue: "Then he is instructed in what is above him. . . . When in innocency, or when by intellectual perception, he attains to say,— 'I love the Right; Truth is beautiful within and without, forevermore. Virtue, I am thine: save me: use me: thee will I serve, day and night, in great, in small, that I may be not virtuous, but virtue;'— then is the end of creation answered, and God is well pleased."[36]

Much of his address sang Unitarian music of this kind. Emerson celebrated the divine indwelling and the practice of firsthand creative spirituality in words that could have been spoken by Channing. What made his address notorious was that, in the chapel of Divinity Hall, in a charge to the church's next class of ministers, he gave voice to some of the most anti-Christian material in his journals. Though many of those he offended assumed otherwise, Emerson did not seek controversy, and he experienced the resulting firestorm as a curse. Seeking, more modestly, to challenge the complacency of his audience and to speak his essential truth without causing unnecessary offense, he had diluted some of his private judgments. In his journal, for example, he enumerated various short-comings of Jesus: "I do not see in him cheerfulness: I do not see in him the love of Natural Science: I see in him no kindness for Art; I see in him nothing of Socrates, of Laplace, of Shakespeare." Because Emerson believed that the perfectly exemplary figure "should remind us of all great men," he could not claim to exalt Jesus above all other figures, without fearing that he was indulging in superstition.[37]

Emerson's Divinity School address spared Jesus and its audience this kind of judgment. He argued that genuine Christianity is about the divine indwelling in all that lives. He portrayed Jesus as a prophet of "the mystery of the soul" who esteemed "the greatness of man" above all others and who lived deeply in the shimmering beauty and harmony of the soul. In Emerson's rendering, Jesus taught with singular spiritual insight "that God incarnates himself in man, and evermore goes forth anew to take possession of his world." In his "jubilee of sublime emotion," Jesus proclaimed his own divinity, taught others to see God in him, and urged them to follow him by seeing God in themselves. This is the original gospel faith, Emerson claimed: "But what a distortion did this doctrine and memory suffer in the same, in the next, and the following ages! There is no doctrine of the Reason which will bear to be taught by the Understanding." Jesus taught and lived the Reason-filled religion of Spirit in which Spirit is seen to indwell all that lives, but a dogmatizing early church reduced the divine indwelling "to one or two persons" "and denied with fury" the divine nature to everything else.[38]

Early Christianity turned Jesus into a demigod and covered him with official titles, thereby violating the memory of Jesus and the spirit of true religion: "The understanding caught this high chant from the poet's lips, and said, in the next age, 'This was Jehovah come down out of heaven. I will kill you, if you say he was a man.'" In this way, Emerson alleged, historical Christianity turned the religion of "Christ" into a regime of violence. True religious feeling is peaceable, appreciative, generous, and attractive, but historical Christianity was preoccupied with dogma and ritual. The church obliterated the soul and exaggerated the realm of the personal: "It has dwelt, it dwells, with noxious exaggeration about the *person* of Jesus," Emerson explained. "The soul knows no persons. It invites every man to expand to the full circle of the universe, and will have no preferences but those of spontaneous love."[39]

He allowed that Jesus and the church both spoke of miracles, but he denied that Jesus thought of miracles in the same way the church did. To Jesus, all of life was a miracle, Emerson explained, "but the word Miracle, as pronounced by Christian churches, gives a false impression: it is Monster. It is not one with the blowing clover and the falling rain." For centuries, the church sought to kill people who gave wrong titles to Jesus; it also tried to convert people by appealing to miraculous events. These practices, he argued, are linked in the logic of bad religion: "To aim to convert a man by miracles, is a profanation of the soul. A true conversion, a true Christ, is now, as always, to be made, by the reception of beautiful sentiments." True religion is open and sympathetic. It is always open to new revelation, but historical Christianity was a closed book. The church restricted the divine indwelling to one or two persons, it limited inspiration to a closed canon, and it claimed that the age of revelation was over. Emerson countered, "It is my duty to say to you, that the need was never greater of new revelation than now."[40]

He dipped into his journal to document his case against historical Christianity. Barzillai Frost, though unnamed, took a dreadful pounding, as Emerson recycled entire paragraphs from his journal that blasted Frost's lifeless preaching. He repeated various withering assaults on the church's dogmatism. He condemned the boring formalism of church services and the church's "fear of degrading the character of Jesus by representing him as a man." He quoted his wife Lidian on the wickedness of going to church and himself on the sad strangeness of people electing to leave their houses to attend bad services. He allowed that he knew a few eloquent preachers, but for the most part, "it is still true, that tradition characterizes the preaching of this country; that it comes out of the memory, and not out of the soul; that it aims at what is usual, and not at what is necessary and eternal." In this way, he judged, historical Christianity eviscerated the spiritual power of Christian preaching "by withdrawing it from the exploration of the moral nature of man, where the sublime is, where are the resources of astonishment and power."

Emerson ended in the only way that he could, urging the young ministers to go off on their own and think their own thoughts. Imitation cannot transcend its model, he warned, invoking a favorite journal theme. The imitator is doomed to mediocrity: "Let me admonish you, first of all, to go alone; to refuse the good models, even those which are sacred in the imagination of men, and dare to love God without mediator or veil." Instead of regarding themselves as caretakers or followers of a tradition, and giving themselves overmuch to pastoral tasks, they were better advised to cultivate their individual souls: "Yourself a newborn bard of the Holy Ghost,—cast behind you all conformity, and acquaint men at first hand with Deity." The remedy to bad religion was "first, soul, and second, soul, and evermore, soul."[41]

NEWBORN BARDS UNDER ATTACK

Emerson's Divinity School address challenged Unitarian decorum to the breaking point, but for the most part, the Unitarian leaders kept their poise in dealing with him. They prized their sobriety and polite manners; they did not fight in public. In delivering the Divinity School address, Emerson became an outsider to them; they denounced him behind closed doors and closed ranks against him. *The Christian Examiner* confirmed this state of affairs by recording its disapproval of Emerson; the Divinity School address ended the paper's journalistic pose of impartiality between the establishment and the Emersonians.

Norton abandoned this decorum by attacking Emerson personally in the pages of a Boston newspaper. Emerson's address represented, in his opinion, a crisis for the church that called for extreme measures: "There is a strange state of things existing about us in the literary and religious world, of which none of our larger periodicals has yet taken notice," he announced. "It is the result of that restless craving for notoriety and excitement, which, in one way or another, is keeping our community in a perpetual stir." Having established the transcendentalists' baleful motive, Norton described their intellectual perspective as a complex of "ill understood notions, obtained by blundering through the crabbed and disgusting obscurity of some of the worst German speculatists." The Emersonians' lack of intelligibility was not aided, he chided, by the fact that they had to get their German pantheism through interpreters.[42]

Norton further charged that besides not knowing what they were talking about, Emerson and his friends were arrogant and willfully irrational: "The characteristics of this school are the most extraordinary assumption, united with great ignorance, and incapacity for reasoning." He admitted that one of the transcendentalists' intellectual heroes, Thomas Carlyle, had some talent as a writer, but he conceded nothing to the Emersonians. For all of their talk about originality, they were shabby imitators at best. At worst, some were heretics who exploited their clerical status to corrupt the faith of the church. To Norton, Emerson's heretical views were less important than the fact that he was invited to express them at a divinity college graduating ceremony: "What his opinions may be is a matter of minor concern; the main question is how it has happened, that religion has been insulted by the delivery of these opinions in the Chapel of the Divinity College of Cambridge, as the last instruction which those were to receive, who were going forth from it, bearing the name of Christian preachers."

Norton did not doubt that the Divinity School's "highly respectable" officers were disgusted by Emerson's performance, but he warned that not only the Divinity College and the church needed to worry about the danger posed by Emersonian heresy. American civilization itself was at stake. If the Divinity College of Cambridge could not protect its graduation ceremony from insults to religion, what would become of Christian America? "The words God, Religion, Christianity, have a definite meaning, well understood. We well know how shamefully they have been abused in modern times by infidels and pantheists; but their meaning remains the same; the truths which they express are unchanged and unchangeable." Norton observed that the community at large understood that a Christian teacher was supposed to believe and teach the faith of the Christian church. Any Christian teacher who believed or taught something else was a fraud. The acid test for American society, he admonished, was to take the minister's private beliefs as seriously as it took his public teaching. American communities could not afford to tolerate careful-speaking ministers who privately questioned the faith. Sooner or later, Norton cautioned, the privately questioning pastor degenerated into "obscure intimations, ambiguous words, and false and mischievous speculation." With Emerson, among others, in mind, he urged that it was not enough to wait until pastors became flaming heretics. Should American society allow the Emerson types to abound, he warned, "and grow confident in their folly, we can hardly overestimate the disastrous effect upon the religion and moral state of the community."[43]

Norton's attack set off a public controversy, which fed later controversies that pitted him against Ripley and Parker. American Unitarianism got the public fight that Norton believed it needed. For nearly a year, while friends and onlookers defended him from blistering criticism, Emerson kept his bitter reaction private. He still believed that faction-fighting was useless and vulgar. *The Christian Examiner* editorialized that the Divinity School address contained "neither good divinity nor good sense." It commended Henry Ware Jr. for his politely phrased rejoinder to Emerson, that either a personal God exists or there is no God. The problem of spiritual deadness in Unitarianism could be cured, he asserted, only when people "come more to realize the presence and the authority of the living Father." Take away the personal Father of the universe, he warned, "and, though every ordinance remain unchanged, mankind becomes but a company of children in an orphan asylum; clothed, fed, governed, but objects of pity rather than congratulation, because deprived of those resting-places for the affections, without which the soul is not happy." *The Christian Examiner* applauded: "This is sense; this is truth; and this is good writing. . . . Here is a style which becomes the subject, simple, manly, straight-forward. Give us such writing and such preaching as this, and defend us from the wordiness and mysticism, which are pretending to be a better literature, a higher theology, and almost a new revelation."[44]

That set the tone for the Unitarian establishment. Mainstream Unitarianism was manly, clearheaded, and Christian; Emersonianism was effeminate, dreamy, and dubiously Christian at best. Having endured the accusation by the preceding generation that their church did not belong to Christianity, the guardians of mainstream Unitarianism insisted that there was such a thing as Unitarian Christian orthodoxy, to which Emerson did not belong. Editorial judgments on this theme kept the controversy stoked for months. Emerson's book on nature received only a handful of reviews in three years, but the Divinity School address received over thirty in a few months. An article in the *Boston Courier* protested incredulously that Emerson apparently believed "that every man was or might be his own god." *The Christian Register* reported that Abner Kneeland, "the convicted blasphemer," was delighted with Emerson's speech and quoted it triumphantly. Closer to home, Mary Moody Emerson bit her tongue at first, having already despaired of Waldo. The exotic mysticism of the Divinity School address made her nostalgic for the days of their early corre-spondence, "when his young Muse was wont to wander into strange 'universes' and find idealised people and alas, 'new laws.'" She prayed that Waldo's "new school may be a wheel within a wheel moving under the Great Mover to give some apprehension of the relation to Himself that the philosophical could not otherwise so highly attain." As the controversy made Emerson notorious, how-ever, Mary Emerson's disposition toward his thinking returned to character. She told friends it was obvious that the address had been written "under the influ-ence of some malign demon." She loved "dear Waldo," but was appalled at what he wrought.[45]

The Transcendental Club took a decidedly more favorable view. Elizabeth Peabody was enthralled by the Divinity School address. Orestes Brownson praised Emerson's free-spirited boldness while allowing that some of his formu-lations were ill-considered. James Freeman Clarke and Christopher Pearse Cranch defended Emerson from his critics—"It is too late in the day to put a man down by shouting Atheist, Infidel, Heretic"—while claiming that Channing, not Emerson, deserved to be recognized as the leader of the Transcendentalist "New School." Jones Very and William Henry Channing became part of Emerson's inner circle after hearing the address. Most important, the Divinity School address had a formative and catalyzing effect on Theodore Parker, who had graduated from the Divinity School the previous year.

Parker, then a West Roxbury pastor, frequent contributor to the *Christian Examiner,* an erudite student of German biblical scholarship, and a gifted linguist, was hoping for an academic post at the Divinity School. His early articles and reviews reflected the discretion of an appointment-seeking scholar, but upon hearing Emerson's address, Parker enthused in his journal, "My soul is roused. . . . So beautiful, so just, so true, and terribly sublime was his picture of the faults of the church in its present position." To a friend, George Ellis, Parker proclaimed that Emerson's address, while "a little exaggerated, with some philosophical untruths," was nonetheless "the noblest, the most inspiriting strain I ever listened to." With the inspired redirection of Parker's largely self-taught mind, American transcendentalism entered a new stage of religious definition. Parker expressed his gratitude to Emerson for the rest of his life. Late in his life he recalled with affection that at the turning point of his career, "the brilliant genius of Emerson rose in the winter nights, and hung over Boston, drawing the eyes of ingenuous young people to look up to that great, new star, a beauty and a mystery, which charmed for the moment, while it gave also perennial inspiration."[46]

DEFENDING TRANSCENDENTALIST CHRISTIANITY

To Emerson, the outcry against his heresies was a form of abuse. He bitterly judged that Norton's polemical violence was symptomatic of the shallow externality of his religion: "The great army of cowards who bellow and bully from their bed chamber windows have no confidence in truth or God," he reflected privately. "Truth will not maintain itself, they fancy, unless they bolster it up and whip and stone the assailants." Connecting the will to persecute and the spirit of religious dogmatism was the only way that Emerson could make sense of Norton's otherwise inexplicable belief that true religion had to be defended. Feeling deeply his victimization as an abused prophet, he ridiculed Norton's "feminine vehemence" in defending Unitarianism. For all of their claims to manliness, he implied, with a chauvinistic squeal of his own, it was the Unitarian rationalists who shrieked and threatened. To Emerson, the underlying problem was that superficial religion is easily threatened: Because Norton's religion could not tolerate any serious external challenge, he and his cohorts felt compelled "to whip that naughty heretic."[47]

Emerson's sense of persecution ended his already-strained relationship with organized religion. The dean of Harvard Divinity School, John Gorham Palfrey, disclaimed any responsibility for the address and spread the word that he was deeply offended by it. It was nearly thirty years before Emerson was again invited to speak at Harvard. Throughout the controversy, he refused to debate his critics. When Henry Ware Jr. respectfully questioned the basis of his position, Emerson replied that he "could not possibly give you one of the 'arguments' on which as you cruelly hint any position of mine stands." As a good transcendentalist, he didn't believe in making arguments and claimed not to understand the point of defending his claims. "I do not know, I confess, what arguments mean in reference to any expression of a thought," he explained to Ware.[48] To Ripley and Parker, however, good transcendentalism did not exclude making arguments on behalf of its truth claims or preclude responding to the likes of Andrews Norton.

Norton insisted that evidence is all that we have. There is no such thing as absolute certainty, he admonished, and mere experience establishes no certainty at all. The fact that historical verdicts are merely probable is no reason to impugn historical reason, for there is no ground of believing in Christianity that transcends the probabilities of historical evidence. Religious feeling and principle are important, he admitted, but both are groundless apart from certain facts: "There can be no intuition, no direct perception, of the truth of Christianity, no metaphysical certainty." Neither feeling nor principle establishes anything in religion. The new infidels therefore had no basis; all they had were catchphrases cribbed from atheist obscurantists like Schleiermacher and philosopher Benedict de Spinoza. Norton countered that the only legitimate means of establishing religious belief is the rational investigative procedure of forming probable historical judgments upon facts. For him, to deny the biblical miracles was to give up Christianity altogether. Without the miracles of Jesus, Christianity has no evidentiary basis for claiming that Jesus was more than an exemplary moral figure. For this reason, he judged, notwithstanding its pious-sounding appeal to the inward evidence of religious experience, Emersonianism was merely "the latest form of infidelity." It wholly embraced the argument of Spinoza, "founded on atheism . . . that the laws of nature are the laws by which God is bound." The Emersonian theology of spiritual intuition appealed to a phantom authority and renounced the only genuine basis of Christian affirmation.[49]

The liberal pedigree of this argument posed special problems for defenders of transcendentalist Christianity. Norton is now remembered as the old-guard bulldog who condemned transcendentalism, but in his time, before Parker stormed the field, Norton was America's leading proponent of biblical criticism. Contrary to the image of the backward-looking reactionary that prevails in the literature on Emerson and American transcendentalism, Norton stood at the left edge of American Christianity. He caused pain in New England by judging that numerous Gospel passages were spurious additions, including the first two chapters of Matthew; he argued that eight New Testament books did not belong in the canon, because they lacked apostolic authority; later he contended that Moses, because he possessed a genuinely religious spirit, could not have written the Pentateuch. Brownson and Ripley understood that Norton, America's most liberal religious scholar of note, and his tradition of Enlightenment empiricism had done valuable work for liberal theology in eroding religious authoritarianism.[50]

But Norton empiricism was reactionary in the present context, they judged. Though Norton took early retirement from teaching in 1830 to devote himself to research, his spirit prevailed at Harvard Divinity School. His brand of liberal Christianity denied that all people possess an inner light of Spirit and truth, more precisely, he denied that all people possess an inherent power of perceiving religious truth by virtue of having souls. Harvard religion made religious truth the province of academic experts, who alone knew how to make sound judgments about the evidences and principles of rational belief. Brownson pressed hard on the point that this religious worldview had a politics. Harvard religion, like Harvard University, was elitist, provincial, out of step with American democracy, and bordering on senility. With cutting understatement, Brownson said that Harvard was not known "for her reverence for the people, her faith in democratic institutions, or her efforts to establish universal suffrage and equal rights." Harvard took no pains to educate her sons "in harmony with those free principles which are the just pride of all true Americans." To put it plainly, Harvard had no democratic spirit, and Brownson was sure that Harvard would never acquire one, either, "so long as Locke is her text-book in philosophy."[51]

Norton would not engage in a direct exchange with such a rough-mannered, self-educated interloper as Brownson. But Ripley, a product of Massachusetts Unitarianism and Harvard Divinity School, a former valedictorian at Harvard College, and pastor of Boston's Purchase Street Church, was not so easy to ignore. He was also Margaret Fuller's managing editor at *The Dial,* and, more impressively to Norton, served as editorial supervisor of the *Specimens of Foreign Standard Literature* series. Norton's attack on "the latest form of infidelity" gave special offense to Ripley by impugning the faith of Schleiermacher, De Wette, and Spinoza, Ripley's intellectual heroes. In three indignant pamphlets in response to Norton, Ripley produced long quotations that showed their deep religiosity. He also took aim at Norton's methodological imperialism. Ripley reported that as a loving son of Harvard, he had hoped that the Cambridge Theological School would respond creatively "to the piercing cry of our country and age for a free and generous theology." As a liberal Christian, he refused to sit in judgment on any Christian's claim to discipleship or the Christian name. "But the doctrine which lies as the foundation of your whole Discourse is a signal manifestation of the exclusive principle," he told Norton. People come to Christ in many different ways, Ripley noted, but Norton sacralized his own empiricist verificationism as the only valid criterion of Christian belief. Any person who did not rest her faith "on a certain kind of evidence" was tagged as an infidel. Despite its Enlightenment pedigree, this criterion was advanced "with the same want of reserve or qualification that a teacher of the Infallible Church would have exhibited before the Reformation." Ripley admired scholars who demonstrated spiritual humility and served the public good, "but if they do not acknowledge a higher light than that which comes from the printed page; if they confound the possession of erudition with the gift of wisdom; and above all, if they presume to interfere in the communion of the soul with God, and limit the universal bounty of Heaven within their 'smoky cells,' I can only utter my amazement."[52]

THEODORE PARKER:
LETTING OFF THE TRUTH

That set the stage for Theodore Parker's entry into the debate over transcendentalism, which he dominated for the next generation. Parker was a singular figure in highly eccentric company. With little formal education, he was a brilliant autodidact and voracious reader, gifted especially in languages. Born in 1810, as a youth he imbibed his mother's deep piety and his father's love of classical literature. Aided by a family friend, he read Homer and Plutarch in translation before the age of eight, began Greek and Latin at the age of ten, and took up astronomy and metaphysics at twelve. He passed the exams at Harvard College with high honors, but was refused a degree because he could not afford the tuition. In 1834, after working as a farmer, carpenter, and teacher, Parker enrolled at Harvard Divinity School, where his rough edges were polished by Henry Ware Jr., for whom he sustained a deep affection for the rest of his life. He also studied under Palfrey and Norton, and by the time he entered the ministry, he could read twenty languages.

His first congregation was a small Unitarian church in West Roxbury, which he chose mainly for its proximity to Boston libraries. Parker came to transcendentalist religion and radical politics during his nine-year pastorate in West Roxbury. In his early career he struggled to define the extent of his theological liberalism, an endeavor that conflicted, at its boundaries, with his hope for a teaching post at Harvard Divinity School. His early writings showed off his vast historical knowledge, including his familiarity with modern German scholarship, while moving between liberal and conservative posititions on various critical issues. His early writings struggled to make sense of scripture and theology, often conveying an unsettled outlook. For years, for instance, he struggled with the doctrine of biblical inspiration. Though he ruled out the idea of verbal inspiration, Parker assumed that Christianity required some kind of affirmation of scriptural inspiration. At the same time, he questioned how the Bible could be inspired in *any* sense if it contained no great moral or religious truth exclusively.

For a while Parker kept the latter question to himself. He judged that the Old Testament contained almost nothing of the religion of love and universal good that the New Testament contained in its better parts. Both testaments contained incredible miracle stories: "some were clearly impossible, others ridiculous, and a few were wicked."

For several years he wrote cautious articles that, contrary to his reputation, sometimes took conservative positions. Parker denied that the apostles predicted the immanent second coming of Jesus; he accepted certain biblical miracles as historical; to his later embarrassment, he defended the Mosaic authorship of the Pentateuch. The fact that he aspired to a Harvard position contributed to his theological muddle; the fact that he wrote for church publications weighed more heavily upon him. Feeling compromised by his ambitions, he worried about his relation to the Unitarian church. How much freedom was it prepared to indulge? Inspired by Emerson's Divinity School address, for him an example of clear and true religious thinking, he began to press the question.[53]

The controversy over Emerson's speech convinced him that Unitarianism had already broken into two parties: "One is for progress, the other says, 'Our strength is to stand still.'" Parker believed that Channing was the "real head" of the first party, while the conservatives had no leader. "Some day or another there will be a rent in the body," he predicted. The following year he attended the annual Berry Street Conference and shook his head in disbelief as Unitarian ministers debated whether they should exclude from Christian fellowship those who denied "the value and authority of miracles." Ripley and Hedge spoke effectively against the proposition, but that night, "a little horrified" at the spectacle he had witnessed, Parker raged in his journal: "This is the 19th century! This is Boston! This among the Unitarians!" Motivated by this clarifying incredulity, he made a resolution: "I intend, in the coming year, to let out all the force of Transcendentalism that is in me. Come what will come, I will let off the Truth fast as it comes."[54]

His first pass at "letting off" the truth was a review of *The Life of Jesus Critically Examined,* by David Friedrich Strauss. The fourth edition of Strauss's explosively controversial work was imminent; its first edition, published in 1835, had ended Strauss's academic career before it began. In the form of a densely detailed, two-volume prolegomenon to his own left-Hegelian constructive theology, Strauss sought to demolish the historical credibility of the Gospel narratives by exposing their pervasive layers of mythology. Parker was probably his first American reader. He stewed over the book for years, argued with it, and measured his own developing beliefs against Strauss's biblical criticism and left-Hegelianism. In 1838 Parker spoke to Channing about preparing an American edition of the book, who advised him against it. The following year, while contemplating his review of Strauss's third edition, Parker fretted that he wouldn't be able to say what he really believed in the Unitarian *Christian Examiner.* Although he did not endorse the book, his review contained ample foreshadowings of his radical future.

Parker judged that Strauss overused the category of myth and ignored evidence that supported the historical credibility of certain gospel narratives. He lauded Strauss for his intellectual energy and sophisticated scholarship, while noting that Norton was a rigorous scholar, too. Even as he asserted that *The Life of Jesus Critically Examined* was "the most remarkable work that has appeared in theology, for the last hundred and fifty years" and that it towered above its field as a model of theological scholarship, Parker acknowledged that it was not a great work of theology, for it lacked a religious spirit. Great theological work required rigorous scholarship and a religious spirit, but Strauss displayed only the former. This did not mean that Strauss was not a Christian; indeed, Parker believed that Strauss was a truly religious spirit, more Christian than his conservative enemies. The problem was that his book didn't show it: "It is colder than ice. It is the most melancholy book we ever read."

By implication, Parker set a high standard for his own work. He intended to combine Straussian critical rigor with a warm religious spirit. Turning to the debate between Norton and Ripley, he gave the Unitarian establishment a strong taste of what it was in for.[55]

In *"The Previous Question between Mr. Andrews Norton and His Alumni,"* a pamphlet authored by one "Levi Blodgett," he assumed a rustic pose, attributing his "uncouth phraseology" to the fact that "much o' my life has been spent at the plough, and ower little at the college or the schule." Its real author was obvious. Parker was the eleventh child of a Lexington farmer. His intervention in the Norton-Ripley debate sought to steer it away from Ripley's tedious and pedantic defenses of transcendentalist heroes. "Levi Blodgett" knowingly took it for granted "that one party in this debate had never read the chief works of Spinoza before this controversy began." He doubted if ten Bostonians had studied Spinoza. As for Schleiermacher and De Wette, it was his understanding that they wrote in German, which hardly anyone in Boston could read. "Now books cannot do much harm unless they are read," he observed. He therefore proposed to shift the debate away from personalities and belief in miracles to the crucial issue, the essential nature of religion.[56]

Farmer Levi had a germ theory of religion. He noted that Norton and Ripley spoke much about the evidence for Christian belief, but it seemed to him there was a "previous question" that had to be dealt with before one could speak intelligibly about the evidentiary basis of any particular religion. This was the question of how people came to have any religion at all: "Gentlemen, we must settle the *genus,* before we decide upon the *species.* The evidence for religious truths in *general,* I take it, cannot be different in *kind,* from the evidence for the *special* religious truths of Christianity." There cannot be two kinds of evidence any more than there are two kinds of right, he reasoned. To his understanding, all religions professed a belief in the existence of God and a sense of dependence on God; this was what made them religions. He could not imagine a religion that did not confess these primary truths. Moreover, to the religious understanding, the existence of God is not something that has to be discovered or proven, but a fundamental truth of human existence. "I reckon that man is by nature a religious being; i.e., that he was made to be religious, as much as an ox was made to eat grass," Parker asserted. "The germs of religion, then, both the germs of religious principle and religious sentiment, must be born in man, or innate, as our preacher says."[57]

Norton claimed that the primary truths of Christianity were established through the senses by historical revelation, but Parker countered that this logically impossible position simultaneously denied and implicitly assumed an innate capacity to receive revelation. Revelation cannot be received by human subjects if they are not disposed by the "germs" of their innate human nature to receive it,

Parker explained: "An outward revelation could only be the *occasion* of manifest-ing these germs, and not the cause of religion in man. It cannot be the creation of a new element in man; as it must be if these germs are not already in him." Religion begins with religious "germs" that are innate in humanity and make pos-sible the appeal to what some religions call "revelation." Moreover, because all religions are rooted in the same innate germs, Parker reasoned, all religions are fun-damentally identical though some are more developed than others. Christianity is developed to perfection—perhaps even to the extent of being the absolute reli-gion—but all religions are "only specific variations of one and the same genus."[58]

This put the evidentialist appeal to miracles in its place. Parker invoked the logical maxim that what is true of the genus obtains also of the species:

> If, therefore, the two fundamentals of religion, which in themselves involve all necessary truths thereof, be assumed by Christ as self-evident, already acknowledged, and therefore at no time, and least of all at that time, requiring a miracle to substantiate them, I see not how it can be maintained, that miracle was needed to establish infe-rior truths that necessarily follow from them.

Norton's evidentialism insisted on the necessity of lighting the sun with a can-dle by turning a merely theological position about the significance of miracles into a matter of essential *religious* concern. This is a category mistake, Parker insisted, for in its essence, religion is not about sense-bound phenomena like miracles. If Socrates did not require historically validated miracles to establish the truth of his teaching, how did it pass as a *Christian* argument that the truth of Christ requires miraculous proofs?

Unitarianism faced a choice between rival liberal perspectives, but Parker implied that only one was genuinely liberal. The first believed that Christianity is the perfection of a religion rooted in the innate spiritual truths of the soul; the second believed that Christianity is the perfection of a religion not rooted in the innate spiritual truths of the soul. Parker appreciated that those who sub-scribed to the latter view often felt a desperate need to "establish the divine authority of the mediator of this religion" by appealing to the historicity of Christ's miracles. But this strategy failed, he counseled, because it held up an authoritarian religious structure with weak arguments at best. Miracle arguments cannot be proven, and they prove nothing. It is not far-fetched to imagine a morally repulsive miracle worker. Parker did not doubt that Jesus performed mir-acles, "but I see not how a miracle proves a doctrine." He suggested that genuine Christianity values the miracles for Christ, not Christ for the miracles. It is the character of Christ that gives value to the miracles of Christ reported in scripture, he explained; Christians rightly regard the miracle claims of other religions as matters of indifference, not as claims that have to be denied or refuted.[59]

"I need no miracle to convince me that the sun shines, and just as little do I need a miracle to convince me of the divinity of Jesus and his doctrines, to which a miracle, as I look at it, can add just nothing," he concluded. Norton's

Unitarianism denied the real basis of Christian truth while making matters of eternal importance rest on evidence too weak to seal a verdict in a minor court case. Parker protested, "You make our religion depend entirely on something outside, on strange events which happened, it is said, two thousand years ago, of which we can never be certain, and on which you yourselves often doubt, at least of the more and less." In this situation, his prayer was, "God save Christianity from its friends, its enemies we care not for."[60]

"Levi Blodgett's arguments" heightened Parker's growing reputation as a provocateur. His intervention in the Norton-Ripley debate confirmed the general Unitarian impression that he belonged to the radical side of the Unitarian divide. Parker's high regard for German theology was a matter of record; he was known to be friendly with rough-looking "Come-outers" from Cape Cod, who disdained all creeds and proclaimed that all nature was a church; politically, he associated with the coalition of abolitionists, pacifists, and other reformers that convened at Chardon Street Chapel in 1840 as the Friends of Universal Reform. *The Previous Question* stirred no immediate controversy, however. Much of its style was tongue in cheek; the pamphlet was ignored by some of its targets; and Parker made several assuring statements about Jesus as the prophet of perfect religion. Parker associated with radical reformers and eccentrics, but so did Channing and Ripley. He was more combative than Emerson, but he also identified with Unitarian Christianity more closely than Emerson. In the flush of his enthusiasm for Emerson's Divinity School address, he had worried over the fact that Emerson left the ministry but resolved to keep Emerson's spirit alive in the church as a Unitarian pastor.

In 1840, this resolve was still a source of assurance to Unitarian leaders in the Boston Association of Ministers whom he otherwise irritated. Emerson drifted out of the church almost casually; in 1840, with deeper anguish, Ripley's ministerial appointment at Purchase Street also began to unravel; but at the end of the year in which Parker began to "let off the Truth fast as it comes," he was still a reasonably respected figure in Unitarian circles.

The resignations of Emerson and Ripley were both crises of conscience, though Ripley was much older when he gave up the security of his pastoral position. His resignation was a question of coming clean with his congregation about his inner beliefs. He explained to his congregation that "the essential principles of liberal Christianity, as I had always understood them, made religion to consist, not in any speculative doctrine, but in a divine life." It was painful to him to see his beliefs derided as heresy by church leaders. "I had a native aversion to human authority for the soul," he confessed. "I could not stand still. . . . The plainest expositions of Christian truth, as it seemed to me, were accused of heresy. Every idea which did not coincide with prevailing opinions, and many which had heretofore always been received by liberal churches, were considered hostile to church and state, were spoken of under various appellations which no man understood, and this caused the uninitiated to fear and the good to grieve."[61]

Ripley's own theology had become clearer, but so had the opposition of the Unitarian establishment and much of his congregation. Personally, his members loved him, but many of them shared his ministerial colleagues' disapproval of his religious views. These reactions reinforced Ripley's inner doubt that his theology belonged in the Unitarian church. In his farewell sermon he listed, as his heresies, "that I was a peace man, a temperance man, an abolitionist, a transcendentalist, a friend of radical reform in our social institutions; and if there be any other name that is contrary to sound doctrine as now expounded by the masters in our Israel, to consent to bear whatever stigma might be attached to it."[62] The latter claim was only half true, for Ripley was too sensitive to endure the resentment of disapproving colleagues and congregants. He preached his last sermon on March 28, 1841, less than two months before Parker set off an explosive theological controversy.

By the time that the furor over Parker's ordination sermon of May 19 played itself out, the Unitarian establishment was deeply chagrined that he insisted on remaining a Unitarian minister.

THE TRANSIENT AND PERMANENT

In the closing months of 1840, Parker began to notice that he was having trouble finding colleagues who would exchange pulpits with him. He took a pledge not to violate "Christian self-respect" by accumulating too many rejections: "I should laugh outright to catch myself weeping, because the Boston clergy would not exchange with me!"[63] The following May, his life turned a corner when he preached at the ordination of Charles C. Shackford in South Boston. "The Transient and Permanent in Christianity" was unusual fare for an ordination sermon, but typical of Parker. It was not meant to provoke a controversy. Parker, unfailingly genuine after Emerson's Divinity address had set him free, always said exactly what he believed and took pride in having no tact. He puzzled over the fact that certain colleagues casually discussed personal beliefs among themselves that they never expressed in public, let alone in the pulpit. Parker rebelled at the notion that certain religious opinions or problems had no place in the pulpit, and did not recognize distinctive obligations and decorum for ordination services. With typical straightforwardness, not calculating any particular effect, he presented his basic theological perspective at the ordination of a colleague not known for any attachment to the church's liberal wing. Nearly every subsequent nineteenth-century liberal theologian worked some version of the distinction between Christian core and husk, which Parker enunciated here. His primer on the essence of true religion claimed that historical Christianity was mostly husk.

"It must be confessed, though with sorrow, that transient things form a great part of what is commonly taught as Religion," he proposed. "An undue place has often been assigned to forms and doctrines, while too little stress has been laid on the divine life of the soul, love to God, and love to man."[64] Parker's definition of genuine Christianity as pure morality and pure religion centered on the latter spiritual realities. He argued that true Christianity is the religion of Jesus: "It is absolute, pure Morality; absolute, pure Religion; the love of man; the love of God acting without let or hindrance." The only creed that true religion lays down, he claimed, "is the great truth which springs up spontaneous in the holy heart—there is a God." The watchword of true religion is the exhortation of Jesus: "be perfect as your Father in Heaven." Parker admitted that true religion requires a form and carries a sanction, but only as attributes of Spirit-filled living. The only outward form that religion requires is divine living; true religion consists of "doing the best thing, in the best way, from the highest motives." It followed that the only sanction that religion requires "is the voice of God in your heart; the perpetual presence of Him, who made us and the stars over our head; Christ and the Father abiding within us." This is the permanent religious core of genuine Christianity; the rest is transient and dispensable theology, ritual, and historical dross.[65]

While the parade of "onlys" made Unitarian leaders wince, and later protest, that is not what made Parker's sermon explosive. His description of true religion, after all, was a page from Channing. What made his address incendiary was that in an ordination sermon, in front of ministers from several denominations, Parker aggressively explained why doctrines pertaining to the authority of Christ and the Bible belonged to the dispensable husk of historical Christianity. He explicitly negated doctrines that his liberal Christian forerunners had implicitly relativized, but not rejected. On the basis of biblical inspiration and authority, he observed, the church insisted for centuries that people believe "impossible legends [and] conflicting assertions." The doctrine of biblical authority required Christians "to take fiction for fact; a dream for a miraculous revelation of God; an oriental poem for a grave history of miraculous events; a collection of amatory idyls for a serious discourse." Because the Bible was presumed to be verbally inspired by God, Christianity was identified with believing that God "gave counsels to-day, and the opposite to-morrow; that he violated his own laws; was angry, and was only dissuaded by a mortal man from destroying at once a whole nation." The primitive notion that God favored one people over others "was originally a presumption of bigoted Jews," Parker assured, but under the pressure of bad religious logic, it became an article of Christian faith which Christians were burned for not believing.[66]

Parker took a brief pass at exempting Jesus and Paul from "this idolatry of the Old Testament" before explaining why doctrines about the authority of Jesus and the New Testament also belonged to the category of idolatry. "Modern Criticism is fast breaking to pieces this idol which men have made out of the Scriptures," he asserted. "It has shown that here are the most different works thrown together. That their authors, wise as they sometimes were, pious as we feel often their spirit to have been, had only that inspiration which is common to other men equally pious and wise; that they were by no means infallible; but were mistaken in facts or in reasoning; uttered predictions which time has not fulfilled; men who in some measure partook of the darkness and limited notions of their age, and were not always above its mistakes or its corruptions." The Gospel narratives, moreover, contradict each other and often "shock the moral sense and revolt the reason." In their attempts to make an idol of Jesus, Parker judged, the Gospel writers frequently lowered Jesus to the level of Hercules and Apollonius. Later the church portrayed Jesus as a half-god, and still later as God himself.[67]

He urged that all of this had nothing to do with Christianity "except as its aids or its adversaries." The questions that pertain to these issues may be unavoidable for theology, Parker allowed, but they have nothing to do with true religion: "If Jesus had taught at Athens, and not at Jerusalem; if he had wrought no miracle, and none but the human nature had ever been ascribed to him; if the Old Testament had forever perished at his birth,—Christianity would still have been the Word of God; it would have lost none of its truths. It would be just as true, just as beautiful, just as lasting, as now it is; though we should have lost so many a blessed word, and the work of Christianity itself would have been, perhaps, a long time retarded."[68]

It followed that Christianity does not rest even on the personal authority of Jesus. Jesus was "the organ through which the Infinite spoke," Parker explained, and what mattered ultimately was not his reality, but the truth that he spoke. Jesus was the exemplar of a religious ideal, but what mattered was the truth of the ideal, not the history of Jesus. Parker pressed this claim to its logical con-clusion. Even if historical criticism were to prove that the Gospels are total fab-rications and that Jesus never lived, he asserted, the truth of Christianity would not be affected: "None of the doctrines of that religion would fall to the ground; for if true, they stand by themselves." Historical criticism will never prove that much, he asserted; neither will it take away much that is beautiful in Christianity. On the other hand, liberal Christianity needed to give up more than it thought or desired. The only permanent religious truths were life-giving moral intuitions.[69]

The Transient and Permanent in Christianity had some rough passages rhetor-ically; Parker was in poor health when he wrote it. He had no clue that it would spark a controversy. Beyond a rather pointed ordination prayer from Brookline pastor John Pierce, who invoked the church's reverence for the authority of Christ and the Bible, the sermon stirred little reaction among Unitarians. Most of Parker's colleagues knew that he relativized Christian doctrine on a weekly basis. Several months later, he reflected that "the sentiments in the South Boston sermon had so long been familiar to me, I had preached them so often with no rebuke, that I was not aware of saying anything that was severe. I thought the sermon would be reckoned tame and spiritless, for it so poorly and coldly expressed what burned in my heart like a volcano."[70]

To some of its non-Unitarian clerical observers, however, the sermon was a shocking mockery of Christianity, and three outraged ministers representing the

Congregationalist, Methodist, and Baptist churches agreed that Parker's heresies had to be exposed. From notes and memory they cobbled together a version of the sermon that they published in several conservative religious journals. Their reconstructed text accentuated the sensational parts, but even a perfect copy would have sparked an uproar. The offended ministers were seeking not merely to expose Parker, but to embarrass the Unitarian church. For twenty years, conservatives had routinely called the Unitarian church "a halfway house to infidelity." With the publication of Parker's sermon and the controversy it set off, Unitarian leaders were challenged to prove that the "halfway" epithet was wrong. Would they break fellowship with Parker and condemn his heresies?

Unitarian leaders were in an impossible situation. Many of them admired Parker even while finding him difficult company; others genuinely liked him; but most were offended by parts of the sermon. His colleagues responded by cutting him off from the privileges of ministerial fellowship. Nearly all of the area ministers refused to exchange pulpits with him, and some refused to speak to him. At Harvard, a divinity student, John Weiss, protested, "Is love to God and love to man, intuition, instinct, the only Permanent? Can Revelation afford us nothing else? Where are all our hopes of repentance, regeneration—our assurances of immortality? And where, too, all this time, is Christ? Our moorings are all cast loose! We had already caught a glimpse of the Holy Land—we felt its celestial breath upon our souls—swiftly and sure each little bark was making for its destined haven, when, with one mighty upheaving from some Tartarean depth, we are cast back into the infinite void—into primeval chaos— no Christ, no religion; only some grim-smiling, sinister Impersonal Reason, brooding over the vast abyss."[71]

Weiss later became Parker's friend and memoirist; in later life, upon warming to a subject, he still averaged five or six metaphors per sentence. In 1841, however, his anxieties were widely shared by Unitarians. The Parker controversy heightened the identity crisis of Unitarian Christianity. Like Emerson, Parker dismissed traditional Christian teaching in an ecumenical setting with little regard for the public implications of his words. Like Emerson, he expounded his personal viewpoint on an occasion that had called him to speak for the common mind of the church. At the same time, his address was both more radical and more church-oriented than Emerson's, which was problematic for Unitarianism on both counts. Parker used his knowledge of biblical criticism to negate scriptural claims that Emerson left alone, but most of his argument adhered more closely than Emerson's to the style and basic claims of mainstream Unitarianism. At a critical point in the furor over his sermon, old-school Unitarian pastor Samuel K. Lothrop acknowledged that most of his homily was typical Unitarian sermonizing. Though he worried that Parker's extremism threatened to "overturn Christianity altogether," Lothrop acknowledged that in the main, he traded on a qualitative distinction between true religion and doctrinal reflection common to Unitarian preaching.[72] This acknowledgment was chastening and anxiety-provoking to many Unitarians. Did Parker represent the future of

American Unitarianism? Was he far enough outside the mainstream to be expelled?

In the winter of 1841–42, cut off from his colleagues in the Boston Association, Parker reluctantly accepted an invitation to present a course of lectures on religion in Boston's old Masonic Temple on Tremont Street. The lectures were a huge success, drawing hundreds of students from Cambridge each week to fill the 750-seat temple. In 1842, these lectures were published under the title *A Discourse of Matters Pertaining to Religion*.

Parker enjoyed the labor of turning his lectures into a book. The circumstances that produced it were grinding him down, however. He ached for a break from every-week sermon writing, but his colleagues refused to exchange pulpits with him. He desperately needed a larger stage than his congregation, Parker confessed to his friend Convers Francis: "If I stay at Spring Street, I must write 104 sermons a year for about 104 people. This will consume most of my energies, and I shall be in substance *put down*—a bull whose roaring can't be stopped, but who is tied up in the corner of the barn-cellar, so that *nobody hears him;* and it is the same as if he did not roar, or as if he were muzzled. *Now this I will not do. . . .* I must confess that I am disappointed in the ministers—the Unitarian ministers. I once thought them noble; that they would be true to an ideal principle of right."[73]

Publication of *A Discourse of Matters Pertaining to Religion* guaranteed that Parker would not be silenced. The book was widely reviewed, to the dismay and embarrassment of Unitarian leaders, and he resumed his highly popular lecturing. In January 1843, a few months after the book was published, the Boston Association of Ministers sought to settle the question of his Unitarian status. At a previous meeting, mindful of his absence, they had delicately criticized the book's flaming heresies. In his presence, under the condition that no catechizing was to be allowed, they presented their charges. Old-guard leader Nathaniel L. Frothingham declared that Parker's book was "vehemently deistical" and "subversive of Christianity," the latter because it aimed "to dissolve Christianity in the great ocean of absolute truth." On these counts, he judged that Parker had forfeited his right to ministerial fellowship. Several others added their resentment of Parker's tendency to claim that their private views were more liberal than the views they proclaimed from the pulpit.[74]

In self-defense, Parker asserted that he had never uttered a public word of complaint about being excluded from ministerial fellowship and that he never intended to accuse anyone of hypocrisy. With regard to his heresy, he requested a clarification of the "precise quiddity" that had to be added to absolute religion to make it qualify as Christianity. There were, he suggested, three logical possibilities about the relation of Christianity to absolute religion: Christianity is less than absolute religion; Christianity is equal to absolute religion, and Christianity is absolute religion and something more. He assumed that no Unitarian minister took the first option; the second was his position; he gathered that they held out for number three. Parker wondered aloud how the guardians of a modern religious tradition that lacked a creedal standard of orthodoxy proposed to establish the precise orthodox "more" that distinguished Christianity from absolute religion.

The Unitarian elders tried to change the subject, but were driven back to Parker's challenge. Finally, after one of them declared that the answer lay in the biblical miracles and the authority of Christ, others agreed that because Christianity was "a supernatural and a miraculous revelation," clearly Parker was not a Christian. One minister judged, "It is plain that we can't have ministerial intercourse with Mr. Parker: he denies the miracles." In reply, Parker rehashed his argument that miracles added nothing to the permanent truth of Christianity. The current battlelines had been drawn "immediately after the South Boston sermon," he noted, and the ministers had a right to expel him if they judged that he was truly harmful to the Unitarian church. At the same time, he reported, it surprised him that the Boston Unitarians were getting into the censorship business and that "the shibboleth of Christianity among the Unitarians was miracles."

After three hours of debate, it was clear that the Unitarian ministers wanted Parker out without having to expel him. Emerson's replacement at Second Church, Chandler Robbins, declared that it was Parker's moral duty to resign from the Association, but Parker firmly refused. The Unitarians would have to expel him to get rid of him. At this exhausted impasse, the meeting suddenly took a bathetic turn when Cyrus Bartol spoke warmly about Parker's moral integrity and good will, which prompted Ezra Stiles Gannett and Chandler Robbins to make clear that they, too, had never doubted his personal character. Parker burst into tears and ran from the room. He could take criticism, but not mixed with tender sentiments.[75]

The first Unitarian heresy trial was over. It confirmed that the Unitarians were shunners, not excommunicators. The Unitarian leaders were acutely aware that they were vulnerable to charges of hypocrisy. They protested when mainline Protestants denied them the Christian name, but they denied it to Parker. They nursed the bitter memory of being excluded from pulpit exchanges with Congregational conservatives, but they excluded Parker. Frothingham and others countered that the two cases were categorically different. The conflict between Unitarianism and Trinitarianism was a conflict within Christianity, they explained, while the dispute between the Association and Parker pitted Christianity against non-Christianity. With this claim, the Unitarian leaders sought to uphold their Christian identity and to establish that their church was closer to traditional Protestantism than to Emerson and Parker. The problem was that "Unitarian orthodoxy" was self-contradictory. They could not invoke a standard of right belief for Unitarian Christianity without denying their opposition to orthodox creeds. Their inability to censure Parker foreshadowed their inability to sustain the Christian identity of American Unitarianism.

MODERN SCHOLARSHIP
AND THE NATURE OF RELIGION

Parker had laid out an ambitious intellectual agenda in May 1840. He felt compelled to make a thoroughgoing case for a critical transcendentalist approach to religion and Christianity, judging, rightly, that American liberal Christianity lacked a single work that compared to his models, Schleiermacher's *Glaubenslehre* and the critical scholarship of Strauss and de Wette. He later explained that Germany was "the only land where theology was . . . studied as a science, and developed with scientific freedom."[76] Parker resolved to raise American religious discourse to the standard of contemporary German theology. "I must do or die," he reflected. "I sit down to hard work, and then only do I feel free from this tormenting spirit; at other times I am consumed by self-reproach for the nothings I have accomplished, for the nothing I have undertaken." He felt so keenly the need of a better American theological literature that when he sat down to write his heart pounded audibly and his hand quivered. His research and writing brought him some relief from the pressure he felt to elevate American theology, but "hard work only relieves me for the time it lasts."[77]

To live with himself, he felt he had to raise the level of American religious scholarship. To do this, he had to rewrite all of its basic literature and had already begun the first installment. In 1836, he had committed himself to produce an annotated translation of de Wette's *Einleitung;* this introduction to the critical study of the Old Testament had opened to him the world of critical German biblical scholarship. Parker's edition of this work, published in 1843, contained extensive notes, editorial revisions, and several short essays, including translations of its Latin, Greek, and Hebrew passages. Parker placed on its title page a rather defiant motto for a scholarly work. "Strike, but hear." In the introduction he lamented that most English and American theologians rejected the historical critical method in favor of a "dogmatic theology" that committed them to "a blind and indiscriminating belief." The book sought to correct this situation by making available to American readers an exhaustive survey of the history and current landscape of biblical criticism. Though Parker disagreed with de Wette on various points, notably de Wette's identification of Leviticus with the Elohist source, he supported de Wette's primary contention that biblical criticism was obliged to go beyond Eichhorn-style textual criticism to critique the canon and teaching of scripture as a whole. In 1840, he reasoned that the publication of de Wette's work would take care of the American need for a substantive critical introduction to the Old Testament.[78]

Parker resolved himself to provide the rest of the major works that he felt were needed: "I must write an Introduction to the New Testament—must show what Christianity is, its universal and its distinctive part. I must write a Philosophy of Man, and show the foundation of religion in him." These works would lay the groundwork for his crowning work of reflective critical theology. He noted that he was currently beginning his research on New Testament scholarship; "still harder work" would be needed before he could write a philosophy of religion; harder work yet would be needed "before the crown of *Theology* can be put on the work." He was determined to pursue the arduous and critical work of religious scholarship, he reflected, "still yielding to the currents of universal being that set through a soul that is pure."[79]

But Parker's life soon became one of constant lecturing and social activism, which put his intellectual goals out of reach. Though his collected speeches, sermons, and articles filled fifteen volumes, he never wrote the major theological works to which he aspired. Keenly disappointed that his edition of De Wette's *Einleitung* gained little attention, he soon realized that he could make a greater impact through his sermons and speeches. Contrary to much that has been written about him, Parker remained, at heart, a churchman and theologian. His later consuming dedication to the cause of antislavery was fueled by the morality of the Absolute Religion that he preached throughout his life. For many years he assumed that he would eventually get back to his academic project. "I will do some good work yet in my study, after the great struggle between Freedom and Slavery is ended," he would say.[80] He intended, in particular, to write a major work on the history of world religions, a subject on which he often preached,[81] and it surprised him that his early lectures on "matters pertaining to religion" became his defining theological work.

For all of his frustrated ambition, however, Parker's *Discourse* did accomplish much of the field-elevating objective that he set for himself. Nothing like it had been written by an American; while the book's footnotes were crammed with references to ancient and modern philosophical, theological, and historical works, its body wore this scholarship lightly. It was steeped in Kant and Schleiermacher, but every sentence was lucid American English. Written as a series of public lectures, it raised considerably the discursive standard of academic American theology and was the first work of American theology that contained nearly all of the defining features of mature American theological liberalism. Parker did not live long enough to confront the implications of Darwinian theory, and he was too rationalistic to take a liberal view of the symbolic/metaphorical nature of religious language; otherwise, in the form of an introduction to "enlightened" thinking about the nature of religion, he gave his readers and listeners an early, if hard-edged, introduction to American liberal theology.

Parker declared at the outset that "our theology is full of confusion." Instead of making truth their authority, theologians routinely took authority for truth, he lamented, routinely calling the best thinkers atheists or infidels, while believers reduced Christianity to idolatry, venerating the Bible and Jesus as idols. "What passes for Christianity in our times is not reasonable; no man pretends it," he judged. Parker proposed to call his readers "from the transient Form to the eternal Substance; from outward and false Belief to real and Inward Life; from this partial Theology and its Idols of human device, to that universal Religion and its ever living Infinite God."[82] He began with proof of the *fact* of a "religious element in Man," borrowed from Schleiermacher, before setting off on a sprawling survey of world history that showed the development of humanity's universal religious sentiment.

Schleiermacher taught that self-consciousness is the reciprocity between a person's feelings of dependence and freedom. Each feeling is relativized by the other; one cannot feel dependence or freedom without feeling the other. In any moment of consciousness, we are made aware of our unchanging identity and its changing character. Self-consciousness includes a self-caused element (*ein Sichselbstsetzen*) and a non-self-caused element (*ein Sichselbstnichtsogesetzthaben*) that Schleiermacher called the Ego and the Other. The Ego expresses the subject for itself; the Other expresses the coexistence of the ego with an other. The core religious feeling that Schleiermacher famously called "the feeling of absolute dependence" is made possible, in his account, by this double constitution of self-consciousness. Only in *relation* to an other does self-consciousness exist; the ground of self-consciousness is its openness to an other. It followed that all moments of the feelings of freedom and dependence comprise a single reality that corresponds in reciprocal relation to an other that makes self-consciousness possible. In Schleiermacher's words, "Hence a feeling of absolute dependence, strictly speaking, cannot exist in a single moment as such, because such a moment is always determined, as regards its total content, by what is *given*, and thus by objects towards which we have a feeling of freedom." At the same time, self-consciousness is also awareness of absolute dependence, "for it is the consciousness that the whole of our spontaneous activity comes from a source outside of us in just the same sense in which anything towards which we should have a feeling of absolute freedom must have proceeded entirely from ourselves."[83]

Parker appropriated his notion of core religious dependence from this theory, beginning his argument with the claim that the wellspring of all religion is the Spirit-endowed "inner Sanctuary of the Heart." He otherwise took his distance from Schleiermacher's theory of consciousness without convincingly showing that he understood it. Parker asserted that the religious element in human beings "first manifests itself in our consciousness by a feeling of need, of want; in one word by *a sense of dependence*." Without explaining that Schleiermacher's relational theory of self-consciousness was irreducibly dialectical, he attributed to Schleiermacher the view that "the ultimate fact of consciousness" is the feeling of dependence. Parker was surely uncomfortable with the religious connotations of dependence language, especially since he failed to grasp that, for Schleiermacher, dependence is always a necessary element in the feeling and movement of freedom. He advised that "consciousness of the Infinite" might be a better way of expressing the intuitive religious sentiment that Schleiermacher meant to describe. In any case, he maintained, his own argument did not depend upon or require acceptance of Schleiermacher's theory of consciousness, but was founded upon the mere "*fact* of a religious element in man."[84]

Parker made use of Schleiermacher in his own way, just as he appropriated Kant to his own end. For years the American transcendentalists had called themselves Kantians without acknowledging that Kant's "transcendental" claims referred to transcendental *categories* of understanding, not innate ideas; Parker was a chief exponent of the notion that American transcendentalism derived its theoretical basis from Kantian philosophy. When Kant, in his *Critique of Pure Reason,* attempted to explain how such diverse entities as the particulars of the external world and the pure concepts of the mind could be related, his "transcendental" solution found the relationship in the universal applicability of time, for both the particulars of the external world and the pure concepts of the mind exist in time. Space and time are not realities that rationality apprehends in the world, he reasoned, but the essential preconditions of thought itself. The essence of Kant's transcendentalism was his contention that human reason makes sense of the world by applying its a priori categories to all phenomena perceived by the senses.[85]

Parker shared the American transcendentalist tendency to read his own belief in innate ideas, especially "intuited moral truths," into Kantian philosophy. Near the end of his life he recalled that his adoption of Kant's transcendental method during his years as a divinity student was the decisive intellectual turning point of his life. Though Kant was one of the world's worst writers, Parker reflected—"even of Germany"—he was nonetheless one of its most profound thinkers; though Kant's conclusions were not always convincing, "he yet gave me the true method, and put me on the right road." The transcendental method he obtained from Kant disclosed the existence of "certain great primal intuitions of human nature, which depend on no logical process of demonstration, but are rather facts of consciousness given by the instinctive action of divine nature itself." For Parker, three of these innate primal truths were crucial to the possibility and phenomenon of religion: (1) the instinctive intuition of the divine creates consciousness of divine reality; (2) the instinctive intuition of moral right creates consciousness of the existence of a moral law that transcends human will; and (3) the intuition of the immortal ensures "that the essential element of man, the principle of individuality, never dies." These primal intuitions comprise the foundation of religion, he reasoned, "which neither the atheist nor the more pernicious bigot, with their sophisms of denial or affirmation, could move, or even shake." For the rest of his life, Parker maintained that true religion rests on these three essential truths. His life and thinking were based on "what was spontaneously given to all . . . the great primal instincts of mankind."[86]

This was not very good Kantianism, because like Emerson and other Americans with a background in Scottish commonsense philosophy, Parker read Kant in the light of Scottish intuitionism. Influenced by Coleridge and the intuitionist "Kantianism" of Harvard German literature scholar Charles Theodore Follen, the American transcendentalists who struggled with Kant tended to read their intuitionist spirituality into Kant's categories of the understanding.[87] Thus Parker declared at the outset of the *Discourse* that knowledge of God's existence is "an *intuition of reason*" that requires "no *argument* whatever." With an Emersonian spirit he assured that certainty of divine reality is established not by reasoning, but by reason: "The fact is given outright, as it were, and comes to the man, as soon and as naturally, as the consciousness of his own existence, and is indeed logically inseparable from it, for we cannot be conscious of ourselves except as *dependent* beings."[88]

The Idea of God is revealed to consciousness by intuition categorically apart from sense experience. For Parker, it does not depend upon or require a posteriori arguments about the order and beauty of the world, nor does it need a priori arguments about the spiritual nature of reality; it does not require any arguments at all. At the same time, he could not rest his argument entirely on the transcendental assurance that the Idea of God is an innate truism like liberty or immortality, for he worried that pure intuitionism is purely subjective. He invoked Schleiermacher's description of religious dependence, but never spoke of religion as absolute dependence. He invoked the Coleridge/Emerson distinction between Reason and the Understanding, but gave a higher creative role to the Understanding than Coleridge or Emerson. Parker theorized that Reason receives its concepts from the Understanding and depends upon the interpretive capacities of the Understanding in rendering its judgments. That is, the Understanding performs a creative function in formulating concepts and delivering them to Reason. Contrary to Emerson's "reasoning machine" picture of the Understanding, Parker theorized that the Understanding formulates, creatively interprets, and supplies to Reason the concepts upon which Reason makes its judgments. The performative function of Reason is merely to affirm or reject the concepts delivered by the Understanding.[89]

In order to establish a guard against subjectivism, Parker's revised schematism turned Emerson's purely intuitional ideas of Reason into *judgments* emerging from the deliberative interaction of the Understanding and Reason. Emphasizing that the Understanding must be educated to perform its interpretive functions, it asserted in good Kantian fashion that the Understanding (and therefore, Reason) necessarily relies upon external data delivered and limited by sense experience. "When the occasion is given from without us, the Reason, spontaneously, independent of our forethought and volition, acting by its own laws, gives us by intuition an Idea of that on which we depend. To this idea we give the name of GOD or GODS, as it is represented by one or several separate conceptions."[90]

Parker's reconceptualization of the ideas of Reason as judgments opened the back door to confirming arguments for God's existence. While holding fast to the claim that arguments are useless as proofs of divine reality, he granted a constructive role to them as confirming support systems for truths established intuitively. "This intuitive perception of God is afterwards fundamentally and logically established by the *a priori* argument, and beautifully confirmed by the *a posteriori* argument," he wrote. Apart from the enlightening perception of intuition, the cosmological and teleological proofs of divine reality give us merely abstract ideas of power and causation, at best; but rational arguments do confirm the intelligibility of religious ideas established by intuition. True belief in God always precedes the proof of God's existence; in Parker's language, intuition provides the ideas that the believer reasons about: "Unless this intuitive function be performed, it is not possible to attain a knowledge of God." Apart from intuition, Parker explained, rational proofs of God's existence prove nothing, because they address a reasoning faculty that cannot originate the Idea of God. Only intuition can originate the religious ideas that theology and philosophy rightly make the objects of their rational inquiry: "As we may speak of sights to the blind, and sounds to the deaf, and convince them that things called sights and sounds actually exist, but can furnish no *Idea* of those things when there is no corresponding sensation, so we may convince a man's understanding of the soundness of our argumentation, but yet give him no Idea of God unless he have previously an intuitive sense thereof."[91]

Parker never carefully defined what he meant by "the religious element in human nature." He spoke of it as a "germ," a fact of nature, a principle, a faculty, an intuition, and an instinct, but he never precisely clarified this central concept in his thought or even explained how it differed from other primal intuitive truths. He claimed to accept Kant's critiques of the classical philosophical proofs of divine reality while countering that "the fact of the Idea given in man's nature cannot be got rid of."[92] In particular, he claimed to accept Kant's refutation of the cosmological argument while basing his own position on a modified version of it. *A Discourse* put it this way: "The existence of God is implied by the natural sense of dependence; implied in the religious element itself; it is expressed by the spontaneous intuition of Reason."[93] The thesis of his essay "Transcendentalism" was closer to Schleiermacher: "I am not conscious of my own existence except as a finite existence, that is, as a dependent existence; and the idea of the infinite, of God on whom I depend, comes at the same time as the logical correlative of a knowledge of myself." Schleiermacher did argue that human beings come into knowledge of God's existence as the One on whom we depend through our experience of dependence. However, Parker's assurance, "So the existence of God is a certainty," was alien to Schleiermacher, as was Parker's summary of his argument: "Of this I am certain,—I am; but of this as certain,—God is."[94]

That was Emersonian transcendentalism, though Parker defended "absolute religion" with rationalistic arguments that Emerson eschewed. Most of Parker's argument rested on a vague concept of intuitional truths as universal elements or principles of human consciousness, not as subjective insights of an Emersonian individual soul. In his later career, Parker loaded his speeches with statistics and evidentialist arguments that contrasted with Emerson's denigration of the Understanding. For all of its argumentative proofmaking and self-defense, however, Parker's major religious work carried forward the Emersonian thesis that the foundation of religion and morality "is in Man, not out of him."[95] While Emerson wrote mystical, neo-Platonist evocations of the Oversoul, Parker carried out the unwelcome rationalist critique of historical religion that Emerson took for granted as a truth of Reason. As a depressed youth, Emerson had awoken from his spiritual lethargy when Edward Everett introduced him to the "new learning" of German criticism, but Parker demonstrated how transcendental religion and critical historical consciousness fit together.

ABSOLUTE RELIGION AND HISTORICAL CHRISTIANITY

In his first edition of *Life of Jesus Critically Examined* (1835), Strauss had sought to destroy the credibility of the Gospel narratives, to clear the field for his own left-Hegelian metaphysical theology. He used historical criticism as a means to negate every form of historically oriented theology, and he destroyed his career prospects in the process. Thus, in the book's second and third editions, Strauss sought to regain academic favor and make his peace with a liberal Protestant theological establishment by making a host of Schleiermacher-style revisions of his argument. This maneuver failed to win him an academic appointment, however, and Strauss hated the watered-down pastiche of liberal theologies that his book had become. With his fourth edition, published in 1840, therefore, he restored the myth-smashing left-Hegelian vigor of the book's original edition and marked the beginning of the end of his theological career.[96]

Parker's thinking about the relationship between history and religious truth was formed during this period, and he was keenly aware of the Straussian controversy. He admired Strauss's historical demolition of the Gospel narratives, while assuring himself that his own "religious spirit" made him a different kind of theologian than Strauss. Compared to Strauss's wide-ranging assault on the Gospel narratives and his slashing insistence that "the true criticism of dogma is its history," Parker considered his own critical perspective moderate and reasonable.[97] Strauss delivered wholesale negative verdicts, while Parker's were more piecemeal. Strauss taught that Christianity is true only as a primitive mythical anticipation of the Hegelian idea of divine-human unity; Parker smelled the trinitarianism in Hegelian dialectics and protested against its speculative mythologization of Jesus.

"The whole question seems to rest on a false position, viz., that Jesus of Nazareth was the Supreme Being," he observed. It is one thing to claim that Jesus knew God intimately or that Jesus is the greatest moral exemplar of how we should live, Parker reasoned; it is something else to rescue Christian Christ-myth with metaphysical spinning about the dialectical procession and return of Absolute Spirit in the world. "I am perpetually astonished that men should reason so—on such premises," Parker wrote in his journal. "Still more, that, starting from such premises, they will plunge into the sea of Deity, and tell us the metaphysics, and the physics, too, of God." The tradition of metaphysical theology epitomized by Hegel "is a game that serves to pass the time and sharpen the faculties, but it is played for straws," he judged. "The victor gains—nothing. It seems, in the history of Theology, as if there was a *tertium quid* between a lie and the truth; as if the opposite of a lie was also a lie, and not truth; as if truth and falsehood were the two extremes of a *tertium quid,* and the real way was deemed to be between them both."[98]

Thus Parker took his leave of the theological tradition most attuned to his own language of Absolute Religion. He wanted nothing to do with Hegelianism. He countered with a blend of transcendentalist spiritual certainty, unsparing historical criticism, and hardheaded rationalist logic. "Any argument is vain when the logical condition of all argument has not been complied with," he admonished.[99] His combination of piety and rationalism struck him as being so attractive—his crowds at the Masonic Temple were overflowing—that he was genuinely unprepared for the outrage that greeted his published lectures, previous controversies notwithstanding. Building up to his call for "real Christianity, the absolute Religion . . . Being Good and Doing Good," Parker detailed why the prevailing Christianity was neither real nor good. Like Strauss, he granted nothing to the notion of Christian truth as in-house narration of particular events. "If Christianity is true at all, it would be just as true if Herod or Catiline had taught it," he insisted. The problem was that scriptural narrative meets none of the modern tests for serious historical writing: "In the case of the Evangelists, they constitute a very serious difficulty. We know the character of the writers only from themselves; they relate much from hearsay; they continually mingle their own personal prejudices in their work; their testimony was not reduced to writing, so far as we know, till long after the event; we see that they were often mistaken, and did not always understand the words or actions of their teacher; that they contradict one another, and even themselves; that they mingle with their story puerile notions and tales which it is charitable to call absurd; that they do not write for a purely historical purpose, relating facts as they were, but with a doctrinal, or controversial aim."[100]

All of the Gospels mix fact and fiction pervasively, he judged; the Gospel authors are unknown, and the fourth Gospel has "scarcely any historical value." In 1840, Parker criticized Strauss for one-sidedly denigrating the historicity of the Gospel narratives, but in 1842 he adopted many of Strauss's critical judgments, including his wholesale rejection of the Gospel miracle stories. He claimed that the author of the fourth Gospel "invents actions and doctrines to suit his aim, and ascribes them to Jesus with no authority for so doing." His picture of the Jewish background to Christianity surpassed German Enlightenment standards for anti-Jewish bigotry: "A nation of Monotheists, haughty yet cunning, morose, jealous, vindictive, loving the little corner of space, called Judea, above all the rest of the world; fancying themselves the 'chosen people' and special favorites of God; in the midst of a nation wedded to their forms, sunk in ignorance, precipitated into sin, and still more, expecting a Deliverer." Out of this squalid background, an exemplar and teacher of true religion somehow emerged; Parker judged that the great themes of Absolute Religion—the truths of divine goodness and the spiritual nature of humanity—were at least implied in the teaching of Jesus. At the same time, he admonished, it was crucial never to forget that Jesus shared some of the worst attributes of his culture: "It is vain to deny, or attempt to conceal, the errors in his doctrine,—a revengeful God, a Devil absolutely evil, an eternal Hell, a speedy end of the world."[101]

Parker sought to provoke, eschewing more temperate ways of addressing these points; and parts of the *Discourse* took on the atmosphere of a shooting gallery: "Now it is a most notorious fact, that the Apostles and Evangelists were greatly mistaken on some points. It is easy to show, if we have the exact words of Jesus, that he also was mistaken in some points of the greatest magnitude— in the character of God, the existence of the Devil, the eternal damnation of men, in the interpretation of the Old Testament, in the celebrated prediction of his second coming and the end of the world, within a few years." To make Christianity stand or fall by the authority of Jesus is to make it look ridiculous, he warned: "If Religion or Christianity rest on his authority, and that alone, it falls when the foundation falls, and that stands at the mercy of a school-boy. If he is not faithful in the unrighteous mammon, who shall commit to him the true riches?"[102]

Parker repeated his arguments against the religious value of miracles, for which he was known—"When Mr. Locke said the doctrine proved the miracles, not the miracles the doctrine, he silently admitted their worthlessness"—and added the ultimate negation that he knew his audience awaited: "Is the testimony sufficient to show that a man thoroughly dead as Abraham and Isaac were, came back to life; passed through closed doors, and ascended into the sky? I cannot speak for others—but most certainly I cannot believe such monstrous facts on such evidence."[103]

The time had come, he exhorted, to sweep away all religious authorities save the authority of reason and spiritual intuition. It was time to finish the work of the Reformation. At his best, Jesus fell back on the goodness of God and taught that the truth is its own authority. The early church fell back on the authority of Jesus; the later church trusted in the authority of the Bible; still later, the church made itself an authority. This degenerative layering of authorities was arrested by the Reformation, in Parker's telling. Protestantism overthrew the tyranny of the church and exalted the authority of the Bible; three centuries later, biblical criticism overthrew the authority of the Bible and exalted the authority of Jesus; the future belonged to transcendental Christianity, which negated all external authorities and restored the authority of the divine indwelling. Parker was at his most Emersonian when he warmed to the theme of true religion. True Christians understood that "a Christ outside the man is nothing." True Christianity is not about the death or divinity of Christ, but about the death of sin and life of holy goodness in our heart: "Each man must be his own Christ, or he is no Christian." Absolute Religion knows nothing of "that puerile distinction between Reason and Revelation," Parker insisted. "Its

Temple is all space; its Shrine the good heart; its Creed all truth; its Ritual works of love and utility; its Profession of faith a manly life, works without, faith within, love of God and man."[104]

As an expression of "the one real Religion," true Christianity was implicitly for everyone, but Parker addressed the special role of the Unitarians, whose situation was disturbing and painful to him. Among American denominations, Unitarianism alone stood within hailing distance of Absolute Religion, but was making little progress in getting there. Recalling Norton's famous essay of the movement's youth, he noted that American Unitarianism began as a "Statement of Reasons for Not Believing" certain unacceptable doctrines, including the Trinity, total depravity, substitutionary atonement, eternal punishment, and a vengeful God. The movement's leaders were reformist and well mannered—"the most reasonable of sectarians"—and thought themselves thoroughly biblical. They thought that a moderately liberalized Christianity was a sustainable third way between Protestant orthodoxy and anti-Christian rationalism.

Parker still believed that a third way was necessary but that the existing Unitarian church was not it. Unitarianism was indeed a halfway house to somewhere, but it was stuck in the contradictions of moderately liberalized Christianity and showed little sign of moving in any direction. It advocated the vestiges of supernaturalism without the supernatural, Parker judged. It humanized the Bible, yet tried to salvage biblical miracles; it believed in humanity's spiritual nature, yet asked for a Mediator and Redeemer; it censured the traditionalism of other churches, "yet sits itself among the tombs, and mourns over things past and gone." By straining to keep its old crutches, the Unitarian movement had failed to keep its faith. "It clings to the skirts of tradition," he protested. "It would believe nothing not reasonable, and yet all things scriptural; so it will not look facts in the face, and say, This is in the Bible, yes, in the New Testament, but out of Reason none the less."[105]

Parker still believed, in 1841, that his denomination was America's best religious hope but would not remain so if the church's leaders failed to commit themselves to Absolute Religion. Unitarian Christianity stood in danger of becoming "God-parent to the fair child it has brought into the world, but dares not own."[106] A few years later, he judged that the Unitarian church was hopelessly mired in its contradictions. American Unitarianism began by affirming a negative, he reflected; it denied the divinity of Christ, but by failing to affirm the humanity of Christ, it represented little more than a negation. In his estimation, because most Unitarian leaders, as cultivated New Englanders, were not very religious, Unitarianism was unattractive to ordinary Christians. Uninterested in Absolute Religion, Unitarian leaders settled, instead, for mediocre theology and the machinery of a theological sect.[107]

In the late 1840s Parker exhorted that the Unitarian church had no hope of becoming "a great sect" if its leaders did not plainly affirm the humanity of Christ. He strongly doubted that they would do so: "They are not now making any advances towards a liberal theology; they stand still, and become more and more narrow and bigoted from year to year." Referring to Norton, he judged that the church's best scholar was "narrow, bigoted, and sectarian." He noted that most of the early movement's impressive figures were no longer preachers; a partial list would have included Emerson, Ripley, Edward Everett, George Bancroft, John G. Palfrey, and Jared Sparks. "There is little scholarship and less philosophical thinking among the Unitarians," Parker concluded. "Some of their members engage in the great moral movements of the day, such as the Temperance Reform, and the Anti-Slavery movement. But the sect as such is opposed to all reforms."[108]

THE POLITICS OF ABSOLUTE RELIGION

This judgment had a political edge. Unitarianism upheld the divinity of human beings in theory, but gave few of its sons and daughters to the struggle against chattel slavery. Parker's *Discourse* made him famous for his infidelity, but his greater notoriety came later, with his commitment to the antislavery movement. In 1848, after moving to Boston, he plunged into abolitionist politics and soon gravitated to the movement's radical, militant wing. Militant enough to become a friend and supporter of John Brown, he gave his best years to the one cause that offended millions of Americans more than apostasy. Though tender-hearted, he was a fierce polemicist, often aggressive in his use of sarcasm and ridicule. In his speeches he denounced slavery as an absolute moral evil while claiming, using statistical evidence, that it was also economically inefficient.[109]

Parker claimed that the purported economic dividends of slavery were not real and was brutally realistic in explaining why slavery was so hard to abolish. He charged that most Americans believed that enslaved blacks had no right to equal treatment and that the entire American political establishment was united in its desire to perpetuate this prejudice. "There are no accidents in politics," he assured. It was no accident that most of America's presidents were slaveholders and that American politics throughout the country was dominated by slaveholder interests. He noted that the press merely reinforced this evil:

> The Anglo-Saxon race, on both sides of the water, have always felt the instinct of freedom, and often contended stoutly enough for their own rights. But they never cared much for the rights of other men. The slaves are at a distance from us, and so the wrong of this institution is not brought home to men's feelings as if it were our own wrong. . . . No "respectable" paper is opposed to slavery; no whig paper, no democratic paper. You would as soon expect a Catholic newspaper to oppose the Pope and his church, for the slave power is the Pope of America.[110]

It grieved Parker that American churches were equally culpable for perpetuating the evils of slavery. Lamenting that the two most popular doctrines in

American Christianity were hell and slavery, he observed that not a single denomination belonged to the abolitionist movement: "The land is full of ministers, respectable men, educated men—are they opposed to slavery? I do not know a single man, eminent in any sect, who is also eminent in his opposition to slavery." The only recent exception paid a cautionary price, he noted: "There was one such man, Dr. Channing; but just as he became eminent in the cause of freedom, he lost power in his own church, lost caste in his own little sect; and though men are now glad to make sectarian capital out of his reputation after he is dead, when he lived, they cursed him by their gods!"[111]

For years Parker preached every Sunday to an enormous "free church" congregation—the Twenty-Eighth Congregational Society—that he organized in 1845; after outgrowing the spacious Melodeon Hall in Boston, his congregation moved to the Music Hall, which seated three thousand. On Mondays he often left on speaking tours that lasted several days, giving a hundred speeches each year on behalf of abolition, women's rights, labor organizing, temperance, education reform, and self-government. He opposed the Mexican War and the annexation of Texas; a passionate believer in self-government, he was the author of Lincoln's description of the American democratic ideal: "of the people, by the people, for the people." His oratory was earnest, felicitous, unadorned, didactic, long-winded even by nineteenth-century standards, laced with sarcastic wit, and too expansive and lacking in images to read well—at least when compared to Emerson or Wendell Phillips. As an orator in the golden age of American oratory, however, he ranked with such larger-than-life contemporaries as Emerson, Frederick Douglass, Henry Ward Beecher, Daniel Webster, Wendell Phillips, Sojourner Truth, Elizabeth Cady Stanton, Charles G. Finney, Philips Brooks, and Abraham Lincoln. As a social activist his comrades included Phillips, Dorothea Dix, Margaret Fuller, William Lloyd Garrison, Horace Mann, and Gerritt Smith.[112]

After the passage of the Fugitive Slave Law of 1850, Parker bitterly concluded that American slavery would have to be smashed by armed force; its evil was too institutionalized in American life to be amenable to moral or political reforms alone. He condemned Daniel Webster as a traitor for selling out the cause of antislavery in the U.S. Senate. Webster, to save the Union, supported the Fugitive Slave Law, advocated no restrictions on slavery in New Mexico, and denounced the abolitionist societies. Parker replied at Fanueil Hall: "He has done wrong things before, cowardly things more than once; but this, the wrongest and most cowardly of them all, we did not look for it." The only comparable deed in American history, he declared, was the treasonous act of Benedict Arnold. After Webster died in 1852, Parker lauded the "orator of Plymouth Rock" as an icon of New England enlightenment, before blasting him as "a tool of the slave-holder and a keeper of slavery's dogs." The sin of the great Daniel Webster was the great evil of debauching the nation's conscience, Parker admonished: "He poisoned the moral wells of society with his lower law, and men's consciences died of the murrain of beasts, which came because they drank thereat."[113] Even some of his friends were shocked by this violation of Unitarian decorum.

In his last years he supported slave uprisings, agitated for the forceful dismantling of slavery, and organized resistance to the Fugitive Slave Law. After John Brown's band of insurrectionists attacked Harper's Ferry, using weapons that Parker helped them secure, Parker insisted that it was morally justifiable to kill the oppressors who maintained America's slave system.

> If you were attacked by a wolf, I should not only have a *right* to aid you in getting rid of that enemy, but it would be my *duty* to help you in proportion to my power . . . If it were a *murderer,* and not a wolf, who attacked you, the duty would be still the same. Suppose it is not a murderer who would kill you, but a *kidnapper* who would enslave, does that make it less my duty to help you out of the hands of your enemy? Suppose he is not a kidnapper who would make you a bondman, but a *slaveholder* who would keep you one, does that remove my obligation to you?[114]

The Unitarian establishment contended that going to war to abolish slavery would be a terrible evil, because war—which is a political instrument, not a moral action—could be justified only by a political motive, not a moral one. Parker shook his head and pleaded the transcendent evil of condemning selected human beings to chattel slavery. The burning moral obligation to destroy slavery consumed his later life. He destroyed his health in his frenetic campaigning against slavery and other social evils and died at the age of forty-nine, in 1860, shortly before America went to war with itself, at least indirectly over the right to own human beings.

THE LEGACY OF PARKER UNITARIANISM

In his lifetime, Parker's constructive religious views were eclipsed by his notoriety as a radical abolitionist and infidel. Though deeply pious in his public prayers, which radiated a sense of serenity and optimistic faith, he was known mostly for his warring spirit and for what he rejected, thereby offending and embarrassing most Unitarian leaders and many others. In his telling, he would have preferred to write elegant Emersonian essays on the life of the soul or, more plausibly, a major work on world religious history, but the crises of his time called him instead to criticism, negation, confrontation, and social struggle.

His friend and biographer, Octavius Brooks Frothingham, aptly noted that as a religious thinker, Parker was compelled "to pay undeserved attention to the dogmas that interested him only as errors to be attacked, and to assail opinions he would greatly have preferred to let die."[115] He preached and lectured to the largest throngs in New England but was deeply alienated from his denomination, spurned as unbearable by most respectable society. Like Channing in his later years, though with a sharper edge, he found many of his closer associates and much of his audience outside the Unitarian church. His Sunday congregation was basically an audience, not a religious community, that gathered to hear his high-powered preaching on religion, history, literature, and current events. Some came and went during the service, many wore casual clothes and read newspapers, others departed early to avoid being seen at Parker's church. Parker scorched the social evils of his country, especially the self-interested hypocrisy of the New England establishment, with blistering rhetorical force, while often grieving privately over the cold hostility he received from political and religious leaders.

At his death he seemed to belong only to the social causes for which he spoke and to a scattered audience of religious individualists, many of them not Unitarians. In the generation that succeeded the Civil War, however, Parker became a figure of Unitarian pride and emulation. The reputational resurrection that he noted regarding Channing happened to him, only more dramatically, for Channing was never widely reviled. In the mid-1860s, many Americans began to repent of having reviled Parker, as the obliteration of American slavery made his opposition to it seem admirable in retrospect. The entry of his followers into Unitarian pulpits accelerated the generational absorption of transcendentalist religion into the mainstream of the Unitarian church.

In 1857 the graduating class of Harvard Divinity School selected Parker as its commencement speaker; only a faculty veto prevented another Divinity School address spectacle. After the war he was widely remembered as "the conscience of the North." Emerson judged that Parker's "commanding merit" was his persistently lived conviction "that the essence of Christianity is its practical morals." For Parker, he explained, Christianity either had a serious ethical meaning or no meaning at all: "It is there for use, or it is nothing; and if you combine it with sharp trading . . . or private intemperance, or successful fraud, or immoral politics, or unjust wars, or the cheating of Indians, or the robbery of frontier nations . . . it is a hypocrisy, and the truth is not in you."[116] In the social and historical context of postwar American Reconstruction, this sentiment set the ideal for the vanguard of a social-turning Unitarianism, and Parker's name was lifted above that of all other Unitarians, except Channing.

As a religious thinker his shortcomings were considerable. Parker had no understanding or appreciation whatsoever of religious symbolism, metaphor, myth, or liturgy. He epitomized the Enlightenment type as reverse-fundamentalist. Only literal propositions were real to him, and he universalized the ones he believed. He denigrated all historical religions, especially Judaism, toward which he displayed the anti-Semitic bigotry that was common to Enlightenment rationalists of his type. The ascendance of a Parker-influenced transcendentalism in the Unitarian church was devastating to the church's old guard. Boston minister Samuel Kirkland Lothrop was a witness to the passing of conservative Unitarianism: "This outbreak, if I may call it so, of Mr. Parker, disintegrated the clergy and the whole body of Unitarians, and dealt a blow from which Unitarianism has not, and probably as a religious denomination never will recover."[117] The routing of old-guard Unitarianism was not effected by Parker's influence alone, or even by the accumulated impact of the transcendentalist movement. Neither did it occur quickly or without an institutional struggle. In 1865, New York minister Henry W. Bellows organized the National Convention (later Conference) of Unitarian Churches to bolster the church's organizational and confessional identity. Spurning more specific creedal proposals, the convention declared in carefully vague language that the Unitarian church was committed to the building up of the Kingdom of God's Son, "the Lord Jesus Christ."[118]

The latter phrase was inflammatory to a group of Parker-quoting activists led by Francis Ellingwood Abbott and William J. Potter, whose protest was turned aside the following year at the first annual meeting of the National Conference in Syracuse. Convinced that American Unitarianism had renounced the principle of freedom by insisting on applying the connotatively supernaturalist title of "Lord" to Jesus, Abbott and Potter organized the Free Religious Association, a freedom-claiming alternative to the National Conference. Felix Adler, Octavius Brooks Frothingham, and John Weiss joined Abbott and Potter as the group's chief intellectual advocates; its core of members and friends included Emerson, Amos Bronson Alcott, Cyrus Bartol, Lydia Maria Child, William Lloyd Garrison, Rowland G. Hazard, Nathaniel Holmes, Lucretia Mott, Wendell Phillips, Elizabeth Cady Stanton, Gerrit Smith, and Edward L. Youmans. Frothingham later recalled that if Parker had lived into his fifties, he probably would have served as the group's leader; in his spirit, the group, led chiefly by Abbott and Frothingham, resolved to work together for "Free Religion."[119]

Free Religion was a "come-out" movement, with some equivocation. It called all religionists and humanists in the Parker mold to break free of Unitarianism and create a more advanced religious society, though many of its advocates remained Unitarian, to the annoyance of church leaders. Some of its key leaders and friends functioned as an independent caucus in the Unitarian Conference at the same time that their movement advocated an exodus from Unitarianism. The Free Religionists strongly asserted their connection to Parker; two of them, Frothingham and Weiss, were longtime Parker associates who later wrote important biographies of Parker. Frothingham also became the major historian of New England transcendentalism and the chief exponent of Free Religion theology.

In a movement loaded with such cases, the oedipal weight in Frothingham's case was particularly significant.[120] His father, Nathaniel L. Frothingham, was the old-guard leader who spearheaded the early Unitarian effort to force Parker out of the ministry. A ministerial patriarch of upper-class Boston Unitarianism, he epitomized its mannered gentility and high-minded moralism. Frothingham later reflected that his father held the clerical profession in high regard on account of its dignity and propriety, "but as much on account of its social position as on account of its sanctity." He loved being a minister because it afforded him "the highest type of gentlemanliness." The younger Frothingham attended Harvard Divinity School while his uncle, Edward Everett, was Harvard's president; as a student product of old-guard Unitarianism, he took for granted that "Strauss was a horror; Parker was a bugbear; Furness seemed an innovator; Emerson was a 'Transcendentalist,' a term of immeasurable reproach." His conversion to freethinking transcendentalism occurred during his early ministry, chiefly under Parker's influence, but he later recalled that he was fifty years old before he completely overcame the influence of his father.[121]

From Parker he learned about developments in biblical criticism, especially Tübingen-school historical criticism, but more important was Parker's personal influence. "He communicated a moral impetus," Frothingham later recalled. Though Parker's ideas were often questionable, and his learning was more copious than discerning, "his singlemindedness was perfect, and his devotion to his fellow-men was almost superhuman."[122] Frothingham became a transcendentalist of Parker's type and modeled his ministries in Jersey City and New York City after Parker's example. In 1863 he founded a Unitarian church on Fortieth Street, Manhattan; four years later he became president of the Free Religious Association, a position he held until 1878; by 1869, he had converted his congregation to Free Religion, breaking away from the Unitarian church. Frothingham renamed his Sunday audience the Independent Liberal Church and moved it, like Parker, to a spacious midtown dance hall, Lyric Hall; later it moved to the new Masonic Temple. The congregation disbanded in 1879 after he took early retirement from the ministry.

Frothingham was widely regarded as Parker's heir, but in crucial respects his later preaching and writing relinquished Parker's religious essentials. Parker unfailingly maintained that Absolute Religion is based on the perfect goodness of a personal God, the immortality of the soul, and the absoluteness of the moral law within.[123] Frothingham relativized these principles in the later 1860s, taking the logical next step beyond Parker's Christian-rooted philosophy of religion and adopting an explicitly post-Christian ideology that he called "the religion of humanity." In 1867, the opportunity to join a radical "come-out" movement offered him a welcome symbol and expression of independence from Christianity.

The Free Religionists advocated a Parker-style philosophy of world religion that was soaked in Parker's post-Unitarian spiritual vision, but drained of Parker's deeply prayerful, God-relating spirituality. Frothingham's "religion of humanity," aspiring literally to its name, affirmed ideas about God, immortality, the moral law, and the like on the basis of a least common denominator that Frothingham named the "faith of mankind." It called for a world-embracing "Bible of Humanity," and declared that every person is a Christ.[124] Abbott's Free Religion was more dogmatic in its humanism, reducing Parker's Absolute Religion to the ideology of barely religious humanism. Abbott proposed that religion is fundamentally "the effort of man to perfect himself," that religion is rooted in universal human nature, and that all historical religions are therefore identical "in virtue of this one common root." He taught that while Christianity was self-abasing and God-oriented, "prostrate on its face," Free Religion was totally self-affirming, "erect on its feet." Christianity was based on faith in Christ, he explained, but Free Religion was based on "faith in Human Nature." Christianity was about self-humiliated devotion to Christ, but Free Religion was about "self-respect and free self-devotion to great ideas." These affirmations yielded a grandiose self-affirmation. Abbott concluded that while Christianity was the faith of the soul's childhood, Free Religion was the faith of the soul's adulthood: "In the gradual growth of mankind out of Christianity into Free Religion, lies the only hope of the spiritual perfection of the individual and the spiritual unity of the race."[125]

This rendering of Parker's legacy was still religious enough to affirm that "the great peace of Free Religion is spiritual oneness with the infinite One," but that was as close as Free Religion came to the religion of Channing. As an organization, the Free Religious Association lasted only a generation, ending with the 1893 World Parliament of Religions in Chicago. Frothingham returned to Boston after his retirement and wrote several filiopietistic works on the heritage of Boston Unitarianism that betrayed more than a bit of regret at its waning.[126] As a way of appropriating the religious legacy of Parker and Emerson, however, his movement played a significant role in later Unitarian and liberal Christian history.

Logically, Free Religionism was an argument for breaking free from all existing institutions, but some of its advocates argued that the Unitarian Conference was the best place to contend for a post-Christian universal religion. Both sides had cause to appeal to Parker's example. For decades, old-guard Unitarians claimed to see no contradiction in the phrase "Unitarian orthodoxy"; more important, Channing insistently called himself a Unitarian Christian, not a Unitarian. Parker's position was the last stop within Unitarian Christianity. He routinely dismissed Unitarianism as hopelessly conservative, but never severed his connection to it, insisting on his right to the Christian name while regarding Christianity as merely a potential example of ideal Absolute Religion. Over the course of the half-century that followed his death and witnessed the elevation of his reputation, some of his spiritual comrades left the Unitarian communion, while others remained within it and became part of its redefined mainstream.

The question whether Unitarianism needed to retain the Christian name, or at least its right to claim it, became a crucially defining issue in the postwar nineteenth century. In the mid-1860s the original American transcendentalist, Frederic Henry Hedge, struggled to persuade Unitarians not to foresake their Christian identity. Hedge had not allowed his friendship with Emerson or his commitment to Transcendentalism to erode his Christian moorings, and his broad knowledge of church history gave him a wider context for thinking about religious issues than most of his colleagues had. More important, he judged that there was no reason to abandon progressive Unitarian Christianity. In 1864, shortly before the organization of the National Unitarian Conference, in a stirring speech at Harvard Divinity School, he warned against the logic of Parker's followers, who dreamed of a Christianity stripped of Christ and a supernatural God: "The cathedral of St. Paul's might then become a church of 'Intuitive Morals,' and Westminster Abbey a chapel of Pure Reason." The actual choice, Hedge countered, was not between corrupted historical religions and a pure religion of Spirit, but between vital and weak historical religions. Parker's Absolute Religion was not "a universal intuition of the soul," as its advocates imagined, but rather a particular form of religious thinking that contained a history and its own limiting historical blinders, like every other religious perspective. Noting that not much of a religion came from Absolute Religion, Hedge implied that even if Parker's followers took over a few cathedrals, they were not likely to build many of their own.[127]

That put it negatively, but the following year Hedge's book *Reason in Religion* made a positive case for keeping Unitarianism Christian. He observed that the defining debate within Unitarianism was no longer over miracles or the legitimacy of historical criticism; the old guard had lost that debate. What was now at stake, he admonished, was whether Unitarianism should remain a form of Christianity: "I am far from maintaining that Christianity must stand or fall with the belief in miracles; but I do maintain that Christian churches, as organized bodies of believers, must stand or fall with the Christian Confession,—that is, the Confession of Christ as divinely human Master and Head." The Unitarian communion had no viable future and no right to expect one if it did not remain Christian in this precise confessional sense, he exhorted: "There must be a line somewhere . . . a line which defines it, and separates those who are in it from those who are without. The scope of the Liberal Church is large; but everything and everybody cannot be embraced in it."[128]

Liberal Christianity seemed to have gone too far; there had to be a line that guarded the liberal church from anything-goes relativism. Unitarianism would not survive—or at least not flourish—as a humanistic fellowship of liberal Christians and non-Christian ethical humanists and naturalists. In the same year and for many years after, Henry W. Bellows made the same argument in seeking to hold the Unitarian Conference together as a Christian body. When told that the conference's constitutional reference to Jesus as Lord violated religious freedom, Bellows implored that American Unitarianism had already reduced its tie to Christianity to the bare minimum; if there was to be any change in the conference's constitution, the change had to be made in the other direction. "We are to consider not only the few on the one side, who may or may not care to unite with us, but the great body of Christians of all denominations, the Universal Church of Christ," he urged. "I demand liberality to them, the liberality which acknowledges their Lord and Leader, and welcomes them to a household whose hearth glows with faith in and loyalty to the personal Saviour."[129]

That is, and is not, what happened. The Unitarian Conference retained its minimal tie to the faith of historic Christianity, but in a way that marginalized the faith language of Christ as Lord and Savior. Unitarianism produced several notable liberal Christian leaders in the succeeding generation, including Harvard social ethicist Francis Greenwood Peabody and Harvard philosopher Charles C. Everett, but as a denomination the Unitarian church gradually relativized its Christian identity. Parker's neo-Christian theology was a marginal position in the Unitarian church at the end of his life in 1860. A half-century later, in a cooler voice, it was the mainstream Unitarian perspective. The transcendentalist philosophy of Parker and Emerson became passé, but their implicitly post-Christian religious humanism reconfigured the church of Channing and the Henry Wares. The Unitarian church liberalized enough to become a comfortable home to a wide continuum of liberal Christian, neo-Christian, and non-Christian ethical humanists, including the humanist successors of the Free Religious Association. In 1932 the spiritual descendants of Free Religion joined John Dewey and others in issuing "A Humanist Manifesto," which dropped the Free Religion interest in world religions and exalted scientific humanism as the only worthy object of religious loyalty.[130] A century after Parker's death, a prominent Unitarian leader, Jack Mendelsohn, reflected that while Parker's outspokenness was an embarrassment to his contemporaries, "it was a godsend to succeeding generations. Parker was the wave of the future for Unitarian religion in America. It was his spirit that has prevailed and thus preserved the only genius for which Unitarianism is fit."[131] This was the genius of beginning a progressive transformation that could be carried out only in the future, by others.

Joseph Henry Allen, a discerning witness of the Parker revolution, in his 1882 lectures on Unitarian history at Harvard Divinity School, reflected on the transition then occurring in his tradition. Having known and admired Parker, he confirmed the increasingly commonplace estimate that Parker was one of the two colossi of American Unitarian history, and he emphasized Parker's great sensitivity and compassion in private relations. While he took for granted Parker's theological achievement in liberating Unitarianism from the confines of a peculiar orthodoxy that was, in 1882, already difficult to explain to Harvard students, Allen also noted, with cool disapproval, that Parker was unceasingly partisan, aggressive, and polemical in his public speaking and attitude. Lacking any capacity to appreciate or even deal with people who disagreed with him, Parker routinely misrepresented the views of his opponents and even in his most scholarly work, was "always anticipating hostility, and in a chronic attitude of fighting."[132]

Allen admonished that this was no longer an acceptable way to think about religion or advocate a religious perspective. In decades past, he explained, theological debates were waged with great learning on both sides, "with the sole aim on each side to get the victory over the other, and on both, to see which could hit the hardest blows. Each combatant spoke for a party,—evangelical, unitarian, rationalistic,—and his business was to do that party the best service and its adversaries the most damage he could." In decades past, even *liberal* theology was positivist and partisan, and liberal theologians adopted a set of ideas and then looked for evidence or modes of interpretation that fit their ideas. But in 1882, he exhorted, the rhetorical mode of party politics was no longer appropriate to religious thinking; theology had to be based on the methods and verdicts of science and historical criticism. Scientific thinking is cool, inductive, and disinterested, he explained: "Science builds together its facts, bit by bit, comparing, explaining, investigating, combining, but keeping as clear as may be from all theories whatever, except as they grow irresistibly out of the facts."[133]

Historically, theologians had for the most part written about other theologians, but in the age of Darwin, theology was obliged to become scientific, or perish: "Darwin, Spencer, Tyndall, Huxley, are names of much more immediate moment to the theological world than the names of Schleiermacher, Strauss, Baur, and Parker. In the field of debate now open, the place of honor is held, not by the advocates of this or that opinion, but by those who, patiently, learnedly, and candidly are doing their best to bring a genuine scientific spirit to bear upon the facts."[134]

Precisely in this sociohistorical context the liberal theology movement exploded far beyond the boundaries of Unitarianism and scattered non-Unitarian forerunners. Although the triumphant liberal movement that emerged in the later nineteenth century often did not share Allen's conception of theological science, all of its advocates agreed that theology had to be carried out differently in the age of Darwin and historical criticism. Modernity presented unprecedented opportunities to Christianize America and the world in a progressive way, but it also threatened to extinguish Christianity. The "mainline" successors of the Unitarians resolved to save Christianity from its secular enemies and Unitarian friends.

3.
Imagination Wording Forth:
Horace Bushnell
and the Metaphors of Inspiration

Mainline liberal theology had more singular beginnings than Unitarianism, but a richer harvest. Channing, Emerson, and Parker were epic figures who provoked their tradition to question and struggle with the limits of its liberalism. In contrast, only one non-Unitarian thinker of their time, Horace Bushnell, made a comparable contribution to American religious thought, and for most of his career he was a sadly isolated figure.

It took two conversion experiences even to keep young Bushnell in the church; his third occurred long after he became a pastor. As a pastor and theologian he had to withstand many years of unrequited ambition, the threat of excommunication, and another long period of lonely rejection, before he heard himself lauded by a smattering of clerical followers as the father of American liberal theology. Although Bushnell was "pre-liberal" on more counts than Parker, in the areas that counted most for the tradition he founded, he was a figure of singular historical importance, grievously in error in certain convictions, but also deservedly remembered as the theological father of mainstream American liberal Protestantism. Bushnell was America's greatest nineteenth-century theologian and the first American to theorize about the metaphorical nature of religious language.

ON CHOOSING CHRISTIANITY

Horace Bushnell was born in 1802, in rural Litchfield County, Connecticut, where his parents made their living as wool carders and weavers. As the eldest son, Bushnell expected to carry on his father's trade, notwithstanding his father's frosty demeanor. In contrast, his warm and devoted mother aspired for him to attend college and become a minister, and, like Parker, he was tenderly eloquent on the subject of mother-love for his entire life. Repelled, as a youth, by the harshness of the Congregationalist Calvinism that he heard in church, Bushnell may have belonged for a time to a local "infidel club," led by a Thomas Paine–quoting Deist. In any case, he was clearly prepared to disappoint his mother, whatever the extent of his disaffection from the prevailing orthodoxy, for to him, higher education represented the path to ordained ministry, a calling he sought to avoid. His first experience of elevated religious feeling occurred as the advent of large-scale textile manufacturing in New England threw into doubt the viability of the family business. In response, he joined the local church in 1822 and at the relatively advanced age of twenty-one, he entered Yale College the following year, at the height of the Congregational-Unitarian schism.[1]

There, in the company of generally younger, better educated, and more urbane classmates, Bushnell lost his newfound religious faith. He also felt acutely his lack of sophistication, reflecting later that his basic problem was linguistic. "I was brought up in a country family, ignorant of any but country society, where cultivated language in conversation was unknown," he explained. "I came to writing with no stock of speech but this. I had no language, and if I chanced to have an idea, nothing came to give it expression. The problem was, in fact, from that point onward, how to get a language, and where."[2]

After college Bushnell turned successively to school teaching, journalism, and law school, spinning words in fields that brought him little satisfaction. His dislike of Calvinist orthodoxy and his educated skepticism made him resist, at first, the waves of religious enthusiasm that swept New England in the 1820s and 1830s. Bushnell's religious feelings were stirred by the revival preaching of the Second Great Awakening, but these feelings were in tension with his skepticism about Christian doctrine and his misgivings about the social spectacle of mass religious fervor. He would later recall that for years he nursed a host of intellectual doubts that prevented him from claiming the faith that his heart desired. Finally, in 1831, upon completing his legal studies at Yale at the top of his class, Bushnell attended a prayer meeting of law school tutors and blurted out his problem. Speaking to admiring acquaintances who envied his academic success and the promising legal career that lay before him, he confessed his personal conflict about religion: "When the preacher touches the Trinity and when logic shatters it to pieces, I am all at the four winds," he disclosed. The conflict between his head and heart had thrown him into a personal crisis, and Bushnell intimated that perhaps the moment had come for him to pay greater heed to his heart: "My heart wants the Father; my heart wants the Son; my heart wants the Holy Ghost—and one just as much as the other. My heart says the Bible has a Trinity for me, and I mean to hold by my heart. I am glad a man can do it when there is no other mooring."[3]

The closest thing we possess to a first-person explanation of Bushnell's conversion is a sermon he preached years later at Yale College Chapel, in which he told his story as a sermon illustration. He asked his college audience to picture a young man whose religious beliefs had gradually shriveled to nothing, despite his prolonged search for religious truth:

> He has not meant to be an atheist; but he is astonished to find that he has nearly lost the conviction of God, and cannot, if he would, say with any emphasis of conviction that God exists. The world looks blank, and he feels that existence is getting blank also to itself. This heavy charge of his possibly immortal being oppresses him, and he asks again and again, "What shall I do with it?" His hunger is complete, and his soul turns every way for bread. His friends do not satisfy him. His walks drag heavily. His suns do not rise, but only climb. A kind of leaden aspect overhangs the world. Till, finally, pacing his chamber some day, there comes up suddenly the question, "Is there, then, no truth that I do believe?"[4]

Bushnell's single affirmative certainty was a moral intuition: "'Yes, there is this one, now that I think of it: there is a distinction of right and wrong that I never doubted, and I see not how I can; I am even quite sure of it.'" He could doubt the reality of God, but not the good, a moral certainty that contained the basis of a life-changing religious faith: "Then forthwith starts up the question, 'Have I, then, ever taken the principle of right for my law? I have done right things as men speak; have I ever thrown my life out on the principle to become all it requires of me? No, I have not, consciously I have not. Ah! then, here is something for me to do! No matter what becomes of my questions—nothing ought to become of them if I cannot take a first principle so inevitably true, and live in it.'" The idea of venturing forth in faith in pursuit of the good struck Bushnell as "a kind of revelation." His spirit lifted at the feeling of conviction that his conversion to right-living religion brought him: "'Here, then,' he says, 'will I begin. If there is a God, as I rather hope there is, and very dimly believe, he is a right God. If I have lost him in wrong, perhaps I shall find him in right. Will he not help me, or, perchance, even be discovered to me?'"

His logic was like that of an Awakening revivalist, though stripped to bare essentials. Bushnell recalled the moment, and its feeling, in which he gave his life to the good and the hope of God within it: "Now the decisive moment is come. He drops on his knees, and there he prays to the dim God, dimly felt, confessing the dimness for honesty's sake, and asking for help that he may begin a right life. He bows himself on it as he prays, choosing it to be henceforth his unalterable, eternal endeavor." He was sensitive to the appearance that this experience fell short of a conversion to gospel Christianity and that he appeared to have come to Christianity by his lack of truth, not by the power of Christ's truth. He countered that there was a more biblical way of construing his conversion—as an example of Christ's command to seek first the kingdom of God and his righteousness alone. "And the dimly groping cry for help, what is that but a feeling after God, if, haply, it may find him, and actually finding him not far off? And what is the help obtained but exactly the true Christ-help? And the result, what, also, is that but the kingdom of God within, righteousness and peace and joy in the Holy Ghost?"

On that slender basis Horace Bushnell enrolled at the Theological School of New Haven to redeem his mother's hope for him.[5]

UPDATING THE NEW DIVINITY:
NEW HAVEN THEOLOGY

Yale Divinity School, founded in 1822 in the midst of the Unitarian schism, was the main theological bastion of a mediating revisionist orthodoxy variously called "The New Divinity," "New School Protestantism," "New Light Calvinism," and "New Haven Theology." Rooted in American Congregationalism, the New Divinity tradition was closely connected to the "New School" wing of American Presbyterianism. In essence, New Haven Theology represented the last phase of the New Divinity tradition of modified Calvinism founded by Jonathan Edwards and Samuel Hopkins and now continued by Timothy Dwight, Edwards's grandson and Yale president. Dwight's protégé, Nathaniel William Taylor (1786–1858) was the theological school's chief theologian and preacher.

Taylor joined the divinity school faculty at its founding and established its claim to the ongoing tradition of Edwards and Hopkins. He argued that a modified New Divinity was more theologically true to the spirit of Calvin and the Puritans than was the fossilized scholastic orthodoxy taught at Princeton Theological Seminary and the insufficiently alleviated Calvinism taught at Andover Theological Seminary. Old Light Calvinism militated against the spirit of revival and evangelism, while the New Divinity tradition traced its origins to Edwards's Great Awakening revival preaching. Classical Calvinist teaching on election, depravity, and atonement made the Reformed churches vulnerable to devastating Unitarian criticism, but the New Divinity tradition gradually developed a theology of "moral government" that modified Calvinist orthodoxy. Taylor believed that a liberalizing extension of New Divinity revisionism held the key to a better orthodoxy. In his view, the Old School Presbyterians at Princeton Seminary were stuck in the seventeenth century, while the Congregationalists at Andover Seminary had set back the cause of orthodoxy a half-century by incompetently polemicizing against the Unitarians. Along with his close friend Lyman Beecher, the evangelistic spellbinder of America's Second

Awakening, Taylor urged that it was not too late to save the Calvinist tradition from Unitarian apostasy and itself.[6]

His essential strategy was to further modify Hopkinsianism. As a student at Yale in the early 1800s, Taylor had felt such a deep and painful conviction of sin that his revered teacher, Timothy Dwight, feared for his sanity. Taylor studied theology with Dwight for four years after his graduation from Yale in 1807; for two years he was a member of Dwight's family and his personal secretary. In his early career Taylor served as pastor of First Church, New Haven, where he succeeded Moses Stuart and remained in close contact with Dwight. Taylor pastored at First Church for eleven years, developed his theology, and built a reputation as a formidable theologian and preacher. He made a name as a controversy-stirring polemicist, chiefly by rejecting Calvinist orthodoxy's doctrine of natural depravity. In 1822 Taylor blasted Andrews Norton for allegedly misrepresenting the orthodox Calvinist theory of original sin; in the same year, with the founding of Yale Divinity School, he made the new divinity school the institutional home of latter-day New Divinity.[7]

Taylor favored a doctrine of "depravity by nature," which described sin as the product of free human choice. Human beings are prone by their nature to choose private interest over God, he affirmed, but they are not compelled by their nature to make sinful choices, for the very notion of moral responsibility for sin requires a human capacity not to sin. He reasoned that if human beings have no power to make good choices, they cannot be held morally responsible for making sinful choices. Rightly understood, therefore, depravity is a moral condition produced by the free choice of evil, not a natural condition passed on as a biological inheritance. Though all moral agents sin by choice, no person is born into sin. To Taylor, this was the appropriate orthodox response to the Unitarian charge that the Calvinist doctrine of imputed Adamic evil made God the author of sin. Against Andrews Norton, Taylor denied that Calvinists "as a class" believed that depravity was a physical property in human nature. In 1828 he spelled out what he did not believe and sparked a factional war in New England Congregationalism:

> To believe that I am one and the same being with another who existed thousands of years before I was born, and that by virtue of this identity I truly acted in his act, and am therefore as truly guilty of his sin as himself—to believe this, I must renounce the reason which my Maker has given me.[8]

Taylor's revised New Haven Theology obtained its philosophical bearings from Scottish commonsense realism; it leaned heavily on a vague distinction between "inevitability" and "necessity"; as a theology of the new Awakening, it emphasized that sinners are active agents in the Holy Spirit's work of spiritual regeneration. With his divinity school colleagues, homiletics professor Eleazar T. Fitch (1791–1871) and chaplain Chauncey Goodrich (1790–1860), Taylor sought to shore up a united Calvinist front against the Unitarian movement. By

1828, however, he was preoccupied with fending off attacks from conservatives. Taylor realized there was no prospect of a Calvinist consensus on *why* human beings are sinful in every moral act, on which the orthodox parties were hopelessly split into five factions. While playing down the significance of this disagreement, he vigorously advocated a comprehensive system of divine moral governance, which held together his various doctrinal modifications, as the basis of a new orthodox consensus.[9]

Traditional Calvinism taught a penal-satisfaction view of Christ's atonement, according to which, Christ's suffering and death on Calvary opened the way for the salvation of the elect by paying the full debt that sinners owed to God; Christ's suffering satisfied God's offended righteousness by appeasing God's wrath. In the sixteenth century, the "governmental" model of theology was developed as an alternative to penal-satisfaction doctrine. Pioneered by legal theorist and theologian Hugo Grotius, a follower of Jacob Arminius, it was appropriated by Arminian Pietists, Anglicans, and Methodists in the seventeenth and eighteenth centuries. A key advocate of moral government theology was Anglican bishop and moral philosopher Joseph Butler (1692–1752), whose *Analogy of Religion* (1736) was revered by New England Protestants as a model defense of Christianity from deist criticism. An equally significant and more influential supporter was Jonathan Edwards.

Though Edwards accepted traditional substitutionary atonement doctrine and famously disbelieved in the freedom of the human will, he respected the moral government model of Grotius and Butler; on various occasions he used rectoral language (moral government) in speaking of faith and atonement as obedience to the laws of the divine Moral Governor. In the middle and later eighteenth century, his disciples increasingly appropriated moral government ideas. Joseph Bellamy defended the rectoral model in a book, *True Religion Delineated*, for which Edwards wrote a favorable preface; Samuel Hopkins cast his theological system within the framework of moral government theory; a generation later, Jonathan Edwards Jr. developed a thorough governmental theory of atonement. By the time of the Unitarian controversy, a host of orthodox theologians, including Taylor, Caleb Burge, Asa Burton, and Nathanael Emmons, supported rectoral atonement theory, often as "the Edwardean theory."[10]

Moral government theory holds that theology should be organized primarily around the question of how moral beings are governed under the influence of divine authority. As an Edwardean tradition theory of atonement, it emphasized the primacy of God's honor and the maintenance of God's absolute law. Eminent Andover theologian Edwards A. Park formulated the classic summation of its teaching: "The atonement is *useful* on men's account, and in order to furnish new motives to holiness, but it is *necessary* on God's account, and in order to *enable* him, as a consistent Ruler, to pardon any, even the smallest sin, and therefore to bestow on sinners any, even the smallest favor."[11]

By conceiving Christ's atonement as the work of making possible God's forgiveness of sin without violating God's absolute law, moral government theologians devised an alternative to classical penal-satisfactionist doctrine. At the height of the Unitarian controversy, Caleb Burge's *Essay on the Scripture Doctrine of the Atonement* spelled out the slightly liberalizing implications of the moral government model. Burge argued that the purpose of Christ's sacrifice on the cross was not to appease the Father's wrath at sinners or increase his love for them, but to enable God to pardon sinners in a manner that accorded justly with his holy honor and law; the "satisfaction" that Jesus gained was only to the demands of general justice. Jesus did not pay the literal debt of sinners; his obedience was not constitutive in his atonement, which was effected by his suffering only; and his pains were not literally the pains of the damned. Moreover, Burge concluded, though God is not obliged to save anyone, Christ's atoning death gained the possibility of salvation for all people.[12]

This revisionist trend was noted by Unitarians and Old Light Calvinists alike at the time of the Unitarian schism; Channing judged that moral government Calvinists were giving up Calvinism while keeping the name. "They adhere to the system as a whole, but shrink from all its parts and distinguishing points," he observed. "This silent but real defection from Calvinism is spreading more and more widely." Channing rejoiced that under the pressure of "the progress of the modern mind," modern Calvinism was "giving place to better views," even among conservatives. At the same time, he cautioned that moral government Calvinism was only slightly less pernicious than traditional Calvinism. While modern Calvinism was dropping some of its most offensive traditional features, it still offended against the goodness and benevolence of God. By claiming that God's reconciliation with sinners could be effected only by the bloody, scale-balancing, infinite sacrifice of Jesus and by picturing God as demanding such a sacrifice, New Divinity Calvinism still conflicted with the spirit of modern progress and "the progress of the spirit of the gospel." Burge strongly suggested that from a rectoral standpoint, God's glory would be diminished if all people were saved, but the religious sensibility behind that belief was odious even to many Unitarians who did not believe in universal salvation. Channing's Baltimore sermon blasted moral government Calvinism as an incoherent and unsustainable revision of a morally repulsive orthodoxy.[13]

Channing was right about the sustainability of New Divinity revisionism, and New Haven Theology lost its hegemonic status, even at Yale, during Taylor's lifetime. By the end of his career Taylor was regarded by Yale students as "a kind of relic of a bygone era," recycling old-style scholastic lectures that belabored the problems and thought forms of a distant epoch. As a strategy of coping with the crisis of the 1820s and 1830s, however, Taylor's New Divinity was a creative third way in theology. The Unitarians underestimated its reorienting potential for the churches that they left behind. With a rhetorical flamboyance and assertive self-regard that offended his opponents, Taylor took the fight to his critics on both sides. He lauded his school's theological project as a watershed correction of Christian theology as a whole and claimed that because theologians of the past had failed to adopt the correct organizing theme, all previous systems were "utter and complete failures." The seeds of good orthodox theology were planted by Augustine, Calvin, Edwards, and Hopkins, he acknowledged, but truly good theology began with himself, although in rare moments of humility, he explained that even a dwarf who stands on the shoulders of a giant can see further than the giant.[14]

By Taylor's lights, the essential theme of genuine Christianity was that God's moral government works to secure the highest well-being of its subjects. Taylor contended that the Bible assumes on every page this great theme, which Calvin and Edwards came near to grasping but obscured with unfortunate speculations. It followed, for Taylor, that instead of being fixated on the inscrutable sovereignty of God or the utter dependence of God's worthless creatures, the appropriate work of theology was to decipher the means by which God's benevolent governance promotes human flourishing. Christ's atoning work was not a satisfaction or penalty for sin, but the expedient that allows for God's pardon of sin. Moreover, arguing that human moral agency and divine moral government fit together not only rightly, but in fact, Taylor appealed to Scottish commonsense intuitionism to buttress his claim that God's moral laws are built into "the very nature and structure of the mind." To decipher the operation of the moral laws within human consciousness, he reasoned, is to read the workings of the divine Mind in creation; to obey the laws of God's moral government is to find happiness, which God wills for his faithful servants. Taylor affirmed that God's moral laws "proffer the highest good of which man is capable—the happiness of being good and doing good." In the Yale Divinity classrooms where New Haven Theology was taught, two generations of theological students were taught that Calvinist orthodoxy was not about coercion, domination, or fear, but about the beneficent influence of a self-limiting divine Governor in the world.[15]

MORAL GOVERNMENT AS SOCIAL THEOLOGY

New Haven Theology was calibrated to appeal to self-affirming citizens of a thriving, expanding, modern republic. Taylor perceived that Channing's moral objections to Calvinism hit a nerve among many churchgoing Americans. He bristled at Unitarian criticism, but felt its sting. Americans were decreasingly tolerant of sermonizing that called them totally depraved and devoid of free will. Traditional Calvinist teaching violated their democratic common sense, their intuitive sense of their moral powers, and, increasingly, their picture of God. Foreign visitors to Jacksonian America were often struck by the self-affirming complacency of common and well-born Americans alike; Alexis de Tocqueville noted at the time that Americans appeared to assume that all problems could be solved by the individual mind. This distinctive cultural trait filtered down to religion, he observed, for Americans treated their religious beliefs less "as a doctrine of revelation than as a commonly received opinion." American theologians across the orthodox/New Divinity/Unitarian continuum found confirmation of their religious worldviews in the moral intuitionism of Scottish commonsense philosophy.[16]

At the same time, New Haven Theology pointedly emphasized the authority of moral law over the shifting social contracts of an expanding republic. In 1832, when Lyman Beecher became founding president and theology professor of Lane Theological Seminary in Cincinnati, a New School Presbyterian institution, his encounters with mob violence on the American frontier were chastening to friends in New Haven, who worried that much of America was morally uncivilized. New England Federalists such as Dwight and Taylor took for granted that a good society requires state-supported churches. The break-up of the Standing Order in Connecticut was traumatizing to these church-establishment Federalists, and Beecher later confessed that he sank into deep despair when Connecticut elected to abolish the Standing Order. New Haven Theology moralism represented, among other things, a latter-day Puritan determination to moralize the public. Beecher and his friends resolved that if the church was to be separated from the state, they would secure the church's future by evangelizing the public and insisting that divine law is the proper basis of government. New Haven Theology was revisionist for decidedly conservative purposes; Taylor added to the New Divinity modifications of Calvinism, but always to save Calvinist orthodoxy. The New Haven theologians made their peace with the separation of church and state while admonishing that America was a biblically rooted, Protestant project, not the fulfillment of a Greek or Roman ideal. In contrast to America's classical-aspiring founding fathers, they interpreted America, like their Puritan fathers, through the lens of biblical history and prophecy. Beecher claimed that the key features of the American republic were prefigured in Hebrew law and religion, especially the rights to personal liberty, private property, election of leaders, and appeals to higher courts; he and Dwight read into the book of Revelation America's Great Awakenings and the triumph of American civilization.[17]

The latter-day Puritanism of New Haven Theology did not shield its proponents from the guardians of an older orthodoxy. Beecher's biblical Americanism was outspokenly reformist on several issues: he opposed slavery, advocated temperance and women's suffrage, and defended America's expanding Midwest civilization from conspiracy-imagining reactionaries. More pertinently, Old Light Calvinists charged that Beecher and Taylor watered down the orthodox faith and that Taylor-style New Divinity was closer to Unitarianism than to genuine Reformed orthodoxy. Taylor insisted that God "demands only a rational faith of rational beings" and that scripture had to be tried "at the bar of reason." Joseph Harvey, a Westchester pastor, countered that this claim exalted reason above revelation and betrayed the duty of Christians to "contend earnestly for the faith once delivered to the saints." He railed against New Haven Theology "with Bible in hand," vowing to "bid defiance to the powers of human reason." East Windsor pastor, Bennet Tyler, a college classmate of Taylor, resigned his pastorate in Maine and returned to Connecticut to lead the fight against "Taylorism." Tyler's Theological Institute of Connecticut (which became Hartford Theological Seminary) was a bastion of orthodox reaction, and Tyler campaigned so ardently against New Haven Theology that "Tylerism" became an interchangeable term for orthodoxy in Connecticut. With Harvey, he condemned Taylor's softening of the doctrines of native depravity and divine sovereignty and vehemently charged that the kind of Christianity taught at Yale retained only the shell of Calvinist orthodoxy while stripping away its essential vision of a sovereign, mysterious, impassible deity.[18]

This was the confessional background to Bushnell's seminary education. His first-hand exposure to the Taylor-Tyler controversy proved to be good training for his pastoral career in a Connecticut congregation and denomination split by it. The protest against Taylor-style New Divinity had simmered for years before exploding in 1828; by the time Bushnell began divinity school, Taylor was consumed by the conflict. His polemical cycle of attack and counter-attack was still consuming him in 1835 (the year Beecher was tried for heresy in Cincinnati). Though Taylor believed that history had left the Old Light Calvinists behind, he criticized them incessantly, fueling the conflict beyond any useful purpose. He told his students that he would never be understood until he wrote a book on the controversy, but the book would have to be so large that no one would read it. A gregarious, handsome, often overbearing figure, he was endowed with powerful rhetorical skills, a rigorous intellect, an unabashedly emotional piety, and an oversupply of defensiveness. Longtime friend and discerning critic Leonard Bacon, who succeeded Taylor as pastor of New Haven's Center Church, later recalled that he rushed to argument "like a war-horse to battle." Taylor made no apology for his bristling lack of tact; even Beecher called him indiscreet. Yale president Andrew D. White recalled from his student days that Taylor's lectures were distinctively thoughtful, racy, and humorous; Theodore Munger similarly recalled that his teacher's classroom arsenal mixed exacting logic with pious tears. More sharply, Munger judged that Taylor "knew no such thing as the personal equation, or another's point of view."[19]

His dogmatic and overbearing nature aside, however, Taylor cleared a path for an American theological liberalism that shared few of his beliefs. Though many of his former students later criticized him for not tending to their feelings, he challenged them to think for themselves and follow the truth "if it carries you over Niagara." He often quoted Joseph Bellamy: "Do not be afraid of investigation and argument—there is no poker in the truth."[20] Taylor raged for intellectual freedom. He defended the right of conscience and biblically informed reason to reinterpret Christian truth, and emphasized his continuity with Calvin, Edwards, and Hopkins while relieving his students of Calvinist doctrines that offended their moral sensibility. While his friend Beecher had to endure a sensational heresy trial before being acquitted by the Cincinnati presbytery and synod, Taylor's eminent stature in New England protected him from a similar treatment by his enemies.

Taylor was supplanted and sharply criticized by "New Theology" Bushnellians in the later nineteenth century, but Taylor-style New Divinity had a crucial impact on Bushnell's religious worldview. Bushnell never doubted Taylor's wisdom in emphasizing God's overflowing benevolence and the moral similarity or kinship between God and human beings. Taylor confirmed his belief that God is knowable in the self's intuitions of the good. Following his teacher, Bushnell assumed that intuitionist moral philosophy is a valuable partner to theology as a means of disclosing the self's inward "movements of the Spirit." Like Taylor, Bushnell conceived pastoral ministry as the work of supporting God's redeeming transformation of souls from the bondage of sin to self-giving love. More selectively than his teacher, he shared Taylor's high regard for Jonathan Edwards.[21]

But their relationship was mutually edgy, critical, and unappreciative, and Taylor alienated his student on the issues that mattered most to Bushnell. Taylor was a logic-chopping scholastic who fervently identified with his tradition's doctrinal intellectualism. He lectured in syllogisms, crafting an intricate theological system that explicated the divine order of the world. His unshakable belief in the moral perfection of the divine order was matched by his belief in his capacity to comprehend it. He recognized that scriptural language is often figurative, but assumed that theologians are required to translate imprecise biblical statements into literally precise propositions. He taught that God cannot break the laws of his own moral government, that scripture is rightly understood as a code of moral laws, and that theology is obliged to bring unbelievers to God by rationally persuading them of the truth of Christianity. Though he believed that the entire history of Christian dogmatics was seriously deficient, Taylor reveled in his kinship to the Reformed tradition of Calvin, Francis Turretin, the Westminster divines, the Puritans, and Jonathan Edwards. To him, conscience was the home of divinely endowed moral certitudes, not a source of moral conflict. He ascribed no value at all to religious doubt. Good theology proved that the best moral system possible is already in place, under the governance of a beneficient deity, who wills the continual and eschatological triumph of the good.

Bushnell resisted his teacher on all these counts. He disliked New Haven Theology, he doubted that Calvinist scholasticism was worth saving, and he was put off by Taylor's constant polemics with conservatives. He especially disliked Taylor's house of syllogisms. To him, Taylor-school theorizing about the divine system of moral governance was neither interesting or assuring. It did not address the burning personal questions that drove him to divinity school and it reduced matters of heart and spirit to mechanics, demeaning the figurative language of scripture. Bushnell was keenly attuned to nature, but New Haven Theology had little feeling for nature, despite its Edwardean heritage. For all his modifications, Taylor was a caretaker of a scholastic tradition, carrying on the idioms of New England Calvinism and, like his theological heroes, affecting an air of certainty. This latter trait, especially, grated on Bushnell; Taylor treated religious doubt as weakness of faith, deficient understanding, or both, but Bushnell had never lived a doubt-free day. Taylor would remember Bushnell as a persistently belligerent student who opposed nearly everything that he tried to teach; Bushnell's only praise of his teacher was that Taylor taught him to think for himself.[22]

THINKING ABOUT WORDS

Bushnell accepted more graciously religious inspiration from another New Haven theologian: Josiah Willard Gibbs (1790–1861), a distinguished philologist and pioneer of American higher-critical scripture scholarship, from whom he took his mandatory Greek and Hebrew courses. Formerly a colleague of Moses Stuart's at Andover, Gibbs attended closely to developments in German linguistic and biblical scholarship. As a biblical scholar and teacher, he played a significant role in legitimizing the use of higher critical methods in American biblical scholarship. He played a similar role as an interpreter of trends in German linguistic theory, especially as a follower of Karl Ferdinand Becker (1775–1849), whose work contributed significantly to the early development of comparative philology as an academic discipline.[23] Gibbs was a meticulous, quietly cautious figure. Because he was devoted to historical and linguistic research, published little, and rarely ventured an unqualified opinion, he was a puzzle to his faculty colleagues. Taylor and Chauncey Goodrich prized conviction; though friendly to Gibbs, they judged him to be timid, pedantic, and vacillating. Tayor made him the butt of his trademark zinger about the superiority of logic over history. Because historical truths are merely probable, Taylor admonished his students, history cannot establish the basis of a credible religious worldview: "I would rather have ten settled opinions, and nine of them wrong, than to be like my brother Gibbs with none of the ten settled."[24]

Gibbs noted various discrepancies in the Bible, accepted the source critical theory of a multiple-document Pentateuch, and judged that the first chapter of Matthew might be a late addition. He rendered these judgments with extreme scholarly caution and ample assurance that no doctrinal commitment was at stake. Gibbs recognized that some Pentateuchal material did not originate with Moses, but, like Moses Stuart, he drew the line at post-Mosaic redaction, claiming that Moses edited the entire Pentateuch. As a legitimizer of modern German scholarship, he sought to demonstrate that Christian orthodoxy was compatible with critical speculation about the historical origins and redaction of the Bible.[25]

On the whole, Bushnell took no more interest in historical criticism than Taylor. He was not impressed by the higher critical claim to recover the historical story behind the canonical narratives of scripture. Even his teacher's modest version of this claim apparently struck him as a departure from the appropriate subject matter of biblical scholarship. Throughout his career Bushnell charged that higher critical scholarship was presumptuous and spiritually destructive, especially in its rejection of the biblical miracles.[26]

It was as a linguist that Gibbs caught Bushnell's imagination and inspired his formative philosophical insight. Gibbs believed that the essential clue to the development of the meaning of words is founded on what he called "the analogy and correlation of the physical and intellectual worlds." All discursive terms have some basis in sense experience, he proposed. The key to the philological discipline he called "semasiology" was the insight that nearly all words express originally physical experiences in the form of "intellectual" ideas. Aside from a narrow category of nouns that refer to sensible objects and mathematical ideas, he contended, all words are metaphorical. There is no apparent physical relation between the sounds we make and the ideas we seek to express in speaking words. At the same time, he reasoned that *some* relation must make it possible to communicate meanings through words and proposed that "every word expressing an intellectual or moral idea originally expressed a physical one."[27]

Though Gibbs's theory of language was not published until years later, he was working out its key principles when Bushnell studied under him. The key question for Gibbs was how to account for the transference from sense experience to intellectualization. His theory was essentially one of faded metaphor that emphasized the role of imagination in creating linguistic meaning. Gibbs argued that words "which originally belonged to the world of sense, and denoted sensible objects, operations, and relations, are transferred, by a metaphor depending on a perceived analogy, to the world of intellect to express mental objects, operations, and relations." The word "spirit" is etymologically related to the word for "breath," for example, the word "transgression" is similarly related to "going over," "comprehension" is related to physical "grasping," "rectitude" derives from "a straight line," and so on. Gibbs cautioned that the faded metaphors of everyday language should not be confused with rhetorical metaphors employed for aesthetic effect. Metaphors designed for adornment are dispensable, he explained, but the concealed connection between intellection and physicality contained within faded metaphors is indispensable to the communication of their particular truth.[28]

As a teacher Gibbs was content to show that linguistic analysis occasionally sheds light on the meaning of difficult scripture texts. Beyond positing "a secret analogy between the intellectual and physical worlds," he did not develop the religious implications of his language theory.[29] But his restless, intuitive student, preoccupied with the problem of finding a language, felt immediately that semasiology had more ambitious work to do in the field of religious understanding. For his ordination exam, instead of writing a sermon, Bushnell wrote a paper that used linguistic arguments to prove the existence of a divine Moral Governor. Though he later gave hazy accounts of the chronology, it was probably during this period that he first struggled with Coleridge's *Aids to Reflection*, which was newly available in the Marsh edition. Bushnell found the book's aphoristic arguments "foggy and unintelligible" at first, but he returned to it repeatedly, drawn by its spirit and basic distinctions, determined to make sense of Coleridge's rendering of Christian truth. As a divinity student and during his early career as a pastor, he pursued, beyond the limitations of his teacher, the religious implications of the metaphorical nature of language. Bushnell reflected deeply on the function of language as the bearer of religious meaning, studying Plato, Goethe, Schleiermacher, Emmanuel Swedenborg, and Victor Cousin for clues to the metaphorical import of language. Eventually he took Coleridge's book from the shelf and discovered that this time, "behold, all was lucid and instructive!" Coleridge exalted imagination as the mind's experience of itself in the act of thinking; for the rest of his life, Bushnell's thinking was pervaded by the Coleridgean picture of imagination as a transcendently perceptive, creative, unifying power.[30]

Bushnell preached eloquent, irenic, metaphorically loaded sermons at North Congregational Church in Hartford, Connecticut. In 1839, six years into his preaching career, he unveiled the concept of language that lay beneath his developing religious thinking in an invited lecture to the Porter Rhetorical Society of Andover Theological Seminary. A miscommunication left him only a day to prepare a lecture titled "Revelation," but, in fact, Bushnell's early career had been spent preparing and waiting for it. He eyed the invitation with anxiety, foreboding, and excitement. He knew that his religious views were provocative; he had recently discovered a "trouble of the throat" that concerned him greatly; he had mixed feelings about his Hartford congregation. Hoping to find a greener pasture in academe, Bushnell welcomed the opportunity to present his theological ideas, but Andover Seminary was conservative. Preparing his wife Mary for a life of religious controversy, he told her (and himself) that the time had come to speak his truth:

> I have been thinking lately that I *must* write and publish the whole truth on these subjects as God has permitted me to see it. I have withheld till my views are well matured; and to withhold longer, I fear, is a want of that moral courage which animated Luther and every other man who has been a true soldier of Christ."[31]

He was conflicted in many ways. Bushnell quietly dissented from New England theology, but yearned to have the social influence and prestige of the old Puritan preachers; he loved to preach, but doubted that he belonged in the ministry; he celebrated the progress of American society, but mourned the passing of America's "age of homespun," when families worked together as organic agricultural households; he celebrated the American republic as a providential experiment in Christian liberty, but denounced the basic political theory of the American Constitution. For the most part he defended the class interests of the prominent Hartford merchants and retailers who dominated his church, but not without stabs of moral censure; Bushnell was sensitive to the insulated elitism of his employers, and his own. These conflicting impulses and realities gnawed at him, especially the first. Bushnell was torn between his spiritual integrity and his desire for worldly security and respectability; he told his wife that he wanted desperately to be a good provider for their daughters and son, but at the same time he felt spiritually compelled to endanger "all their worldly comforts" by giving voice to his religious truth. He acknowledged the apparent contradiction between wanting to protect his family and choosing to jeopardize their security, "but I am under just these contending impulses." Plaintively asking, "Has my dear wife any of Luther's spirit?" was his way of disclosing his resolve to be a good father and husband by choosing the path of worldly danger and spiritual truth: "How more, for example, for our dear boy than to give him the name and example of a father who left him his fortunes, rough and hard as they were, in the field of truth?"[32]

In that mood Bushnell journeyed to Andover to proclaim that human speech and divine self-expression are best perceived under the single category of "revelation." He proposed that God's grandeur is best apprehended not in God's awesome power or knowledge, but in God's self-expressive publicity, which is given "to communicate to creatures that which is their life—the warmth, light, beauty, and truth of the Divine Nature." Revelation is not a thing, Bushnell contended; it does not create truth or even establish truth. Truth exists before it is revealed; revelation is the active revealing of truth. Put differently, revelation is God's publicity, the bringing of truth "into outward exhibition." Having no color or shape or voice or tangibility, he reflected, revelation can be communicated "only by some manifestation or apparition which presents her to view." Revelation requires forms that function more or less as the signs or "outward bodies" of truth, and it requires self-conscious subjects who are capable of receiving revelation. While accepting the Bible as a revelatory vehicle, Bushnell declared that beyond the revelation of God contained in scripture "the whole temple of being around us and above us is written over with spiritual hieroglyphs all radiant with his light."[33]

In the very language of truth, we communicate God revealed. In Coleridge's spirit, Bushnell made a qualitative distinction between the language of sense or fact and the language of thought or truth. The language of sense is simple enough to be used to some extent even by animals, he observed, but the language of thought requires reflective subjects, it expands as thought expands, and its possibility depends on God's provision of "a vast storehouse of types or images fitted to represent thoughts" in the outward world. With Jonathan Edwards, he viewed nature as a type or figure of God's mind. Our very capacity to communicate thoughts is testimony to God's self-expressive creation in nature of the forms necessary to represent and express thought, he proposed: "I stand here then a thinking creature in a vast temple of being. The sky is over me, the earth is beneath, and around me I gaze on the floor and the walls and the shafted pillars of the temple and behold all overlaid and inlaid with types of thought. Whose thought? If I am intelligent so is the world. I live here— amazing thought!—embosomed in the eternal intelligence of God." To the

Psalmist, he noted, the heavens declared the glory of God and the firmament his handiwork; more recently, William Wordsworth confessed that he read "the Eternal deep Forever haunted by the Eternal mind" in the signs of intelligence around him. Bushnell urged that these were emblems of the same perception that "in language we have a revelation of God which shows as in a mirror one vast and varied image of his intelligence."[34]

It was an audacious beginning, close to the spirit of Emerson's Divinity School address of the previous year, fully as fresh, Coleridgean, and breathless as the transcendentalist manifestos of its period. Bushnell did not bother to defend his deduction that because images convey thoughts, they must be natural signs; his claim that nature contains analogies of the divine mind undoubtedly counted on Andover's memory of Puritan nature theology, especially the nature imagery of Jonathan Edwards. Self-inspired by his liberation of "revelation" as a category, he rushed to a vision of all reality as God's self-expressive language. Much of his Coleridgean discussion of the differences between languages of sense and thought resembled Emerson's account of words as signs of natural facts and nature as the symbol of spirit.[35] These connections to Emerson were unknown to Bushnell; Emerson's *Nature* had only a handful of readers in 1839. Bushnell worried and hoped that his life had turned a corner upon speaking his truth. "Revelation" contained the seeds of his field-challenging mature theology. But it was another decade before he found the occasion and inspiration to challenge New England Christianity in Luther's spirit. While warning his wife to brace for "hazards and reproaches, and perhaps privations, which lie in this encounter for the truth," he devoted himself in the 1840s, with conflicted feelings, to the problems of internal and external church politics.[36]

Bushnell struggled for years merely to hold together his Hartford congregation, which was deeply split between Old School and New School factions. His two leading deacons were opposing factional leaders. While assuring conservatives that his theology was not as novel or heterodox as it seemed, he used his rhetorical skills to lift North Church above the theological controversies of its time. He avoided the Taylor-Tyler debates about the precise nature of depravity, which he regarded as fruitless, and bypassed the entire discussion of the differences between natural, moral, and gracious ability that fueled New England theology from Hopkins to Taylor. His early preaching featured aesthetically refined meditations on spiritual topics, extended commentaries on current events, and, especially, earnest reflections on the moral basis of religion. Bushnell's preaching took a more deeply spiritual turn in 1848, but its basic sensibility and purpose remained constant throughout his career. He later recalled that upon entering "the vein of comprehensiveness" in his early ministry, he sought to speak a unifying religious truth that broke free of unsolvable scholastic debates. In his words, "the effect of my preaching never was to overthrow one school and set up the other; neither was it to find a position of neutrality midway between them; but, as far as theology is concerned, it was to comprehend, if possible, the truth contended for in both; in which I had, of course, abundant practice in the subtleties of speculative language, but had the scriptures always with me bolting out their free incautious oppositions." This strategy worked at North Church, which enabled Bushnell to survive his notoriety after New England Congregationalism found him neither irenic or comprehensive.[37]

SOCIAL CHRISTIANITY AFTER DISESTABLISHMENT

Bushnell was slow to unveil his alternative theological rhetoric. Although he gained his notoriety, and his later influence, as a theologian of Wording-forth imagination, for much of his career he sought to make his mark as an advocate of civic and social causes. While doctrine was controversial, social issues were energizing and unifying. Bushnell's ambitions for himself and the church found numerous outlets in ecclesiastically disestablished New England. He never doubted either the Puritan conception of the state as a moral instrument or his clerical duty to hold the state to its moral responsibilities. His first published sermon, given after the Boston antislavery riot of 1835, argued that Protestantism is purified Christianity, Congregationalism is purified Protestantism, and Protestant religion rightly translates into a politics of republican government. His sermon "The Crisis of the Church" gave voice to his belief in America as the world's redeemer nation while it identified America's worst problems as "slavery, infidelity, Romanism, and the current of our political tendencies." For better and worse, this list contained the germ of American social Christianity. His list of the worst problems evolved over time. He subsequently judged that Wild West barbarism was America's greatest problem; after that he complained that America's moral character was undermined by its rising cult of fashion and materialism; still later, he introduced the notion that certain aspects of American society were "Christianized" while others remained to be Christianized—a concept that performed heavy labor for the social gospel movement.[38]

Bushnell never accepted the basic political theory of the American Constitution or the variant of Calvinist teaching that supported it, holding out for the Puritan dream of a Holy Commonwealth. The American Founders' theory of government as a system of checks and balances to control atomistic self-interests seemed, to him, to resign the public realm to corruption. Bushnell objected that a genuine Calvinism could not make its peace with this theory of government. Samuel Hopkins bravely opposed slavery, but he also allowed that sin is sometimes the necessary means of the good.

Bushnell repeatedly protested that American politics was corrupted by slavery and its own theory of government. Though he voted Democrat until the mid-1850s, when the Republicans emerged as an antislavery party, he denounced the Jeffersonian republican heritage of the Democratic Party and its acceptance of slavery. Jefferson was a deist, a slaveowner, an individualist, and a social contract theorist who viewed government as a trustee of rights-bearing individuals; he even claimed that nations needed occasional revolutions. Bushnell was repulsed on all counts. He protested that Jeffersonian social contract theory undermined the moral basis of the state: "We have taken up, in this country, almost universally, theories of government which totally forbid the entrance of moral considerations. Government, we think, is a social compact or agreement—a mere human creation, having as little connection with God, as little of a moral quality, as a ship or war or a public road." He countered that the commonwealth of good sanctioned by divine law is a normative organic order that precedes any social contract negotiated by elections. Bushnell believed that the proper function of legislation was to ensure the virtue of the state and create a good society. He refused to accept Nathaniel Taylor's realist admonition that, unavoidably, politics is often about choosing the lesser of evils. The presidential campaign of 1844 offered a grim case in point. Taylor argued that there was a lesser evil worth supporting in the choice between James Polk, a proslavery Democrat, and Henry Clay, a slaveowning Whig who authored the Missouri Compromise; Bushnell replied that to vote for a bad person is to institutionalize and endorse immorality and to violate the greater good. That greater good, he admonished, is served always by following the path of righteousness, and he therefore urged his congregants to submit a blank ballot as an act of national repentance.[39]

Bushnell's logic was abolitionist, but he never came close to joining the abolitionist movement. He frequently condemned American slavery as evil, stridently denounced the Fugitive Slave Law, passionately opposed the Missouri Compromise, and, because it threatened to expand the territory open to slavery, railed against the Mexican War. His social gospel admirers later pointed to these positions as proof of his righteousness on the issue of racial justice, but Bushnell was far from righteous with regard to race. To put it plainly, he embraced and expressed the racism of typical nineteenth-century white Americans. His opposition to slavery was profoundly distorted by his conviction, frankly expressed, that blacks were products of an inferior civilization and stood in the way of America's own progress. For decades after his death, Bushnell's followers and biographers whitewashed his related prejudices against Jews, Catholics, Asians, Celtic Irish, American Indians, and people of other "alien" cultures. In the same year that his Emersonian lecture on revelation celebrated his reflective participation in God's vast temple of being, Bushnell delivered a weekday evening sermon, published as a pamphlet, that explained why some races ranked higher in the temple of being than others. *A Discourse on the Slavery Question* contended that the vexing issue of slavery could be settled by instituting reforms on both sides. Slavery was a crime, he acknowledged, but "if there was ever a people on earth involved in crime, who yet deserved sympathy and gentleness at the hands of the good, it is the slaveholding portion of our country." This sentiment guided his idea of racial reform.[40]

Bushnell worried about the prospect of Northern states having to put down a slave insurrection and cautioned, "We are linked with slavery, by duties of mutual aid and defense." To defuse the threat of a black uprising and the prospect of Northern intervention on behalf of slavery, he asked the Southern states to reform the slave system by ending its three most obnoxious features— the refusal to recognize the "moral and intellectual nature" of slaves as human beings, the refusal to protect slaves from violence, including rape, and its hostility to family life. Anything beyond this, he assured them, was none of a Northerner's business: "I say to the South, this institution is your own, not ours. Take your own way of proceeding. Modify your system as you please. Invent any new fashion of society as you please, or introduce any old fashion. Create you a serfdom, or a villein socage, or sweep the whole fabric away." Slavery itself was not necessarily evil, he judged; what was evil was the maintenance of a chattel system that violated the basic rights of slaves as human beings. Without doubting that American slaveholders were resolved "to face out the odium of the human race," Bushnell asserted that history was in the process of sweeping away the chattel system. "The moral position of the world begins to reflect a peculiar disgrace on your institutions," he observed. "You feel it now; you will feel it more; you will be compelled to yield to the feeling."[41]

His proposed reform on the Northern side called for the elimination of abolitionist societies. The abolitionists were badly mannered, unwise, and lacking in clerical direction, he pronounced; to put it mildly, "they did not go to work like Christian gentlemen." Moreover, they cherished "egregious expectations" for the good that abolition would accomplish "in behalf of the colored race." The abolitionists dreamed of "a new created, enlightened race of Christian freemen," but this dream was even more misguided than their claim to righteousness. The verdict of history was clear about the possibility of a racially integrated civilization:

> There is no example in history, where an uncultivated and barbarous stock has been elevated in the midst of civilized stock; and I have no expectation that there ever will be. . . . The ancient Britons, the primitive stock of the island, being a barbarous race, soon dwindled to extinction under their Saxon conquerors. The Aborigines of our own continent, both in South and North America, are rapidly hastening toward the same fate. In British India, New Holland, and South Africa, a like result is also approaching.[42]

Bushnell derived a morally contorted case for opposing slavery from this reading of the lesson of history. On the formal issues of the day that led to the Civil War, he took righteous positions against the existing slave system. He condemned chattel slavery as "an essentially barbarous institution" and an offense against God's moral law; in 1844 he pronounced that "we have made a farce of American liberty long enough" by giving political sanction to slavery; in 1851, he vowed that he would rather let the Union he cherished disintegrate than obey "this abominable Fugitive Slave Law." Bushnell also denounced the Mexican War as a slaveholder grab for expanded slavery and barbarism; in the 1850s he wished aloud that he had a son to give to the antislavery struggle in Kansas; and in the 1860s he fervently admired and supported Abraham Lincoln. Bushnell's criticism of the Missouri Compromise and Henry Clay, its author, made him an inadvertent partisan player in the presidential campaign of 1844. Without naming Clay, Bushnell blasted the author of the Missouri Compromise for bringing "moral desolation" on America and thereby taking upon his soul "the sorrows of untold millions of bondsmen." His sermonic broadside offended many of Bushnell's friends and congregants, who could not bear the thought of James Polk as president, and who viewed Clay as the savior of the Whig Party after the tragic death of William Henry Harrison. The sermon was used against the Whigs in the campaign, and it played a significant role in the state electoral campaign. It also inspired a bitter counterattack that accused Bushnell of betraying his ministerial calling. In a tone of wounded special pleading, he replied that he criticized Clay only as America's leader in "a national sin," not as a partisan candidate. His bruised feelings caused him to avoid partisan politics for the next dozen years.[43]

Bushnell's sensitivity to the charge of political overreaching contained a crucial clue to his antiabolitionism. He prized his respectability in polite society and his hard-won esteem at North Church, which generally reflected the prevailing sentiments of a state noted for its hostility to abolitionism, but which also contained a smattering of abolitionists and assorted fence-sitters. The leadership ideal that Bushnell set for himself, in this context, was to be a great reconciler who led America to righteousness, the same ideal by which he defined the church's social mission.

He was capable of warning his privileged congregants that their exclusive gentility was sinful in its own way, cautioning, "Our range of life is so walled in by the respectability of our associations, that what is on the other side of the wall is very much a world unknown. . . . Sin is here, and sin that wants salvation, but it is sin so thoroughly respectable as to make it very nearly impossible to produce any just impression of its deformity." The seed of a serious critique of his own whitebread notion of "comprehensiveness" was there, but Bushnell never let it grow. He cherished the virtue of comprehensiveness—among upright non-aliens—but despised the kind of comprehensiveness that Henry Clay symbolized—the kind that compromised with evil—while dreaming that America could become a unified nation as a holy commonwealth. Christianity does not choose between tradition and vision, he preached; it embraces both in searching for the good, "for the new must be the birth of the old, and the old must have its births, or die." On the transcendent moral issue of his time, he rationalized that he belonged to a church-influenced establishment that was gradually undermining the slave system more effectively than was the shrill opposition of misguided abolitionists.[44]

The fact that he reflected and perpetuated the racism of the establishment gave him little pause before the Civil War. Believing that blacks were inferior to white Anglo-Saxons by virtue of their grossly inferior acculturation, Bushnell judged that American blacks were doomed to "dwindle towards extinction" after slavery was abolished. "At present they are kept from a decline in population, only by the interest their masters have in them," he explained. "Their law of population, now, is the same as that of neat cattle, and as the herd will dwindle when the herdsman withdraws his care, so will they." Bushnell's racism was expressed without malice; never a hater, he had cordial relations with the few blacks he knew, and readily acknowledged the extraordinary achievements of certain individual blacks. He cautioned, however, that survival as a class was another matter: "The difficulty is to elevate the race, *as a race,* among us." Estimating that it would require "five hundred or a thousand years of cultivation" before blacks could be expected to acquire even a chance of surviving in America, he judged that American blacks had virtually no chance of holding out that long. The scant progress of most nonenslaved Northern blacks sealed the point for him. For many years, he observed, benevolent Christians in Hartford had struggled to raise the condition of their city's black population, but, overwhelmed by "the deficiencies of an uncultivated race," achieved little success. As a firm believer that backward races impeded cultural progress, Bushnell was inclined to favor the extinguishing logic of history. This amounted to a perverse rationale for antislavery politics. On the eve of the Civil War, he continued to believe that slavery (and therefore, American blacks) would wither away under God's providential timetable and the demographic trends of American life.[45]

There is some evidence that his racial views changed after the war. In the aftermath of the war, Bushnell worried that emancipated blacks were confronted not only with the handicaps of their brutal American history and cultural deprivation, but also by the hateful resentment of American whites. His belated reflection on this problem lifted his theorizing on race to a higher moral level. *The Moral Uses of Dark Things* (1868) affirmed the "equal and sublime right which inheres" in the humanity of people of African descent. More personally, Bushnell confessed that he found it difficult to believe in Providence when he considered the terrible fate of American blacks, "a condition so unhopeful, so nearly impossible to them, and so perplexing and full of oppressive concern to us." He puzzled at why God "put a race into existence encumbered with such disadvantages." The dark faces of blacks veiled a darker mystery, he reflected: "The more we are drawn to them, by their free good nature, and the warm humanities we often learn to admire in their friendship, the more heavily are we oppressed by the very hard lot so mysteriously put upon them, in the unfavored type of their race."[46]

In this perplexity, Bushnell found reason to affirm that God was at work in the counterimages of racial diversity. If the various families of the world looked alike, he reasoned, "the immortal, spiritual nature, the real man, would be swamped to a great degree under the reigning similarities." The racial diversity of humankind underscored the fact that external qualities are secondary, "while the unreducible diamond of the moral nature, that which forms absolute ideas and receives their immutable stamp in its character," exists in people of all colors. Bushnell's torturously executed defense of this claim criticized race-hierarchy "science" in a way that confused numerous interpreters who attributed to him exactly the racist view he rejected.[47]

Even at his worst, Bushnell never viewed blacks and whites as different kinds of human beings; he affirmed that blacks and whites alike possessed "plainly godlike affinities" in their moral nature. Turning to gospel faith, he prophesied that blacks were likely to possess a promising future in salvation history, if not ordinary history. "Perhaps the Africans will come up late enough to be last," he reflected; in the gospel spirit of "the last shall be first," he envisioned an eschatological kingdom in which "our long ago despised African brothers, now despised no longer, will reveal the meaning of their late-maturing, last-day gifts, their capacities of vision, and music, and song, and will let us hear the harps they carried in their bosom strike into play in the customary inspirations of religion." That was the closest he came to treating blacks as equals. Bushnell broke through to a partial-gospel perspective on the souls of black people, but when he was not depicting them stereotypically as genial singers of simple religion, he continued to place them in a theodicy-category of "dark things" that included plagues, mysterious diseases, and animal infestations. Neither did he take back a word of his reproaches against abolitionism.[48]

The abolitionist movement galled Bushnell more than other social movements, but only slightly; like many disestablished preachers of his generation, he was agitated by social movements that were not led by clergy, even when they promoted Puritan causes such as prohibition of alcohol and tobacco. In *A Discourse on the Slavery Question* he lamented that popular social movements were filled with "conceit of their own superior wisdom." In reality, these movements revealed to clergy their own dwindling social role and influence. The following year, Bushnell preached his first sermon against a reform movement he found disastrously stupid—the emancipation of women. He preferred to keep silent on this issue, he reported, but "the revolution which is beginning to appear in the manners of the female sex in a certain section of our country" forced him to speak. Bushnell protested that women were supposed to help men, not compete with them, and he called for "a place of quiet, and some quiet minds which the din of our public war never embroils." It was not too late to save "a little of the sweetness and purity" of life, he noted, warning that giving women the right to vote threatened to destroy domestic peace: "Do save us one half of society free of the broils and bruises and arts of demagogy!"[49]

In succeeding years his antifeminist appeals emphasized "nature" as much as civilization and family politics. Bushnell was routinely rhapsodic on the feminine ideal. Gender differences impressed him greatly as emblems of a divinely created natural order. He found that women and men "are a great deal more like two species, than like two varieties." To Bushnell, the look of a man said, "Force, Authority, Decision, Self-asserting Counsel, Victory," while women by nature responded, "I will trust, and be cherished and give sympathy and take ownership in the victor, and double his honors by the honors I contribute myself." Men are ruled by the force principle, and women by the beauty principle, he explained: "One is the forward, pioneering mastery, the out-door battle-ax of public war and family providence; the other is the indoor faculty, *covert,* as the law would say, and complementary, mistress and dispenser of the enjoy-abilities."[50]

Bushnell pleaded with reformists not to violate the natural blending of men and woman as positivity and receptivity, providence and use, strength and beauty. He believed that the duality of male and female reflected God's norma-tive order of creation; at the same time he believed in Lamarckian-model evo-lution, and therefore worried about the inheritability of bad acquired characteristics. He warned that women were sure to become deformed if they entered the public sphere as colleagues, voters, and competitors: "The look will be sharp, the voice will be wiry and shrill, the action will be angular and abrupt, wiliness, self-asserting boldness, eagerness for place and power will get into the expression more and more distinctly, and become inbred in the native habit." Bushnell encouraged his daughters' education, principally as an aid to the domestic cultivation of virtue, but exhorted them not to seek public influence or the right to vote. Female suffrage was a "reform against nature" that threat-ened the natural basis of marriage, and therefore the basis of civilization.[51]

None of this disqualified him from being claimed a generation later by the founders of the social gospel movement, because few Americans of any kind were abolitionists, and much of the social gospel movement shared Bushnell's Victorian gender politics and his Anglo-Saxon chauvinism. His racism and anti-Semitism reflected commonly held prejudices, and so raised few eyebrows dur-ing his lifetime. Bushnell's positions on issues pertaining to racial justice were more progressive, on the whole, than the views of his audiences; moreover, his prejudices helped him remain on reasonably good terms with audiences that opposed his theology. A generation later, the liberal social gospelers were gener-ally less prejudiced, but they were also inclined to view his racism as customary for his time and even plausible within it. At the same time many of them shared his conviction that gender equality would be a bad thing for women, America, and men, not necessarily in that order.

One aspect of his chauvinism, however, nearly did disqualify him, his anti-Catholic sentiment. The subject arose in his first published sermon and nearly consumed him in the mid-1840s. Bushnell believed throughout his life that freedom-cherishing Protestants were morally obliged to repudiate the repressive politics and religious dogmatism of the Catholic church. In 1843 he joined Lyman Beecher and First Church pastor Joel Hawes in founding an anti-Catholic activist organization called the Protestant League, later renamed the Christian Alliance of the United States. The Protestant Leaguers aggressively attacked the Vatican on religious and political grounds and declared forthrightly that their objective was to march on Rome and overthrow the papacy. Bushnell drew large crowds for his anti-Catholic speeches, getting his first taste of extra-local fame. He argued that the menace of America's expanding-frontier bar-barism and the problem of Romanism were linked by America's overly generous immigration policy, although later he revised his ranking of America's worst problems, giving first place to the "wild race of nomads roaming over the vast western territories of our land." For several years, he found anti-Catholic activism exciting; he never gave up believing it was liberal.[52]

To Bushnell it was morally and politically unacceptable that Catholic nations still existed, and he saw barely greater reason to tolerate Catholicism as a religion. Protestant Christianity was supposed to be a movement that struggled for religious freedom the world over, he preached. In 1846, while taking the obligatory nineteenth-century sabbatical in Europe to recover his health, he wrote an open letter to Pope Gregory XVI that later qualified for inclusion on the *Index Expurgatorius*. Bushnell granted the pontiff the same allowance he gave Henry Clay—the distinction between office and person—before laying a blistering indictment on the papal office. The Vatican was "arrogant and offensive," it maintained "the worst government in Christendom," and routinely violated the rights of non-Catholics. With a sharper edge, Bushnell portrayed the Catholic system as an insidious hierarchy of priestly police that destroyed family trust and required secrets and deceit: "You have a confessor between every wife and her husband, and between both and their children; so that if one lisps a free thought, or vents a sigh at the table, the story, he knows, will be wormed out of some one in the family." Catholicism turned the family table into "a gathering of spies," he claimed; it turned the sublime religion of Jesus into an oppressive regime of dogma and ritual; not surprisingly, it therefore made its victims "cruel, servile, faithless to a proverb, and mournfully destitute of all habits of industry, order, and providence."[53]

A Letter to His Holiness, Pope Gregory XVI was widely reprinted as a pamphlet in England, Italy, and the United States. Bushnell's chief biographers and advocates, who usually agreed, later took instructively different tacks on his anti-Catholic activism. Mary Bushnell Cheney described her father's polemic as "pungent, keen, and unsparing of the truth" and speculated that its wide circulation in Italy may have helped "to liberate the thought of the Italian people." Closer to home and her expertise, she judged that whatever its historical effect may have been, "we may call the writing of this letter to the Pope one of the most characteristic things which Horace Bushnell ever did." Nearly twenty years later, Theodore Munger reduced the letter to an aberration. In a single sentence, he declared that it deserved to be "lightly passed over" as an unfortunate lapse in judgment and that fortunately for Bushnell's reputation, the Christian Alliance was later taken over by conservative evangelicals, causing Bushnell to resign. Had he not resigned from the Evangelical Alliance, Munger implied, it would not have been possible for a succeeding generation of liberal Christians to claim him as their spiritual father.[54]

NURTURING SENSITIVE, SUPERIOR CHRISTIANS

Well into his middle age, Bushnell regarded himself as a professional failure. He knew he was gifted with rare insight and eloquence, but felt he had little to show for his endowments or hard work. His feelings were justified. His civic activism was satisfying only to a point for he could not find an absorbing social cause, and bruised by partisan criticism, he vowed to stay out of politics. He kept vowing to take greater interest and satisfaction in his pastoral tasks, but yearned for a larger public. His robust health gave way to chronic fatigue and various bronchial and pulmonary illnesses, and he undoubtedly brooded over his agonized decision, during a period of especially poor health in 1840, not to accept the presidency of Middlebury College. Bushnell was widely sought as a public speaker, but for many years a defining message eluded him. He was respected as a thoughtful, eloquent, spiritually uplifting preacher, but he had few conversions to show for it. For nineteenth-century Congregational preachers, this was not insignificant.

Mainline American Protestantism lived off its revivals. The churches were spiritually and financially dependent on revival conversions, as clergy well knew. Bushnell disliked the aesthetics and theology of revival preaching, and it showed. For years he gave his best imitation of "come to Jesus" preaching but relatively few conversions occurred at his church. He confessed to friends that it was depressing to be judged by conversion numbers, and in 1836 he became so discouraged that he considered returning to teaching, which he hated. Two years later he published "The Spiritual Economy of Revivals of Religion," in which he criticized American churches for placing too much emphasis on successful revivals. Bushnell cautioned that the phrase "revival of religion" had no scriptural basis and that, as a churchly enterprise, revival religion was too individualistic, episodic, and reductionist. On further reflection, he judged that it also reinforced a mistaken way of dealing with children. In 1847 he published *Discourses on Christian Nurture,* a pair of essays that criticized the prevailing view of children as pagan slaves of sin who stand alienated from God until they repent and commit their lives to Jesus. Bushnell countered that children should grow up as Christians and never know themselves as anything else. This notion had a history in the covenant theology of early New England Congregationalism, but in revival-awakened nineteenth-century New England, it shook the dominant theology to its foundations.[55]

New Divinity orthodoxy was a tradition of Calvinist accommodations to revivalism and modern humanism, in that order. From Bellamy and Hopkins to Emmons and the younger Edwards to Dwight and Taylor, a succession of Edwardean modifiers made room for a Calvinist affirmation of free will and a less fearsome doctrine of divine sovereignty. But New England Theology was still a form of Calvinism, with an emphasis on human depravity, even as it made room for revivalist appeals to make a "decision for Christ."

The result was the kind of Second Awakening theology preached by Lyman Beecher and a host of lesser revivalists that vigorously asserted both the necessity of repentance, conversion, and spiritual rebirth and the Calvinist view of young children as unregenerate captives of sin. The problem, rarely voiced but undoubtedly felt to some degree by many parents, was that young children were thus excluded from the saving benefits of Christ. Salvation was individual, each soul was isolated from every other, and children were left out. Young children were told they could not be good, or Christian, until God gave them "a new heart," but they could not receive a new heart until they were old enough to truly comprehend what they were supposed to pray for. Nineteenth-century literature abounded in images of the home as a virtue-producing haven of purity and familial nurture, but the dominant theology undermined the very notion of the child as a moral subject. Over the course of a decade, while thinking about the practical problem of how children should be nurtured in the faith, Bushnell found himself attacking the entire system of New England Theology at its weakest point.

Discourses on Christian Nurture was ecclesiastically brave and culturally attuned. It challenged the established religion with the sentiments of a rising cult of domesticity. In the 1830s and 1840s, popular literature celebrated middle-class family life as society's haven of virtue and care. With uncharacteristic understatement, Bushnell enthused that his subject was "beginning to attract new interest, and excite a spirit of inquiry." In the face of criticism, the book was soon suppressed by its intimidated Sunday school publisher, but Bushnell issued an aggressive second edition, *Views of Christian Nurture,* which became the theology of the cultural trend it reflected.[56]

Its author was a devoted father and husband who regretted that clergy were not leading the movement to valorize the organic, nurturing, virtue-producing qualities of family life. He noted that American churches perversely undermined the same qualities in church life and for this he blamed the prevalence of revivalism: "We hold a piety of conquest rather than of love,—a kind of public piety that is strenuous and fiery on great occasions, but wants the beauty of holiness, wants constancy, singleness of aim, loveliness, purity, richness, blamelessness, and,—if I may add another term not so immediately religious, but one that carries, by association, a thousand religious qualities—wants domesticity of character." Modern American Christianity compared poorly to popular novels and gift books in valuing the virtues of domestic nurture. The church lacked a "Christian atmosphere" of other-regarding fellowship because its theology militated against the development and honoring of the tender virtues. Bushnell assured readers that revival preaching had a necessary role in the church's life, but not at the expense of its deeper everyday mission.[57]

Against the prevailing theology, Bushnell protested that the church and family are fundamentally organic institutions. Moreover, though his expanded second edition admitted that "all our modern notions and speculations have taken a bent towards individualism," he contended that even the modern state and school retained an organic basis: "There is a spirit in each of these organisms, peculiar to itself and more or less hostile, more or less favorable to religious character, and to some extent, at least, sovereign over the individual man." The individuated self pictured in revival preaching does not exist, he admonished: "We possess only a mixed individuality all our life long. A pure, separate, individual man, living *wholly* within and from himself, is a mere fiction." He scolded that a church that took its organic spiritual character seriously would not picture its children as sinful aliens needing to be "dragged into the church of God by conquest." Neither would a Christian family teach its children they must receive a new spiritual heart before they can be good:

> They should rather seek to teach a feeling than a doctrine; to bathe the child in their own feeling of love to God and dependence on him, and contrition for wrong before him, bearing up their child's heart in their own, not fearing to encourage every good motion they can call into exercise; to make what is good, happy and attractive; what is wrong, odious and hateful; then as the understanding advances, to give it food suited to its capacity, opening upon it gradually the more difficult views of Christian doctrine and experience.[58]

Bushnell's book unpacked the good-parenting specifics of this prescription; his two succeeding editions expanded upon them. Every family needs discipline and careful government, he counseled, "but there is a kind of virtue, my brethren, which is not in the rod, the virtue, I mean, of a truly good and sanctified life." He judged that many who equated the rod with orthodoxy and parental duty "might really as well be heathens as Christians." Bushnell censured those "who only storm about their house with heathenish ferocity, who lecture, and threaten, and castigate, and bruise, and call this family government. They even dare to speak of this as the nurture of the Lord." It was painful to him to reflect on "how they batter and bruise the delicate, tender souls of their children, extinguishing in them what they ought to cultivate." His third edition elaborated why overbearing, disapproving parents rarely produced children of warm piety: "Nothing will set a child farther off from religion, or make him utterly incapable of sympathy with it, than to have had it put upon him in a whining and misgiving way." More provocatively for a mid-nineteenth-century church leader: "No parent has a right to put oppression on a child, in the name of authority. And if he uses authority in that way, to annoy the child's peace, and even to forbid his possession of himself, he should not complain, if the impatience he creates grows into a bitter animosity, and finally a stiff rebellion."[59]

For the most part, *Views of Christian Nurture* exemplified the sentimental virtue ethic it preached. It was surprisingly short on gender statements; Bushnell held back his personal concern to preserve an idealized women's sphere. While assuming the authority of husbands over their wives, he spoke of families and parenting mostly in gender-neutral terms. Even his amplified third edition taught that fathers and mothers hold their familial authority together as an indivisible unity and that parents must never undercut each other's authority in front of their children. For all of its reserve on the theme of women's redeeming domestic mission, however, in a wider sense the book was pervaded by it. Bushnell was not effeminate in his personal bearing—notwithstanding Ann Douglas's influential portrait to this effect—but in all its editions, *Christian*

Nurture was a showcase example of feminized mid-nineteenth-century religious discourse.[60] It exhorted that "religion never thoroughly penetrates life, till it becomes domestic." The world worships power and material success, Bushnell argued, but Christianity nurtures spiritual refinement. The world lives by competition and conflict, "proposing money as the good thing of life; stimulating ambition for place and show," but Christian nurture is training in sanctification, enjoyment, appreciation, and fellowship. It "satisfies your wants, contents your ambition, beautifies and blesses your character." On this theme, once he overcame the book's suppression by its original publisher and several years of hostile reviews, he found a sizable public.[61]

Originally published by the Massachusetts Sabbath-School Society, *Discourses on Christian Nurture* was suppressed after Bennett Tyler and other conservatives at the Theological Institute of Connecticut protested against it. Tyler warned that children are depraved sinners who become Christians only by being born again, not by education. In eight public letters to Bushnell, he criticized the book's appeal to spiritual nurture as an audience-flattering betrayal of the gospel. Some reviews were insulting; *The Christian Observatory* editorialized that Bushnell had "a vicious taste for originality," while *The Christian Review* judged that his organic church amounted to "downright socialism." In a more academic spirit, Princeton Seminary stalwart Charles Hodge and German Reformed Church theologian John Williamson Nevin objected that Bushnell explained away depravity and supernatural grace on naturalistic grounds. If nature and supernature are so closely correlated, they protested, how is God's supernatural redemption to be distinguished from a mere possibility within history open to every well-meaning person?[62]

Bushnell puzzled over this question for years; he may have perceived that his argument was overly naturalistic. In the heat of his first theological controversy, however, he lashed back at Tyler and the Sabbath School publishing committee, protesting "the very singular outrage I have suffered." His sharply worded rejoinder, *An Argument for "Discourses on Christian Nurture,"* strengthened his claim to orthodoxy, claimed Samuel Hopkins as an ally, settled a few personal scores, and chided, "Brethren, whether you will believe it or not, a new day has come." Taking control of his suppressed book, he added this rebuttal and four articles, publishing this new edition as *Views of Christian Nurture and of Subjects Adjacent Thereto.*[63]

Engulfed in controversy, Bushnell aggressively defended his position, referring to himself as the victim of "this outrage" and pressing hard on the religious implications of believing that children are condemned sinners. Unlike the book's famous third edition, in the second Bushnell defended his nurture theme with only glancing references to Anglo-Saxon virtue. A dozen years later, however, he heightened his sociopolitical claims, buoyed by a shifting popular tide in favor of the book's nurture theme, and in the third edition of *Christian Nurture* (1860), he dramatically expanded on the connection between Christian nurture and Anglo-Saxon power.[64]

Munger later recalled that Bushnell possessed a distinctive "ethical cleanness" in every aspect of his life, but, like many of his liberal comrades, Munger white-washed the racist dimension of his hero's ambitions for Christian America. Bushnell's moral perspective was distorted by a streak of chauvinistic will to power that he never recognized. He not only claimed that good Christian nurture is life-giving, beautiful, and true to the spirit of Christ; he also insisted that it was the only effective basis of securing Anglo-Saxon Protestant power over the world. Wedged between his tender, aesthetically refined descriptions of Christian love and fellowship, he inserted an excursus on "the out-populating power of the Christian stock" that slurred Catholics, Jews, blacks, and virtually all other groups not belonging to the world's "Puritan stock." *Christian Nurture* aggressively asserted that the great cause of winning the world to Christ was better served by building up the world's Puritan stock than by trusting in revivals.[65]

"The populating power of any race, or stock, is increased according to the degree of personal and religious character to which it has attained," he announced. Put differently, the power of a race is primarily a function of its spiritual and cultural strength, built up by "century-long reaches of populating force," and only secondarily a function of its military might: "Any people that is physiologically advanced in culture, though it be only in a degree, beyond another which is mingled with it on strictly equal terms, is sure to live down and finally live out its inferior. Nothing can save the inferior race but a ready and pliant assimilation." Bushnell spelled out the pertinent lessons of Western history. For centuries the "Christian and Mohommedan races" appeared to be locked in a rivalry that favored the latter, he observed, but history proved "that one religion was creating and the other uncreating manhood; one toning up a great and powerful character, and the other toning down, steeping in lethargy, the races it began to inspire; till finally we can now see as distinctly as possible, that one is pouring on great tides of population, creating a great civilization, and great and powerful nations; the other, falling away into a feeble, half-depopulated, always decaying state, that augurs final extinction at no distant period." The superiority of the "Christian race" ensured its eventual capacity to "completely expurgate the world" of its inferior rivals.[66]

Bushnell's pre–Civil War chauvinism was imprecise; he made no attempt to distinguish race from ethnicity or nationality. Even his criticisms of prejudice were sloppy and bigoted. *Christian Nurture* "explained" that modern Jews were miserly and corrupt as a consequence of the prejudice that Jews suffered for centuries under Christian governments: "The old Jewish stock of the Scripture times, whatever faults they may have had, certainly were not marked by any such miserable, sordid, usurious, garbage-vending propensity, as now distinguishes the race. But the cruelties they have suffered under Christian governments, shut up in the Jews' quarter of the great cities, dealing in old clothes and other mean articles for their gains, hiding these in the shape of gold and jewels in the crevices of their cellars, to prevent seizure by the emissaries of the governments, and disguising their prosperity itself by the squalid dress of their persons—these, continued from age to age, have finally bred in the character we so commonly speak of with contempt." Bushnell took for granted that modern Jews were as repugnant as "common" contempt for them supposed. His idea of moral reflection on this subject was to caution his Christian audience that "our children, treated as they have been for so many generations, would finally reveal the marks of their wrongs in the same sordid, miserly instincts."[67]

At the request of the Bushnell family, Yale theologian Luther Wiegle excised Bushnell's anti-Semitic comments from the 1916 edition, but all of the book's other slurs remained. In Bushnell's telling, the contrast between North and South America provided a chastening reminder that even the Christian world was divided between superior and inferior races. "What a lesson could also be derived, in the same manner, from a comparison of the populating forces of the Puritan stock in this country, and of the inferior, superstitious, half Christian stock and nurture of the South American states. . . . And the reason of the difference is that Christianity, having a larger, fuller, more new-creating force in one, gives it a populating force as much superior." World progress depended upon the world's superior race prevailing. Bushnell occasionally cautioned that Saxon Protestants were capable of degenerating into barbarism, as had, he noted, the Dutch Boers in South Africa. America was the hope of the world because it was founded and built by a superior Christian race devoted to liberty and Christian civilization. To believe in America was to have faith that American Protestants and their northern European families of origin would remake the world in their image, progressively pushing the weaker races "out of the world, as in the silence of a dew-fall." Bushnell's anxiety to see American slavery end— in God's out-populating time—was tied to this vision of the inbreaking king- dom of God on earth. Slavery impeded the realization of America's moral greatness, which had no room for blacks at all.[68]

Bushnell cautioned that this did not mean that Americans no longer needed to try "to convert the heathen nations." It was not enough to simply outstrip and inherit the world. Missionary evangelism still had its place, because it was "for God to say what races are to be finally submerged and lost, and not for us." The chief moral responsibility of American Protestants was to keep themselves worthy of their superior status. The way to achieve this end was to strengthen the nurturing institutions and theology of the church: "I only say that, when we set ourselves to the great work of converting the world, we are to see that we do not miscondition the state of childhood, and throw quite away from us, mean- time, all the mighty advantages that God designs to give us."[69] Accustomed to preaching of this kind, many readers took in stride Bushnell's presumption that a chapter on Anglo-Saxon superiority belonged in a spiritual theology of Christian nurture. He never doubted that his racial views were progressive, and this attitude was slow to die in the progressive theological tradition he founded. Bushnell received a torrent of criticism in his later career, but not on the cluster of issues on which he most deserved it.

SEEING AND SPEAKING THE GOSPEL

Views of Christian Nurture brought Bushnell recognition, but not much satisfaction. His book gained him the public audience he sought, but it ended his
career in the Sunday School movement. Spurned by the Sabbath-School Society,
he had no spiritual home apart from a congregation toward which he continued
to have mixed feelings. Bushnell reeled from the controversy that his book
unleashed. He felt adrift and conflicted and turned increasingly to devotional
fare, especially Catholic mystical literature. His wife believed that the death of
their four-year-old son in 1843 pushed him toward mysticism. In 1847, at the
outset of what became a close friendship with Boston Unitarian pastor Cyrus
Bartol, Bushnell apologized that he barely had time for an exchange of greetings,
being "just now so deep in heresy, or the repute of it thrown upon me." On
Bartol's Unitarianism and his own seemingly muddled position, he reflected: "I
consider myself to be an orthodox man, and yet I think I can state my orthodox
faith in such a way that no serious Unitarian will conflict with me, or feel that
I am beyond the terms of reason."[70]

Bushnell believed he could mediate the schism that had torn Congregationalism apart. Bartol must have been astonished: How could Unitarianism
and orthodoxy be compatible? One either believed in the Trinity or not, or in
Christ's atoning sacrifice or not. On *that,* all parties agreed. In February 1848,
preoccupied with thoughts about how he should clarify his position; wounded
by recent attacks on his person and position; increasingly convinced from his
devotional reading that a deeper sense of God's presence was attainable,
Bushnell had a convicting mystical experience of Christ as a living, personal
power. Upon waking and seeing his expression, his wife asked, "What have you
seen?" He replied, "The gospel."[71]

Later that month he spoke of this experience as a revelation of Christ as "the
form of the soul." Though he never described his experience explicitly,
Bushnell's preaching became more incarnational and transformationist as a consequence of his mystical encounter with Christ. His emphasis on the primacy of
will gave way to an emphasis on what he called "inspirability." His experience
enabled him to link his themes of nurture and divine indwelling to a more
explicitly supernaturalist Christianity. He attested that the Spirit of Christ is not
merely an idea or the basis of exemplary religion, but the very life of one's soul
brought to life by supernatural grace. In phrases that resembled Jonathan
Edwards's descriptions of his "new sense of divine things" and "new sense of the
glory of Christ," Bushnell increasingly emphasized the transforming work of
God's Spirit in rendering visible, to believers, the self-expression of God in creation. Thematically, he focused on the representation of God in Christ, the
indwelling of Christ in the soul, and the spirit-transforming mission of the Holy
Spirit.[72]

Daring to preach what he called "a simple outspeaking" of his spiritual experience, Bushnell testified with renewed spiritual vigor that "the grand object of the gospel plan" is to incarnate Christ in the spirit of every person; Christ was incarnated in the world for this purpose. With grateful surprise, Bushnell found that his experience of mystical illumination heightened his desire to inspire his congregation. Against Edwards—whom he rarely cited, mainly for this reason—he proclaimed that "the very spirit and beauty of Christ himself" is available to all who sincerely desire Christ. Urging his congregants not to settle for a "dreary and cheerless" religion of duty based on morality and moral will, Bushnell enthused: "What a joy and relief it should be to the soul to find the incarnate Word descending to its aid, to go out of herself and rest herself in a love not her own, and thus to form herself unto a new and noble life by adherence to another!" To preach such an expectation is a kind of daring, he allowed, but faith is precisely an exercise in daring that expects the Spirit: "The great design of God in the incarnation of his Son is to form a divine life in you. It is to produce a Christ in the image of your soul, and to set you on the footing of a brother with the divine Word himself."[73]

His first two conversions had merely, and barely, kept him in the Christian church; by his accounting, this one made him a friend of Christ and theologian of Christ's indwelling Spirit. He later recalled, "I seemed to pass a boundary. I had never been very legal in my Christian life, but now I passed from those partial seeings, glimpses and doubts, into a clearer knowledge of God and into his inspirations, which I have never wholly lost. The change was into faith,—a sense of the freeness of God and the ease of approach to him." His friend Cyrus Bartol tellingly remarked that Bushnell's later spiritual countenance closely resembled Channing's.[74] Renewed by fresh inspirations in his later career, he preached Channing's theme of the intimate communion between divine Spirit and human spirit, but as a Trinitarian theologian. More precisely than Channing, though lacking Channing's charity to "aliens" and the poor, he theorized about the possibility of continuous spiritual growth into the character of Christ. Intuitively akin to Emerson, but with vastly greater theological concentration, Christian identity, and a decidedly non-Emersonian sense of the "dark side" of God and nature, Bushnell became America's theologian of the gospel as a gift to the poetic imagination. Though he never resolved the tension between the authority he ascribed to inspirations and his theory of language, he significantly advanced Emerson's early vision of theology as a poetry of the divine.

LANGUAGE, GOD, AND CHRIST

Bushnell's post conversion opportunities to define his theological position arrived with remarkable timeliness when in March, 1848, he received nearly simultaneous invitations from Harvard, Yale, and Andover to give major theological addresses. The serendipity of these invitations was too perfect not to make an impression in the afterglow of his mystical experience. These were the academic centers of the competing theologies of a broken Congregationalism, and Bushnell was anxious to pursue constructive dialogue with all of them. Pursuing his ideal of Christian comprehensiveness, he sought to promote Christian reconciliation, not by synthesizing the church's rival theologies, but by moving the field of theology beyond its fixed disagreements. Learning that he was being considered for the Hollis chair at Harvard, he wrote and presented three major addresses: "A Discourse on the Atonement" in July at Harvard, "A Discourse on the Divinity of Christ" in August at the Yale commencement, and "A Discourse on Dogma and Spirit; or the True Reviving of Religion" in September at Andover.

Written for decidedly different yet theologically sophisticated audiences, Bushnell's addresses made a rough fit when joined together. They were short on accessibility and expository flow, but more important, he perceived, they lacked an explanation of the theory of language that underlay his theologizing. In preparing the lectures for publication, he therefore composed an introductory essay on language in which he tried to help readers make sense of his constructive claims. For twenty years, this prolegomenon merely provoked liberals, conservatives, and Taylorites alike, who resisted his emphasis on the metaphorical nature of language, which undercut their certainties. Bushnell anticipated that this book, *God in Christ: Three Discourses,* would be controversial, noting that "a somewhat evil notoriety" preceded its publication. Refusing to apologize to conservatives for daring to speak at Unitarian Harvard, he claimed not to understand why so many people found his religious thinking offensive. He vowed to stay out of the furor he knew was coming: "I advertise it beforehand, to prevent a misconstruction of my silence, that I am silenced now, on the publication of my volume." Bushnell disavowed this pledge shortly after *God in Christ* made him notorious.[75]

His approach to theology offended virtually the entire field, from left to right, of American religious thinkers, who assumed that theology was the science of drawing and systematizing logical deductions from literal assertions of fact. Notwithstanding his various debts to Emerson, even Theodore Parker approached the Bible as a storehouse of ostensibly factual assertions and literal propositions and never doubted that "a passage of Scripture can have but one meaning." In contrast, Bushnell contended that American religious thinking was deficient and overly dogmatic on this account. Building on his early account of religious language, with occasional citations of Coleridge and Gibbs, he explained the theory of faded metaphor and the distinction between linguistic physicality and thought before summarizing his Wordsworthian conclusion of a decade earlier: "If the outer world is the vast dictionary and grammar of thought we speak of, then it is also itself an organ throughout of Intelligence." An organ of whose intelligence? Bushnell proclaimed that this question drives us directly to the divine Author, "no more to hunt for Him by curious arguments and subtle deductions, if haply we may find Him; but He stands *expressed* every where, so that, turn whichsoever way we please, we behold the outlooking of His intelligence." The revelation of God in language is "an amazing fund of inspiration" that outshines all other evidences.[76]

God in Christ boldly picked up where his 1839 Andover lecture had left off. Like most philosophers and even many philologists, Bushnell observed, theologians routinely assumed that some terms of thought are literal and others figurative. But terms of thought are always figurative, he objected. The distinction between literal and figurative pervades the very body of language and creates the qualitatively different linguistic departments of sensation and thought. While allowing, with qualification, that "literal" terms are factual, belonging to the department of sensation, he emphasized that the language of thought is always figurative: words of thought and spirit are always signs or images; they cannot be univocal equivalents of truth, no matter how many evidences are piled up in their support.

As a provocation to "our younger theologians," he explained his neo-Platonist theory of the analogical relationship between thought and the external world. Bushnell proposed that words of thought and spirit are possible only because their cognitively apprehended forms are provided in the world of sensation "by reason of some hidden analogy"; moreover, words of thought and spirit are *names* of these outwardly existing forms or images. He did not claim to understand how God does it: "All we can say is, that by a mystery transcending in any case our comprehension, the Divine Logos, who is in the world, weaves into nature types or images that have an inscrutable relation to mind and thought." Form is somehow brought to represent the formless by a process that deepens in mystery with our attempts to understand it.[77]

Bushnell played up the impossibility of settling the meanings even of everyday terms. "Literal" words are slippery and inexact, representing only certain sensations of sight or taste or the like, he observed. From either a nominalist or realist standpoint, factual terms are merely names of genera, not exact representatives of particular things. More important for theology, words of thought and spirit are hopelessly fluid; words such as bitterness, love, and justice are endlessly various in their range of significations. We tend to avoid thinking about the indeterminacy of our language, he noted, because we cannot get along without such words, "and it is uncomfortable to hold them in universal scepticism." Bushnell sympathized with this reaction while exhorting against it. Instead of ignoring the open-ended, never-settled nature of signification, he proposed, it is better to think of words as mere signs by which thought is expressed: "They do not literally convey, or pass over a thought out of one mind into another, as we commonly speak of doing. They are only hints, or images, held up before the mind of another."[78]

Bushnell exempted a sizable class of thought-words from indeterminacy, allowing that geometrical figures, numerals, and other "necessary ideas" such as time, space, cause, truth, and right possess determinate meanings. In its idea, truth cannot be anything different from truth, he reasoned, just as a circle must be a circle. The problem in theology was that religious thinkers routinely presumed the rights of necessary ideas for words such as sin, hope, salvation, and love. Against the implicit assumption that merely figurative words of thought can be turned into determinate ideas with sufficient repetition, he inveighed that "there could not be a greater mistake." The word "sin" made an instructive example. Endlessly repeated, the word bears a different meaning to every mind: "The whole personal history of every man, his acts, temptations, wants, and repentances; his opinions of God, of law, and of personal freedom; his theory of virtue, his decisions of the question, whether sin is an act, or a state; of the will, or of the heart: in fact, his whole theology and life will enter into his impression of this word *sin,* to change the quality, and modify the relations of that which it signifies."[79]

Words of thought and spirit are necessarily indeterminate by virtue of being figurative, and, he cautioned, they are also unavoidably falsifying with respect to the truth they are meant to express. Thought-words impute forms to formless truths; they relate to the truth "only as form to spirit." On this theme Bushnell loved John Bunyan, who confessed that his "dark and cloudy words" held the truth only in the way that cabinets enclose gold. If religious thinkers were to bear in mind that words are mere signs or images of realities that have no sensible quality, Bushnell reasoned, the church would be spared many useless fights over creeds. The same recognition would help Christians appreciate that the Bible is a cryptic text loaded with truth-revealing paradoxes and outright contradictions.[80]

"Probably, the most contradictory book in the world is the Gospel of John," Bushnell asserted, but too sensitive to his audience to pile up evidence, he moved quickly to the claim that John's Gospel contains "more and loftier truths" than any other book in the world *because* it is pervaded with paradoxes and contradictions. Like any good writer possessed by the desire to express truth, he explained, John refused to let matters of fact or rational coherence get in the way of his witness to truths of spirit: "It is nothing to him that a quirk of logic can bring him into absurdity." The artful witness to spiritual truth may use logic-chopped definitions, Bushnell allowed, but a good writer uses definitions only as "multiplying forms or figures of that which he seeks to communicate." Possessing mere words for definitions, the spiritually attuned religious thinker understands that definitions can never be determinate measures of thought; the discerning thinker thus employs them "only as being *other forms* of the truth in question, by aid of which it may be more adequately conceived." Implicitly, this statement signaled that Bushnell had no objection to creeds, rightly understood. On the other hand, taking a shot at New England theology, he wrote that "a writer without either truth or genius, a mere uninspired, unfructifying logicker, is just the man to live in definitions. He has never a doubt of their possibility." The dogma-based theologian ignored the instability of his own definitions, and thus worked out a Christian system that was both consistent and false, "false because of its consistency."[81]

Bushnell complained that dogmatic theologians were highly peculiar as a class. For example, they granted Goethe the right to contradict himself when he explained poetic truth, but refused the same right to themselves or, more important, the Gospel writers. The Gospel of John is "a vast compilation of symbols and forms," he observed. What was to be done with such a richly literary work of imagination? "Shall we say, with the infidel, this is all a medley of contradiction—mere nonsense, fit only to be rejected? Shall we take up these bold antagonisms, as many orthodox believers have done, seize upon some one symbol as the real form of the truth, and compel all the others to submit to it; making, thus, as many sects as there are symbols, and as many petty wars about each truth as it has sides or inches of surface? Or shall we endeavor, with the Unitarians, to decoct the whole mass of symbol, and draw off the extract into pitchers of our own; fine, consistent, nicely-rounded pitchers, which, so far from setting out any where towards infinity, we can carry at pleasure by the handle, and definitely measure by the eye?"[82]

Conservatives and Unitarians alike reduced the rich polyphony of scripture to singular propositional meanings; Bushnell countered that good scripture scholarship needed to approach the Bible closer to the way that aesthetically sensitive literary critics studied literature: "There is no book in the world that contains so many repugnances, or antagonistic forms of assertion, as the Bible," he asserted.

> Therefore, if any man please to play off his constructive logic upon it, he can easily show it up as the absurdest book in the world. But whosoever wants, on the other hand, really to behold and receive all truth, and would have the truth-world overhang him as an empyrean of stars, complex, multitudinous, striving antagonistically, yet comprehended, height above height, and deep under deep, in a boundless score of harmony; what man soever, content with no small rote of logic and catechism, reaches with true hunger after this, and will offer himself to the many-sided forms of the scripture with a perfectly ingenuous and receptive spirit; he shall find his nature flooded with senses, vastnesses, and powers of truth, such as it is even greatness to feel.[83]

Bushnell held out for a conception of Christian truth as the expression of God, or, more precisely, God coming into expression "through histories and rites, through an incarnation, and through language—in one syllable, by the *Word.*" It requires all the media of God's self-expression to begin to suggest the meaning of Christ's mystic life and death, he urged. Put negatively, it offends true piety and intelligence alike to claim that the meaning of God's self-expression in Christ can be defined by "a few dull propositions." Much of the Bible is poetry, he noted; much of the rest is narrative, "which is equally remote from all abstractions, and, in one view, equally poetic; for history is nothing but an evolution or expression of God and man in their own nature and character." In both cases, the kind of truth claimed by the scriptural witness is spiritual and poetic, not appealing to reasons, rational proofs, or historical evidence, but self-authenticating. "The teachings of Christ are mere utterances of truth, not argumentations over it," Bushnell explained. "He gives it forth in living symbols, without definition, without *proving* it, ever, as the logicians speak, well understanding that truth is that which shines in its own evidence, that which *finds* us, to use an admirable expression of Coleridge, and thus enters into us."[84]

The true Christian witness is a seer, not a logician; she emits spiritual fire, "not formulas for the mere speculative understanding." Bushnell often told acquaintances that he owed more to Coleridge's *Aids to Reflection* than to any other book except the Bible,[85] explaining in *God in Christ* that "the most fructifying writer I ever read, was one in whom I was, at first, able only to see glimpses, or gleams of truth." Only after many years of patient intellectual struggle with the issues treated by Coleridge, and a long period of "laborious self-questioning," could he claim for himself the truths to which Coleridge gave witness. And once Coleridge made sense to him, he stopped reading *Aids to Reflection* altogether, "save in a chapter or two, which I glanced over, just to see how obvious and clear, what before was impossible, had now become." With Coleridge he proclaimed that Christian truth is spirit and life, "as Christ himself declared," not a datum of the natural understanding. Like the writer of the Gospel of John, he interpreted the outward form of Christ's life "only as a manifestation of his indwelling glory, by which this may be brought home to the heart."[86]

God in Christ was widely denounced as a Unitarian-leaning attack on creeds, but Bushnell insisted that he surrendered no Christian truth to the Unitarians and did not dispute the church's need of creeds. As long as the church did not absolutize any single doctrinal formula, he explained, he felt no sympathy for Unitarian anticreedalism and favored a multiplicity of creeds, "as many as are offered," because the existence of many creeds reminded the church that all theology consists of the relative interpretation of symbols. Understood as "a kind of battle-dooring of words, blow answering to blow," he thought the church's various creedal statements played a healthy role in Christian life. Neither did he concede any substantive claim to the Unitarians about the nature of God or salvation. The Unitarians were right to oppose certain forms of orthodox dogmatism, he suggested, but they were wrong to strip Christianity of spiritual truths that gave the gospel its tonic energy, including the doctrines of the Trinity, the person of Christ, human depravity, vicarious atonement, and the Spirit of God as a supernatural grace.[87]

To rescue these great truths from unimaginative orthodoxies and Unitarianisms alike, "We must think ourselves together, not as fixing our minds on some halfway place, where we may meet, but simply as striving after the divine verities of the gospel, and the unity of the spirit." Although Bushnell coveted the Hollis chair, he spared the Unitarians no criticism and dared to bore them, lecturing at length on atonement theory. He defended the doctrines of the Trinity and atonement as belonging to the sphere of metaphorical expression, not the sphere of logic: "They are forms of truth which have their reality in and through the imaginative and morally aesthetic powers—truths of form and feeling, not of the logical understanding." At Yale he rejected tradi-tional dual-nature Christology, arguing that Christ "stands before us in simple unity, one person, the divine-human, representing the qualities of his double parentage as the Son of God, and the son of Mary." At Harvard he gave an early version of what became his signature theory of vicarious atonement, interpret-ing the saving work of Christ as subjectively regenerative and as the fulfillment of objective Jewish ritual-religion. Against the grain of Unitarian Christianity, Bushnell insisted that objective atonement language is indispensable to Christianity and that Christianity and Judaism are intimately connected on this account. To the Andover conservatives he contrasted the spirit of dogmatism unfavorably to the spirit of true piety, singing exactly the kind of liberal Christian music that might have won the Hollis chair, had he played the game that way.[88]

DEFENDING AND RETHINKING IN EXILE

As it was, Bushnell offended nearly everyone. Aside from a smattering of individual pastors, *God in Christ* had no constituency at all. It alienated the Harvard Unitarians, who dropped him as a candidate for the Hollis chair; it out-raged conservatives and Taylorites of all kinds, who condemned his relativizing approach to church creeds and his characterization of biblical discourse. Conservatives Chauncey Goodrich and Enoch Pond reached immediately for the epithet "pantheist." Pond and conservative evangelical David Lord blasted Bushnell for failing to prove that all words are sensibly derived or that spiritual subjects must be designated universally by figures. Catholic convert Orestes Brownson dismissed the book's approach to religion as "an old acquaintance" from his transcendentalist days.[89]

Charles Hodge condemned the book as a transcendentalist-lurching con-coction of "Rationalism, Mysticism, and the new Philosophy." By his count, the book's heresies included Sabellianism, Docetism, Apollinarianism, Eutychianism, Pelagianism, and semi-Pelagianism. Though he found nothing objectionable in Bushnell's general theory of language, Hodge charged that his arguments about the implications of language indeterminacy for theology were so exaggerated and transparent "that we can hardly give him credit for sincer-ity." He derided Bushnell as "a man who would leave the ark to ride out the del-uge on a slimey log." That was mild language compared to that of some reviewers, who gave Bushnell an accusatory pounding.[90]

But many of the book's outraged opponents were Connecticut Congre-gationalist pastors not satisfied with slashing book reviews. For five years a coalition of conservative pastors centered in the Congregationalist Association of Fairfield West campaigned to put Bushnell on trial for heresy, and with few allies outside his congregation, he barely survived their efforts. He was ostracized by his colleagues, all but one of whom refused to exchange pulpits with him; wounded by their scorn, he tried to defend his orthodoxy. His legal training proved useful as he fought off repeated procedural challenges; mostly he relied on the fierce loyalty of his congregation, which grew in his affection. Any three members of his congregation could have forced him to endure a heresy trial, an unsettling fact to Bushnell, given that three prominent congregants were early trustees of Bennet Tyler's Theological Institute of Connecticut. At least one of them was a key source of Bushnell's denominational trouble, but his accusers were unable to enlist the necessary threesome, and the Hartford Central special committee that handled the first phase of the case split 3–2 in his favor. In the struggle to retain his clerical standing, Bushnell lost his Protestant Alliance optimism that American Protestantism was remaking the world in a good way.[91]

Two defenders helped him survive his days of accusation. Writing under the pseudonym "C.C." (later explained as "Criticus Criticorum," critic of the critics), Chester, Connecticut, pastor Amos S. Chesebrough published ten articles in the Hartford *Religious Herald* that turned the tables on Bushnell's accusers. Under such titles as "Do They Understand Him?" "What Is Orthodoxy?" and "A Divine Person—What?" he showed that Bushnell's accusers interpreted his work in contradictory ways and invoked conflicting standards of orthodoxy. Some of Bushnell's ostensible heresies excluded each other, he noted; in every case, Bushnell's true offense was his refusal to absolutize certain "speculations that have been tacked upon God's truth." Pressing both points, Chesebrough suggested that Reformed "orthodoxy" was a phantom. He later recalled that he could not stand to see Bushnell condemned "by hard names fished up out of ancient theologic rubbish—a Socinian, a Sabellian, an Apollinarian, a Docetist—as if calling a man opprobrious names answered for evidence of heresy." He noted the emotional stress of the controversy: "It is impossible for those who have come upon the stage of public life within the last thirty years to realize the intense excitement and tremulous apprehension caused by these charges of heresy against so prominent a character."[92]

Bushnell and Chesebrough became close friends, as did Bushnell and North Church deacon Henry M. Goodwin. A seminarian at Andover, Goodwin published a strong defense of Bushnellian language theory at the height of the controversy that helped some readers see the issues more clearly. Bushnell gratefully reported that he was one of them. Tiring of public controversy, he confessed to Goodwin that he was beginning to consider the possibility of devoting himself entirely to pastoral tasks. "I seem to be now very much cut off from access to the public; not so, I trust, from access to God. . . . God is left, and he is the best public to me, the only public in which I have any satisfaction; and I think with the highest delight of going apart with him into a desert place to rest awhile." The following year, in 1852, on its own accord, North Church voted unanimously to withdraw from the Hartford North Consociation. Bushnell saved his status as a Congregational pastor, but the controversy cost him what should have been his most productive years.[93]

God in Christ was flawed on several counts. It ignored technical problems and ambiguities in Gibbs's theory of language; it followed Coleridge in categorizing imagination as a faculty of mind, while making no attempt to develop a faculty psychology of mind; it ignored pertinent scholarship on virtually all its themes; it was dubiously Trinitarian; it made little attempt to address the problem of naturalism raised by critics of *Discourses on Christian Nurture.* The book was often condemned for its strengths, however, a fact that depressed its author for years. Bushnell grieved that his sincerely Christian spirit was routinely disregarded or denied. He despaired that critics such as Pond, Lord, and Brownson dismissed the book entirely, as though he had failed to show—minor problems notwithstanding—that theology rightly speaks in a different kind of language from the factual discourse of science. He complained to William Patton, the only colleague who exchanged pulpits with him, that his opponents wrote about the human spirit "as if it were a machine under the laws of mechanics." To Cyrus Bartol he confessed that the furious reaction to his book inflicted an "angel of dryness" upon him.[94]

Feeling wrongfully attacked, he was disposed to concede nothing. With a wounded spirit, he broke his promise not to answer criticism and set out to correct his opponents. His thinking about the atoning work of Christ was still in an early phase. Though he noted the liturgical objectivity of the Bible's atonement language, his atonement theory was rejected by the Fairfield West conservatives, who assailed it vehemently, and by the bare majority of theological moderates on the Hartford Central Association special committee, chaired by Noah Porter, who handled the heresy charges against him.[95] On this issue, Bushnell held his ground and put his likely inner misgivings on hold. He tried to say the same thing with different words in a way that at least made a few converts. He insisted that the language issue was the key to everything else, threatening his opponents' sense of security by saying that religious language is suggestive and symbolic, not factually descriptive. He pleaded that those who misconstrued his language principle were bound to misunderstand everything else.

Seeking to clarify the language principle, he explained in *Christ in Theology* (1851) that all religious truth "is and must be presented under conditions of form or analogy from the outward state." In a transcendentalist aside, Bushnell appeared to concede the possibility of directly intuited truth, knowable independent of words or other acts of communication. He may have meant to allow only that the content of any truth conveyed by language into the mind is possessed by consciousness independent of the communicative symbols that convey it.[96] In either case, what was crucial to him, and clearly expressed, was the clothing of thought in signs or analogies. At the moment that a conscious subject thinks discursively, he explained, the subject dresses its truths in forms that are not equivalents of its truths, but merely signs or analogies. Even doctrinal definitions and abstract philosophical principles are true only figuratively: "They will carry their sense, not by simple notation, as in arithmetic or algebra, but as offering it to the critical power of the eye and heart in symbols naturally expressive."[97]

This was the core of the language principle. Bushnell grasped the difference between core and secondary commitments. He was committed to a Gibbsian account of the origin of language but did not rest the argument for his language principle upon it. He believed there was an "eternal connection" between the forms of things in being and the contents of the divine mind, but treated this belief as a speculative aside. The language principle, elementary and practical for him, concerned the significance of language as an expression of mind and did not require a full-blown theory or metaphysics of language to correct bad arguments in theology. Bushnell admonished that "all our difficulties and controversies" regarding the truths of revelation were caused by a basic failure to face up to what was known about the clothing of truths in signs and analogies. The problem was not peculiar to New England theology, he suggested; it was an "almost universal sin that infests the reasonings of mankind concerning moral and spiritual subjects." Throughout the world, people treated the symbolic forms of their truths as the truths themselves.[98]

This mistake is the root of all dogmatism, he admonished: "It was not my design to make an assault upon logic itself as a science. I was not ignorant that all the sublime results of the calculus are fruits of genuine logic. I only meant that as soon as we carry this method into moral and religious philosophy, and subject our mind to it as a dominant influence there, we are sure to be enveloped in sophistries without end or limit; for words, in this case, have a wholly different relation to their truths—a relation of form or symbol, and not of mere notation." Bushnell understood that this claim and his appeal to the play of metaphor as the appropriate language of faith were incomprehensible to most of his literally trained clerical audience: "I was well aware that the views of language expressed in my book would be generally looked upon as fantastic and extravagant." But in truth, he urged, it was hardly extravagant to observe the distinction between the formless truths conveyed in language and the forms in which they are inevitably conveyed. It was not right to count him a despiser of theology merely for having reflected on the difference. He did not doubt that "we must have something, somehow held and exercised, that may be called theology. We must define, distinguish, arrange and frame into order the matter of our knowledge." At the same time, he did believe that the desire to make theology as notational as possible was profoundly misguided: "If it were possible to get religious truth into shapes and formulas having an absolute meaning, like the terms of algebra, as clear even to the wicked as to the pure, and requiring no conditions of character in the receivers, it would very nearly subvert, it seems to me, all that is most significant and sublime in the discipline of life."[99]

Bushnell debated various doctrinal points with his adversaries, claiming always that their disagreements were about language usage, not lack of belief:

"All my supposed heresies, in reference to these great subjects, are caused by the arrest of speculation and the disallowance of those constructive judgments, or a priori arguments, by which terms that are only analogies, and mysteries that are most significant when taken only as symbols, are made to affirm something wiser and more exact than what they express."[100] For example, attributing to him a literalist position that he never adopted, Fairfield West conservatives accused Bushnell of denying that Christ possessed a human soul "distinct in its actings from the Divinity."[101] God in Christ denied only that the human soul of Jesus was to be spoken of, "or looked upon, as having a *distinct* subsistence, so as to live, think, learn, worship, suffer, by itself." He rejected Chalcedonian dual-nature Christology because of its tendency to fracture the personal unity of Christ, making Christ an unreal and conflicted figure: "This theory of two distinct subsistences, still maintaining their several kinds of action in Christ,— one growing, learning, obeying, suffering; the other infinite and impassible —only creates difficulties a hundred fold greater than any that it solves." The Nestorian drift of New England orthodoxy offered a telling example in his time. Bushnell opposed the New England Reformed tendency to deny that the divine nature of Christ was directly involved in his sacrificial suffering and death. He warned that in its overreaction to Unitarian Arianism and Socinianism, New England theology stood in danger of losing the principle of Christ's consubstantial humanity.[102]

Christ in Theology rehashed this doctrinal debate, but this time in a way that pressed hard on the language problem. Bushnell declared that as long as its language was not regarded as an analytical or speculative description, he could live with the orthodox formula "two natures and one person." He affirmed as a truth of revelation that Christ is divine; he affirmed also that the incarnation is properly described as God's assumption of humanity, the Word made flesh, not merely as the coming together of the Word and some man. "But whether the assumption included the assumption of a human soul; or whether, if it does and that soul lapses into the divine person so as to have, no more, any personality or character of its own, it would really *be;* or so far different from the state of not being, that a true account of the one person would require us to notice at all the presence, or trace the historic fortunes of an entity so ambiguous,—what, in a word, the assumption involves, how the one person thus resulting is interiorly constituted, what part the human occupies in him or is, who speaks, obeys, suffers, dies,—these are questions we are never to raise. They are by the supposition excluded, both as being impossible and irrelevant." The way to show the self-authenticating divinity of Jesus is not by drawing the metaphysical boundaries of his wills and natures, he contended, but by reviewing Christ's life and character. We know nothing about Christ save that which is expressed. Liberal Protestantism in the succeeding generation took this prescription to heart.[103]

The same sensibility informed his approach to Trinitarian doctrine. Bushnell was accused by Hodge, the Fairfield West group, and various others of denying God's immanent Trinity "as involving a tripersonality in the Divine nature."[104]

For decades afterward he was routinely identified as a Sabellian, sometimes by followers.[105] This was never quite right, as he struggled to explain in *Christ in Theology;* more important, this attempt to clarify his position contained the first sign of a significant shift in his thinking toward classical Trinitarianism. He began by identifying Schleiermacher as a modern proponent of the Sabellian tradition. For Schleiermacher, as for Sabellius, he observed, the doctrine of the Trinity made sense only as a statement about the three modes or manifestations by which the one God has been revealed. Sabellian modalism affirmed a trinity of manifestations while rejecting the orthodox doctrine that God exists as an immanent trinity of persons. Against a host of accusers, Bushnell denied that he had ever denied the immanent Trinity; he therefore disputed his identification as a Sabellian. His view was that taking any position about the inner nature of God is wrong. Orthodox Trinitarianism taught that because God has been revealed in three manifestations, God must be a triunity of persons; the Sabellian tradition countered that God's three manifestations are modes or media of revelation only. The one God has been revealed in three ways; it is wrong to reason that God must not be a single person if God has been revealed in three modes.[106]

Bushnell believed that both positions claimed too much. His emphasis on expression and his critique of orthodox dogmatism led many to identify him with the Sabellian view, but he noted indignantly that he never denied the immanent Trinity: "The very tenor of my argument required me *not* to deny it." The entire business of taking normative positions on the nature of God's inner mystery is misguided, he urged. The approach he advocated was to "stay by the Scripture and trust ourselves to *no* constructive reasonings on the subject." He observed that the Trinity we know is a Trinity of revelation; it is given to humankind for use, not for theory. This sounded like Sabellianism to many, but the Sabellians also claimed to know more than is known. Bushnell declared, "Any attempt to solve or conceive God's interior mystery, by reasonings cast in the molds and categories of our human consciousness, is presumptuous, possibly even absurd." It is better to seek after God "in the simple *use* of that by which he is offered to knowledge." Against the violating presumptions of theology, he pleaded, it should be enough to receive the three manifestations of God under the conditions of revealed expression without claiming that the "tiny molds of our discursive understanding" enable us to understand God's inner being.[107]

This was the view that informed *God in Christ,* though it was not stated as clearly, and it was the view that Bushnell tried to settle upon and that fit the rest of his theology. *Christ in Theology* made effective polemical use of it in defending his right to the Christian name. In preparing his defense against the accusation of heresy, however, Bushnell's historical research proved unsettling. Scholarship was never his mode. Though capable of doing scholarly work, he was primarily a seer; for him, books were repositories of inspiration for his own ideas, and he told friends that he rarely read a book straight through. *God in*

Christ was written in the style he preferred, "a simple outspeaking of myself." The prospect of researching his defense of *God in Christ* was distasteful to him, but sometime after he grudgingly embarked upon it, Bushnell found himself admiring, to his astonishment, the Nicene Creed. He studied Athanasius's defense of the creed and found surprising spiritual wisdom in the formulas of the Nicene fathers. *Christ in Theology* duly reported: "I feel obliged to confess that I had not sufficiently conceived its import, or the title it has to respect as a Christian document." Having conceded that, undefinable as it may be, the Trinity has to be more than a "dramatic show," Bushnell developed a chastened respect for the efforts of the Nicene fathers to think about the ontological ground of the instrumental Trinity confessed by scripture.[108]

His unexpected admiration for Nicene orthodoxy yielded the judgment that New England orthodoxy was decidedly inferior by comparison. Nicene orthodoxy developed a sophisticated doctrine of the coinherence (*perichoresis*) of each person of the divine triunity with the others, but New England theology had no conception of triune coinherence at all. On the ground that the Nicene doctrine of eternal generation implied a subordination of the Son to the Father, the eighteenth-century fathers of New England theology eliminated the entire concept of the eternal generation and procession in the Godhead. This was a disastrous negation, Bushnell admonished, and showed the totalizing distortion that ensues from confusing truth with its form. Lacking any concept of the identity of each person of the Godhead with each other, New England theology lost the dynamic actualism of Nicene orthodoxy. Instead of viewing the Trinity as dynamic and relational, grounded in interrelating action, New England conservatives and Hopkinsians "began to assert a trinity of persons in the divine essence itself, which is plain tritheism."[109]

This irony was galling to Bushnell. He bitterly reflected that he was being accused of heresy by the guardians of a regnant theology that was significantly less orthodox than his own. "The truth is, that what we call orthodoxy on this subject, in New England, is wholly unhistorical—a provincialism, a kind of theological *patois,* quite peculiar to ourselves," he chided. The New England fathers were active thinkers, "but they were too little historic, in their theological studies, to keep their circle of thought duly expanded." So Bushnell refused to accept judgment from people whose idea of orthodoxy included the impossible notion that trinitarianism is a doctrine about God's threefold essence. "I do then peremptorily refuse to justify myself, as regards this matter of trinity, before any New England standard," he announced. "We have no standard, better than a residuary tritheistic compost, such as may be left us after we have cast away that which alone made the old historic doctrine of trinity possible."[110]

But his own ground was shifting. Bushnell asserted that he still rejected the metaphysical presumptions of the Nicene fathers, since he still believed it was wrong to commit the church to propositions about the inner life of God. The appropriately modest way to speak of the Trinity is in the scriptural mode as God's expressive activity, he urged. Instead of beginning, like the Nicene Creed, on the ontological plane, "within the active life of God," it was better to start with the evidence of God's expressive activity in the world, before making any propositional inferences about the nature of the divine mystery behind it. *Christ in Theology* opened the door to the latter enterprise, however. Having established his agreement with Nicene orthodoxy that God is always engaged in the creative process of "eternally threeing himself" in history, Bushnell agreed that theologians are entitled to make certain inferences about the reality behind God's manifestations.

If God is always relationally active in revelation, he reasoned, the church's theology may confess that God is pure act or even that God is "eternally and immanently three." Cautioning that statements about God's being must always be made "more timidly and with larger reservations of modesty," he thus accepted the legitimacy of moving from revelational knowledge to qualified statements about God's being "eternally self-revealing in his nature." His new respect for Nicene orthodoxy pushed him in an unexpected direction, claiming that New England theology lost its right to the orthodox name by replacing the doctrine of eternal generation—"precisely that on which the church doctrine hangs"—with the doctrine of three substances condemned at the Nicene Council. As for himself, Bushnell reflected, "While I have as little care as possible to secure a shelter under any form of orthodoxy, it is, I confess, a most refreshing surprise to me to find that I can so heartily approve the general truth of what I supposed I had rejected."[111]

Convinced that New England theology had "slidden competely off the basis of historic orthodoxy," he resolved to accept neither instruction nor correction from it and, as always, to find his own way. In his own fashion, however, the course that he followed brought him closer to key aspects of historic orthodoxy. His breakthrough realization that orthodox Trinitarianism described the mystery of God in a more compelling manner than either New England orthodoxy and Unitarianism moved him to reflect more deeply on the church's experience of the Trinity as God's outpouring language. Embroiled in controversies over his novel religious claims, he plunged into the problem of the relation of God's Trinitarian self-expression to time and eternity. Bushnell would pursue his steadily deepened, though selective and critical, appreciation of orthodoxy as a spiritually compelling way of speaking the divine mystery. He began with the mystery of God's triune self-relation, moved to the long-deferred problem of the relation of nature and supernature, and ended his career with an extended rethinking of God's atoning self-sacrifice in Christ.

SPEAKING THE DIVINE TRIUNITY

Bushnell's Sabellian-leaning position was eroded by the insight that the Trinity did not begin with the incarnation or end with Christ's atonement. Without a doctrine of eternal generation, he reflected, Christian churches inevitably reduced the triune mystery to a static monotheism that barely made room for a time-begotten Jesus. In his coming-out declaration of 1854, "The Christian Trinity a Practical Truth," Bushnell lauded classical Trinitarianism as a bulwark against the competing reductionistic theisms and pantheisms that posed as superior alternatives. The doctrine of the Trinity has immense practical value, he argued, because it upholds the sublime mystery of God's ineffable infinity and personality. Trinitarian doctrine is routinely misconstrued and ridiculed by people who misunderstand the metaphorical nature of religious language; but properly understood, the language of triune mystery upholds and communicates, like no other, the transcendent glory and personality of God.

This argument was framed by a pantheist-Unitarian dialectic. To Bushnell, pantheist strategies exalt the infinity of God at the cost of negating God's personality and make God "a vast platitude; or, if not this, a dreary, all-containing abyss; a being unconscious, a fate, a stupendous *it*, without meaning or value to our religious nature." Unitarian theism took an opposite tack, picturing God as a personal, universal Father, a simple unit of reason who created and rules the world for the benefit of his children. "But the difficulty now is that the dimensions are lost, the infinite magnitude is practically taken away," he remarked. The fathers of Unitarianism undoubtedly realized that the word *person*, applied to God, is merely a figure derived from the analogy of human personality, but they failed to anticipate the deadening spiritual effect of constantly invoking this single figure. The Unitarian emphasis on God's singular personality had the effect of turning the figure of "person" into a literal affirmation. Insistently identifying God as a unified person, the Unitarians reduced God to human dimensions: "Their one God, their Great Father, would be a name without magnitude or any genuine power of impression."[112]

Bushnell argued that some version of this fate awaited every Christian tradition that lost its feeling for the play of metaphor and the ineffable mystery of God's triune self-expression. The doctrine of the Trinity is the answer to "the great problem of the practical life of religion," he asserted, which is the problem of how to keep alive a spiritually vital sense of the glorious infinity and personality of God: "By these cross relations of a threefold grammatic personality, the mind is thrown into a maze of sublimity, and made to feel at once the vastness, and with that the close society also, of God." Trinitarian theology upholds the personality of God without reducing the figure of person to a literal affirmation, "for God cannot become either one person or three, in any literal sense, when steadfastly held as both." From a rhetorical standpoint, he enthused, the idea of the Trinity is "at once the profoundest practical expedient ever adopted, and the highest wonder ever accomplished in human language." The Trinity is the infinite communicative sign by which God enters the world of finite signs and spirits, and only a spiritually bankrupt church would give it up.[113] Bushnell proclaimed that no experience in this life is more beatific "than to have found and fully brought into feeling the practical significance of this eternal act or fact of God, which we call the Christian Trinity. Nowhere else do the bonds of limitation burst away as here. Nowhere else does the soul launch upon immensity as here." The great themes are never easy or obvious, he reflected: "The mind labors and wrestles after them, and comes into their secret slowly." Without claiming to stand on the plane of understanding claimed by the Nicene fathers, he knew assuredly that worship of God as triune holy mystery is the heart of vital Christian piety: "Let no shallow presumption turn us away then from this glorious mystery, till we have given it time enough, and opened to it windows enough by our praises and prayers, to let in the revelation of its glory."[114]

Though couched in formulas, Trinitarian piety practices the play of metaphor; though often ridiculed as an embarrassment, it is actually the church's greatest spiritual treasure. Bushnell hoped that it was also unifying. While claiming not to care whether his theology was judged to be orthodox, he cared very much about his relations with conservative colleagues. The frosty shunning that he endured from them deeply pained him. In the winter of 1851–52, during a Hartford revival that featured famed revival preacher Charles Finney, Bushnell was wounded by the refusal of his Hartford colleague Joel Hawes to treat him as a fellow Christian. He pleaded with Hawes that they were both orthodox in the sense of the term that preceded New England orthodoxy, for to his mind, *Christ in Theology* had substantiated this claim. Later he assured Hawes that he fully accepted the Nicene doctrine of the Trinity and an "equivalent expression" doctrine of the atonement. Bushnell's reflections on Trinitarian piety, conceived at the height of his successful effort to win Hawes's acceptance as a Christian brother, won him a modicum of peace in the closing years of his ministry.[115]

NATURE, SUPERNATURE,
AND THE REDEMPTION OF EVIL

He was loaded with talent, but short on health and, in his lifetime, an appreciative public. Bushnell traveled widely in his search for a cure for his vaguely tubercular lung disease. Searching for health in California, he selected and surveyed the site for the University of California at Berkeley, but declined its presidency. Cut off from his church-based public, he politicked for a city park in Hartford and then designed one of the masterpieces of American landscape architecture, Bushnell Park. He held two U.S. patents on home heating devices and frequently charted routes for railroad lines and canals.[116] An avid mountaineer and explorer despite poor health, his travel letters gave stunning descriptions of favorite landscapes that reflected his perceptive attunement to nature.

Bushnell could never resign himself to his avocations; like Jonathan Edwards, his profound interest in nature was always religious in a way that inspired theological reflection. The mystic stream that flowed through his writings reflected his acute sense of nature as analogous to spirit and his deep interest in its workings. During the period in which he confronted the prospect of an early end to his pastoral career, made necessary by worsening health, Bushnell composed a major treatise, *Nature and the Supernatural,* on the relation between nature and supernature. This book made a sprawling, discursive, apologetic case for his picture of the world as the medium of divine and human self-communication. Though early reviewers flattened his high hopes for it, the book found a sizable audience in the years that followed, and, to his surprise, he lived to witness, during and after the Civil War, a partial restoration of his reputation, chiefly as the author of *Christian Nurture* and *Nature and the Supernatural.*[117]

Christian Nurture had been pummeled for its naturalism. In *Nature and the Supernatural* Bushnell set the record straight about the extent of his attachment to naturalistic explanation, arguing for a theological third way between orthodoxy and naturalistic materialism. It owed much of its long-running popularity to its accessibility and religiously assuring tone. Written on the level of apologetic religious philosophy, decidedly removed from the scholastic quarrels of New England theology, the book was shrewdly attuned to the religious anxieties of a de-Christianizing American middle class. Speaking directly to the religious perplexities of Americans unsettled by what he called "the naturalistic tendencies of our time" and employing various proofs that he spurned in other contexts, he defended the credibility of the Christian world picture, arguing that nature and supernatural power are complementary poles of God's universal economy. *Nature and the Supernatural* proposed to find "a legitimate place for the supernatural in the system of God, and show it as a necessary part of the divine system itself."[118]

Using arguments briefly sketched in Coleridge's *Aids to Reflection,* Bushnell elaborated this concept of nature as a symbol of God's regulative mind, an idea expressed in his earlier writings, but never quite explained.[119] *Nature and the Supernatural* defined "nature" as the sense-apparent world of substance in which events transpire, in orderly succession, under the law of causality. It defined "the supernatural" as the hypothetical "range of substance" that acts upon nature's chain of cause and effect "from without the chain," producing results that unaided natural processes cannot bring to pass. Countering David Hume, Bushnell admonished repeatedly that the latter definition ruled out the notion of supernatural agency as a suspension of the laws of nature: "It is only said that we, as powers, not in the line of cause and effect, can set the causes in nature at work, in new combinations otherwise never occurring."[120]

Crucial to this argument was Bushnell's emphasis on the immanence and variable agency of the supernatural realm. Supernatural acts do not violate the laws of nature, he explained; they are not performed only by God, and they do not consist primarily of marvels, apparitions, or like phenomena. Supernatural power meets us "in what is least transcendent and most familiar, even in ourselves." The very idea of human personality, a being not bound by the law of cause and effect, is supernaturalist, he argued; human subjectivity contains powers that have power over the laws of nature. Every act of will turns the laws of nature to ends that would not be affected by the unaided operation of nature: "Nature never built a house, or modeled a ship, or fitted a coat, or invented a steam-engine, or wrote a book, or framed a constitution. These are all events that spring out of human liberty, acting in and upon the realm of cause and effect, to produce results and combinations, which mere cause and effect could not."[121]

Appropriating Coleridge's distinction between powers and things, Bushnell maintained that the supernatural realm is the realm of acting powers, while nature is the realm of things acted upon, and that the relation of these two realms is like the relation of mind and body. The Coleridgean concept of super-nature as a system of free, expressive, will-powering selves that relate to nature, in effect, as its mind, brought Bushnell to the unfinished theme of "The Christian Trinity a Practical Truth." There he argued that while nature is a grand and awesome piece of God's universal economy, it has no redemptive power. Nature provokes and raises up, but is not transformative. It cannot heal the world of its evil. Salvation depends upon the other pole of the divine economy, which is supernatural grace.[122] Staking his apologetic case on this claim, Bushnell charged in *Nature and the Supernatural* that naturalistic philosophies are incapable of dealing with evil. His third way was still a form of supernaturalism, though he conceived supernatural power in a different way from orthodoxy. For him, only a supernaturalist Christianity can establish the reality of evil and only a supernatural God can save the world from it.

On both counts, Bushnell cast his position as an alternative to Theodore Parker's hollowed-out religious naturalism, selecting the strongest or, at least to him, most impressive opponent he could find. A cordial acquaintance of Parker's, he took care to distinguish the "new infidelity" championed by Parker and David Friedrich Strauss from the Christianity-hating "old school of denial and atheism" led by David Hume and the French deists. The Parker school was more respectful of religion, he observed, and did not condemn Christianity in the "crude-minded and malignant" tones of the old deism. Generally it spoke in the cooler voice of academic historical criticism, treating Christianity as an example of religious mythology. Moreover, undoubtedly with Parker in mind, Bushnell conceded that "the new infidelity" even had its genuinely good points: "It finds a religious sentiment in all men, which, in one view, is a truth. It finds a revelation of God in all things, which also is a truth. It discovers a universal inspiration of God in human souls . . . [and] rejoices also in the discovery of great and good men."[123]

But this made the Parker school more threatening and destructive to Christianity than the old deism, he warned. Despite its good points, the new infidelity, like the old, was thoroughly committed to naturalism. With better manners than their atheist forerunners, the new infidels plied their trade in a culture increasingly infected by the naturalizing mentality. "All atheists are naturalists of necessity," Bushnell explained. "And atheism there will be in the world as long as sin is in it. If the doctrine dies out as argument, it will remain as a perverse and scoffing spirit. Or it will be reproduced in the dress of a new philosophy."[124]

An example of this was Parker's Absolute Religion. The new infidels were united in their rejection of the supernatural: "All pretenses of a supernatural revelation, inspiration, or experience, it rejects; finding a religion, beside which there is no other, within the terms of mere nature itself; a universal, philosophic, scientific religion. In this it luxuriates, expressing many very good and truly sublime sentiments; sentiments of love, and brotherhood, and worship; quoting scripture, when it is convenient, as it quotes the Orphic hymns, or the Homeric and Sibylline verses, and testifying the profoundest admiration to Jesus Christ, in common with Numa, Plato, Zoroaster, Confucius, Mohammed, and others; and perhaps allowing that he is, on the whole, the highest and most inspired character that has ever yet appeared in the world." The new infidelity admired Jesus, to a point, as an inspiring moral exemplar, but it ruled out incarnation, resurrection, new creation, "or any thing above nature."[125]

To Bushnell, the writings of Parker, Strauss, and a series of lesser figures were distinguished by "their virtual annihilation of the gospels." Taking no instruction at all from their biblical criticism, Bushnell warned that "the assault upon Christianity, in which they agree, is the one from which the greatest harm is now to be expected." He bitterly lamented that the Parker-types did not acknowledge "the true genealogy of their doctrine, and that, hovering over the gulf that separates atheism from Christianity, they take away faith from one, without exposing the baldness and forbidding sterility of the other." Acknowledging that orthodox Christianity promulgated many things that deserved to be criticized by the likes of Parker and Strauss, he cautioned that this fact held no reassurance to those who loved the gospel. The fact that Christianity was badly represented merely heightened the threat to its future.[126]

The theologian of inspirability found that naturalism was instructively lacking in spirit; surveying a wide range of naturalist literature, he judged that even the most creative naturalists failed to inspire in a deep or convicting way. Ralph Waldo Emerson was a primary example: "Intoxicated by his brilliant creations, the reader thinks, for the time, that he is getting inspired. And yet, when he has closed the essay or the volume, he is surprised to find—who has ever failed to notice it?—that he is disabled instead, disempowered, reduced in tone." Emerson wrote sparkling prose, but he had no convicting thoughts or purpose; "the force or capacity for it seems to be gone." Bushnell blamed this on a spiritually impoverishing naturalism, which grew stronger in Emerson's later work. "Grazing in the field of nature is not enough for a being whose deepest affinities lay hold of the supernatural, and reach after God. Airy and beautiful the field may be, shown by so great a master; full of goodly prospects and fascinating images; but, without a living God, and objects of faith, and terms of duty, it is a pasture only—nothing more." In the case of Emerson, he judged, a devitalizing naturalistic outlook became a warrant for aesthetic self-absorption;

Emerson's aching incapacity to *do* anything or stand for any self-transcending purpose was a by-product of his self-surrender "to the luxury of watching the play of his own reflective egoism."[127]

This did not mean that all naturalists are spiritually and ethically enervated; Bushnell knew at least one who was not. But in the case of this exception, a pointed lack of consistency explained a great deal. Most naturalists, he noted, reduced "evil" to ignorance, deriding the Christian notion of sin as impossibly reactionary, if not primitive. The one naturalist who tried to take evil seriously was Theodore Parker, not coincidentally the one who cared most about social justice. Parker burned with ethical passion; he gave his life to abolitionism and other social justice causes; he excoriated "the hatefulness of sin and the terrible evils it brings upon the world." The prophetic indictment of human sinfulness raged through his life and teaching. In the same book in which he sought to destroy "every thing supernatural in Christianity," Bushnell observed, Parker blasted liberal Protestants for reflecting "too little on the evil that comes from violating the law of God."[128]

But Parker's naturalism undermined the religious impulse of his ethic: Parker retained the ethical passion of the biblical prophets while stripping away the basis of their (and his) rhetoric about the law of God. Bushnell countered that "the whole matter of supernaturalism, which he is discussing, hinges on precisely this and nothing else; viz., the question whether there is any such thing as a real 'violation of the law of God,' any 'hatefulness in sin,' any 'terrible evils brought on the world' by means of it." To violate the law of God, he explained, "is itself an act supernatural, out of the order of nature, as truly even as a miracle, else it is nothing." The very concept of a "law of God" is extranatural; what makes sin *sinful* is that it violates the supernatural law of a divine, supernatural power. The idea of sin is coherent, he exhorted, only as the acting of a soul, or personal power "against the constituent frame of nature and its internal harmony." The Bible teaches truly that sin causes "a real disorder of nature, which nothing but a supernatural agency of redemption can ever effectually repair." Bushnell's later thinking concentrated on the latter theme; in the meantime he rejected Parker for taking "no manner of notice" of his fundamental incoherence: "Admitting the existence of sin, his speculations still go on their way, as if it were a fact of no significance in regard to his argument."[129]

Shortly before America erupted in civil war, Bushnell emphasized in *Nature and the Supernatural* that sin is real, historical, and organic. He was keenly attuned to the reality of what he called "dark things" in history and creation and observed that while scripture takes no interest in the metaphysics of sin, it is emphatic that the entire human race is sinful. Bushnell affirmed this assertion, with appeals to physiological science and social history. His Lamarckianism made a strong appearance; his appeal to social science was better founded. Bushnell contended that sin is transmitted generationally through social structures and acquired characteristics. Because mind and body are inseparably linked in nature, he argued, the entire order of nature is thereby deformed; the intersubjective bond that links each individual to every other infects all of creation with sin. If it were possible to bring together the complete inventory of sinful inventions, shapes, and structures that passed through the generations of the world's history, he wrote, "means of self-indulgence, instruments of violence, shows of pride, instigations of appetite, incitements and institutes of corrupt pleasure—all the leprosies and leper-houses of vice, the prisons of oppression, the hospitals and battle-fields of war, we should see a face put on the world which God never gave it, and which only represents the bad conversion it has suffered, under the immense and ever-industrious perversities of sin."[130]

Bushnell gave his last years to the problem of the relation of Calvary to this historical inheritance. In the manner of New Haven Theology, *Nature and the Supernatural* pursued a larger theme, urging that all questions and issues pale before the question whether there is such a thing as divine supernatural power. The questions of moral law and miracles are both secondary to that of God's existence, he argued; There is no "law of God" without a divine lawgiver, and the possibility of miracles depends entirely on the truth about divine reality. Repeatedly he cautioned that the issue of miracles, rightly understood, has nothing to do with suspensions or violations of the laws of nature. "Miracles" are supernatural acts that operate on the chain of cause and effect within nature "from without the chain," events that produce a sense impression that evinces the presence "of a more than human power." Maintaining the idea that supernatural action operates *upon* the natural chain of cause and effect meant that divine and human agency are essentially similar. In effect, Bushnell believed that the accounts of Christ's walking on water and changing water to wine testified to events that belong on the same continuum as a woman's act of building a house or raising her arm; all of these acts overpower laws of nature through the force of spirit and will. If God exists, the differences between divine and human supernatural agency are merely matters of degree, he reasoned.[131]

Without claiming that every miracle attested by the Bible actually occurred, Bushnell thus contended that all were possible as signs of God's active will: "Agreeing that the laws of nature will not be suspended, any more than they are by our own supernatural action, will they yet be so subordinated to his power, as to permit the performance of signs and wonders, in which we may recognize a superhuman force?" He chided that it was ridiculous to believe in a personal God but disbelieve in miracles: "Any religion too absolute to allow the faith of miracles, is a religion whose God never did any thing, and is therefore no God." While affirming that Christianity needed to give up the orthodox doctrine of scriptural inspiration and infallibility, Bushnell defended the essential reliability of the Gospel narratives. With offended astonishment, he cited Parker's claim that "few facts" are known about Jesus and that, in certain things, Hercules and Vishnu were equal or superior to him: "Few facts about Jesus! all the miracles recited of him, as destitute of credibility as the stories of Hercules and Vishnu! And yet these evangelists, retailing so many absurd fictions and so much childish gossip, have been able to give us a doctrine upon which the world has never advanced, a character so deep that the richest hearts have felt nothing deeper, and added nothing to the sentiment of it."[132]

That was the heart of the matter for him. *Christ in Theology* urged that Jesus' self-evident divinity is best revealed not by theorizing the boundaries of Christ's natures, but by reviewing the Gospel record of his life and character. *Nature and the Supernatural* contained a classic prototype of this liberal genre.[133] Bushnell made no claim to prove the historical verity of the Gospel narratives in their entirety, but rather claimed to show "that Christ was a miracle himself, in his own person, and performed miracles." Parker emphasized that Jesus believed in demons and heaped invective on the Pharisees; Bushnell tartly replied that demons might well exist and that some people deserved to be chastised. Parker dismissed the virgin birth as myth; Bushnell replied that even here, the Gospel story appeared in a different light to those who knew Christ as the Word incarnate: "If the objector will but let his imagination rise to the real pitch of the subject, it will be strange, if he does not even begin to feel himself kindled, with Mary, in her song of triumph, and accept the whole history, as one transcendentally beautiful and sublime." Bushnell was prepared to yield aspects of the Bible to scientific or historical correction, if necessary, but conceded nothing to those who sullied the character or deity of Jesus. This was where progressive orthodoxy drew the line.[134]

SCIENCE AND THE LAW OF SACRIFICE

Imbued with this perception of the gospel of Christ as a supernatural gift to the imagination, Bushnell retired from his Hartford pastorate in 1859. He recalled to his congregation that when he began his ministry with them, he possessed only a "very small mustard seed of Christian experience"; his meager early faith was mostly a philosophy, but later it became "a faith luminous, glorious, vital, and clear," with little philosophy. He regarded *Nature and the Supernatural* as his magnum opus. For years his determination to complete the work helped him struggle for life, but the book's early reviews depressed him. Most were guarded or equivocating in their praise, and even his friend Cyrus Bartol criticized the book as "supernaturalism run mad" and complained that its negative view of human nature was insulting to God.[135]

Despite a warm review of Bushnell's sermon collection, *Sermons for the New Life*, by his friend Henry Goodwin, the apparent critical failure of his major work heightened Bushnell's regret at lacking a theological constituency.[136] Sadly he told Goodwin, "My day has not yet come, and will not till after I am gone." He mused that, perhaps, "I should fare better if I would get up a school or sect, or raise a party of *ites,* have a publication, etc." At the same time he told his brother George Bushnell, a Congregational pastor, that he preferred to be known as a person of charity than a liberal; it seemed to him "that Jesus, so abundant and free in the charities of his life, had yet the more than human wisdom to assume no airs of liberalism. No man or denomination of men can make a flag of that word, I am perfectly certain, without being injured by it."[137]

Thus he retired with little expectation of founding a liberal school of followers. For years the champion of domestic Christian virtue had left his family behind while he gave lectures and took extended health tours. Now he told his wife that their long separations were over: "I hope we shall be able to be enriched, and comforted, and filled with each other, as with Christ, and make our downhill hand-in-hand, with great peace and ever-helping sympathy." He vowed to be thankful for their blessings and leave behind "anything not to be thankful for," and he gave the appearance of retiring for a while, "playing in the water, and waiting, in sublime inefficiency, for time to run away." Bushnell followed national events keenly, grieving over "those wretched slave-holding sections of the country," dreading that the Union was being torn apart and cheering for Abraham Lincoln, whom he admired enormously. Shortly before Lincoln's inauguration, he gave thanks for the opportunity to be led by a figure—"even if we go to pieces"—who combined "wisdom, weight, and even the highest statesmanship" with "a simply honest mind."[138]

All the while he struggled inwardly with his "heaven-given thought of a book" on the experience and doctrine of vicarious sacrifice, a hope expressed in the closing pages of *Nature and the Supernatural.* Bushnell observed that the modern scientific discovery of the laws of nature had created, quite literally, a new world, "displaying new and vastly higher possibilities," and in need of the parallel development of the laws of God's supernatural kingdom. Christians commonly gave the impression that God is totally capricious in dispensing grace, he noted; it followed from this impression that God must be sought "by no certain method, but only by a sort of adventure, that will some time chance to find him." He countered that this was the mentality of superstition, not genuine faith, which lives by the perception "that God works by laws in the supernatural, in the incarnation and the miracles of Jesus, in his sacrifice and death, in the mission of the Spirit and all spiritual gifts." Just as science attains knowledge of the laws of nature, he argued, theology must devote itself to gaining knowledge of the laws that regulate God's supernatural kingdom.[139]

This was an ambition or goal of New Haven Theology, but Bushnell accentuated the difference between science and theology. In a scientific world, he urged, theology needed to become more scientific, but always in a way "that pertains to the higher realm of the Spirit." Genuinely Christian thinking can never consist of mere observer knowledge or theoretical proofs addressed to the natural intellect: "It must, therefore, stand in terms of analogy and figure, which can fully unfold their meaning only to minds enlightened, in a degree, by holy experience. It must be a contribution to faith, of the laws by which it may address itself to the supernatural forces of grace, and the manifestations of God." Bushnell was too empirically minded to go all the way with Coleridge's transcendentalism; at the same time, the rationalistic proof-making of his

New Haven teachers never ceased to repulse him as a claim to *Christian* meaning. In the year of his retirement, he wrote hopefully to a friend, "I think the day is at hand when something can be done for a better conception of the work of Christ. Here is the great field left that I wait for grace and health to occupy."[140]

He devoted seventeen unexpected years to this work. Made secure by a gift of ten thousand dollars from his congregation, and no longer distracted by competing demands and ambitions, including his frenetic efforts to regain decent health, Bushnell gave himself to his subjects. On his bad days he admitted that only the love of his family and the hope of writing another major work kept him from desiring "to adjourn"; on better days he wrote gratefully, "I don't know what I have done that God should bless me so, in giving me such a call, and work, and subject, and leisure, and means, at the closing of my days, that I may fill up my measure."[141]

His consuming central subject had two sides. Bushnell committed his later life to the theme of vicarious sacrifice well before the Civil War. Throughout the war years, the stunning violence of America's fate reinforced his conviction that the Christian drama of salvation uniquely narrates and incarnates the true story of the world. Relieved at being no longer required to choose between supporting the established government and supporting the abolition of slavery, he condemned the Confederate states for "this horrid rebellion,—a whole third of the nation renouncing their allegiance, even as by right, without so much as an apparent thought of crime!" He reasoned that malevolent forces in American politics had degraded the divine image in human nature to the point of national dissolution. He pounded the slaveholding/individualist/infidel Thomas Jefferson and praised and defended Lincoln assiduously. At the low point of the war from the Union perspective, shortly before the battle of Gettysburg, he exhorted that giving up was morally unthinkable: "We have no time now for heart-sickening or low regrets of any kind. Our mourning should have thunder in it." Like Lincoln, he believed that America's violent fate was comprehensible only in Christian categories: "For a long time we have been trying, as it were, to shake off Providence and law together, and we have so far succeeded that even the conception of government was beginning to be a lost conception." Against the grain of his culture, he preached that the pertinent Christian categories were fallenness, judgment for sin, and blood atonement; America had come to the point "where only blood, much blood, long years of bleeding, can resanctify what we have so loosely held and so badly desecrated."[142]

Bushnell's deeper interest in the experience and doctrine of Christian sacrifice, however, was personal, theological, and religiously transcendent. Absorbed by his late-life perception of love as essentially vicarious and sacrificial, he described this theme as the keynote of "Christly experience," and, more personally, as the subject of his fourth and last conversion. Several mystical illuminations between his third and fourth conversions merely added to his sense of Christ's inward presence. His fourth conversion, over several years, gave him a new perspective on the meaning of Christian discipleship, and he reflected that the story of his life was the story of his conversions to Christly experience:

> First, I was led along into initial experience of God, socially and by force of the blind religional instinct in my nature; second, I was advanced into the clear moral light of Christ and of God, as related to the principle of rectitude; next, or third, I was set on by the inward personal discovery of Christ, and of God as represented in him; now, fourth, I lay hold of and appropriate the general culminating fact of God's vicarious character in goodness, and of mine to be accomplished in Christ as a follower. My next stage of discovery will be when I drop the body and go home, to be with Christ in the conscious, openly revealed friendship of a soul whose affinities are with him.[143]

Possessed by his subjects sequentially, Bushnell aspired to no system. Contrary to a common misreading, he did not turn from theological liberalism to conservatism in his later career; his late-life atonement phase marked no significant change in his theology and did not come from any single moment of illumination. For years he pushed atonement issues to the side while developing his views of social theology, nurture, language, incarnation, divine triunity, and the supernatural; his concentration on the supernatural as redemptive spiritual power led to his last theme, the meaning of Christ's saving work. While Bushnell continued to pour out sermons and articles on a wide range of other themes, his later preaching and systematic work centered on the theme of "Christ and His Salvation."[144] In pursuing this theme, he rightly claimed a continuity of perception over his career.

His theological project was a liberal-leaning experiment in progressive orthodoxy. In his later works Bushnell played up the dualism of nature and supernature, but expounded an immanental conception of supernature; he affirmed the ancient creeds of the church, but emphasized that creedal language is metaphorical; he pursued the meaning of vicarious atonement, but in a way that developed earlier intuitions. The position that provoked "a considerable impeachment of heresy" in 1849 remained his essential position, and he was roundly condemned again for it.[145] Bushnell was right: his day would have to wait. What he could not have anticipated—and would have neither appreciated nor approved of—was that his theological project would be claimed by later liberals who shared very little of his preoccupation with the theme of God's self-sacrifice in Christ.

The Vicarious Sacrifice (1866) declared at the outset that "the thing most wanting to be cleared in Christianity is still, as it ever has been, the principal thing."[146] The meaning of Christ's saving work, the most important subject that any Christian thinker can address, he observed, is both more elusive and more controverted than any other in Christian theology. In his previous attempt to make sense of the problem, *Christ in Theology,* Bushnell argued for a third way in atonement theory: most atonement theories were objectivist, and the "moral influence" tradition exemplified by Coleridge was subjectivist; what was needed was a subjectivist account that saved and refashioned certain objective aspects of the biblical witness to Christ's vicarious sacrifice.

His dismissal of classical objective theory was notoriously blunt. What makes an atonement theory "objective" is that it makes God the recipient of Christ's saving action, he explained. Substitutionary atonement theorists spoke of Christ's suffering and death as propitiating God, satisfying God's justice, and appeasing God's wrath. New Light Calvinism softened these images by adopting the juridical concepts of "moral government" theory, in which Christ's death maintained God's rectoral honor by expressing God's hatred of sin. In the latter case, Christ was viewed as actually bearing the penalty of transgression; New England theologians construed the biblical image of Christ bearing the sins of the world as God's execution of justice on his person.[147]

Bushnell chided that in both cases orthodox atonement theory was less objective than it claimed. For Old Light Calvinists, who increasingly spoke of Christ's death as the satisfaction of God's justice, not God's wrath, the question of audience was unavoidable. If Christ suffered and died to maintain God's rectoral honor and express God's hatred of sin, to whom were these actions addressed? If the purpose of Christ's death was not to give immediate satisfaction to God, who else was left? "Expression to subjects is impression in subjects," Bushnell observed. "It is made for impression and in that has its end." New England theology claimed to uphold the objectivity of Christ's atonement, but in effect, it made public impression the object of Christ's penalty and amounted to a repulsive form of subjective moral influence theory.[148]

The latter judgment was plainly expressed. Orthodox atonement theory offers no gospel at all, he charged, "but only a dull mechanical contrivance of theology." By his count, the "moral influence" passages of scripture pertaining to Christ's atonement outnumbered the merely juridical proof texts by fifty to one. In the New Testament, Bushnell observed, but not in classical orthodoxy, Christ is proclaimed to be our redeemer as the wisdom and power of God, as the image of the invisible God, as the light of the knowledge of the glory of God.[149] By his reckoning, the subjectivist moral influence tradition, in which he later counted Abelard, Peter Lombard, John Wycliffe, Locke, Kant, De Wette, Schleiermacher, and Coleridge, was therefore closer to the spirit of biblical faith.[150] To Coleridge, he explained, the entire effect and value of Christ was subjective; no effect on God was claimed. Moral influence theory captured the "divine warmth and power" of the biblical witness with no offense to moral sensibility. As a theory of atonement, it conceived a change in God's mind or attitude "only in and through a change of character operated in us; even our spiritual renovation in goodness." Bushnell plainly affirmed that this was his tradition.[151]

He sought to give this tradition a stronger biblical basis, however. Coleridge-style moral influence theory interpreted the objective terms of the altar used in scripture as merely figurative, stripping away the objectivity of the liturgically rooted language of debt, payment, and sacrifice used to describe Christ's atonement. The Gospel of John, for example, speaks of Christ's death as a sacrifice, an offering, and a propitiation; declares the remission of sins in Christ's blood; and calls Christ the Lamb of God who takes away the sins of the world. Bushnell admonished that by completely subjectivizing these images, moral influence theology lost the doctrine of justification and thereby lacked any basis of conceptualizing justification except as a conversion of the soul from sin into faith by a change of spiritual character. A great deal of Unitarian preaching took this tack, conflating the Reformation doctrine of justification and spiritual conversion and, in effect, treating justification language as an inferior way of speaking about the new life in Christ.

Bushnell charged that this was not enough, that righteousness and sanctification are not the same thing, and that sinners must be justified before God before they can be sanctified in God's Spirit. Salvation requires pardon of sin as a precondition of the new life in Christ, he argued; without some objective notion of divine government and authority, the spiritual force of God's graciousness in forgiving sin and the very sense of moral law that convicts sinners to seek a new life in Christ are both eroded. In a purely subjective account of Christ's saving work, there is no structure of divine moral government to sustain either a sense of law or an inner voice of conscience. Warning that justification cannot be spiritually serious and merely subjective, Bushnell rejected the Unitarian option: "Having no care for our sins, no impression of them or trouble on account of them, we shall be as indifferent to mercy as to sin, and the whole work of Christ will fail of its power."[152]

What was needed was a "subjective-objective" account of the atonement that communicated the divine love behind Christ's saving work. Absorbed by this spiritual concern, in which he had little company, he contended against theological liberals and conservatives alike that only a suffering God can relate to suffering human beings and save them. On mostly secondhand grounds, Bushnell assured himself that Schleiermacher was a spiritual brother; more directly, he drew encouragement from the cosmic incarnationalism and patripassionism of his English Anglican contemporary, Frederick Denison Maurice, whose books he devoured. Maurice's theology centered on the theme of God's incarnational redemption of the world through fellow-suffering love; his *Doctrine of Sacrifice* (1854) affirmed that the union of Father and Son sustains the world "beneath all the evil, beneath the universe itself." Maurice's explicit affirmation of divine passibility reassured Bushnell that his own belief in God's fellow-suffering was not insane.[153]

Bushnell described Christ as a mediator only in the figurative sense of being a *medium* of God to us as a being in humanity. Put differently, he explained, Christ is not separate from God, even as a mediator: "Whatever we may say, or hold, or believe, concerning the vicarious sacrifice of Christ, we are to affirm in the same manner of God. The whole deity is in it, in it from eternity, and will to eternity be." It followed that we are not to conceive of Christ as the "better side" of God, as satisfying God's wrath, or as mediating *between* God and us in any literal way. It is *God* who enters the world in Christ, shares our condition, and suffers and dies for us: "There is a cross in God before the wood is seen upon Calvary; hid in God's own virtue itself, struggling on heavily in burdened feeling through all the previous ages, and struggling as heavily now even in the throne of the worlds."[154]

This sentence scandalized reviewers across the theological spectrum, as Bushnell expected it would. Unitarianism lost the heart of the gospel message when it renounced the Trinity, he observed; orthodoxy lost it when the church drove a wedge between God and the work of Christ. Theological liberals rejected anything that smacked of anthropomorphism or Trinitarian metaphysics; conservatives rejected anything that "humanized" God's transcendent personhood. In both cases, a cultivated abhorrence of divine passibility negated the church's communication of the stupendously gracious love behind Christ's atonement and led to spiritual bankruptcy. Bushnell proposed to take the cross more seriously as the expression of *God's* outreaching fellow-suffering love: "Let us come then not to the wood alone, not to the nails, not to the vinegar and the gall, not to the writhing body of Jesus, but to the very feeling of our God and there take shelter."[155]

Nature and the Supernatural had lamented that "what is properly called religious experience runs low in our time"; *The Vicarious Sacrifice* urged that part of the problem was that the church made God remote and unaffected by human suffering. "Abstract descriptions given of holiness or holy virtue, do not signify much to those who never knew them inwardly by their effects," Bushnell observed. "We want no theologic definition of God's perfections; but we want a friend, whom we can feel as a man, and whom it will be sufficiently accurate for us to accept and love."[156] In Christ's humble identification with suffering humanity and his acceptance of obscurity and execution, the law of God's supernatural kingdom was expressed.

Bushnell insisted that the way of Christ both reveals God's supernatural law and defies propositional definition. "It is not a theorem, or form of thought, but a process, and the process includes all the facts of a life," he explained. "He is no quantitative matter, like a credit set in a book, or a punishment graduated by satisfaction. His reality is what he expresses, under laws of expression." The way of Christ subverts common sense and eludes dogmatic definition. "Men consciously feel, that a strong power is somehow gathering about his person, but will only know, by and by, what it is," Bushnell observed. "It is the power, in great part, of sorrow, suffering, sacrifice, death, a paradox of ignominy and grandeur not easily solved." The law of God's supernatural kingdom is God's astoundingly self-sacrificial and indiscriminate love of humanity and the world; in brief, it is the law of vicarious sacrifice, poured out for the sake of all in the life and suffering of Christ.[157]

Bushnell affirmed as an implication of this law that God suffers "with and for created beings" in their affliction under evil. "He would not be perfect, if he did not feel appropriately to what is bad, base, wrong, destructive, cruel, and to every thing opposite to perfection," he reasoned. "If the sight of wrong were to meet the discovery of God, only as a disgusting spectacle meets his glass eye, his perfection would be the perfection of a glass eye and nothing more." Moral suffering is genuine agony, he reflected. While declining to speculate on the metaphysics of Christ's physical pain on the cross—Bushnell acknowledged that God is a being physically impassible—he urged that the cross is the ultimate symbol and expression of God's moral suffering. The importance of Christ's suffering lies not in what it is, metaphysically, but in what it expresses and morally signifies. Good Friday is the ultimate symbol of God's fellow-suffering love: "The moral tragedy of the garden is supplemented by the physical tragedy of the cross; where Jesus, by not shrinking from so great bodily pains . . . shows the moral suffering of God for sinners more affectingly, because he does it in the lower plane of natural sensibility." In its revelation of a suffering God, Good Friday makes the name of Jesus "the embodied glory and the Great Moral Power of God."[158]

Bushnell wanted to believe in universal salvation. He affirmed that the logic of his account of Christ's saving work led to the hope of universal salvation, if not its expectation. The notion that eternal punishment is the fate of any soul, he remarked, "does not bring out the kingdom of God, in that one state of realized unity, and complete order, which we most naturally desire, and think to be worthiest of his greatness and sovereignty." It therefore seemed to him that scripture should teach the doctrine of universal salvation. The problem, he noted, was that scripture, Christ especially, plainly asserted the reality of eternal punishment. "It certainly would be more agreeable, if we could have this hope; and many are resolved to have it without Christ's permission, if they can not have it with," he observed. "They even make it a point of merit, to seize this honor bravely for God, on their own responsibility, and for it, if they must, defy the Scripture." Bushnell sympathized, but admonished that Christians are supposed to follow Christ, not improve his teaching: "I think otherwise, and could even count it a much braver thing, to willingly be less brave, and despite of our natural longings for some issue of God's plan that is different, follow still the lead of the Master."[159]

He seemed to fear that certain subjects were off limits to his theory of language. The theorist of figural interpretation felt obliged to affirm a view of eternal punishment that violated his understanding of the gospel, while making nothing of the highly figurative, scattered, unsystematic nature of the Bible's references to this subject. At the same time, in opposition to legalistic understandings of Christ's atoning sacrifice as a payment for sin, he aggressively emphasized the figurative character of the New Testament's sacrificial language. Atonement is a change wrought in its human subjects through which they are reconciled to God, he argued; though clothed in the metaphors of the altar, it is not an expiation for sin. Elsewhere Bushnell observed that while the execution of Jesus featured no lamb, fire, altar, lustral ceremony, or literal sacrifice, it is rightly called the divine sacrifice.

"The people of the law were put in training under these patterns of the heavenly things, till the very mind of their nation should be stocked with images and metaphors thence derived for the heavenly things themselves," he explained. "Who could ever have conceived the ministry and death of Jesus in these words of atonement, sacrifice, and cleansing, whose mind had not first been Judaized in the stock images of its thinking?" Hebrew religion alone was suited to provide the "types and metaphors of God's mercy" that evoked the way that God recomposed the breach of sin through Christ. For that matter, he exhorted, while it is dreadfully mistaken to take any of these images literally, they remain indispensable to gospel speech: "No living disciple, having once gotten the sense of these types of the altar, will ever try to get his gospel out of them and preach it in the common terms of language."[160] Later he argued that atonement concerns not only ordinary human forgiveness, but also the possibility of genuine self-propitiation as a precondition for reconciliation.

The Vicarious Sacrifice argued that God forgives us in the way that humans forgive each other, by caring for the offender; its sequel, *Forgiveness and Law* (1874), reasoned that a further step is required to secure genuine reconciliation. In between, Bushnell had two intense mystical experiences, the second of which gave him a revelation of "a new and most grand element in the conception of Christ's reconciling mission" and burned in him "as a most welcome fire." Essentially, it was an inspiration of the need and divinity of empathic self-sacrifice. Thinking about how it is possible to forgive one's enemies, Bushnell reflected that genuine reconciliation is not possible if the offended party does not take on the experience of the offender and give up one's right to righteous anger. As he explained in *Forgiveness and Law,* "I was brought squarely down upon the discovery that nothing will ever accomplish the proposed real and true forgiveness, but to make cost in the endeavor, such cost as new-tempers and liquefies the reluctant nature. And this making cost will be his propitiation of himself."[161]

Without a self-sacrificing identification with the offender, the offended party burns with the bitterness of wounded feeling, even if she offers forgiveness. Genuine reconciliation requires a resolution of truly willing, unreserved self-sacrifice on the part of offended parties to relinquish their right to resentment, he argued. Put differently, reconciliation requires a deeper process of self-sacrifice than the ethic of care explicated in *The Vicarious Sacrifice.* This realization had implications for Christian atonement, for previously Bushnell had affirmed the notion of Christ's sacrifice as a propitiation for sin only from the standpoint of Christian experience; propitiation language objectivized the grateful feelings of forgiven sinners. But if human forgiveness and reconciliation always require some measure of self-sacrifice on the part of offended parties, he reasoned, "why not of the Great Propitiation itself?"[162]

Just as human reconciliation requires self-sacrifice on the part of offended human agents in preparing to offer forgiveness, Christian atonement must consist, in part, of God's self-propitiation in the sufferings of Christ. Propitiation is common to God and humankind; God had to identify with sinners in their condition to become free of righteous anger against them. Within the framework of what remained a moral influence theory of atonement, Bushnell's last book thus found a novel way of reclaiming the objectivising motif of divine propitiation. He found what he had always looked for: a way to affirm orthodox teaching in his own language and spirit. *Forgiveness and Law* maintained that God *is* an object of Christ's saving action, but only as a triune self-sacrificing lover who yearns for genuine reconciliation with all sinners. God's love for humanity is great precisely in God's tragic suffering: "He lives in everlasting countertides of struggle and victory—victory both over others without and violated good within." The key to the meaning of the cross is a suffering God: this notion had an ample future in late-twentieth-century theology, but no future at all in the nineteenth century, even among Bushnellians.[163]

SHOOTING IN THE DARK, FINDING A PUBLIC

The critical response to *The Vicarious Sacrifice* was lukewarm and occasionally hostile. Unitarian reviewer E. C. Towne sharply denounced Bushnell's "wild fancies about God's burdened heart and wounded sensibility," while Unitarian theologian James Freeman Clarke patronized Bushnell, treating the book as a rehash of Noah Worcester's 1829 Unitarian tract, *The Atoning Sacrifice,* and considering it a laborious attempt to rescue atonement theory for the few who still needed it. Conservatives Charles Hodge and W. G. T. Shedd blasted Bushnell's "humanizing" patripassionism, which Shedd called a "vicious annihilation of the difference between the Infinite and the Finite." Noah Porter, setting the tone for moderate conservatives, claimed that Bushnell diluted the faith and distorted the biblical concept of penalty, and various reviewers dismissed his atonement theology as a blend of familiar moral-influence heresies. A more chilling blast was delivered from another public that Bushnell wanted to reach. Writing in the *North American Review,* Henry James Sr. pronounced Bushnell's construal of Christian love ridiculous. Love is neither heedless nor essentially sacrificial, he lectured; it has nothing to do with pretending to care for bad people; it pays attention to consequences and is always proportionate to merit. To claim that love responds to evil with self-sacrificing care was a perverse "outrage upon all love, Divine as well as human."[164]

It was probably this scathing review that moved Bushnell to think about the meaning of loving one's enemies; James was sure that it did not mean his *agapic* sentimentalism. As Bushnell may have sensed, however, his deep absorption in the true meaning of Christian atonement made him increasingly remote even from his traditional audience. At least his earlier books were controversial; the light response to *The Vicarious Sacrifice* was worrisome. Shortly after the publication of *Forgiveness and Law,* Bushnell confessed to Amos Chesebrough that he had "never published a book that brought such a load on my feeling as this has brought." He had no misgivings about the truth of his position, he explained, but "I have been suffering real oppression of mind from the uncertainty I am in." His uncertainty pertained to expression and impression; Bushnell had lost confidence in his ability to "adjust myself rightly in the statement" and sensed that he was beginning to appear quaint: "What position other minds are in, I have not been sure enough, to set my points accurately, as true address requires," he admitted. "Where is my public? how shall I put this and that to be rightly taken? has been my constant question. It has been with me as with one shooting in the dark, and I have been tormenting myself lest I may have lost my truth by resolving it faultily."[165]

He took solace in the friendly support of Chesebrough, and in his closer, though less supportive, friendship with Cyrus Bartol, and he knew that he was widely admired and influential as a preacher. He had at least a few pastoral followers in Chesebrough, Theodore Munger, Henry Goodwin, Leonard Bacon, and Washington Gladden; Gladden believed that Bushnell had already won the battle "for the moralization of theology."[166] Bushnell made no claim to victory in the field of theology, however, believing that his constructive theologizing was almost completely rejected by academics and church leaders. His books were routinely condemned, he was shunned and isolated through most of his ministry, and pastors who embraced his views were forced to be discreet.

He had to trust that his day would come in a subsequent generation. In his own life, his public seemed to shrink; *Forgiveness and Law* was completely ignored. Bushnell realized that his preoccupation with atonement made him appear quaint to a generation transfixed by evolution, Charles Darwin, and Herbert Spencer. He protested that he had always believed fervently in progress, but as a convinced supernaturalist and Lamarckian, he held out against Darwinism, which embarrassed even the hardiest Bushnellians of the next generation.

In 1867 Bushnell preached at Washington Gladden's installation at the Congregational church of North Adams, Massachusetts; Gladden would later recall that their personal relationship began after he disputed Bushnell's "heretic" label in an article that defended Bushnell's atonement thinking. In fact, the installation service occurred first. During his early ministerial career Gladden had read Bushnell's *God in Christ* and relinquished his inherited religious conservatism. He later recalled that the book had delivered him "at once and forever from the bondage of an immoral theology." Upon beginning his ministry at North Adams, he asked his theological hero to preach the service of installation. In Gladden's recollection, Bushnell tried to warn him off: "It might make trouble for me; it would put the heresy-hunters on the scent; it would be far wiser for me to invite a safer man." Upon realizing that Gladden knew his mind, however, and had no intention of shading his views, Bushnell gladly journeyed to North Adams; his sermon, "The Gospel of the Face," proclaimed that the church needed more preaching on the gospel *of* Christ and less preaching *about* Christ.[167]

The occasion allowed Bushnell and his young follower to spend several leisurely days together, as Gladden would later recount: "Those were great days, driving over the Berkshire Hills, lying in the shade, talking of things visible and invisible, meditating upon the mysteries of the heavens above and the earth beneath. Horace Bushnell was one of the great talkers. There was something Carlylean in his rugged rhetoric and the raciness of his metaphors; and his homely speech was lit up with poetic touches which made it a delight to listen." Shortly afterward, Gladden publicly criticized an Illinois Congregationalist council for refusing to ordain a young minister who embraced Bushnell's atonement theology. This public letter, "Are Dr. Bushnell's Views Heretical?" elicited a warm and, to Gladden, overly thankful reply from its subject. Gladden was both touched and chastened by the depth of Bushnell's gratitude to him. "It was evident that he needed, even then, such comfort as my poor letter could give him," he later recalled. "It was good to know that a word from such a source had comforted him, but it was tragical that he could have needed it."[168]

Gladden, understanding better than his hero that the Protestant orthodoxies were reeling, knew that most Congregational associations contained at least a few Bushnellians and many pastors preached a version of the gospel that quietly appropriated Bushnell's ideas. While Gladden recognized that conservatives still controlled most church institutions, his perception that mainstream Protestantism was opening up kept him in the ministry. By the early 1880s, an influential vanguard of liberals felt secure enough to claim Bushnell as their Moses. Affirming their genuine—and a few imagined—connections to him, leaders of the "New Theology" liberalism of the 1880s and 1890s fashioned an immanentalist perspective informed by historical criticism that took stock of Bushnell's perceived weak spots and anachronisms.

For Munger, Gladden, and the first generation of evangelical liberals, Bushnell's resistance to Darwinism was obsolete; Darwinian evolution was the dominant concept of their generation, and they began by adapting Christianity to it. Some of them found ample grist for their blend of natural selection and social gospel idealism in Bushnell's "Christianizing" Anglo-Saxonism. His opposition to historical criticism was equally out of bounds to them, for after decades of abortive and tentative beginnings, American biblical scholarship took a decidedly historical-critical turn in the 1880s. Most of Bushnell's later theological work was also lost to the ascending liberal movement that claimed his name. Writing off a sizable inheritance, Munger explained, "We are not now interested, except in the antiquarian's way, in the discussion by which one view or another of the atonement was upheld, and we feel almost as little interest in the discussion by which it was redeemed from them. The age has its own point of view, and does not depend upon that of the past."[169]

Munger was Bushnell's leading advocate in the 1880s and 1890s, when Bushnell's books became required reading for seminarians at Yale, Oberlin, Drew, Union, Andover, Bangor, and General Theological Seminary. As a Yale divinity student in 1848, he had witnessed Bushnell's controversial lecture on the divinity of Christ; as a struggling Congregationalist pastor in the 1850s and 1860s, he had kept his faith on the strength of Bushnell's influence; in 1876, the news of Bushnell's death caused him to return to New England and begin his public theological career, but his subsequent relation to Bushnell was complex. Munger idolized Bushnell, praising him effusively as the brightest light of American Christianity; at the same time, on some issues he read too much of his own evolutionary monism into Bushnell, and on other issues he rejected Bushnell's thinking while calling for a Bushnellian redirection of theology.[170]

Munger argued that Bushnell's theory of divine propitiation detracted from God's simple love, "which needs nothing to complete itself." He regretted that Bushnell's atonement theorizing obscured his emphasis on the exemplary life and teaching of Jesus; he rejected Bushnell's reluctant affirmation of eternal punishment, judging that he labored under the sway of a dying theory of biblical inspiration; he appreciated that Bushnell treated the Adamic story of the Fall as mythical in form, but protested his emphasis on depravity. Among Bushnell's theological books, Munger believed that *Christian Nurture* and the early, pure moral influence chapters of *The Vicarious Sacrifice* stood the best chance of becoming classics; to him, the rest of Bushnell's atonement theorizing was ill advised: "Thought is not moving in that direction, but rather away from it, and is grounding itself more and more on the 'moral view,' which accords so well with the great duties and capacities of humanity."[171]

On these and other counts, Munger spoke for a movement and age, as he claimed. Like the "New Theology" movement that he championed, he made the most of his commonalities with Bushnell; on a few issues he wrongly cast Bushnell as a Munger-style liberal; on issues where he acknowledged their disagreement, he explained that theology had to keep up with modern knowledge and culture. Munger liked *Christian Nurture* for its naturalism and played down Bushnell's later Trinitarianism, feeling compelled to explain away the "apparent dualism" of *Nature and the Supernatural*. He grieved that Bushnell rejected Darwinism, but claimed that this failing was "pathetic" chiefly because Bushnell's theology was perfectly adaptable to it. Had Bushnell given Darwinism its due, he claimed, "few would have so fully grasped its central meaning, and so clearly traced it to its divine conclusion," but Bushnell left this project to a succeeding generation of New Theologians. Never fathoming the depth of Bushnell's opposition to Darwinism, Munger played down Bushnell's dualism of nature and supernature. Bushnell was serious in conceptualizing divine reality as *super*natural power and perceiving the totalizing naturalism in Darwinian theory. Worried that Darwinism threatened to eliminate the supernatural realm altogether, he opposed it resolutely.[172]

The New Theology movement was determined to make its peace with Darwinism. It lifted Bushnell's vision of reality as a singular divinely infused organism above his emphasis on paradox, disruption, and the dualism of nature/supernature. Barely a generation younger than Bushnell, and familiar with the church culture that rejected him, Munger lived to see the liberalization of American theology in the age of Darwin, with the triumph of a liberal movement that outgrew its founder.

The evangelical liberals took much from Bushnell while taking over the churches' elite seminaries and divinity schools. Emboldened by his theory of language and emphasis on imagination, many broke free of dogmatic religion; they wholly embraced his gospel-centered emphasis on the figure of Jesus, except for his atonement theorizing. Various offshoots of the social gospel movement adopted his cluster of themes pertaining to Christian nurture, especially growth in virtue, the organic centrality of family life, the ethos of feminized patriarchy, and the connection between prosperity and virtue—sometimes in aggressively chauvinist forms that might have made even Bushnell blush. Liberals embraced his insistence that God is bound by the moral laws of the kingdom; they saw his strong defense of the incarnation and Trinity as a guard against Unitarianism, though many preferred his early near-Sabellianism to his later position. Gladden spoke for many in recalling that if not for the brave words of *God in Christ* and *Christ in Theology,* he would have given up the ministry: "Dr. Bushnell gave me a moral theology and helped me to believe in the justice of God. If I have had any gospel to preach, during the last thirty-five years, it is because he led me into the light and joy of it."[173]

ENJOYING THE GOSPEL

Transcending any arguments that Bushnell bequeathed, fortunately or not, to American Christianity were the qualities of light and joy that he found in the gospel and vividly communicated. All his work was charged with testimony to the inspirations of Christ. Bushnell was opinionated, irascible, prejudiced, chauvinistic, infected with power-lust, and sometimes self-pitying. He also possessed, in extraordinary measure, the faculty he called "inspirableness," which he described as "the faculty of being permeated or interiorly and receptively visited by the higher nature of God, communicating somewhat of his own quality." He had no interest in writing memoirs, revisiting old arguments, or straightening out inconsistencies in his positions. To him the point was always fresh *discovery* of the ways of God's subject-transforming revelation.

His daughter Mary recalled that in his last years, when he came to the dinner table engrossed in thought, "his very hair stood on end, electric with thought; his eyes had a fixed and absent look, and he forgot the name of a potato." In his last year of life, Bushnell worked on "The Inspirations," a manuscript that proposed to illuminate the past and ongoing work of the Holy Spirit in character, story, and scripture. From personal experience he reflected that the experience of God's Spirit as permeating holy presence is rightly called inspiration "because it inbreathes something of a divine quality and configures the subject in some way to itself."[174] Bushnell relied on his inspirations and waited for them; his intellectual work followed them in step. He was emboldened by his inspirations to speak his truths in the name of truth and church unity, always convinced that somehow these ends intertwined.

His private correspondence was pervaded by the same spirit of joyful, expectant, Christ-seeking discovery that filled his sermons. Upon learning from one of his daughters that she did not get life from reading the Bible, Bushnell tenderly expressed his regret and gave her this window on his own piety:

> My own experience is that the Bible is dull when I am dull; and that
> when I am really alive, and set in upon the text with a tidal pressure
> of living affinities, it opens, multiplies discoveries and reveals depths
> even faster than I can note them. The worldly spirit, in some form
> of indifferentism, shuts the Bible; the Spirit of God makes it a fire,
> flaming out all meanings and most glorious truths. Great love to
> you all. God bless your Sunday nights, and set our hymns all singing
> in your feeling.[175]

As a poet and theologian of the glorious truths of the Spirit he belonged to a class by himself among nineteenth-century American theologians; as a preacher he was nearly in a class with the famed Brooklyn spellbinder and forerunner of evangelical liberalism, Henry Ward Beecher. Younger than Bushnell by eleven years, and less intellectual, Beecher was helped by *Christian Nurture* to break away from the New Haven Theology Calvinism of his father, Lyman Beecher. With occasional reservations, mostly intellectual, Bushnell appreciated the younger Beecher's extraordinary capacity to receive and express inspiration. On various occasions he made his way to Plymouth Church, Brooklyn to hear Beecher's brilliantly expressive preaching. Together these preachers of the Christ within prefigured the rise of a triumphant liberal Protestantism,[176] and Bushnell had friendly relations with several Beechers, including Harriet Beecher Stowe.

To Bushnell and Henry Ward Beecher, however, unlike much of the movement they inaugurated, theology made sense primarily as a spiritual art form; theology was essentially poetry of the divine and human spirits. Lyman Beecher's famous son taught that the gauge of true religion "is the intensity and the productiveness of the love principle" and preached that the test of a person's growth in grace "is not whether he likes or does not like the instruments and accessories of religion, but whether or not he likes religion itself, with all its gentleness, all its self-denial, and all its fruits."[177] Bushnell believed that, in its own way, theology needed to become scientific, but to him the caveat was enormous. He emphatically disbelieved that theology should attempt to discover and formulate the laws of God's supernatural kingdom by empirical, dogmatic, or metaphysical means. "Is there any hope for theologic science left?" he asked rhetorically in his later years. "None at all, I answer most unequivocally. Human language is a gift to the imagination so essentially metaphoric, warp and woof, that it has no exact blocks of meaning to build a science of. Who would ever think of building up a science of Homer, Shakespeare, Milton?"[178]

Scriptural meaning is no less figurative or poetic than *Paradise Lost*, he insisted: "The Bible is not a whit less poetic, or a whit less metaphoric, or a particle less difficult to be propositionalized in the terms of the understanding." The parables of Christ, for example, "what are they but images and figures visible given to the imagination?" Bushnell conceded that the parables inspired a

thousand varying interpretations, heightening the dogmatic anxiety for definitions and creeds, "but we revere them none the less and hold them none the less
firmly, that they are rich enough to justify this liberty." The gospel outshines
and outlives all systems erected in its name. Expressed in its own voice, gospel
truth is convictingly self-authenticating and does not acquire greater solidity or
security by being propositionalized.[179]

His relativizing acceptance of creeds— "the more the better"—galled his clerical enemies to the end. Bushnell allowed that creedal formulations are fine, as
long as the church retained several to play off against each other, and as long as
"we duly understand that they are standards only as being in metaphor, and not
in terms of exact notation." On this theme, he loved to contrast Francis
Turretin's monumental system of Reformed orthodoxy, *Institutes of Elenctic
Theology*, and John Bunyan's classic Puritan allegory, *Pilgrim's Progress*. Turretin's
once-dominant dogmatics, built as a temple for the ages, was already "crum-
bling visibly away, like the stones of Tyre," he observed, but *Pilgrim's Progress*
remained a powerful and beloved expression of gospel faith. Turretin obsessed
about securing solid definitions, but Bunyan eschewed the appearance of solid-
ness, expressing God's laws, in the manner of the gospels, "by shadows, types,
and metaphors."[180]

Thus did Bushnell claim to recover the voice of genuine gospel speech from
centuries of theologic dogmatizers. He called modern Protestants to complete
the recovery of biblical faith begun by the sixteenth-century Reformers and set
back by centuries of Protestant dogmatism. American liberal Protestantism
claimed this mission and self-understanding in the succeeding generation,
though with crucial differences from its theological founder. Bushnell opposed
historical criticism as anti-Christian, but his successors embraced it as a tool of
the project to recover the authentic message of scripture. Bushnell took his basic
philosophical categories from Coleridge, as did Beecher, but their successors,
while appreciating Coleridge and Schleiermacher, judged that they had little
choice in making evolution their philosophical master concept. A few social
gospelers maintained Bushnell's emphasis on the sinful condition of humankind
and the organic social transmission of evil, but many rejected his view of the
human condition as a morbid hangover from Puritanism. A fourth basic difference was more subtle, but theologically loaded: Evangelical liberalism took its
picture of Jesus from Bushnell, but dropped his centering theological emphasis
on the self-sacrifice of God in Christ. The social gospelers accentuated the teaching and exemplary moral character of Jesus, while relegating Bushnell's thinking
about why any of this mattered to the category of bygone atonement theories.
Throughout its glory years, the liberal tradition regarded itself as considerably
more advanced than its founder; afterwards, liberal theology was forced to question whether it had truly improved on Horace Bushnell.

4.

Victorianism in Question:

Henry Ward Beecher, Elizabeth Cady Stanton,
and the Religion of Reform

The liberal Protestant option seeped into American culture in the mid-nineteenth century among a new class of adherents and in the face of heightened challenges to religious belief. The theologians of early American theological liberalism were cultured intellectuals who quoted Kant and Coleridge, censured rationalists as infidels, and aspired to a religion of enlightened moral and spiritual feeling. None of them made a convincing claim to speak for common people; most belonged to a cultural elite. The Unitarians were Harvard-educated, Boston-oriented products of a distinctive religious and cultural tradition, while Bushnell, though aspiring to "comprehensiveness," was virtually a sect unto himself. In the middle decades of the nineteenth century, a period of heightened religious uncertainty, a burgeoning new middle class of Americans created a larger and different kind of religious constituency. Bushnell's Hartford congregation approximated the type, but the type was epitomized by Plymouth Church in Brooklyn Heights, New York, where Henry Ward Beecher prefigured a new kind of mainline Protestantism.

In New York, between 1847 and 1867, as huge numbers of Irish and German immigrants poured into Manhattan, the upper class and the rapidly growing middle class fled to Brooklyn. Brooklyn Heights attracted a predominantly middle-class population of upwardly mobile merchants and professionals, along with a sizable number of wealthy "old money" newcomers. Brooklyn's population skyrocketed from 30,000 to 295,000 in barely twenty years. The new American middle class was newly educated, culturally middle-brow, insistently Protestant, mostly Anglo-Saxon, and uneasy about its nouveaux riches status. It believed in its own progress but disliked the flood of current immigrants, especially the Irish Catholics. It worried about accelerating urbanization, declining public morals, and eroding religious faith; on the last front, at least, there was much to worry about.[1]

This new middle class was a product of the very expansion of modern commercial society and cultural pluralism that was undermining the authority of America's dominant Protestant churches. It benefited from modernity while wringing its hands over the social effects of modernization, and similarly it benefited from advances in scientific knowledge while fretting about their effect on religion. The old rationalism was philosophical and ideological; even to Theodore Parker the infidel was a godless blasphemer. But in Parker's later lifetime, scientific rationalism, speaking in a cooler voice and pointing to a growing body of scientific evidence, became harder to stigmatize. Mid-century critics of Christianity spoke less about rationalistic worldviews and the impossibility of miracles and more about geological data pertaining to the age of the earth, archaeological discoveries that contradicted biblical history, and the increasingly settled conclusions of modern biblical criticism. A bit later, Darwinism raised the stakes in this argument to new heights; American culture was slow to absorb the science behind Darwinian theory, but by the 1870s, Darwinism epitomized the challenge of modern science to every existing religious worldview.

This challenge, joined together with biblical higher criticism and a secularizing trend in American society, inspired a fundamentalist reaction and decades of intense controversy in the churches. Even for fundamentalists, however, the debate was always complicated by the enormous benefits that accrued for all people from gains in scientific knowledge. In the mid-nineteenth century, communities like Brooklyn Heights prefigured the change in mainline Protestant consciousness: Americans became less willing to submit to the inscrutable will of God or the external authority of the Bible after science broke their submission to disease and pain. In 1859 Henry Ward Beecher recalled that as a youth, he had listened to long moralistic sermons about why God had plagued the world with cholera. As a pastor and religious thinker, Beecher keenly perceived that he was living in a profoundly different world, in which the religion of authority and unfathomable divine decrees had lost its credibility to people who felt that they had gained power over nature.[2]

In this social context, Henry Ward Beecher gave voice to the hope of a modernized Protestantism. His was a voice keenly attuned to the anxieties, prejudices, and ideals of its audience, and American liberal Protestantism gained its first popular leader and its first sizable following through his evocative sermonizing. Though outspoken in his disregard for disciplined theoretical reflection, especially formal theology, Beecher made a singular contribution to the development and legitimization of American liberal Protestantism as a whole. In his journalism, lecturing, and preaching, mid-Victorian middle-class Americans took heart that religion, science, and American progress all worked together.

OUTGROWING LYMAN BEECHER: THE REFUGE OF PERSONAL RELIGION

Henry Ward Beecher was the ninth of Lyman Beecher's twelve children, and the next to last of his children with Roxana Foote Beecher. Henry's cultivated, deep-spirited mother died when he was three years old, though his sermons and orations later spoke of her as if he had known her well. As a youth he was treated coldly by his aristocratic stepmother, Harriet Porter Beecher, while Lyman Beecher overwhelmed all of his children with the idea of their need of salvation from eternal punishment. Henry, who craved love and approval for the rest of his life, became highly skilled at avoiding conflict and thus escaped an outright theological break from his father until middle age, all the while sustaining his father's fervant preaching zeal.

Lyman Beecher was called to the Congregational church of Litchfield, Connecticut, in 1810, three years before Henry's birth. He was America's greatest revival preacher, during what came to be called the Second Great Awakening, until Charles G. Finney surpassed him in the 1820s. Lyman Beecher's hyperkenetic preaching and exceptional organizational skills kept the fire of revival burning in New England from 1812 to 1824, bringing thousands of souls into the church. He emphasized the hygienic effects of religion as an aid to public order and the traditional Reformed lineage of his theology, though he preached the modified "free to sin" Calvinism of his friend Nathaniel Taylor. He pressed for the conversion of his children, sometimes raging in prophesy, sometimes cajoling and subtle, always the hound of heaven who spoke the language of the chase. Though all of his children eventually obliged him, for many years Lyman Beecher despaired that Christ would return before they were saved. As a youth, Henry wilted under the pressure; afraid of his father and disappointed by his own religious confusion, he developed a close friendship with his older sister, Harriet, to whom he confided the secrets of his spiritual struggle and with whom he sustained a deep spiritual kinship for the rest of their lives. At the age of sixteen, he told her that he was finally ready to join the church; in later life he would recall, "I do not know how or why I was converted. I only know I was in a sort of day-dream, in which I hoped I had given myself to Christ."[3]

Perceiving that his son was insecure, imaginative, and a mediocre student, Lyman Beecher sent him to Amherst College instead of Yale, with the hope that Amherst would protect him from self-indulgence. Harriet later recalled that her brother's student years were spent roving the forests "lost in dreamy contemplation." He scrawled his Latin verbs into the crown of his hat, "an exercise whence he reaped small profit, mentally or morally"; in college he remained a weak student. Beecher lacked the discipline for memorization or intensive study, and was easily distracted, but inherited his father's tremendous physical energy. During his sophomore year he was attracted to the sister of a friend, Eunice Bullard, who reminded him, as he explained to Harriet, of the idealized image that he carried of his mother; Beecher and Eunice were engaged just as he began to identify with his father's messianic yearning to go west. Lyman Beecher and Charles Finney were both convinced that if the West, the key to America's future, were lost to Catholicism or anarchy, Christian America would be finished. Lyman Beecher worried that even a Methodist takeover of the Ohio River Valley would ruin America's Puritan heritage, and his exhortations on this theme fueled a family preoccupation and helped to enliven a national one. Henry's brother Edward moved west first, assuming the presidency of Illinois College; in 1832 Lyman Beecher led a procession of Beechers, who had not lived together since their Litchfield years, to the frontier. The patriarch became the founding president of Lane Theological Seminary and pastor of Second Presbyterian Church in Cincinnati, two Beechers started pastorates in Ohio, two others entered Lane Seminary, Catherine Beecher founded the Western Female Institute in Cincinnati as a bulwark against infidelism and Catholicism, and Harriet joined her in this work.[4]

Henry enrolled at Lane Seminary fresh out of Amherst in 1834, just after his father's seminary erupted in a controversy over abolitionism and just before his father was put on trial for heresy. Both events, but especially the latter, were stirred by issues that deeply influenced Henry's later thinking and reformism. Lyman Beecher despised slavery and was not shy about preaching against it; unlike Finney, however, whose perfectionist revivalism was egalitarian in its politics and militantly abolitionist, Lyman Beecher kept his distance from abolitionists. His idea of a good antislavery movement was the American Colonization Society, established in 1817, which proposed to resettle freed slaves in Africa. Beecher joined this movement in 1826, and among other activities, he helped the Society obtain a physician for the colony of Liberia. In 1829, one of his Boston congregants, William Lloyd Garrison, made a speech at Edward Beecher's Park Street Church that embraced colonizationism; Garrison famously recanted two years later.

Upon moving to Cincinnati, Lyman Beecher tried to walk an antislavery tightrope. The seminary's founder, Arthur Tappan, was a liberal abolitionist philanthropist from New York, and most of the students were Finney-style evangelical abolitionists; but much of the local population was sympathetic to the South, and nearly all the trustees were conservative, some with sizable economic interests in the South. This muddle approximated Beecher's own conflicted feelings; he opened Lane Seminary to black students and spoke against slavery, but his position was too tepid for Lane students inspired by Finney's abolitionism. To the dread and loathing of white Cincinnati, the Lane students insisted on relating to black townspeople as social equals, and in the spring of 1834, faculty radical Theodore Weld and student leader Henry B. Stanton challenged Beecher to commit the seminary to the cause of immediate abolition. Beecher pleaded that the colonizing alternative was less violent than abolitionist insurrection and more practical as a means of negotiating with Southerners, but the abolitionists held their ground. The following fall, while Beecher raised money in New England, the trustees, taking the matter into their own hands, abolished all nonacademic societies at the seminary, and censured Weld and the students for consorting with local blacks. To the trustees, this racial mixing revealed a "spirit of insubordination" that conjured revolting images of "France and Hayti." In response to the trustee crackdown, Weld and Stanton led a walkout in which fifty-three seminarians left Lane and enrolled at the seminary of the new Oberlin College, just before Arthur Tappan installed Beecher's rival, Charles Finney, as Oberlin's second president and first professor of theology.[5]

Henry Ward Beecher leaned toward abolitionism as a college student, but he was deferential to authority, eager to be liked, and mindful of his father's maxim that the wise reformer pushes only as far as the prevailing community will allow. After graduating from Amherst he moved to Cincinnati and became one of a handful of students left at Lane Seminary, which averaged five students during the years that Henry studied there. Lyman Beecher's school was hurt by the "Lane Rebellion" for years, scorned by the Finney-abolitionist stream of evangelicalism and reviled by townspeople who resented its experiments in race mixing. By the time that he enrolled at seminary, Henry knew a good deal of theology simply by virtue of being a Beecher, but he never warmed to the academic study of doctrine or scripture. His chief instructor was his father; more agreeably, he also studied under Calvin Stowe, who later married Harriet. Since he found that studying theology only heightened his doubts and torment, his consuming academic interests became poetry and literature; his favorite poets Byron, Coleridge, and Wordsworth; his favorite writers Sir Walter Scott and Robert Burns, mainly on moral grounds; and he judged that the German romanticists (especially Goethe and Lessing) were superior to their New England transcendentalist imitators. Though he questioned for most of his seminary career whether he belonged in the ministry, he decided early that if he did become a minister, he would never preach doctrinal sermons. Style, imagination, and feeling were important to him; he studied popular orators and worked hard at developing his own speaking style. It was instructive to him that Coleridge, Wordsworth, and Scott meant more to him religiously than any theological writer.

This perception was reinforced in 1835 by the spectacle of his father's trial for heresy.[6] Lyman Beecher had moved to Boston in 1825 to save the city from being completely routed by Unitarianism; then he moved to Cincinnati to save America from being de-Christianized by Catholics, Methodists, and infidels, and to remove himself from the Taylor-Tyler controversy. The dispute over New Haven Theology cut him deeply; though Taylor was his closest friend and theological soulmate, it grieved him that Taylor and Tyler insisted on splitting the church over small theological differences. Beecher told his Boston congregation that he could not bring himself to enter a theological controversy between friends of Jesus Christ; thus he left New England Congregationalism and became a Presbyterian pastor and seminary leader, but at the near breaking point between the Presbyterian "Old School" and "New School" factions. His indictment for heresy played a role in the schism between the two schools that broke American Presbyterianism into two churches in 1837. The simultaneity of the New Haven and Presbyterian controversies was not coincidental; the American Congregationalist and Presbyterian denominations were closely related, often blending together in federated congregations, and the two conflicts were essentially denominational variants of the same controversy. In its Presbyterian form, the Old School tradition was deeply conservative, dogmatic, wary of pietistic fervor, and rooted in seventeenth-century Reformed orthodoxy; it had a strong institutional home at Princeton Theological Seminary. The New School tradition was pietistic, evangelical, less defined by church dogma, and more inclusive in its ecclesiology; its institutional bastions were Union Theological Seminary, Auburn Theological Seminary, and Beecher's new home.[7]

The Cincinnati Old Schoolers wasted little time in going after Beecher. He was brought to trial in 1835 by Joshua L. Wilson, pastor of Cincinnati's First Presbyterian Church, who charged that Beecher taught heresy on the subjects of human ability, original sin, and Christian perfection. In the spirit of "one heresy leads to another," Wilson reasoned that because Beecher was guilty of apostasy on these issues, he was also guilty of hypocrisy in claiming to believe in the Westminster Confession of Faith and guilty of slander in claiming that his opinions were traditional church orthodoxy. Theologically, Wilson was no match for Nathaniel Taylor's best friend. Defending himself in his own congregation, Beecher turned the trial into a theology seminar and secured a verdict of innocence from the Cincinnati presbytery. This verdict, coupled with Beecher's supremely confident ability to avoid censure, intensified the resentment of his Old School opponents toward him, and Wilson appealed to the local church synod, which held a second trial in Dayton, Ohio. This time the proceedings were much tougher for Beecher; his accuser was better prepared, the site was less friendly, the charges were pressed in a bitterly accusatory spirit, and the trial lasted nearly a week. The episode was traumatic for the Beecher family, especially for Henry—his father's companion throughout the grinding, insulting, often tedious ordeal—and his younger brother Charles, who took the invective against their father personally. Though Beecher beat the charges again, to the family's distress, Charles dropped out of seminary and moved to New Orleans. Henry, his faith shaken, had doubts about his ministerial calling and renounced all pretensions to an interest in theology, vowing that he would never join or speak for any theological faction.[8]

By his lights, Henry remained true to this vow for the rest of his life. How Beecher resolved his crisis of faith and committed himself to lifelong Christian service is unclear, since he was uncharacteristically reticent about it. His most telling account was given many years later, through the lens of his later theology. Beecher recalled that on a "blessed morning of May" in the Ohio woods, after the period in which he had studied theology, he had an experience of God's moral nature that settled his troubled mind and heart:

> It pleased God to reveal to my wandering soul the idea that it was his nature to love a man in his sins for the sake of helping him out of them; that he did not do it out of compliment to Christ, or to a law, or to a plan of salvation, but from the fullness of his great heart; that he was a Being not made mad by sin, but sorry; that he was not furious with wrath toward the sinner, but pitied him—in short that he felt toward me as my mother felt toward me, to whose eyes my wrong-doing brought tears, who never pressed me so close to her as when I had done wrong, and who would fain with her yearning love lift me out of trouble. And when I found that Jesus Christ had such a disposition, and that when his disciples did wrong he drew them closer to him than he did before—and when pride, and jealousy, and rivalry, and all vulgar and worldly feelings rankled in their bosoms, he opened his heart to them as a medicine to heal these infirmities; when I found that it was Christ's nature to lift men out of weakness to strength, out of impurity to goodness, out of everything low and debasing to superiority, I felt that I had found a God.[9]

This remarkable statement is too filtered and imprecise to be taken literally as historical information, but it perfectly expresses the essential understanding of Christianity that Beecher preached, with an increasingly liberal slant, throughout his ministry. His lifelong question was Luther's: How can I find a gracious and loving God? Family tension played a role in determining his answer. He could not be a Christian if that required him to subscribe to his father's theological tradition, but neither could he break from his father. Throughout his childhood he coped with the lack of parental love and warmth that he craved by idealizing his departed mother, whose self-giving and unconditional love was what he needed. Christ could be a savior to him only if Christ loved him in the way that his mother had loved him. New England Theology—abstract, legalistic, and barely alleviated in its Calvinism—knew nothing of this Christ; Henry could never preach that, but he also could not preach against it without sabatoging his career and his relationship with his father. Thus he accentuated the revivalist core of his father's own preaching and developed a style of evangelical preaching that focused on personal religion and morality while avoiding formal theology as much as possible.

This strategy shrewdly capitalized on Beecher's personal feelings. Projecting from his experience, he reasoned that even very conservative churches were probably filled with people who yearned to hear a gospel of personal religion shorn of theology, church doctrine, and partisan politics. After a brief stint as a journalist in Cincinnati, he accepted a pastoral call to a small Presbyterian church in Lawrenceburgh, Indiana, with the intention of preaching a saving gospel of divine love and minimal theological superstucture. His immediate problem was that he had to pass muster with the presbytery of Oxford, Ohio, to become an ordained minister. Beecher feared that his candidacy would not survive his examination before the Oxford presbytery, which was controlled by Old Schoolers. He was doubly unfortunate in having the question arise in 1838, the year that the Presbyterian Old School, upon gaining control of the church's General Assembly, set off a denominational schism by voting to remove four New School synods that were theologically liberal and opposed to slavery. In Cincinnati, Beecher had no choice; the only presbytery was Old School, and his Lawrenceburgh congregation was aligned with this presbytery. Moreover, upon accepting his call to the Lawrenceburgh congregation, he had married Eunice Bullard and brought her from Boston to Lawrenceburgh. Assuring himself that he knew enough theology to get past an ordination exam, he gave a sharp performance and won the presbytery's approval. The Oxford Old Schoolers set one condition, however; they passed a resolution that required all new ordination candidates to be affiliated with the Old School Presbyterian church, a measure intolerable to all the Beechers. Henry told his congregation that he was "unwilling to be hemmed in by the narrow lines of schools and parties"; his congregation responded by cutting its ties to the Oxford presbytery. He was thus ordained at his own church in a ceremony conducted by his father and his brother-in-law, Calvin Stowe. Though opposed to all theological factions, Beecher was ordained as a New Schooler.[10]

Henry struggled for years with the contradictions of both being and not being a protégé of Lyman Beecher. He inched away from his father's belief in the colonization strategy, but regarded immediate abolitionism as a destructive, insurrectionist fantasy. While vowing to avoid atonement doctrine and the burning fire of hell, Beecher tried to start a revival in Lawrenceburgh, convinced that good revival preaching required no message beyond the saving love of God and the companionship of Christ. To his regret, he could not get even the semblance of a revival going without warning about the terrors of hell; his rural Indiana listeners were accustomed to vivid hellfire harangues from Methodist and Baptist preachers, and they puzzled over his damnation-free sermons. They sensed that he cared little for his pastoral duties outside the pulpit and criticized him for spending too much time on his sermons, not making pastoral calls, and spending money too freely. Beecher was kindly in casual conversations, they acknowledged, but they wanted pastoral seriousness and salvation preaching. He had problems at home, as well; his wife protested that he spent much of his limited income on personal indulgences. She also resented local manners, her isolation in Lawrenceburgh, her tiny two-room house, and the West in general.[11]

Eager to please, Beecher took most of these complaints to heart. He worked hard in Lawrenceburgh, tried his hand at hellfire preaching, and made a few converts. He honed his pulpit skills in the course of learning how to make the gospel come alive to Indiana farmers, though he never sparked a revival. His proficiency as a preacher gained the attention of Indiana state treasurer Samuel

Merrill, a deacon at the newly formed Second Presbyterian Church of Indianapolis. This congregation, a product of the Old School/New School schism, had broken away from an established Old School congregation in 1838. The following year, after six ministers rejected the offer, Beecher accepted a call to be the congregation's first pastor. He was thrilled to move to a city, though in fact Indianapolis was a country village with stump-lined roads. He anticipated that his wife would miss Boston less in the state capital of Indiana, and he exulted that Indianapolis had fine houses, large yards, several public buildings, and educated people. He vowed that he was now finished with hellfire evangelism and could preach the love-and-morality religion that his heart embraced.[12]

This religion was emphatically revivalist; Beecher was no less committed to evangelistic preaching than his father. By his third year in Indianapolis, despite poor health, he had launched major revivals in Terre Haute and in his own church, which boosted his reputation across the state. More than two hundred new communicants joined his church, he started revivals in several more area churches, and he was soon accepting preaching invitations on a scale like that of his father. He preached long, engaging, rhetorically overheated sermons on personal religion and morality that called sinners to confess their sinfulness and let Christ into their hearts. His sermons were short on politics, atonement doctrine, and theology in general, but very long on the ways of sin, the moral righteousness of God, and every person's need of a redeemer. Allegorical narrative was a favorite trope. Beecher won his first taste of fame in 1846, when he published a series of talks on the moral vices of the day that typified his revival preaching.

In *Seven Lectures to Young Men on Various Important Subjects* he focused on two pressing subjects: the moral temptations of youth in the new Western cities and the perversion of business caused by speculation and gambling. Beecher dramatized these problems as related assaults on Christian civilization: America was based on the Protestant work ethic of industry, temperance, thrift, and piety, but American cities, especially in the West, were work-despising moral sewers that subverted the Christian basis of American society. In the city, Beecher observed, young men were invited to gamble, get drunk, slough off, and fornicate with prostitutes. Beecher focused always on the moral character of the tempted individual. Employing his favorite revival technique, he described various moral choices as the responses of different character types and issued a slippery-slope warning: Once a young man took a first wrong step, he was bonded to degeneracy, like the johns at a local house of prostitution, "with red and swoln faces, or white and thin; or scarred with ghastly corruption; with scowling brows, baleful eyes, bloated lips and demoniac grins." Beecher took a closer look: "Here a shuddering wretch is clawing at his breast, to tear away that worm which knaws his heart. By him is another, whose limbs are dropping from his ghastly trunk. Next, swelters another in reeking filth; his eyes rolling in body sockets, every breath a pang, and every pang a groan. But yonder, on a pile of rags, lies one whose yells of frantic agony appall every ear. Clutching his rags with spasmodic grasp, his swoln tongue lolling from a blackened mouth, his bloodshot eyes glaring and rolling, he shrieks oaths; now blaspheming God, and now imploring him." Having relinquished hellfire, Beecher compensated with lurid descriptions of the personal hell of living in sin, and the entertainment value of his revival preaching rested heavily on this device.[13]

His preaching was well received for more than its value as entertaining evangelism, however; Beecher affirmed both the anxieties of small-town church-people about the ways that their country was changing and their traditional moral values. *Seven Lectures* favored farmers over merchants, villages over cities, and common people over intellectuals. It blasted high culture, modern novels, the circus, the racetrack, and especially, the theater: "The Theatre epitomizes every degree of corruption," he pronounced. "If you would pervert the taste— go to the Theatre. If you would imbibe false views—go to the Theatre. If you would efface as speedily as possible all qualms of conscience—go to the Theatre. If you would put yourself irreconcilably against the *spirit* of virtue and religion—go to the Theatre." The worst playwrights and novelists were French, he assured, but England was no slouch at degeneracy; even Shakespeare was often lewd. "These men of pleasure are, the world over, *corrupters of youth*," he charged. "Upon no principle of kindness can we tolerate them; no excuse is bold enough; we can take bail from none of their weaknesses." Beecher appreciated the anxieties of his audience about the weakness of prevailing social restraints against gambling, intoxication, prostitution, speculative profiteering, wildcat banking, and other moral ills. He affirmed that the heart of any society worth building lay in the Protestant ethic of piety, hard work, and frugality and that wealth was a moral good if it was gained by morally worthy means. In Indiana, he gave no sign of doubting that the small-town rural life was the best life of all.[14]

The year 1846 was a breakthrough year for him. Beecher's book was well-received, he was increasingly treated as a star preacher, and he grew in confidence, which allowed him to venture gingerly into dangerous territory. He was further motivated by embarrassment after his blistering attack the previous year on the moral hypocrisy of a Lawrenceburgh distiller, C. G. W. Comegys, who was a church member. Righteously Beecher made the case for Christian condemnation of the alcohol industry, but his choice of Comegys as a moral target soon backfired. Comegys recycled some local complaints about Beecher's arrogance, waited for Beecher's fulsome self-defense, and then acidly countered that while Beecher was very righteous about the evils of distillers—who forced themselves on no one—he was instructively delicate on the subject of slavery. This cutting reply embarrassed Beecher into speech, and two months later he preached three sermons on the religion and politics of slavery. He repudiated the Southern scriptural defense of slavery and laid out his own position, which was attuned to his audience and solicitous of it. Beecher rejected colonization (it would never work) and abolitionism (it would never work, and it incited violent insurrection) before identifying himself with a larger, vaguely defined third group. This third group constituted the majority of Northern citizens, and, he claimed, wanted slavery to end but had no acceptable strategy to bring about its termination. Clear, at least, that he had no answer, Beecher declared that he was ready to support any nonviolent economic or political strategy that was devised by the moral majority of the North. As usual, his claim to majority sentiment was the key to his appeal; by attributing strong moral feelings on the subject to most Northerners, he sought to shield himself from criticism while delegitimizing the two positions he rejected. He flattered the audience that he sought to influence, and his sermons were warmly received, which confirmed him in his view that this was the right tack for church leaders to take. Two months later, a hometown mob celebrated the Fourth of July by beating to death a well-known elderly man who had bought his own freedom from slavery. Pleading the need to keep civil peace, Beecher persuaded a local abolitionist leader not to publicize the incident. It was not his finest moment, but it surely revealed that he knew the real state of the majority's moral feeling.[15]

Beecher came into his own in other ways during his Indianapolis pastorate. He studied phrenology (which he had studied in college) and mesmerism (which his sister Harriet pressed upon him as a cure for various nervous diseases); most important to his spirit, he cultivated beautiful flowers. All the family attested that Beecher's lifelong love of gardening was a sign of his special connection to his mother, who was an outstanding gardener. In Indianapolis, his prodigious vegetable and flower gardens impressed some locals and made others grumble about his misplaced priorities; he won prizes at state fairs and became the chief speaker and ringleader of the Indiana Horticultural Society. His sermons linked the cultivation of flowers and the cultivation of a healthy spiritual life; Beecher saw no tension, as yet, between these analogies and the theology of revivalism. One of the people that his ministry touched was his brother Charles, his mother's last child. In 1842, alarmed by Charles's continuing crisis of faith, Lyman Beecher asked Henry to give Charles a job as a church music director. It is a telling measure of his regard for Henry's ministry that his father turned to him at the point of the family's deepest distress about the one Beecher male who was not a minister. Charles moved to Indianapolis, was soon swept up in the revival taking place at Henry's congregation, and the following year became a candidate for ordination in the presbytery of Indianapolis. This was not the last time that Henry came to the rescue of his sensitive younger brother or other siblings; to Lyman Beecher's surprise, it was his dreamy, mother-starved ninth child who became the family mainstay.[16]

Beecher's Indianapolis career had a chastening downside, however. Upon accepting his call to Second Presbyterian, he apparently assured his wife, the daughter of a prominent New England physician, that malaria was unknown in Indianapolis, where, in fact, nearly everyone in Indianapolis had it. The region was notorious for the mosquito-breeding swamps, boggy forests, and river valleys that produced a chronic plague of malaria every summer. Upon arriving in Indianapolis, Eunice Beecher was horrified to learn from Samuel Merrill's wife that "everyone has 'chills and fever' more or less constantly" and within a few weeks so did she and her husband. The Beechers and their children suffered debilitating attacks of "the shaking ague" for the next eight years, and Eunice Beecher never recovered from the experience. After her second child was born dead in 1840, in search of health, Henry took her back to her parents' home in West Sutton, Massachusetts, where she remained for nearly a year. The Indianapolis Presbyterians did not miss her. Samuel Merrill reported to his brother at the time that Mrs. Beecher was commonly regarded as being "as ill disposed as indisposed." The locals did not care for her sharp tongue and New England mannerisms. Merrill remarked at the time, "Mr. Beecher is still popu-lar but his wife is a great weight on him whether from mere ill health or some-thing else I cannot say." He worried that Beecher's effectiveness "will be much impaired wherever he may be by the difficulties alluded to." Later he became less circumspect about the difficulties.[17]

Eunice Beecher's years in Indianapolis defeated her. She hated Indianapolis and made no secret of it; her husband was driven by his work and enabled by his prodigious energy to shake off his illnesses, but she could not do the same. She often missed church, had no friends to speak of, and was frequently accused of untruthfulness. Many congregants believed that her illnesses were strategi-cally timed. "Full of large tales, and enormous exaggerations," John Ketcham judged with hyperbolic emphasis. "No one believes a word she says." Her phys-ical and emotional suffering made little impression on fellow Presbyterians, and years later, they would resent her even more when her novel, *From Dawn to Daylight,* portrayed them as dirty, lazy, and callous. In truth, Eunice Beecher was worn down by five pregnancies, her continual struggle with malaria, her family's financial problems, and her personal loathing of Indiana. Having lost one child at birth, her spirit was nearly crushed in 1845 by the death of her two-year-old son, George Lyman. "My heart is almost broken," she told Harriet Beecher Stowe. "I have the wildest longings to look into his grave and see if he is indeed there, or if this be not a horrible dream from which I may one day wake." Two years later, after her husband received an attractive offer to become pastor of a new Congregational church in Brooklyn Heights, Eunice wrote to him: "Do not, do not let my health have any influence in your decision. I shall never be well any where. George's death has destroyed all that was left of my constitution. I despair of ever being of much use to any one. Let me then—my love—wear away what remains of life—in *any place,* where you can do the most good. It matters little to me—so that I can be with you while I live."[18]

Beecher wavered for months about resigning from Second Presbyterian. He finally resigned before deciding whether to accept an associate pastorship at Park Street Church in Boston or the pastorate of Plymouth Church in Brooklyn Heights, telling his Indianapolis congregation that he needed to move to the eastern seacoast to "save the life and restore the health of my wife." There were few expressions of regret in Indianapolis; Merrill noted that everyone admired Beecher's preaching but resented his lack of attention to other pastoral tasks. With weaker spelling, but more colorful expression, Ketcham further explained:

"The truth is, we, as a *town,* feel that we are loosing a valuable citizen; but he has never endeared himself as a pastor to his church—he has not been a pastor at al—only a brilliant preacher—and brilliant he is." For all of his sensitive effusions from the pulpit, Beecher had never connected personally to his parishioners. Always vowing to become a better pastor, he was not sufficiently disciplined to subordinate his personal interests to his pastoral responsibilities. As long as revivals were popular and his father lived nearby, he was eager to preach revivals, but he could not face up to the grinding demands of hands-on pastoral care. Beecher's style of ministry was not appreciated in Indiana, his sensational preaching notwithstanding.

He opted for the newness of Plymouth Church, and upon moving to Brooklyn Heights, he found the audience he was seeking, in and beyond Brooklyn.[19]

VICTORIAN MORAL POLITICS:
PREACHING TO THE MIDDLE CLASS

In Brooklyn Heights Beecher put liberal Protestantism on the map. The city of Brooklyn was only thirteen years old in 1847, and Plymouth Church was the city's second Congregational church. Beecher enjoyed his new environment from the outset and gradually adjusted his preaching style to it. In his later Indianapolis ministry he had begun to address controversial social issues; upon arriving at "the Heights," as it was called locally, he asserted his right to speak on social topics, explaining that he aimed to preach Christ "in his personal relations to individual men," but this did not mean that he had nothing to say about social issues. Every Christian preacher was obliged to address the social aspects of Christian moral teaching, such as the morals of politics or commerce. Beecher promised to keep an especially sharp eye on commerce: "It is here that the Devil teaches Christians to use the world's selfish maxims; it is here that he persuades them to smother their conscience, to abate its circuit." His rough manners, unkempt appearance, and racy style of speech initially startled his new acquaintances, and one parishioner observed, "There is something of the power of growth peculiar to the great western wilds about this young man, but somewhat of its rudeness also." The wife of a church trustee reported, "Don't ask me what I think of him. I can't tell you for the life of me. I only know that I am intensely interested. There is a sort of fascination about the man which I should think was produced in a good measure by his earnestness, his fervor, his seeming naturalness."[20]

His revival campaigning set off similar reactions. Brooklyn's nouveaux riches had little acquaintance with revival religion, and local pastors were appalled by its introduction to their upwardly mobile neighborhood. For several weeks his efforts elicited only blank looks and head-shaking, but Beecher kept calling for conversions, and soon Plymouth Church was growing with revival. Catherine

Beecher visited her younger brother and reported to their father that Henry was giving the most inspired sermons she had ever heard. Her brother was comfortable with educated New Yorkers, he liked the cosmopolitan feeling of his new congregation, and he acquired a stronger circle of friends than he had managed in his earlier pastorates. Though never one to form intimate friendships aside from his bond with Harriet, he enjoyed and respected his new parishioners. Their friendly criticism of his tendency to gush improved his preaching; their outpouring of sympathy when he lost an infant daughter, Catherine, bonded him to the church. He remarked to Harriet that his congregants in Indiana had not known how to offer sympathy. Swiftly Beecher became convinced that the middle-class life was the best life of all.[21]

This judgment extended to middle-class religion. To the extent that he had a theology, Beecher preached a watered-down New School revivalism rooted in his belief in the love and righteousness of God, the regenerative influence of Christ, and the moral capacity of human beings to turn from sin. "I do believe that man is corrupt enough, but something of good has survived the wreck," he told his audiences. Beecher began to rethink the assumptions of revival religion shortly after he moved to a more cosmopolitan area, however. His early theological minimalism was a way of coping with orthodoxy and his disagreements with his father, but in Brooklyn Heights, he quickly perceived that his revivalist gospel seemed quaintly out of step. For the first time since he was ordained, he allowed himself to think about the questionable theological underpinnings of his religious message. Having discarded "so many technical views," he told Harriet, he had given up thinking about theology during his Indiana ministry. But upon moving to Brooklyn Heights, he read a recently published book that caused him to rethink the theology of revivalism: Horace Bushnell's *Views of Christian Nurture*.[22]

Bushnell was too strident and negative for Beecher's taste, and the book's attack on the revival system denigrated much that was precious to every Beecher. A few months later, Beecher shuddered at the storm of controversy that Bushnell set off in his 1848 lectures at Yale and Harvard. Although Beecher did not wish to become, or be known as, a follower of Horace Bushnell, he recognized that Bushnell was a kindred spirit in important ways. Bushnell shared and expressed his sense of the moral nature of God, his concept of Christ as moral redeemer, his disaffection from theological orthodoxy, and his belief that language is flawed as a vehicle of religious truth. Beecher loved and preached the gospel of the garden; Bushnell made him reflect on the contradictions between the cultivating, organicist metaphors of the garden and the theology of revivalism. Revival religion had a dreadful view of children, no theology of nurture at all, and—Jonathan Edwards notwithstanding—little sense of nature as the vehicle of sacred presence. Confronted by Bushnell's powerful text, and moved by it, Beecher reached at first for his usual evasion: "Although I cannot agree with Bushnell, I can as little with his respondents; nor do I see any benefit in a controversy," he told Madison University professor John Howard Raymond.

"When will ministers learn that putting up fences and disputing about land-marks is not an equivalent for the careful cultivation of the soul?"[23]

This sentiment was Bushnellian, however, and Bushnell hooked Beecher more deeply than he let on. Beecher felt the importance of Bushnell's brave attempt to bridge the gap between nature and the supernatural. When his younger half-brother, Thomas Beecher, informed him that Bushnell's theology was strongly attractive to him, Henry rejoiced that Thomas seemed to grasp that in religion feeling is deeper and more important than thinking. He appreciated that Bushnell's writing had encouraged this conviction in his younger brother, but he cautioned that Bushnell was still essentially an intellectual. "It seems to me that it is this outward sympathy, springing from an inward sympathy with God, that Bushnell principally lacks," Beecher explained. "He lives toward God, toward truth, toward the good, the beautiful, the perfect. But that tremendous sweep, which the Pauline, because Christlike, mind takes, when from the crystal mountains it descends . . . he is not ignorant of—but *it is not the* force of his life." As Beecher saw it, Bushnell came close to expressing the life-truth of true religion, but because his approach to religion was still essentially intellectual, he invested too much significance in his negations and distinctions and battled for theological victories. Bushnell's religious message was half-romanticist; Beecher's romanticism was wholehearted. In writing or speaking, Beecher explained to a friend, "I do not seem to think, *I see*. If I speak of images it is because they glow, I see landscapes or cliffs—or forests, or prairies and the *impression* is as minute and vivid as if it were really before my eyes."[24]

With increasing forthrightness he preached on the superiority of imagination over intellect and on the basis of religion in feeling. Contradictions did not faze him; when informed one Sunday that his sermon had contradicted what he said the previous week, Beecher shrugged, "Oh, yes! Well, that was last week!" Elsewhere he counseled, "Life is a kind of zig-zag." He continued to think of himself as a theology-minimalizing revivalist and reformer, not a theological critic like Bushnell, but he attained a crucial inner clarity about the religious differences that separated him from his father. Beecher was a theological minimalist only by a formal definition of theology; he had minimal interest in "theology" as a dogmatic system or formal discipline; in a wider sense of the term, however, he was thoroughly, effortlessly theological. Beecher had a deeply theological imagination, and his extemporaneous sermonizing overflowed with reflective religious insights. To his mind, true religion was the life of love, not the life of love mixed with fear or hedged by it. He wrote to a friend, "I do not see why a man of fine feelings, who receives impress from superior motives rather than from the lower, may not be blessed to his conversion without the use of fear at all." The most loving and grace-filled people that he knew were not brought to God by fear, and the purest forms of religion did not rely upon it. Lyman Beecher warned his son that he had no right not to tell sinners of the wrath of God, but in Brooklyn Heights, Henry realized that he believed in a different religion from his father's. It was not merely a matter of playing down theology, or even a matter of theology alone; it was a matter of preaching a different kind of religion. Henry did not explicitly say this until 1867, but implicitly, the differences pervaded his sermons long before he wore the liberal badge.[25]

His fame as the voice and symbol of a new kind of American Protestantism was made possible by a confluence of circumstances peculiar to his time and place. Beecher's congregation expanded in its first two decades nearly in step with the soaring population of Brooklyn Heights. The church was destroyed by a fire in 1849, which proved to be fortuitous, since the church had already outgrown its first home. Beecher designed a new sanctuary that featured a central platform, no pulpit, and seating arranged in a large semicircle surrounding the platform. The new sanctuary, fittingly called "the auditorium," was ideal for him. Without stained-glass windows or ecclesiastical adornments, it seated more than two thousand people and had room for an additional five hundred seats that were usually occupied on Sundays. The novel seating arrangement, which allowed Beecher to be heard without raising his voice, gave the impression of intimacy and informality and accentuated the role of the preacher as performer. Beecher was not shy in describing the latter advantage:

> It is perfect because it is built on a principle—the principle of social and personal magnetism, which emanates reciprocally from a speaker and from a close throng of hearers. I want them to surround me, so that they will come up on every side, and behind me, so that I shall be in the center of the crowd, and have the people surge all about me![26]

His exuberant personality thrived in Brooklyn Heights. Churchgoers were attracted to his overflowing buoyance; many helped him indulge his expanding appetites for expensive paintings, engravings, jewelry, rare books, and the like. Beecher admitted to friends that he often had to sneak new indulgences into the house because his wife disapproved of them. Eunice Beecher also disliked his new friends and parishioners, from whom she remained coldly distant, but privately, he noted that at least her health had stopped deteriorating in Brooklyn Heights. Of his early years at Plymouth Church, Beecher later recalled, "I had a very strong impression on my mind that the first five years in the life of a Church would determine the history of that Church, and give to it its position and genius; that if the earliest years of a Church were controversial or barren, it would take scores of years to right it; but that if a Church were consecrated and active and energetic during the first five years of its life, it would probably go on for generations developing the same features. I went into this work with all my soul, preaching night and day, visiting incessantly, and developing, as fast and far as might be, that social, contagious spirit which we call a revival of religion."[27]

Beecher was opposed to controversy, but he believed in challenging Americans to live up to their highest ideals; always he negotiated between his conscience and his sense of the mood and will of his audience. His younger brother Charles, who had lived in Louisiana for ten years and been more deeply affected by slavery than other Beechers, prodded Henry's conscience on the issue. Now serving as a pastor in Terre Haute, he warned Henry and Harriet that America was about to suffer an explosive retribution for its sins. At the outset of Henry's gradual rise to fame, four years before Harriet exploded into the national consciousness, neither gave preeminence to the struggle against slavery. Harriet was not a minister only because she was not male; as compensation, while struggling to find her own work and voice, she dabbled for years in mesmerism, spiritualism, the water cure, electricity treatments, and the movement cure. She and Henry, encouraged by each other and moved by current events, especially the passage of the Fugitive Slave Bill of 1850, took up the cause of antislavery at approximately the same time. In 1848, Henry did not share his brother's apocalyptic sense of crisis, but he did resolve that the time had come to join the antislavery resistance, and he sought to find his own way of entering the struggle without joining the insurrectionists. He found it in the Edmondson case.[28]

Emily and Mary Edmondson were daughters of Paul Edmondson, a free black man, and Milly Edmondson, a slave, who lived in Washington, D.C. Upon reaching the age of their optimal market value, the sisters made a failed attempt to escape from bondage and were sold by Milly Edmondson's owner to a trader for the New Orleans market. While his daughters were held captive in an Alexandria jail, awaiting the transport to New Orleans, Paul Edmondson journeyed to New York to plead for assistance from antislavery activists. He was advised to seek help from Beecher, whom he informed, after making his way to Beecher's house, that he needed $2,250 to buy his daughters' freedom. Beecher responded by staging a piece of electrifying political theater. Taking the father with him to his speaking engagement at the Broadway Tabernacle, he staged a mock auction that dramatized the revolting barter of human beings and made a dramatic appeal for the Edmondson girls' freedom. A witness later recalled, "He made the scene as realistic as one of Hogarth's pictures and as lurid as a Rembrandt." Beecher raised the necessary funds, the sisters were set free, and the case gained national attention, thrusting him to the forefront of the non-abolitionist wing of the antislavery movement. Three years later, a year after the Fugitive Slave Law drove her into the movement, Harriet Beecher Stowe assumed personal responsibility for the education of the Edmondson sisters. The following year, in the early weeks of her fame from *Uncle Tom's Cabin*, she met Milly Edmondson for the first time and bought the freedom of two more of her children. In succeeding years Beecher used the mock auction technique several more times to raise money and goad the conscience of the North.[29]

Beecher's rising public stature was made possible by the success of his church, his emergence as an antislavery reformer, and what the *Independent* called the "unreportable pyrotechnic splendors" of his public speaking engagements at places like the Broadway Tabernacle and the Tremont Temple. It was enhanced nationally by his association with the *Independent*. Middle-class Americans had a distinctively Victorian anxiety about the moral condition of their country in the mid-nineteenth century. They worried about America's slavery problem, the implications of America's westward expansion, and its growing industrialization and early social modernization. One important venue to address these concerns was the denominational newspaper, which provided responsible reporting and moral guidance on the issues of the day. *The Independent* epitomized the genre. It was founded in 1848 by publisher Henry C. Bowen, a prominent New York merchant, son-in-law of Lewis Tappan, and trustee of Plymouth Church, who had convinced Beecher to move to Brooklyn Heights. The paper's editors were respected, moderate, Congregational ministers: Leonard Bacon, Richard S. Storrs, and Joseph P. Thompson; from the beginning, its star attraction was Beecher. The editors vowed to take a stand on all important issues while remaining committed to nonpartisanship in church and party politics. This editorial ideal proved to be rather taxing in the troubling national politics of the 1850s, but, owing to these national troubles, *The Independent* developed into a journalistic powerhouse.[30]

The paper's early success owed much to a fire-alarm crisis over slavery and to Beecher's rising celebrity. *The Independent* supported the Free Soil position without, at first, taking a line on the Free Soil Party; led by Beecher, it blasted the Missouri Compromise and the Fugitive Slave Law as betrayals of Christian and American moral principles; at Beecher's urging, the paper criticized the role of business leaders in the enactment of both measures. The passage of the Fugitive Slave Bill set off the political fire alarm that established the paper's early identity and constituency. By criminalizing all acts of passive and overt assistance to escaped slaves, the Fugitive Slave Law of 1850 directly implicated Northerners in the maintenance of the slave system and inflamed the antislavery sentiments of church leaders who had never expected to promote civil disobedience. By giving voice to these outraged moral feelings, *The Independent* became a major political voice in its second year of existence.

All the paper's editors were more moderate than Beecher, and even Beecher was initially cautious about lawbreaking. His first response to the new fugitive law condemned its immorality and effrontery while calling for merely passive disobedience to it: "We shall not attempt to rescue, nor interrupt the officers if they do not interrupt us." A month later, strengthened by Harriet's exhortation to "be the champion of the oppressed," he made a case for proactive disobedience. It was a Victorian Christian argument for the transcendent right to protect one's virtue; the Fugitive Slave Law could be obeyed only by violating a higher moral law, he observed, and because the law of the land in this case was an occasion of sin, Americans were morally obliged to disobey it. Beecher opined that the law contained provisions odious enough "to render an infamous thing consistently infamous throughout." Thereafter he pressed this line of argument against the slave system itself; slavery was evil because it subverted America's Christian virtue and poisoned American politics. Beecher was especially concerned about the virtue of the commercial sector. With blistering moral censure he charged that the Fugitive Slave Law was fueled politically by the greed of Northern business leaders who sold out their moral principles to make money off slavery. After the *Independent's* editors affirmed their support of this view, the paper lost 1,500 subscribers but gained 5,000 new subscribers, thereby settling in-house debates about its audience and political orientation.[31]

Beecher's antislavery activism drew him into cooperative efforts with abolitionists in the 1850s, though he repeatedly proffered his reasons for not being one of them. He later recalled that during those years, "a man that was known to be an Abolitionist had better be known to have the plague. Every door was shut to him." Beecher averted that fate; at times he even commended colonization as a better alternative, with the same blend of paternalism, romanticizing idealization, and otherwise unremarked realism that marked the writings of his soon-famous sister. For all his flattering words about the refined moral feelings of Northern whites and his often-patronizing descriptions of blacks as backward victims, Beecher realized that most Northerners did not share his sympathy for the victims of America's original sin. He possessed a core inner awareness of the majority's shabby contempt for blacks. This awareness came into view on the few occasions that he spoke about colonization. He realized that the North had done next to nothing for its own black population. "Here is a class downcast and downtrodden among us—the poor, the despised, the weak," he observed. "The doors of the schools and colleges are shut against them, and the doors of the trades are shut." Beecher doubted that emancipated blacks would ever be able to flourish in a society so deeply prejudiced against them; so he proposed to "educate them, Christianize them, and *then* colonize them." In 1852, at the end of the sensational novel that made her world famous, Harriet Beecher Stowe closed *Uncle Tom's Cabin* with the same prescription. Brother and sister Beecher played roles in the antislavery movement that were far more radicalizing than the politics of their obstensible objective. "When I came here [to Brooklyn Heights] you could get no great missionary society, Bible society, or tract society to say one solitary word for the slave," Henry later reflected. "Such were the interests of the mercantile classes of the South that it was extremely difficult to exert there any anti-slavery influence."[32]

Beecher played a key role in changing that fact, while giving his voice to a host of related reform movements. In the 1850s he used his ascending moral influence to advocate temperance, political reform, and the abolition of poverty and disease; in the 1860s he added women's rights to this list of causes. He tried to oppose slavery without committing himself to a political party, but the passage of the Kansas and Nebraska Act in 1854 and the subsequent violence in Kansas convinced him that partisan political struggle was morally unavoidable. The Kansas and Nebraska Act effected a division between the territories of Kansas and Nebraska under the assumption that Kansas, despite lying above the Missouri Compromise's benchmark latitude 36°30′, would be a slaveholding state. Beecher condemned the measure as a betrayal of Christian and American moral principles. While he persisted in his claim not to be an abolitionist, his intervention in the Kansas civil war outflanked many abolitionist leaders to the left. Many abolitionists were pacifists; Beecher spoke widely on behalf of the antislavery forces in Kansas and contributed directly to their struggle by sending rifles to them. His campaign at Plymouth Church to arm the Kansans with Sharp's rifles earned an unlikely name for his protosuburban congregation: "Church of the Holy Rifles." In the 1856 presidential campaign, while speaking continually on behalf of "bleeding Kansas," Beecher gave up his remaining pretensions to a strategy of mere moral persuasion. Obtaining a leave from Plymouth Church, he campaigned for the newly formed Republican Party and its presidential candidate, John C. Frémont, giving three-hour speeches two or three times a week to open-air audiences of between eight and ten thousand. Repeatedly Beecher urged that both of the established political parties, the Whigs and the Democrats, were slavery parties; the Democrats were simply more honest about it. There was no significant moral or political difference between the Democrat, James Buchanan, and President Fillmore, the Whig, since both were determined to betray Kansas, implicate Northerners in the guilt of slavery, and thus make obedience to the law an occasion of sin. These speeches were derided by Bushnell and other intellectuals, notably Henry James Sr., for their rhetorical excesses; Beecher embarrassed Bushnell by playing to the crowd. With a common touch and an appealing mixture of idealism and ebullient opportunism, however, Beecher read the signs of the times more shrewdly than many of his intellectual betters.[33]

CRUSADING FOR LIBERTY:
THE MEANING OF THE CIVIL WAR

Beecher had a hand in the revival of 1858, but by then he no longer shared his father's faith in revivalism as the golden key to national reform. Though often identified as a radical abolitionist, he remained essentially a moderate in the antislavery movement. He expressed concisely his view of John Brown's 1859 raid at Harper's Ferry: "His soul was noble; his work miserable." Beecher sympathized with Brown while disapproving "his mad and feeble schemes." Against his own abolitionist allies, Beecher refused to advocate breaking all religious ties with slaveholders, and he opposed abolitionist demands to withdraw mission-church support for slaveholding Cherokee Indians. Claiming to speak for the majority of Northerners, he insisted until the outbreak of the Civil War that the North wished no harm to Southern commerce, schools, churches, and families. As the war grew near, however, Beecher made no attempt to hide his excitement at the coming assault on Southern civilization. On Thanksgiving Day, 1860, in a sensational address he explained the meaning of America's Civil War: "The Southern States and the Northern alike found poisonous seed sown in colonial days. The North chose to weed it out. The South determined to cultivate it, and see what it would bear. The harvest-time has now come. We are reaping what we sowed. They sowed the wind, and they are about to reap the whirlwind." The North was prosperous by virtue of the seed that it had sown, he declared: "Ours is wholesome; theirs is poisonous."[34]

That set the tone and theme; around the world the Christian nations were growing stronger: "The nations of Christianity are a vigorous stock, and have a future. Already Christian nations rule the world." In the North, but not in the South, the United States was keeping up: "We know it by the victory of ideas, by the recognition of principles instead of mere policies, by the ascendency of justice, and by the witnessing and ratifying rage of all who love oppression and oppressors." The social order of the North was organized as a regime of liberty, but Southern society was based on slavery, "a rotten core." God held the two Americas, in their maturity, up to judgment. The day of judgment was at hand, Beecher preached: "Two queens are not to rule in this land." One regime or the other had to go: "There is a Divine impulsion in this. Those who resist and those who strive are carried along by a stream mightier than mere human voli-tion. Whether men have acted well or ill, is not now the question; but simply this: *On which side will you be found?*"[35]

Beecher was elated when the war finally started. During the siege of Fort Sumter he paid obligatory regret at the "wretchedness and wickedness and mon-strosity of war" before turning to his theme that there are worse evils than war and America was the proof: "I hold that it is ten thousand times better to have war than to have slavery. I hold that to be corrupted silently by giving up man-hood, by degenerating, by becoming cravens, by yielding one right after another, is infinitely worse than war." Compared to the wretchedness of the slave system, "war is resurrection." He dismissed the notion that the Southern states had a right to leave the Union: "It is a right that invalidates all power in government." Warning that there was no negotiable peace that did not "suppress every manly sentiment and every sympathy for the oppressed," Beecher pressed hard on both themes, while giving priority to the former. "They have fired upon the American flag!" he raged. Believing that his compatriots would fight for the cause of restoring the Union, but not for immediate emancipation, he called for a nation-actualizing crusade for liberty: "Give me war redder than blood, and fiercer than fire, if this terrific infliction is necessary that I may maintain my faith of God in human liberty, my faith of the fathers in the instruments of lib-erty, my faith in this land as the appointed abode and chosen refuge of liberty for all the earth!"[36]

The slaveholder states had disowned liberty both by perpetuating slavery, he preached, and now by becoming traitors. The war was a crusade: "We must not stop to measure costs. . . . We must put our honor and religion into this struggle."

Beecher set a vigorous example of putting religion into the struggle. He spoke at recruiting meetings, blessed flags, and raised $3,000 from Plymouth Church for the regiment of his son, Henry Jr., who enlisted for three years.

Beecher crusaded for a new kind of American political religion while reserving, and amply exercising, his individual right to criticize the government. He reasoned that the American Puritan model was no longer sufficient to produce public virtue for its fragmented country; what was needed was an explicitly nationalist public religion. The American state and church shared the same destiny and moral responsibility; America had to become a single nation, belatedly, and the church had to play a major role in uniting the United States. Addressing two companies of the "Brooklyn Fourteenth," many of whose members he had recruited, Beecher tied together the state and church as tightly as he bound the evils of slavery and secession: "Remember, citizen! Remember, Christian soldier! The American flag has been fired upon by Americans, and trodden down because it stood in the way of slavery! This is all that you have reaped for your long patience, for your many compromises, for your generous trust and your Christian forbearance. You may now see through all the South just what kind of patriotism slavery breeds!" To the middle-ground states of Kentucky, Tennessee, and Missouri, he quoted the Apocalypse. Christ hated lukewarm religion and so did Beecher: "We do not believe in hermaphrodite patriots. We want men to be men from the crown of their head to the sole of their foot, and to say *no* to oppression, and *yes* to liberty, and to say both as if thunder spoke!"[37]

Beecher thundered across the North to raise its fighting patriotic spirit, never doubting that the war was fought for idealistic reasons, and enraged at President Lincoln's refusal to declare them. In 1861, Beecher knew that the North was unwilling to fight for emancipation; he also doubted the constitutionality of dismantling the South's institutions: "This conflict must be carried on *through* our institutions, not over them." By the following summer, however, under the influence of Theodore Tilton and other abolitionist friends, he exhorted the president to commit the nation to emancipation. Not to admit that the war was about slavery was to degrade the war effort. "The gist of the war is slavery. This is the pivot on which the whole history turns." Week after week he hammered on the subject from the pulpit, his lecture platforms, and in the *Independent*. His attacks became increasingly strident and personal, on a par with Garrison's standard fare. By the end of the summer, against the objections of his sister Harriet and his half-brother Thomas, who pleaded that white America would not fight for emancipation, Beecher attacked Lincoln fiercely for failing to commit the Union to the abolition of slavery. He also complained that the war was dragging on because the president had no sense of the value of time. He was greatly relieved the following January when Lincoln finally issued the Emancipation Proclamation. Beecher rejoiced, "Blessed be God, he has sent a porter. He has opened the door by the hand of the President. He has lifted the silver trumpet of liberty, and the blast is blown that rolls through the forest, and goes along the mountain-side, and spreads wide over the prairies." He had no patience with those who protested that Lincoln lacked any constitutional authority to abolish slavery: "We are going to have the Union as it never was, but as it was meant to be. The Union as it was meant to be, and not the Union as it was, is to be our doctrine; because the Union as it was, was a monstrous outrage on your rights, and on mine."[38]

The Independent, Beecher's chief vehicle of communication through the war years, was also his albatross. The depression of 1857 hit Bowen hard and hurt the paper financially. Like many Northern merchants, he was financially ruined four years later by the war and was forced to make ends meet by hiking the paper's advertising revenue. This alienated its genteel ministerial editors, who also did not like the radical drift of what was ostensibly their publication. When they resigned in 1861, Beecher took over as editor-in-chief; Bowen banked on Beecher's fame; both of them relied on Beecher's close associate and protégé, Theodore Tilton, to keep the paper running as managing editor. Tilton was already doing most of the drudge work, but under Beecher's editorship, he essentially took over the paper. Politically and professionally the two ministers were tightly bonded to each other and to Bowen. Emotionally Tilton and Beecher shared a kind of friendship that was not uncommon for nineteenth-century heterosexual men of their class. Expressions of loving affection and intimacy passed easily between them, and they hugged and kissed each other and showered each other with flowers. "I toss to you a bushel of flowers and a mouthful of kisses!" Tilton typically effused to Beecher, whom he called "my Dear Bishop"; Beecher reciprocated lavishly to Tilton and to numerous male and female friends. Years later Tilton recalled that "I loved that man as well as I ever loved a woman." He owed his career to Beecher, having begun as Beecher's sermon transcriber and an *Independent* copyboy, but now he was coming into his own. In 1860, while Beecher looked down on Lincoln, Tilton vigorously supported his presidential candidacy in the *Independent*. His reward was a warm relationship with the new president and a lucrative patronage appointment for Bowen as collector of the port of Brooklyn. Two years later, when Beecher's son lost his commission in the army, Tilton promptly secured a better commission after a personal visit to the secretary of war. Henry was deeply gratified, while Eunice Beecher declared that Tilton was never to enter her house again.[39]

Together they kept the *Independent* going through the war years. Beecher enlisted his sister Harriet as a regular contributor, whose renown gave the paper a boost, but its biggest draw by far was Beecher's sermons. Beecher rarely took the time to write out his sermons—he explained that he preferred to serve them hot—but Tilton recorded his extemporaneous Sunday effusions and published them in the *Independent*. In 1863 Beecher took a six-month vacation in England and the Continent, noting that he was exhausted from years of speechmaking and a year of newspaper management. In England, while keeping up with the war news, Beecher declined invitations to give speeches and tried to relax. He encountered a great deal of anti-Union sentiment, but told friends that it didn't matter what England thought of America's fratricide; England was self-centered anyway.

In truth, Beecher shied away from facing hostile British audiences; emotionally drained, he was wary of instigating a public relations disaster for himself and the Union. Tilton assured him soothingly that his "golden" silence pleased their American friends, but the news of the summer changed Beecher's mind. The Union won major victories at Vicksburg and Gettysburg, and Tilton's encouraging letters informed Beecher that popular opinion in New England was swinging in favor of oppressed blacks: "A friend of mine, just from Grant's army, says that every officer and soldier in it is an abolitionist—made so by the progress of the war." The Irish-instigated New York draft riots helped the abolitionist cause, Tilton reported: "In New York, the result has been a wonderful change of sentiment (more than I can describe) in favor of the Negroes, and against the Irish." In September he told Beecher that public support for the government had risen dramatically, "far stronger than when you left." Even Lincoln was popular: "The old man is showing the strong hand, and every loyalist is cheering him. . . . He is the most popular man in the country." A recent chat with the president revealed to Tilton "a great growth of wisdom in his ugly head." Lincoln had informed Tilton that he no longer supported colonization and exhorted, "Tell your anti-slavery friends that I am coming out all right." By mid-September Beecher was convinced that the war and American opinion had taken a decisive turn and judged that the moment had come to make a pro-Union pitch to the British. A word of encouragement from the American ambassador to England, Charles Francis Adams, set him into motion.[40]

He approached audiences warily, but they in fact were primed to give him the benefit of the doubt, and his rousing speeches in Manchester, Glasgow, Edinburgh, Liverpool, and London received highly appreciative publicity back home. In Edinburgh he teased, "We have so much English blood in our veins that when we began this war we blundered and blundered; but we are doing better and better every step." In London, when asked why the Union would not simply let the Southern states go, Beecher replied, "Because they would be still less peaceable when separated. Oh, if the Southerners only would go! They are determined to stay—that is the trouble." In Manchester, when asked to assess the antislavery movements, Beecher explained that one group, "very small and able," proposed to save the country by disunion; he belonged to the other group, which proposed to abolish slavery without destroying the Union: "I would not burn a barn in order to get rid of the rats. We have always said, the thing is bad enough, but not so bad but we can cure it by moral means."[41]

When the *New York Times* and the *Independent* published his speeches with parenthetical indications of jeers, loud applause, and, mostly, cheers, New Englanders were elated and Beecher was enthralled: "I have not, in a single instance, gone to the speaking halls, without, all the way, breathing to God unutterable desires for inspiration, guidance, success," he told Tilton. "And in all this time, I have not had one unkind feeling toward a single human being." Upon returning to America in November, he was hailed as a national hero; mass meetings were held, and many exaggerated things were said about his great achievement, some of them by him. Writing in the *Atlantic Monthly*, Oliver Wendell Holmes cheered, "When have Englishmen listened to nobler words, fuller of the true soul of eloquence?" Having endured weeks of anti-Union sneers with uncharacteristic silence, Beecher believed that he had turned the tide of British public opinion. The English parliament had been on the verge of declaring for the Confederacy before he spoke out, he boasted, a claim that was repeated by his admirers for decades afterward. For historical parallels to Beecher's achievement, William Taylor reached back to Demosthenes pleading the cause of Athens against King Philip; Lyman Abbott invoked Cicero against Catiline; John Henry Barrows titled his chapter on the episode, "The American Demosthenes Triumphs." Historian E. D. Adams later provided some needed perspective in a footnote: "He was a gifted public orator and knew how to 'handle' his audiences, but the majority in each audience was friendly to him, and there was no such 'crisis of opinion' in 1863 as has frequently been stated in order to exalt Beecher's services."[42]

Tilton's veneration of his mentor intensified in Beecher's absence and peaked during his English triumph. "My love multiplies for you every day," he emoted. Bowen was more conflicted about Beecher. *The Independent* hailed Beecher's speaking tour in issue after issue, despite Bowen's attempt to deflate Tilton's regard for the American Demosthenes. The year before, Bowen's thirty-eight-year-old wife, Lucy Bowen, the mother of ten, had mysteriously taken ill and died. On her deathbed, she reportedly confessed to Bowen that she and Beecher had been lovers and even worse, she was still in love with Beecher, who had at least one other extramarital lover that she knew of. Beecher probably had fled to England to let Bowen cool off; now Bowen turned to Tilton, who had already saved his magazine and his bank account. "I sometimes feel that I must break silence," he told Tilton. "One word from me would make a revolution throughout Christendom. . . . Beecher would be driven from his pulpit and from Brooklyn in twelve hours." Not even Bowen wanted that, at least not yet, for Beecher was his source of income, in addition to the kickbacks and bribes that Bowen shook down from supply ships as a wartime port collector. For his part, Tilton had to take into account that Bowen was justly regarded as the most treacherous man in Brooklyn; he stayed close to Beecher, strengthened his own power base, and encouraged Beecher to work on his relationship with President Lincoln.[43]

By the time that Beecher returned from England, Tilton was a formidable figure in Beecher's world. He was connected to the entire antislavery and radical Republican movement, he controlled the *Independent* (though Beecher was still formally its editor-in-chief), he had a friend in the White House, and he was surrounded by a clique of Plymouth Church members who controlled Brooklyn's political patronage. Though a sharp writer, Tilton recognized that his power derived from personal connections and organizational position, not from public esteem, as in Beecher's case. In the closing months of the war, Beecher tested his own standing in the Republican party with requests for favors from government officials, including President Lincoln, all of which were promptly granted. "I very much wish to oblige Beecher," the president replied on one occasion. In January 1865, during a cordial meeting with Lincoln, whose honesty and shrewdness impressed him greatly, the president assured Beecher that, contrary to rumor, he had no intention of holding a peace conference with Confederate emissaries; Beecher later assured friends that the president would not betray the principles for which the war was fought. He apparently did not press for a confirmation that Lincoln no longer planned to colonize blacks in Latin America. Three months later, at Lincoln's request, Beecher delivered the oration at the ceremonial lifting of the Union flag over the ruins of Fort Sumter; Lincoln told his cabinet that without Beecher in England, there might have been no flag to raise. At Fort Sumter, Beecher called for just punishment of the "ambitious, educated, plotting, political leaders of the South," but no retaliation against ordinary Southerners: "Our hearts wait for their redemption. All the resources of a renovated nation shall be applied to rebuild their prosperity, and smooth down the furrows of the war." Editorialists across the country hailed the speaker as a fitting and inspiring choice for the occasion. Beecher's fame was nowhere near its peak, but his enjoyment of it was.[44]

He and Tilton and other dignitaries departed from Fort Sumter on a steamer on April 15, 1865. That night the president was assassinated. The presidency was now in the hands of Andrew Johnson, a Southerner and former Democrat who passionately believed in states' rights, a former slaveowner whom Lincoln had chosen as a running mate in hopes of uniting the country after the war. He supported the not-yet-ratified Thirteenth Amendment to the Constitution, which abolished slavery, but he took a minimalist position on Reconstruction and the legal protection of former slaves. Johnson's plan, which he called Restoration, called for the creation of loyal state governments that repudiated Confederate debt and ratified the Thirteenth Amendment; that was all that he required to revoke martial law and withdraw federal troops. In the first two years of his presidency he granted over twenty thousand pardons to former Confederates. In 1866 his radical Republican enemies in the Congress joined with moderate Congressional Republicans to pass the Civil Rights Act over his veto and propose the Fourteenth Amendment, which he furiously denounced. Johnson opposed virtually all uses of federal government power to force states to educate black Americans or allow them to vote or to use public facilities.

As late as November 1865, several months after he had assumed formal editorial control of *The Independent,* Tilton was still writing letters of grateful, almost gushing devotion to Beecher: "The intimacy with which you honored me for twelve years has been, next to my wife and family, the chief affection of my life. By you I was baptized; by you married; you are my minister, teacher, father, brother, friend, companion. The debt I owe you I can never pay. My religious life, my intellectual development, my open door of opportunity for labor, my public reputation—all these, my dear friend, I owe in so great a degree to your own kindness that my gratitude cannot be written in words, but must be expressed only in love." By then, Beecher had already been warned by New York *Ledger* editor Robert Bonner that Tilton routinely denigrated him behind his back, but Beecher found it too painful to consider that Tilton's professions of affection might be self-promoting or hypocritical. By the time that Tilton wrote his last adoring thank-you note to Beecher, however, the two Congregationalist leaders were on opposite sides of the nation's defining postwar battle, and Beecher had made his first serious misjudgment of the public mood. Though he fancied that he was at the top of his game as a political player, he was in the process of destroying his political reputation and efficacy.[45]

During the war Beecher had straightforwardly urged that blacks deserved equal rights of suffrage and citizenship, but after the war he hedged on this commitment and struggled to sort out the politics. How was a war-ravaged United States to integrate thousands of ex-slaves into a society pervaded by deep feelings of hostility on all sides? The "spirit of Lincoln" was no help; Lincoln believed that blacks were inherently inferior to whites, wanted to colonize U.S. blacks somewhere in Latin America, and in 1858 famously declared, "I will say then that I am not, nor ever have been in favor of bringing about in any way the social and political equality of the white and black races, that I am not nor ever have been in favor of making voters or jurors of negroes, nor of qualifying them to hold office, nor to intermarry with white people." In the weeks that followed Lincoln's death, Beecher reflected on the political situation, sent conflicting signals, and then declared that while he still believed in the principle of equal rights for ex-slaves, he opposed the way that his usual allies were endeavoring to secure these rights. He judged that the radical and moderate Republicans were overplaying their hand. Though he insisted that he was not "a Johnson man," the prospect of extensive federal control over the defeated Southern states collided with his belief in limited government and repulsed him nearly as much as it repulsed Johnson. Worried that the enforcement of the Civil Rights Act was sowing the seed of a white backlash, he wanted the ex-slaves to be able to vote and to enjoy other civil liberties, but not as the beneficiaries of coercive federal intervention.[46]

Beecher therefore supported most of Johnson's Restorationist program and campaigned for it, with minor caveats, on a lengthy speaking tour in the fall of 1865. In October he told a crowded gathering at Plymouth Church that he did not support the anti-Johnson editorials appearing in the *Independent,* that Johnson was a great president, and that America needed to rely upon the kindness of white Southerners, "which is more important to the blacks than all the policies of the nation put together." Tilton replied with furious disbelief that the politics of the situation obviously required massive coercion: The South had annulled the ordinances of seccession and abolished slavery only because it lost a civil war, and it would accept equal suffrage only if it was similarly coerced. Beecher rejected the latter claim, arguing that suffrage belonged to a different category, because democracy could not be imposed from without. The following summer, he declined an invitation from the president to appear with him at a convention in Cleveland but delivered a public letter that explained why state governments needed to be allowed to work out their own approaches to civil rights.[47]

With "The Cleveland Letter" Beecher separated himself from the controlling mainstream of the Republican Party and became friendlier to the Democratic Party, with which Johnson had begun to cooperate. In the letter, he called for an indefinite moratorium on enfranchisement and a general pullback from coercive federal intervention and pleaded that "nothing is so dangerous to the freedman as an unsettled state of society in the South." Though he vigorously called for the integration of African Americans into American society, Beecher's description of the integrationist process contained a whiff of Bushnellian racism: "Civilization is a growth. . . . None can escape that forty years in the wilderness who travel from the Egypt of ignorance to the promised land of civilization. The freedmen must take their march. I have full faith in the results. If they have the stamina to undergo the hardships which every uncivilized people has undergone in its upward progress, they will in due time take their place among us." This was a more hopeful sentiment than the chauvinist supremacism of Bushnell and Lincoln, but Beecher veered perilously close to it. He lectured that American blacks could not be given their equal place in American society: "It will come to sobriety, virtue, industry, and frugality."[48]

That did it. Many of Beecher's usual allies had held their noses until then, but the Cleveland Letter, reprinted in newspapers across the country, demanded a response, and it got a massive, angry, withering one. Newspaper baron Horace Greeley excoriated Beecher's patronizing, supremacist intimations and his support of Johnson. Tilton denounced his former idol as a Johnsonian traitor, charging that Beecher had done more harm to the republic than any American other than Johnson. Tilton had already called for Johnson's impeachment, and Beecher felt the rage that impeached Johnson the following summer. Various Beechers pleaded with him to amend his position; brother Edward and brother-in-law Calvin Stowe censured him publicly. Even Plymouth Church turned against him, as Bowen organized a committee that nearly got him fired. While numerous friends and relatives lectured him publicly, Harriet lectured him privately that he had underestimated the anger of the conquerors, who were "sore with suffering."[49]

Beecher never conceded that they were right. He warned that democracy cannot be imposed by force and that Reconstruction was a recipe for a white backlash. "No army, no government, and no earthly power can compel the South to treat four million men justly, if the inhabitants (whether rightly or wrongly) regard these men as the cause, or even the occasion, of their unhappiness and disenfranchisement," he insisted. The racist terrorism of the Ku Klux Klan, founded in 1866, soon strengthened his convictions. Beecher held out for a soft-Reconstructionist politics, protested that he was not a Democrat, urged that the Republican Party needed a genuinely moderate wing, and took his lumps. Retaliating against Bowen and Tilton, he withdrew his sermons from the *Independent* and hurt the magazine financially. At Plymouth Church he was fortunate to attain the aggressive support of financier John Tasker Howard, a church founder, who lobbied undecided church members on his behalf. Beecher retained his job on the strength of his penitent assurance that he was not a Democrat, taking comfort that a few Christian liberals, including young Washington Gladden and Lyman Abbott, agreed with him about Reconstruction.

His chief concern at the moment was not to misread his public for a second time. The previous fall, at the end of a sermon, Beecher had dramatically asked his congregation to pray "that I may not be seduced from the work of this ministry." He had heard rumors that a Cabinet post was in the offing. Beecher was burned by his lust for political power, or, at least, by his lust for proximity to it. He badly underestimated the anger that Republicans felt at seeming to lose the peace to an enemy that refused to accept the implications of its defeat. Harriet advised him to find another venue; he was not cut out for party politics. Beecher made the right choice, opting to go back to religion.[50]

IMAGINING LIBERAL CHRISTIANITY

He resolved to rethink and express the religious center of his life in a way that represented a move forward, not a retreat. Beecher could not return to the old-time religion any more than he could imagine or desire a religion shorn of sociopolitical commitments. These nonstarters were related. He extricated himself from the Johnson mess, but not from political activism. He returned to thinking and writing mostly about religion, but now in a plainly liberal, cosmopolitan voice. His explicitly liberal turn, a declaration of theological independence, was issued in the form of a novel. Not a theoretical or scholarly type, Beecher was never tempted to systematic theology. He may have figured that no novel could be the basis of a heresy trial. Shortly after his Fort Sumter speech, he signed a contract with Robert Bonner to write a good Victorian novel (filled with "good moral purpose and effect") for serialization in Bonner's mass-circulation newspaper, the New York *Ledger*. With an eye on Beecher's popularity and the staggering success of *Uncle Tom's Cabin,* Bonner gave him a whopping $24,400 advance, even though this Beecher had never written a novel. After dallying for two years, caught in the firestorm over Reconstruction, he settled down in the sitting room of Tilton's home to write *Norwood,* with Elizabeth Tilton's soothing companionship to help him work through his writing block. To an anxious Bonner, he described his project: "I propose to delineate a high and noble man, trained to New England theology, but brought to excessive distress by speculations and new views. . . . The heroine is to be large of soul, a child of nature, and, although a Christian, yet in childlike sympathy with the truths of God in the natural world, instead of books. These two, the man of philosophy and theology and the woman of nature and simple truth, are to act upon each other and she is to triumph."[51]

Beecher's rendering of this theme was a revelation to readers unschooled in Melville and Hawthorne. Philosophically he taught a second-hand Emersonianism to churchgoers who would not have taken it from Emerson; *Norwood* became a best-seller, went through four editions in ten years, was dramatized in a successful New York play, and appeared serially in the *Ledger*, despite harsh reviews. The story focused on the courtship of Barton Cathcart and Rose Wentworth, a young couple from Western Massachusetts, but Beecher gave its key lines and saving actions to Rose's father, the town doctor, Reuben Wentworth, a warm-hearted, Coleridge-quoting sophisticate who had graduated from Harvard and received his medical training in Europe. To his "sensibility of exquisite taste" was added, by training and reflection, "a rational element, and then a moral sympathy, until he found himself united to the organized system of nature with every part of his being." In other words, he represented Beecher. In conversations with the town's Congregational pastor (a Yale-educated Lyman Beecher Calvinist) and a local judge (a materialist and skeptic), he spoke for a new possibility, modern liberal Christianity.[52]

Wentworth's long, overflowing discourses sounded suspiciously like excerpts from Plymouth Church sermons, showing that neither the dogmatic Christian nor the skeptical materialist understood the first thing about true religion. He explained the Coleridgean difference between Reason and Understanding, paid his respects to science, and identified religion with Reason: "I accept the facts which appeal to my senses as the lowest possible truth and as appealing to the lowest avenue of my mind. Nature is more than a vast congeries of physical facts, related to each other as cause and effect, and signifying nothing else." The factual truths of the Understanding had their place and value, "but they create in my breast, besides all that, such heights and depths of sensibility that I know that they have a moral relation to my moral sentiments, and that while science, like the mole, knows the root and bulb, faith alone, acting in a spiritual sphere, recognizes the developed stem and blossoms." Wentworth taught that the wellspring of all good theology is poetic inspiration: "Prose is the work-day dress in which truths do secular duty. Poetry is the robe, the royal apparel, in which truth asserts its divine origin. Prose is truth looking on the ground; eloquence is truth looking up to heaven. Poetry is truth flying upward toward God!" Every great theologian is a poet at heart, he believed, "indebted for fame to those very elements of poetry."[53]

Beecher distinguished the doctor's religion from the pastor's orthodoxy: "Your God is historic—mine is living. Your God is in a temple—mine every where. You have excogitated and built up, element by element, attribute by attribute, a conception of God, to which by resolute concentration you direct your thoughts, without help in symbol, natural object, or any instrument whatever, but wholly by will-force. Now and then there will arise out of this stretching void some dim image or sense of Divinity. But even at that your conscience, not love, clothes Him. You have little help from your affections; less from ideality; none from taste and beauty; and, really, you worship an *abstract thought*—a mere projection of an *idea*—not a whole Mind, a *Living Being!*" For Wentworth, the Savior was everywhere, "in the book and out of the book. I see Him in Nature, in human life, in my own experience as well as in the recorded fragments of His own history. I live in a Bible. But it is an unbound book!"[54]

Wentworth was an Emersonian pantheist, but he had a surprisingly good word to say for revivals. "In every department of life men are moved in masses, and, as it were, with social contagions," he reasoned. "Few men in any thing act alone. They kindle themselves in the simplest employments by social contact. Social enthusiasms have characterized the progress of the race in every department of society." On this ground, he believed, revivals were a good thing for society, for the kind of people who needed revivals. When his friend, the judge, objected that revivals were "got up," Wentworth replied that so was the rest of culture and society: "Is not education 'got up?' Is not art culture 'got up?' Is not your own profession and mine, 'got up?' Why should men be afraid to speak of moral states as the result of deliberate and intentional effort? Why should not men apply the term education to moral faculties as well as to others?" The moral sentiments are as much subject to laws as any other parts of the mind, he reflected, and in pressing for a moral result, the revivalist was no more to be denigrated than the poet or dramatist who pressed for an aesthetic result.[55]

Thus did Beecher come to terms with his early ministry. *Norwood* marked a turn in his religious pilgrimage, but he was committed to seeing his life as a continuous unfolding of a singular conversion experience and religious sensibility. This commitment required Beecher to keep revising the memory of his early career as he moved to an increasingly explicit liberalism; in his sermons of the later 1860s and 1870s he confirmed and developed the speeches of Reuben Wentworth. Beecher's definition of true religion was Parkeresque: "The essence of religion is love to God and love to man. It is toward God a whole and continuous sympathy and love." This was the ideal of Christ and the key to Christ's significance, he taught:

> Christ's ideal is neither philosophy, nor war, nor statecraft, but love—love to God, and love to man. When that spirit predominates in the soul, you have struck the keynote; you have got hold of the radical principle; you have touched the line of direction. And all unfolding, all growth, that is true and perfect, in time, is to take that direction. And when the perfect man shall appear on the earth—the *coming man* that we hear so much about, and that is so slow a traveller—it will be found that he is a man who has perfectly entered into this divine conception of love, reaching upward toward all things high and pure and noble, and reaching outward toward all sentient beings.[56]

Without equivocation Beecher asserted that doctrine plays a merely secondary role in true religion. The main thing in Christianity is "a heart that breathes

kindness and love." When people objected that this claim undermined traditional religion, Beecher replied that so did Christ: "When men say what I have
said, and what I say again, and what I will testify to so long as the breath of life
is in me, that the spirit of Christ is love; and that he who truly loves God and
men is a Christian, no matter in what church he is found, nor in what circumstances he is placed, men say, 'You are knocking the foundation out from under
things.'" Traditional religion invests its trust in the instruments of religion, he
explained, but religion itself is the life of love, the loving spirit of Christ. "Now,
I take religion; and if I am let alone I will not deny its instruments; I believe in
instruments; I believe in doctrine; I believe in church organization; I believe in
the utility of wisely administered ordinances. These things are important. But I
say that wherever the two come in conflict, I must take religion."[57]

Beecher did not dispute the need for church doctrine, but he refused to
believe any doctrine that offended against the spirit of love. "People say to me,
'Can a man be a Christian and not believe in this, that and the other thing?'"
He was usually careful not to name the specific things. "It is very difficult to say
what a man may not lack and yet be a Christian," Beecher replied. People come
to Christ from all manner of cultural backgrounds and belief systems, and what
matters is not their theology of Christ's nature, but their growth in Christ's
spirit: "I do not care what point you start from—whether from the naturalism
of Persia, or from the starting point of truth and lies among the Brahmin, or
from the naturalists of scientific times, or from the outer circle of the Christian
sects—from among those that are remotely orthodox, or almost orthodox, or
quite orthodox, or more than orthodox, or super-hyper-orthodox; no matter
where you start, the fact is just this: You have human nature in you; and that
human nature has the seeds of this grand Christian development. And you may
start where you will, so that you *start,* so that you put yourself under the drill of
the divine spirit of love and peace and joy in the Holy Ghost." If one seeks to
grow in and under Christ's spirit of love, he taught, everything else that is good
and saving will follow, including appropriate beliefs. If one does not follow the
way of Christ's spirit, no "correct" religious belief that one may hold is worth
anything.[58]

In his sermons Beecher increasingly resorted to horticultural metaphors to
explicate the theme of growth in Christ's spirit. Though he now had less time
for gardening, he compensated by talking about it more, while keeping an elaborate greenhouse at his summer residence in Peekskill, New York. One of his
books was titled *Plain and Pleasant Talk about Fruits, Flowers, and Farming.*
From the pulpit he reminisced that in a small town—Indianapolis—where he
served as a young minister, "there were but two or three gardens, and I undertook to preach the Gospel by the garden as well as by the pulpit." One year, he
recalled, he had cultivated a bed of three thousand hyacinths that were much
admired by his neighbors, especially the local German population, though
one of his parishioners opined that he had never seen anything as "purty" as a

cabbage. Undeterred, Beecher continued to grow his bright flowers in the otherwise dismal Indianapolis, "and the love of flowers grew, and it was not more
than two or three years before there were ten times as many flowers in that town
as there ever had been before." The moral of the story: "Let your flowers shine
that men, seeing how beautiful they are, will go and make gardens for themselves." Beauty is natural and material, Beecher allowed, but it does not belong
to the world of things that will pass away, for beauty is firstly spiritual and
divine; it inheres in the nature of God and all spiritual existence. In the teaching of Jesus, it is called the kingdom of God. "My friends, we are living an invisible life," Beecher exhorted. "There is a kingdom of God within us. There is a
work of God going on there."[59]

Confident in his message and person, he proclaimed his willingness to let the
fruit of religious beliefs be the only test of their truth. Horticulturalists do not
brag about their flowers or argue about their supposed superiority, Beecher
observed, nor do they care about the names that people assign to them. Real gar-
deners simply bring forward the fruit of their labor to be judged and accept
Christ's standard of judgment, which is the standard of every horticulturalist
committee: "By their fruits you shall know them." By that standard, Beecher
reasoned, the truest religion is the one that produces the most loving, healthy,
and ethical people: "If the Roman Catholics can prove that they make better
men than we protestants do, that ends the argument with me. I am going in for
the sect that makes the greatest number of men of the best sort." Calvinism had
a record of making "magnificent, strong men," Lyman Beecher's son reflected,
but it showed a clear tendency to make only a few of them and to crush the spirits of the rest. This was not his ideal of a church: "Show me the sect that makes
the largest number of men high and noble, and I am for that." To his mind this
was the proper ground for the Calvinist-Arminian dispute: "I do not care for
arguments. Go away with your texts. Show me the men that you have made."[60]

Religions are either life-giving and compassionate, or they are false, Beecher
argued; the tests of worthy belief are practical. As a youth Beecher had listened
to his father sermonize on the causes of disease and chronic illness, and always
the misfortunes of suffering people were attributed to God's punishment of sin.
Beecher still believed that sin was the cause of most of the world's trouble, but
he could not believe it in quite the same way, once science explained the biology of illness. Neither did he mourn the loss of things that he could no longer
believe. In his maturity he perceived that bad religion, not a vengeful deity, was
the cause of much of the world's evil and a great deal of its chronic illness.
Speaking to a generation of Americans who struggled with illness constantly yet
no longer accepted chronic illness or disease as their God-given fate, Beecher
challenged them not to give in to poor health or bad religion. His volume on
preaching contained an entire chapter on the religious importance of health.
"There are few men in the ministry who live at one half their competency or
power," he observed disapprovingly. "They do not know how to make their

machines work at a high rate of speed, with great executive energy, without damage to themselves. It is an art to be healthy at all; but to be healthy when you are run at the top of your speed all the time is a great art indeed."[61]

To be truly healthy is not merely to be not sick, he admonished. "I divide people into, first, the sick folk; secondly, the not-sick folk; thirdly, the almost-healthy folk; and fourthly—and they are the elect—the folk that are healthy. What I mean by 'health' is such a feeling or tone in every part of a man's body or system that he has the natural language of health." Young children have it, and puppies too; they cannot eat or run or wrestle enough: "They are just *full*. It is buoyancy. It is the insatiable desire of play and exertion." Nearly all the great speakers have it, he exhorted aspiring preachers: "They are almost always men of very large physical development, men of very strong digestive powers, and whose lungs have great aërating capacity. They are men of great vitality and recuperative force." Since he was describing himself, Beecher noted that it was not a good idea to do a lot of muscle-building exercise. His own chunky body had done little of it. Good religion, good moral habits, and zest for life are more important for health than weight-lifting, he counseled. Christianity and good health go together: "If there was ever a system of joy and hope in the world, pre-figured by the prophets, and afterward characterized by the Sun of Righteousness, it is that ardent and hope-inspiring gospel that you are to preach."[62]

Unfailingly, untiringly he insisted that Christianity is not about "the dungeon and the pit," except as suffering, death, and the pit are redeemed by the power of Christ. Christianity is the "science of right-living," Beecher taught: "Consider the intrinsic beauty and moral power of a nature in which the malign element is subdued, and the whole emissive force of the soul is genial, benevolent, and helpful. Looking upon an individual as you would upon a picture, a statue, or a fine piece of architecture, is there anything that men so much admire as a strong, grand nature that acts invariably in the line of kindness?" This was his ideal: great-souled vibrancy, love-inspired magnanimity, which he called "the new manship of the world." His romantic Christian Victorianism called anxious middle-class achievers to their higher selves: "The world groans and travails in pain because it is under the dominion of the animal nature that is in the old man, and not under that of the nature of kindness which is in the new man."[63]

New England Theology proceeded by doctrinal argument and scriptural proof; Beecher countered that "the power of the gospel does not lie in historical statements; neither does it lie in systematic arguments; it lies in the living force of the higher moral nature of the church and of the community at large." For him, the church had never tried Christianity, but Christianity was precisely something meant to be *tried*, not believed in. Beecher estimated that 90 percent of the church's energy and soul-power since the advent of Christ "has been expended upon the external, accidental concomitants of the gospel," a terrible waste for the world. More to the point, it was a terrible waste of the kingdom of Christ's spirit that already exists in the world: "There has never been a time in which the whole force of any considerable body of Christians has been mainly and enthusiastically directed to the production of the real gospel—a manhood which has laid aside all malice, and is acting in the full power and enthusiasm of divine love." The power of positive thinking found its first platform at Plymouth Church, Brooklyn.[64]

Beecher routinely invoked the highest moral ideals while daring to speak from his own experience. His condemnation of nighttime entertainment was a typical example. "I protest against the use of night for social pleasures, to the extent which, in cities and in fashionable circles especially, it is prostituted," he sermonized. In case any listeners needed the reminder, Beecher assured them that he was no drudge and did not believe in solitude, asceticism, or melancholy: "I believe in gaiety and joyousness." He wished to be known "as a friend of liberty and a friend of pleasure." At the same time, he knew that "all men at night are pigs." Even within moral bounds, he judged, pleasures are not wholesome in the untimely hours of night. The turning of night into day, amid the glare of artificial lights and excitements—"these things are not wholesome. They are not wholesome either to the body or to the soul." More precisely, these nighttime "dancings and feastings and fooleries" were a waste of time and "utterly unpardonable" as a sin against God-given health and wholesomeness. He gave thanks for his own contrasting upbringing: "I never became acquainted with wickedness when I was young, by coming in contact with it. I never was sullied in act, nor in thought, nor in feeling, when I was young. I grew up as pure as a woman. And I cannot express to God the thanks which I owe to my mother, and to my father, and to the great household of sisters and brothers among whom I lived. And the secondary knowledge of these wicked things which I have gained in later life in a professional way, I gained under such guards that it was not harmful to me."[65]

That was in 1870, near the height of Beecher's prestige as America's favorite moralist. Two years later, he changed his tune, after his congregants learned enough to read between the lines. In 1872 Victoria Woodhull, the radical feminist journalist and avatar of free-love spiritualism, published a story well known in certain circles, that Beecher had committed adultery with Elizabeth Tilton. Woodhull was condemned by polite society as a malicious liar, but her story inspired months of heated gossip. Beecher knew the rumors, and in 1873 he and Theodore Tilton signed an agreement, published in the Brooklyn *Daily Eagle,* not to contribute further to them. The following January Beecher reflected homiletically on the case of John Stuart Mill, while hoping that his own was behind him: "I am sorry that he was not better than he was. That is the way I feel about all of you. People are criticizing him, finding fault with him, shaving him down; and doubtless he was imperfect, as we all are. Nobody ever thought he was an angel; he never thought himself to be one; but laying aside all incidental questions, he had admirable traits." This was the minimal standard that Beecher desired for himself, while protesting that he was still as pure as the ideal woman.[66]

THE RIGHTS OF WOMEN:
ELIZABETH CADY STANTON
AND THE FEMINIST MOVEMENT

Despite the vehement opposition of his sisters, Beecher was a staunch advocate of women's rights and a vice-president of the Women's Rights Society. He wrote articles in support of woman suffrage, gave speeches and sermons that pressed the case for women's equal rights, and raised money in 1863 to help found the National Woman's Loyal League, which elected Elizabeth Cady Stanton as its first president and Susan B. Anthony as secretary. As a feminist he had little company among Protestant leaders of his generation; American Protestantism was slow to give up its idealization of the true woman as a husband-owned, motherly keeper of domestic virtues. Feminist activism was doubly controversial in the mid-1860s, especially among progressives, because it conflicted politically with the other great cause of the moment. The fact that Beecher and Tilton were leaders in the feminist movement of their generation had much to do with the scandal that later engulfed them. The fact that a women's rights movement existed in this generation in the first place owed much to Cady Stanton, the woman who, in the mid-1860s, epitomized the conflicting cross-currents between the cause of equal rights for women and the cause of equal rights for black males.[67]

Elizabeth Cady Stanton was the chief publicist and theorist of the radical wing of nineteenth-century American feminism. Born in Johnstown, New York, in 1815, she was a child of privilege who struggled throughout her early life to overcome her considerable inner turmoil and her outward exclusion. Her father, Daniel Cady, a former blacksmith and son of a farmer, rose to become a distinguished attorney, judge, and member of the New York state legislature. Her mother, Margaret Livingston Cady, was related to New York's richest old-money families—the Beekmans, Schuylers, Van Rensselaers, and Livingstons. The Cadys' home dominated one end of the town square of Johnstown, and in location and proportion it equaled the local courthouse and the Scotch Presbyterian Church, where the children, especially Elizabeth, learned to fear the devil and their own depravity.[68]

Ten children were born to Margaret and Daniel Cady, five girls and five boys. Six survived early childhood, but only one boy, Eleazor. Elizabeth's earliest memory was the reaction to the birth of her sister Katherine: "I heard so many friends remark, 'What a pity it is she's a girl!' that I felt a kind of compassion for the little baby." When Elizabeth was ten years old, Eleazor, who had recently graduated from Union College, suddenly took ill and died. Her mother took it bravely, but her father was devastated; he had lost his only son, the bearer of his fondest dreams. Elizabeth tried to console her father: "With my head resting against his beating heart, we both sat in silence, he thinking of the wreck of all his hopes in the loss of a dear son, and I wondering what could be said or done to fill the void in his breast. At length he heaved a deep sigh and said: 'Oh, my daughter, I wish you were a boy!' Throwing my arms about his neck, I replied: 'I will try to be all my brother was.'" By her account, she spent her adolescence pursuing paternal ambitions that only her father's son was qualified to fulfill. After she became famous, she told this story every time she recounted the story of her life.[69]

Elizabeth Cady's parents were conservative down the line: staunch Federalists in politics, Old School Presbyterians in religion, aristocratic in manners. They believed in the sanctity of law and private property, though Daniel Cady had a streak of noblesse oblige; Cady Stanton's later recollections always emphasized her father's kindly, impressive paternalism and her mother's disapproving coldness. She saw a tender side of her father that went undetected by outsiders and felt rejected, or at least not loved, by her aristocratic mother, who found her volatile personality too much to deal with. After her parents were dead, she told a biographer, "My father was truly great and good—an ideal judge; and to his sober, taciturn and majestic bearing he added the tenderness, purity and refinement of a true woman." Her mother, on the other hand, "was inclined to a stern military rule of the household—a queenly and magnificent sway; but my father's great sense of justice, and the superior weight of his greater age . . . so modified the domestic government that the children had, in the main, a pleasant childhood." Other witnesses found her mother a bit warmer and her father quite severe. Cady Stanton struggled throughout her life to assimilate the lack of approval that she felt from both her parents, especially her mother. Even as an adult she kept trying to win the praise from her father, but she also took pride that her own children suffered no lack of maternal affection.[70]

Cady Stanton throughout her life was plagued by a morbid introspection that the family religion aggravated. The Cadys were serious Calvinists, God-fearing and morally upright, and she absorbed the element of fear in her youth. She had recurrent nightmares and rages about death, devils, and judgment; for a time she believed that she was a secret child of the devil: "To me he was a personal, ever-present reality, crouching in a dark corner of the nursery." Though her pastor was kind to her, perhaps the warmest personal influence in her early life, her affection for him may have heightened her tendency to take his sermons too literally. In her telling, his sermons chiefly communicated the certainty of her total depravity, the threat of eternal punishment, and the "machinations of the devil stirring to turn one's heart from God and his ordinances."[71]

This religious worldview was reinforced by her exposure to revival preaching during her years at finishing school. In 1830, Cady Stanton enrolled at Emma Willard's Troy Female Seminary, which she hated for its mediocrity and mixed messages. She wanted to study at Union College, but her parents were devoted to the cult of true womanhood, and in 1830 no college admitted female students. Four years later, Oberlin became the first institution to offer collegiate education to women. Even the Willard school seemed pointless to Daniel Cady;

his ambitious daughter had to beg for permission to study there. Cady Stanton later claimed that she learned nothing new at the seminary aside from French, music, and dancing, though her curriculum included algebra, Greek, logic, botany, history, chemistry and psychology. Cady Stanton admired Madame Willard personally, and the school was a better educational institution than she claimed, but her dislike for it was genuine. She bristled at its mannered, rule-laden, finishing-school atmosphere and resented the educational differences between collegiate and female schooling. Willard exhorted her students to become teachers, but Cady Stanton had no interest in schoolteaching, and the Troy Female Seminary was short on other reasons for women to pursue higher education.[72]

Unsettled, annoyed with her school, and nurtured in high Calvinist religion, in 1831 she accompanied her classmates to the great spectacle currently taking place in Troy: Charles Finney preaching in what came to be called the Great Troy Revival. The Troy area was flush with apocalyptic religion in the 1830s; the Millerite and Mormon movements were just beginning, the Shakers had a community nearby, and upstate New York was well tended by revivalists. Finney was the greatest of the revival preachers; his abolitionist disciples, Theodore Weld and Henry Stanton, were both converted by his perfectionistic evangelism. Every day for six weeks young Elizabeth Cady listened to Finney with a mixture of half-believing fascination, moral compulsion, and dread. His scorching, spell-binding evangelism finally overwhelmed her, and she came to the "anxiety bench" and pleaded for salvation. She later recalled that Finney was surely the equal of Savonarola as a "terrifier of human souls." He flapped his arms, rolled his eyes, and prophesied about the wrath to come; sometimes he spotted the devil. His preaching seized Cady Stanton's soul with fear of judgment, driving her to a nervous breakdown: She later recalled that Finney's preaching haunted her dreams with visions of the lost. Her friends became alarmed that she was losing her mind.[73]

Upon learning that his daughter had been victimized by a camp meeting revivalist, Daniel Cady forbade any discussion of religion or Finney until she regained her equilibrium. In June she accompanied her father, sister, and brother-in-law to Niagara Falls, where her brother-in-law, Edward Bayard, a lawyer who soon gave up law for a distinguished career in medicine, explained to her the psychology of delusion. Bayard gave her books on phrenology and rational philosophy, and assigned novels by Charles Dickens and Sir Walter Scott. This soaking in realism cured her of her conversion: "After many months of weary wandering in the intellectual labyrinth of 'The Fall of Man,' 'Original Sin,' 'Total Depravity,' 'God's Wrath,' 'Satan's Triumph,' 'The Crucifixion,' 'The Atonement,' and 'Salvation by Faith,' I found my way out of the darkness into the clear sunlight of Truth. My religious superstitions gave place to rational ideas based on scientific facts, and in proportion, as I looked at everything from a new standpoint, I grew more and more happy, day by day." Though she periodically struggled with her religious identity for many years, she remained true to the moral she derived from her exposure to revival preaching. Near the end of her life she justly claimed, "The memory of my own suffering has prevented me from ever shadowing one young soul with any of the superstitions of the Christian religion."[74]

Being well-to-do, Elizabeth Cady did not have to teach or sew or labor in a factory after graduating from seminary in 1833. Having neither plans nor husband, she spent seven years riding horseback, reading, partying, and visiting friends and relatives. She especially enjoyed visits to the Bayards at Seneca Falls and her cousin Gerrit Smith in Peterboro, New York. Edward Bayard introduced her to homeopathy and sustained a close, lifelong, nearly conjugal friendship with her. Each was in love with the other, but he was already married to her sister, and after she became a radical feminist, her feeling that she had been deprived of romantic happiness fueled Cady Stanton's rage against the institution of marriage. Her relationship with Smith was of a very different sort, and it changed her life. Gerrit Smith was a Livingston cousin whose father, Peter Smith, made his fortune as a speculator. Peter Smith founded the town of Peterboro (near Syracuse) and built a baronial mansion there in 1806. His son Gerrit used his inheritance as a base for numerous radical Christian causes, beginning as an advocate of the home missions and Sunday school movements; moving on to the prison reform, peace, and temperance movements; by 1835 he was a fervent abolitionist. An eccentric figure, generous to a fault, cultured, fun-loving, and highly compulsive, his creed was simple: God is love. At various times he was president of the New York chapter of the American Anti-Slavery Society and vice-president of the American Peace Society. With his equally reform-minded wife, Ann Fitzhugh Smith, the daughter of a wealthy Maryland slaveholder, Gerrit Smith welcomed to his home a steady stream of Southern in-laws and abolitionist leaders alike. More important, his estate was a well-known station on the underground railroad for slaves escaping from bondage, and he founded a nondenominational abolitionist church and a seminary for black ministerial students. A founder of the abolitionist Liberty Party, he ran for several offices and was elected to the House of Representatives in 1852 but quit in disgust after eighteen months.[75]

Being financially dependent on her father, Cady Stanton was careful not to join any of her cousin's causes, but she loved Peterboro. The Smiths were joyful entertainers, especially after they gave up Calvinism in the early 1830s; their home was a constant scene of dancing, games, and fascinating company. At her cousin's estate Cady Stanton met reformers, abolitionists, runaway slaves, Oneida Indians, old Dutch aristocrats, temperance advocates, Southerners, seekers, and politicians. On one occasion, which she often described in later life, she heard an eighteen-year-old runaway slave give a breathtaking account of her sale in the New Orleans slave market for prostitution. Virtually all of America's abolitionist leaders moved in and out of Smith's home, among them Henry B. Stanton, whom Cady Stanton later would describe as "the most eloquent and impassioned orator on the anti-slavery platform."[76]

The same Henry Stanton had led the abolitionist student rebellion at Lane Seminary in 1834. By 1839 he was a dashing, heroic figure who faced down angry mobs, gave stirring speeches for immediate abolition, and converted hostile crowds to antislavery politics. Listening to him speak for the first time, Cady Stanton judged that he was not quite as eloquent as abolitionist spellbinder Wendell Phillips but had a warmer and more attractive spirit. "Mr. Stanton was then in his prime, a fine-looking, affable young man, with remarkable conversational talent, and was ten years my senior, with the advantage that that number of years necessarily gives," she later recalled. One morning after a long ride on horseback, while they were walking through a grove, he asked her to marry him. She later recalled that he proposed to her with the charming revelation of feeling "which brave knights have always found eloquent words to utter." With stunned delight she accepted his proposal; with agonized second thoughts, she broke the engagement four months later.[77]

The implications of marrying the abolitionist movement were daunting for her. Henry Stanton was an agent for the American Anti-Slavery Society and one of Theodore Weld's "Band of Seventy" abolitionist preachers. His life was filled with hardship and danger. He was committed to a moral cause, while she merely socialized with activists, enjoying a carnival of fascinating characters. He proposed to rescue her from "a giddy whirl of fashionable follies," but she liked her life of coming and going. Though all her sisters had married law students, and she had not lacked opportunities for marriage, she was nearly twenty-four years old, had sought neither marriage nor a life-binding cause, and was enjoying her father's money. Upon hearing of the engagement, Cady Stanton's father blasted her choice of a lowly antislavery agent, for he despised radicals and did not trust one with his daughter. Edward Bayard weighed in with the legal problems, reminding her that New York marriage law gave almost no protection to married women and stripped them of their rights to inherit property, keep earnings, sign contracts, initiate lawsuits, or establish credit. Even children were legally controlled by their fathers. Still claiming that her romance with Henry Stanton was the "sweetest" event of her life, Cady Stanton, deeply conflicted, gave up the engagement. The real love of her life was Edward Bayard, but he was not available, and she risked losing her inheritance if she married her second choice. But then, learning that Stanton would be going abroad for eight months, to the upcoming World Anti-Slavery Convention, she changed her mind again. They eloped shortly before he sailed for London.[78]

Thus Elizabeth Cady married the abolitionist movement, which owed her husband two years' back salary. At that moment the movement was splitting into two main factions, with other splinter groups forming as well. One group, the Garrisonians, held out for the strategy of moral suasion and welcomed women as full members of the American Anti-Slavery Society. Some of them argued that party politics was inherently compromising; some contended that electoral politics was repugnant in the case of slavery because the Constitution was a slaveholder document; as a group they agreed that male and female abolitionists should work together as equals in the same organization. An anti-Garrison faction led by Stanton, Gerrit Smith, Theodore Weld and James G. Birney, arguing for political realism, countered that the cause of immediate abolition needed a political party. The Liberty Party was their first resort. Fearing that any direct link with feminism would hurt the political viability of their cause, the anti-Garrisonites advocated separate men's and women's abolitionist societies. Stanton attended the inaugural World Anti-Slavery Convention in London as a member of the American movement's anti-Garrison faction, which meant that he was newly committed to electoral efficacy. It also meant that he had no job.

In London, Cady Stanton listened to antislavery leaders debate whether the female members of Garrison's delegation should be allowed to vote. It was a life-changing spectacle, to which she later traced her conversion to women's rights activism: "It was really pitiful to hear narrow-minded bigots, pretending to be teachers and leaders of men, so cruelly remanding their own mothers, with the rest of womankind, to absolute subjection to the ordinary masculine type of humanity. I always regretted that the women themselves had not taken part in the debate before the convention was fully organized and the question of delegates settled." To the surprise of her husband and Garrison's delight, Cady Stanton expressed her rage that the debate took place at all. She was inflamed; internal political factors meant nothing to her, because her sense of justice was offended. It was very much a Garrisonian reaction. Though Henry Stanton spoke in favor of seating the American women, he maneuvered against it behind the scenes, for the anti-Garrisonites had a vested interest in seeing Garrison lose the debate. After the anti-slavery champions voted against female delegates, Garrison sat with the exiled women and refused to address the convention. This gesture deeply moved Cady Stanton even though it was made by her husband's opponent: "After coming three thousand miles to speak on the subject nearest his heart, he nobly shared the enforced silence of the rejected delegates. It was a great act of self-sacrifice that should never be forgotten by women." It was also an action that her newly opportunistic husband would not have taken.[79]

Cady Stanton agreed with her husband that the abolitionist movement needed to get political. In the company of antislavery reformers, however, her outrage at the treatment of female abolitionists gave her the first glimmering of another transcendent moral cause. Her conversion to this cause—women's rights—created an uneasy tension in her relationship with Henry Stanton, who temporized on women's rights after he opted for political pragmatism in 1840. In later life he even temporized for a while on the politics of abolition. In London Cady Stanton made the acquaintance of Lucretia Mott, a Garrisonian delegate, Quaker, and outspoken feminist. Mott belonged to the radical Hicksite faction of the American Society of Friends, which applied the Quaker doctrine of the "inner light" equally to men and women; she would later recall that she grew up "so thoroughly imbued with women's rights that it was the most important question of my life from a very early day." Her favorite religious writer was William Ellery Channing, whom she studied and quoted avidly. Cady Stanton approached Mott gingerly, having been admonished by James Birney, the Southern abolitionist, that Mott's fervent feminism was divisive and that she was a chief cause of the bitter schism in the antislavery ranks. Cady Stanton was further predisposed to regard Quaker women as not quite human, "ready to be translated at any moment." She worried that Mott and the other female abolitionists would be hostile to her, being married, as she was, to the wrong side of the argument.[80]

But Mott was kindly and courteous to her, and as the convention unfolded, Cady Stanton was powerfully drawn to Mott's side of the argument, and then to Mott herself. "I soon found that the pending battle was on woman's rights, and that unwittingly I was by marriage on the wrong side," she later recounted. At dinner a group of Baptist ministers kept the argument going. "In spite of constant gentle nudgings by my husband under the table, and frowns from Mr. Birney opposite, the tantalizing tone of the conversation was too much for me to maintain silence. Calmly and skillfully Mrs. Mott parried all their attacks, now by her quiet humor turning the laugh on them, and then by her earnestness and dignity silencing their ridicule and sneers. I shall never forget the look of recognition she gave me when she saw by my remarks that I fully comprehended the problem of woman's rights and wrongs. How beautiful she looked to me that day." To Cady Stanton, Mott was "an entire new revelation of womanhood." A world of new possibilities opened to her, and she sought every opportunity afterward to be at Mott's side, "and continually plied her with questions." Mott revealed to her the possibility of thinking for herself, especially about religion and the rights of women. On the day that the abolitionist convention voted not to recognize female delegates, Cady Stanton and her mentor left the hall together, arm in arm, "reviewing the exciting scenes of the day." She later recalled that they agreed to hold a convention on women's rights when they returned to the United States, "as the men to whom they had just listened had manifested their great need of some education on that question." Eight years elapsed before the "ladies of Seneca Falls" were able to redeem that pledge.[81]

The labors of marriage and family intervened. Lacking means of support, the Stantons returned to Johnstown, where they moved in with the Cadys, and Stanton served an apprenticeship with Daniel Cady. Having opted for the political road to abolition and decided to become a lawyer as a logical next step, Stanton won the favor of his father-in-law, though his comrades taunted him for selling out. In 1842, several months after the Stantons' first child was born, Stanton began his law career in Boston, which he chose in order to challenge Garrison on his home turf. He made a meagre living and threw himself into Liberty Party politics; fortunately for their growing family, Daniel Cady purchased a home for them. Cady Stanton spent her Boston years caring for their children—three of them by 1845—and entertaining a roster of friends that included Lydia Maria Child, Elizabeth Peabody, Nathaniel Hawthorne, Frederick Douglass, Ralph Waldo Emerson, and Theodore Parker. She corresponded with Mott, attended Parker's lectures, and consumed Parker's writings. "I have heard a course of lectures from him and am now reading his discourses," she told a friend in 1846. "He finds my soul—he speaks to me or rather God (through him) to me." In Parker's *Discourse of Matters Pertaining to Religion* she found the union of transcendentalism, rationalism, and radical Christianity that both inspired her and made sense to her. Cady Stanton rehearsed Parker's arguments in her mind, still haunted by what she called her "dark Scotch Presbyterian days." Parker shared her passions and lifted her self-esteem. He provided the overall religious worldview that she was seeking, which confirmed her central intuitions while leaving room for the development of her own thinking. When she and Stanton moved to Seneca Falls, New York, in 1847, she left her fulfilling Boston years behind with the hard-won assurance that in matters of religion and philosophy, she had found her way.[82]

Cady Stanton was happy in Boston, but Stanton suffered from poor health and tough political competition. Seeking health and opportunity in a less crowded environment, by moving his family to Seneca Falls, he inadvertently launched the modern feminist movement. In 1848 he helped organize New York state's Free Soil Party, but the following year he ran for the state Senate as a Democrat and won. Reelected three years later by five votes in a special election, he never held another elected position; all of his later positions were by appointment, as a Republican. Publicly his wife defended him stoutly, looking past his opportunistic failure to speak out for women's rights; privately she resented her isolation in a rural village of four thousand people. "Up to this time life had glided by with comparative ease, but now the real struggle was upon me," she later recalled. She was miserable in Seneca Falls; she felt buried in housework, her boys caught malaria, even her servants came down with chills and fever, and she was lonely: "I suffered with mental hunger, which, like an empty stomach, is very depressing. I had books, but no stimulating companionship." For the first time she reflected on "the practical difficulties most women had to contend with in the isolated household, and the impossibility of woman's best development if in contact, the chief part of her life, with servants and children." Even in later life she had difficulty remembering that "most women" did not have servants.[83]

In her isolated misery she received a saving invitation to spend a day with Lucretia Mott, who was visiting friends in nearby Waterloo while attending the yearly convention of Hicksite Quakers. Sitting at tea with four sympathetic Quaker women, Cady Stanton poured out "the torrent of my long-accumulating discontent with such vehemence that I stirred myself, as well as the rest of the party, to do and dare anything." They wrote the call of the Seneca Falls convention that night and published it the following day. Lucretia Mott was the oldest of the group at fifty-four, Cady Stanton the youngest at thirty-two. Mott was the only member who had any experience as a conference organizer or speaker; Cady Stanton was the only one who was not a Quaker or Garrisonian abolitionist.[84]

The women agreed to model their "Declaration of Sentiments and Resolutions" on the Declaration of Independence, substituting "all men" for the tyrant King George; their resolutions were explicitly political, owing to the fact that Cady Stanton wrote them. Eleven were presented to the convention, which attracted more than a hundred men and women. Cady Stanton's resolutions spelled out the implications of the ruling sentiment that all men and women are created equal and are endowed by their Creator with the inalienable rights of life, liberty, and the pursuit of happiness. Despite the objections of Henry Stanton, who did not attend the convention, her ninth resolution called for female suffrage. Three of the Quaker organizers also opposed the suffrage plank, but Mott overruled them out of affection for her protégé. Mott subsequently added a twelfth resolution that called for the overthrow of the male monopoly of the pulpit "and for the securing to woman an equal participation with men in the various trades, professions and commerce." Abolitionist leader Frederick Douglass attended the convention; he and Cady argued forcefully that suffrage was the one right that secured all the others. The Seneca Falls convention debated this claim at length before passing the suffrage resolution narrowly; the other resolutions passed unanimously. At Cady Stanton's initiative, women's rights became something to talk about in the United States.[85]

The organizers were stunned by the insults they inspired. The *Worcester Telegraph* called them Amazons "bolting with a vengeance." The *Rochester Advertiser* called them "extremely dull and uninteresting, and, aside from their novelty, hardly worth notice." The Philadelphia *Public Ledger and Daily Transcript* declared: "A woman is nobody. A wife is everything. A pretty girl is equal to ten thousand men, and a mother is, next to God, all powerful." The "ladies of Philadelphia" therefore resolved "to maintain their rights as Wives, Belles, Virgins, and Mothers, and not as Women." Much of the publicity caricatured the organizers as angry radicals or sour old maids, conveniently overlooking the fact that all of them were devoted mothers and wives who had not, as Cady Stanton observed, "experienced the coarser forms of tyranny resulting from unjust laws, or association with immoral and unscrupulous men." The Seneca Falls organizers were not enraged victims speaking from their experiences of abuse, yet they perceived an immense wrong. In Cady Stanton's phrase, they were "fortunately organized and conditioned," yet they bravely spoke against the wrong done to women, because "they had souls large enough to feel the wrongs of others, without being scarified in their own flesh." She also reminded her comrades that at least people were finally talking about women's rights.[86]

For the next dozen years the initiatives belonged to others. While Cady Stanton's family expanded to seven children, she received little domestic help from her husband, who was absorbed in political maneuverings. Though not overwhelmed, she was certainly burdened with "the woman's problem" that she vividly described in personal letters and calls to action. In the spring of 1850 a group of abolitionists meeting at the American Anti-Slavery Convention in Boston issued a call for a national women's rights convention in October; one of the organizers was Lucy Stone, a recent graduate of Oberlin College. For the next decade the movement existed only as a series of ad hoc local initiatives, some of them called "national" conventions. Throughout the 1850s each convention of what came to be called the Women's Rights Society opened with a letter from Cady Stanton, but she did not attend a national meeting until 1860, and she gave as much energy to the cause of temperance as to women's rights. The feminist movement remained undefined and effectively leaderless as Cady Stanton coped with her boisterous children, and Mott and Lucy Stone kept low profiles. Susan B. Anthony, an unmarried Rochester activist, fumed that the movement's leaders were absorbed in their children and home-improvement plans but needed several years herself to develop into a movement leader. Cady Stanton befriended Anthony and wrote speeches for her, but the movement floundered in the mid-1850s, as the Kansas crisis and the controversy over the Supreme Court's *Dred Scott* decision pushed women's rights to the margin of consciousness even for many feminists.[87]

Between 1854 and 1860 Cady Stanton delivered only one speech, a stemwinder to the New York state legislature that made a case for the equal rights of women. In her official version of this event, her father Daniel Cady was moved to tears by the eloquence of the first draft and helped her strengthen its legal arguments. He asked her where she had learned to feel so keenly the wrongs of her sex; she replied that it was in his office, listening to the complaints that women brought to him. Other sources tell a different story: Judge Cady tried to bribe her into not giving the speech, then threatened to disinherit her if she gave it, then stormed out of the room. Whether he carried through on his threat to disinherit her is unknown, but Cady Stanton stopped giving speeches on the subject until after her father's death in 1859, and she confided to Anthony in 1855: "I passed through a terrible scourging when last at my father's. I cannot tell you how deeply the iron entered my soul. I never felt more keenly the degradation of my sex." Then she moved to the subject of her husband. "Henry sides with my friends who oppose me in all that is dearest to my heart. They are not willing that I would write even on the woman question. But I will both write and speak." She ended by noting that these confidences were strictly confidential. Long after she became famous for protesting "the prolonged slavery of woman," Cady Stanton would claim for the record that at least her conservative father, if not her abolitionist husband, was on her side all along.[88]

In 1859, at the age of forty-three, she gave birth to her seventh child, with considerably less enthusiasm than she had felt for the previous six. Her normal exuberance was gone; she was ill and depressed; she wanted to energize her foundering movement; Anthony's bitter complaints about her breeding habits were beginning to sink in. "You need expect nothing from me for some time," she wrote to Anthony, trying to head off her criticism: "All I had & was has gone into the development of that boy." While she made her slow recovery, her father died, unreconciled to her, and John Brown raided Harper's Ferry with weapons bought by Theodore Parker, Gerrit Smith, and four others. The following year, with her father no longer alive to hear of it, she made a dramatic return to the public arena with a blistering attack on the institution of marriage.[89]

At the Tenth National Woman's Rights Convention at the Cooper Institute in New York City, Cady Stanton asserted that marriage was not a divine institution, but rather a human artifact that "has ever and always been a one-sided matter, resting most unequally upon the sexes." A man gave up nothing in marriage, she noted, but a woman gave up everything, "even the most sacred of all, the right to her own person." From the beginning of recorded history, "man has had the sole and whole regulation of the matter. He has spoken in Scripture, he has spoken in law. As an individual, he has decided the time and cause for putting away a wife, and as a judge and legislator, he still holds the entire control. In all history, sacred and profane, the woman is regarded and spoken of simply as the toy of man." Cady Stanton therefore urged that the right to divorce was essential to any movement that supported the rights of women. After various feminists protested that this was exactly what they did not believe, and that her entire speech had no place in a women's rights convention, Anthony rose to her friend's defense. For women, she argued, the law was a tyrant; for men it was an instrument of domination: "Woman has never been consulted; her wish has never at all been taken into consideration as regards the terms of the marriage compact. By law, public sentiment, and religion, from the time of Moses down to the present day, woman has never been thought of other than as a piece of property, to be disposed of at the will and pleasure of man."[90]

That put women's rights back into the news. The New York press hammered Cady Stanton for weeks. The *New York Daily Tribune* found it "simply shocking" that she could think of marriage "as a business." The *Evening Post* condemned her "exceedingly loose view" of marriage and her advocacy of the right of divorce; it was "suicidal" for women to propose the abolition of marriage, since the whole point of marriage law was to protect women. The *New York Herald* found it "difficult to believe that the speakers were females." Condemning the speech as "infidel and licentious," the *New York Observer* reported that resolutions "which no true woman could listen to without turning scarlet, were unblushingly read and advocated by a person in woman's attire, named in the programme as Mrs. Elizabeth Cady Stanton." Having set off a media firestorm in New York, Cady Stanton returned to Seneca Falls just as her husband was preparing for an unusual experience of his own. Having picked more than his share of losers in politics, even when he was selling out one cause or another, Stanton picked a winner in 1860, when he backed Abraham Lincoln for president and worked hard on his campaign. After Lincoln was elected, Stanton hoped for a major cabinet position; in the end he received a minor Treasury post as deputy collector of the customs house in New York City. His wife rejoiced that at least she was finally leaving Seneca Falls. She was already known in New York, and her children would not imprison her in America's greatest city.[91]

Against Anthony, who viewed the Civil War as a setback for the women's movement, Cady Stanton insisted that the war was a crusade for freedom. In New York, she could lead and speak for a feminist movement that welcomed the war. This was the historical turn for which the political abolitionists had struggled. "I have an unwavering faith in the endurance of the Republic," she wrote to Secretary of State William H. Seward. "This war is music to my ears. It is a simultaneous chorus for freedom; for every nation that has ever fought for liberty on her own soil is now represented in our army." She exulted that the turmoil and confusion of the moment were but "the noise and dust of the wagon bringing the harvest home." The war would create new possibilities in America for black males and all women alike, and this proposition was worth fighting for. After the war was over, however, and a Southerner was in the presidency, she judged that the moment had passed for the American sons of Africa.[92]

THE RIGHTS OF CITIZENS
AND THE FEMINIST SCHISM

Despite his considerable success, Henry Ward Beecher never really put the disaster of the Johnson mess behind him. He was too politically engaged for that to be possible; his world was too politicized, and he made unfortunate enemies. At the height of the controversy over Reconstruction, when Tilton furiously attacked Beecher for political apostasy, relations cooled between the two ministers, though not to the point of outward unfriendliness. Tilton remained a member of Beecher's congregation (though he rarely came to church), and Beecher continued to socialize with Tilton and his wife Elizabeth, often visiting them in their home. Beecher's withdrawal from the battle over Reconstruction made it easier for the two ministers to deal with each other. Beecher's adoption of women's suffrage as one of his causes made dealing with each other unavoidable, for Tilton moved to the culturally radical edge of liberal Republican politics in the later 1860s, becoming a champion of women's rights, divorce reform, and, arguably, free love.

The conflicting claims of two great causes and the politics of the Fourteenth Amendment fractured American reform politics after the Civil War. The Fourteenth Amendment was bitterly opposed not only by the likes of Andrew Johnson, but also by the founding mothers of American radical feminism, Elizabeth Cady Stanton and Susan B. Anthony. This historical development was complicated by the fact that essentially the same group of people belonged to both the Anti-Slavery Society and the Women's Rights Society. In the early months of 1866, while the Fourteenth Amendment was being drafted, many activists made a slogan of the phrase "this moment belongs to the Negro." Longtime abolitionist leader Wendell Phillips was prominent among them. Cady Stanton countered that the daughters of Jefferson and Adams were not going to defer to uneducated black males. "We have fairly boosted the negro over our own heads, and now we had better begin to remember that self-preservation is the first law of nature," she resolved. To Phillips she scolded, "It is better to be the slave of an educated white man, than that of a degraded, ignorant black one." Her letters began to press the point with tartly bigoted phrases. On her better days she still agreed with Tilton that the two causes needed to be fused together, but she increasingly signaled her readiness to abandon "Sambo," as she put it, for educated white woman suffrage alone. In the spring of 1866, Tilton proposed that the Anti-Slavery Society and the Women's Rights Society merge into a new organization called the American Equal Rights Association. He pitched this idea to Frederick Douglass, who immediately approved, but Phillips and Cady Stanton both disapproved. The question was publicly debated at the succeeding conventions of both groups, which took place on the same day, May 10, 1866, at the same place, the Church of the Puritans in Union Square, New York.[93]

The Fourteenth Amendment, which had been officially introduced into Congress ten days earlier, granted citizenship to ex-slaves, curbed the president's pardoning power, and sharply reduced the congressional representation of any state that denied the vote to any male citizen. Cady Stanton and Anthony agreed that the gender restriction was disastrous for women; it reinforced the legal status of women as nonpersons at the very moment when feminists had hoped to gain all the rights of citizenship. After consulting with Tilton, Anthony resolved to press the idea of a merger. Her resolution was voted down at the Anti-Slavery Society, where it was opposed by Phillips; but at the Women's Rights Society meeting that followed, Phillips explained that he still supported both causes; he insisted only that priority had to be given to suffrage for black males. As a gesture in the direction of universality, Anthony proposed changing the name of the Women's Rights Society to the American Equal Rights Association. The resolution passed and solidarity was gained. Although the two causes were still represented by different organizations, the women had made a statement for inclusivity.[94]

Then it was Beecher's turn to speak. Since he was virtually a member of the Johnson administration, Beecher had little credibility in these circles on the subject of antislavery politics, though he still considered himself an antislavery leader. He strongly supported the Tilton-Anthony proposal to merge the two organizations. In the guise of humor, with an icy edge, Tilton displayed hostility toward his mentor for the first time, introducing Beecher as a man of great modesty and shyness. Bristling with performance excitement, Beecher mounted the platform and launched a speech on "Woman's Duty to Vote." Moving straight to the question of the moment and asking why advocates of voting rights for former slaves should press the issue of female suffrage in 1866, he answered, "Because the question is one and the same." Beecher passed on the current politics of the former issue—"That is the case in court"—before assuring the crowd that he supported giving the vote to Americans of African descent and Americans of Irish descent alike: "We shall give it to them." The convention applauded and Beecher turned to his theme.[95]

The "greatest development of the suffrage question" was the movement for women's suffrage, he asserted: "It is more important that woman should vote than that the black man should vote." Giving the vote to males of African or Irish descent was important, he explained, but feminism was a revolutionary restoration; it was not merely a reform, but transformative, returning things to their true form. Beecher reached for the strongest way of saying it: the movement for women's rights sought to restore the divine order of things. "I claim that woman should vote because society will never know its last estate and true glory until you accept God's edict and God's command—long raked over and covered in the dust—until you bring it out, and lift it up, and read this one of God's Ten Commandments, written, if not on stone, yet in the very heart and structure of mankind, *Let those that God joined together not be put asunder.*"[96]

This was not a religious occasion, however, and Beecher quickly returned to politics. The vote is a schoolmaster, he reflected; it teaches and requires citizenship. In America, the vote was not the representative of class privilege, "as it is in England, worn like a star, or garter, saying, 'I have the king's favor or the government's promise of honor.'" In America, voting was like breathing: "It belongs to us as a common blessing. He that does not vote is not a citizen with us." That was the point: American women deserved to be citizens, and more important, had a duty to exercise citizenship. America's leading preacher of Victorian virtue blasted its cult of domesticity, even as he took women's maternal nature for granted as an argument for his side: "I say that more and more the great interests of human society in America are such as need the peculiar genius that God has given to woman. The questions that are to fill up our days are not forever to be mere money questions. Those will always constitute a large part of politics; but not so large a portion as hitherto. We are coming to a period when it is not merely to be a scramble of fierce and belluine passions in the strife for power and ambition. Human society is yet to discuss questions of work and the workman. Down below privilege lies the masses of men." To deal rightly with these issues, he asserted, America needed its women to be citizens: "Is there a man who does not know, that when questions of justice and harmony are blended, woman's instinct is better than man's judgment?"[97]

Beecher gave short shrift to "woman's place" arguments: "A woman that is content to wash stockings, and make Johnny-cake, and to look after and bring up her boys faultless to a button, and that never thinks beyond the meal-tub, and whose morality is so small as to be confined to a single house, is an undergrown woman, and will spend the first thousand years after death in coming to that state in which she ought to have been before she died." He gave thanks that his own mother was not the kind of woman who "never thought of anything outside of her own door-yard." To those who claimed that politics was too vulgar for women, he replied that politics was unspeakably vulgar because the political sphere was entirely dominated by men. Female citizens would make it less vulgar. To those who persisted that a woman's place was in her home, Beecher offered two more arguments. First, the American public welfare needed the informed judgment, care, and virtues of its women: "Universal beneficence never hinders anybody's usefulness in any particular field of duty. Therefore, woman's sphere should not be limited to the household. The public welfare requires that she should have a thought of affairs outside of the household, and in the whole community." His second argument was tongue in cheek: "It is said, 'She ought to stay at home, and attend to home duty, and minister to the wants of father, or husband, or brothers.' Well, may all orphan women, and unmarried women, and women that have no abiding place of residence vote? If not, where is the argument?"[98]

To those who objected that a woman might vote for herself and take office, Beecher struggled to take the problem seriously: "Women, you are not educated for these offices. I hear bad reports about you. It is told me that the trouble in giving places to women is that they will not do their work well; that they do not feel the sense of conscience. They have been flattered so long, they have been called 'women' so long, they have had compliments instead of rights so long, that they are spoiled." Beecher asserted that these reports would cease after women became citizens. Women already worked harder than men, he admonished; the issue was citizenship, not comparative strength of will or conscience. He clinched his case by invoking the name of the world's most admired figure. "If I now, here in your midst, shall mention the name of Queen Victoria, your cheers will be a testimony to your admiration of this noble woman." The feminists cheered thunderously. Beecher continued, "Though it be in a political meeting, or any other public gathering, no man can mention her name without eliciting enthusiastic tokens of respect. And yet, the same men that cheer her will go home, and put on their spectacles, and argue that woman ought not to hold office?"[99]

This performance held the convention spellbound for an hour. The leaders of the newly named American Equal Rights Association may have taken Beecher's public standing too seriously as they applauded him uproariously, for his arguments were going nowhere in 1866, even if they played well at Plymouth Church. Determined to gain the rights of citizenship for women, Cady Stanton and Anthony organized campaigns to strike the word "male" from the Fourteenth Amendment and from the revised New York State Constitution; Cady Stanton ran for Congress in the Eighth District of New York; later, she, Anthony, Lucy Stone, and Henry Blackwell campaigned tirelessly for the vote in Kansas. In each case they were not only defeated, but subjected to a barrage of ridicule, condescension, and invective.

The frustrations of dealing with constant misogyny brought out the worst in Cady Stanton, and she undermined the movement's attempts to work cooperatively with antislavery radicals. Her strong sense of class and race superiority found voice in her speeches, and she was not above race-baiting in her frustration at being told to wait her turn. Cady Stanton and Anthony were both aggressively confrontational, self-righteous, and culturally radical in their advocacy of women's rights, and in Kansas they made a fateful alliance with a deep-pocketed racist showman, which sparked a schism in the feminist movement.[100]

George Francis Train made his fame by traveling around the world in eighty days, inspiring the novel by Jules Verne, and his fortune as the chief organizer of the Crédit Mobilier, a holding company for the stock of the Union Pacific Railroad. He wore purple jackets, lime-green satin vests, and red boots, and he supported white woman suffrage as a weapon against black political power. In Kansas he teamed with Cady Stanton and Anthony to campaign for female suffrage; in his case, the cause included vile speeches that denounced suffrage for "low-down nigger men." With his money, Cady Stanton and Anthony founded a brash weekly newspaper called *The Revolution,* which showcased the hate mail it received, especially about Train, and Cady Stanton's sharp editorial replies. Her alliance with Train enraged Phillips, William Lloyd Garrison, and other antislavery leaders, as well as feminist leaders Lucy Stone and Mary Livermore. Garrison protested to Anthony that Train was a "crack-brained harlequin and semi-lunatic," among other things; his letter was not written for publication, but it was printed in *The Revolution,* along with an editorial that ridiculed Garrison and praised Train. In 1867, the Fifteenth Amendment became the issue of the day. It stipulated that a U.S. citizen's right to vote cannot be denied or abridged on the grounds of race or previous condition of servitude. After feminist leaders were asked by their political "allies" not to oppose it for its gender exclusivism, Cady Stanton howled her doubt that the likes of Phillips and Greeley would be willing "to stand aside and trust their individual interests, and the whole welfare of the nation, to the lowest strata of manhood." If this was a plausible doubt, she asked, then how could it be that they asked "educated women" to stand aside "while 2,000,000 ignorant men are ushered into the halls of legislation?"[101]

This controversy over the politics of suffrage produced a schism between the New York and Boston branches of the American Equal Rights Association. The Boston branch, led by Lucy Stone, Mary Livermore, and Julia Ward Howe, was appalled by Cady Stanton's racism and opposed to the aggressively radical politics of Cady Stanton, Anthony, and their supporters. Stone's group spoke more mildly for the most part, was more moderate in its politics, and was strongly opposed to racist opportunism; it was also more friendly to mainline Christianity, males, and the notion that the present hour "belonged to the Negro." The New England feminists agreed with Clara Barton that if the door "was not wide enough for all at once—and one must wait, or *all* must wait, then I for one was willing that the old scarred slave limp through before me." Renaming their organization the New England Woman Suffrage Association, Stone's group declared the existence of a breach in the American Equal Rights Association, threatened an irrevocable schism in the national organization, and demanded that Stanton and Anthony break their association with Train.[102]

That set the stage for the last united convention of American feminists. The American Equal Rights Association convened on May 9, 1869, at Steinway

Hall, near Union Square in New York City. All three of its vice-presidents sat on the platform: Elizabeth Cady Stanton, Frederick Douglass, and Henry Ward Beecher; its president, Lucretia Mott, stayed home with the flu. Parkerite minister Octavius Brooks Frothingham in an opening statement declared that he expected a "generous, sweet atmosphere" to prevail at the meeting, but the fireworks began as soon as he finished speaking. Cady Stanton and Anthony were accused of harming the organization by associating with Train, while Anthony was accused of misusing the organization's funds by paying Train for his speeches. Having assumed the presiding chair in Mott's absence, Cady Stanton called for a vote of confidence; after she won the vote, she proceeded to defend herself and Anthony with a stunningly bigoted appeal.[103]

Cady Stanton and Train had already agreed to a parting of ways—Train left New York the following day—but she conceded nothing on the political substance at issue. The Republican Party had recently secured the addition of the Fifteenth Amendment to the Constitution (which was enacted the following year), she observed. This meant that "the lower orders of men" had become lawmakers, while women were forced to live under "the legislation of the ignorant African." Cady Stanton told the abolitionists to stop congratulating themselves on this achievement: "Think of Patrick and Sambo and Hans and Yung Tung, who do not know the difference between a monarchy and a republic, who cannot read the Declaration of Independence or Webster's spelling book, making laws for Lucretia Mott, Ernestine L. Rose, and Anna E. Dickinson." She condemned the amendment in the harshest possible terms: "On all the blackest pages of history, there is no record of an act like this, in any nation, where native born citizens, having the same religion, speaking the same language, equal to their rulers in wealth, family, and education, have been politically ostracized by their own countrymen, outlawed with savages, and subjected to the government of outside barbarians."[104]

The most ignorant men were always hostile to the equality of women, she noted; it was up to the Republicans, who were presently in power, to overcome the savages and barbarians: "It is an open, deliberate insult to American womanhood to be cast down under the iron-heeled peasantry of the Old World and the slaves of the New, as we shall be in the practical working of the Fifteenth Amendment, and the only atonement the Republican party can make is now to complete its work, by enfranchising the women of this nation." She pleaded the elementary justice of her case: "Shall American statesmen, claiming to be liberal, so amend their constitutions as to make their wives and mothers the political inferiors of unlettered and unwashed ditch-diggers, bootblacks, butchers and barbers, fresh from the slave plantations of the South, and the effete civilizations of the Old World?" What America needed was an infusion of new virtue into its public life, without which, she warned, postwar America was doomed to destruction. The crucial question was the kind of people to whom America would turn: "Will the foreign element, the dregs of China, Germany, England,

Ireland, and Africa supply this needed force, or the nobler types of American womanhood who have taught our presidents, senators, and congressmen the rudiments of all they know?"[105]

Frederick Douglass spoke next. He had not meant to speak at this convention, but he could not bear to remain silent. He had spoken at the Seneca Falls convention, had repeatedly advocated woman suffrage, and had long admired Cady Stanton, but he could not abide "the employment of certain names, such as Sambo, and the gardener, and the bootblack, and the daughters of Jefferson and Washington and all the rest that I cannot coincide with. I have asked what difference there is between the daughters of Jefferson and Washington and other daughters. I must say that I do not see how anyone can pretend that there is the same urgency in giving the ballot to woman as to the negro. With us, the matter is a question of life and death, at least in fifteen states of the Union. When women, because they are women, are hunted down through the cities of New York and New Orleans; when they are dragged from their houses and hung upon lamp-posts; when their children are torn from their arms and their brains dashed out upon the pavement; when they are objects of insult and outrage at every turn; when they are in danger of having their homes burnt down over their heads; when their children are not allowed to enter schools, then they will have an urgency to obtain the ballot equal to our own."[106]

Anthony immediately objected that all of this was true for black women; Douglass agreed, but admonished that it was true for them because they were black, not because they were women. Anthony held her ground, conceding nothing and insisting unequivocally that the higher class of nonenfranchised persons deserved to be enfranchised first: "The old anti-slavery school say women must stand back and wait until the negroes shall be recognized. But we say, if you will not give the whole loaf of suffrage to the entire people, give it to the most intelligent first. If intelligence, justice, and morality are to have precedence in the Government, let the question of woman be brought up first and that of the negro last."[107]

The radical feminists were finished with putting themselves second; if they had to insult the intelligence of blacks to be first, they were ready to do so. Fearing that their historical opportunity was slipping away, they cut their ties to the abolitionists and created a new organization, the National Woman Suffrage Association, which worked at the national level for a universal suffrage amendment. The group's founding leaders were Cady Stanton and Anthony; Tilton gave up his unity ideal and went with them as a fellow-travelling male supporter. Lucy Stone's New England group responded by forming its own national organization, the American Woman Suffrage Association, which supported the Fifteenth Amendment and continued the state-by-state strategy to attain women's suffrage.

The American Equal Rights Association was finished except for a handful of branches that declined to affiliate with either of the two new organizations. In a plot that proved to be too cunning by half, Cady Stanton and Tilton briefly changed the name of the National Association to the Union Woman Suffrage Society, absorbed some of the old Equal Rights Association branches, and then restored the name, National Woman Suffrage Association, after the group's 1870 convention. Strategically, Cady Stanton and Anthony judged that the state-by-state approach to suffrage politics was too arduous; philosophically, they judged that their former allies in the American Equal Rights Association were too preoccupied with postslavery issues, too Christian, and too conservative on cultural issues to press the case for women's rights.

Having friends on both sides of the feminist conflict, Beecher tried to mediate between them before the movement broke apart. There was a genuine political basis for him to do so; Beecher's claim that woman suffrage was more important than the immediate enfranchisement of former slaves gave ballast to the radical feminist side on the chief dispute at issue. At the same time, Beecher knew that his better friends were on the other side. Fitting better with the feminists who still believed in Victorian ideals and gentility, Beecher cringed at Cady Stanton's strident attacks on the evils of marriage, Christianity, and men in general. Cady Stanton dismissed scriptural teaching as male supremacist ideology; she gave increasingly unbridled expression to "my continuous wrath against the whole dynasty of tyrants in our political, religious, and social life"; she thundered that "the male element is a destructive force, stern, selfish, aggrandizing, loving war, violence, conquest, acquisition, breeding in the material and moral world alike discord, disorder, disease, and death." Upon launching the National Association in 1869, she and Anthony announced that their new organization would exclude males and attack the tyranny of church and law.[108]

Later that year, the American Woman Suffrage Association dramatized its markedly different sensibility by electing Beecher as its first president. Lucy Stone's moderate feminists highlighted their propriety and respectability by choosing a famous minister as their leader and positioned themselves as a good-spirited, inclusive alternative to Cady Stanton's exclusivist, anti-Christian organization. The factional nature of his new position caused Beecher some embarrassment; he felt the irony of his agreement to lead the side he had recently stood against. He was the one who had urged the American Equal Rights Association to replace expediency with the principle of "manhood and womanhood suffrage for all." His rationale for his new position was less convincing: "If there are two general associations for the same purpose, it is because we mean in this great work to do twice as much labor as one society could possibly do." Nobody believed that. Resolving to make a show of force in the National Association's home base, with a good deal of anger at the member-stealing of its rival, the American Association held its 1870 national convention in New York City during the same week that the National Association/Union Society held its own national convention there.[109]

Beecher's New England feminists drew huge crowds and favorable press; Cady Stanton's New York feminists got neither. On the second day of their convention, the New York feminists made a desperate countermaneuver, resolving to change their image by installing "a popular man" as a counterweight to Beecher. Under the leadership of Beecher's youngest sister, Isabella Beecher Hooker, the convention asked Cady Stanton and Anthony to resign their offices. Cady Stanton had tired of organization politics and was eager to develop her burgeoning lecture career on James Redpath's national Lyceum circuit, which followed the new railroad. By then most of her children were grown, her marriage was effectively finished, and the Lyceum circuit was enormously popular and lucrative. With ideological reluctance, but a stronger sense of personal relief, she resigned the presidency and agreed to rescind the organization's ban on male members. Her decision galled Anthony, who reluctantly resigned her office. The "popular man" was never in doubt, as the National Woman Suffrage Association elected Theodore Tilton as its next president. Having cultivated close relationships with all the players on the movement's radical wing, Tilton agreed to front for it. Since Anthony was incurring great debt trying to keep *The Revolution* going, Tilton arranged to have his friend, heiress Laura Curtis Bullard, take over as owner and editor of the paper. *The Revolution* was now in the hands of the heiress of Winslow's Soothing Syrup, who bought an extra house in Brooklyn so she could be closer to Tilton and her new hobby.[110]

For the next twenty years, the National and American suffrage organizations were rivals, as personal and ideological conflicts kept the two organizations from working together or even communicating very much. The National Association was also plagued with internal leadership conflicts after relations between Cady Stanton and Anthony soured in the early 1870s. Anthony resented Cady Stanton's egotism, her various self-indulgences, her frequent thoughtlessness, her popularity with Lyceum audiences, her embrace of Victoria Woodhull, and her obesity, approximately in that order; Cady Stanton wearied of being scolded. Referring to rumors of their "dissolved partnership," she asked Anthony in 1870, "Have you been getting a divorce out in Chicago without notifying me? I should like to know my present status." In 1871, Victoria Woodhull's sensational call for free love and cultural revolution heightened the National Association's reputation for cultural radicalism; at the same time, Cady Stanton grieved at the ascension of Isabella Beecher Hooker to leadership status. Hooker, a headstrong, culturally mannered devotee of spiritualism, smitten with Woodhull, steered the National Association away from Cady Stanton's harsh rhetoric and nativist prejudices; Cady Stanton complained that Hooker shared the Beecher family egotism. The National Association got off to a weaker start than its organizational rival and was nearly destroyed by its backing of Woodhull's bizarre 1872 presidential campaign on the Equal Rights Party ticket. It never made much headway among working-class women; on the strength of Anthony's activist organizational labors, Cady Stanton's lecture circuit fame, and its own institutional maturation, however, it made significant gains among previously unpoliticized professional-class women, especially in the fields of education and journalism.[111]

By contrast, the American Association kept the faith that the Republican Party would enact woman suffrage after it enfranchised all males regardless of color. Lucy Stone's New England feminists were sadly mistaken about the Republicans; woman suffrage got a brief mention in the 1872 Republican convention platform and nothing afterward. Stone and Cady Stanton disliked each other and disagreed about the social and political goals of feminism. With each organization accusing the other of making morally unacceptable alliances, leaders on both sides rarely spoke to each other, except to argue; Beecher and Tilton were the exceptions, but not for long. The Beecher scandal unfolded against this background. The radical feminists with whom Tilton allied himself were horribly wrong to descend to nativist race-baiting and outright racist bigotry, but they were right to protest, in 1870, that a precious opportunity for woman suffrage was slipping away.

THE GREAT BEECHER SCANDAL

The Great Beecher Scandal is something like the O. J. Simpson case of the 1990s and something like the Alger Hiss case of the 1950s. Like the former, it transfixed the nation for months; like the latter, many who entered it never came out. In Beecher's time there were three main versions of the story and many attempts to hammer out bridges to link these versions; 125 years later the bridge-building is still going on. To search for the historical truth is to confront a maze of self-serving fictionalizing, since all three of the main versions are loaded with unverifiable claims and personal agendas. To explain the Beecher scandal concisely is impossible; even to try, one must begin by getting a fix on Beecher's immense public stature in the early 1870s. In 1872, Yale University launched an endowed lecture series called the Lyman Beecher Lectures on Preaching. The first, second, and third Lyman Beecher lecturer was Henry Ward Beecher, who had not been sufficiently studious as a youth to attend Yale. For three years, he dispensed fascinating advice to Yale theology students on how to write sermons, conduct prayer meetings, choose appropriate hymns, and the like. He opined that Calvin's doctrine of God was not Christian, he dispensed homely advice on staying healthy, and he urged that love is "the central element of the ministry." The latter theme yielded his most revealing remark: "When you kindle to a full sympathy with God and man, you can preach anything you please. You can say anything you please; if it goes with a reasonable degree of wisdom and a great degree of sympathetic love, it will be warmly received."[112]

Certainly that was his own experience. Beecher's powers to inspire lifted him to new heights of public admiration and spurred him to assorted new ventures after his disastrous dalliance with Andrew Johnson. He wrote *Norwood* and severed his connections with the increasingly radical *Independent*. He repaired his relations with establishment Republicans and supported President Grant. His friendship with financier John Howard Tasker, an investor in the John B. Ford publishing syndicate, led to lucrative contracts for several volumes of sermons and a best-selling book on the life of Christ. His friendship with Samuel Wilkeson, who was Cady Stanton's brother-in-law and a chief agent for the rapidly expanding Northern Pacific Railroad, garnered him $15,000 worth of stock for the purpose of "influencing the public mind to favor the new railroad." He became a featured performer on the Lyceum circuit and thus enriched himself doubly off the new railroad. His new chief lieutenant, District Attorney Benjamin Tracy, organized a tightly knit group of Plymouth Church Republicans that vied for control of Brooklyn's political patronage; onlookers called them "Beecher's Boys." In 1870, Beecher and Ford launched a new journal, *The Christian Union* (later renamed *The Outlook*), with help from Howard and Wilkeson. The fact that Tilton took a radical-left turn during this period confirmed Beecher in his moderate self-image, though Tilton cautioned various critics that Beecher's theology and politics were not much different from his own. The fact that Beecher launched a rival journal after withdrawing his popular sermons from the *Independent* made Tilton and Bowen furious.[113]

Beecher's new magazine swiftly capitalized on his fame, and by the end of its first year, *The Christian Union* had 30,000 subscribers; by 1872, it had 132,000. Beecher gave every appearance of being too big to bring down. Prosperous and admired, he sloughed off attacks from religious conservatives; he became a national champion of an old cause, temperance, and a new one, women's rights. *Scribner's Monthly* described him as a national treasure, noting that his style was "unconstrained, free, full, flowing, exuberant, and spontaneous . . . [yet] with all his ideality, he never ceases to teach common sense." Buoyant and charming, Beecher was the master of the powerhouse speech that conveyed the appearance of intimacy. At critical points stretching over a five-year period, however, the shower of adulation that fell upon him became hard to bear for certain insiders who knew about his sexual indiscretions. Tilton seethed in silence for four years before giving in to the urge to bring him down. The following year he showed that Henry Ward Beecher was not too big to bring down at least a few pegs.[114]

His decision to engulf Beecher, himself, and his wife in scandal was linked to Tilton's left-wing criticism of the Grant administration. The actions behind the scandal began at what appeared to be the height of Tilton's power. By 1870, after nine years of managing *The Independent,* he had tripled the paper's subscription and advertising revenue and made it the most influential religious weekly in the country, with over half a million readers. His success was a problem for the paper's owner, Henry Bowen, because Bowen wanted to ingratiate himself with President Grant, while Tilton repeatedly blasted the Grant administration for its corruption, its opportunism, and its failure to carry out a progressive Reconstruction of the former slaveholding states. On more than one occasion, in a notoriously corrupt political environment, Tilton showed himself to be personally incorruptible, spurning political bribes and refusing to be intimidated by power brokers whom Bowen was eager to please. This gave Bowen plenty of reason to want to get rid of his successful and powerful editor; doing it was another matter.

The Beecher scandal began on July 4, 1870, when Elizabeth Tilton confessed to her completely surprised husband that her "passionate fondness" for Beecher had developed into a fifteen-month sexual affair. In the version of the story that circulated among radical feminists, chiefly on Victoria Woodhull's telling, Elizabeth was also pregnant with Beecher's child. Theodore Tilton later emphasized that his wife began the affair shortly after the death of their infant son Paul, when she was "in a tender frame of mind" and that Beecher was her pastor. In Woodhull's version of the story he also claimed that he took the news quite well at first. He and Elizabeth Tilton did not have a good marriage, and they knew very well that Beecher's marriage was a disaster. Tilton may have informed his wife that he indulged himself sexually on the lecture circuit, and his sexual relationship with Laura Curtis Bullard was widely presumed in their circle of friends. Cady Stanton later claimed that on another occasion during the same year, in the presence of Susan B. Anthony, both Tiltons heatedly confessed to adultery. In the Woodhull version Tilton resolved, at first, to remain a free lover, telling his wife that there was no reason why they couldn't all enjoy themselves. He felt so uplifted by his own magnanimity—"For two weeks I lived a kind of ecstasy"—that he decided to introduce his wife to his lover. Tilton was delighted when Bullard and Elizabeth became friends, and the three of them felt very progressive for several weeks, until Tilton noticed Elizabeth's thickening body, quickly did the math, and "realized" that his wife was pregnant with Beecher's child. "It is his!" he shouted; soon thereafter, Tilton renounced his "advanced social theories," at least for his wife.[115]

Something like this is the way the scandal started, though Elizabeth Tilton probably was not pregnant with Beecher's child. Theodore Tilton's subsequent version of the story made no claim about a Beecher pregnancy and admitted to no free-love enthusiasm on his part; Woodhull's version (recently championed by Barbara Goldsmith) is more convincing in its claims about Tilton than about Beecher's impregnation of Tilton's wife; in Beecher's version the cause of the scandal was Tilton's professional downfall and his bizarre tryst with Woodhull. Woodhull got her original story from Cady Stanton and feminist activist Paulina Wright Davis; later Theodore Tilton was a prime source of her information. But it remains a matter of conjecture exactly what she heard from them and what she made up. She claimed that Davis told her of Elizabeth's pregnancy, but Davis and Elizabeth Tilton both denied that they discussed Elizabeth's personal life. She probably heard the accusation from Tilton, who raged at home that he didn't know which of his children belonged to him, but Tilton never publicly charged that Beecher impregnated his wife. In December 1870 Elizabeth Tilton did lose a child, probably to miscarriage; she called it her "love babe." Woodhull reported that Elizabeth suffered a miscarriage and that the child was Beecher's; Goldsmith claims that Beecher was the father and that Elizabeth went to an abortionist. At the Beecher trial, however, Tilton testified that his wife's affair with Beecher began on October 10, 1868, and ended fifteen or sixteen months later. If the affair ended in early February or earlier, the child could not have been fathered by Beecher. Moreover, Elizabeth's nurse Lucy Mitchell testified at the Beecher trial that Elizabeth suffered a miscarriage when she was three months pregnant. At the Beecher trial, only Frank Moulton suggested that Beecher and Elizabeth might have conceived a child three months after Elizabeth confessed the affair to her husband. When pressed on the matter, Cady Stanton defended Woodhull's version of the story, calling it "substantially true." At the same time she implied that Woodhull's account was fictionalized at the edges. "Victoria's story is exaggerated, rather higher-colored than I heard it," she reported.[116]

The version that Cady Stanton heard and passed on to Woodhull was offered by Theodore Tilton on the day after he reportedly recognized his wife's pregnancy and jumped to conclusions. Cady Stanton, the Tiltons, Anthony, and Bullard had planned to have dinner together at Bullard's home, but a miscommunication (or, Elizabeth believed, a bit of deception on Cady Stanton's part) left Anthony and Elizabeth on their own. At dinner, in Woodhull's rendering, Tilton told Cady Stanton and Bullard that Beecher, "that abominable man," had ruined his life. He could accept free love, he assured; his own indiscretions showed that; what he could not accept was Beecher's lecherous deceit in crawling like a snake into his home and impregnating his wife. Upon returning home, Tilton found Anthony in the parlor with Elizabeth; his wife had told Anthony everything. An ugly scene followed; Tilton told Anthony to leave, but Anthony feared for Elizabeth's safety. Anthony, standing up to Tilton, spent the night at his house and was told by him the following morning, in a snarling voice, "Never enter my house again." For years afterward Anthony frustrated reporters and comrades alike by refusing to tell what she knew, but she did tell Cady Stanton, who replied that Theodore Tilton told the same story. Shortly after Anthony left the Tiltons' home, Elizabeth's mother, Mrs. Morse, entered the picture. She clubbed Tilton with her parasol and shouted that none of this would have happened if he had not spent his evenings at meetings on women's rights.[117]

By November the story had multiple versions and an impossible maze of subplots. Elizabeth later recounted that Tilton grew morbid and bitter at home, wondered aloud which children were his, and railed against Beecher and herself for betraying him. He was inclined to believe the worst about Beecher, having been warned for years by Bowen that Beecher was a sexual predator. Elizabeth begged him to stop maligning Beecher and herself: "When you say to my beloved brother—'Mr. B. preaches to forty of his m[istresses] every Sunday,' then follow with the remark that after *my* death you have a dreadful secret to reveal, need he be told any more ere the sword pass into *his* soul?" The following month Mrs. Morse sent word to Beecher that Theodore Tilton had made immoral proposals to a young female boarder and that Elizabeth needed advice about separating from her husband. This story strengthened Beecher in his dealings with Bowen and later raised doubts about Tilton at the Beecher trial. In the early going, though, the key player was Bowen. Elizabeth Tilton suffered a miscarriage on December 23, 1870; later that day, Mrs. Morse wrote a blistering letter to Bowen that accused her son-in-law of being a lecherous philanderer, drunkard, and heathen. The letter stoked Bowen's deepening resentment of Tilton; Bowen hated Tilton's increasingly radical politics, which caused trouble for Bowen's Christian magazine on cultural issues and alienated the *Independent* from the Grant administration. Tilton was rumored to have a mistress—Laura Curtis Bullard—and a supply of lecture circuit paramours. In recent weeks he had editorialized in the *Independent* that marriage without love is sinful and that, by this standard, most marriages were adulterous. Bowen was ready to fire him. After consulting with Beecher, he confronted Tilton with his mother-in-law's accusations, the editorial, and the story about the female boarder. Tilton countered that the real issue was that Beecher had seduced his wife.[118]

For a moment Bowen and Tilton bonded; both had been cuckolded by Beecher. They agreed that Beecher had to resign from Plymouth Church and leave Brooklyn; Tilton wrote a letter to Beecher demanding his resignation for unspecified reasons, and Bowen delivered the letter personally. Tilton naïvely trusted Bowen to represent their shared position on the matter. Bowen's foremost consideration was President Grant, however, for his falling-out with Beecher had hurt him badly. Tilton belonged to the radical Republican wing that disapproved of the Grant administration's corruption and the machine politics of Brooklyn's Republican establishment; Beecher was a Grant-supporting regular Republican who found Tilton overly moralistic on the subject of machine politics. Bowen wanted desperately to be readmitted to Beecher's social and political circle, and so he gave Tilton's letter to Beecher under the guise of neutrality; he was just the deliveryman. Beecher was dumbfounded by Tilton's demand. The letter made no sense to him, he said; it was pure insanity. He asked for Bowen's position on the matter; Bowen surmised that Beecher still did not know that Elizabeth Tilton had confessed everything to her husband. He judged that his best chance to ingratiate himself with the Grant administration was to sell out Tilton and cut a deal with Beecher. He was finished with Tilton anyway; *Independent* readers were filling his mailbox with complaints about Tilton's heathenish cultural opinions. The bargaining commenced immediately: Tilton was to be fired as editor of *The Independent* and the *Brooklyn Daily Union,* while Beecher agreed to say nice things about Bowen to Grant, give Bowen a financial interest in the J. B. Ford syndicate, and allow Bowen to publish his sermons in *The Independent.*[119]

That night Elizabeth Tilton advised her husband that Beecher was undoubtedly confused by the letter demanding his resignation, because she had not carried out her promise to inform him of her confession. The next day, Bowen and

Beecher had long overdue confrontations with Tilton. Bowen threatened to fire Tilton if he told Beecher about Bowen's role in composing the letter demanding his resignation, but Tilton apparently realized that he was going to be fired anyway. He, in turn, arranged a meeting with Beecher and accused him of corrupting Elizabeth. Producing a written confession from Elizabeth Tilton, Tilton read it to Beecher, whose face, head, and neck turned "blood-red," in Tilton's account: "I feared for the moment that there would be some accident to him. He burst out with these words: 'Theodore, I am in a dream; this is Dante's inferno.'" Elsewhere Tilton recalled that Beecher began to blubber about killing himself, not for the last time. "You have a right to kill me," he declared. "I have forfeited my life to you. Take it." Beecher later admitted at Plymouth Church that the news of Elizabeth's confession "fell like a thunderbolt on me." Tilton told Beecher that they were obliged to make peace and that Beecher would have to live with his guilt as his punishment. Beecher asked for permission to see Elizabeth again "for the last time": Admonishing him not to scold her for confessing their adulterous relationship, Tilton warned: "I have hitherto spared your life when I had power to destroy it; I spare it now for Elizabeth's sake; but if you reproach her I will smite your name before all the world." Beecher proceeded directly to Elizabeth's bedroom, began to cry at her bedside, and dictated a letter that revoked her confession, which she obediently wrote. Leaving Tilton's house, according to Tilton's testimony, Beecher staggered down the stairs and moaned to him, "This will kill me." He entrusted the letter of retraction to his friend Frank Moulton, who offered to serve as a mediator between Beecher and Tilton; Beecher also wrote to Moulton that he wished he were dead.[120]

All of this took place in December 1870, the mere beginning of the Beecher scandal. On New Year's Eve, Bowen told Beecher at a party that he had fired Tilton. Beecher later recalled that he winced upon hearing the news. It may have occurred to him that he had overplayed his hand. What he needed most was Tilton's silence, and he had not helped his cause by extracting a retraction from Elizabeth Tilton. Enraged by Beecher's manipulation of his wife, Tilton confronted Beecher in Moulton's home on January 3; he later testified that Beecher offered to resign his ministry, if Tilton required, with one request: "That if it be necessary for you to make a public recital of this case, that you will give me notice of your intention to do so, in order that I may either go out of the world by suicide, or else escape from the face of my friends by a voyage to some foreign land." Beecher had no travel plans. He counted on Tilton's unwillingness to be responsible for a scandal that would include the public disgrace of his wife. For the next three years Beecher struggled to secure Tilton's silence and cooperation. He stiff-armed Mrs. Morse and enlisted Moulton to stifle her threats to expose him. He financed a new magazine for Tilton called the *Golden Age* by forwarding $7,000 to him through Moulton; Beecher raised the money by mortgaging his house, although Moulton told Tilton that it came from anonymous admirers. As long as Beecher and Tilton agreed to keep the matter private, Moulton posed as their mutual friend, but in the days of accusation he took Tilton's side and produced incriminating evidence against Beecher.[121]

For several years Tilton alternated between spilling his story to various acquaintances and scrambling to keep it private. Having told it first to Cady Stanton, he went to extraordinary lengths in 1871 to keep Victoria Woodhull from publishing it. Besides running for president as an advocate of free love, women's rights, and communicating with departed spirits, Woodhull published a weekly newspaper that promoted these causes; in partnership with her sister, Tennie C. Claflin, she also operated a brokerage firm. She was a flamboyant public speaker; friends and critics alike called her "The Woodhull." Born Victoria Claflin in Homer, Ohio, Woodhull and her sister achieved their success by attaching themselves to Cornelius Vanderbilt, who grieved for his deceased mother and son. Woodhull helped Vanderbilt search the spirit-world, Tennie C. effected a sexual liaison with him, and Vanderbilt financed their enterprises. In 1871, having heard the details of the Beecher fiasco from Cady Stanton's long-time associate, Paulina Wright Davis, and from Cady Stanton, Woodhull threatened to publish the story as an example of Victorian hypocrisy. She wanted Beecher to publicly champion free love, and Tilton and Beecher took her threat very seriously. They and Moulton devised a suppression strategy and agreed to appease her with friendship. Tilton resolved "to make her such a friend of mine that she would never think of doing me such a harm." Beecher made only token gestures in this direction, but Tilton more than fulfilled his assignment, becoming inseparable from Woodhull for more than a year. He published a fawning biography of her in the *Golden Age* that breathlessly lauded her brilliance, her ineffable beauty, and her extraordinary psychic powers; Woodhull was a magnificent champion of free love and a remarkable spiritual phenomenon, he declared. She frequently spoke to Demosthenes, among other departed spirits; her second marriage was decreed by the spirits in heaven; and she often performed miracles. On Woodhull's insistence Tilton reported that her miracles included at least one resurrection from the dead. In Indiana "she straightened the feet of the lame; she opened the ears of the deaf; she detected the robbers of a bank; she brought to light hidden crimes; she solved physiological problems; she unveiled business secrets; she prophecied future events." Tilton spent entire days and nights with her, and he may have been her lover; Woodhull practiced what she preached. She chided Tilton and Beecher for lacking the courage to preach what they practiced.[122]

For the most part Beecher avoided Woodhull, despite being exhorted by Tilton and Moulton to befriend her. He spurned Woodhull's demands for an interview on the grounds that he did not want to provoke conflict between the two wings of the women's rights movement. He finally agreed to be interviewed in June 1871 only after she renewed her threat to expose him. Some of Woodhull's reporting was clearly unreliable. She insinuated a carnal relationship with Beecher, for example; later she claimed not only that Tilton was her lover, but that for three months he slept in her arms every night; still later she insisted that she would never make the latter claim, even if it were true. However, Woodhull's later account of her June discussion with Beecher contained several quotes that sounded like him in his gender-bending expressionist mode. In her telling, he told of his early interest in mesmerism and confided that he kept a spirit table at Plymouth Church. He reported that he supported divorce reform: "Marriage is the grave of love. I have never married a couple that I did not feel condemned." When she asked why he didn't preach this conviction, Beecher replied that he did not wish to preach to empty seats. He preached the truth as fast as people could take it: "Milk for babies, meat for strong men."[123]

Holding to the hope that Beecher would support her cause, if not her presidential candidacy, Woodhull kept his confidences and bided her time. The year 1872 was a cruel one for her, however. Her campaign went badly, she was ridiculed and then shunned by the press, Cady Stanton switched her support to Grant and campaigned for him, Woodhull went bankrupt. Her relationship with Tilton damaged his reputation, and faced with cancelled lectures and financial ruin, Tilton ended their relationship. "I suddenly opened my eyes to her real tendencies to mischief, and then it was that I indignantly repudiated her acquaintance," he explained. He leaped at the chance to manage Horace Greeley's presidential campaign, which didn't help. Greeley was trounced by Grant in one of the ugliest campaigns in American history, and shortly after the election Greeley died. To outward appearances, Beecher seemed to be riding higher than ever, but inwardly he trembled at Tilton's power over him, confiding to Moulton that he was terrified by the prospect of being exposed. In his "ragged edge" letter to Moulton of February 1871, which became famous after the case went to court, he confided, "Nothing can possibly be so bad as the horror of great darkness in which I spend much of my time. To live on the sharp and ragged edge of anxiety, remorse, fear, despair, and yet put on all the appearance of serenity and happiness, cannot be endured much longer."[124]

On November 2, 1872, in a *Woodhull & Claflin's Weekly,* Woodhull and her sister published the story as she knew it in the form of an interview with herself by an unnamed reporter. She characterized her report as "aggressive moral warfare on the social question." Salacious details were provided and three sources were named: Isabella Beecher Hooker, Paulina Wright Davis, and Elizabeth Cady Stanton. Woodhull reported that Tilton's rage at being cuckolded was the cause of his wife's miscarriage and that Beecher preached to at least twenty of his mistresses every Sunday, an estimate that cut Tilton's in half. Cady Stanton judged that some of Woodhull's reporting was exaggerated but gave no specific examples. Editorializing on the meaning of it all, Woodhull asserted that marriage belonged to the same category of outmoded institutions as monarchy and slavery. She felt compelled to "ventilate" what she knew about the Beecher scandal's "putrid mass of seething falsehood and hypocrisy." Her conscience obliged her to "destroy the heap of rottenness which, in the name of religion, marital sanctity, and social purity, now passes as the social system." For a man of such powerful "amative impulses" as Beecher, she urged, free love was a necessity: "Every great man of Mr. Beecher's type, has had in the past and will ever have, the need for and the right to the loving manifestations of many women." Beecher's failing was hypocrisy, she insisted, not lechery. The 100,000-copy run sold out quickly, single copies selling for as high as $40. With the paper's appearance the scandal threatened to erupt far beyond Beecher's social circle. His lieutenants moved quickly to punish the offenders and intimidate would-be imitators. District Attorney Benjamin Tracy arrested the sisters on the day that their paper hit the streets, charging them with sending obscene matter through the United States mails, a federal offense. They spent six months in prison before the indictments against them were dismissed; in the meantime, Victoria Woodhull received no recorded votes in the presidential election.[125]

Beecher won the early battle to control the story, but not entirely. He dismissed Woodhull's newspaper as the ravings of two prostitutes and wrote a disavowal of the story for Tilton's use. He apparently took it for granted that Tilton shared his desire to discredit Woodhull's claims; instead he got a chastening preview of the nightmare to come. Refusing to disavow Woodhull's story, Tilton begged off on the curious ground that, as the husband of the slandered wife, he was not the "proper person" to issue a denial. In truth his resentment was eating at him. His life had exploded. He had lost both *The Independent* and his Christ-centered faith; his relationship with Woodhull had soiled his credibility; people looked the other way when they saw him; and his new periodical was doing poorly. In a few months he had lost his reputation and his national audience. His refusal to defend Elizabeth cut her deeply; she wailed against his "heartless" abandonment: "To you I owe this great injustice of exposure, such as has never before befallen a woman. Blow after blow, ceaseless and unrelenting these three years! O cruel spirit born of the devil of anger and revenge!" Tilton stewed in his resentment for a year and then slowly, fitfully moved toward a formal confrontation. For a while he tried to turn up the heat on Beecher while protecting his wife's reputation; temporarily reconciled to Elizabeth, Tilton told various acquaintances that Beecher made immoral proposals to her that she rebuffed. In 1873, however, he gave up his wife's reputation, obtained a fresh confession from her, and passed it on to a young journalist, Edward H. G. Clark, who published a single-edition newspaper on the scandal titled *The Thunderbolt*. The paper took its name from Beecher's reaction to Elizabeth's confession. Though Clark was appalled by Woodhull—he reported that she was enough of a menace to society to deserve hanging—he blasted the "monstrous conspiracy" that silenced and imprisoned her for publishing a story that needed to be told.[126]

Tilton incurred the wrath of Plymouth Church leaders for slandering their pastor, though Beecher conspicuously kept silent on the matter. After the church dropped Tilton from its rolls, his response set off a chain reaction that produced the Beecher trials. To Beecher's great distress, Tilton initiated an inquiry by the local Congregational church council that dragged Beecher's disapproving rival, Richard Storrs, into the picture. The inquiry backfired on Tilton—prominent churchman Leonard Bacon attacked him publicly as "a knave and a dog"—but it did produce a judgment that Plymouth Church needed to investigate its pastor. That judgment and Tilton's humiliation at being dropped from the rolls of Plymouth Church and attacked by Bacon set the Beecher trials into motion. Tilton resolved to defend his reputation by exposing Beecher. Needing the sympathetic ear of a woman, Beecher confided to Moulton's wife that the time had come to kill himself; Frank Moulton was not a Christian, but his wife Emma was a member of Plymouth Church. According to her subsequent testimony, Emma Moulton asked her pastor if, instead of killing himself, it wouldn't be better for him to confess his sin and ask Plymouth Church for forgiveness. Beecher ruled out that option: "I cannot do that; for the sake of the woman who has given me her love, for her children, for my family, for my church, for my influence throughout the whole world, that I can never do. I will die before I will confess it." When Emma Moulton counseled that the truth would eventually come to light anyway and it was better for him to con- fess it, Beecher was adamant that confession and forgiveness were out of play: "My children would despise me. I could not go back to my home, and my church would not forgive me, they would not deal with me as you have done. There would be nothing left for me to do. My work would be finished. It would be better that I should go out of life than to remain any longer in it." Beecher realized that he had a better chance of beating the charge than he had of living a postconfession life that he could stand to endure. He could not live without adulation; he could barely stand to imagine it. After four years of rumors, subplots, changes of position by both Tiltons, and vows of silence, he thus defended himself against the charge of seducing Elizabeth Tilton, first at Plymouth Church.[127]

At the Plymouth Church hearing, Theodore Tilton had the misfortune of being contradicted by his wife, who renounced her confession. This change of position, her next to last, was the decisive one for the Beecher trials. Elizabeth Tilton was dreamily vague on exactly how far she and Beecher had gone roman- tically, but she clearly denied that they had sexual relations. She defended her honor and the man she still loved against the accusations of her husband. She denied that she had confessed to any affair with Beecher on July 4, 1870; as for her written confession the following December, she explained that it was dic- tated to her by Tilton "when I was pretty nearly out of my mind" with emo- tional duress. Elizabeth admitted that she was guilty of a sin, not of having sex with Beecher, but of opening her heart in love to him. She confided that Tilton continually put her down, but Beecher always made her feel good about herself: "With Mr. Beecher I had a sort of consciousness of being more; he appreciated me as Theodore did not; I felt myself another woman; I felt that he respected me; I think Theodore never saw in me what Mr. Beecher did." Plymouth Church welcomed her spirited self-defense and the smooth assurances of its pas- tor, who confirmed that he and Elizabeth Tilton had never had improper relations. Beecher provided the story line for the press in his opening paragraph: "Four years ago Theodore Tilton fell from one of the proudest editorial chairs in America, where he represented the cause of religion, humanity, and patriotism, and in a few months thereafter became the associate and representative of Victoria Woodhull and the priest of her strange cause. By his follies he was bankrupt in reputation, in occupation and in resources." He had felt sorry for Tilton and tried to help him, but was abused for his trouble: "I can now see that he is and has been from the beginning of this difficulty a selfish and reckless schemer, pursuing a plan of mingled greed and hatred, and weaving about me a network of suspicions, misunderstandings, plots and lies, to which my own innocent words and acts, nay, even my thoughts of kindness toward him, have been made to contribute."[128]

Beecher admitted that he put too much trust in Frank Moulton, who conspired on Tilton's behalf. His version of the "thunderbolt" evening had Elizabeth Tilton explaining to him that she had made a confession of adultery as a ploy to win her husband's "reformation" by lowering herself to his level. As for Woodhull, Cady Stanton, Anthony, and other radical feminists who supported Tilton's accusation, Beecher explained that he had associated with them in recent years only because Tilton and Moulton had convinced him that it was necessary "to maintain friendly relations with the group of human hyenas." That insult enraged Cady Stanton and set off a windfall of bad press for the feminist movement. Isabella Beecher Hooker, having dared to cast aspersions on her brother's innocence, was another problem; Beecher's defenders took care of that problem by characterizing Hooker as a deluded misfit driven by an "unnatural" affection for Victoria Woodhull. Plymouth Church exonerated its pastor of all guilt, condemned Tilton as a vicious scoundrel, and censured Moulton for betraying Beecher's loyalty. Against her will, Anthony was dragged into the scandal by Cady Stanton, who publicized their role in it. After the Plymouth Church verdict, Cady Stanton apologized to Anthony for betraying her confidence, but exhorted her: "When Beecher falls, as he must, he will pull all he can down with him. But we must not let the cause of women go down in the smash. It is innocent."[129]

Defeated at Plymouth Church, Tilton took his accusation to civil court. Seeking to refute Elizabeth's portrait of him as cold and unappreciative, he published a sizable cache of excerpted Tilton-Tilton love letters from the late 1860s. Theodore's 112 letters to Elizabeth, like her 89 letters to him, were filled with fervent expressions of affection. The following year, in 1875, the case went to trial and created a national sensation. It was a front-page story for six months; the parallels with Nathaniel Hawthorne's *The Scarlet Letter* were labored repeatedly. Beecher was tried for alienating the affections of Elizabeth Tilton, a criminal offense. The main evidence against him consisted of his self-pitying nearly confessional letters, Elizabeth Tilton's love letters, and Beecher's various attempts to appease Theodore Tilton and keep the scandal out of public view. The prosecution emphasized that Beecher did not deny Tilton's accusation on the night of the thunderbolt; four years passed before he publicly denied it. Beecher countered that Tilton never explicitly charged him with adultery on the thunderbolt night and that he made no such accusation for four years. Eunice Beecher was one of the ninety-five witnesses who testified on her husband's behalf. She affirmed his simple goodness after hearing herself described day after day as cold, shrewish, and inhospitable; Tilton claimed that she scowled constantly. Members of Plymouth Church decorated the courtroom with flowers as a tribute to their pastor, who sniffed them to comfort himself. Tilton testified for fifteen days and Beecher for fourteen. The lawyering was spectacular on both sides; Beecher's six-attorney team was headed by superlawyer William M. Evarts, who had defended President Johnson from impeachment charges; Tilton's three-attorney team was led by William A. Beach, who approached Beecher with a studied mixture of worldly respect and moral contempt. Beecher spent more than $100,000 in his defense. On the basis of the trial testimony, his guilt must be judged as reasonably certain, though not proven; adding Elizabeth Tilton's last confession, the certainty hardens. But the prosecution lacked a smoking gun, all its key witnesses had credibility problems, and Beecher's lawyers tied up Tilton's testimony with legal objections pertaining to marital confidentiality. Aside from Tilton, the strongest prosecution witness was Frank Moulton, who testified that, having lied for Beecher and schemed with him for years, he was now telling the truth in testifying against him. Beecher defense lawyer John Porter quickly got the audience laughing at Moulton over his claim to being a truthful person.[130]

The key to the trial was Elizabeth Tilton, the witness who never testified. She had changed her position four times in the years that led up to the trial; she had set the legal process in motion with her confession of 1873, only then to recant her confession at the church hearing. At the civil trial she appealed for the opportunity to testify, but, by then, neither side wanted to hear from her. After the judge denied her request to read a statement, she gave it to the press. Shrewdly crafted from a legal standpoint, her statement bore the imprint of Beecher's lawyers. Elizabeth Tilton declared that she was innocent of the charge, but added, tantalizingly, that she wanted the opportunity to tell the story in her own words without revealing "the secret of my married life." Both sides preferred their chances without her testimony. The prosecution called only a dozen witnesses and failed to refute Beecher's story. Cady Stanton and Anthony were not called to testify, and Victoria Woodhull made a very brief appearance; Tilton's lawyers steered clear of the radical feminists. While Moulton gave precise accounts of conversations that seemed to presume Beecher's guilt, Beecher's memory was conveniently weak or vague on almost nine hundred occasions.

The summations alone lasted five weeks; Evarts and Beach gave dueling orations on good and evil that were heartily applauded by overflow audiences. In his charge to the jury, the judge instructed Beecher's Brooklyn peers not to be influenced by Tilton's idiosyncrasies—his relationship with Woodhull received much attention—or Beecher's exoneration at Plymouth Church. The twelve jurors, all small-business merchants, argued and voted while reporters climbed lampposts for a glimpse of their deliberations. After eight sweltering days, the jurors gave up: on their first ballot, they voted eight to four against Tilton; on their fifty-second ballot, they voted nine to three against Tilton. A mistrial was declared, and the church scandal of the century was over.[131]

Plymouth Church treated the verdict as an acquittal and celebrated Beecher's survival as a great victory for all things good. Most of the mainstream press took the same line, the dominant theme being that Tilton was a raving egotist who smeared a great man to avenge his own failures. *Harper's Weekly* judged that the entire case reduced to Tilton's resolve "to smite Mr. Beecher to the heart." More than a year later, an extraordinary representative council of the American Congregational churches was called to investigate the case and judged that Beecher was innocent. Two years after that, Elizabeth Tilton changed her story for the last time, asserting that she and Beecher had committed adultery: "The lie I had lived so well the last four years had become intolerable to me." Her letter was widely published, but the press and public dismissed her as hopelessly dishonest.

In his closing argument to the jury, William Beach had spent two days trying to reduce Beecher's exalted religious standing by convicting him of theological liberalism: Beecher believed in Darwinism, didn't believe in the divine inspiration of scripture, dismissed many of the biblical miracles, and taught that "men need not the blood of Christ." Was it so hard to believe that he also did not practice or believe in Christian morality? Beach pleaded with the jurors not to confuse Beecher with their concern for the moral influence of Christianity. The church had survived many worse catastrophes than the loss of a famous preacher like Henry Ward Beecher, he assured.[132]

But to Brooklyn and much of America, Beecher epitomized the progress of Christian influence. He was Mr. Christianity. It could not be that a man of such refined nobility and loving Christian kindness could be guilty of the cunning deceits attributed to him. It was much easier to despise Tilton. Moulton told Plymouth Church that he intervened in the case because he feared that the scandal would "undermine the very foundations of social order." America shared his original intuition about the meaning of the Beecher case. Beecher was tainted and personally wounded by the scandal, but the Beecher industry, which had climbed to new heights during the scandal, continued to thrive after it. Wilkeson bragged to his sister-in-law, Cady Stanton, that the scandal lifted Beecher's book sales "higher than a kite." To Cady Stanton, that boast effectively summed up why Beecher was too big to bring down: Victorian America could not convict its fondest self-image or silence his voice.[133]

Beecher understood what he lost in the process of prevailing over his accusers. Though his outward fame, his book sales, and his audiences grew after the trial, even Beecher's admirers acknowledged that the scandal had diminished his genuine religious authority. "I have not been pursued as a lion is pursued, I have not been pursued even as wolves and foxes," he lamented after the trial. "I have been pursued as if I were a maggot in a rotten corpse." His wife observed that he lost his "old cheery smiles" as a consequence. High-spirited by nature, Beecher continued to deliver scintillating sermons and orations, but without his former joy. For years he preached that all love is good, generative, and godly; the world is redeemed by the synergy of divine love and all manner of human loves, he taught. Elizabeth Tilton had been eager to embrace his assurance that all loves are harmonious; afterward, however, she was reduced to lonely silence, as her ebullient idol struggled to repair his damaged moral authority and wondered at times whether he had any self left: "For so many years I have read of myself and heard of myself, that I have ceased in some moods to have any actual self, and am projected as an idea before my own mind." Chastened by years of accusation, Beecher retreated from the idea of himself as a gender-bending sexual expressivist. He made clear that his romanticist progressivism upheld the sanctity of marriage. It pained him to see Washington Gladden and others search for a new spiritual leader in what should have been his glory years. For years he had to deal with messy aftershocks; he and Moulton took passes at mutual lawsuits; he expunged Emma Moulton from the rolls of Plymouth Church; and he informed reporters, after she made her final confession, that Elizabeth Tilton was mentally unbalanced. Henry Bowen also made a final scene, alleging, to a packed Plymouth Church, that he knew of another woman with whom Beecher had an affair. Since he would not divulge the name of the (obvious) woman, Bowen made it easy for Plymouth Church to expel him from its membership for slandering the pastor.[134]

Though he had to put up with a fair amount of heckling in the process, Beecher hit the Lyceum circuit hard in the years following his trial, which revived his public reputation. He drew huge crowds, stumping for political reform, women's suffrage, and liberal religion, and against alcohol and trade unions. Trade unions had nothing to do with his kind of progressivism; he was a romantic individualist to the core. The more that he traveled, the more enthused he became. He seemed to grasp that the cultural basis of his fame had changed. He was admired for his sparkling celebrity, not for his goodness. Politically he supported Republicans until 1884, always with an eye out for an ambassadorship; for a while he even fancied that a deadlock in Republican ranks might produce a "draft Beecher" movement for the presidency. In 1884, however, he switched to Democrat Grover Cleveland with more than a twinge of personal identification; Cleveland, accused of fathering a child out of wedlock and of hiring a succession of sexual partners, admitted the former but denied the rest. Beecher dared to defend him as the victim of a sexual smear, letting loose at a campaign rally in Brooklyn: "Men counsel me to prudence lest I stir again my own griefs. No! I will not be prudent. If I refuse to interpose a shield of well-placed confidence between Governor Cleveland and the swarm of liars that nuzzle in the mud, or sling arrows from ambush, may my tongue cleave to the roof of my mouth, and my right hand forget its cunning. I will imitate the noble example set me by Plymouth Church in the day of my own calamity.

They were not ashamed of my bonds. They stood by me with God-sent loyalty. It was a heroic deed. They have set my duty before me, and I will imitate their example."[135]

Meanwhile, in 1877, Theodore Tilton fled to Paris, abandoning his wife and four children. He lectured a bit and wrote poems; mostly he played chess at the Café de la Régence. During the trial he seemed to fathom what had happened to him. He recalled from the stand that after the war ended, and slavery was abolished, and his occupation was taken from him, "I turned to examine the theology in which I had been trained from childhood, and it gradually faded away before my inquisition." He stopped believing in Christ during the same period that he stopped believing in Beecher. He lurched after new causes—feminism and divorce reform—but they filled his spiritual void only for a while. When Beecher died in 1887, the mayor declared a public holiday in Brooklyn, the state legislature adjourned, and fifty thousand people lined the streets for his funeral procession to Greenwood Cemetery. While playing chess, Tilton was told of Beecher's death by a reporter; he stared into space for a moment, looked down, and resumed his game without a word. When he died in 1902, his daughter Florence issued a statement that no one in the family would attend his funeral or seek to have his body returned to America.[136]

DEALING WITH DARWIN:
LIBERAL THEOLOGY AS RELIGIOUS EVOLUTIONISM

Beecher attained the kind of celebrity that fed on itself; he became famous for being famous. His later career was distinguished by more than his heightened fame, however, or his overpowering resolve to prevail over personal scandal, or even his immense contribution to the popularization and legitimization of theological progressivism. He also made an important intellectual contribution to a beginning liberal theology movement. Fond of noting that theological conservatism was dethroned in America by pastors, not by academics, and having played a major role in the redirection of mainline American religion, he was not surprised that the theological movement his preaching prefigured and legitimized was led mainly by pastors. Beecher had little feeling for the sociological consciousness of the dawning social gospel, but he keenly sensed the importance of evolution for the next generation of Christian thought. In the early 1880s, when Beecher was at the end of his career and Congregationalist pastors Theodore Munger, Washington Gladden, Newman Smyth, and George Gordon were promoting what they called "the New Theology movement," Beecher led and encouraged the movement's embrace of Darwinian evolutionary theory.

He was not the first American to call for a theological accommodation with Darwinian theory, but he was the first theological and church leader to do so, and as such, he had a major influence on the development of American theology. With Beecher's increasingly explicit endorsement of evolutionary theory, all the Bushnellians gave up Bushnell's theological opposition to Darwin. Beecher did not talk them into it; the Bushnellians perceived on their own the futility of resisting Darwinism. What Beecher did was change the environment in which theology was done; his influence and the modernizing turn that he represented made it possible for a New Theology movement to arise.

American Protestantism was slow to deal with *The Origin of Species,* which was published in America on the eve of the Civil War. The first American Darwinist was Harvard botanist Asa Gray, who corresponded with Darwin throughout the 1850s about his investigations and published five articles on Darwinism in 1860 and eight more over the next fifteen years. He described the general theory of natural selection and grappled with the philosophical and religious implications of evolutionary theory, maintaining that while design can never be demonstrated in nature, the Darwinian system as a whole rested upon its novel conception of a purpose in nature. Oberlin geologist and Congregational minister George Frederick Wright was another early American adherent of Darwinian theory, though more qualified in his endorsement. For a dozen years, while American scientists debated the seriousness of Darwinian theory and gradually crossed over to the Darwinian camp, American theologians said very little about Darwinism. For a decade after that, they debated whether Charles Hodge was right that Darwinism and Christianity are incompatible. Hodge's *What Is Darwinism?* (1874) judged that Darwinism is inherently antiteleological, Asa Gray notwithstanding, and that "the denial of design in nature is virtually the denial of God." This verdict was reduced to a soon-famous slogan that hundreds of Christian apologists and many more fundamentalists repeated after Hodge: "What is Darwinism? It is atheism."[137]

Though diverted by his personal drama, Beecher kept up with the popular science and philosophical literature on Darwinism. He read the chief apologists of Darwinism, especially Thomas Huxley, John Tyndall, and Herbert Spencer, and was attracted to Spencer's evolutionary philosophical system. Gradually, with audience-sensitive subtlety, his sermons employed evolutionary concepts, especially with reference to the evolution of consciousness, the development of the biblical understanding of God, and the progressivity of revelation. Like many liberal theologians after him, Beecher drew encouragement from the writings of polymath evolutionist John Fiske, whose vivid descriptions of the life process introduced many Americans to Darwinism. Fiske expounded an essentially Spencerian vision of cosmic evolutionary process while emphasizing, unlike Spencer, that Darwinian theory is compatible with personal theism. Beecher's sermons conveyed a similar faith in the 1870s, though always implicitly and without any citation of sources. In the early 1880s, his evolutionism became explicit.[138]

He made the turn with his usual explanation about serving the truth as fast as people could take it. Beecher noted in 1882 that American Christianity was not friendly to endorsements of Darwin or Spencer from the pulpit. A preacher had to take care of himself first: "He must therefore not be expected to come in like an equinoctial storm; he will rather come in like a drizzle; he will descend as the dew." The church had been slow to make its peace with Darwin, he acknowledged, and he had been cautious about calling for a theology accommodated to Darwin, but the time had come "to revolutionize theology from one end to the other." The old theology had to go, especially the old concept of a God who punished human beings "for sins they never committed" and the claim that Darwinism had to be false because it contradicted biblical revelation. Personally, it was all right with him to have descended from a monkey, as long as he had descended far enough. More seriously, he exhorted that to believe in revelation is not to believe only that God inspired the Bible or wrote on stone for Moses: "He made a record when he made the granite, and when he made all the successive strata in the periods of time. There is a record in geology that is as much a record of God as the record on paper in human language. They are both true—where they are true. The record of matter very often is misinterpreted, and the record of the letter is often misinterpreted; and you are to enlighten yourselves by knowing both of them and interpreting them one by the other. It is no more a quarrel between science and religion, than a discussion over family matters is a quarrel between the husband and wife; it is simply a thorough adjustment of affairs."[139]

His drizzling sermons turned to a steady downpour after that. Repeatedly Beecher urged that for the church to hold out against the science of its time and identify Christian truth with a premodern worldview was theological suicide: "No great development can be made in these modern times of universal intelligence and democratic liberty, and not be felt everywhere by all men. The attempt to repress investigation, to keep out of the hands of our sons and daughters the books of the day, written by great men, full of honest and inspiring thought, expressed in lucid and attractive style, is not only wrong but impracticable." While Darwinian theory was still unproven in numerous respects and perhaps unprovable in some of them, the time had passed in which the church could afford to take an adversarial or even neutral position toward it. Beecher offered his own experience as a model for the adjustment that the church needed to make in its thinking. "In my earliest preaching I discerned that the kingdom of heaven is a leaven, not only in the individual soul, but in the world; the kingdom is as a grain of mustard-seed; I was accustomed to call my crude notion a *seminal theory* of the kingdom of God in this world," he recalled. "Later I began to feel that science had struck a larger view, and that this unfolding of seed and blade and ear in spiritual things was but one application of a great cosmic doctrine, which underlay God's methods in universal creation, and was notably to be seen in the whole development of human society and human thought."[140]

· He counseled that the truth of this impression was now unavoidable for the entire church:

> That great truth—through patient accumulations of fact, and marvelous intuitions of reason, and luminous expositions of philosophic

relation, by men trained in observation, in thinking, and in expression—has now become accepted thoroughout the scientific world. Certain parts of it are in dispute, but substantially it is the doctrine of the scientific world. And that it will furnish—nay, is already bringing—to the aid of religious truth as set forth in the life and teachings of Jesus Christ a new and powerful aid, fully in line with other marked developments of God's providence in this His world, I fervently believe.

Beecher left the specific problems and implications to others, making no attempt to rethink the meaning of creation or providence in the light of evolutionary theory and leaving it to others to refute Charles Hodge on the relation of evolution to teleology.[141]

What he did proclaim was the necessity of doing so. This was the main agenda for the new theology that was needed. There had to be a third way between Hodge's reactionary supernaturalism and the various atheisms that claimed Darwinism as an ally. Spencer and Fiske had begun to show the way on a philosophical level; what was needed was a fully developed theology of evolutionary process. Beecher made his contribution to this project by seeking to remove various obstacles to it, like the distinctions between natural and revealed religion, and between morality and spiritual religion, which he claimed were "obliterated" by evolution: "There is no spirituality itself without morality; all true spirituality is an outgrowth, it is the blossom and fruit on the stem of morality. It is time that these distinctions were obliterated, as they will be, by the progress and application of the doctrine of Evolution."[142]

The orthodox doctrine of biblical inspiration and infallibility was another obstacle. Eschewing the perils of an inductive approach to this problem, Beecher simply observed that the doctrine failed to make good on its promise. Conservatives always argued that the church needs a verbally inspired Bible in order to have doctrinal certainty, he explained, but history was a chastening teacher on this matter. In the history of Protestantism, the doctrine of the single and absolute authority of scripture led to an unending process of doctrinal and ecclesiastical splintering. Instead of securing doctrinal certainty, it fueled a sectarian mania of Protestantisms. "There is scarcely a square league that has not a separate sect in it, and all of them cry, 'Thus saith the Lord!'" Beecher chided. The doctrine sabatoged its ostensible purpose. "It did not end all controversy; it never has ended controversy; it never will end controversy. You must find some larger formula than that."[143]

A better theology was in the making, he promised in 1885, the theology of a better Christianity:

> I believe that there is rising upon the world, to shine out in wonderful effulgence, a view of God as revealed in the history of the unfolding creation that men will not willingly let die—partly through a better understanding of the nature of God in Christ Jesus, and partly also through a growing knowledge of the universal God,

the all-present God, the spiritual God, pervading time and space
and eternity.

The heart of this advanced religion was an echo of Channing:

> The frowning God, the partial God, the Fate-God, men would fain
> let die; but the Father-God, watching, caring, bearing burdens,
> whose very life it is to take care of life and bring it up from stage to
> stage—that thought of God will quench utterly the lurid light of
> Atheism. We are coming to a time when we shall be so assailed by
> Atheistic philosophy, that men will be forced back upon this nobler
> view of God; and so, indirectly, God will restrain the wrath of men,
> and cause the remainder thereof to praise him.[144]

A LIBERAL LEGACY:
BEECHER, CHANNING, AND FEMINISM

Beecher's theology became more clearly liberal in his later career, but he never relinquished his trademark double-mindedness. In his liberal old age he liked to think that Channing and Lyman Beecher were soul mates: "I see [them] standing together, and travelling in precisely the same lines, and towards precisely the same results. For did not Lyman Beecher feel that, as the doctrine of God and of moral government was presented in the day in which he lived, the glory of God was obscured, that men were bound hand and foot, and that the sweetness and beauty of the love of Christ in the Gospel were misunderstood, or even veiled and utterly hidden?" Not wanting to say that he had become exactly what his father fervently opposed and condemned, Beecher had to distort his father beyond recognition as a spiritual ally of Channing. At least he remembered Channing more accurately: "It is enough glory to say of Channing that he understood the day in which he lived, and understood that he was appointed to be a pilot to the times that were to come after; and that whatever he did administratively he did intelligently, that the young and the vital wood that carried the sap and the life of the tree might have a chance." Henry Ward Beecher hoped for a similar remembrance.[145]

The ascending progressive movement of his later years produced no religious thinker who compared to Bushnell and no inspiring preacher who compared to Beecher. Surprisingly, the liberal theology movement did not require a towering figure to conquer the American Protestant establishment in the closing years of the nineteenth century. But the scandal that tarnished Beecher's later career did cost the movement the striking example of a male religious leader who took seriously the disenfranchisement and oppression of women as a class. Beecher was not the only liberal minister to support the early woman suffrage movement; Channing, Emerson, Parker, and Frothingham supported women's rights, as did Tilton and various mainline Protestants in the orbit of the *Independent*. However, Beecher's active support meant more to the suffrage movement than that of any other half-dozen ministers combined. Before the outbreak of the scandal, which he never dealt with honestly and never completely overcame, he was a leading spokesperson for one wing of the feminist movement and a friend to the other. By the time the case went to trial, he was no longer friendly with anyone in the radical wing of the movement, and he resigned his presidency of the American Woman's Suffrage Association.

The worst loss was to liberal Protestantism. Beecher's feminism was unusual in his family and did not take root in the religious movement that succeeded him. Eunice Beecher despised the movement for women's rights and refused to allow Cady Stanton into her home; Catherine Beecher publicly contended against her brother on woman suffrage; Harriet Beecher Stowe belonged to the Connecticut Woman Suffrage Association, but was deeply conflicted about feminism. All of the women closest to Beecher argued that women best exert their power as domestic, virtue-nurturing wives and mothers. The entire family shunned Isabella Beecher Hooker after she accused her half-brother of adultery; she had become an enemy, an ally of the "human hyenas." During the period that Beecher respected his pledge of silence to Tilton, the radical feminists disseminated inside information that made him look guilty. When Harriet protested that their publication of private letters entrusted to their safekeeping was an outrageous betrayal, Cady Stanton shrugged that it was just politics as usual. Harriet attacked them bitterly as a "free love roost of harpies," and nineteenth-century liberal Protestant leaders made little contact with radical feminism after that.[146]

For all their social idealism, the social gospelers of the generation that succeeded Beecher were conflicted about women's rights. They produced few feminists of any kind and precious few feminist leaders, since many of them believed that the Beecher women were right about the social role of women. Though they tended to support women's suffrage, few of them had any concept of a feminist theology. The only example they knew, the product of Cady Stanton's later life, was something to be shunned.

A BIBLE FOR WOMEN:
THE IDEA OF FEMINIST RELIGION

In her later life Cady Stanton turned to religion, or at least the problem of religion. For ten years after the feminist schism of 1869 she worked the same Lyceum speaking circuit as Beecher, building up her name, earning up to $200 per appearance, and "stirring up women to rebellion," as she liked to say. A typical tour took her to forty towns and cities every six weeks, speaking once per day and twice on Sundays. She wrote Anthony's speeches but left the problems of the National Woman Suffrage Association to Anthony, who ran the organization after the Woodhull/Hooker debacle of 1872. Of the fifteen National Association meetings held in the 1870s, Cady Stanton attended only five. She

She began with a speech on "The Solitude of Self" that defined her feminist ideal as individual self-reliance and independence. "No matter how much women prefer to lean, to be protected and supported, nor how much men prefer to have them do so, they must make their voyage of life alone, and for safety in an emergency they must know something of the laws of navigation," she observed. This was not a feminist issue only; Cady Stanton liked Emerson on the theme of self-reliance. All people are on their own. She argued that the special problem for women was that they were forced to live as though they were not on their own. Since women were not allowed to be independent, they were forced to live a lie: "The talk of sheltering women from the fierce storms of life is sheerest mockery, for they beat on her from every point of the compass, just as they do on man, and with more fatal results, for he has been trained to protect himself, to resist, to conquer." In this, her last speech to a feminist convention, she did not try to rouse the convention to rebellion but spoke somberly to each individual about her existential fate.[152]

Then she turned to religion. For years it had disturbed her that religion so often played a reactionary role in American life. Well acquainted with the liberal stream of American religion, Cady Stanton was a member of Frothingham's Free Religious Association, had many friends who were liberal Protestant pastors, and often spoke in their churches. "My experience has been that clergymen are much more liberal than their people, particularly if they have to do with liberals, even of my advanced school," she reflected. She knew many pastors whose religious views were much like her own; her list included Beecher, Parker, Frothingham, William Henry Channing, Henry Bellows, Wiliam Henry Furness, Moncure Daniel Conway, and numerous others. She believed in what she called "the God of Justice, Mercy, and Truth." Cady Stanton's God was the ethical ground of her belief in the universality of equal rights, whose ethical laws "govern the universe of mind and matter alike in the moral and material world." Like Parker, she dreamed of an egalitarian civil religion that bound Americans to right action through the force of its rationality and goodness.[153]

But most of the religion that she encountered on the Lyceum circuit was insistently Bible-quoting, authoritarian, and inimical to feminism. To her mind it was the enemy of rationality and goodness. Cady Stanton urged that it was tragically misguided for the women's rights movement not to confront the problem. Many suffragists were not feminists; others, like Anthony, believed that suffrage was the key to all other feminist goals; Cady Stanton set herself against both groups. "Miss Anthony has one idea and has no patience with anyone who has two," she told Clara Colby, her colleague in theological subversion. The song of suffrage was not enough for Cady Stanton: "I am deeply interested in all the live questions of the day."[154]

The Woman's Bible began with her resolve in 1886 to produce a feminist Bible commentary, written by women equipped with the requisite knowledge of Hebrew and Greek. Cady Stanton invited numerous women to participate, but their responses were deflating. There were almost no trained women Bible scholars to invite (the Society of Biblical Literature had a single female member, Anna Ely Rhoads, in the 1890s), and educated churchwomen declined to be associated.[155] Cady Stanton made an abortive beginning on the project, gave it up for several years, and then returned to it in 1895, this time with scaled-down ambitions. With the assistance of her friend Clara Colby, editor of the *Women's Tribune*, she enlisted a handful of women to contribute commentaries on selected biblical passages that referred to women or in which the absence of reference to women was especially notable. These contributions rounded out a volume that was written mostly by Cady Stanton, who felt she was nearly alone, with little support and no models. *The Woman's Bible* made no reference to predecessors such as Maria Stewart or Sarah Grimké.[156] Neither did she enlist the perspective of any contemporary black feminist, though Anna Julia Cooper's *A Voice from the South* (1892) offered a model of black feminist engagement with the Bible that advocated sexual equality, racial equality, and the social gospel.[157] Taking up the problem of the Bible in collaboration with a few academically untrained, white, female contributors, Cady Stanton unleashed the first volume of *The Woman's Bible* in November 1895.

The book was actually a commentary on selected passages, but she liked the shock value of its title, which, Cady Stanton figured rightly, would draw attention to it. "From the inauguration of the movement for woman's emancipation the Bible has been used to hold her in the 'divinely ordained sphere,' prescribed in the Old and New Testaments," she declared at the outset, summarizing the problem. "The Bible teaches that woman brought sin and death into the world, that she precipitated the fall of the race, that she was arraigned before the judgment seat of Heaven, tried, condemned and sentenced. Marriage for her was to be a condition of bondage, maternity a period of suffering and anguish, and in silence and subjection, she was to play the role of a dependent on man's bounty for all her material wants, and for all the information she might desire on the vital questions of the hour, she was commanded to ask her husband at home." To Cady Stanton, this was the legacy of biblical religion for women and the greatest obstacle that modern women confronted in their struggle for independence.[158]

In her attack on conservative biblicism, Cady Stanton shared a crucial presupposition with a rising fundamentalist movement; like the fundamentalists, she denounced figurative interpretation of the Bible as an obfuscating liberal ploy. Commonsense literalism was good enough for her, and she sided with the old rationalist infidels who viewed the Bible as a sourcebook of mostly bad propositions. A school of modern divines tried to save the Bible by transfiguring "this mournful object of pity" into literature, she observed; they loved to talk about the metaphorical or mystical meaning of scripture. Cady Stanton countered that commonsense literalism is more truthful and progressive: "The plain English to the ordinary mind admits of no such liberal interpretation. The unvarnished texts speak for themselves. The canon law, church ordinances and Sciptures, are homogeneous, and all reflect the same spirit and sentiments." This explained why it wasn't necessary to understand biblical languages or history in order to write *The Woman's Bible*. In the preface to the second volume, published in 1898, Cady Stanton elaborated, "As the position of woman in all religions is the same, it does not need a knowledge of either Greek, Hebrew or the works of scholars to show that the Bible degrades the Mothers of the Race. Furthermore, *The Woman's Bible* is intended for readers who do not care for, and would not be convinced by, a learned, technical work of so-called 'higher criticism.'"[159]

The factual meaning of a book that was plainly hostile to women was enough to deal with. Cady Stanton dismissed the charge of presumption. "Why is it more audacious to review Moses than Blackstone, the Jewish code of laws, than the English system of jurisprudence?" If the state can be compelled by modern standards of moral decency to change its laws, why not the church? In the spirit of Theodore Parker, she admonished that the notion that scripture is God's inspired Word is exactly what cannot be believed: "Bible historians claim special inspiration for the Old and New Testaments containing most contradictory records of the same events, of miracles opposed to all known laws, of customs that degrade the female sex of all human and animal life, stated in most questionable language that could not be read in a promiscuous assembly, and call all this 'the Word of God.'" With a plainness that she commended to pastors, Cady Stanton asserted that the Bible was written by men, not inspired by God, and therefore reflects a male bias against women: "The spirit is the same in all periods and languages, hostile to her as an equal." She conceded no more than Parker, and no less. "There are some general principles in the holy books of all religions that teach love, charity, liberty, justice and equality for all the human family, there are many grand and beautiful passages, the golden rule has been echoed and re-echoed around the world," she acknowledged. There was such a thing as good religion, and even the Bible was sometimes progressive, but women needed to deal with the fact that even with its good parts, the Bible was the chief instrument of their enslavement.[160]

The idea of *The Woman's Bible* was more important than anything in it. Aside from its Cady Stanton firecrackers, much of the book was rather cursory and impressionistic at best. Cady Stanton liked the egalitarian spirit of the first creation story and noted that Genesis 1:27 implies a feminine element in the Godhead ("in the image of God he created them; male and female he created them"). Her gloss on the second creation story did surprisingly little with it. "My own opinion is that the second story was manipulated by some Jew, in an endeavor to give 'heavenly authority' for requiring a woman to obey the man she married," she offered. "It is evident that some wily writer, seeing the perfect equality of man and woman in the first chapter, felt it important for the dignity and dominion of man to effect woman's subordination in some way." Repeatedly she criticized the primitive, narrow, tribal spirit of Hebrew religion, often remarking on the absurdity of trying to model one's behavior on biblical characters, and offering Deuteronomy 2:34 as a case in point: "In making war on neighboring tribes, the Jewish military code permitted them to take all the pure virgins and child women for booty to be given to the priests and soldiers, thus debauching the men of Israel and destroying all feelings of honor and chivalry for women. This utter contempt for all the decencies of life, and all the natural personal rights of women as set forth in these pages, should destroy in the minds of women at least, all authority to superhuman origin and stamp the Pentateuch at least as emanating from the most obscene minds of a barbarous age."[161]

Convinced that scripture denigrates and oppresses women, Cady Stanton fought against scriptural authority in order to chip away at the power of Christianity to subjugate women. Her knowledge of German biblical scholarship was mostly secondhand, but she made effective use of Anglican bishop John William Colenso's pioneering historical critical work on the Pentateuch. Sometimes she exaggerated Colenso's critical edge to make the Pentateuch's history look as bad as its morals. In her description, Colenso showed "that most of the records therein claiming to be historical facts are merely parables and figments of the imagination of different writers, composed at different periods, full of contradictions, interpolations and discrepancies." Persistently she tied the fate of oppressed women in the modern age to the continuing moral influence and authority of the Bible: "There are many instances in the Old Testament where women have been thrown to the mob, like a bone to dogs, to pacify their passions; and women suffer to-day from these lessons of contempt, taught in a book so revered by the people."[162]

Cady Stanton gave short shrift to the notion that the New Testament is any better, aside from the example of Jesus. She judged that early Christianity had the same degraded view of women that she loathed in the Hebrew Scriptures, though her specific comments on the New Testament were very truncated. *The Woman's Bible* ran out of steam halfway through its New Testament section; Cady Stanton barely took a pass at Ephesians and 1 Timothy, and her glosses on the Gospels and Acts were uninspired. To her, the New Testament made life even worse for women than the Old. In the pastoral epistles, she explained, the early church codified female subordination with an even higher degree of specificity. The Gospel picture of Mary and Joseph offended her sense of class privilege and her feminism: "The questionable position of Joseph is unsatisfactory. As Mary belonged to the Jewish aristocracy, she should have had a husband of the same rank." The virgin birth story was nonsense; if Jesus needed a heavenly Father, why not a heavenly Mother? "These Biblical mysteries and inconsistencies are a great strain on the credulity of the ordinary mind."[163]

Christology was alien to her, but Cady Stanton affirmed the moral exemplariness of Jesus. Though she did not press the claim, she upheld the liberal Jesus as a counterpoint to biblical tyranny: "Jesus is not recorded as having uttered any similar claim that woman should be subject to man, or that in teaching she would be a usurper. The dominion of woman over man or of man over woman makes no part of the sayings of the Nazarene. He spoke to the individual soul, not recognizing sex as a quality of spiritual life, or as determining the sphere of action of either man or woman." Cady Stanton sought to speak to the individual soul, as well; she was a feminist Parker in religion. She could affirm Jesus in the way that Parker managed, though in her case, feminism was the critical principle. By this principle the church of Jesus was mostly enemy land; Cady Stanton accepted the religion of the liberal Jesus, but not the Christianity of the churches. She called for a new canon that retained only the justice-claiming, woman-affirming parts of the Bible: "Verily, we need an expurgated edition of the Old and the New Testaments before they are fit to be placed in the hands of our youth to be read in the public schools and in theological seminaries, especially if we wish to inspire our children with proper love and respect for the Mothers of the Race."[164]

Cady Stanton did not ask why some version of the Christian Bible needed to be salvaged or why a feminist religion needed any canon at all. Those questions remained for a later generation of feminist theology. While *The Woman's Bible* stirred a sensational public reaction, it inspired no tradition of feminist theology in its time. The first volume went through seven printings in six months and made the best-seller list. It was widely condemned for its intemperate attacks on Christianity and Judaism, most of which Cady Stanton expected. It was nearly condemned in very forceful language at the 1896 convention of the National American Woman Suffrage Association. That was another matter. Anthony and Colby were prepared for the push to condemn Cady Stanton and her book. They skillfully removed the first resolution from consideration, but they could not turn back a censure resolution. Despite an impassioned appeal from Anthony not to censure the mother of American feminism, "one who has stood for half a century the acknowledged leader of progressive thought and demand in regard to all matters pertaining to the absolute freedom of woman," the National American feminists did exactly that in January 1896. They renounced any connection on their part to "the so-called Woman's Bible."[165]

Infuriated, Cady Stanton tried to convince Anthony that they should both resign from the association. But Anthony would not resign; the movement was her life. She told the press that women had the right to "interpret and twist the Bible to their own advantage as men have always [done] to theirs." Cady Stanton perceived that this was not exactly a ringing endorsement. She appended the censure resolution to the next edition of *The Woman's Bible*, wearing it like a medal. Liberal theology made room for milder feminisms in the succeeding generation, but it was not forced to confront any that assaulted the canon. Anthony promoted the speaking career of Methodist minister Anna Howard Shaw while expressing relief—with some exaggeration—that Shaw was theologically orthodox. Cady Stanton's rage against the Jewish and Christian contributions to the oppression of women had no place in the liberal theology movement of her time or even the suffrage movement. The idea of a feminist theology, as distinguished from a theological liberalism that accommodated women's rights reformism, had to wait for more than a half-century.[166]

William Ellery Channing   Arlington Street Church

William Ellery Channing

Ralph Waldo Emerson   Theodore Parker

Horace Bushnell

Henry Ward Beecher

Elizabeth Cady Stanton

Theodore Munger

Washington Gladden

Newman Smyth

Charles A. Briggs

Borden Parker Bowne

5.

Progressivism Ascending:

Theodore Munger, Washington Gladden,
Newman Smyth, the New Theology,
and the Social Gospel

For many years the pioneers of what came to be called the "New Theology" movement gained little or no influence in their churches and seminaries. Plymouth Church provided a cosmopolitan big-city launching pad for Beecher's public career, but there were few congregations like Beecher's in the mid-nineteenth century, and even he waited until after the Civil War to identify himself explicitly as a theological liberal. In 1880, aside from newly founded Johns Hopkins University, the modern American research university did not exist. The major chairs of theology were housed at such church-affiliated institutions as Yale, Andover, Union, Princeton, Chicago, and Oberlin, and all were still held by conservatives. Some were distinguished theologians, especially Andover's Edwards A. Park; most were modifying guardians of New England Theology, committed to carrying on the intellectual legacy of Reformed orthodoxy. Congregational, Presbyterian, and Baptist theologians sharply debated the merits of Old School orthodoxies and the orthodoxy of various "New Divinity" or "New School" currents. Repeated disagreements between Congregationalists and Presbyterians severed various ties of cooperation and kinship between these denominations; Old School Calvinists at Princeton charged that American Protestantism as a whole was rampant with Arminianism and Pelagianism. To the end of its reign, New England Theology did not lack intellectual energy, but all its debates were safely ensconced in the Protestant house of authority.[1]

In this religious environment, for the first twenty years of his ministry, Theodore Munger muddled through a succession of pastoral assignments with mounting disappointment. He was nearly fifty years old before he found a congregation and cultural epoch in which his spirit flourished. Not coincidentally, Munger's transformation into a theological leader began at the same North Adams, Massachusetts, congregation at which Washington Gladden overcame his own dubious beginnings. In their early careers, Munger and Gladden both struggled with religious doubt, criticism, and poor health; later, both acquired inner conviction and public hostility when they became Bushnellians; in late middle age, both became revered leaders of an ascending liberal Christian movement. To Munger's surprise and Gladden's expectation, the New Theologians found that they did not share their hero's chief problem. These pioneers lived long enough to see that they were not born in the wrong generation. By 1895, their movement dominated the discourse and institutions of the American Protestant establishment.

TWO ROADS TO LIBERAL PROTESTANTISM

Munger and Gladden both grew up in subsistence-scraping farm families, though under significantly different circumstances. Born in 1830 to Ebenezer and Cynthia Selden Munger, Theodore Munger was the fifth child in a personally warm, tightly bonded, supportive family. His mother, who married well below her social class, came from a long line of New England ministers; his father was a physician, lover of books, and farmer who chose the tiny central New York communities of Bainbridge and later, Homer, as home for his growing children, the latter because it offered schooling. Munger was close to both his parents, especially his mother, who were religiously devout, but without the preoccupation with sin of the prevailing religion. As a young man his father had relinquished his studies for the ministry because he could not profess assurance of his election to salvation. Munger later recalled that as a child he heard a great deal about natural wickedness, wicked children, and the sin of Adam, but never at home. He also recalled loving the simplicity and wholesomeness of his family life and the beauty of the Tioughnioga valley in which he grew up.[2]

His college experience was less inspiring. Munger attended Yale College during the period that Bushnell's *God in Christ* sparked a religious furor in New England; he witnessed Bushnell's discourse on the divinity of Christ but gave little attention to the controversy it sparked. The official curriculum at Yale interested him even less. Though outwardly an agreeable and successful student, Munger disliked both Yale's classroom-drill pedagogy and its conventionalized revival religion. The college's various weekly religious services and its curriculum were equally uninteresting to him; Munger's heart was in literature, and he shared his father's belief that literature and religion are deeply linked expressions of spiritual experience. During his college years he derived greater intellectual enrichment from his wealthy, cultured aunt, Gertrude Richards Selden, who lived in New Haven, than from his professors. He spent much of his time studying Shakespeare and a host of contemporary writers not mentioned in his classes, especially Tennyson, the Brownings, Dickens, Emerson, and Lowell, later reflecting that he "made up for what the tutors did not teach me by rather wide reading in literature."[3]

Upon entering Yale Divinity School in 1852 he tried to absorb himself equally in New Haven Theology. Munger admired Nathaniel Taylor greatly, enthusing to a friend that Taylor was "the strongest, clearest, most convincing thinker I ever met with, and I may say, ever read." It delighted him that Taylor "has a system of mental philosophy of his own which is unlike any other." Challenged by Taylor to rethink his entire worldview, he reported that he could not imagine a better teacher for a prospective minister or lawyer: "All my old opinions are completely cast adrift, yet I hope to get foundations that will stand the test of logic, and will not fail in unlooked-for crises." Munger never quite embraced Taylor's theological system, but he greatly admired his teacher's intellect and passion. It took him several years to judge that Taylor gave him the wrong foundations. After he graduated from divinity school, he undertook a postgraduate term at Andover Seminary, which afforded him a comparative perspective on the two giants of contemporary American theology. Edwards A. Park knew as much theology as Taylor, Munger observed, and taught more clearly and systematically, but he did not edify like Taylor: "Park is perfectly round and smooth. Nothing strikes you. He makes everything clear—infant baptism, and the plan of redemption—but, he *impresses* you no more with one than the other. He floods you with proof and illustrations, but somehow they never get further than your note-book." Park had logic, but no emotive power; Taylor had both: "He is a genius in theology—an enthusiast, and he makes you feel. Somehow he plants a truth within a man and it becomes life and power."[4]

Munger entered the ministry a bit unsettled with Taylor's theological scheme but determined to preach, like his teacher, with inspiriting force. Ordained as a pastor of Village Church in Dorchester, Massachusetts, in 1856, he worked hard at sermon writing and performance, took speech lessons from a local college instructor (who later instructed President Lincoln), and devoted entire days to writing and study. "I had spent all my adult life thinking and dreaming of *sermons*," he later recalled. "I must confess that I did not then believe with Professor Drummond that 'Love is the Greatest Thing in the World.' I thought the *sermon* was the greatest thing." Unmarried and still substantially unformed theologically, he was pressed by the demands of the weekly sermon to get clear about what he believed. As at Yale, where he formed a close bond with his erudite Aunt Gertrude, Munger forged deep friendships with two older women, one a devout, prosperous widow who took him in as a house guest; the other a girls' school headmistress who shared with him her keen interest in progressive

Anglican theology. From the latter friend, whom he called Miss Haines, Munger gained his first acquaintance with the writings of Frederick Denison Maurice and Frederick W. Robertson. These thinkers greatly aided his sermon writing after he became a Bushnellian.[5]

His career had two turning points; the first occurred in 1859, with his reading of two recently published works: Bushnell's *Nature and the Supernatural* and *The Life and Letters of Frederick W. Robertson*. The essentially conservative tone of Bushnell's major work aided Munger's receptiveness to the liberal immanence motif that he took from it. He was deeply drawn to Bushnell's conception of the supernatural as personal power and embraced Bushnell's Coleridgean maxim that the relation of supernature and nature is analogous to that of mind and body. Exhilarated by Bushnell's picture of reality as a single divine system composed of interacting personal and natural forces, Munger renounced what he later called "the already yielding theology" of traditional supernaturalism. Judging that supernaturalist dualism was untrue to inward experience and outward fact, and shaped by years of reading Romanticist poetry and novels, he left behind what remained of his attachment to Calvinist orthodoxy and adopted a religious perspective that better fit his religious sensibility.[6]

His immediate problem was the sermon: how and what should he preach? Bushnell's sermons aided him greatly, but during the weeks that Munger rethought his theology and approach to preaching, he was crucially influenced by a two-volume narrative of Robertson's letters, recently published, that told the story of Robertson's struggle to find a living faith. Recommended by Miss Haines, these volumes spoke powerfully to Munger and numerous American liberals of his generation. Frederick Robertson, a liberal Anglican preacher and social activist, spent most of his brief career as rector of Trinity Chapel in Brighton and died in 1853 at the age of thirty-seven. His collected letters, skilfully edited, contained a moving account of his rebellion against the "unreality" of Christian dogmatism, his pointed debates with establishment Anglicans and Oxford Movement Tractarians, and his struggle to find a "real," vibrant, personal faith. Though linked to Frederick Denison Maurice, the leader of nineteenth-century Broad Church Anglicanism, whom he fervently admired, Robertson was intellectually independent of Maurice, Charles Kingsley, and other progressive Anglican leaders. A powerful preacher whose published sermons, after his death, went through many editions, Robertson proclaimed that Christianity is the revelation that "man is God's child and the sin of man consists in perpetually living as if it were false." His story and message affected Munger so deeply that near the end of his life Munger would recall that the publication of Robertson's letters was, for him, a singularly providential event: "This volume of Robertson met the need of vast numbers of the people; and it met mine with such a fulness that I have never since felt a doubt over what I should think, or what I should preach. If I were asked today what is the most important thing in theology for a preacher, young or old to know, I would answer:

'The six principles of Robertson's thought.' From that day to this preaching has been a constant joy."[7]

Robertson's first three principles established the spirit of progressive Christianity before saying anything about its content: Christian proclamation is rightly constructive and positive in its spirit, not negative; truth is found in the holding together of opposite propositions, not in a mediating position between them; because spiritual truth is discerned by spirit rather than by discursive propositions, truth should be taught suggestively, not dogmatically. The fourth and fifth principles pertained specifically to Christian belief: belief in Christ's exemplary human character rightly precedes any belief in Christ's divinity, and Christianity rightly works from inward reality to outward reality. Robertson's last principle pledged adherence to "the soul of goodness" in struggling against evil.[8]

For the rest of his career Munger's sermons were guided and shaped by these principles; sometimes he invoked them explicitly. He made it a rule not to polemicize with critics, and, most of the time, not to answer attacks at all. To his congregants at Village Church this approach to Christianity offered a welcome contrast to New England Theology, and they supported him strongly, finding spiritual enrichment in his graceful preaching and irenic temperament. Munger nursed private doubts throughout his first pastorate, however; though his increasingly explicit liberalism provoked remarkably few complaints from conservatives, he questioned whether he belonged in the Congregational church. Aside from Bushnell, whose controversial stature in Congregationalism was chastening, his favorite religious thinkers were Anglicans. He shared Miss Haines's enthusiasm for Robertson and Maurice. Compared to the spirit of Broad Church Anglicanism, he found that Congregationalism lacked a sense of catholicity and historical continuity. At the same time, his closest friend, Elisha Mulford, having left the Congregational church, was in the process of becoming an Episcopal priest. Shortly before he resigned from Village Church, Munger confessed to Mulford that he found Congregationalism spiritually thin: "We cluster about great preachers, and call great audiences strong churches. But when the power of a church is measured by the mental calibre of a preacher, or the pleasurableness of his tones, where and what is the *church?*" Henry Ward Beecher epitomized the problem. Munger admired Beecher for his progressive spirit and eloquent preaching but doubted that Beecher was building anything that would last: "One cannot help asking what is to become of the immense power of such a man as Beecher. He is doing wondrous things for individuals but scarcely anything for the lasting church of Christ. If his energy and power could be caught up by some organic body and perpetuated it would seem to me more in accordance with the genius of Christianity."[9]

The Broad Church movement of Maurice and Robertson seemed to fit his requirements, though Munger worried that it might fall short of redefining the Anglican mainstream. In 1860 he announced to a disappointed congregation that he felt compelled to resign from Village Church, take a break, and reconsider certain "important questions." As the unmarried house guest of Mrs. Walter Baker, he had no pressing financial concerns except to support his widowed mother. He spent most of the Civil War years sermonizing in Boston-area churches, where his friendliness and rhetorical felicity made him a popular guest preacher, though lacking in a way that his hero aptly identified. Hoping to succeed Bushnell as the pastor of North Church, Hartford, he preached several sermons to Bushnell's congregation. Afterward, in a kindly letter Bushnell warmly praised his preaching but noted that Munger seemed too much the "literary gentleman," and "not enough of an apostle." For his part, Munger rejoiced at the opportunity to become friends with Bushnell, enthusing that he "never before had the opportunity of conversing with so great a man." For three years he provided pulpit supply and short-term service to Boston-area churches and made his peace with Congregationalism. For better or worse, Munger resolved, the Congregational church was his group; he later reflected that he had "too much Puritan blood in his veins" to become an Anglican. In 1864, newly resettled in his ecclesial identity, he accepted the pastorate of Centre Church in Haverhill, Massachusetts, and married Elizabeth Duncan, daughter of a prominent Haverhill family. During the war years, Munger's sermons acquired a deeper maturity, but not the maturity of an apostle or reform leader.[10]

Gladden's early career was equally faltering and less prepared. Solomon Washington Gladden was born in Pottsgrove, Pennsylvania, in 1836 to Solomon and Amanda Gladden. Family tradition held that his great-grandfather was one of George Washington's bodyguards, which explained the middle name by which he later chose to be called. His father moved the family to Lewisburg, Pennsylvania, in 1840 upon becoming headmaster of the village school. Solomon Gladden was ambitious for his son, making him memorize etymological definitions at the age of three; though a Congregationalist by background, he was also a Methodist lay preacher in Pennsylvania, having no Congregational church to attend. Gladden later recalled that his father could not abide the strict Calvinism of Pennsylvania Presbyterianism and thus subjected himself to wildly uproarious revival services that pained him with embarrassment. A warm, highly engaged father, Solomon Gladden suddenly fell ill from an intestinal malady and died in 1841; sixty-eight years later, Gladden wrote that his father's death "has never let go of my heart; the pain of it is poignant yet. This man had so wound himself into the life of this child that they could not be torn apart without lasting suffering."[11]

Upon giving up her brief struggle to teach her husband's classes and keep her two sons, Amanda Gladden sent Washington to live with an uncle, Ebenezer Daniels; later she placed him with his paternal grandparents; a year later, he returned, as a family apprentice, to Daniels's rugged farm in Owego, New York. With the understanding that he would work for his uncle until the age of twenty-one, Gladden was adopted into Daniels's family and promised an education. A devout Presbyterian, Daniels had only a slight education, attained under Solomon Gladden, but he was an avid reader, encouraged Gladden's growing intellectual interests, and took advantage of an enlightened state public library system. Intellectually, Gladden thrived under his uncle's care; though the demands of farm work restricted his formal schooling to four months per year, his evenings were absorbed with private study and family readings.

His religious upbringing was more ambiguous. Owego was in the "burned-over district," so named for its overcultivation by Charles Finney and other revival preachers. Gladden found Presbyterian services repressive and boring, later recalling that he would have welcomed a vigorous theological argument from the pulpit but heard only religious platitudes. For several summers he attended a Baptist Sunday school as an alternative. Though his youthful religious experiences were mostly desultory, he studied religion obsessively, memorizing the Westminster Shorter Catechism and much of the Bible; with little outside counsel he struggled to make sense of morally troublesome passages in the catechism and Old Testament. He took an interest in other churches, but found that "sectarian jealousies were fierce; ministers of the different churches were hardly on speaking terms." He later recalled that despite being unusually pious in his youth, "I cannot lay my hand on my heart and say that the church-going helped me to solve my religious problems. In fact, it made those problems more and more tangled and troublesome." Gladden listened to people describe the peace they had found with God, repeating the steps and words they recounted, but never found the assurance of God's favor.[12]

The symbiosis between religion and politics claimed his early interest. In 1848, when Gladden was twelve, his church's youthful new minister ventured a prayer "that we might remember our brethren in bonds, as bound with them." Gladden later recounted the moment: "I well recollect how the faces of some of the elders, standing in prayer time, grew red as they listened to the petition. It looked as though he must be an abolitionist. Called to account, he failed to clear himself of the imputation, and he had to go. We wanted no such incendiary praying as that in our pulpit." As closely as he listened to their conversion experiences, Gladden paid attention to his respectable Presbyterian elders as they explained political reality: "Abolitionists were a kind of vermin. The slaves were better off where they were. Were they not fulfilling the divine decree? How about Canaan? Were not the negroes his descendants, and had it not been said of him, 'A servant of servants he shall be unto his brethren'? And what would become of them if they were set free? Did we want them overrunning the North?"[13]

These were the ruling sentiments of the church of his youth, but America began to change in the same years that Gladden came of age. In 1852 his uncle arranged an apprenticeship for him at the Owego *Gazette,* the local Democratic newspaper. Gladden left the farm, started work as a manual laborer, and soon advanced to journalism. He joined a breakaway Congregational church, which had recently hired its first pastor—Samuel C. Wilcox, the abolitionist fired by Gladden's Presbyterians. Under terms of an 1801 Plan of Union, early nineteenth-century Congregationalists and Presbyterians had established congregations together on America's expanding frontier, but by 1850 little ecumenical spirit remained between these denominations. Because Presbyterians were often more aggressive, theologically defined, and denominationally self-conscious, and because their system of polity provided stronger administrative cohesion, many federated churches evolved into outright Presbyterian congregations. Congregationalists became more self-assertive in response, sometimes blaming Presbyterians for their own shortcomings. In the 1830s Congregational leaders began to organize their own churches, and in the early 1850s this trend accelerated, partly as a consequence of rising antislavery sentiment; in 1852 the Plan of Union was terminated.[14]

Gladden's Owego Congregational church exemplified the incipient social gospel version of this story. The first church established in Owego was Congregational, in 1810; the Owego Congregationalists subsequently federated with local Presbyterians and later were swallowed by them. In 1850, forty-six dissidents from the Presbyterian church reestablished an autonomous Congregational society, principally to take a stand against slavery. Gladden's decision to join them marked a turning point in his life. Though his church soon lost its young pastor, whose health was broken, it attracted others who impressed him as brave and inspiring leaders. Gladden converted to Congregationalism and gained his first gleanings of the social gospel:

> It was not an individualistic pietism that appealed to me; it was a religion that laid hold upon life with both hands, and proposed, first and foremost, to realize the Kingdom of God in this world. I do not think that any other outlook upon the work would have attracted me. I had known the history of this little Congregational church from its beginning; I had been in keenest sympathy with all for which it stood. . . . I wanted to be—if I could make myself fit—the minister of a church like that.[15]

His first cause was the finally burgeoning antislavery movement; Gladden declared his Republican party loyalty before turning old enough to vote. In 1856, however, after studying for a year and a half at Owego Academy, he enrolled at Williams College in Willamstown, Massachusetts, where he found little outlet for social activism. Williams College exuded New England respectability and Congregational seriousness; like its community, it was privileged, historic, and thoroughly settled. The college's faculty consisted of nine professors; its curriculum featured a single elective in four years (French or German in the junior year); pedagogically it emphasized classroom memorization and recitation. Future U.S. president James Garfield was a senior at Williams when Gladden entered the freshman class; a Garfield biographer recounts that "not a breath" of America's heightening national crisis disturbed the secluded calm in the 1850s at Williams, where "all was abstract, elegant, classical, philosophical." Gladden certainly found it so; his memoir, otherwise drenched in politics, described his college days as a delightful walled-off oasis of study and socializing. He wrote songs and poetry, took long hikes in the surrounding hills, accepted classroom drill more readily than Munger, and took years to decide which of his girlfriends to marry, finally settling on his Owego sweetheart. Williams students spent most of their senior year studying philosophy and theology under Mark Hopkins, a legendary teacher and paragon of Congregational conservatism, whose classes included Saturday morning seminars on the Westminster Shorter Catechism. Gladden later reflected that "what his best students got from him was not so much conclusions or results of investigation, as a habit of mind, a method of philosophical approach, a breadth and balance of thought." What Gladden got was the only theological training of his career.[16]

He graduated reluctantly, leaving behind his happiest years and associations, and returned to Owego, where he taught school for several months, very unhappily, suffering miserably from nervous tension. At the urging of his friend Moses Coit Tyler, the new pastor of Owego Congregational Church, Gladden applied for a preaching license from the Susquehanna Congregational Association. It helped that one of Lyman Beecher's least theological sons, Thomas K. Beecher, was moderator of the assembly; though lacking in professional training, Gladden received a certificate in Beecher's handwriting. For the rest of his life he claimed that Thomas was a better preacher than his famous brother. Gladden's early preaching was a crude imitation of Charles Finney's flaming blend of abolitionism and evangelical revivalism. "That it was very crude preaching hardly needs to be said; the theology was raw, and the rhetoric was ragged; the only thing that rescued it from contempt was the saving grace of a youthful enthusiasm and a real wish to help men find the way to a better life," he would later reflect. After preaching for two months at Le Raysville, Pennsylvania, he accepted a call from a metropolitan congregation in Brooklyn, New York, that called itself the First Congregational Methodist Church; Gladden later doubted that a more "foolhardy undertaking" could be imagined.[17]

His first congregation, the product of an angry split in a local Methodist congregation, had few members, no leaders, and no natural constituency, and was burdened with a huge church-building debt. Equally troubling to Gladden was the traumatizing confusion of his first urban experience. Brooklyn, with approximately 275,000 people in 1860, to Gladden seemed "a thing stupendous and overpowering, a mighty monster, with portentous energies." The city's seemingly godlike powers left him stupefied, especially its power "to absorb human personalities and to shape human destinies." Having lived only in quiet villages and farm communities, he was bewildered by the rushing complexity of the city: "Everything was alive, yet there was a vivid sense of the impersonality and brutality of the whole movement, of the lack of coordinating intelligence." His professional inadequacies compounded his sense of being under seige. Gladden attended Henry Ward Beecher's sensational Thanksgiving Day oration on the liberty-loving faith of the North, which he found exhilirating, though also chastening. He felt keenly his lack of stature and sophistication in a Congregational Association that included such eminent preachers as Beecher, Richard S. Storrs, and Henry J. Van Dyke. He worked hard to raise the condition of his church, but failed; his marriage in December 1860 to Jennie Cohoon merely added to his problems. Overwhelmed by his environment, burdened with difficult administrative problems, poorly compensated, anxious about his inadequacies, and frightened about his country's impending war, Gladden quickly unraveled emotionally; he suffered a nervous breakdown and, in June 1861, resigned his position.[18]

Thus did his career get off to an even poorer and less promising beginning than Munger's; Gladden entered the ministry ill-prepared for a clerical vocation in a modern, industrializing society. Like Munger, he was slow afterward to find his prophetic voice; the flood of his books that inspired much of the social gospel movement did not begin until 1876, the year of Bushnell's death and Munger's middle-aged awakening. Well before Munger became a movement leader, however, Gladden transformed himself into a pioneer of modernizing social Christianity.

FINDING THE SOCIAL GOSPEL

Gladden's emotional breakdown mirrored the trauma of American society in the spring of 1861: the nation had descended into civil war. Business was paralyzed, Brooklyn merchants stood idle in the marketplace, church attendance dwindled to nothing. "A nervous collapse left me in a crippled condition," he later recalled, but within a few days he found rescue in Morrisania, New York, then a secluded suburban village; later it became part of the Bronx. The tiny congregation of Morrisania was located two miles north of the Harlem River; its members invited Gladden to regain his health as their pastor in a low-pressure environment. Sailing up the East River with his wife, "we found ourselves at the end of our journey in green country lanes, with no noise of wheels or whistles, with time to work in our gardens, and birds and bees and butterflies filling the air with life and color and music." There Gladden found healing and enrichment; working only part-time at first, he attracted new members to the congregation, built a new church building, and launched new programs. He created an ambitious lecture program that brought Ralph Waldo Emerson to Morrisania as a guest speaker; Gladden found Emerson thoroughly gracious and genial. Sensitive to his lack of theological training, Gladden wanted to study at Union Theological Seminary, but managed to attend only a few lectures, to his disappointment. As in his youth, he made up for sparse circumstances by devoting himself to independent study, finding his reward in the sermons and theological writings of Bushnell and Frederick Robertson.[19]

By his account, Robertson opened his eyes, and Bushnell taught him how to use them: "Here were men to whom spiritual things were not traditions but living verities; men who knew how to bring religion into vital touch with reality." From Robertson he learned to preach with imagination and daring; to Bushnell he owed his deliverance from the religion of hellfire and capricious divine judgment. Bushnell's *God In Christ* was a revelation for Gladden, convincing him that the social-ethical Christianity to which he was predisposed made sense only as a form of liberal-ethical theology. Under the force of Bushnell's conviction that God is morally just, he found that the gospel became good news to him: "That there was a gospel to preach I had no longer any doubt, for I had been made to see that the Judge of all the earth would do right. That was the foundation of Bushnell's faith; his heresy was the unfaltering belief that God is just. What he denied was simply those assertions and implications of the old theology which attribute to God injustice." In his view, Bushnell was controversial because he had the courage to reject offensive teachings, chief among them the claims "that men should be judged and doomed before they were born; that men should be held blameworthy and punishable for what was done by their ancestors; that justice could be secured by the punishment of one for the sin of another." These propositions were "unthinkable" to Bushnell, Gladden observed: "He dared to say so, and by his courage he opened the way to a larger liberty for a great multitude."[20]

The last of these propositions, about the atonement, was the one that New England Theology defended to the end of its reign. Gladden noted that some conservatives eventually yielded the language of penalty, but even to them, the heart of the gospel was the claim that God the Father inflicted suffering on his Son to satisfy the ends of general justice. This was the final-stand orthodoxy that Bushnell routed from the field, he observed: "This was his heresy,—this explicit and unflinching denial that there could be in a just government any such thing as a judicial substitution of the innocent for the guilty." Bushnell mightily affirmed the vicarousness of love and Christ's identification with the alienation and afflictions of the sinner, Gladden allowed, but he denounced penal and rectoral atonement theories alike "with the wrath of the great love that was kindled in his soul." Persistently, Gladden read Bushnell as America's prophet of ethical piety: "The motive that inspired him was his passionate sense of the divine justice, his determination to preach none other than a right God,—a God whose judgments would commend themselves to every man's conscience." To carry on the work of theology and preaching in Bushnell's spirit was to reformulate Christian teaching from an ethical standpoint, he urged. Modern, forward-looking theology must not try to refurbish doctrines that Bushnell rightly left behind; it must seek instead to harmonize Christian teaching "with the ethical convictions and the spiritual needs of men."[21]

To this straightforward task, Gladden dedicated his long career of preaching, ministry, journalism, and social activism; in his later career, a torrent of plainly written books explained liberal social Christianity to a mass audience. He pastored for five years in Morrisania, developed his theology, and regained his health, while keenly following the events of the war. For a time he traveled to the front lines as a volunteer in the Christian Commission hospital service, searching for his brother, a lieutenant in the Eighth New York Heavy Artillery, whose body was never found after the battle of Cold Harbor. At General Grant's headquarters before the battle of Petersburg, Gladden caught a glimpse of President Lincoln, whom he admired enormously. In 1865, invited to speak at the Williams College commencement, he delivered a war poem that caught the attention of several Congregationalists from North Adams, Massachusetts. The following year, with a growing family to support, he assumed the pastorship of North Adams Congregational Church.

The differences between Morrisania and North Adams expanded Gladden's ambitions and horizon almost immediately. Morrisania was homogeneous and suburban, but North Adams was a New England factory town and democratic community. People of different social classes regularly interacted in North Adams, sometimes antagonistically; the strains of industrial conflict and disorder were part of its social makeup. In Morrisania, Gladden's influence was restricted to his suburbanized congregation, but in North Adams, he had access to an entire community. The opportunity to practice a genuinely social ministry lifted his spirits; he embraced the opportunity to reach a wider public. From the beginning his social ministry was linked to his ideals of simplicity, frugality, and the right of constructive work. Gladden was slow to perceive the structural downside of New England's booming industrialization; with no grasp of labor politics at all, his early writings on labor-capital relations emphasized the moral responsibilities of workers and enthused about the growth of machine production in New England. His 1869 travel guide, *From the Hub to the Hudson,* celebrated the region's growing industries without a whiff of concern about working conditions, child labor, or labor rights. At the same time, Gladden's early writings did prefigure some of his later core themes: he emphasized the necessity of a strong work ethic and the dignity of constructive work; he worried about the corroding effects of commercial society on the virtues of honesty, integrity, and frugal living; in response to a local YMCA dispute, he defended the right of workers to enjoy such innocent amusements as backgammon, checkers, bowling, billiards, and square dancing. The latter venture plunged Gladden into a bitter, long-running controversy within a few months of his arrival in North Adams. The following year, on the occasion of his installation service, he invited the notorious Bushnell to sermonize on the meaning of Christian faith, which offended the same people scandalized by his position on square dancing.[22]

Gladden was opinionated, verbal, and politically engaged; his aggressive civic and religious activism put off many of his new neighbors; but he was never an ideologue. Long after he became a sharp critic of the social ravages of capitalism, he took a pragmatic approach to economic policy, emphasized the primacy of individual responsibility, and was unfailingly passionate on the necessity of a strong work ethic for a healthy society. His moralism was more yielding than many ministers on the right of workers to innocent recreation, but he categorically condemned gambling, alcohol imbibing, polka dancing and waltzes, sure that sexualized dancing of the latter sorts derived from the gutter depravity of Paris. Though he kept plunging into controversy, Gladden was sensitive to the antagonism he inspired and was convinced that his liberalizing theology was centered in the life and teaching of Christ. Less than a year after his arrival in North Adams, he felt compelled to preach a very personal sermon defending his morality from sensational rumors. At the low point of his social ostracism, when he feared that Jesus was his only sure friend, he wrote a yearning, wistful hymn, "Oh, Master Let Me Walk With Thee," that became a classic of liberal Christian piety. The qualities of Christ-following vulnerability and good will that it expressed struck deep chords of feeling in what became the American social gospel movement. On the strength of these qualities and his outward-reaching pastoral activism, Gladden won the respect and affection of his congregation, which he shaped to his religious sensibility, while members took pride in his growing reputation as a writer. His support from the congregation was so deeply appreciative that he found it difficult to leave even after a long-dreamed of position was offered to him. Gladden gave slightly more than four years to North Adams and then seized a larger public.[23]

During his North Adams ministry his lucid meditations on current events and the modern meaning of Christianity attracted a sizable audience well beyond North Adams, including Theodore Tilton. In the late 1860s Gladden became a frequent contributor to *The Independent;* from its founding in 1870, he was also a mainstay of the legendary national magazine *Scribner's Monthly* (later renamed *The Century*). In 1871, after Henry Bowen fired Tilton from *The Independent* and reorganized the paper's editorial staff, he offered Gladden a position as its religion editor, which meant he offered a substantially larger salary, an environment of high-powered acquaintances, and a national audience. Gladden later recalled that "it cost me a pang to separate myself from the associations and companionships of my Berkshire home." North Adams had enriched and strengthened him; in its meeting halls he had begun to model a new kind of liberal social ministry, and in the Berkshire mountains and streams he had found an inner peace that seemed akin to the nature mysticism described by Wordsworth in "The Prelude." Now he was heading back to the monster metropolis of Brooklyn. The irony gave Gladden pause, but only briefly; he now had a sense of self and calling that made him eager to seize a larger public. When a cleric chided him that God called ministers to preach, not edit, Gladden retorted that if printing presses had existed in the first century, the apostle Paul surely would have published a newspaper.[24]

The *Independent* was at the height of its influence in 1871, thanks to Tilton and Beecher, who had both recently departed. Gladden was reticent for the rest of his life about the circumstances that brought him to the newspaper. Though he eventually rebelled against Bowen's commercialization of the paper, for four years he exulted in the work and associations of prestige journalism, interpreting trends in American religion to a mass audience with no pressure to hide his own viewpoint. Without title he also served, in effect, as one of the paper's managing editors. "There was never any lack of subjects to write about; there was never an hour when any number of significant things were not taking place," he later recalled fondly. The office traffic alone was fascinating; visitors included Schuyler Colfax, the vice-president of the United States; Massachusetts Senator Henry Wilson, who succeeded Colfax as vice-president; and William Lloyd Garrison, whose late-life serenity impressed Gladden greatly. Contributors to the *Independent* included Garrison, Wilson, Horace Bushnell, William Cullen Bryant, Henry James, William Dean Howells, and John Greenleaf Whittier. In Gladden's telling Garrison was a delightful, perfectly at-ease companion who joked about the eccentricities of reformers and never doubted that formerly enslaved blacks would thrive under emancipation. "It was interesting to note the atmosphere of quiet content by which he was always surrounded; he had fought the good fight and had entered into peace," Gladden reflected.[25]

Surrounded by such company, Gladden thrived and dissented. He filled his section with topics he cared about and celebrated the progress of liberal Protestant religion in American life. At the same time, with little success, he tried to persuade his colleagues to report more objectively on the machinations of the Grant administration, the failures of Reconstruction, and the election of 1872. Under Bowen's direction, the paper assumed a party line on current politics. The *Independent* proclaimed its fidelity to "the three R's—Right, Radical, and Religious," while Bowen steered the paper's editorial policy firmly into line with the Grant administration. Good Republicanism supported the Republican currently in power; Gladden shared the paper's general politics, but not its committed partisanship. He wrote its blistering editorials against New York City's corrupt and despotic Tweed Ring, but he protested against the paper's contemptuous treatment of Horace Greeley in the 1872 presidential campaign. The *Independent* made little pretense of objectivity in skewering Greeley and his campaign, which was managed by Theodore Tilton. Unlike under its previous editor, the paper also turned a blind eye to signs of corruption in the Grant administration. Gladden later reflected that Grant's presidency was ruined by the cultural aftershocks of the Civil War, and that the scandals and disasters of his second term were byproducts of the "serious loss of national probity and honor" caused by the cultural ravages of the war, especially its violence and buckraking opportunism. In his own section of the *Independent*, Gladden, concerned about America's cultural resources, sought to renew and redirect the moral power of American religion. His articles deplored the segregating effects of Catholic parochial schools, lauded the progress of Darwinian theory in America, and defended the virtue of people who liked to square-dance or play whist. Most important to him, the *Independent* vigorously defended a Chicago

Presbyterian pastor, David Swing, after he was formally accused of heresy in a watershed ecclesiastical trial.[26]

THE RIGHT TO GOOD THEOLOGY: THE SWING TRIAL

Gladden had a clear concept of the difference between good and bad theology, which he expressed frequently: good theology conformed to the moral good, and bad theology attributed morally offensive beliefs or attributes to Christianity or God; everything else worth debating in religion is secondary to this moral test. From his surveyor's perch at the *Independent,* he judged that American Christianity was generally improving, but still contained sizable factions that preached an immoral theology. It was a sign of progress that even many conservatives no longer held that Christ's sacrifice on Calvary satisfied the wrath of the Father, or that Adam's sin is imputed to all people, or that God condemns infants to hell. At the same time, Gladden cautioned, many preachers and seminaries still taught these dreadful doctrines. "To teach such a doctrine as this about God is to inflict upon religion a terrible injury and to subvert the very foundations of morality," he admonished. "To say that God may justly punish a man for the sins of his ancestors, that God does blame us for what happened long before we were born, is to blaspheme God, if there be any such thing as blasphemy. To say that any such thing is clearly taught in the Bible clearly teaches a monstrous lie. Yet such theology as this is taught in several of our theological seminaries and preached from many of our pulpits."[27]

When outraged clergy challenged him to prove this accusation, Gladden readily provided evidence. He acquired a different kind of critic in Francis Patton. Patton, a twenty-nine-year-old product of Princeton Theological Seminary, taught by Charles Hodge, was newly appointed to the chair in didactic and polemical theology at the Presbyterian Theological Seminary of the Northwest (later, McCormick Theological Seminary). In a righteously blistering response to Gladden, Patton charged that Gladden showed an unchristian disrespect for doctrines taught by Protestant orthodoxy for centuries. His disagreements with Gladden were limited by their physical distance and Gladden's Congregationalism; Gladden soon learned, however, that Patton had already found a better target in Chicago Presbyterian pastor David Swing. He and Swing were members of the same presbytery. Patton's charge that Swing was a heretic led to the most significant American heresy trial of the 1870s and, as the *Independent* editorialized, a watershed event in the history of American theological liberalism.[28]

David Swing was a kindly, buoyant figure, eloquent in the pulpit, who preached a plainly liberal version of the faith without seeking fights with conservatives. He was a classics professor at Miami University of Ohio before he moved to Chicago, in 1866, to become pastor of Westminster Church (later renamed Fourth Presbyterian Church). His trial for heresy took place in 1874, when he was forty-four years old. Highly popular in Chicago, beloved by his congregation, and respected by his clerical colleagues, he gave evocative, poetic sermons that epitomized Frederick Robertson's ideal of preaching as irenic Christian expression. Gladden would later describe him as a poet "with a reverent insight into the deep things of the Spirit, a tender sympathy with every-thing human, a streaming humor, a radiant optimism, a keen delight in all things beautiful." Swing's accuser firmly believed, however, that none of this had any significance to the issue at hand and that Swing was merely a prominent example of the scandal of American Presbyterianism. Since Presbyterianism was a creedal faith, Patton reasoned, Presbyterian ministers were obliged to preach every doctrine taught by the Westminster Confession; the fact that most of the church's ministers were shying away from this obligation heightened his deter-mination to make an example of Swing.[29]

Swing made himself an inviting target by emphasizing the cultural relativity and rhetorical multivalence of scriptural teaching. Clearly pained by the impre-catory psalms, he used the concepts of "temporary inspiration" and progressive revelation to explain why some portions of scripture lacked enduring religious authority. Some Old Testament "hymns" were more deeply inspired than oth-ers, he judged, and many were quite faltering by comparison to the "grand melody" of the Sermon on the Mount and the "divine chants" of Christ's fol-lowers. His rejection of biblical literalism was plainly expressed: "Always distrust any one who rigidly follows the letter of God's word, for thus you will be plunged into a world of discord, and the Bible will lie at your feet a harp, bro-ken, utterly without music for the sad or happy hours of life." He provoked Patton further by claiming that the church's creeds, entirely the work of fallible human minds, were even more questionable. The word "heterodoxy" should be reserved for such spiritual maladies as "selfishness, or uncharity, or primeval vio-lence," he contended. Swing allowed that there is "such a thing as Christian doc-trine," but he exhorted that the kingdom of God is built by Christlike moral goodness, not Christian doctrine: "The final peace of society is to come not by the path of Christian theology, but by the more flowery path of Christian love and Christian good manners." Because God is the ideal of justice, he preached, "it becomes the Christian world to see to it that His character is so painted that the human mind can look up to Him and feel the grandeur of the ideal, not to be repelled, but charmed and conquered."[30]

Patton prosecuted Swing for heresy, acknowledging at the outset that the case was loaded with personal factors. "I realize the responsibility of my position, and the difficulty of my undertaking," he declared. "Grave charges are preferred against a popular minister. He is beloved by his congregation, and he has the sympathies of the city." Then, ignoring the personal factors, Patton launched a strident attack on Swing that disregarded his colleagues' affection for him and their likely identification with him. His twenty-eight-point indictment lumped major and trivial claims together. He accused Swing of ridiculing the Trinity, denigrating the Westminster Confession, dismissing double predestination, and refusing to preach Christ's objective atonement. He further charged that Swing admired John Stuart Mill, that his poetic language was vague, and that he "gave his name and influence to Unitarianism" by taking part in the dedication of a Unitarian chapel. Possessed by his doctrinal certainty, Patton insisted repeatedly that personal feelings about Swing or any doctrine—for example, everlasting punishment—were irrelevant: "I cannot help it if that is a doctrine which is unpleasant to the feelings. It is in the Confession of Faith." His occasional threats gained few friends in Chicago. "Are you going to put these charges out of court as frivolous?" he asked. "No, you will not. If you do I will impeach Professor Swing before the Synod, and I will impeach the Presbytery for its infidelity." At the end he implored the Presbytery to turn away from infidelity, charging that Swing was heretical on the plenary inspiration of scripture, justification by faith, the Trinity, and "one or more of the five points of Calvinism." The future of Presbyterian creedalism was at stake, he exhorted. The eyes of American Protestantism as a whole were on Chicago to see if the Presbyterian Church would reaffirm Calvinist orthodoxy or degenerate into "broad churchism."[31]

Swing's defenders were openly outraged, and some criticized Patton as an interloper and fanatical dogmatist. J. T. Mathews urged that the real issue was Patton's overweening pride and lack of heart: "There are many men in the Presbyterian Church to-day who are prouder of their theology than they have reason to be of their virtue." Swing's preaching was inspiring and meaningful, Mathews judged, while Patton's preaching gave the impression of "old dry hay . . . stored away for ages in the old Confession." Arthur Swazey observed that Patton made no attempt to find mutual understanding with Swing: "The first move was an onslaught, as upon an enemy of divine revelation." Several pastors agreed with Walter Forsyth that Swing did not contend against Christian doctrine, as accused, but contended "against a spirit of dogmatism, against a narrow bigoted use of doctrine." The eldest Beecher brother, William Beecher, asserted that Swing stood in the tradition of New School Presbyterianism that Lyman Beecher preached against a decaying Old School Calvinism. Barring a complete takeover by "the extreme Old School," he implied, with folksy asides, the era of heresy trials should have ended with his father's vindication in 1835. The New School leader, Robert W. Patterson, spoke for many in affirming the very "broad-church" view that Patton condemned. The church needed to allow interpretive latitude in dealing with its scripture and creeds, Patterson urged; moreover, though he did not always agree with Swing, he found none of Swing's beliefs heretical. The most piercing words of defense belonged to the defendant. Swing observed that in Patton's theology, everything proceeded from God "as a simple despot." Patton's orthodoxy stood for the worship of brute force and permitted no critical questions, he protested: "This dreadful hostility to reason has robbed Prof. Patton of almost the entire world, apart from his little narrow church world." Swing affirmed that he was a gospel-centered evangelical, not an orthodox Calvinist. He challenged his clerical colleagues to admit the same of themselves: "Not one of you, my brethren, has preached the dark theology of Jonathan Edwards in your whole life. Nothing could induce you to preach it, and yet it is written down in your creed in dreadful plainness."[32]

The Presbytery of Chicago supported Swing by a vote of 48 to 13, affirming interpretive latitude, broad-churchism, a respected colleague, and itself. Swing felt little sense of vindication, however, and even his relief was short-lived; Patton appealed the case to the Synod of Illinois, promising another round of aggressive contention. Swing, emotionally drained and disheartened from his month-long trial, wanted peace more than anything else. He resigned his Presbyterian pulpit, and at the urging of numerous followers, conducted services at Chicago's Music Hall and later organized an independent congregation named Central Church. He remained a popular preacher in Chicago until his death in 1894. For Gladden, however, Swing's retreat from the battle was a bitter loss. One of Gladden's favorite themes was that liberals needed to be "stay-inners, not come-outers." The key to religious progress in America was to liberalize its existing denominations, he contended. At his insistence, the *Independent* covered the Swing trial as the religious event of the decade, helping to fuel the trial's massive media coverage.[33]

But the Presbytery of Chicago had barely rendered its verdict when Swing recused himself from any further battles. Gladden expressed his disappointment bluntly: "Mr. Swing has made a great mistake." While appreciating that Swing was sensitive, exhausted, and not "a man of war," Gladden protested that his leadership was needed desperately in the liberal movement's fight against reaction. "Nearly everybody knows that an attempt to enforce a literal acceptance of the terms of the [Westminster] Confession would drive out of the Presbyterian church at least half of its ministers," he observed. "The Confession was framed two hundred and thirty years ago, and it is ridiculous to suppose that the light which has been shed upon Biblical and theological science since that day has revealed no flaw in this old document, or that its phrases, many of which, when they were adopted, were shrewd compromises between conflicting opinions, are all in this year of grace the exact and scientific expression of the faith of the living Presbyterian church." David Swing was the church's brightest light, Gladden editorialized; thoughtful and inspiring, with an "unblemished" reputation, he was "the best loved and the most influential Presbyterian minister in the Northwest." Had he chosen to fight Patton's appeal, "there would have been light all around the sky, and thousands who are chafing in the bonds of old-time creeds would have rejoiced in the liberty wherewith Christ makes us free."[34]

The latter claim was at least half wrong, as the subsequent heresy trials of Charles Briggs and Henry Preserved Smith made clear. The Presbyterian church made biblical inerrancy its chief article of faith in the 1880s and reaffirmed it periodically for forty years afterward. Gladden's deep identification with Swing's cause and way of thinking skewed his journalistic judgment and led him to underestimate the extent of conservative control in the northern Presbyterian church. Gladden could not claim to have made the personal sacrifice that he wanted Swing to make; moreover, his hope and disappointment in Swing had a crucial subtext, the *Independent*'s search for a new liberal champion. Knowing readers noticed Gladden's praise of Swing's unblemished reputation, just as the good name of the liberal movement's greatest public figure, Henry Ward Beecher, was gravely imperiled by an increasingly public swirl of rumors and accusations. Gladden owed his position at the *Independent* to this scandal, and a month after the Swing trial, the main accusation exploded into a formal charge of adultery. Beecher lost his unblemished status as a progressive hero at the very moment that the social preconditions for an American progressive movement in religion had come into being.

IMAGINING LIBERAL PROTESTANTISM

The country that made Beecher a national icon was ready for a liberal theology movement, but mainline American Christianity had no liberal theologians in 1876. The Swing trial took place in 1874; the Beecher trial occurred in 1875; Bushnell died in 1876. The Bushnellians were not well placed at the time. Theodore Munger was then a much-travelled Congregational pastor serving a tiny flock in San José, California. He founded his new congregation in 1875, having journeyed to California, as nineteenth century New Englanders usually put it, "in search of health." Known for his quietly gracious personality and highly literate preaching, his increasingly explicit Bushnellianism had brought an early end to his pastorate in Haverhill, as Munger had no will or desire to quarrel with conservatives. What bothered him more was that progressive Christianity barely existed in America; on his more depressed days he lamented that liberal theology had no American existence at all. "There is no man to defend liberal ideas in theology who believes in Christ," he complained to Elisha Mulford, apparently forgetting Bushnell. "At least I know of no one. Unitarianism is on one side. Infidelity on the other. Between, there is no defender of liberal theology, of modern Christian thought." The Congregational church had some liberal pastors and congregations, but no progressive theologians worthy of the name. Munger's personal situation was equally bleak. After nearly four years serving a congregation in Lawrence, Massachusetts, that generally supported him, his struggles with nervous depression and related physical maladies forced him to resign. At forty-five, hoping to creep back to health in the California sun, he moved to San José, where the Congregational board assured him that he would find other health-seeking New Englanders.[35]

Washington Gladden's situation was barely more promising. The commercialization of the *Independent* had weighed heavily on his moral sensibility. He had protested against Bowen's blurring of the distinction between the paper's editorials and its advertisements, and when his protest was ignored, he resigned in November 1874. Though he later made less of the transition, Gladden was disheartened at the time, because he loved journalism and the large audience it accorded him. Left without a journalistic perch, he wrote a dismal letter to Beecher protégé Lyman Abbott that lamented his lack of options: "Of course I shall go back into the pulpit. Nothing else is left to me." He sought a new pastoral assignment and was fortunate to be called to North Congregational Church in Springfield, an attractive western Massachusetts city of 31,000, which contained six Congregational churches and a wide variety of others. There Gladden began to write books for the progressive religious movement that he and Munger believed was long overdue.[36]

All his books were written for lay audiences; a journalist by training and temperament, Gladden had a knack for explaining religious issues in everyday language. Most of his early books were thematical collections of sermons and adult education lectures. *Being a Christian* (1876) argued that the heart of religion is its effect on personal character, not its ritual forms or dogmas, or the feelings it evokes: "You become a Christian by choosing the Christian life, and beginning immediately to do the duties which belong to it." *The Christian Way* (1876) elaborated his ideal of character development, arguing that Christianity takes its goal from the teaching and way of Christ, who taught that "the highest attainable beauty of character is only reached by those who aim at perfect goodness." Gladden described the conventional character-shaping practices of prayer, Bible study, Christian fellowship, and church work before expounding the role and formation of Christian character in secular life. "In every system of morals, in every estimate of character, we must put truth first," he declared. Truthfulness is the fundamental virtue in every area of life; even in business, a Christian is called to "shine forth as a light" of truthfulness. Because truthfulness creates bonds of trust, community, and sociableness, he explained, Christianity acquires its essential social meaning by being truthful. For Gladden, creedal orthodoxies fail the test of truthfulness by requiring ministers to hide the truth that they really believe.[37]

He gave seven fulfilling years to Springfield, throwing himself into the life of the city, editing a magazine called *Sunday Afternoon* (later renamed *Good Company*), and publishing several books and articles that heightened his reputation. Increasingly drawn to labor/capital issues, Gladden defended the right of workers to form unions and persistently argued that the key to industrial peace was cooperation between workers and employers. He also formed an important friendship with Munger, who, upon hearing of Bushnell's death in 1876, realized that he was homesick for New England. For the first time in his California sojourn he wrote a new sermon, a meditation on the significance of Bushnell's career, which later became the nucleus of his influential book on Bushnell. A published edition of this sermon caught the attention of pastorless Congregationalists in East Hartford, across the Connecticut River from Bushnell's home, who invited him to be their pastor on a trial basis. Accepting their invitation, Munger soon found himself clashing with reactionaries again, but the following year salvation arrived in a call from North Adams Congregational Church, where Gladden's successor, Lewellyn Pratt, had accepted a professorship at Williams College. Munger's life turned a corner once he got past the North Adams Congregationalist Council.[38]

North Adams Congregational Church was a progressive oasis in a Congregationalist Berkshire Hills region that had long prided itself on its uncompromising resistance to Unitarianism. This tradition of vehement orthodoxy was reasserted in nearby Indian Orchard in November 1877, a month before Munger's council examination, when a church council refused to approve the installation there of a mildly liberal pastor, James F. Merriam; the key issue was Merriam's view of eternal punishment. Deeply involved in the debate over Merriam's installation, Gladden insisted that conservatives had no right to exclude ministerial candidates on the basis of their supposed creedal deficiency, because Congregationalism had no creeds. After Gladden was out-voted, the Indian Orchard Church ordained Merriam anyway and sacrificed its Congregational standing. A month later, Gladden worried that the same thing might happen to his beloved North Adams congregation.[39]

The council that examined Munger was chaired by Gladden's former profes-sor and the ex-president of Williams College, Mark Hopkins, and included Gladden and Yale president Noah Porter. Munger gave a carefully composed summary of his theology that stressed the Bushnellian theme of the wisdom of multiple creeds. He rejected the doctrine of endless punishment, but accepted the "awful certainty" taught by Christ that persistent sinners dwell in "outer darkness" separated from God. With apparent inkling of the case's historic sig-nificance, the council deliberated for four hours after his presentation. Gladden defended Munger's position; more important, Porter contended that the func-tion of a Congregational council was not to establish a dogma, but to examine a candidate's apparent fitness to preach the gospel. A grateful Munger later recalled that "President Porter carried the council. Men who had voted one way in the Indian Orchard Council voted another here." Equally grateful to Gladden, who repeatedly brought him to Springfield to showcase Munger's progressive thinking, Munger likened himself to "the man in the Bear-fight who slid into the garret while his wife fought the beast—he was very encouraging but not very helpful." Because of its timing and Munger's well-known Bushnellian standpoint, the North Adams decision marked a crucial precedent in Congregationalist history: a door had opened, and not only for Munger.[40]

Gladden had one more career move to make. In 1882, offered a position at *The Century* by his friend Roswell Smith, he considered returning to full-time journalism, but at the same time, he was invited to the pastorate of First Congregational Church in Columbus, Ohio. Gladden was hesitant to leave New England, but Smith convinced him to take the Columbus position, urging that "every man ought to go west" for a few years. "If God calls, you go to the

largest Congregational church in the name of Congregationalism at the West,"
Smith exhorted. "You have no conception of the power of such a position in
Ohio. You would tower up there, head and shoulders above other men, in influ-
ence." That was assurance enough for Gladden. "The areas were larger, and so
were the opportunities," he later recalled. "I might want to come back to the
East, some day, but for the next ten years, at least, that was the place for me."
He stayed for the remaining thirty-six years of his life, and amply fulfilled his
friend's prediction.[41]

Meanwhile Munger flourished in North Adams, and later in New Haven.
After his retirement he reflected that life began for him in North Adams: "It was
then I really took start in life—a rather late beginning, but better than if made
before. In hardly any other parish in New England could I have had the peace
and the forbearance and the support that were necessary to protect me while I
was making my way out into the New Theology. North Adams may claim not
a little share in this, first through Dr. Gladden, and then through me." However,
it was Munger who made the first important contribution to the New Theology
movement, and both were slightly preceded by a fellow Congregationalist pastor and theologian, Newman Smyth. Though shy about publishing, Munger
was more reflective than Gladden, and a more stylish writer. During the early
years of his North Adams ministry, his thoughtfully eloquent sermons were
often published in a local newspaper, *The Transcript*. Elisha Mulford shared two
of these sermons with a respected acquaintance, who marveled at Munger's
exceptional felicity. Told that Munger's age was "some way beyond forty," the
acquaintance declared, "It is time he began to garner his wheat." Munger started
with a volume of practical advice to young people, *On the Threshold*, that sold
more than 25,000 copies. In 1883, at the age of fifty-three, he published his
manifesto for a "New Theology movement," *The Freedom of Faith*.[42]

THE HOPE OF PROGRESSIVE ORTHODOXY:
NEWMAN SMYTH

Munger's landmark text, often described as the keystone of the liberal theology movement, was not quite the first work of its kind. Newman Smyth got
there first. In 1877, Smyth's slender volume titled *The Religious Feeling* offered
the first attempt by an American mainline theologian to integrate the theology
of Schleiermacher with Darwinian evolutionary theory. Two years later, Smyth
published a second work, *Old Faiths in New Light*, that made a cautious case for
the legitimacy of higher critical biblical scholarship. Smyth's third book,
Orthodox Theology of To-Day, published in 1881, played an important role in the
liberal movement's breakthrough into academe. With these books, liberal theology in a fully-orbed sense of the term took root in American mainline
Protestantism.

Smyth exemplified a generational trend and pioneered one for American liberals, by drinking deeply from German theology. Born in 1843 in Brunswick, Maine, and thus younger than Munger by thirteen years, he was raised in a nurturing, academic, broadly evangelical family. His father, a professor of mathematics and natural philosophy at Bowdoin College, was an outspoken antislavery activist; his devout, cultured mother was the dominant influence at home. In his later life Smyth would recall that his mother "had a happy art in guiding us by a word in season, and her gracious, intelligent influence, like an atmosphere, pervades still all my memories of my childhood and youth." Smyth's father counted Harriet Beecher Stowe and Calvin Stowe among his closest friends; as a youth Newman studied in a private school run by Mrs. Stowe. One day she read a portion of *Uncle Tom's Cabin* to him; the Smyth family rejoiced when the novel became famous a few years later. Newman Smyth grew up well adjusted and intellectually curious, as did his older brother Egbert, who became a prominent church historian at Andover Seminary. Educated at Philips Academy in Andover, the younger Smyth enrolled at Bowdoin College in 1859 at the age of sixteen, where he kept up the record of his family and graduated at the top of his class.[43]

The empiricist bias that marked Smyth's later theology was established in college. He spent a good part of his college career haunted by Sir William Hamilton's philosophical skepticism. It bothered him greatly to think that he could not prove even his own existence, much less the existence of God. He made a practice of venting his frustration in the college gymnasium, until the day it occurred to him, after an extended workout, that he could not seriously question the existence of his own aching body. "I have never questioned my existence since," he later reflected. "I solved it by exercise." The most vivid memory of his college experience was Lincoln's election to the presidency. As a boy he was keenly aware of his father's minority status as an abolitionist; it seemed to Smyth that his father was nearly the only one in Maine. More than sixty years later he recalled feeling intensely excited for his father after Lincoln's victory in Connecticut won the presidency. Near the end of the war, upon graduating from Bowdoin in 1863, Smyth received a commission as a first lieutenant in the Sixteenth Maine Regiment of the Fifth Army Corps, stationed outside Petersburg, where he fought in the siege of Petersburg and rose to the rank of acting captain. After the war, he proceeded straight to Andover Seminary, where his brother Egbert had recently joined the faculty. The appointment of Egbert C. Smyth to Andover's chair of ecclesiastical history in 1863 proved to be a turning point in the history of Andover Seminary and American theological liberalism, but all of that was far off when Newman Smyth enrolled there. The defining figure at Andover was Edwards A. Park, who impressed the younger Smyth as a brilliant apologist for an outdated scholastic system. "The minds of some of us were not satisified with his method of reasoning," Smyth later recalled. "It seemed to us that he shaped Edwards to conform to his system of

New England theology rather than leading us to understand Edwards' deeper spiritual thinking."[44]

Like Munger and Frederick Robertson, Smyth was frustrated with the sheer unreality of orthodox dogmatism. His older brother gave him the essential clue to a better alternative, but Egbert Smyth was in no position either by training or position to give his younger brother the true-to-life theology that he was seeking. Egbert Smyth was just beginning to find his way in a new field at a new institutional home when his younger brother arrived at Andover. Egbert had graduated from Andover in 1854, spent six years as a professor of natural religion and revealed religion at Bowdoin College, and studied at the universities of Berlin and Halle for one year before assuming the Andover chair in church history. At Berlin he studied under the eminent neo-Schleiermacherian mediationist theologian Isaak Dorner, who gave him a historically oriented model of theological teaching that was deeply rooted in Athanasian Christology and Schleiermacher's modern Christocentrism. Like Dorner and his closer intellectual model, Union Theological Seminary historical theologian Henry Boynton Smith, Egbert Smyth taught that no doctrine can be understood apart from its history. At Andover Seminary, he taught his younger brother to understand the orthodox doctrine of the Trinity as a product of the early church's prolonged struggle with its inherited neo-Platonism.

Egbert Smyth's methodological refusal to subordinate history to dogma eventually effected a revolution at Andover Seminary. In 1865, however, he was a junior member of a faculty that still defined itself as a bastion of militant anti-Unitarian orthodoxy and had to prove his orthodoxy while legitimizing an historical approach to it. His younger brother judged that the problem with Andover Seminary wasn't merely Andover's history, but the state of American theological education as a whole. "Theological learning seemed to me at that time to have come to a pause in America," he later reflected. Park and Charles Hodge had both studied in Germany, but Park appropriated only the most conservative aspects of German mediation theology, and Hodge militantly opposed the entire school of Schleiermacher. The example of his older brother was more instructive to Newman Smyth; he was intrigued by the possibility of gaining a modern theological education in Germany. After his graduation from Andover in 1867 and a brief pastoral stint in Providence, Rhode Island, he thus headed for Germany, where he and Charles A. Briggs launched a generational trend.[45]

Following his brother's path and the European custom of lecture-grazing, Smyth attended lectures for several weeks at the University of Berlin and then moved to Halle. At Berlin he studied under Dorner and became friends with the American biblical scholar Charles Briggs. Dorner showed him that theology did not have to resemble an acrobatic balancing act or scholastic tournament in the manner of New England Theology. It was possible to pursue theology in a reflective, nondefensive, historical manner that was both modern and evangelical. Smyth found his model of this ideal at Halle, where he studied under renowned neo-Pietist theologian Friedrich August Tholuck, an extraordinarily engaging teacher and spiritual mentor. Theologically he belonged to the evangelical-Pietist wing of the Schleiermacher school of mediating theologies, trimming the radical aspects of Schleiermacher's thought while retaining his emphasis on the centrality of religious experience.

Schleiermacher organized theology into three divisions—philosophical, historical, and practical—and taught that the Bible must be understood by the same scientific methods that apply to all other literature. Following his example, the mid-century German theorists of theological encyclopedia folded biblical scholarship, Christian history, and dogmatic theology into the single controlling discipline of historical theology. Tholuck incorporated much of Schleiermacher's system into his own thinking, but he restored the separate disciplinary status of exegetical theology and reinstated apologetic arguments that Schleiermacher eschewed. His theological encyclopedia contained four divisions. On the ground that the Bible has special authority, Tholuck classified biblical study as a discipline unto itself, and he appealed to historical and philosophical arguments that supported the supernatural authority of scripture. Rightly conducted, he argued, theological apologetics "secures faith in the higher dignity of Christ, and also in the authority of the gospels, for it confirms their narratives." While urging that biblical scholarship is obliged to employ the methods of modern historical criticism, Tholuck insisted that good biblical scholarship is an inside discipline. No interpreter can understand biblical history or meaning from a purely outside perspective: "It must be remembered that the scientific apprehension of religious doctrines presupposes a religious experience. Without this moral qualification, it is impossible to obtain a true insight into theological dogmas."[46]

Tholuck was sufficiently conservative that Edwards A. Park enlisted him as an ally of New England Theology. Park launched his influential journal *Bibliotheca Sacra* in 1844 with a three-part translation of Tholuck's lectures on theological encyclopedia. The elements of Tholuck's thinking and personality that made a life-changing impression on Newman Smyth, however, were the liberal ones. Tholuck was gospel-centered and modern at the same time. Though he trimmed the implications of this commitment, he taught his students not to fear modern historical criticism. He insisted that religious experience, not doctrine, is central and saving; more important, he inspired students by personal example. "The memory of Tholuck is like a benediction," Smyth gratefully recalled in later years. "He was one of the most learned, acutely critical, comprehensively informed, and at the same time the simplest and most spiritual of the evangelical teachers and preachers in Germany. To those students who came under his personal influence he gave himself freely, fully, with a child-like simplicity in his impartation of his learning such as I have hardly known in any one else. In his preaching he was the simple evangelist, but his was the simplicity of wisdom, and when he preached the students flocked to hear him. In his personal conversations with students whom he took under his special guidance, he was the keen questioner and a most stimulating conversationalist. He would be sure to send one back to his studies with a fresh eagerness in the pursuit of truth. And his humility was deep as his faith was high and his knowledge comprehensive." From Tholuck's example, Smyth learned that theology could be beautiful. Tholuck dispelled his fear of German historical criticism, taught him to read scripture from a critical standpoint, and explained how Schleiermacher approached theological problems. For many years after he studied in Germany, Smyth's personal library consisted almost entirely of German works. Though he lamented that German scholars often veered to radical extremes, to him it was self-evident that they owned the field of theological studies in the mid-nineteenth century. He regarded himself throughout his long career as a thinker in the progressive-evangelical tradition of Tholuck and Dorner, especially Tholuck.[47]

In more functional terms, Smyth regarded himself as a progressive evangelical pastor with theological and scientific interests. He never aspired to an academic position. For seven years after his return from Germany he pastored a Congregational church in Bangor, Maine, where he married and started a family. In 1877, shortly before moving to a Presbyterian pastorate in Quincy, Illinois, he composed a programmatic account of the faith that he believed and preached. *The Religious Feeling* embraced Schleiermacher's experiential approach to religion, sustained a lengthy conversation with Charles Darwin and various Darwinists, and called for a thorough integration of theology and evolutionary theory. Two years later, *Old Faiths in New Light* amplified these arguments and offered a mildly written brief for the modern historical-critical approach to scripture. It was still a bit early to advocate the social gospel, which he also supported, but in these two books Smyth laid the foundation for what Munger soon called a transforming theological movement.

Smyth introduced his first book as a modest departure from standard apologetics. His personal faith had survived, he reported, only by virtue of his direct acquaintance with modern German thought, but most Americans lacked the opportunity to attend German universities, and there were no English-language works that adequately explicated the new German thinking. Moreover, even German theologians and philosophers did not pay enough attention to modern science, especially Darwinian theory; to Smyth's perception the Germans were creative, but too narrowly focused on historical problems, philosophy, and theological reinterpretation. What was needed was a complete adjustment of Christian belief to modern knowledge, especially the modern evolutionary understanding of the natural world.

Smyth proposed to take scientific empiricism seriously without restricting his imagination to its limits. Theologians are obliged to deal with evidence, he affirmed; the antireligious wing of the Darwinist movement, led by Thomas Huxley, was right to insist on that point. But the Huxley types were wrong to invoke David Hume on the uselessness of speculative theology, since "there *are* heights and depths of being" that scientific reason cannot grasp. Science investigates the natural world, theology investigates the religious nature of human subjects, and in both cases the point of departure is feeling. All human knowledge of the external world is given in and through sensation. In a few deft strokes, by beginning with the modern scientific challenge to religious conviction as such, Smyth cleared the ground for his anthropocentric theological turn. Theology is not the explication of abstract propositions decreed by authority or metaphysical proof; it is, rather, the scientific investigation of the "perennial source of religion" identified by Schleiermacher, the feeling of absolute dependence. "We have not made ourselves, we found ourselves in existence; and our earliest, and our latest, our only consciousness of ourselves is a consciousness of dependent being," Smyth explained. "We feel our dependence upon something other than ourselves and the things that appear, over which we have no power even in thought, and with regard to whose orderings we have no will but to obey. This is the religious feeling in its simplest form, the feeling of absolute dependence." Because the religious feeling is real, theology has its own crucially important work to do.[48]

Smyth emphasized that the field of religion belongs to theology; religious feeling, the given in this field, has an irreducible integrity that cannot be explained away by other modes of explanation, such as evolutionary theory. Smyth accepted Darwinian theory as a true account of natural evolutionary process, but he denied that Darwinian biology explained either religious feeling or the moral sense: "You have not told what the ripe ear is when you have described the blade and the husk. Both have grown from a hidden root, and in accordance with a law which made each after its kind." Smyth offered John Stuart Mill as a witness, however unwitting, against the notion that moral feeling is merely one social instinct among others. In his famous protest against the idea of a God whose will made something morally abhorrent right, Mill declared that he would never worship such a God, even if such a being sent him to hell for it. Smyth questioned how this commendable sentiment squared with Mill's ethical utilitarianism: "Upon what conceivable principle of utility should Mr. Mill go to hell? How will it profit him? What conceivable good will come of it to others?" Mill's objection reflects the existence of a transcendent moral law that is not merely a social instinct or social construction, Smyth contended, but Mill's own moral theory cannot make sense of his protest. His objection to traditional Christian theism is admirable, but not on a secular basis. Utilitarianism does not explain his own most cherished belief, and neither does Darwinism.[49]

Concerning the relation of science and religion, Smyth affirmed that biology and theology are different fields, but they do interact. Modern theologians rightly continued to speak of a "design" in nature, for example, but they were obliged to reinterpret the meaning of design in the light of Darwinian theory. He urged that in similar ways, theologians were obliged to use modern historical-critical tools in interpreting the Bible, without relinquishing their reverence for the Bible as God's Word. Smyth admonished that a poorly informed fear of historical criticism was doing more harm to American Christianity than the wildest German scholarship: "The mere suspicion that the advanced scholarship and the old faiths are to-day at variance, is itself a fruitful cause of popular indifference and unbelief. Indeed, the Christian faith suffers more from a certain vague mistrust, or undefined unbelief, among the people, than it does from any one positive and definite form of infidelity."[50]

Smyth called for a confident spirit of Christian openness to the modern world. His tone was measured and hopeful; he did not press far on any issue; his point was always to establish the legitimacy of interpreting Christianity in the light of modern science and historical-critical scholarship. He dismissed the traditional doctrine of biblical inspiration as "mechanical" and traditional theology itself as "orthodoxism," but his rendering of the historical-critical account of biblical history was very cautious. As a work of literature that grew out of the life of an ancient people, he counseled, the Bible is best understood by studying the historical process through which it was produced: "The Bible is not the Koran, and we are not called upon to tear revelation from its historical surroundings." Smyth explained that from a modern historical-critical perspective, the Old Testament contains three great currents of Hebrew life: prophetic teaching, priestly lore, and wisdom literature. These three traditions are sometimes blended in the scriptural witness, sometimes are separated, and at still other times flow side by side. Some modern scholars deconstructed the biblical text into a more complex array of literary strands, Smyth allowed, "but it is enough for our purpose, and safer, to keep here well within the limits of the facts generally admitted by those biblical scholars whose opinions are of weight."[51]

Old Faiths in New Light was an invitation, not a manifesto. Its first concern was to show that biblical criticism is safe, enlightening, and spiritually enriching. Smyth acknowledged that a rationalistic stream of contemporary German scholarship, championed by Abraham Kuenen, gave a thoroughly naturalistic account of the rise of Hebrew religion, but he assured that this was a minority position even among German scholars. Source and redaction criticism were perfectly compatible with the biblical belief that God acted directly in the history of Israel; Assyrian scholar George Smith was an example of a biblical critic who employed the tools of higher criticism wisely and reverently.

Smyth responded directly to the objection that biblical criticism is a slippery slope: "If we go with them one mile, will they not compel us to go with them twain? Is it not safer, it will be asked, not to yield an inch to this destructive German criticism—to stand firmly in the old ways? But we cannot, without covering our own eyes, and deafening our own ears, refuse to confess that we have received from modern biblical scholarship some new light, and that voices which we may not mistrust call us to advance to some fresh views of the providence of God in revelation." Smyth knew that higher criticism had to be legitimate if Isaak Dorner and August Tholuck accepted it, and he knew from personal experience that source criticism made the Bible more comprehensible and interesting. What American Christianity needed was a generation of pastors and seminary professors who accepted modern knowledge without apology as a means to a stronger, better-established religion.[52]

Smyth's piety and judicious tone saved him from much hostility in his early theological career, but his dismissive references to "orthodoxism" set off alarms on the theological right. His third book proposed to set the matter straight. "I would still retain and use as descriptive of a reverent, but progressive, Christian theology the old word orthodoxy," he declared. His project was not to leave orthodoxy behind, but to distinguish between the spirit of genuine orthodoxy and a regnant, now-tottering orthodoxism. "By orthodoxy I would mean the continuous historical development of the doctrine of Jesus and His apostles; and the orthodox habit or temper of mind I would consider to be simply fidelity to the teachings of the Spirit of Truth throughout Christian history." Just as interpretation is necessarily open-ended and ongoing, he urged, so is genuine orthodoxy. What it means to follow Christ today is always a somewhat new question. This is an orthodox truism, but it is exactly what the spirit of orthodoxism cannot tolerate. "Orthodoxism, on the other hand, is the dogmatic stagnation and ecclesiastical abuse of orthodoxy," Smyth explained. "Orthodoxism is an orthodoxy which has ceased to grow—a dried and brittle orthodoxy. Orthodoxism offers a crust of dogma kept over from another century; it fails to receive the daily bread for which we are taught this day to pray." True orthodoxy is progressive; it is the orthodoxy of today, not merely of yesterday.[53]

This was the spirit of Bushnell, as Smyth confirmed in his discussion of the atonement, and the spirit of Isaak Dorner, whom Smyth described as the world's "greatest living theologian." Smyth embraced Bushnell's essentially moral concept of the saving work of Christ without completely giving up the idea of atonement as divine satisfaction. Atonement is the perfect self-satisfaction of divine love in the forgiveness of sin, he proposed. With Dorner, he found such fullness of love in his experience of God "as to make both mind and heart rejoice in the glory of the Lord." Smyth rejoiced to be living in the age of church history that produced its healthiest, most beautiful and morally regenerative theologies: "Where else in the whole field of theological literature can be found nobler, worthier, more thoroughly ethical conceptions of God than the orthodox theology of to-day is giving through its living masters? Escaping the limitations both of Calvinism and humanitarianism, it would have us worship God as infinitely majestic, and holy, and yet unspeakably beautiful and attractive." The hope of progressive orthodoxy was the faith of the modern age that God is love.[54]

With a deep breath, Smyth turned from this buoyant declaration of faith to its most troubling difficulty. How should progressive orthodoxy deal with the biblical doctrine of everlasting punishment? The notion that God punishes sinners in hell forever is morally repugnant, but doesn't the Bible plainly teach this? Smyth surveyed the usual interpretive options—"eternal" doesn't mean "forever"; immortality could be conditional; damnation might imply annihilation of souls, not everlasting punishment; all of the biblical language about damnation is metaphorical—and admitted that he had no sure answer: "I see many of these teachings as one might see the colours of a painter on his palette; they are all true colours, they all will be needed; doubtless they are complementary colours; but I do not now, at least, see them combined and harmonized as I shall hope to do when the divine Idealist shall have finished His picture of human history, and it shall be unveiled at last, in that day of revelation, ready for the judgment."[55]

In the meantime he proposed adding a third option to the usual choice between heaven and hell: the doctrine of a future probation, supported by various church fathers and strongly affirmed by Dorner, which Smyth called "a third truth which seems to be left in the shadows of the gospel of the kingdom." Scripture refers to a period of waiting between one's death and the day of judgment in a place of departed spirits, he observed, an intermediate spiritual state with its own range of interpretive possibilities. Smyth enlisted against the assumption that the processes of life can be brought to a sudden halt by death. Death is merely an accidental circumstance, he noted; it is not an inward change: "All the analogies of experience would seem to compel us to believe that disciplinary processes of life must be continued after death; and in this intermediate period, suggested by some Scriptures, room would be found for the play of those forces of moral development whose working we observe in the present life. Not, then, until the day of revelation shall disclose to our eyes the secrets of Hades, are we warranted in raising one question of our troubled understandings, or one doubt of our beating hearts, concerning the just judgments of God in eternity." The possibility of a progressive sanctification after death deserves to be part of the faith of a progressive Christian orthodoxy.[56]

All of these arguments were attractive and unsettling to different factions of Smyth's seminary alma mater, as he expected. The argument that ignited the greatest furor was the one that he considered comparatively innocuous. This was the doctrine of a future probation, which later singed Charles Briggs as well. To Smyth's surprise, shortly after the publication of *Orthodox Theology of To-Day*, he was invited by Andover Seminary to succeed the retiring Edward A. Park in its chair of systematic theology. He had never aspired to an academic position, and he would not, in the end, attain this one or any other. His failure to secure his alma mater's theological chair was a watershed event in modern American theology, however, and it set off the defining liberal theology controversy of the 1880s. The spectacle of Andover Seminary turning liberal convinced Theodore Munger and many others that the future belonged to the New Theology movement.

TURNING LIBERAL: THE CASE OF ANDOVER THEOLOGICAL SEMINARY

Andover Seminary's liberal conversion was ironic, but not implausible. Though founded in 1808 as a militantly orthodox alternative to Unitarianism, the seminary contained both Old School Calvinists and New Divinity

Hopkinsians nearly from its founding, while tilting to the Hopkinsian side. America's first critically trained biblical scholar, Moses Stuart, belonged to the Hopkinsian group at Andover and generally subscribed to Nathaniel Taylor's revisions of the New Divinity tradition. In the mid-nineteenth century Andover took pride in its reputation as the Congregational church's intellectual power-house institution. It averaged one hundred fifty students at a time when no other seminary except Princeton enrolled more than a hundred. With the arguable exception of *The Biblical Repertory and Princeton Review,* Andover's *Bibliotheca Sacra* was the most respected theological journal in the United States. The school attracted New School teachers like Calvin Stowe and was often referred to, even by non-Congregationalists, as America's greatest semi-nary. In 1863 the seminary hired one of its most promising alums, Egbert Smyth, to strengthen and slightly modernize its teaching of church history; for several years Smyth gently resisted the dogmatism of Andover orthodoxy, but by the mid-1870s he had like-minded colleagues. In 1878 he became the faculty president; in 1881, the seminary's appointment of Newman Smyth to Park's theology chair vividly confirmed that Andover no longer subordinated history to dogma. Smyth's appointment by Andover's board of trustees was strongly supported by a core of liberal-leaning faculty leaders that included Egbert Smyth, Charles M. Mead, Joseph H. Thayer, John P. Gulliver, and the recently appointed William Jewett Tucker. Andover Seminary was opting for progressive orthodoxy.[57]

The old-guard conservatives understood very well that "progressive ortho-doxy" was a trojan horse for liberalism. Park, viewing the appointment as a betrayal of the seminary's heritage and his own, conferred with the denomina-tion's secretary of the Board of Foreign Missions, who organized a protest against the appointment, charging that Smyth's notion of a future probation was disastrous for foreign missions. At Park's urging, *The Congregationalist* also edi-torialized against Smyth, fueling a denominational controversy over academic freedom, liberalism, and the purpose of foreign missions. Seeking to quell a con-troversy that they believed the seminary had been wrong to instigate, Andover's Board of Visitors, a self-perpetuating supervisory board with parallel trustee-like authority, revoked Smyth's appointment on the ground that he lacked teaching experience. While the Board of Visitors succeeded in keeping Newman Smyth off the faculty, they did not stop Andover Seminary from turning liberal. In 1882 Newman Smyth accepted the pastorate of a prominent Congregational church, Center Church in New Haven, Connecticut, which he served for the rest of his career, exercising an influential ministry to Yale students and faculty. In 1884 Egbert Smyth and his faculty colleagues launched a journal, *Andover Review,* that quickly became a major journal of the liberal theology movement. Edited by Egbert Smyth, William Jewett Tucker, J. W. Churchill, Edward Y. Hincks, and Park's successor in theology, George Harris, the journal secured key faculty support from John P. Gulliver, John Phelps Taylor, Frank Woodruff, and George F. Moore and attracted such outside contributors as Newman Smyth,

Francis H. Johnson, Borden Parker Bowne, George A. Gordon, Francis G. Peabody, George F. Genung, Lewis F. Stearns, Bliss Perry, John Wright Buckham, and Hamilton Wright Mabie.[58]

Andover Review was far from radical; none of its editors blasted the old orthodoxy with the critical bite of Levi Paine, who taught church history at Bangor Seminary. To greater effect, however, they pressed hard for a New Theology that made peace with modern science, especially evolutionary theory, and for continued progress in theology and society. They called for a Christian appropriation of Darwinian theory that opposed orthodoxism and scientistic rationalism alike, appealed for a morally acceptable understanding of Christ's atonement, and questioned the logic of substitionary atonement. Most provocatively, they defended the doctrine of a future probation for those who did not hear the gospel in this life. Their belief that Christianity required a new theology to survive and flourish in the modern age was offensive to the Andover old guard; Park denounced the apostasy of the new faculty, and in 1866, Andover's Board of Visitors launched heresy trials against Egbert Smyth and his coeditors that dragged on for six years.[59]

Andover Review took the offensive after being charged with heresy. In 1888, the editors published a collection of unsigned editorials that quickly acquired the status of a movement primer. *Progressive Orthodoxy* convinced many readers that the new theology was a recovery of pure Christianity. While conceding that there was probably such a thing as "novelty of doctrine without progress, as well as progress without entire novelty," the editors proclaimed that believing in the possibility of genuine progress through new thinking was part of what it meant to have faith in the ongoing work of the Holy Spirit. From any standpoint, they admonished, theologians were obliged to make their case with reason and evidence. "Prove all things" was an apt injunction for theology. Scripture was honored more, not less, they exhorted, when Christian thinkers opened their faith to the facts of reason and history: "They are life; the human mind feels their vivifying power in the world of thought and theology, and cannot be held back from larger conceptions of God and his kingdom and human destiny, because everything it cherishes in hope and expectation was not definitely uttered by an Apostle in writing a practical letter to the Romans, or the Corinthians, or the *Diaspora*." They defended the universalistic hope of a future probation with unbending liberal zeal: "Our belief is that somewhere and sometime God will reveal himself to every one in the face of Jesus Christ, and that the destiny of each and all is determined by the relation to Christ. If we did not believe this, Christianity would no longer be for us the universal religion, and the teaching that Christ is Son of Man, the universal man, the Head of humanity, would be robbed of its significance."[60]

None of the Andover theologians acquired the status of a major movement thinker. Most readers of *Progressive Orthodoxy* had no idea which editors had written the book's various chapters, and by the turn of the century, Andover liberalism seemed quite mild compared to developments at Union Theological

Seminary, Boston University, and the newly founded University of Chicago. The liberalization of Andover Seminary was an historical watershed, however. For more than seventy years, Andover faculty were required to sign a strict creedal statement every year, but this determined policy failed to stop the Congregational church's showcase conservative institution from turning liberal. Subsequently the Andover theologians kept their teaching positions and accented the progressive aspects of progressive orthodoxy. Most galling of all to the seminary's former constituency, in 1922 Andover Seminary merged with Harvard Divinity School. The institutional heritage of Andover's protest against the Unitarian takeover of Harvard, including its massive library, ended up belonging to Unitarian Harvard.

THEOLOGY FOR A LIBERAL
MOVEMENT: THEODORE MUNGER

Munger's apologia for a New Theology movement was published in the midst of the Andover controversy. Like most of the Andover liberals, he considered himself a peaceable broad-church type, not a factionalist or party ideologue of any sort. Identifying with the progressive-orthodoxy liberals at Andover and sympathizing with their plight at finding themselves in a faction fight, he explained at the outset that this was not how the New Theology movement wanted to proceed. The New Theology was "a definite movement," but not a party, Munger claimed; its spirit was constructive and interpretive, not factional: "It is not a disturber of the peace in the realm of belief, but comes forward to meet the unconscious thought and the conscious need of the people, and if possible, do something towards quelling the anarchy of fear and doubt that now prevails." The New Theology was not really interested in faction fights with conservatives, but spoke to the doubts and anxieties that all Christians felt, simply by virtue of living in the modern age. It sought to link the truth of the Christian past to the truth of the Christian present. It affirmed God's triune self-expression, but not "a formal and psychologically impossible Trinity"; it affirmed the divine sovereignty, but not as a theoretical cornerstone, "preferring for that place the divine righteousness"; it believed in the incarnation, but not as "a mere physical event" separated from God's indwelling presence in humanity; it accepted the atonement as a divinely enacted process of redemptive ethical import, not as a suprahistorical transaction. The forerunners of the New Theology were Bushnell, Robertson, Maurice, and a few others, Munger noted. He gave no list of contemporaries, suggesting that the movement had too many proponents to list individually: "If we enumerate its representatives among the living, we must recite the names of those who are eminent in every form of thought and in every work of holy charity."[61]

The New Theology was thus understood to be a sizable movement fully in tune with the genuine progress of modern culture. At the same time, Munger distinguished between the wants and needs of modern culture: cultured modern people wanted broad enlightenment, an educated "mental largeness" that grasped and comprehended the world, but they also needed "height," the spiritual wisdom of a modernized, but anciently rooted Christian religion. With stylish felicity he sought to explicate what made modernized New Theology new: it believed in revelation, inspiration, and scriptural authority but was distinguished by its refusal to conceive these categories in dogmatic ways. Munger explained that revelation, the unveiling of God's thought and feeling, has a cognitive element but is not essentially propositional. Revelation is not something *from* God that can be *known* as factual information; it is something *of* God that its recipients rationally *interpret.* The New Theology therefore correlated reason and revelation, giving first place to reason: "We accept the Christian faith because of the reasonableness of its entire substance, and not because we have somehow become persuaded that a revelation has been made." The critical work of reason does not cease at the point of revelatory unveiling; acceptance of revelation rests on reason—"it is impossible to conceive of it as gaining foothold in the mind and heart in any other way, nor can faith in it be otherwise secured." Through every moment of its reception, interpretation, and appropriation, revelation appeals to reason, "playing into it as flame mingles with flame, and drawing from it that which is kindred with itself."[62]

Munger acknowledged that reason is limited and contains elements of faith; good theology does not claim to exclude everything that cannot be understood, for reason cannot comprehend eternal truth: "But this is quite different from silencing reason before questions that have been cast upon human nature, yet are so interpreted as to violate every principle of human nature." Reason appropriately corrects theologies that contradict science or moral goodness in the name of revelation. "To trust is a great duty; but as reason has an element of faith, so faith has an element of reason, and that element requires that the fundamental verdicts of human nature shall not be set aside." Any theology that denigrates reason ultimately denigrates faith and revelation, he warned. Reason is limited, fallible, and dependent on faith elements of its own, "but so far as it goes, it goes surely and firmly; it is not a rotten foundation, it is not a broken reed, it is not a false light." New Theology took no interest in strategies that removed religion from the logic and tests of scientific rationality.[63]

Neither did it treat the Bible as God's literal words. Though he made little use of biblical scholarship in his arguments, Munger was clear that the theory of verbal inspiration had no place in the New Theology. Inspiration is "the breathing of God upon the soul," he observed. "Who can put that into a theory?" The New Theology strongly affirmed that the biblical writers were inspired, while regarding the biblical text as a history of revelation, not revelation itself. Munger explained that "we are getting to speak less of the inspired *book,* and more of the inspired *men* who wrote it." New Theology revered scripture as a witness to revelation, "but it also holds that the Scriptures were written by living men, whose life entered into their writings; it finds the color and temper of the writer's mind in his work; it finds also the temper and habit of the age; it penetrates the forms of Oriental speech." In a word, modern theology read the Bible as literature: "It is not a diviner's rod; it is not a charmed thing of intrinsic power, representing a far-off God." As a modern Christian standpoint, critical yet faithful, New Theology interpeted the Bible as a record of God's continually unfolding revelation in history. Like most nineteenth-century liberals, Munger subordinated the narrative character of scripture to the ideas he found within it, believing that the Bible is essentially "a book of eternal laws and facts that are evolving their truth and reality in the process of history."[64]

Munger repeatedly emphasized that New Theology differed from old orthodoxies principally on account of its immersion in real life. New Theology, finding its methods "in the every-day processes of humanity," dealt with human life in the manner of poetry and drama, viewing humanity "by a direct light, [looking] straight at it, and into it." His favorite examples were Robertson sermons: "See how every sentence rests squarely on human life, touching it at every point, the sermon and human experience meeting as if cast in a mould." In contrast, said Munger, every orthodoxy builds up a theoretical system that is far removed from the rich complexity of actual life, and stands on an alien structure of abstractions built up logically from a single premise such as human depravity or divine sovereignty. The New Theology was realistic and experiential by contrast. It modeled itself on literature and poetry more than logic, making no claims about God, salvation, or the natural world not consonant with human experience. It rejected the traditional dichotomy between sacred and secular realms, finding no experiential or scriptural basis for supernaturalist dualism. It insisted that God is moral in a morally uncompromised sense of the term and that faith is a moral act, "an actual entering into and fellowship with the life of Christ." In all these ways, Munger affirmed, the New Theology awakened a sense of living *reality*, and thus allied itself with scripture and modern scientific consciousness. More deeply than orthodoxy, modern theology asserted the incarnational presence of God in human life and the goodness of God's relational character.[65]

"It is the characteristic thought of God at present that He is immanent in all created things,—immanent yet personal, the life of all lives, the power of all powers, the soul of the universe; that He is at most present where there is the most perfection," Munger asserted. With this conception of divine reality, he reasoned, trinitarian language begins to make sense again; if God is the spiritual power whose being is constitutive of all reality, it is reasonable to believe that God should make himself known as a Son of man and ever-present Spirit. Revelation and reason fit together when God's immanence is emphasized; formal notions of trinity and unity fall away, "and God in Christ, filling the mould of humanity to the full, becomes a great, illuminating truth." Munger reflected that "we may or may not pronounce the ancient phrases, but we need no longer hesitate to say, 'Father, Son, and Holy Spirit,' meaning a paternal heart and will at the centre, a sonship that stands for humanity, a spiritual energy that is the life of men, and through which they come into freedom and righteousness."

Supernaturalist conceptions of divine reality bring Christianity into conflict with science and moral feeling, he admonished, but the New Theology supported science and moral feeling by bringing God's self-expressions into life.[66]

Munger's carefully calibrated rhetoric was crucial to the effect of his argument. *The Freedom of Faith* was a manifesto for a field-transforming movement in the form of irenic self-expression; it made audaciously presumptuous claims with modest disclaimers. While denying that he spoke for any party, Munger claimed to speak for the spirit of the age. He named not a single living thinker as a proponent of New Theology, but argued that the New Theology movement included all the best thinkers currently active in all fields of inquiry. The New Theology brushed aside all previous theologies as unworthy of science and the good, but it claimed to speak "no word of contempt for those who linger in ways it has ceased to walk in." It was scarcely "more than a movement" thus far, Munger admitted, and it had no taste for partisan brawling: "It is not an organization, it is little aggressive, it does not herald itself with any Lo here or Lo there." Determined not to fight, at least not directly, the New Theology expected nonetheless to prevail, precisely because it was a forward-moving attempt "to meet the unfolding revelation of God."[67]

The New Theology represented the epochal shift in thinking that modern Christianity needed. Munger believed that the New Theology deserved to overtake the field of theology, and he hoped it might do so with a minimum of party wars and bitterness. He noticed, in 1883, that the academic guardians of New England Theology were all reaching retirement age. While Munger's well-mannered Victorianism made him temperamentally averse to conflict, his concern to minimize in-house theological warfare had a further cause. For all his praise of modern science, he dreaded scientism as a philosophical worldview. He felt deeply that the life-or-death enemy of liberal Christianity was secular materialism, not religious orthodoxy. The crucial question for him, as for his movement, was whether human beings belong ultimately to God or nature: "Is mind a gradation of matter? Is spirit the essence of matter, or is it something *other* than matter, over it and inclusive of it?" The New Theology was prepared to defend God and immortality against an ascending atheistic materialism, Munger vowed, while religious orthodoxy, being alien to modern consciousness, was bound to lose the argument to an overpowering enemy.

"We talk of Waterloos and Gettysburgs; they were petty conflicts in comparison with this battle now going on in the realm of thought, one side claiming that the material world includes man, the other side claiming that he cannot be summed up in its category and is but partially adjusted to its methods." The highest principle of materialism is unvarying law, Munger observed, while the highest principle of the human subject is freedom. All other questions pale before this one. Is God the ultimate reality, or matter? Do freedom-claiming subjects belong wholly to the material world, or is their claim to freedom grounded in spiritual reality? "If the material world includes me, then I have no shield against its relentless forces, its less than brute indiscrimination, its sure finiteness or impersonal and shifting continuance," Munger wrote. In that case, freedom, meaning, and personal identity are all illusions. "But if spirit has an existence of its own, if there is a spiritual order with God at its head and with freedom for its method, then I belong to that order, there is my destiny, there is my daily life."[68]

Munger embraced Darwinian evolutionary theory as science, but not as ethics or a substitute theology. Darwinism taught the survival of the fittest, but Munger countered that the "inmost principle" of Christianity, "its entire significance, is the salvation of the weak." Darwin admitted that naturalism cannot solve the mystery of free will; Munger added that it cannot solve the mystery of personal identity, either. "Matter cannot uphold the consciousness of identity," he explained. On a naturalistic account, the "I am" of self-consciousness is the illusion of a mere "conglomerate of atoms." Naturalistic materialism does not account "for the difference between the instincts of the brutes and the mental and moral faculties of man, nor for the sense of personal identity; nor can any theory account for it that is limited by matter with its universal law of constant flux and atomic change." By contrast, Christianity is the religion of personal identity par excellence, because Christianity teaches the resurrection of the dead. Early Christianity took its stand as a claim that identity is real and continues after death. Munger cautioned that the Pauline meaning of this claim was distorted by various church fathers, who pressed it into a false doctrine of the resurrection of the flesh; a chief task of the New Theology was "to clear away the slight rubbish left by them." Easter faith is not about the resuscitation of corpses, he admonished, but about the reality and endurance of personal identities forged in God's image. Personal identity is the central idea of Christian resurrection and the key to its meaning. In this life we possess matter-feeding bodies adapted to gravitation, time, and space; in the next life our spirits will build about themselves bodies adapted to spiritual conditions. This is the faith that gave birth to Christianity, Munger exhorted, and remains our best living hope.[69]

The Freedom of Faith went through eight editions in its first year and made Munger an unlikely movement leader. It was denounced as semi-Christian novelty by *Bibliotheca Sacra,* which moved to Oberlin during the Andover controversy, and by the likes of *Biblical Repertory and Princeton Review,* but by 1883 American conservatives had lost much of their power to confer odium on revisionists. Fortunate in its timing, the book exemplified Robertson's principles—especially that truth should be taught suggestively, not dogmatically—and helped to engender the field-changing movement that Munger imagined. Beginning as a new style of preaching, the New Theology was thoroughly Victorian. One of its enthusiasts was Queen Victoria herself, who praised "Newman Smyth's and Munger's wonderful books" and reported that she was "encouraged and strengthened" by *The Freedom of Faith.* As she appreciated, the New Theology, a product of the pulpit, showed that a new kind of theology already existed in the preaching of modern Christianity's more

forward-thinking clergy. Munger and Newman Smyth expressed their content-
ment to remain in parish ministry, where they were free to develop their thinking without ecclesiastical censure. Aside from his opening apologia for a
modernizing, life-oriented theological movement, Munger's book was a collection of sermons on immortality and resurrection. He noted shortly afterward
that the movement for which he spoke could only have sprung from the pulpit,
since all other fields of instruction in religion and the sciences were "dominated
by the inductive method." The pulpit was ahead of theology, and both trailed
literature, drama, and poetry. The rhetorical pitch and focus of his thinking
were the keys to its inspiring effect; belonging more to literature than theology,
Munger sought to evoke and speak to people's life experiences rather than to
expound traditional dogma.[70]

Persistently he sought to explicate Christian ideas by reflecting on the experiences behind them, and his reinterpretations of Christian ideas were usually
linked to judgments about changes in modern consciousness. His later sermons
bore such titles as "The Witness from Experience," "Truth through and by
Life," "Life Not Vanity," "The Gospel of the Body," "The Defeat of Life,"
"Trust and Righteousness," and "Music as Revelation." Like Emerson and
Bushnell, Munger embraced Coleridge's maxim that Christianity "is not a theory or speculation, but a life—not a philosophy of life, but a life and a living
process." Like Queen Victoria, he advocated the triumph of spirit over nature
within culture and the life process. His favorite theme was that Christianity is
concerned primarily with living because God is immanent in the world and
human life; since the object of theology is the living Spiritual power that sustains all life, theology is obliged to "think in harmony" with other disciplines.
Since it was not credible to ask modern people to be loyal to "two equally
authoritative methods of thought," theology could not claim exception from the
authority of modern critical consciousness.[71]

Since no theologian can be interested in everything, Munger had a clear criterion for choosing his subjects: usefulness in pursuing his theme. Though
accepting of historical-critical Bible scholarship, he made little use of it, apparently because he did not think it helped bring Christian subjects to life. "We are
under no obligation to accept any truth until it is serviceable," he asserted; truth
is important, but only utility makes truth interesting. Evolution was the crucial
example to Munger. Newman Smyth, in *Old Faiths in New Light,* interpreted
the six-day creation story in Genesis as a metaphorical description of evolution
and argued that scripture is "scientific" in its empirically sensible descriptions of
nature. Taking a similar approach to the relation of science and Christianity,
with less special pleading, Munger judged that evolutionary theory was sufficiently established scientifically that Christians should not resist it. This was not
the reason, however, that theologians needed to be seriously interested in evolution; evolution was crucially important to modern Christianity because evolutionary theory served important interests of living Christian faith.[72]

First, evolution reaffirmed and bolstered the Christian idea of the unity of creation. Christianity has always argued that nature is unified and that the ground of nature's unity is found in God, Munger observed, but in earlier centuries Christian thinkers merely asserted this principle as a faith. In the later nineteenth century, evolutionary theorists confirmed the Christian belief in the unity of nature with scientific evidence, as Darwinian biology showed that nature works by a single principle. "As knowledge broadens and wider generalizations are made, we find a certain likeness of process in all realms that indicates one law or method; namely, that of development or evolution," Munger explained. "One thing comes from another, assumes a higher and finer form, and presses steadily on towards still finer and higher forms." Rightly viewed, this was a welcome discovery for Christianity, for evolution refuted dualistic and polytheistic religious worldviews and confirmed the immanental, monotheistic picture of a unified universe created by a single world-embracing Creator: "With one principle or method in all realms, we have a key that turns all the wards of the universe, opens all its doors in the past, and will open all in time to come." The basis of science is the Christian idea that the world is composed of a singular rationality; evolution confirms this religious idea, and opens a path in every direction to the harmony of knowledge.[73]

Second, evolution confirmed Christianity's "highest hopes" for the world, "for the process tends steadily towards the moral." The Christian community prays and struggles daily for the spread of righteousness throughout the earth, he explained; evolutionary theory demonstrates that the story of the world is, in fact, a story of continuing moral progress. The church is right to equate the moral progress that evolution brings about with the moral progress that Christians pray for in seeking the fulfillment of righteousness: "It is not amiss to see men in prehistoric ages forsaking caves and living in huts, using first a club and then a bow, ores and then metals, nomadic and then in villages." Related to Christian hope is the human joy "to see despotism yielding to a class, and the class yielding to the people; personal revenge passing into social punishment of crime by law, and justice slowly creeping to higher forms; penalty first as vindictive, then retributive, and now at last reformatory; first a conception of God as power, then as justice, and finally as love." These examples of evolutionary process in action are deeply constitutive of the church's moral hope and vision, Munger argued. Growth in righteousness cannot be something different from the world's actual moral progress, for "no truth is perfect that is cut off from other truths."[74]

Third, evolutionary theory strengthened the teleological argument for divine existence and goodness. The argument from design, classically put forth by William Paley, contends that a holy Creator is reflected in the beauty, complexity, and goodness of creation; teleological apologists typically based their case on some conflation of claims about the beauty and complexity of the natural world, the progress of civilization, the intricacy of perception, the mystery of consciousness, the dynamics of love, and the like. Munger noted that evolution bolstered and expanded these claims: "If we can look at the universe both as a whole and in all its processes and in all ages, and find one principle working everywhere, binding together all things, linking one process to another with increasing purpose, and steadily pressing towards a full revelation of God's goodness, we find the argument strengthened by as much as we have enlarged the field of its illustration." Evolution perfects the church's faith in the God-given unity of the world and strengthens its faith in the world's divinely charged goodness.[75]

Munger had good company; Henry Ward Beecher, Newman Smyth, and John Fiske made similar arguments in urging the church to face up to the truth of evolution. These arguments were important, Munger urged, but they did not speak to people's feelings, the deeper source of religious resistance to evolution. People change their beliefs more readily than their feelings, he noted, and in the case of evolution, a sizable "readjustment of our feelings of reverence" was required. Christian leaders were still struggling to comprehend basic facts and details about natural selection. Beecher waited for years before he endorsed evolution explicitly; in his later career he merely began to think about evolution in a religious way. Most theologians were still struggling to catch up to Beecher, and more important, the church had almost no experience of learning how to feel its new conception of creation. "When a meteor falls to earth, men at first take more heed of its shape and composition than of its origin," Munger analogized. Modern Christian leaders no longer challenged evolution as a scientific description, and some had begun to think about evolution in a religious way, but thus far, Christian feelings were being left behind.[76]

Munger made a beginning with favorite lines from Goethe and Tennyson that illumined his own panentheistic romanticism. Tennyson's saying, "Closer is he than breathing, and nearer than hands and feet," conveyed the true sense of God's presence in creation better than the whole of Milton's *Paradise Lost,* he judged. Munger looked forward to a modernized church that shared this sentiment. When God becomes known to feeling as the Spiritual power of evolutionary process, he predicted, "the old sense of reverence will come back to us and become a finer, deeper, intenser feeling than it was under the old concept of creation. It will also be a more intelligent and better-proportioned reverence." The old concept of creation engendered spiritual respect and assurance, he explained, but not a deep, life-giving reverence, which is stirred only by creation as an ongoing whole, not by the part of creation that lies behind us. Munger exhorted: "It is only under a theory of evolutionary creation that we can truly wonder and adore God." Modern knowledge makes known the God of life-giving, creative process who directed evolution, over millions of years, toward the emergence of created moral beings.[77]

He disputed the common sentiment that evolution denigrates human uniqueness. "If the conclusion disturbs us, if we shrink from linking our nobler faculties with preceding orders, it is because we have as yet no proper conception of the close and interior relation of God to all his works," Munger argued. The organic relation of humankind to the material and animal worlds does not wholly determine human nature or destiny, for as long as human beings have souls and spiritual freedom, he reasoned, it does not matter from where human beings evolved in the world's prehistory. The "cord of origin" that binds human beings to physical nature does not bind their destiny: "As we find God in destiny, so we may find him in origin,—present at both ends of his own process and in equal power." If evolution is viewed as a process directed by God's laws of action, and not as an unsupervised, inexorable system of mere natural selection, he counseled, there is no reason to fear that evolution will swallow up human distinctiveness in matter and brute life. Evolution is about the uniform working of force in nature, but evolution by itself cannot explain the force of nature, which has its only possible origin in will. Will is an attribute of personality, Munger noted; it is also the basis of freedom and religion. Humankind bears an organic relation to the process of creation, but human beings possess freedom by virtue of their absolute relation to the spiritual Power that indwells and enlivens the process of creation. On this ground Munger exhorted modern Christians to be thankful for their freedom-blessed existence, "however it came about, and let us not deem ourselves too good to be included in the one creation of the one God."[78]

Thus did the liberals of Munger's generation make their peace with evolution, if not Charles Darwin. Evolution discloses the process by which humanity has emerged from necessity and instinct, Munger reasoned, but religion belongs to the realm of humanity becoming free. Only spirit is wholly free; absolute freedom is impossible for finite human beings, and human beings are obliged to carry along some of their evolutionary inheritance while moving toward spiritual freedom. Developing this consummately Victorian vision of the triumph of spirit over nature, many social gospelers went further than Munger in linking evolution to progress in democracy and political reform; some explicitly identified modern progress with the kingdom of God; a few sought to Christianize social Darwinism; others developed the evolutionary monist implications of Munger's theology.

Taking advantage of his proximity to Yale University, Newman Smyth spent much of the 1890s in biology laboratories, seeking to understand evolution as an admirer of what he called the "patient and ingenious researches" of modern scientists. His many years of labor in university laboratories bore fruit in two books, *The Place of Death in Evolution* (1897) and *Through Science to Faith* (1902), both of which surveyed the current state of scientific research on evolution. *Through Science to Faith* contained a Mungeresque vision of the evolutionary process as God's process of revelation, which throughout natural and human history has unfolded through the struggle of life: "It has been gradual and progressive; and it continues still to be increasing manifestation of the Spirit of the Christ to the growing Christian sense of the world." He ended with an evolutionary vision of immortality: "We are not yet born into this larger world, but nature has formed and nourished us for its liberty. Man's life, still cherished in nature's womb, feels the stirrings within it of unknown powers, and has present embryonic consciousness of its immortal worth. First is that which is natural; and afterwards—its sure fulfillment—is that which is spiritual."[79]

The New Theology movement lacked a towering field-shaping figure. Munger made no attempt to be one. An every-week preacher throughout his career, he spoke mostly through sermons and essays, lacking time and strength for scholarly work, and deflected requests from friends to write movement-building major works. His pulpit voice was perfectly suited to aid his movement's take-off, however. In the early 1880s Munger gave notice that liberal Christianity had ambitions for the field of theology. He exemplified the movement's sermon-oriented literary sensibility at a time when the New Theology was almost entirely a preacher's movement. With Bushnellian conviction he insisted that literary imagination is the privileged interpreter of Christianity, because "both are keyed to the spirit." Like the spirit of Christ, he argued, great literature reveals the nature and meaning of things. Inspired by truth, the literary imagination stands upon and shows humanity at its ethical and spiritual best.[80] In the course of explicating these Bushnellian themes, Munger helped create a generation of Bushnellian liberals. More than any individual, he lifted Bushnell to a place of honor in American theology. At the same time he marked and defended the ways that an ascending liberal movement distinguished itself from its major forerunner.[81]

Increasingly showered with praise and honors for his theological leadership, Munger made a homecoming of sorts in 1885 by accepting the pastorship of United Church in New Haven, where he became Newman Smyth's next-door neighbor and friend. Center Church and United Church stood side by side, adjacent to the Yale campus, giving area residents an ample supply of liberal Congregationalist preaching. Though his return to New Haven provoked protests from conservatives, two years later Munger was elected to the Yale Corporation, which confirmed the new respectability of theological liberalism. Between these events he coped with the deaths of his two dearest friends: his wife, Elizabeth Duncan Munger, and Elisha Mulford. Munger offered what he could to an ascending liberal movement during this period, while pleading lack of time and emotional vigor to do more. Urged by his Houghton & Mifflin publishing friend, Horace E. Scudder, to write a major work on Bushnell, he begged off for ten years. "The fact is my place and pulpit require all my time and strength," Munger explained. "Each is as sharply determined as the other. I *must* keep my pulpit up to the mark. Every consideration demands this. And then there is no end to the other time-consuming and strength-exhausting work." He still doubted his standing and qualifications. Amos Chesborough and various others whom Scudder could approach were closer to Bushnell personally, he noted. "My hesitation is chiefly a matter of conscience," he confessed finally. "If I felt that I had a right I would gladly undertake the work and see what I could do with it, though to tell the truth I have not much heart for anything."[82]

He had little heart for anything while burdened with overwork and the depressing loss of loved ones. *The Freedom of Faith* observed that people undertake great things only in their twenties, thirties, and forties, when strong health and "a certain simplicity" allow them to sail through life without reflecting on their inevitable end. At fifty, Munger reflected, we are overtaken by a different sense of ourselves. A sense of mortality "peculiarly real" dawns upon us as we cope with shrinking frames, shriveled skin, and increasing weakness and infirmity: "Heretofore life, the world, the body,—all have been for us; now they are against us, they are failing us; the shadow of our doom begins to creep upon us."

Munger was describing his own experience, yet his own great things began only at fifty-three, with this book. Widely sought afterward as a leading religious thinker, he gave his voice to the New Theology, remarried, and inspired many with his felicitous, graceful sermonizing. Just before his retirement in 1900, he also wrote his major work on Bushnell, *Horace Bushnell, Preacher and Theologian* (1899), a hymn of appreciation that occasionally blurred the lines between subject and author. In its closing lines, Munger predicted that Bushnell would continue to grow in importance. A theology that fit modern thought was clearing the field of premodern conceptions of divine reality and redemption, he observed, and when this transformation was completed, Bushnell's epochal achievement would stand out in clearer view: "Then it will be seen how pivotal was his work in a transition that will grow more significant as the contrast deepens between what was driven out and what was brought in. It will be said of him as Harnack has said of Luther: 'He liberated the natural life, and the natural order of things.'"[83]

Munger's friends routinely described him as deep-hearted, profoundly spiritual, and prophetic; church historian George L. Walker observed that he had "a poet's fire and a prophet's vision." Munger's greatest contribution to American Christianity was his deep spiritual earnestness, Walker recounted; beyond his formative intellectual contributions to theological liberalism, Munger made his readers feel that the New Theology movement "was a progress in piety no less than in knowledge." Congregational pastor and theologian George A. Gordon testified that Munger was "the wisest, gentlest, most winning, and in many respects the most availing of the religious leaders of his generation." Religion was his life, Gordon recalled; Munger lived in the Spirit and helped others perceive its truth and beauty. As a preacher he sought to be seen through, like a window, not to be seen; thus he was known for his sincerity and faithfulness. He preached simple, eloquent sermons that eschewed showy mannerisms. As a pastor and theological leader he was "full of compassion, slow to anger in the conflict of thought, of great patience and of great and precious power," and in retirement he seemed, to Gordon, only to deepen in spiritual serenity: "He became richer in heart and more beautiful in spirit. He moved in a deep and constant atmosphere of peace. The mystery of life was always with him, but it was a mystery of light because of his faith in the compassionate God and Father of man."[84]

Never a quietist, Munger was a man of causes whose compelling character grew out of the other-regarding causes he adopted. Gordon noted that many people were attracted to the New Theology after being attracted to Munger personally. But Munger was much less a prophet than a pastor, spiritual exemplar, and theological reformer. Though sympathetic to various progressive social causes, he was not a social gospeler, much less a social gospel leader. He had little energy for political activism, especially political economy or social policy. Like many liberals who quietly supported social gospel reforms, but kept their distance from the social gospel movement, he believed that one struggle was enough. While supporting social gospel opposition to revivalist individualism, he gave only token support to the idea of social salvation. Like many well-stationed liberal preachers, Munger took little interest in the tasks that social activism outside his class required, and his preaching contained nothing to offend privileged parishioners who agreed with him on theology. He repeatedly asserted the church's obligation to make its theology pertinent to "real life," but chose not to address labor organizing, property rights, social policy, and other real-life socioeconomic issues. To judge from his writings, the chief social problem of his time was America's growing materialism. In Munger's time, however, in the very movement his preaching and writing helped to engender, a strikingly different kind of Christian social witness came to life.

THE SOCIAL GOSPEL AS POLITICAL ECONOMICS: WASHINGTON GLADDEN

Washington Gladden was its prophet. Though he was slow to concede the point, Columbus, Ohio, was a good place to conjure the social meaning of modern Christianity. A city of 53,000, Columbus was crude, mostly unpaved, and poorly lit when Gladden arrived there in 1882. The city's domestic architecture was depressing to him; the flatness and monotony of the Ohio landscape, "a perpetual weariness . . . hard to bear," were even more so. Ohio State University barely existed, with just over three hundred students. Gladden cheered himself with the fact that Columbus was Ohio's capital city, "pervaded by the atmosphere of politics," and that some of its wide streets contained "large possibilities of beauty," but in his early Columbus years he gave more attention to national Congregationalist controversies than to local social concerns. In the early 1880s, Congregationalists fiercely debated the liberalization of Andover Seminary, the "Creed of 1883," and the New Theology of Munger and Newman Smyth. Gladden took special interest in the national Congregationalist attempt to devise a nonbinding creed, which broke down over the question of repentance after death. Conservatives argued that no genuinely

Christian creed could endorse the possibility of a "second probation" or "probation after death," for to leave room for such a possibility was to "cut the nerve of missions" by undercutting the motive for evangelism. The most effective progressive response to this charge came from missionaries who countered that soteriological exclusivism was far more damaging to Christian missions, because people in the "heathen nations" were often horrified by the claim that their ancestors were condemned to hell. With typical social gospel appreciation for the progressive missionary as a social type, Gladden later noted that much of the church's best thinking on the relation of Christianity and other religions came from missionaries.[85]

Gradually he became a Midwesterner, while pastoring an upscale church that stood across the street from Ohio's state capitol. A product of the complex interrelationship of Central Ohio Congregationalism and Presbyterianism, First Congregational Church had its roots in a blended Congregational-Presbyterian congregation named First Presbyterian. In 1852, a group of antislavery Congregationalists and Presbyterians broke away from First Presbyterian; four years later, following the trend of similar antislavery splinterings, they changed their name from Third Presbyterian to First Congregational. Long accustomed to social activism and progressive religion, the Columbus Congregationalists welcomed Gladden warmly, well beyond the standard of New England cordiality, and he worked hard for them, visiting nearly every family each year. On Sunday mornings he preached about personal religion; on Sunday evenings and various weekday occasions he preached on social and theological topics. All but a few of his thirty-eight books were collections of his favorite sermons. Gladden was kindly, genial, and somewhat shy, with a keen sense of irony. Beloved by his Columbus congregation, he maintained cordial relations with most parishioners, though with a definite formal reserve; his personal correspondence extended to only a handful of parishioners. Occasions of intimate self-revelation were extremely rare for Gladden in any context; his memoir barely mentioned his wife, gave little insight into his inner life, and said nothing at all about his personal life after the Civil War.[86]

Typically for him, his memoir was long on discussions of "the industrial problem," "the municipal problem," "the Negro problem," and the merits of America's recent presidents. He recalled that the 1880s "was an interesting period in which to exercise the function of the Christian ministry. The spirit of inquiry was in the air." The official theologies of American churches were still very conservative, he recalled, but "it was evident that the Christian world was getting ready for a forward movement." For Gladden, the Hocking Valley coalminers strike of 1884–85 was a major turning point. Numerous strikes took place in the coal regions of southeastern Ohio during the mid-1880s, but the strike against the Columbus and Hocking Valley Coal and Iron Company affected Gladden personally, because most of the company's top executives were members of his congregation. Beginning as a demand for higher wages, the strike soon grew into a battle over trade unionism. Two of the company's vice-presidents, Walter Crafts and Thaddeus Longstreth, were members of Gladden's board of trustees. Longstreth was militantly hostile to unionism; Crafts was a milder personality, "one of the kindest and fairest-minded of men," in Gladden's estimation, yet he vowed to Gladden, "We'll kill that union if it costs half a million dollars." In the end, both sides suffered heavy losses, and the eleven-month strike ended with an abject surrender by the miners. The miners reorganized shortly afterward, forced the company to submit to outside arbitration, and won an arbitrated wage agreement. Crafts later conceded to Gladden that the company was better off dealing with an organized union than a mob; though he claimed no credit for the company's turnabout, Gladden strongly advocated collective bargaining and mutually negotiated settlements.[87]

His lectures during this period launched the explicitly "social gospel" phase of his career. Certain that liberal Protestantism possessed the solutions to America's social problems, Gladden proclaimed that the church had a great deal to say about wealth, inequality, labor, unions, socialism, and war, "and it is high time that the Church of God were saying it from hearts of flame with tongues of fire." The Puritan and evangelical roots of the social gospel showed through whenever he warmed to the theme of Christian America: "We must make men believe that Christianity has a right to rule this kingdom of industry, as well as all the other kingdoms of this world." The Christian gospel recognizes no political or national boundaries on its claims, he exhorted; morally serious Christianity claimed "that her law is the only law on which any kind of society will rest in security and peace; that ways must be found of incorporating good-will as a regulative principle, as an integral element, into the very structure of industrial society."[88]

A qualifying assurance invariably came next. Gladden prized his carefully cultivated reputation for objectivity and fairness. He wanted the church to be the conscience of an expanding industrial society without taking sides in the class struggle. He emphasized that both sides of the labor-capital wars often bargained in bad faith, considered only their own interest, demonized their opponents, and resorted to unjustified coercion. A characteristic speech on these themes, his most significant lecture of the mid-1880s, was composed as an attempt to mediate an 1886 strike in Cleveland. Calling for negotiated settlements and pledges of cooperation as an alternative to the ongoing war between labor and capital, Gladden firmly endorsed trade unionism while censuring the warlike tactics of both sides: "Is not this business of war a senseless, brutal, barbarous business, at best? Does either side expect to do itself any good by fighting the other?" He made personal appeals and assurances: "Permit me to say that I know something about this war; I have been in the thick of it for thirty years, trying to make peace, and helping to care for the sick and the wounded; and I know that the wrong is not all on one side, and that the harsh judgments and the fierce talk of both sides are inexcusable." He allowed that both sides had strong arguments; the working class could not win the class struggle without uniting, and "the masters" could not win without smashing the unions. The problem was the shared assumption that winning and warfare were necessary. Gladden ended with a blend of personal and religious appeals: "Is it well, brother men, is it well to fight? Is it not better to be friends? Are you not all children of one Father? Nay, are you not, as the great apostle said, members one of another? Your war is not only wholesale fratricide, it is social suicide."[89]

This speech was widely praised for its fair-mindedness and its demonstration that the church could be an honest broker of labor-capital conflict. When he delivered it to the affluent Law and Order League of Boston, at Tremont Temple, Gladden got a rousing ovation and an invitation to return the following week to give it again to a working-class audience in the same auditorium, where he was cheered heartily. Gladden loaded his social addresses with enough figures and topical references to assure outsiders that he knew what he was talking about. Nearly every address also preached his social philosophy, which expounded the primacy of the Golden Rule, a dualistic view of human nature, and the practice of cooperation as both means and end. Gladden's ideas of the good society and social salvation were still essentially individualistic in the 1880s; just as individuals should practice the Golden Rule of loving one's neighbor as oneself, employers and their employees should practice cooperation, disagreements should be negotiated in a spirit of other-regarding fellowship, and society should be organized to serve human welfare rather than profits. He opposed business corporations and corporate unionism alike, arguing that the virtues of altruistic cooperation are practicable only for individuals and small groups. Gladden taught that all individuals combine traits of egotism and altruism and that both are essential to the creation of a good society; without self-regarding virtue, society would have no dynamism or vigor. The problem with American society was that its economic basis was based on competitive vigor alone.[90]

"The industrial system as at present organized is a social solecism," Gladden charged. "It is an attempt to hold society together upon an anti-social foundation. To bring capitalists and laborers together in an association, and set them over against each other, and announce to them the principle of competition as the guide of their conduct, bidding each party to get as much as it can out of the other, and to give as little as it can,—for that is precisely what competition means,—is simply to declare war—a war in which the strongest will win." This was the heart of the matter for Gladden. Throughout his social gospel career he clung to a cooperativist critique of the wage system. He argued that because the wage system was thoroughly antisocial, it was also immoral and anti-Christian. By his lights, there were three fundamental options in political economy: relations of labor and capital could be based on slavery, wages, or cooperation. Gladden allowed that the wage system marked a crucial improvement on slavery, but fell far short of anything acceptable to Christian morality. The first stage of industrial progress featured the subjugation of labor by capital, he explained; the second stage was essentially a war between labor and capital; the third stage was the social and moral ideal, the cooperative commonwealth in which labor and capital shared a common interest and spirit.[91]

Gladden believed during his early and middle career that this ideal was imminently attainable. "It is not a difficult problem," he assured, speaking of the class struggle. "The solution of it is quite within the power of the Christian employer. All he has to do is admit his laborers to an *industrial partnership* with himself *by giving them a fixed share in the profits of production,* to be divided among them, in proportion to their earnings, at the end of the year." Profit sharing was the key to the making of a good society in the realm of political economy: it rewarded productivity and cooperative action; it channeled the virtues of self-regard and self-sacrifice; it socialized the profit motive and abolished the wage system; it promoted mutuality, equality, and community. To the "Christian man," the strongest argument for cooperative economics was its simple justice, Gladden contended: "Experience has shown him that the wage-receiving class are getting no fair share of the enormous increase of wealth; reason teaches that they never will receive an equitable proportion of it under a wage-system that is based on sheer competition; equity demands, therefore, that some modification of the wage-system be made in the interest of the laborer. If it is made, the employer must make it."[92]

To this respected Protestant pastor, who preached every Sunday to the business class and very few workers, the crucial hearts and minds belonged to the employers. The ideal solution was to convince the capitalist class to set up profit-sharing enterprises, not to abolish capitalism from above or below. In an age of ascending socialist movements, Gladden repeatedly cautioned that most employers were no less moral than the laborers they employed. It was too soon to give up on a decentralized, cooperative alternative to the wage system. Defining socialism as economic nationalization, he judged that socialism would require a large, overcentralized, and inefficient bureaucracy that placed important freedoms in jeopardy. Socialists who proposed to pull down the existing order were right to condemn the greed and predatory competitiveness of capitalism, Gladden argued, "but they are foolish in thinking that humanity will thrive under a system which discards or cripples these self-regarding forces." A better system would mobilize good will and channel self-interest to good ends. The reform that was needed was "the Christianization of the present order," he insisted, not its destruction. The "principal remedy" for the evils of the prevailing system was "the application by individuals of Christian principles and methods to the solution of the social problem."[93]

Gladden was slow to acknowledge the structural limitations on social justice. He sought to appeal to the rationality and moral feelings of a capitalist class increasingly pressured by embittered workers; only gradually did he perceive the irony of his assurances that business executives were at least as moral as their employees. If this assurance was true, the crisis of the prevailing order was about more than the morality of individuals, but as late as 1893, he defended his basic strategy of appealing to the moral feelings of the business class. In *Tools and the Man,* Gladden presented his most developed case for a "third way" profit-sharing model, which he called the "industrial partnership" model: "I would seek to commend this scheme to the captains of industry by appealing to their humanity and their justice; by asking them to consider the welfare of their workmen as well as their own. I believe that these leaders of business are not devoid of chivalry; that they are ready to respond to the summons of good-will." The same work clearly signalled that he was moving to a more explicitly pro-union perspective, however—"I confess that I am strongly inclined to take the workingman's view." Gladden allowed that cooperative ownership represented a plausible and attractive basis for a third way between capitalism and socialism, though he judged that profit-sharing "industrial partnerships" were better suited to capitalist America. Most important, he dropped his assurances that the class struggle could be easily remedied. The deepening chasm between labor and capital that Gladden witnessed in the 1890s drove him to a more realistic, structural view of political economy. His judgment that working people were losing the class war drove him to support unionism more decisively, albeit with a host of criticisms of union violence and featherbedding. By the end of the decade, though he was heartened by the ascendancy of liberal theology and the social gospel, Gladden realized that his hope for a nonsocialist, decentralized economic democracy had less and less of a material basis in a society increasingly divided along class lines.[94]

Like most of those in the social gospel movement, he took pains to dissociate himself from "socialism," by which he meant centralized state ownership of all or most business enterprises. Like much of the social gospel movement, however, he adopted a politics that combined a "monopoly enterprises" state socialism with an economic democracy model of profit sharing and cooperativist enterprises. Gladden's critique of state socialism was sensible and prescient. He objected that socialism denigrated the spirit of individual creativity and invention. "It ignores or depreciates the function of mind in production—the organizing mind and the inventive mind." The stream of the socialist movement that followed Karl Marx invested unwarranted faith in the dogma that labor creates all value, he observed: "It is not true that labor is the sole cause of value or wealth. Many substances and possessions have great value on which no labor has ever been expended." He disapproved of the socialist promise to provide meaningful work for everyone. "Socialism takes away the burdens that are necessary for the development of strength," Gladden explained. "It undertakes too much. It removes from the individual the responsibilities and cares by which his mind is awakened and his will invigorated."[95]

Most important, he protested that socialism, which required enormous governmental power and virtually infinite human wisdom, was too grandiose and bureaucratic to work. "The theory that it proposes is too vast for human power," he objected. "It requires the state to take possession of all the lands, the mines, the houses, the stores, the railroads, the furnaces, the factories, the ships,—all the capital of the country of every description." Under a socialist order, he noted with incredulity, American government bureaucrats would be vested with the power to set wages, prices, and production quotas for a sprawling continent of consumers and producers: "What an enormous undertaking it must be to discover all the multiform, the infinite variety of wants of sixty millions of people, and to supply all these wants, by governmental machinery! What a tremendous machine a government must be which undertakes, in a country like ours, to perform such a service as this!" Americans were not accustomed to viewing government as an agent of redemption, and while Gladden linked arms with the socialists in seeking to make American society less stratified and antisocial, he carefully kept his distance from socialist promises to make centralized government "the medium and minister of all social good."[96]

Gladden's social gospelism was essentially moralistic, cooperativist, and predisposed to make peace. It was allergic to Marxist rhetoric about smashing the capitalist state and skeptical even toward the milder state socialism of European social democracy. The social gospelers sought to Christianize society through further progress, reforms, and evangelization, not through revolutionary schemes to collectivize the economic order. For all of his determination to stand for a third way, however, Gladden drifted to the left in the 1890s, as he recognized that the greatest threat to his social vision came from a burgeoning corporate capitalism. He counseled that socialists should be respected, and respectfully corrected, as long as they didn't promote unnecessary violence; he called himself "enough of a Socialist to believe" in a foreign policy opposed to war and based upon international treaties with all nations. His judgment that working people were losing ground in the class struggle caused him to defend the union movement most of the time. He insisted that the right to property is subordinate to the rights of life and freedom and significantly qualified his opposition to state socialism. Gladden persistently rejected state collectivism as an economic strategy, but he made exceptions for the entire class of economic monopolies. In the early 1890s, these included the railroad, telegraph, gas, and electric companies; he later judged that mines, watercourses, water suppliers, and telephone services also belonged to this category. The railroad companies in particular were "gigantic instruments of oppression." In any industry where no effective competition existed, he argued, the only just recourse was state control. The railroad and electric companies did not operate under the law of supply and demand, nor offer their commodities or services in an open market; in effect, they closed the market. "This is not, in any proper sense, trade; this is essentially taxation," Gladden argued. "And, therefore, I think that all virtual monopolies must eventually belong to the state."[97]

His steadily deepening support for trade unionism deepened all of his leanings toward realism and decentralized socialism. In *Social Facts and Forces* (1897), Gladden recognized that unionists had legitimate reasons to intimidate scab laborers, though he still argued that the goal of trade unionism must be human solidarity, not proletarian solidarity. In his memoir, *Recollections* (1909), he judged that America was probably headed for an imminent plunge "into a Socialistic experiment," though he warned that socialism was inferior to cooperative strategies and that American society was insufficiently educated and prepared for either approach. By the time that he wrote *The Labor Question* (1911), the American social gospel movement was at high tide, but Gladden shared little of Walter Rauschenbusch's faith that the last un-Christianized sector of American society—the economy—was in the process of being Christianized. The triumph of corporate capitalism and the rise of aggressive labor organizations—such as the National Association of Manufacturers and the revolutionary Industrial Workers of the World—ended Gladden's fantasy of a paternalistic share-economy; he realized that his hope of a nonsocialist, decentralized economic democracy had little material basis in a society increasingly divided along class lines. Giving up on profit sharing and cooperatives, he took his stand with a flawed labor movement. Unorganized labor was "steadily forced down toward starvation and misery," he observed. Elsewhere he lamented that corporate capitalism was becoming utterly predatory and vengeful toward unions, "maintaining toward them an attitude of almost vindictive opposition." In this context, unionism was the only serious force of resistance against the corporate degradation of labor. If the dream of a cooperative economy was to be redeemed, Gladden argued, it would have to be redeemed as a form of union-gained industrial democracy. The partnership between labor and capital that America needed more desperately than ever would have to be gained through union-organized collective bargaining, gaining for workers their appropriate share of economic control.[98]

SOCIAL SALVATION:
THE SOCIAL GOSPEL DIFFERENCE

The social gospelers, products of the evangelical reform movements, advocated various reforms, some of them quite novel in American religion, but this is not what made the social gospel distinctive in Christian history. The social gospel movement inherited its active social reformism from the antiwar, antislavery, and temperance movements of evangelical Protestantism and gained much of its missionary impulse from the Home Missions movement. Social gospelers like Gladden, Shailer Mathews, and Walter Rauschenbusch were raised in evangelical traditions, converted to theological liberalism, and gave liberal Christianity an energizing social mission through their gospel-centered desire to Christianize America. While they promoted various social reforms as aspects of the church's Christianizing mission, however, what made the social gospel distinctive in Christian history was not its reforms, but its theology of social salvation.

In substantial measure, Gladden owes his title "father of the social gospel" to his theorizing and exemplifying of social salvation theology. "The end of Christianity is twofold, a perfect man in a perfect society," he wrote in 1893, giving a liberal twist to postmillennialism: "These purposes are never separated; they cannot be separated. No man can be redeemed and saved alone; no community can be reformed and elevated save as the individuals of which it is composed are regenerated." The message of the gospel is addressed to individuals, Gladden allowed, but the gospel addresses each individual as a member of a social organism, which creates the medium through which individuals respond to the message: "This vital and necessary relation of the individual to society lies at the basis of the Christian conception of life. Christianity would create a perfect society, and to this end it must produce perfect men; it would bring forth perfect men, and to this end it must construct a perfect society." The themes of genuine Christianity are the themes of Christ, Gladden insisted: repentance, regeneration, and the presence of the kingdom. Christ taught, "Be ye perfect as your Father in heaven is perfect." He also taught, "Repent, for the kingdom of heaven is at hand." Gladden admonished that the link in the latter statement is never to be broken; repentance is intrinsically connected to the presence of God's kingdom: "The opportunity, the motive, the condition of repentance is the presence of a divine society, of which the penitent, by virtue of his penitence, at once becomes a member."[99]

The social gospelers thus claimed to recover the meaning of Christ's petition, "Thy kingdom come." For Jesus, as for genuine Christianity, the purpose of God's inbreaking kingdom was to regenerate individuals and society as coordinate interests. Gladden preached that neither form of regeneration is possible without the other: "Whatever the order of logic may be, there can be no difference in time between the two kinds of work; that we are to labor as constantly and as diligently for the improvement of the social order as for the conversion of man." The crucial test of the church's witness is its success in maintaining an equilibrium between personal and social regeneration. Having grown out of, and beyond, an evangelical tradition fixated on individual salvation, modern Protestantism needed to emphasize "the social side of our Christian work" and dedicate itself to Christianizing America. Gladden urged that the church's social mission was to claim the kingdoms of this world for the kingdom of Christ, including "the kingdom of commerce, and the kingdom of industry, and the kingdom of fashion, and the kingdom of learning, and the kingdom of amusement; every great department of society is to be pervaded by the Christian spirit and governed by Christian law."[100]

To Christianize society was to suffuse its sentiments, doctrines, customs, institutions, and laws with the Christian spirit. "This is what is meant by the coming to earth of the kingdom of heaven," Gladden preached. "We pray every day that it may come, but we do not by this prayer imply that its advent is still to be awaited." For Christ, as for the Christ-following church, the kingdom of God has already broken into nature and history. It is the spirit that inspires historical progress and the ongoing progress of evolution:

> It was present then, this divine society, this kingdom of truth and
> love; and the centuries have but enlarged its dominion and con-
> firmed its peaceful sway. Mighty have been the changes wrought

through its gentle influence; the world in which we live is a vastly better world than the brightest dream of the best man who had lived in the world two thousand years ago. Through faithful witnesses, through brave confessors, through loyal soldiers of the cross, Christian truth and love have been steadily gaining possession of the hearts of men and of the life of society; the opinions, the feelings, the maxims, the usages, the organized activities of men have been gradually suffused with Christian motives and principles; the leaven has been working silently but pervasively upon the mass.[101]

"Thy kingdom come" is a powerful petition, but Gladden observed that it makes all the difference whether one perceives the kingdom of Christ as Christ's ongoing progress-inspiring presence or as his "future arrival from some distant scene." The liberal postmillennial spirit of the social gospel was growing in America, but so was the spirit of otherworldly, antisocial, apocalyptic premillennialism. The nineteenth century was even creating powerful new forms of premillennialist Christianity in the vast profusion of Darbyite dispensationalist movements, spin-offs of Millerite apocalypticism, and the like.[102] Gladden shook his head sadly: "It is a dismal and dreadful spectacle to see men standing in the dawn of this new day and crying that there is no light. Strangely do they honor their Master and Lord when they fail to discern anything but evil in the bright displays of his power of which the world is full." To the social gospelers, progress in democracy, culture, and science showed traces of the working of Christ's spirit and signs of his power. They gave short shrift to the premillennialist objection that Jesus and his apostles did not address sociopolitical subjects. "Those to whom they spoke had no political responsibilities," Gladden explained. "They were not citizens, they were subjects; to preach politics to them would be like preaching about dancing to people with amputated limbs." The early Christians did not ask themselves how they should exercise power in a morally responsible way, but to modern Christians this was the central ethical question.[103]

Gladden pioneered a new kind of social ministry in the course of addressing this question. Devoted to the church, he was deeply involved in ecumenical concerns while also serving on the Columbus city council, the Columbus board of trade, and, for many years, the labor committee of the National Council of the Congregational Churches. He took part in nearly every organization launched by the social gospel movement, including the Inter-Denominational Congress, founded by Josiah Strong in 1885, and the Evangelical Alliance, which became a social gospel vehicle under Strong's leadership in the late 1880s. With economists Richard T. Ely and John Bates Clark, Gladden was one of the founders of the American Economic Association, which began, in 1885, as a staunch opponent of laissez-faire economics. In the early 1890s, under the influence of Gladden, Ely, and Lyman Abbott, the Chautauqua Society became a major social gospel institution, spawning the American Institute of Christian Sociology, led by Ely, which in turn sponsored a significant outreach vehicle, the

Summer School of Applied Christianity. Gladden wrote frequently for the *Dawn,* a Christian Socialist monthly founded by Episcopal social gospeler W. D. P. Bliss, and the *Kingdom,* a major social gospel periodical founded by Congregationalists. He also endorsed the American Institute of Social Service, founded by Strong in 1898 after the Evangelical Alliance failed to endorse his ambitious educational outreach plans. The primary work of the latter institute was carried out by another educational vehicle that Gladden supported as a contributing member, the National Committee for Studies in Social Christianity.[104]

Near the end of his long ministerial career, Gladden's successor in Columbus, Carl S. Patton, told him that he had two absorbing interests: liberal theology and the social gospel. Gladden looked at him quizzedly and asked, "Well, what else *is* there?" To have made this a plausible question was a sizable achievement of his generation. In his later career, after liberal theology acquired a generation of well-positioned academic leaders, Gladden played a significant role as a popularizer of the new theology. His book *Present Day Theology* (1913) gave a guided tour of New Theology thinking to lay readers; an earlier work, *Seven Puzzling Bible Books* (1897), addressed to "the plain people," gave reassuring explanations of the meaning of assorted Old Testament books; his popular adult church school textbook, *Who Wrote the Bible?* (1891), offered a quite conservative introduction to modern biblical criticism. Gladden worried that the mildly critical judgments of the latter work would prove controversial, but the book was widely embraced by pastors and Sunday school teachers, teaching him that the churches were genuinely opening up.

Much of his work erased any distinction between the liberal theology and social gospel movements, as Gladden argued effectively that they belonged together as two facets of the same faith. His effectiveness as an advocate of liberal social-gospel theology owed much to his relatively conservative version of it. Though he embraced modern knowledge and plainly declared his refusal to accept any religious idea that offended his moral sensibility, Gladden held a pastor's aversion to what he called "the fields of destructive criticism." He appropriated modern biblical criticism with a very light touch; more important to him was the challenge of evolutionary theory and his conviction that modern evolutionary theory confirms and explains the existence of a personal God.[105]

DEALING WITH DARWIN: LIBERALISM AND THE THEOLOGY OF EVOLUTION

The most important thinker with whom Gladden's generation had to contend was Herbert Spencer. Every liberal theologian of the late nineteenth century struggled to accommodate Darwinism, which required coming to terms with Spencer's influential system of evolutionary philosophy. For the liberals who were social gospelers, this project had special hazards, for Spencer was the chief theorist of social Darwinism. American historian Richard Hofstadter remarked that in the generation following the Civil War "it was impossible to be active in any field of intellectual work without mastering Spencer." The architects of American philosophical pragmatism, idealism, and personalism—notably William James, Josiah Royce, John Dewey, and Borden P. Bowne—all struggled with Spencer in the 1880s and 1890s, as did the founders of American sociology: Lester Ward, Charles Cooley, and Albion W. Small. Another major American sociologist, William Graham Sumner, was an outright Spencer-style social Darwinist. Spencer's system was a mechanistic world-systems philosophy that combined Darwinian natural selection theory with laissez-faire economic ideology, anarchist politics, early thermodynamics theory, the geology of Sir Charles Lyell, Lamarckian developmental theory, Malthusian population theory, and Samuel Taylor Coleridge's idea of a universal pattern of evolution. As a philosophy of evolution it described life as a continuous process of development from incoherent homogeneity (protozoa) to coherent heterogeneity; as a political philosophy it opposed all state-supported poor laws, education, sanitary supervision, and other measures that impeded the beneficent natural process that Spencer called "the survival of the fittest."[106]

The New Theologians—though intimidated, attracted, and appalled by Spencer's influential system all at once—took much of it as an authoritatively scientific description of the way the world works. Munger, Gladden, and Newman Smyth found evolutionary theory inspiring as proof of the unity and rationality of nature; though he never developed the point, this was evidently one of Beecher's reasons for admiring Spencer also. On the other hand, much of Spencer's worldview was impossible from a Christian standpoint; Munger, Gladden, Newman Smyth, and various contributors to *Andover Review* rejected Spencer's theological agnosticism and his heartless social Darwinism. Drawing upon the writings of Scottish philosopher Henry Drummond and "mutual aid" theorist Peter Kropotkin, Gladden insisted that life is not, and never has been, a purely predatory struggle for existence; evolutionary science demonstrates that life is also a struggle for the life of others, its ruling principle cooperation, not individual competition. Even animals and prehistoric tribes were self-sacrificing and cooperative in some of their everyday practices. More important, Gladden urged, the spiritual force that builds the kingdom of God is self-sacrificing love, not survival of the fittest. In 1885 he joined Richard Ely in founding the American Economic Association, which took aim at an ascending social Darwinist movement in its statement of principles: "We regard the state as an agency whose positive assistance is one of the indispensable conditions of human progress." Elsewhere Ely contended that the modern trade union was second only to the church as a force for human community. The social gospelers righteously opposed what Ely called the misuse of science "as a tool in the hands of the greedy and avaricious for keeping down and oppressing the laboring classes."[107]

The social gospelers and liberal theologians accepted evolution as science, while disputing social Darwinism as moral, social, and political theory. Gladden and other religious liberals addressed the latter issues readily on their own authority. They needed help with a third set of questions, however: What was the proper relation of religion to evolutionary science? In what way should theology accept correction from science? Most important, did evolutionary science leave room for God? The New Theologians took comfort that Darwin expressly left room for God, but they were well aware that many Darwinists did not, as they watched higher education move steadily away from God. On this matter, and as a model of dialogue between religion and science, they took grateful guidance from America's leading popularizer of Darwinian evolutionary theory, John Fiske. Gladden was fond of quoting Darwin's estimate that Fiske was his best American expositor. An accomplished polymath, Fiske expounded the Darwinian science in Spencer's philosophy, but rejected his claim that the reality behind the universe is unknowable; at a banquet in Spencer's honor he noted that even Spencer spoke of a "Power" in life that is revealed "in every throb of the mighty rhythmic life of the universe." Fiske proposed that evolutionary theory and religion are both concerned with the manifestations of this single, infinite, and eternal Power. Assuming a Spencerian conception of life as "the continuous adjustment of inner relations to outer relations," he explained elsewhere that living things are fundamentally characterized by their response to external stimuli. The eye, for example, began with pigment grains in a dermal sac, making the spot sensitive to light, "then came, by slow degrees, the heightened translucence, the convexity of surface, the refracting humors, and the multipliction of nerve vesicles arranging themselves as retinal rods." The result of this complex adjustment of inner relations to outer relations was an immense expansion of life, he observed: "Then came into existence, moreover, for those with eyes to see it, a mighty visible world that for sightless creatures had been virtually non-existent."[108]

In Fiske's telling, the evolution of the eye was a paradigmatic process of preparation for the revelation of the glory of creation. It provided, like all examples of evolutionary process, a telling analogy of the human impulse to worship, which is constitutively human, a universal aspect of the human response to the indwelling of human beings in creation. Genuine atheism is modern and very rare. Aside from a handful of intellectuals and cranks, he claimed, virtually all human beings have taken for granted the existence of a psychical reality approximately similar to that of humanity, a belief that links modern humanity to human beings of the primitive ages. Fiske contended that the human impulse to worship, a fact of evolutionary process that conforms to all other analogies of nature known to evolutionary science, happened to be "the largest and most ubiquitous fact" of human existence. All the analogies of evolutionary science confirm the existence of a human impulse to reach out to an unseen world, he argued; all the analogies of nature "fairly shout against the assumption" of a breach of continuity between human evolution and all other evolution: "So far as our knowledge of Nature goes the whole momentum of it carries us onward to the conclusion that the Unseen World, as the objective term in a relation of fundamental importance that has coexisted with the whole career of Mankind, has a real existence; and it is but following out the analogy to regard that Unseen World as the theatre where the ethical process is destined to reach its full consummation." Fiske's verdict, "here advanced for the first time," was a godsend to the New Theologians: "The lesson of evolution is that through all these weary ages the human soul has not been cherishing in Religion a delusive phantom; but, in spite of seemingly endless groping and stumbling it has been rising to the recognition of its essential kinship with the ever-living God. Of all the implications of the doctrine of evolution with regard to Man, I believe the very deepest and strongest to be that which asserts the Everlasting Reality of Religion."[109]

The New Theologians took their bearings from this assurance. Fiske's value to the liberal theology movement was heightened by the fact that he established his reputation as an evolutionary thinker before addressing the implications of evolution for religion. Gladden called Fiske's writings "a veritable evangel to many groping minds" and rested his own arguments for theistic evolution on Fiske's authority. The "greatest fact of human history," he argued, following Fiske, is "this universal belief in an unseen world and in a God who is the Father of our spirits. *It is this fact, which evolution, through countless ages, has been producing.*" Fiske taught the religious liberals that the first great truth of evolution is the fact of immense variation; in his words, evolutionary science demonstrated that the existence of highly complex organisms is "the result of an infinitely diversified aggregate of circumstances so minute as severally to seem trivial or accidental." Yet this truth is no threat to religious belief, Fiske assured, for the intelligent believer "will always occupy an impregnable position in maintaining that the entire series, in each and every one of its incidents, is an immediate manifestation of the creative action of God." The New Theology embraced evolution on that basis: "That is the last, the sanest, and the strongest word that evolution has to speak respecting the fundamental truth of evolution," Gladden declared.[110]

His tone was appreciative and assuring. Gladden was sure that religion is too deeply insinuated in the nature and evolutionary history of humankind to be obliterated by a handful of atheist orators. It was true, and a good thing, that science had dismantled traditional religious ideas and driven modern theology to an immanent conception of divine reality, but science also needed religion as a corrective to its tendency to merely rip things apart. Religion reminded science not to ignore the Power "by which all these fragments are knit together in unity." By his reckoning, science-informed modern theology was more attractive and rested on a stronger intellectual foundation than any theological perspective in Christian history: "I firmly believe that modern thought is laboriously building up a foundation for our faith far more firm and broad than that on which men rested their souls in what were known as the ages of faith." Some of his social gospel friends went further in turning evolution into a virtual god-term. Lyman Abbott, for example, a prolific social gospel journalist and successor to Henry Ward Beecher at Plymouth Church, in his *Theology of an Evolutionist* (1897), enthused that "it would be difficult to find anywhere a nobler statement of the profound mystery of life than is to be found in the writings of Darwin, Huxley, and Herbert Spencer." This sentiment yielded the Christian qualification that evolution has room for "an Energy that thinks, feels, and wills—a self-conscious, intelligent, moral Being." Reading Spencer into Darwin, Abbott cautioned further that evolution should not be identified unequivocally with Darwinism; we know that evolution is true as a scientific description of the process of life, while the politics of "survival of the fittest" was another matter entirely.[111]

Fundamentally there were three options for modern Christianity in dealing with evolution, in Abbott's view. The first option was resistance, which rejected evolutionary theory as a form of atheism and exploited whatever gaps could be found in its scientific record. The second option was the separate-realms strategy, which argued that religion and science belong to qualitatively different fields of inquiry and discourse. Abbott judged that this strategy had a grain of truth, but failed to do justice to the divinely charged unity of spiritual and natural reality: "If we believe that there is one God—God of the physical and material nature, God of the spiritual and intellectual nature—we shall be more and more inclined to believe that His method of work in the world is one," he contended. The future of theology belonged to a third option, which faced up to the truth of evolution and accepting it wholeheartedly. Abbott drew another kind of distinction in pressing the latter claim. Though he rejected the liberal dichotomy between religion and science, he drove a Parkeresque wedge between religion and theology. "Religion is a spiritual life; theology is the science of that life," he proposed. True religion is love toward God and humanity, while theology is the intellectualization of the reality known in true religion. It followed, for Abbott and many other liberals, that evolution was essentially a theological problem, not a problem for religion. The purpose of changing the church's theology was to keep evolution from becoming a religious problem. Because modern people were conflicted between their traditional religious beliefs and their belief in evolution, what was needed was a change in their theology so they could hold fast to their religion.[112]

EVOLUTION AND MANIFEST DESTINY: THE POLITICS OF THE KINGDOM

The social gospelers and liberal theologians invested heavily in John Fiske's description of evolution as a scientific and religious account of the process of life. Some of the liberal theologians were not social gospelers, and a few social gospelers of Josiah Strong's type were not theological liberals, but all of them faced up to Darwinism in the late nineteenth century. Fiske helped them greatly with their chief concern, which was to save a role for God in evolutionary process. His brand of evolutionism produced a darker legacy in other respects, however, for it was Fiske who made famous, in the early 1880s, the evolutionary case for Anglo-Saxon superiority and expansion. Fiske belongs to history chiefly as the theorist of "manifest destiny." A generally pacific figure, he embraced Spencer's claim that militarism and violence belonged to the pre-industrial stages of civilization. His ambitions for the race that created industrial civilization were world-embracing, and by pressing on the Darwinian logic of race fertility, he came to symbolize the narrow difference between evolutionary ideology as progressive idealism and predatory chauvinism. Like the social gospelers, Fiske meant to promote social progress and idealism, but, like some of the social gospelers, he lapsed into racism and imperialism, usually for liberal reasons. With lapses and blinders of his own, Gladden generally upheld a better social gospel in struggling with the moral paradoxes and divided loyalties of American Christian progressivism.[113]

The "manifest destiny" of Anglo-Saxon America was a favorite theme of Fourth of July orators long before Fiske endorsed it. His contribution was to enlist evolutionary science on its behalf, and thus make it respectable and historic. In *The Descent of Man* Darwin predicted—and then hedged on his prediction—that the advance of higher civilizations would gradually extinguish the world's backward races. Fiske did not hedge. Brushing away Darwin's equivocations on Social Darwinism, he nominated "the English race" (Fiske eschewed the term Anglo-Saxon) as the civilizing hope of the world. The imperial outreach of England and the growing population of the United States put the entire planet within reach of English civilization, he observed; by his "extremely moderate" estimate, America's population would exceed 700,000,000 by the end of the twentieth century, and he saw a similar "civilizing" in Africa: "No one can carefully watch what is going on in Africa to-day without recognizing it as the same sort of thing which was going on in North America in the seventeenth century; and it cannot fail to bring forth similar results in course of time." Within two or three centuries, the African continent was sure to be occupied "by a mighty nation of English descent."[114]

Fiske enthused that American civilization combined the exact qualities of democracy, federal-system diversity, and industrialism that were needed to peaceably civilize the world. If America would only drop its backward, shameful tariff system and openly compete with the rest of the world, it would transform the world through commerce and the power of its superior civilization. America and England possessed the power to remake the world in their own image, and this was the hope of world peace and prosperity. Fiske counseled that the world was bound to be afflicted by war as long as it remained partly barbarous, because for the barbarous races, war was "both a necessity and a favourite occupation." For this reason, civilized countries had to maintain the capacity and will to wage war: "As long as civilization comes into contact with barbarism, it remains a too frequent necessity." On the other hand, the notion that two civilized Christian nations might go to war against each other was "a

wretched absurdity." Civilized peoples do not kill each other; Christian civilization was the solution to war. The settlement of America was the symbol and
beginning of the world's salvation, Fiske believed. To have established American
democracy and federalism over the entire American continent was "to have
made a very good beginning towards establishing it over the world," and the
manifest destiny of the English race was to make all of humanity civilized and
Christian.[115]

Originally delivered to the Royal Institute of Great Britain, where it was
heartily praised, "Manifest Destiny" was published in *Harper's Magazine* in
1885 and made Fiske famous. He repeated the lecture more than twenty times
in American cities; at the request of President Rutherford B. Hayes, General
William T. Sherman, and a host of politicians, he gave it in Washington and
made a great success, heightening his reputation among Anglophile social
gospelers. More important, all of it was a mere overture to the explosive impact
of Josiah Strong's *Our Country,* also published in 1885, which mixed the same
argument with a strong blend of rural Protestant virtues and prejudices. Strong
was a restless, energetic, but little-accomplished ministerial activist in 1885; one
of his stops as a cleric was a five-year stint as Secretary of the American Home
Missionary Society in Ohio, Kentucky, West Virginia, and western
Pennsylvania, where his work produced his electrifying rewrite of a stock Home
Missionary theme. For more than forty years, the American Home Missionary
Society published a running series of articles and two major booklets titled *Our
Country* which detailed the challenges to American missions posed by "heathen"
Indians, Catholic immigrants, Mormons, rationalist infidels, and Wild West
barbarism in general. Bushnell's *Barbarism the First Danger* was published as a
Home Missionary Society pamphlet. Culling information from a wide range of
sources, including some that were quite new to missionary literature, Strong
compiled a powerful appeal for home missions. *Our Country,* written to raise
money for the missions movement, also launched a sizable segment of the social
gospel movement and turned Strong into the movement's key organizational
leader.[116]

Like its namesake publications, *Our Country* was long on the numerous "perils" that stood in the way of a Christianized America, especially immigration,
Romanism, Mormonism, intemperance, socialism, concentrated wealth, and
cities. Unlike most early social gospel literature, much of the book was pervaded
by a spirit of crisis: The American experiment showed signs of going seriously
wrong. For reasons that Lyman Beecher would have recognized, Strong worried
that "glory is departing from many a New England village, because men alien in
blood, in religion, and in civilization, are taking possession." At the same time,
he acknowledged that the "marked superiority" of the Anglo-Saxon race owed
much to its "highly mixed origin"; the Anglo-Saxons were not only Saxons,
Normans, and Danes, as Tennyson poetically suggested, but also Celts and
Gauls, Irish and Welsh, Frisians and Flamands, French Huguenots and German
Palatines. This fact explained a great deal about the vitality and superiority of

the Anglo-Saxon race, Strong asserted. It showed that the superiority of Anglo-Saxonism was tied to its success in assimilating inferior races. Ralph Waldo Emerson once remarked that "the best nations are those most widely related." Strong boasted that by this criterion the United States was already by far the world's best nation: "There is here a commingling of races; and, while the largest injections of foreign blood are substantially the same elements that constituted the original Anglo-Saxon admixture, so that we may infer the general type will be preserved, there are strains of other bloods being added." If American immigration was carefully controlled, he counseled, the Anglo-Saxon race would rise to a "higher destiny" in America and the world.[117]

Strong observed that every great race is defined by one or two great ideas; for the Greeks, it was beauty; for the Hebrews, purity; for the Romans, law. What Anglo-Saxonism stood for was civil liberty and pure spiritual Christianity: "Without controversy, these are the forces which, in the past, have contributed most to the elevation of the human race." It was fortunate for the world, therefore, that the Anglo-Saxons were also "the great missionary race." In a single century, the United States had increased its territory by tenfold while the English built a global empire: "This mighty Anglo-Saxon race, though comprising only one-thirteenth part of mankind, now rules more than one-third of the earth's surface, and more than one-fourth of its people." Moreover, by the end of the twentieth century, he expected Anglo-Saxons to outnumber "all the other civilized races of the world." Believing that the course of history reflected God's providential will for the world, Strong insisted that the meaning of the Anglo-Saxon ascendancy was theological: "Does it not look as if God were not only preparing in our Anglo-Saxon civilization the die with which to stamp the peoples of the earth, but as if he were also massing behind that die the mighty power with which to press it?"[118]

The Anglo-Saxons were the savior race, and America was destined to be "the great home of the Anglo-Saxon, the principal seat of his power, the center of his life and influence," for England's "pretty island" was too small to transform the world. Anticipating Frederick Jackson Turner by a decade, Strong predicted that the approaching American settlement of the world's last great frontier would be an important turning point in American and world history. "There is no other virgin soil in the North Temperate Zone," he observed. "If the consummation of human progress is not to be looked for here, if there is yet to flower a higher civilization, where is the soil that is to produce it?" He celebrated the stunning size of the American continent, showing that all of France could fit into New England, Japan fit into California, Norway and Sweden fit into Arizona and New Mexico, Germany and Spain into the southeastern corner states, six countries into Texas, and so on. "Our continent has room and resources and climate, it lies in the pathway of the nations, it belongs to the zone of power, and already, among Anglo-Saxons, do we lead in population and wealth."[119]

By virtue of their Anglo-Saxon heritage, Americans also possessed a fervent colonizing spirit, he judged. As a race, Anglo-Saxons possessed "an instinct or genius for colonizing." The Anglo-Saxon was typically energetic, persevering, and independent; "he excels all others in pushing his way into new countries." Strong allowed that there was a down side to all of this pushing and colonizing; the world's great races have all been chiefly occupied with warfare, and the Anglo-Saxons, like others, had to kill a lot of people to get ahead. But the world was progressing beyond the stage of war and conquest, through the progress of Anglo-Saxon Christianity and industrialism: "We are leaving behind the barbarism of war; as civilization advances, it will learn less of war, and concern itself more with the arts of peace, and for these the massive battle-ax must be wrought into tools of finer temper." Citing battlefield statistics from the Civil War, Strong showed that Americans were growing taller and stronger and that the "superior vigor" of the American people confirmed Darwin's suggestion in *The Descent of Man* that the "wonderful progress of the United States, as well as the character of the people, are the results of natural selection."[120]

Strong's conclusion combined God and Darwin. Through the evolutionary process of natural selection, he explained, God was "training the Anglo-Saxon race for an hour sure to come in the world's future." His concluding authorities were Darwin and Horace Bushnell. Darwin taught that "civilized nations are everywhere supplanting barbarous nations," chiefly through the power of intellectual superiority. Before Darwin, Bushnell predicted that the world's culturally advanced civilizations were sure to "live down and finally live out" its inferior races. Strong believed that the Anglo-Saxon race was superior because it was stocked by freedom-loving, pure Christians, but he admonished that it was not protected from its destructive elements by racial advantages alone: "The Anglo-Saxon race would speedily decay but for the salt of Christianity." At the same time, as long as the Anglo-Saxons remained Christian, the "dark problem of heathenism among many inferior peoples" had a divine solution. God's "final and complete solution" was contained in what Bushnell called "the outpopulating power of the Christian stock." The divine solution to history was the Anglo-Saxon Christianization of America and then the world.[121]

Our Country struck a deep cultural nerve; the intense reaction to it was comparable to the one set off by *Uncle Tom's Cabin*. As a reflection of American Gilded Age anxieties, it remains singularly revealing; Strong understood very well the mind and feelings of his country's dominant culture. His position at the right edge of the social gospel movement, theologically and politically, made him an effective proponent of the social gospel in mainstream church circles. The book sold 175,000 copies in English and made its author a major movement figure. In December 1885, while serving as pastor of Central Congregational Church in Cincinnati, he organized an "Inter-Denominational Congress" that proposed to discuss America's current social problems. Speakers included Gladden, Ely, Abbott, and Amory H. Bradford; major topics included the urban situation, socialism, immigration, and the need of a religious census; key friendships were forged, especially between Strong and Gladden. The following year, Strong left the pastorate to become Secretary of the American

Evangelical Alliance, the organizational forerunner of the Federal Council of Churches. Under his leadership the Evangelical Alliance became an institutional vehicle of the social gospel, convening highly influential conferences in 1887, 1889, and 1893. The 1887 conference in Washington attracted nearly 1500 delegates; the 1889 conference in Boston focused on urban problems and progress in industrial cooperation; the 1893 conference in Chicago, held in connection with the World's Columbian Exposition, featured such new social gospel leaders as socialist author George Herron and social reformer Jane Addams. In the same year, the social gospel movement was represented at the World's Parliament of Religions by Gladden, Ely, University of Chicago sociologist Albion W. Small, and Harvard ethicist Francis G. Peabody.[122]

The rise of a socially oriented Christian movement allied with a triumphant liberal theology created a new demand for sociology in American seminaries. The newly founded University of Chicago led the way in this area, featuring work in "Christian sociology" by Albion Small, Graham Taylor, and Shailer Mathews; other prominent early social gospel sociologists and social ethicists were Francis Peabody at Harvard and William Jewett Tucker at Andover Seminary. Concentrating mostly on urban problems, Strong founded and directed the League of Social Service and, in 1902, the American Institute for Social Service. In his second major work, *The New Era, or, The Coming Kingdom* (1893), speaking with the commanding voice of a movement leader, he made a detailed plea for greater church cooperation, proposing that Protestant churches should stop competing with each other and agree to divide the territory of their communities among themselves, "no church taking more than it can work thoroughly." Noting that many towns had too many churches, especially in prosperous areas, while many poor communities had no church at all, Strong scolded that America would never be Christianized as long as the churches perpetuated this competitive evil.[123]

All of his now-famous themes were prominently displayed in *The New Era,* especially "The Destiny of the Race," "The Contribution Made by the Three Great Races of Antiquity," "The Contribution Made by the Anglo-Saxon," and "The Problem of the City." Strong confirmed that he regarded the United States as the world's redeemer nation, though he also sought to clarify what his Anglo-Saxonist Christian-Americanism did not mean. He believed that the forces of good had "a longer leverage" in the United States than any other country, but he also believed the same thing about the forces of evil. The crisis had not passed; America's immense capacity for good was rivaled by its capacity to harm the cause of righteousness on earth. The race question was a key example; the Anglo-Saxon race was strengthened by its racial diversity, but there were sharp limits to this openness. Strong warned that American immigration policy was ignoring this reality, and thereby running down America's Anglo-Saxon stock: "There is now being injected into the veins of the nation a large amount of inferior blood every day of every year." Immigration was also corrupting America, and so was alcohol. Strong admonished that temperance was a great progressive cause. The cause of the kingdom required Americans to annihilate the saloon "and every other agency which is devitalizing and corrupting our population." Lastly, he exhorted, the key to Christianizing the world was first to Christianize the United States. "I do not imagine than an Anglo-Saxon is dearer to God than a Mongolian or an African," he declared, in a single-sentence qualification that cried out for a chapter. He did remark earlier that the unique meeting of races in America "is peculiarly favorable to the eradication of race prejudice and the cultivation of a broad sympathy which must precede the coming brotherhood of man." Since Anglo-Saxonism was essentially a cultural category for him, he did not regard himself as a racist, and was not taken as one by black associates such as Booker T. Washington. To Strong, the point of the social gospel was always the Christianization of the world: "My plea is not, Save America for America's sake, but, Save America for the world's sake."[124]

RIGHTEOUS EMPIRE: THE STRUGGLE OF NATIONS AND THE CRUCIBLE OF RACE

World events soon brought further clarifications about what the social gospelers meant. For more than a century America resisted the siren's call of empire, but in 1898 President William McKinley committed the United States to war with Spain, took the Philippine Islands, and formally annexed the Hawaiian Islands, and the American empire was launched. The following year the United States partitioned the Samoan Islands by agreement with Germany; the year after that America helped to suppress the Boxer Rebellion in China. What was a social gospeler to think? Was the cause of the kingdom served by America's stepping onto the world stage? With marginal caveats and a gentler voice, the quintessential social gospeler shared Strong's view of the struggle for the world. Gladden agreed that immigration needed to be sharply limited, he struggled to find a Christian third way between the hardline imperialist and anti-imperialist factions of the day, and he supported all of his country's foreign interventions. In all of this, he led and reflected the mainstream of the social gospel movement.

Though milder spoken and more carefully reflective than Strong, Gladden shared his friend's Anglophilia and his enthusiasm for Anglo-American solidarity; like Lyman Abbott and many American pastors, he embraced Strong's theology of Anglo-Saxonism. He traveled to England four times between 1888 and 1898 and found that England and America were essentially alike. Continental Europe, on the other hand, felt truly alien and often repulsive to him, even in the Protestant countries. Gladden preached the essential message of *Our Country* from his pulpit, contending that England and America needed to stand together to defend and extend Christian civilization. Though he was more deeply committed to nonviolence than Strong, he accepted Strong's argument that civilized countries were sometimes morally obliged to fight wars against barbarism. Shortly before the outbreak of the Spanish-American War, Gladden was deeply repulsed by reports that Spanish soldiers were butchering Cubans involved in the Cuban rebellion. Though he judged that the Cubans were too "ignorant, superstitious, brutal and degraded" to be capable of self-government, he supported the Spanish-American War as a humanitarian commitment to repel their oppressors. His chief concerns in 1898 were that America needed to maintain pure motives in fighting the war and also maintain its friendship with England. He rejected imperialist and anti-imperialist rhetoric alike on the same ground; both groups assumed that American policy was based on selfish motives. "We are not going to be dragged into any war for purposes of conquest—neither for the acquisition of territory nor for the extension of trade," Gladden countered. "And those who are preaching this jingoism to-day should be warned that the Nation has a conscience that can speak and make itself heard, and that will paralyze its arm whenever it is lifted to do injustice to any weaker people."[125]

That was the voice of the mainstream social gospel at the turn of the century. While some of his colleagues, notably Strong and Lyman Abbott, crossed the line into outright Christian imperialism, and a significant group of others stoutly opposed America's imperial turn, Gladden held out for the primacy of good intentions. He insisted that American intervention wasn't imperialism if it was prosecuted for benevolent reasons, and that the third way between imperialist chauvinism and anti-imperialist irresponsibility was the Christian moral way. All the social gospelers laid claim to the Christian moral way, of course, but they parted ways on the choices of America's deepening interventionism. Protestant leaders such as Graham Taylor, George Herron, Edward E. Hale, Henry van Dyke, Leonard W. Bacon, Henry C. Potter, Charles R. Brown, and Charles H. Parkhurst firmly resisted America's new military activism. On the other side, Strong wrote in *Expansion under New World Conditions* (1900) that it was no longer possible for Americans to "drift with safety to our destiny." America was God's chosen nation, "shut up to a perilous alternative," and was now obliged to accept moral responsibility for its redeemer status. *The Outlook,* a major liberal Christian magazine, took the same line, enthusing that "the army among Anglo-Saxon peoples is no longer a mere instrument of destruction. It is a great reconstructive organization." Throughout the Middle East and Asia, the *Outlook* explained, Anglo-Saxon armies were "promoting law, order, [and] civilization," fighting famine and building railroads, and "laying the foundations of justice and liberty."[126]

True to its roots in the home missionary movement, the social gospel was interventionist, outward-reaching, and explicitly mission-oriented. Its most aggressive and prominent advocates insisted that "blessed are the peacemakers" had nothing to do with staying home. *Outlook* editor Lyman Abbott pronounced that it was "the function of the Anglo-Saxon race" to confer the civilizing gifts of law, commerce, and education "on the uncivilized people of the world." His rejoinder to William James, Graham Taylor, and other anti-imperialists spelled out the moral basis of this function: "It is said that we have no right to go to a land occupied by a barbaric people and interfere with their life. It is said that if they prefer barbarism they have a right to remain barbarians. I deny the right of a barbaric people to retain possession of any quarter of the globe. What I have already said I reaffirm: barbarism has no rights which civilization is bound to respect. Barbarians have rights which civilized people are bound to respect, but they have no right to their barbarism."[127]

Gladden said essentially the same thing with nicer words. In the name of peace and humanitarianism, he supported all of his country's imperial maneuvers in Latin America, the Philippines, the Middle East, Africa, and East Asia. Like Shailer Mathews and even (for a time) Walter Rauschenbusch, he viewed American intervention as invariably civilizing, constructive, and, therefore, Christian; it was "morally unthinkable" to him that the United States might set free the Philippines, Puerto Rico, and Guam after these colonial possessions were relinquished by Spain. He lectured that "degraded races" never worked their way up to civilization; history showed that "inferior races" had to be lifted up to civilized standards of behavior by stronger races, and he exulted that his country was beginning to join England in this humanitarian mission. He vigorously supported America's suppression of the Philippine independence rebellion of 1899, contending that the Filipinos were too backward for independence; he judged that Cuba needed "many years" of careful guidance and sharply criticized President Theodore Roosevelt for withdrawing from Cuba; anxious for Christian access to "the vast mongolian population," he took pride in America's role in establishing an open door to China.[128]

His optimism was immense, and, to many, inspiriting. Gladden began each year with a sermon on the ways that America and the world had improved over the past year. Equating divine providence with progress, he found ample evidence of progress. In his later career, before the Great War made a horrible mockery of it, he dreamed that the world's progress and its frightful new weapons were making war obsolete. Civilized nations did not fight each other, he reasoned, and the new machinery of mass destruction functioned as a deterrent to war. At the same time, Gladden threw himself into a host of causes where progress lagged: he advocated municipal ownership of public-service industries as an antidote to monopoly corruption; he supported numerous municipal and antipoverty reforms, as well as the municipal church movement; he persistently spoke against anti-Catholic prejudice, which cost him the presidency of Ohio State University in 1893; more than most social gospelers, he also welcomed numerous African American speakers to his pulpit and worked for many years to create new educational and industrial opportunities for American blacks.[129]

The primary vehicle for his outreach to blacks was the American Missionary Association, a consolidation of several Congregational antislavery missionary societies that was founded in 1846. Before the Civil War, the A.M.A. worked entirely among Northern blacks, but after the war, when Gladden joined it, the organization moved into the South and established numerous schools and churches open to blacks. The schools included Hampton Institute, Fisk University, Berea College, Tillotson Institute, Atlanta University, Howard University, Tougaloo University, Straight University, and Talladega College, as well as scores of primary and secondary schools. In its early postwar ministries, the A.M.A. fought against segregation; later it acquiesced to the demands of a dominant segregationalist culture. Over the course of his long association with the organization, Gladden served in a variety of capacities, including vice-president and president. For nearly thirty years, he accepted the line on black development eventually identified with Booker T. Washington, which empha-sized industrial education and economic security. He told wary audiences that the A.M.A. was not seeking integration or political equality for blacks; it was enough to help blacks get on their feet after the ravages of slavery.

Gladden never stopped believing that Reconstruction was a catastrophe that unnecessarily alienated white Southerners; for years he insisted that genuine reconstruction had to begin with "civilizing" education programs and take into account the bruised feelings of Southerners; he never fully absorbed the fact that America's terrible racial problems after the war were caused chiefly by white racism. In the 1890s, however, his optimism that American race relations were improving was belatedly chastened by the persistence of violence against blacks. In 1895 Gladden urged the A.M.A. to condemn racist lynchings; the following year he admonished the A.M.A. that conditions for blacks in America were not much better than slavery. One measure of the latter fact was the outcry against President Roosevelt's welcome of Booker T. Washington to the White House. At the same meeting that elected Gladden to its presidency, in 1901, the A.M.A. solemnly approved of Roosevelt's widely condemned hospitality to a black American. Two years later, upon reading W. E. B. DuBois's newly published book, *The Souls of Black Folk,* Gladden converted to a racial politics that sought equality. He had met DuBois at Atlanta University and was greatly impressed; *The Souls of Black Folk* pressed upon him that blacks were oppressed in the South as a class and that uplift programs supported by Booker T. Washington wrongly denigrated the importance of higher education for blacks. Gladden her-alded DuBois's book to Christian audiences. While assuring that the A.M.A. stood "for no unnatural fusion of races, for no impracticable notions of social intercourse," he urged that political equality was another matter entirely. Social equality was negotiable, but justice was not; Christian morality and the demands of justice required nothing less than "perfect equality for the Negro before the law, and behind the law." With his conversion to this belief, Gladden got a strong taste of the state of American race relations by reading his mail. He later admitted that the "bitter and violent" letters he received gave him a new realization of what blacks were up against in his beloved country.[130]

On this issue, as on others, Gladden landed in the middle of the social gospel movement, leaning left. A few social gospelers—such as Thomas Dixon Jr., Alexander McKelway, and Charles H. Parkhurst—were outright racists in the precise sense of the term: they believed that blacks are biologically inferior.

Many were right-leaning cultural chauvinists, like Strong and Abbott, who elevated Anglo-Saxonism to the level of an absolute assimilationist ideal. At the left end of the spectrum, a significant group of social gospelers—notably Algernon Sidney Crapsey, Herbert Seeley Bigelow, Newell Dwight Hillis, and Charles B. Spahr—militantly defended the rights of black Americans to social and political equality. Gladden championed the racial politics of a left-leaning mainstream claimed by such social gospelers as Joseph Cook, Quincey Ewing, Benjamin Orange Flower, William Channing Gannett, Jenkin Lloyd Jones, Henry Demarest Lloyd, and William Hayes Ward. For Gladden, as for most of the social gospel movement, the crucial lines at issue were established by the debate between Washington and DuBois, and Gladden was determined to affirm both.[131]

Lyman Abbott's *Outlook* was decidedly pro-Washington. In 1899, Abbott invited the Tuskegee principal to tell his personal story; the result, composed by Washington, Abbott, and ghostwriter Max Bennett Thrasher, became a classic of American autobiography: *Up from Slavery*. Serialized to the *Outlook*'s 100,000 subscribers, this book established the model of a black leader for much of black and white America. *The Outlook* praised Washington effusively for years afterward, and took strong exception to the rise of a competitor armed with a dissenting message, when DuBois criticized Washington for selling out the rights of blacks to higher education and equal standing before the law. *The Outlook*, the leading organ of liberal Protestantism, countered that DuBois was ashamed of his race: DuBois made the white man the standard, but Washington looked for a standard in the ideals of his own race; DuBois sought social equality for blacks, but Washington was too self-respecting for that; DuBois was university-oriented, but Washington emphasized industrial schools; DuBois wanted blacks to read the Ten Commandments in Hebrew, but Washington wanted blacks to obey them in English; DuBois tried to push his race into a higher place, but Washington sought to make the race stronger; DuBois demanded the right to vote, but Washington sought to make blacks competent for the duties of citizenship. For the kind of Christian liberalism represented by Abbott, Strong, John R. Commons, Edgar Gardner Murphy, and Francis G. Peabody, the choice between DuBois and Washington was no contest.[132]

Gladden objected that this was a false choice, because it wrongly denigrated DuBois and it wrongly dichotomized the politics of race. He judged that DuBois's *The Souls of Black Folk* was singularly revealing, illuminating the consciousness and subjection of an oppressed minority. Gladden did not dispute America's need to restrict the franchise to men who were educationally qualified to exercise it, "but when one law is made for black men and another for white men, the injustice is so glaring that it cannot endure." He believed it was wrong to emphasize industrial education to the exclusion of higher education; industrial education was appropriate for the masses, he reasoned, but America needed black leaders also. "I fear that Mr. Washington is putting too much weight on economic efficiency as the solvent of race prejudice," he declared. "All that

Booker Washington is doing we may heartily rejoice in, but there are other things that ought not be left undone." Gladden stuck to this "both-and" for the rest of his life: "There is no reason why there should be any quarrel between these two classes of educators; each needs the other's aid." With equal passion, he also praised "the glorious company" of his numerous white Southern allies and unfailingly kept in mind that cultivating the goodwill of white Americans was part of the work of struggling for racial justice. The saving work of the A.M.A. would not have been possible, he remarked, without the goodwill of white Southerners "whose eyes are open to the ethical principles involved in our most serious social question." Though he acknowledged in 1909 that most Southerners did not yet share his view of the race problem, "it is the opinion that must prevail, because this is a moral universe."[133]

THE GREAT WAR AND THE SOCIAL GOSPEL

His belief that the good was prevailing held firm until the year of his retirement, 1914. In 1909, Gladden ended his autobiography with a stirring affirmation of the moral universe. The nations were piling up weapons, he admitted, and organized capital and labor were waging class war, but these were the last gasps of a discredited principle. It was not possible that the world would indulge the "howling farce" of violence for much longer. The civilized nations were converting the world to "the possibility of cooperation as the fundamental social law," and the kingdom of God was growing in modern history. "It is impossible that the nations should go on making fools of themselves," Gladden assured. The world was getting better, under the influence of the United States; America was Christianizing its own politics and culture and increasingly bringing light to the rest of the world. "We turn our faces to the future with good hope in our hearts," Gladden exhorted. "There are great industrial problems before us, but we shall work them out; there are battles to fight, but we shall win them. With all those who believe in justice and the square deal, in kindness and good will, in a free field and a fair chance for every man, the stars in their courses are fighting, and their victory is sure."[134]

Five years later he retired from First Church, Columbus, shortly before Europe descended into war. His sermons afterward repeatedly condemned the war and tried to make sense of it. Gladden claimed at first that the world was still getting better; the Great War was proving the futility of war and the necessity of a great federation of nations. At the same time, he attributed the war to the lust and corruption of Europe's ruling classes, privileged egotists who refused to take moral responsibility for their power. What was called "war fever" was nothing but ruling-class manipulation of the hatred and nationalistic fears of ordinary people. Gladden's Anglophilia did not extend to solidarity in war, at least not in the early years of the Great War, and against Lyman Abbott and other early proponents of American preparedness and participation, he campaigned against preparedness. He gave numerous antiwar speeches and joined a host of anti-interventionist organizations, including the American Peace Society, the Church Peace Union (founded by Andrew Carnegie), the American Alliance for International Friendship, and, more ambivalently, the League to Enforce Peace. The last organization, led by William Howard Taft, promoted the idea of a league of nations, which Gladden liked, while containing a wider range of political ideologies than most peace organizations. By 1915, Gladden's opposition to American intervention was so fervent that he made allies wherever he could find them.[135]

"I am a pacifist myself," he announced in the *New Republic.* "At the beginning of this war my pacifism was mild and moderate, but with every month it has grown more radical and more irreconcilable; the one lesson I have learned is the insanity of militarism." He allowed that self-sacrificial love is a beautiful virtue, "but to kill for one's country is neither sweet nor beautiful"; he was ready to give his life for America, but he would never be ready to kill for it—"that does not invite me." War is madness, Gladden exhorted; "it is the reversal of the nature of things; it is a social solecism." This was not quite absolute pacifism; he granted that wars fought to resist some horrendous evil could be justified morally. He reasoned, however, that the Great War was not a last resort to avert some terrible, threatening evil; the ongoing catastrophe in Europe was fueled on all sides by aggression, corruption, and greed, and it lacked a redeeming or justifying moral purpose. None of the warring parties showed any interest in brokering terms of peace; England and France entered the war ostensibly as a protective measure against German conquest and tyranny, but now both countries were clearly determined to conquer Germany. In "A Plea for Pacifism," published in the *Nation,* Gladden implied that the warring nations preferred war to peace partly because the war was great for science and technology; it created "new machinery for maiming and mangling and brutalizing men; new methods of inflicting torture," and new devices "for erasing the beauty of the earth and ruining its fairest monuments."[136]

Until December 1915, President Wilson was an ally of the "peace and unpreparedness" forces, but on December 7, Wilson announced in his State of the Union address that the cause of American peace could no longer afford American unpreparedness. Wilson's military buildup called for a standing army of 142,000 and a reserve force of 400,000. Three days later, Wilson addressed the Federal Council of Churches in a speech that stroked familiar chords and affirmed Wilson's affinity with the social gospel; Christianity is not important as a body of doctrines, he told the liberal Protestant leaders, but as "a vital body of conceptions which can be translated into life for us." Just as cooperation was "the vital principle of social life," Christianity was "the most vitalizing thing in the world." Gladden took a diplomatic tack in responding to the president; in a personal letter he thanked and praised Wilson for commending the social gospel—"the best of it was that you knew what it was that you were trying to commend." And he enclosed a copy of his recent manifesto for pacifism. "It is not often that your policy fails of my hearty approval," he assured, "but here is a matter in which I wish I might have a hearing." Wilson graciously replied that it gave him second thoughts to be opposed by someone like Gladden and promised to read the pamphlet; in the meantime he assured Gladden that he was determined to conduct his policies in accordance with Gladden's ideals.[137]

Gladden was not reassured on the issue that overshadowed everything else. From the pulpit he declared, "Just now it appears probable that our nation is going to be sucked into the maelstrom; and plunged into a conflict with a people with whom we have no legitimate quarrel. The people of the United States and the people of Germany are not enemies. We bear them no grudges." The following January he warned that public sentiment was shifting in the direction of going to war, even though Americans had no concept of what they might hope to accomplish by intervening. "What is going to happen at the close of this war?" he asked. "What will be the condition of the Great European nations when they stop fighting?" Gladden resolved to campaign against Wilson's military buildup. Joining forces with Jane Addams, Unitarian pacifist John Haynes Holmes, and other members of the Anti-Preparedness Committee, he appeared before military affairs committees of the House and Senate and made numerous antiwar speeches. For several weeks he toured New England as a featured speaker of the anti-preparedness movement. He pleaded that war is abominable, that America had no reason to fight against Germany, and that America lacked a coherent vision of postwar Europe. His book of that year, *The Forks of the Road,* insisted that it was not too late for America and the rest of the world to accept the law of love as the governing law of the world.[138]

"If you eat poisonous or indigestible food, the retribution is not deferred until after death and judgment, nor is there any scheme of substitution by which you may evade the penalty; it follows the transgression instantly and inevitably," he admonished. "No less swift and certain are the consequences of every violation of the moral law." Every selfish act breeds deeper selfishness, selfishness breeds hate, and hate, "as Jesus told us, is incipient murder." Gladden refused to believe that humankind might fail to absorb this lesson amid the carnage of the Great War. "I confess that I am unable to entertain such a benumbing conception," he confessed. "I cannot even imagine that this bloody lesson will be lost upon the world." At the same time, he warned that a host of "sinister and infernal influences" were at work to push America into the war. Some "hysterical alarmists" were scaring Americans with invasion fantasies; others, "a good many partly developed human beings," found the smell of blood exciting and were anxious not to miss out on the thrill of killing. Then there was the sinister influence of war capitalism: "There are tremendous financial combinations involving billions of capital, which stand to make immense profits out of war, and out of the preparation for war, and they are moving heaven and earth today to drive this nation into the complications which will put money in their purses."[139]

Gladden was fond of contrasting the "ape and tiger psychology" of barbarism and the animal world to the cooperative psychology of civilization. Civilized relations are based on mutual trust, he observed, and in civilized societies, men do not carry weapons or live by the law of retribution; yet in the present war, civilized nations were reverting to animal violence and living by retribution. Meanwhile the United States moved steadily closer to plunging into this "Gehenna of militarism." The prospect of American intervention filled him with revulsion: "God grant that I may not live to see it!"[140] Without calling for unilateral disarmament, he pleaded, instead, to see his country take the lead in organizing a "League of Peace" that outlawed war and enforced the moral law with international police power: "This war is the most astounding development of history; should not the reactions which follow the war be equally astounding?"[141]

Except for 1912, when he supported Theodore Roosevelt's Progressive ticket, Gladden had voted Republican all his life. Like most reformers, however, he supported Wilson in 1916, mostly on the ground that he was the candidate most likely to resist interventionist pressure. A month after the election, Wilson asked the warring powers to state their war aims, and Gladden took heart that the president was determined to obtain conditions for peace negotiations and keep America out of the war. Shortly afterward, he met with Wilson, who apparently expressed his resolve to broker terms of peace; Wilson then appeared before the U.S. Senate on January 22 to call for the creation of a "League of Peace" and urge the warring parties to negotiate a "peace without victory." The war needed to be resolved in a way that did not produce bitter losers, Wilson exhorted, and the proposed federation of peace-loving nations would keep the peace: "The equality of nations upon which peace must be founded if it is to last must be an equality of rights. Only a peace between equals can last. Only a peace the very principle of which is equality and a common participation in a common benefit."[142]

It was a stirring moment for Gladden-style social gospelers, progressives, and liberal internationalists. Wilson's dramatic address was a page from the diplomatic sections of *The Forks of the Road;* the president seemed to be sincere about living up to Gladden's social gospel ideals. But the warring powers on both sides were determined to gain victory, and on January 31, Germany declared that it would resume unrestricted submarine warfare against all ships, armed or unarmed, that sailed into a German war zone. When three days later the American steamship *Housatonic* was sunk without warning, Wilson broke off diplomatic relations with Germany, declaring that Germany's attack was an intolerable act of aggression.[143]

Gladden sadly accepted that Wilson had no alternative. In February, the British secret service intercepted a telegram from the German foreign minister Zimmerman to the German ambassador in Mexico in which the German official schemed for Mexican entrance into the war on the side of the Central Powers in return for New Mexico, Texas, and Arizona. The following month, when five American ships were sunk without warning, Gladden, struggling with his conscience while most Americans decided for war, wrote a book titled "Killing Wrong-Doers as a Cure for Wrong-Doing." The title brought a smile to Walter Rauschenbusch's face just before America went to war, but the book was never published. Gladden mused from the pulpit that perhaps this war—"the darkest cloud that has ever obscured the sky"—contained a glimmer of light; to judge from their recent words, he observed, the world's leaders were beginning to sicken of war: "All the great people in the world, the kings, kaisers, czars, emperors, chancellors, presidents, princes, foreign ministers—all the people who make wars—are now with one voice declaring and proclaiming that there are to be no more wars; that this is the last war." The idea of going to war to put an end to war was the kind of rationale that Gladden needed.[144]

On April 2 Wilson expressed this rationale in political terms, telling a joint session of Congress that America needed to join the war against Germany to serve the world's greater good. "The world must be made safe for democracy," he declared. "Its peace must be planted upon the tested foundations of political liberty." Like most social gospelers, Gladden made a convincing reversal as soon as America entered the war; the call of country and Wilson's soaring idealistic rhetoric were irresistible to him, and to them. Lyman Abbott, who converted early, called the war "a crusade to make this world a home in which God's children can live in peace and safety, a crusade far more in harmony with the spirit and will of Christ than the crusade to recover from the pagans the tomb in which the body of Christ was buried." Shailer Mathews, who traveled the same path as Gladden, soon exulted that America at war was proving to be "a glorious super-person, possessed of virtues, power, ideals, daring, and sacrifice."[145]

Gladden was never as jingoistic as Abbott, but he matched Mathews for wartime myth-making, quoting Wilson's idealistic claims repeatedly and insistently in defense of America's intervention. The other nations had gone to war for the sake of their material self-interests, he declared, but America intervened for the sake of democracy and world peace, a mission that was necessary, though awful: "War, even when a nation accepts it with chagrin and without any expectation of exclusive gain, is a devilish business. He who sups with the devil must fish with a long spoon." Seeking additional assurance, Gladden claimed that Wilson's declaration of war against Germany was not really a declaration of war; it was merely "an acceptance of the belligerency which has been thrust upon us."[146]

Wilson pledged that America desired no conquest or dominion, that America acted out of concern for justice, peace, and human rights, not for revenge, and that America had no selfish ends to serve: "We seek no indemnities for ourselves, no material compensation for the sacrifices we shall freely make. We are but one of the champions of the rights of mankind. We shall be satisfied when those rights have been made as secure as the faith and the freedom of nations can make them." These assurances became Gladden's scripture: "I believe that these words are true. And I thank God that I have lived to hear them spoken. They can never be recalled. They can never be forgotten. They will live as long as freedom lives. They will be emblazoned on the banners of the Universal Brotherhood. And when their full meaning is grasped by the great nations of the earth war will be no more." Americans had a "right to believe" that the purpose of their intervention was to put an end to war, he insisted, for Americans were entering the war "to make the world safe for democracy, to defeat a monstrous aggression, [and] to create a new organization of mankind." Wilson's pledge to make the world safe for democracy was "the greatest word I think that this generation has heard," Gladden enthused. "It defines our destiny."[147]

He looked forward to a League of Nations and never doubted that the United States was fighting for democracy. Persistently he preached on these themes in the remaining months of his life.[148] He claimed never to doubt that his country was seeking to create a world order based upon the golden rule: "All that is needed to bring permanent peace to earth is that every nation trust all other nations just as it wishes to be trusted by them." Gladden accepted and preached Wilson's vision of the war as a social gospel cause; he seemed to forget his belief that war belonged to the jungle phase of human existence: "This war needn't be a curse; it may be the greatest blessing that has ever befallen this land." His optimism endured. Gladden and Rauschenbusch died in the same war-ending year, 1918, but their mood in their last days was very different. Rauschenbusch was devastated by the war, which he saw as the death of social gospel idealism; Gladden, asked near the end of his life if he knew of any reason not to be hopeful, replied, "Not one." His entire life had been a miracle, lived through eighty-three years of transforming American Christian progress.[149]

"With the Bible in our hands and the Christian hope in our hearts, it is not hard for us to explain where the idea of progress comes from," Gladden reflected near the end of his life. "It is a spurious kind of Christianity of which it is not the vital element."[150] Progress was the name and description of his faith, and also the atmosphere that he breathed throughout his career. "I have never doubted that the Kingdom I have always prayed for is coming; that the gospel I have always preached is true," he declared in 1912, in a sermon published shortly before his death. "I believe that the democracy is getting a new heart, and a new spirit, that the nation is being saved. It is not yet saved and its salvation depends on you and me, but it is being saved. There are signs that a *new way of thinking, a new social consciousness,* are taking possession of the nation." To Gladden, cooperation, democracy, and progress were god-terms; he never lost faith that the kingdom of God was an ongoing American project.[151]

6.

Enter the Academics:

Charles A. Briggs, Borden Parker Bowne,
Biblical Criticism, and the Personalist Idea

The academics came late to progressive Christianity. Liberal theology had a sizable presence in mainline American Protestantism before it attained a foothold in America's elite seminaries and divinity schools. In the 1880s a handful of liberal academics gained a foothold at such schools as Union, Andover, Yale, Bangor, and Drew. They belonged to an in-between generation. Like the generation that succeeded them, the figures who opened the door of academe to liberal theology were trained in Germany, usually the University of Berlin. They used their German university training to legitimize the legacies of Bushnell, Beecher, the Bushnellians, the early social gospelers, and to a lesser extent, the Unitarians. Under their influence, American religious thinking became closely tied to trends in German theology, but for that reason their idea of modern progressive orthodoxy did not hold the field for long.

The academics who paved the way to the academic triumph of liberal theology in America were schooled in the neoromanticism, idealism, and historicism of mid-century German mediation theology. For this reason they were transitional figures. Egbert C. Smyth was one of them; although he lacked an academic position, Newman Smyth was another; the most important was

Charles A. Briggs. To these figures, the exemplary theologian was Isaak August Dorner; they believed they had a clear idea of what American theology needed to become by virtue of having studied at Berlin. Convinced that German mediation theology was both modern and orthodox, the founders of American academic theological liberalism effected a crucial turn in American religious thinking.

They were slow to call it liberalism; some were slow to admit even to themselves that they were liberals, and the movement they engendered did not speak the language of mediation theology for long. The transitional generation of Briggs and the Smyths and their allies changed the field of American theology but never ruled over it. In their lifetime they witnessed the sweeping away of mediation theology in Germany and its replacement by the ethical historicism of Göttingen theologian Albrecht Ritschl. By the turn of the century, the youthful leaders of a thriving American liberal theology movement labored to stay up to date in their progressivism. Though some were more directly tied to the Ritschlian school than others, and some later became post-Ritschlians, nearly all of the early-twentieth-century leaders of American liberal theology—among them Arthur C. McGiffert, William Adams Brown, William Newton Clarke, Shailer Mathews, George Burman Foster, and Walter Rauschenbusch—were Ritschlians. They imbibed the personalism, historicism, biblical dualism, and socioethical orientation of a field-dominating Ritschlian school. For decades before the Ritschlian ascendancy, the chief debate in American theology was between orthodoxy and some kind of neoromanticism. Hegel had no American following to speak of in the nineteenth century; American liberals spoke the romanticist language of immanence and transcendental unity until it gave way to the Ritschlian language of personalist ethical idealism.

In the early twentieth century, American theologians took the difference very seriously. Thinkers like William Adams Brown were keenly impressed by the changes in consciousness that separated them from the preceding generation of liberals. There was one American philosopher and theologian from the transitional generation who taught the youthful Ritschlians a great deal, however: Borden Parker Bowne, who founded a school of his own. Though not a full-fledged Ritschlian, Bowne expounded the personalist philosophical idealism of the Ritschlian school with a brilliance that equaled any of Ritschl's German or American followers. Briggs and Bowne, as academics teaching in church-related institutions, were more vulnerable to heresy hunters than most pastors and paid for their novelty. Both of their careers were marked by formal heresy charges; the Briggs case is the most famous heresy proceeding in American religious history. Though neither figure had the star power of a Beecher, Bushnell, or Channing, liberal theology needed no stars to conquer the field in the generation of Briggs and Bowne. Through their writings their movement acquired a new level of intellectual maturity and institutional leverage.

MEDIATING THEOLOGY FROM GERMANY
TO AMERICA: CHARLES A. BRIGGS

The more controversial figure, Charles Briggs, was the one who long resisted any identification with theological liberalism. Born in New York City in 1841, Briggs attended the University of Virginia, where he embraced the evidentialist empiricism of Francis Bacon with a convert's fervor.[1] His teachers convinced him that in the study of history, no less than chemistry, scientific method holds the key to disciplinary progress. Briggs's second conversion took place during the Great Revival of 1858, in his sophomore year. To the delight of his parents and his uncle Marvin Briggs, he accepted the faith of evangelical Protestantism. Briggs's mother, Sarah, was a devout Presbyterian, as was his uncle Marvin, who had recently graduated from Princeton Theological Seminary. Though equally ardent in evangelical conviction, his father, Alonson, was not much of a church-goer, confessing to his son that as a young man he nearly "set out to be a Christian," but then postponed his decision "for a more convenient season" that never came. He advised his son to join the Methodists, "for they are the safest [group], and are doing more to convert the world than all the other denominations put together." Briggs joined the Presbyterians instead, and soon nettled his father by announcing his intention to study for the ministry.[2]

Alonson Briggs was the owner of America's largest barrel-making company. Widely known as "the barrel king," he wanted his son to succeed him in the family business, not pursue the ministry. Briggs held him off while moving under the wing of his Uncle Marvin. Before his nephew's conversion Marvin worried that "Charley" was too studious, bought too many books, and didn't get enough exercise; after his conversion, while still fussing about insufficient exercise, Marvin admonished him not to neglect his studies "both on your own account, and on account of the cause of religion."[3]

Marvin Briggs was an orthodox Calvinist with a warm-blooded evangelical streak. "The Christian is a new creature in Christ Jesus," he exhorted Charley. "This is what it means to be a Christian." He also tried to steer his nephew to Princeton Seminary, assuring him it was the best seminary for serious-minded evangelicals; for one thing, it had America's best theologian, Charles Hodge. In 1859 Marvin reported to his nephew that he had heard Henry Ward Beecher speak the night before on "Christian Commonwealth." Like many Princeton alums, he was of two minds about Beecher. "The lecture abounded and over-flowed with force and beauty," he observed; at the same time it was "full of Abolitionism, distasteful alike to my friend and myself." Marvin Briggs favored the stolid Reformed orthodoxy of his seminary over the emotionalism and antislavery enthusiasms of New School evangelicalism. Charley Briggs leaned the same way, but not as decidedly. In 1861, responding to President

Lincoln's appeal for volunteers to defend the capital from an expected Confederate attack, he spent three months in the New York Seventh Regiment. While waiting for a battle that never materialized, Briggs wrote passionately evangelistic letters to his sisters, inviting them to come to Jesus. Meanwhile he made up his mind about seminary. In the fall, instead of enrolling at the bastion of Old School Presbyterian orthodoxy, Princeton, Briggs headed off to the citadel of New School Presbyterianism, Union Theological Seminary in New York.[4]

Union Seminary, then located on Park Avenue, was a product of New School evangelical piety. Founded in 1836 as the New York Theological Seminary— just before the Old School and New School factions of American Presbyterianism broke apart in 1837—and renamed during its incorporation in 1839, Union was a pietist-leaning New School alternative to the rationalistic orthodoxy and ecclesiastical conservatism of the Old School. Although the seminary's founders bitterly resented the Old School's abrogation of the Plan of Union that held the two kinds of Presbyterianism together, Union Seminary was generous in dealing with the strains of a divided church. Its founders described themselves as church people "of moderate views and feelings, who desire to live free from party strife." Temperamentally and theologically, the founders of Union Seminary were moderates who pledged to resist "all the extremes of doctrinal speculation, practical radicalism, and ecclesiastical domination." After the Presbyterian church broke apart, the seminary retained both of its Old School professors, including its lone systematic theologian, Henry White. Thirteen years later, shortly after White's death, Union hired another theologian, Henry Boynton Smith, initially to teach church history, who soon epitomized the seminary's reconciling spirit.[5]

Smith was the quintessential New School moderate. Later famed as "the hero of Presbyterian union," he was raised a Unitarian, converted to evangelical Congregationalism as a student at Bowdoin College, and joined the New School Presbyterian church upon joining the faculty of Union Seminary. His contributions to American theology and church relations were strongly influenced by his graduate training in German mediation theology. Smith was not the first American to pursue graduate theological studies in Germany, but more than any other figure, he initiated the shift in American theology from a Scottish and English orientation to a German orientation. After dropping out of graduate programs at Andover and Bangor Seminaries on account of poor health, he attended lectures in Paris, regained his health, and enrolled at the University of Halle in 1838.

At Halle he studied under evangelical pietist icon Friedrich August Tholuck, who befriended him. The following year Smith studied at Berlin under eminent church historian J. August Wilhelm Neander and biblical scholar Ernst Wilhelm Hengstenberg. At the time, five years after Schleiermacher's death, Neander was the leader of the mediationist school; a dozen years later, Isaak August Dorner became the movement's leading thinker. German mediating theology was a modernizing project that sought to establish a third way, more or less in the manner of Schleiermacher, between strict confessional orthodoxies and the kind of rationalist radicalism advocated by David Friedrich Strauss. It was strongly incarnationalist and experiential, it viewed doctrine as secondary to God's ongoing work of redemption in history, and it emphasized the notion of the church as a developing, living organism.[6]

In 1847 Smith began his teaching career at Amherst College, joining the faculty at Union Seminary three years later. In 1855, he succeeded to Union's chair of systematic theology. In both positions he taught "divinity through history" in the manner of his teachers. Exemplifying the possibility of a mediating American Presbyterianism that was orthodox, irenic, and open to historical change, Smith was Egbert Smyth's role model during Smyth's early career at Andover. As an orthodox Presbyterian, Smith believed that scripture is infallible when interpreted "by its real spirit," which allowed him to speak of biblical inspiration as plenary "divine influence," not verbal divine superintendence. He respected the religious integrity of Princeton Old School orthodoxy and Taylor-school New Haven Theology, but judged that both schools failed to work out a balance between faith and philosophy, partly because both were insufficiently historical in their thinking.[7]

Smith's version of a mediating alternative blended ideas from Neander, Tholuck, Horace Bushnell, and, especially, Isaak Dorner. Temperamentally irenic, he pursued theology to build bridges, not refute others. His inaugural lecture at Union expressed this sensibility explicitly: "To mediate between our extremes is our vital need, and such mediation can only be found in Christ, and not in an ethical system." To Smith, incarnation and redemption belonged together as ground and consequence; the incarnation of God's Son for the redemption of all people was the grand principle of Christianity, with a crucial implication for Christian piety: "As the central idea of the whole Christian system is in mediation, so should this be the spirit of our theology, the spirit of our lives." With these words Smith expressed the essential self-understanding of Union Seminary. His mediating Christ-centered piety was shared by most of his colleagues, especially biblical scholar Edward Robinson, who made a deep intellectual and personal impression on Briggs that was second only to Smith's influence.[8]

Edward Robinson, Union Seminary's first major scholar, having joined its faculty in 1837, was the only American to achieve an international reputation in biblical studies before the Civil War. A protégé of Moses Stuart at Andover Seminary, he studied under Tholuck and renowned Hebrew grammarian Friedrich H. W. Gesenius at Halle, and subsequently under Neander and Schleiermacher at Berlin. In his early scholarly career he founded the journal *The Biblical Repository* and published an English edition of Gesenius's landmark Hebrew lexicon; early in his career at Union, he became the world's foremost biblical geographer. Theologically, Robinson was slightly more conservative than Smith; on certain issues he was even more conservative than Moses Stuart.

His idea of good mediation theology was the conservative confessionalism of German Lutheran biblical scholar Ernst Wilhelm Hengstenberg.[9]

Like Hengstenberg, he covered his critical training with a tight creedal orthodoxy. Robinson defended the Mosaic authorship of the Pentateuch and the historical credibility of scriptural narrative; with Hengstenberg, he accepted the single authorship of the book of Isaiah and the messianic interpretation of Isaiah, though he rejected Hengstenberg's mechanical notion that God uttered predictions through the prophets of which they were unaware. Robinson rarely used his critical training to correct biblical history, but for him, the "monkish traditions" of postbiblical lore belonged to another category. In this area his major work, *Biblical Researches in Palestine* (1841), demolished centuries of pious lore and tradition. Using the methods of historical criticism to reconstruct the geography of ancient Palestine, Robinson laid the foundation of all modern geographical and archaeological study pertaining to the land of the Bible. In 1842, his major work won the gold medal awarded by the Royal Geographical Society of London; by 1856, it had grown to three volumes, setting an impressive standard of scholarly excellence for Briggs. Together, Smith and Robinson taught Briggs that American evangelicalism needed and had nothing to fear from first-rate scholarship. They also convinced him, mostly by example, that to become a first-rate scholar, it was necessary to study in Germany.[10]

Two years after he began his studies at Union, Briggs was forced by his father's illness to leave seminary and assume management of the family barrel business, which he raised to a new level of profitability. He married Julie Valentine in 1865. After recuperating from his illness, Alonson Briggs urged his son to stay in the family business, but Charles had his sights set on Germany. He and his wife headed for Berlin in 1866, armed with a preaching license from the (Old School) First Presbytery and a letter of introduction from church historian Philip Schaff, who occasionally lectured at Union. Briggs's acquaintance with Schaff was fortuitous and long-lasting. Schaff, then on leave from Mercersburg Seminary in Mercersburg, Pennsylvania, had many friends in Germany. A Swiss-born German product of Tübingen, Halle, and Berlin, he was a cofounder, with John Williamson Nevin, of the Catholic-leaning, German Reformed "Mercersburg Theology." His richly ecumenical orthodoxy contained a strong Romanticist flavor that reflected his training in German mediating theology. Schaff's numerous German teachers included C. F. Schmid, J. A. Dorner, and Ferdinand Christian Baur at Tübingen, Friedrich August Tholuck and Julius Müller at Halle, and Ernst Hengstenberg and August Neander at Berlin. In the 1860s and 1870s these became increasingly familiar names in American theology.[11]

In Berlin Briggs studied under Robinson's scholarly exemplar, Hengstenberg, who inveighed against higher criticism, and under Smith's model, Isaak Dorner, who taught him the theological principle of unity in diversity. Briggs greatly preferred the latter. Dorner was at the height of his scholarly influence and creativity in the late 1860s, having moved from Göttingen to Berlin in 1862. A post-Kantian mediationist, his theology synthesized traditional Lutheran confessionalism and Schleiermacher's experientialism. He impressed Briggs deeply as a creative thinker, faithful churchman, and scholarly seeker of the truth, and his emphasis on unity in diversity and his doctrine of progressive sanctification left lasting imprints on Briggs's thinking; Hengstenberg, in contrast, impressed him as a special-pleading relic of authoritarian religion. Briggs was a biblical conservative when he arrived in Berlin; in the manner of his teacher, Edward Robinson, he approached the Bible with a lightly critical touch. Upon being exposed to trends in Continental source criticism, however, he found it impossible to share Robinson's high regard for Hengstenberg. With typical candor, Briggs later reflected that Hengstenberg "was not seeking the truth, but battling for a lost cause."[12]

He relinquished his biblical conservatism, though not his full-blooded evangelicalism, within a few months of arriving in Germany and began to express his faith in sanctificationist language that was alien to Old School Presbyterianism. "The world needs new views of truth," he wrote to Marvin Briggs. "The old doctrines are good, but insufficient. They need the light that must dawn on them from a more advanced Christian truth." He still believed in "the standards of our church," he assured, but standard Reformed orthodoxy gave "no light at all" on the nature of the regenerated life. "I cannot doubt that I have been blessed with a new divine light," he reported to his uncle. "I feel a different man from what I was five months ago. The Bible is lit up with a new light." Two months later he lamented Marvin's misfortune in having attended Princeton Seminary, "where there is an incarnation of doctrine and everything is looked upon from that standpoint." To his mother, Briggs enthused that his current studies made him feel "much nearer to God, more under the Divine guidance and protection than I did last year at this time." In his twenty-sixth year he felt "that I am better, that Christ has revealed himself more to me and that I have been drawn nearer to Christ."[13]

This was the holiness language of New Light Presbyterianism, but nothing in the background of American New Light Presbyterianism suggested that historical criticism could be the agent of sanctifying renewal. Briggs took the latter assurance from his teachers, especially Dorner, who convinced him that historical-critical scholarship was a friend to evangelical faith. He told Henry Boynton Smith that Dorner was "not only a thorough scholar but a pious and kindhearted man. He is very much beloved by his students and influences them to good." Dorner taught that the objective methods of biblical criticism confirmed the historical reliability of biblical faith and liberated Christianity from the straitjacket of scholastic orthodoxy. This conviction was reinforced by Heinrich Georg Augustus Ewald, who taught Old Testament at Berlin, and by Aemilius Roediger, who taught Semitic languages and pressed hard on the theme that all theology must proceed from careful historical exegesis. To Briggs, Dorner was the teacher who pulled everything together. He reported to Smith that Dorner's "magisterial methodology" began with historical exegesis of scripture, moved to historical analysis of church doctrine, and culminated with his own systematic formulation.[14]

Dorner's combination of critical rigor and sanctificationist piety was a revelation to Briggs. By temperament and family background Briggs was an Old School Presbyterian, but Dorner made the "New School" language of sanctification accessible and compelling to him, and raised modern theology to a new level of Christian maturity. The pre-Dorner generation of German theologians was highly rationalistic, Briggs judged, and German theology was still saddled with this inheritance. Much of it featured "too great an exaltation of human reason." To Briggs's mind, the mediation theologians, especially Dorner, were bringing about a new balance of critical and evangelical elements. "The great men of Germany are now endeavoring to reconcile the demands of human reason with the claims of Scripture, and they are doing this," Briggs enthused.[15]

Dorner taught his students to discern and appreciate the theological unity that pervades the diversity of Christian scripture and tradition. Briggs found his vocation in this call; he called it biblical theology, which blended biblical criticism and theological reflection. "I feel confident that I can return to America and use the material I have gathered for the advancement of this [field]," he told Smith. "My studies abroad have assumed a direction in which they will probably continue unless I am called into other fields of thought." What was needed in American theological scholarship was a critically informed biblical theology that blended modern exegesis with Dorner's theology of the thematic unity of scripture. Near the end of his graduate studies, Briggs worried that no American seminary was prepared to underwrite this job description. American scholarship gave little attention to exegesis, much less to biblical theology, he reflected; worse yet, higher criticism was a scare word in America. "I have sometimes thought I would like a position in a theological seminary—but I fear I could do little more than the languages," he told Smith. He also believed that Smith was making a mistake by sending his best students to Halle. "Tholuck and Müller are the only lights of Halle in theology, and these are both dimmed," he counseled. Müller was too ill for serious work and Tholuck was going blind; both were well past their creative years. On the other hand, "Dorner is in his prime and glory as the great leader of the Evangelical Union party."[16]

Like many Americans of the succeeding generation, Briggs attained a definite conception of what biblical scholarship needed to look like from his graduate training in Germany. He began his career strongly convinced that American scholarship was grievously outdated, and he was not shy in expressing this view—a fact that later obscured, for many, his essential evangelical orthodoxy. Equally important to Briggs was the broad-church spirit that he shared with his teachers, Smith and Dorner. Shortly before the Civil War, the Northern and Southern branches of New School Presbyterianism broke apart; four years later, at the outset of the war, the Northern and Southern branches of the Old School separated from each other. This schism made it possible for the Northern branches of the New and Old Schools to renegotiate their relationship. New

School Presbyterianism had never gained much of a foothold in the South, but the Northern/Southern schism in the Old School was very significant, for it opened the possibility of a reunited Presbyterianism in the North. During and after the war, especially at the end of his term as moderator of the Northern New School, Smith pursued this objective, insisting that "the questions between us are about shades of orthodoxy, and do not reach the dilemma, orthodoxy or heterodoxy."[17]

The presence of an Old School theologian on Union's faculty—William G. T. Shedd—helped to sell this argument. The fact that Smith was more comfortable with the Westminster Confession than many New Schoolers made him the ideal figure to negotiate a reunion. Under the leadership of Smith and Union Seminary cofounder William Adams, the Northern New Schoolers convinced their separated Northern brethren to accept only the Westminster Confession and the Presbyterian system of church order as the material basis of Northern Presbyterian reunion. This agreement was ratified in 1869; the year before, Briggs wrote from Germany to his newly celebrated teacher: "I feel very thankful for your efforts on behalf of Union. Dr. Dorner has read all the essays with satisfaction; especially did he admire the Christian charity displayed between Dr. Hodge and yourself. I am connected with the Old School and would prefer that side to the other, but I feel more sympathy with the mediating theology which it seems to me you advocate."[18]

Smith's mediating orthodoxy was still Briggs's model of ideal Presbyterianism. Upon beginning his ministry as pastor of the First Presbyterian Church of Roselle, New Jersey, Briggs promised that he would preach only genuine evangelical faith: "What the Church needs today is the strong meat, the good, old, strong Calvinistic, Augustinian, and Pauline doctrines reiterated in all their sublimity and power," he declared. "It is a mark of our degeneracy . . . that these grand doctrines of the Reformation expressed in our Catechism are not brought out in as much force and prominence as heretofore."[19]

He was no liberal, except as a broad-church supporter and vigorous advocate of historical criticism, and it troubled Briggs greatly that the critical methods he regarded as tools of evangelical preaching were usually identified with theological liberalism. "It is not a good sign of the times that men boast of having thrown off the restraint of our pious ancestors in praise of a 'liberal Christianity'—one that will allow people to believe whatever they choose," he complained. "Liberal Christianity" was a phrase that he spoke only with a scornful edge; at the same time, however, the legitimacy of higher criticism was the central divisive issue in his field, and on this question, Briggs outflanked many liberals of his time. In 1870, Philip Schaff was appointed to Union's chair in theological encyclopedia and Christian symbolism. Two years later, Schaff asked Briggs to translate and edit Karl Moll's *Commentary on the Psalms* for the American edition of the Lange biblical commentary series. Briggs's skillful work on this project caught the attention of his former teachers, and in 1874, after failing health forced Smith to retire, Schaff and Smith urged Union to hire

Briggs as a provisional professor of Hebrew and cognate languages. Thus began his nearly forty-year career at Union, where he succeeded to three endowed chairs, wrote twelve books, cofounded an epochal biblical commentary series, and spent many years as the object of intense partisan controversy.[20]

EVANGELICAL AND SCHOLASTIC ORTHODOXIES

Briggs made his early reputation by insisting that English and American theology had wrongly held out against Continental biblical criticism. "We have thus far been, at the best, spectators of the battle that has raged on the continent of Europe over the biblical books," he admonished. On occasions he allowed that in the decades before the Civil War a few Americans made "occasional and cautious use of German criticism." These exceptions included Moses Stuart, S. H. Turner, Addison Alexander, Samuel Davidson, and his own beloved teacher, Edward Robinson, who died in 1863. Briggs never cited Unitarians like Theodore Parker, Andrews Norton, and George Rapall Noyes in this honor roll, not thinking of himself as belonging to a tradition that included them, and not wishing to be confused with them. He exhorted that the time had come to begin a tradition of critical scholarship in mainstream American Protestantism. "The Providence of God now calls us to take part in the conflict," he declared. "Our Anglo-American scholars are but poorly equipped for the struggle. We should prepare ourselves at once."[21]

In that mood, and for his entire academic career, Briggs vigorously labored to inspire and create an American tradition of biblical criticism. Elected in 1876 as Union's Davenport Professor of Hebrew and Cognate Languages, in his inaugural Davenport address he maintained that biblical criticism and belief in supernatural revelation belong together. Higher criticism repealed various traditions about the Bible, he explained but did not threaten biblical revelation itself: "So long as the word of God is honored, and its decisions regarded as final, what matters it if a certain book be detached from the name of one holy man and ascribed to another, or classed among those with unknown authors?" Textual and higher criticism brings us closer to the scriptural Word that God wants us to have, he assured. Biblical criticism secures unfettered access to the actual Word of God, and is thus a crucial aid to evangelical faith.[22]

He found a difficult venue for this claim in 1880. The rise of an assertive premillennialist movement with substantial Presbyterian leadership led in 1875 to the founding of the later-named Niagara Bible Conference, the first important vehicle of American fundamentalism. Though not overwhelmingly dispensationalist or premillennialist at first, by 1878 the Niagara Conference movement was firmly committed to the position that the premillennial second coming of Christ is a fundamental doctrine of Christianity on the same level as Christ's incarnation. Most conference leaders—including Baptist pastor A. J. Gordon and Presbyterians Nathaniel West, James H. Brooks, William J. Erdman, and Henry M. Parsons—further accepted some form of the dispensationalist interpretation of the Bible pioneered by apocalyptic sectarian leader J. N. Darby (1800–82). According to the dispensationalist scheme that these figures espoused as essential Christian orthodoxy, the Bible teaches one plan of salvation for an earthly people (Israel), another plan for a heavenly people (the Christian church), and the certainty of Christ's return to establish a millennial kingdom in Jerusalem.[23] Premillennialists further taught that world conditions will inevitably degenerate until Christ comes to establish his earthly kingdom.

The spectacle of a modern Christian movement that spoke about biblical "dispensations" and the "any-moment secret rapture" of the church was deeply troubling to Briggs, as it was to the Old School Calvinists at Princeton Seminary. He and they were disturbed by the crude literalism and ahistorical exegesis of the premillennialist movement, which lowered the level of genuine biblical literacy in the churches. They were especially alarmed that American premillennialism was attracting a substantial Presbyterian base. Briggs therefore attacked the movement's essential claim to orthodoxy: "It shows a weakness of judgment and a historic pessimism to leap over 16 centuries to find in the three earliest a purer life and a sounder doctrine," he scolded. "The Church of Christ has *not* gone from bad to worse through 19 centuries, but with the Holy Spirit it has advanced in life and doctrine all through the centuries." Hatred of history and the world have nothing to do with orthodoxy, Briggs admonished, for Christian orthodoxy holds fast to the ongoing guidance of the Holy Spirit through history. The Presbyterian church needed to build upon its recent reunification; instead, it was faced with a strange outbreak of apocalypticism that threatened to create new ecclesiastical factions.[24]

To demonstrate the essential evangelical unity of the Reformed tradition, Briggs reached out to an unlikely ally. His lifelong passion was the cause of church reunion, first within the Reformed tradition, and later among all Christian denominations, and he regarded the reunion between the Presbyterian Old School and New School factions as a work of the Holy Spirit. Ten years after that event he judged that his denomination needed to demonstrate the spiritual unity of genuine Reformed evangelicalism without dodging critical modern questions. At Briggs's urging, Union president William Adams thus asked Princeton theologian A. A. Hodge if his seminary would care to join forces with Union in copublishing a new theological journal. Hodge replied with customary cordiality that it was "both the right and the interest of the Presbyterian Church to be represented by a Theological Review." Later Hodge tried to back out of the journal's editing chores—"I have not the gifts, the experience, or the health," he pleaded—but the fateful experiment named *Presbyterian Review* needed Charles Hodge's son. He and Briggs served as the journal's first coeditors; later, and less agreeably, Briggs shared editing duties with Princeton's Francis Patton; still later, and even less agreeably, Briggs teamed with Benjamin B. Warfield.[25]

This was a difficult partnership for both sides. Union was moving in a liberal direction, but Princeton gloried in its fidelity to seventeenth-century Reformed orthodoxy. Charles Hodge famously boasted near the end of his career that no theological novelty was ever taught during his fifty-plus years at Princeton. He and his successors regarded themselves as custodians of traditional Reformed orthodoxy, and fundamental to their concept of orthodox authority was the doctrine of biblical inerrancy. Until the publication of Hodge's own *Systematic Theology* in 1872, the theology curriculum at Princeton was based on Francis Turretin's seventeenth-century scholastic system, *Institutes of Elenctic Theology*. The Princeton theologians exhorted American Presbyterians to remain faithful to the inerrancy-orthodoxy of Turretin (1623–87), the Helvetic Consensus Formula (1675) and, they claimed, the Westminster Confession of Faith (1647). A. A. Hodge in his *Outlines of Theology* (1860) taught that the original autographs of scripture were "absolutely infallible when interpreted in the sense intended, and hence are clothed with absolute divine authority." In an early issue of *Presbyterian Review*, A. A. Hodge and Warfield spelled out what it meant to claim absolute infallibility for the Bible. In words that defined what came to be called the "fundamentalist" position, they argued for a "perfect inerrancy" doctrine of scripture that recognized only minor blemishes in the Bible as we have it and no blemishes of any kind in the ostensible, extinct "autographs" inspired by God.[26]

Hodge explained: "The historical faith of the Church has always been, that all the affirmations of Scripture of all kinds, whether of spiritual doctrine or duty, or of physical or historical fact, or of psychological or philosophical principle, are without error, when the *ipsissima verba* [exact unaided words] of the original autographs are ascertained and interpreted in their natural and intended sense." Warfield, warning against any deviation from perfect inerrancy, reasoned that since all scripture is verbally inspired by God, it is impossible that the Bible contains errors of any kind. If a single error in a scriptural autograph were to be proven, the entire Protestant structure of authority would collapse. Warfield's precise words were cited by fundamentalists for a century afterward: "A proved error in Scripture contradicts not only our doctrine but the Scripture claims and, therefore, its inspiration in making those claims."[27]

These aggressive assertions about what Protestant orthodoxy had supposedly always claimed had a context. The *Presbyterian Review* was launched in the year of William Robertson Smith's sensational first heresy trial before the General Assembly of the Scottish Free Church. A professor of Old Testament at Aberdeen's Free Church College, Smith was an early advocate of the source critical theories of Karl Heinrich Graf, Abraham Keunen, and Julius Wellhausen. In 1875, three years before Wellhausen published his famous *Geschichte Israels*, Smith introduced English readers to Wellhausen's fourfold documentary hypothesis, which distinguished among the Yahwist, Elohimist, Deuteronomic, and Priestly literary strands of the Pentateuch. More provocatively still, in 1870, Smith observed that "the fundamental principle of the higher criticism lies in the conception of the organic unity of all history." The only genuine history is the critical account that breaks through the "outer shell of tradition into the life of a past age," he contended. Any "historical" account that violates the continuity of history and the conditions of life as we know it must be untrue. Armed with this unflinching principle of modern historiography, Smith embraced the conclusions of source and early redaction criticism, endured two highly publicized heresy trials in 1880 and 1881, and set off an explosive factional debate in American Protestantism.[28]

Like Briggs, Smith insisted that he was a theologically orthodox adherent of the Westminster Confession. Like Briggs, he also claimed that historical criticism enables the Holy Spirit to work directly on modern readers by clearing away the clutter of tradition that stands between readers and God's Word. Briggs perceived that Princeton Theology was, among other things, a desperate attempt to rule out the very idea of biblical higher criticism, and taking aim at his co-editor's classic formulation of inerrancy doctrine, he left no doubt were he stood on the headline religious controversy of the day. Briggs believed that Hodge's conservatism was wrong as history and as theology. There is such a thing as a Protestant tradition of biblical inerrancy doctrine, he allowed, but it was a product of Continental Protestant scholasticism, not the classical Reformed tradition. It had Francis Turretin and the Helvetic Consensus Formula on its side, but not John Calvin or the Westminster Confession.[29]

Briggs explained that the historic Reformed doctrine of the Bible affirms scripture as the only infallible rule of faith and practice, not as a perfectly errorless revelation. Calvin and the Westminster divines affirmed the infallibility of scripture on matters pertaining to salvation, but not on incidental details. Smith repeatedly emphasized that Calvin claimed infallibility for scripture only as the scriptural Word is illuminated by the internal witness of the Holy Spirit, and Briggs pressed the same point to the same effect. The Bible contains numerous errors, he cautioned, and by extending the test of infallibility to matters of science and historical details, Princeton scholasticism jeopardized Christian belief in the name of defending it. "There is a constant tendency in all religions, and especially in the Christian religion, to constrain the Symbol as well as the Scriptures into the requirements of a particular formative principle and the needs of a particular epoch," Briggs lamented. "Not infrequently the constructed system becomes an idol of the theologian and his pupils, as if it were the Divine Truth."[30]

He implied that scholastic inerrancy doctrine was a form of idolatry. To the Westminster divines, Briggs observed, it was enough to speak of the scriptures as lamps or vessels of the Word, not as the Word itself; the clerk of the Westminster assembly, John Wallis, plainly affirmed that these vessels came into contact with "human weakness, ignorance, prejudice and folly" during their production. A generation later, Puritan guardian Richard Baxter argued that there was no reason to doubt the truth of Christianity if one merely doubted the truth of "some words" or "circumstances" in the Bible. This is authentic Reformed orthodoxy, Briggs insisted, which does not identify the external, written word of scripture with the immanent, saving Word of God that scripture contains. To rest the authority of scripture on the denial of "one proven error" was to deny the Confession of Faith. Against the scholastic doctrine of verbal inspiration promoted by Princeton Theology, Briggs endorsed the classical doctrine of plenary inspiration that he learned from Henry Boynton Smith. Plenary inspiration theory extends only to the inward, spiritual sense of scripture, not to its external words, he explained: *"Verbal* Inspiration is doubtless a more precise and emphatic definition, than *plenary* Inspiration; but this very emphasis and precision imperil the doctrine of Inspiration itself by bringing it into conflict with a vast array of objections along the whole line of Scripture and History."[31]

An epochal battle for the mind of the Presbyterian church was thus joined, in what became a leading Protestant journal of the 1880s. Newman Smyth was amazed that Hodge allowed Briggs's article to be published, "for it is a pretty strong historical lever under the load imposed upon apologetics by that side of the church." Briggs was similarly cheered on by Robertson Smith, Henry Preserved Smith of Lane Theological Seminary, Willis Beecher of Auburn Theological Seminary, and other liberals and moderates. Persistently Briggs insisted that he embraced biblical criticism in a way that was consistent with traditional evangelical doctrine and demanded by the facts. He and his allies were not relinquishing the doctrine of biblical authority or giving up the more recent evangelical tradition of appealing to factual evidence and common sense. The best evangelicals were true Baconians committed to the principles of scientific induction.[32]

By this criterion, the best evangelicals included Robertson Smith, Henry Preserved Smith, Newman Smyth, and, at least formally, Willis Beecher, who told Briggs, "As to the question of turning aside to club the bad boys who are throwing stones at the procession, I hardly know what to say." He did not question that "these fellows need snubbing. They have been outrageous past all patience." At the same time, Beecher judged that "Auburn men ought not to be too precipitate in rushing to the front." Auburn, Union, and Lane were the denomination's three seminaries that derived from New School Presbyterianism, but Beecher judged that Union and Lane made better candidates for movement leadership. Preserved Smith gave an example of movement leadership in his review of Wellhausen's recent work. He argued that because Old Testament studies had been "greatly enlarged by the advance in linguistic and historical science which marks our century," evangelical scholars were obliged to appropriate the evidence culled by modern criticism. It was simply a fact that "all questions touching the age or authorship" of the Pentateuch's different parts had been unsettled by modern criticism. Beecher's personal views were more conservative, but he defended the right of biblical critics to academic freedom. He and Preserved Smith squared off in *Presbyterian Review* against Princeton Old Testament scholar William Henry Green and Samuel Ives Curtiss of the Congregational Seminary in Chicago, though the latter noted that even Franz Delitzsch, a prominent conservative evangelical, accepted a multiple-source account of Pentateuchal origins and made no claim for the historicity of the Bible's pre-Mosaic narratives.[33]

The latter fact gave ballast to Briggs's claim that biblical criticism had already swept the field. He exhorted that the time had long passed for biblically faithful scholars to hold out against biblical criticism in the name of truth or scriptural fidelity: "It is significant that the great majority of professional Biblical scholars in the various Universities and Theological Halls of the world, embracing those of the greatest learning, industry, and piety, demand a revision of traditional theories of the Bible on account of a large induction of new facts from the Bible and history." In a subsequent article, Briggs made clear that he regarded modern historical criticism as a better method of understanding how God acts in history than the Old School method of reading scripture as a sourcebook of factual propositions. He admonished that this had nothing to do with giving up the inductive method of science. The developmental historicist methods of modern criticism were yielding new facts, and it was suicide for evangelical scholarship to ignore these facts and condemn the higher critical methods that yielded them.[34] Briggs could not believe that American evangelicalism was determined to hold out against the facts; Preserved Smith advised him to believe it. "I am much less sanguine than you as to the magnificent victory (to use your own words) to which we are marching," he remarked. Later he felt obliged to remind Briggs that he was not bound by Briggs's agreement with "the Princeton men" to keep their disagreements out of the daily newspapers.[35]

THE WORD SET FREE:
DEFENDING BIBLICAL CRITICISM

For twenty-five years Briggs urged the Presbyterian church that historical criticism and evangelical faith are allies: "It is a misfortune that they should ever be divorced." Warfield and the Hodges claimed that modern biblical scholarship was a perfidious outgrowth of rationalist atheism, but Briggs countered that rationalism was a reaction against the kind of orthodox scholasticism that Princeton Theology unfortunately kept alive. Biblical criticism was not a product of unbelief, he contended; it was rather the church's best corrective to orthodox overbelief and the unbelieving rationalism that orthodoxy spawned.[36]

Central to this argument was his claim that modern biblical criticism was a freedom movement in the tradition of the Reformers and the Puritans. Higher criticism posed no threat to biblical faith, he maintained; it stripped away various mistaken notions about the Bible that tradition assigned to faith, but it did no harm to the content of genuine biblical teaching. Like the Reformers and Puritans, modern biblical critics liberated the voice of the biblical witness from the suffocating authoritarianism of orthodox scholasticism and ecclesiasticism. Luther and Calvin recognized various errors in the Bible and emphasized the dynamic interaction of Word and Spirit; by contrast, their scholastic followers made biblical inerrancy a fundamental article of faith and turned the scriptural text into a sourcebook of divine propositions. Following Newman Smyth,

Briggs called the reigning church theology that derived from the seventeenth and eighteenth centuries "orthodoxism" and urged that the best antidote to this distortion of the Reformationist faith was historical-critical interpretation. At the same time, he asserted, modern criticism was also the church's best antidote to the atheistic reaction that orthodoxy inspired: "As Scholasticism is the chief provocative to Rationalism, it can never by any possibility overcome it. The evangelical spirit of the Biblical authors, the vital and experimental religion of the Reformers and Puritan fathers is the only force that will be at all effective."[37]

His effectiveness as a movement leader owed much to this claim to the mantle of Luther, Calvin, and the Puritans. Briggs persistently contended that modern biblical criticism merely worked out the principles of the Reformation and the Puritan movements, "carrying them on to higher and grander results." To his mind, he was a good evangelical Calvinist, faithful to scripture and the Westminster Confession. After history forced him to choose between orthodoxism and liberalism, Briggs sided with the liberals, but always with a tinge of regret; he would have preferred to defend a right understanding of Westminster evangelicalism. It was, to him, a precious fact that the English and Scottish divines who formulated the Westminster Confession in 1647 were good enough Calvinists not to make an idol of the biblical text.[38]

The Westminster divines resisted the ascending inerrancy-literalism of Turretin and other Continental scholastics; against the scholastic trend, they affirmed that only the dynamic interaction of biblical word and the Holy Spirit make scripture God's Word. In the words of the Westminster Confession, the "infallible and divine authority" of the Bible derives ultimately "from the inward work of the Holy Spirit, bearing witness by and with the Word in our hearts." A leading Westminster divine, Samuel Rutherford, inveighed against a rising rationalistic orthodoxy by warning that the Bible is not a rule "in things of Art and Science . . . to demonstrate conclusions of Astronomie"; rather, the Bible is a rule of faith "in fundamentalls of salvation."[39]

This was the tradition of Reformed orthodoxy that Briggs claimed to speak for and extend. In his judgment, the central problem of modern theology was to work out the relation of the divine Word to the work of the Holy Spirit: "This is the problem left unsolved by the Reformation, in which the separate churches of Protestantism have been working, and which demands a solution from the church of the nineteenth century." Briggs believed that if this problem could be solved, "all the other questions will be solved." It could be solved, not by making logical deductions from creeds and dogmas in the manner of scholastic theology, but by making an inductive study of scripture and theology, in the manner of the Reformers and Puritans, under the searchlight of modern knowledge.[40]

Briggs repeatedly exhorted that this project required a conception of inspiration that derived from Luther and Calvin, not from Continental scholasticism. Put differently, it required thinking of inspiration as Spirit-moved inspiredness, not verbal dictation: "Inspiration lies back of the external letter—it is that which gives the word its efficacy, it is the divine afflatus which enlightened and guided holy men to apprehend the truth of God in its appropriate forms; assured them of their possession of it; and called and enabled them to make it known to the church by voice and pen." Inspiration makes the utterances and writings of the biblical figures holy, "but only as the instruments, not as the holy thing itself." Henry Boynton Smith expressed it best, for him, in explaining that inspiration was "an influence within the soul, divine and supernatural, working through all the writers in one organizing method, making of the many one, by all one book, the Book of God, the Book for man, divine and human in all its parts."[41]

By distorting this dual nature of scripture and the character of the inspiration behind it, Briggs contended, inerrancy-scholasticism distorted the witness of the church. A church that took seriously the pervasive human component of scripture would not have controversies over the question whether the Bible contains errors. Biblical criticism conflicted only with "false views of inspiration." It respected the biblical text, but only as the vehicle of the Word, not as the Word itself: "True criticism never disregards the letter, but reverently and tenderly handles every letter and syllable of the Word of God, striving to purify it from all dross, brushing away the dust of tradition and guarding it from the ignorant and profane." With apparent chagrin, Briggs noted that scholarly progress in his field was lagging behind New Testament scholarship; his explanation was that modern Old Testament scholars were guilty of "servitude to the Jews." Writing in 1883, he claimed that Christian scholars were oversensitive to Jewish religious feelings and that, in particular, Old Testament scholarship suffered from the reluctance of Christian scholars to treat the Masoretic text with the same critical vigor that they applied to the New Testament. Briggs admonished that until Old Testament scholars gave up their "old superstitious reverence for Masoretic tradition," Old Testament scholarship would continue to lag behind.[42]

The lag was real; critical work on the Masoretic text compared poorly to the flourishing field of German textual and higher-critical scholarship on the New Testament. Briggs had a sense of the moment, as well. He implied that his field was about to take off; later that year, Julius Wellhausen published his field-transforming *Prolegomena zur Geschichte Israels*. Briggs's portrayal of the field was surprisingly one-sided, however. It shortchanged Wellhausen's already sizable contributions to the understanding of Israelite history and religion and gave an ungenerous view of the achievements of Johann Gottfried Eichhorn, Karl David Ilgen, Alexander Geddes, W. M. L. de Wette, Heinrich Ewald, Friedrich Bleek, Hermann Hupfeld, August Dillmann, Karl Heinrich Graf, and Abraham Kuenen in laying the groundwork for the modern source- and redaction-critical picture of Hebrew religious development. Moreover, his sneer against Christian "servitude" reeked of anti-Jewish chauvinism—which was standard fare in German scholarship. The fathers of modern biblical criticism were notably lacking in regard for Jewish feelings; Wellhausen and his predecessors routinely denigrated Hebrew religion in their writings.[43]

On stronger ground, like his German teachers, Briggs made a compelling case for biblical criticism as a disturbing prod to freedom, noting that the work of criticism on a new shore is always unwelcome: "It disturbs the inspiration of versions, the inspiration of the Massoretic text, the inspiration of particular letters, syllables, and external words and expressions." Biblical criticism appears to be destructive, he allowed, but in truth it is purgative and spiritually liberating. It drives disturbed inquirers "from the letter to the spirit, from clinging to the outer walls, to seek Him who is the sum and substance, the Master and King of the Scriptures."[44]

Predictably, relations between Briggs and his *Presbyteran Review* coeditors were strained by their battle for the mind of the Presbyterian church. Briggs got along reasonably well with the gentlemanly Hodge, but in October 1882 Hodge was succeeded as coeditor by David Swing's accuser, Francis Patton. The following spring Patton ended the journal's series on higher criticism and inerrancy with a tartly phrased arrow at Briggs, Henry Preserved Smith, and Willis Beecher. He allowed, with a show of doubt, that his fellow Presbyterians were *probably* sincere in advancing their mistaken arguments on behalf of evangelical orthodoxy. Patton countered that sincerity was not an adequate test of orthodoxy, however, especially when it paraded views that violated doctrinal standards established by the Westminster Confession. Foremost in the present case was "any opinion inconsistent with the inerrancy of Scripture, or belief in the non-Mosaic authorship of the Pentateuch." In 1885 a heated dispute between Briggs and Princeton Old Testament professor William Henry Green, over Green's work on the Revised Version of the Old Testament (American edition), further strained Briggs's relationship with his Princeton colleagues. Three years later, after Patton was named president of Princeton College, the editorial partnership between Union and Princeton seminaries frayed to the breaking point as Briggs and his new coeditor, Benjamin B. Warfield, battled over the politics of a revision movement in the Northern Presbyterian church.[45]

THE POLITICS OF REVISION: EMBRACING THE MODERN SPIRIT

The most significant heresy controversy in modern American religious history began as a proposal for creedal reform. In 1888, following the example of various Scottish and English presbyteries, the Presbytery of Nassau (Long Island) petitioned the church's General Assembly for a revision of the third chapter of the Westminster Confession of Faith, which affirmed the Calvinist doctrines of predestination and election. This overture was received by the Assembly's committee on bills and overtures, which recognized at once the peril of any prospective debate over the Confession. If debated at General Assembly, the committee feared, the Nassau overture would cause a firestorm in what remained a tenuously reunited denomination. The bills and overtures committee thus tabled Nassau's overture and watched it gain support, the following year, from presbytery to presbytery. Fifteen presbyteries committed themselves to the cause of revision. Upon realizing that the revision question could not be stifled again, the committee formally asked the church's 209 presbyteries whether the time had come to revise the Westminster Confession.[46]

This turn of events exposed Briggs's central inner conflict. Part of him was predisposed to find the revision movement "premature and impracticable," for he disliked the presumption that modern Presbyterians should improve the work of the Westminster divines. As he remarked in October 1889, "the statements of the Calvinistic system in the Westminster symbols are the most cautious, firm, and carefully guarded that can be found, and I would not trust any set of divines now living to revise them or improve them." Briggs preferred "simply to emend the strictness of the formula of subscription," and in *American Presbyterianism* (1885), he called for recognition of the right of interpretive flexibility in determining the meaning of subscription to the Westminster Standards.[47]

He loved the motto, "In necessariis unitas, in non necessariis libertas, in utrisque caritas" ("In essentials unity, in nonessentials liberty, in all things charity"). In his heart, Briggs preferred to fight for interpretive freedom and his own understanding of the confession. He believed, as he explained in August 1889, that the confession was significantly "more comprehensive, more catholic, more scriptural, more liberal and more progressive than the doctrines that now prevail in the Presbyterian Church." The rapid growth of the revision movement caught him by surprise; he later recalled that three parties sprang into existence practically overnight: "One in favor of revision; one opposed to revision; and a third in favor of a new and simple consensus creed."[48]

Briggs was conflicted, but linking arms with the antirevision reactionaries was out of the question for him. He therefore took the third option. By the time that he published his "would not trust" article in *Presbyterian Review*, he was committed to the most radical strategy, which reconciled his conservative and liberal selves. From the beginning of the revisionist petition, he had sensed its potential for evangelical renewal and modernization and enthused with various friends that the revision movement contained great spiritual and intellectual potential for the church. In his view, it contained the possibility of a genuinely forward move in Reformed orthodoxy. Instead of tinkering with the Westminster Confession, or merely opposing the bowdlerizers, Briggs committed his considerable energy to the more promising cause of devising a new creed: "Would it not be far better to let the historical document alone and give our strength to the construction of a new and simpler creed that will give us exactly what we need at the present time?"[49]

His spirited attack on the church's reigning "orthodoxism," *Whither? A Theological Question for the Times,* offered a book-length campaign document in support of this cause. Briggs contended that the church's Confession of Faith had been substantially "revised" already by a distorted scholastic orthodoxy; modern Presbyterianism had already departed from the Westminster Standards "all along the line," he charged. The serious question was not whether the Westminster Standards could be changed, but whether they could be changed back and improved, "to overcome the false orthodoxy which has obtruded itself in the place of the Westminster orthodoxy."[50]

Whither? blasted Charles and A. A. Hodge repeatedly. With ample warrant, Briggs feared that his attacks would seem personal to many readers, and he assured at the outset that no personal animus was involved. In fact, he greatly respected both Hodges, but believed that these men and their school had led the northern Presbyterian church astray, and now Princeton Seminary was predictably leading the church's opposition to the revision movement. "It is the theology of the elder and younger Hodge that has in fact usurped the place of the Westminster theology in the minds of a large proportion of the ministry of the Presbyterian Churches, and now stands in the way of progress in theology and a true Christian orthodoxy," he remarked. Given this fact, there was no way to advance in truth "except by removing the errors that obstruct our path." Briggs asserted that he did not wish to exclude people with bad theologies from the church. He believed in generosity and broad-mindedness. His ideal was a comprehensive church "in which not only these divines shall be tolerated, but all other true Christian scholars shall be recognized, and wherein all Christians may unite for the glory of Christ."[51]

Briggs perceived that the church's controversy over revision had created a teachable moment, and he resolved to drag his denomination into the nineteenth century. Referring to the scholastic theory of biblical inerrancy, he wailed, "What an awful doctrine to teach in our days when Biblical criticism has the field!" Citing Warfield's already-famous warning about "a proved error," he condemned the "peril to precious souls" that Princeton Theology paraded as orthodoxy. "No more dangerous doctrine has ever come from the pen of men," he charged. "It has cost the Church the loss of thousands. It will cost us ten thousand and hundreds of thousands unless the true Westminster doctrine is speedily put in its place." Especially offensive to Briggs was the fact that the Princeton theory of inerrancy was being circulated "in a tract bearing the imprint of the Presbyterian Board of Publication, among our ministers and people, poisoning their souls and misleading them into dangerous error." In this environment, he reflected, it was no wonder that modern biblical criticism could not get a fair hearing. Biblical criticism did indeed destroy the inerrancy theory of scripture, just as Warfield complained, but it did not destroy the claims of scripture: "It rescues the Westminster and Reformation doctrine of the Scripture, and saves the faith of the Church in the Word of God."[52]

Charging that the dominant orthodoxism convinced outsiders and insiders alike that Christianity fears the truth, Briggs unleashed a searing protest: "Orthodoxism assumes to know the truth and is unwilling to learn; it is haughty and arrogant, assuming the divine prerogatives of infallibility and inerrancy; it hates all truth that is unfamiliar to it, and persecutes it to the uttermost." Genuine orthodoxy is progressive and variable, he countered; true orthodoxy loves the truth and is unfailingly open to it. "True orthodoxy is brave, manly, and aggressive; it marches forward," Briggs declared. "The man who has within him the spirit of truth, will hail the truth and embrace it whether he has seen it before or not; and he will not be stayed by the changes, that he fears may be necessary, in his preconceptions or prejudices, or his civil, social, or ecclesiastical position. A traditional attitude of mind is one of the worst foes of orthodoxy." It followed for Briggs that the Westminster Standards spoke no "final word" in theology. "We must recognize that there are inadequate statements and even errors of doctrine in the Westminster Standards and the great creeds of the Reformation." The only way forward in orthodoxy was to advance into the whole truth yielded by modern knowledge and faithful devotion to the Spirit-illuminated Word: "Theological progress is not in the direction of simplicity, but of variety and complexity."[53]

Whither? was loaded with specific charges of excess and failure. Briggs alleged that orthodoxism was excessive in its elaboration of the Westminster doctrines of election, predestination, depravity, and the damnation of infants, and that the confession was flawed on these issues in the first place. "We do not hesitate to express our dissent from the Westminster Confession in this limitation of the divine electing grace," he asserted. "We base our right to differ from the Westminster divines on their own fundamental principle, that the electing grace of God is not tied to the administration of the ordinary means of grace." Calvinism is reformable, he insisted, but not along any line that restricts the universality of Christ's saving death, and thus, the universality of divine grace: "Relief is to be found in a more comprehensive view of redemption, and an extension of the gracious operations of God into the middle state, between death and the resurrection, where the order of salvation, begun for infants and others in regeneration, may be conducted through all the processes of justification by faith, adoption, sanctification by repentance, and glorification in love and holiness, in the communion of God and the Messiah." Briggs implied that Calvin was wrong to deny that Christ died for everyone; more explicitly, he called for a comprehensive theology of redemption and sanctification that was rooted in, but improved upon, the redemption theology of the Reformers.[54]

The latter claim led to his critique of the outright failures of orthodoxism, including its neglect of the middle chapters of the Westminster Confession dealing with sanctification, good works, assurance of grace, and Christian liberty. The confession was problematic on some of the finer points of these topics, Briggs allowed, but at least it treated them all positively, unlike the cold sterility of Hodge, Hodge, and company. "Entire sanctification is commanded and held up as the ideal of Christianity; and we must recognize that it is a possibility under divine grace; and that possibility will ultimately be attained," he exhorted. Like Isaak Dorner, Briggs believed that the souls of the regenerate grow into a state of sanctity after death. He protested that orthodoxism turned sanctification into an immediate act of God, thereby negating its essentially progressive character. Though his critique of the scholastic conscience was comparatively light, he also made the crucial point that modern Christianity was making progress, not only in science and critical understanding, but also in ethics.[55]

Briggs was now moving into new territory, beyond the mere defense of source criticism and broad-churchism and his teacher's pet theory of sanctification. "There are general principles of Christian ethics given in the Scriptures that lead to a higher Christian morality in our century than was possible to the Christian mind several centuries ago," he asserted. Though he believed that modern conceptions of equality, freedom, and just treatment derive from scriptural principles, he pressed the point that they are not laid down in the Bible or anywhere else in premodern Christian tradition. Modern notions about individual rights and equal treatment represent genuine ethical progress, he affirmed, but they cannot be required of Christians on the authority of scripture alone. Briggs did not doubt that "the coming centuries will have enlightened consciences that will be far beyond our highest conceptions of Christian holiness."[56]

He seemed to warm to his own rhetoric of progress. Briggs became increasingly comfortable with "progressive" as a self-description; late in the book he described his position as "progressive theology." He got quite specific in identifying subjects on which modern theology had progressed; chief among them was its openness to criticism and new knowledge. The modern age is the age of criticism, he observed, and criticism is a method of knowledge: "It reviews and re-examines all the processes of human thought and tests all its products." Briggs cautioned that premodern Christianity had nothing to compare to the modern critical spirit. The scholars of earlier centuries accepted their inherited Christian traditions without any genuinely critical consciousness or tools. They had no concept of criticism as a necessary discipline, both destructive of error and constructive of truth, that is the very heart of the modern approach to religion, he observed. Under its probing searchlight, modern theology relinquished its appeals to miracles and predictive prophecy as "evidences" of Christian truth, deemphasized appeals to external evidence and authority in general, secured a critical text of the Bible, destroyed the doctrine of verbal inspiration, devised multiple-source theories of the Bible's composition, emphasized the literary features of the Bible, and established the disciplines of biblical criticism and biblical theology. Modern criticism has destroyed much that long seemed intrinsic to Christianity, Briggs allowed, but it has also constructed superior methods of ascertaining Christian truth and revived "the older and better doctrine of the Reformation" about the relation of scriptural words to the divine Word.[57]

Whither? electrified the Presbyterian church and made Briggs both famous and notorious within it; it went through three reprintings in six months and was reviewed in nearly every denominational journal, often with alarm. Liberals welcomed a high-powered new champion; many conservatives echoed the *Presbyterian Quarterly* in charging that Briggs was out to destroy the church;

some reviewers followed the example of Princeton University's James McCosh, who treated Briggs's religious intentions respectfully, while warning that the book was nonetheless essentially destructive.[58] Warfield, Briggs's last coeditor at the *Presbyterian Review,* also considered the book harmful. *Whither?* was published at the near breaking point of the increasingly bitter acrimony between Briggs and Warfield that made it impossible to carry out the practical tasks of managing a journal and maintaining policy agreements. In the aftermath of the 1889 General Assembly, Warfield insisted that the revision issue was too hot to allow the journal to maintain its policy of alternating editorship; later he charged that Briggs abused his editorial authority; both sides repeatedly charged that the other was doing serious harm to the church. Warfield resigned from the journal first, which produced a hurried negotiation and brief reconciliation between the two institutions; but Briggs resigned in October 1889, citing irreconcilable differences with Warfield. This time the Union faculty agreed, Princeton concurred a few days later, and *Presbyterian Review* ended with its October issue.[59]

The ending of his editorial relationship with Princeton Seminary was dangerous for Briggs, though he eschewed diplomacy in dealing with it; in December he debated Patton before the Presbyterian Social Union of New York and provoked Princeton's already-smoldering resentment. "We are in the beginnings of a theological reformation that can no more be resisted than the flow of a great river," Briggs announced. "It is one of those movements that are long in preparing, but suddenly burst forth with irresistible might." He chided Patton that the mainstream of the church had significantly advanced "in religion, in doctrine, and in morals" since the seventeenth century, and only the antiquarian guardians of a distorted orthodoxy continued to hold out against the modern world. He reflected that it sometimes seemed to him "that our ultraconservative friends do not believe in the Holy Ghost." How else was one to explain their refusal to learn anything from modern science, historical criticism, and humanist morality? "These brethren are mistaken," Briggs declared. "The divine Spirit has been more active in the past three centuries than ever before." Recycling his favorite points from *Whither?* he argued that a new creed was needed to spark a new reformation of the church.[60]

That sparked the beginning of an organized protest against him. Briggs and Union Seminary were furiously denounced the following day in a conservative Protestant newspaper, *Mail and Express,* whose Presbyterian editor sent copies of the editorial to pastors across the country. A campaign for disciplinary action against Briggs and Union at the following General Assembly began to build, aided by a bitter personal attack on Briggs by Union colleague W. G. T. Shedd. In an aggressive reply, Briggs refuted his critics and presented a case for a new creed. The revision movement seemed to be growing rapidly. At the church's General Assembly of May 1890, in Saratoga, New York, 134 presbyteries called for a revision of the Confession of Faith, and 25 offered models of a Briggs-style new creed. At Saratoga, however, the conservatives regrouped and vowed to take control of their denomination and deal appropriately with Briggs. An obliging Union Seminary student, John McComb, aided their cause by funneling damaging information about Briggs to the *Mail and Express*. The following January, upon assuming the newly endowed Edward Robinson Chair of Biblical Theology at Union, Briggs obliged them even more, pouring gasoline on a raging church fire.[61]

A COMPEND OF HERESIES

The Authority of Holy Scripture is one of the landmark addresses of American religious history, though Briggs's original intention for it was uncharacteristically modest. Because his new position was named in honor of Edward Robinson, and because he judged, against his usual disposition, that he should avoid provoking conservatives on this occasion, he decided to devote his inaugural address to issues in biblical geography. But the donor of the Robinson chair was Charles Butler, president of Union's board of directors, who admonished Briggs that the Robinson inaugural was a showcase event, no occasion to avoid controversy. Yielding to Butler's appeal out of gratitude to him and Union Seminary, Briggs wrote a rhetorically blistering address on the nature of scriptural authority. He would later recall that the speech was fired "to some degree of passion after more than a year of unjust attack."[62]

In it, he voiced all of his signature claims on the topic: the gospel-centered evangelicalism of the Reformers, the interaction of Word and Spirit, the wisdom of the Puritan divines, the distortions of scholastic orthodoxy, the liberating promise of biblical criticism. Briggs praised his German teachers for creating a modern critical tradition of theology and his Union teachers for paving the way to a modern, critical, American theology. He gave long lists of higher critical certainties: "Moses did not write the Pentateuch or Job; Ezra did not write the Chronicles, Ezra, or Nehemiah; Jeremiah did not write the Kings or Lamentations; David did not write the Psalter, but only a few of the Psalms; Solomon did not write the Song of Songs or Ecclesiastes, and only a portion of the Proverbs; Isaiah did not write half of the book that bears his name." He called the doctrine of biblical inerrancy "a ghost of modern evangelicalism to frighten children" and declared that scripture contains various errors "in the circumstantials and not in the essentials." He argued that "nothing essential would be lost" to Christianity if all the biblical miracles were to be explained on naturalistic grounds. He posited that scripture, the church, and reason are the "three great fountains of divine authority" and provocatively cited the English Unitarian James Martineau as an exemplar of rational religion.[63]

"There are those who would refuse these Rationalists a place in the company of the faithful," he observed, speaking of Martineau-type Unitarians. "But they forget that the essential thing is to find God and divine certainty, and if these men have found God without the mediation of Church and Bible, Church and Bible are means and not ends; they are avenues to God, but are not God." He declared that he revered the mediating theology of his teachers, Henry Boynton Smith and Isaak Dorner, but he had no respect at all for the "dogmatism of mere traditional opinion and of the dogmaticians." He defended Dorner's theory of progressive sanctification after death, arguing that while scripture contains a conception of a "Middle State of conscious higher life," it contains no notion of immediate sanctification at death. Briggs rejected the traditional concept of a judgment immediately following death: "The bugbear of a judgment immediately after death, and the illusion of a magical transformation in the dying hour should be banished from the earth." His blazing call to battle for the triumph of a genuinely modern Christianity topped all of his previous summonses: "We have undermined the breastworks of traditionalism; let us blow them to atoms. We have forced our way through the obstructions; let us remove them from the face of the earth, that no man hereafter may be kept from the Bible, but that all may freely enter in, search it through and through, and find God enthroned in its very centre."[64]

That did it. His enemies were undoubtedly appalled and delighted at the same time by his performance; they eventually judged that no other evidence was needed to convict him of heresy. Faced with Briggs's rhetoric and flagrant disregard for orthodoxy, it was impossible for conservatives to take seriously his fervent claim that he cared about the evangelical unity of the church. The inaugural address set off an explosion of condemnations and pushed into motion the machinery of ecclesiastical punishment; for church conservatives, it offered a conveniently arresting example of the danger of the revision movement. The speech was criticized by a wide range of secular and denominational publications, including the *New York Tribune, New York Sun, The Christian Intelligencer, The Observer, The Twentieth Century, The Presbyterian*, and the *Mail and Express*. The *New York Evangelist* and *Christian Union* bravely defended Briggs's learning and eloquence, but even the *Independent* decried his seemingly dark, polemical spirit. Briggs struck back with replies that confirmed his reputation for aggressiveness and modernizing radicalism.[65]

"It must be evident to every thinking man that the traditional dogma has been battling against philosophy and science, history and every form of human learning," he declared. Traditional Christian ways of thinking about religion and the world were no longer credible. It was simply a fact that modern Christianity was in crisis, and he had become controversial by proposing to deal with this fact. "There can be little doubt but that the traditional dogma is doomed," Briggs insisted. "Shall it be allowed to drag down into perdition with it the Bible and the Creeds?" Elsewhere he protested that he had never equated or coordinated the Bible, the church, and reason as religious authorities. He still believed that scripture is the only infallible rule of faith and practice. At the same time, he also believed that those who granted no religious authority to reason or the church were grievously wrong: "Those who question the fact that the Church and the Reason are sources of divine authority go in the face of history and the creeds of the Church." Only a distorted Protestant orthodoxy took a low view of church and sacraments, he admonished, or denigrated the gift of the divine light in the faculty of human reason.[66]

Then he took on his major accusers, Shedd and Green. An Old School dogmatist and longtime Union theology professor, Shedd had a romantic side that puzzled generations of Union students. In his early career, he taught English literature at the University of Vermont under president James Marsh, adopting Marsh's interest in Coleridge. He subsequently edited the first American edition of Coleridge's complete works. Shedd allowed his kindly, Coleridge-loving heart one wrinkle in teaching a dogmatic system that otherwise descended straight from the seventeenth century; this was his invention of the doctrine of "classical election," which taught that God elects all dying infants to salvation as a class. In Shedd's later years at Union his students inquired how old a dying infant had to be to miss the cutoff and go to hell.[67]

Shedd confessed not to know the answer to that question, but he was indignantly dogmatic about the evils of higher criticism, protesting that higher criticism leaves us with a Bible authored by uninspired writers. We cannot affirm the inspiration of the biblical books if we cannot say who wrote them, he contended. Briggs replied that the chief virtue of higher criticism was precisely its deliverance of modern Christianity from the tyranny of speculative dogmas of this type and that Shedd's orthodoxy made mistaken traditions about the Bible more fundamental than the biblical message itself: "Dr. Shedd cannot name the author of the Epistle to the Hebrews or of the book of Job. Logically, he should cast these out of his Bible." In his verdict, Shedd-style dogmatism was more harmful to the church and the Bible "than all that Baur, Kuenen or Wellhausen have ever said."[68]

He was equally cutting in dealing with Green, despite Green's immense prestige in the Presbyterian church. Briggs defended his practice of ignoring "the American Hengstenberg" and explained that when he referred to modern scholarship and its various assured conclusions, he spoke only "for the science of the Higher Criticism." By this standard, Green and his conservative American colleagues did not qualify as modern scholars: "When the Professors in the Old Testament department in all the universities of Europe, without an exception, so far as I know, are on one side of a question that only specialists can decide; and when these are sustained by large numbers of American Old Testament scholars, I crave pardon if I do not consider that the name of the venerable Dr. Green is a sufficient reason for me to modify the statement given above." It was his privilege to have studied higher criticism "with the German Hengstenberg himself, in Berlin," Briggs noted, and he found it sad enough that Hengstenberg wasted his spirit and intellectual gifts "battling for a lost cause." Briggs left hanging the implication that he would not waste his own spirit on Hengstenberg's lesser American kin.[69]

THE BRIGGS TRIALS
AND THE IMAGINARY BIBLE

The first round of formal heresy accusations against Briggs began in April 1891, when the Presbytery of New York appointed a committee to determine if disciplinary action should be taken against its most prominent biblical scholar. Five presbyteries had already overtured the General Assembly to take action against Briggs and Union Seminary; the number grew to sixty-nine by the time of the General Assembly convention. The accusation against Union was that by unilaterally promoting Briggs to the Robinson chair, the seminary had violated the 1870 Old School-New School agreement that gave General Assembly the right to veto all appointments of professors to Presbyterian seminaries. Union countered that Briggs was a longtime faculty member who was merely being transferred from one faculty chair to another. The original accusation against Briggs, as formulated by an appointed committee of the Presbytery of New York, was that he had equated the divine authority of scripture, the church, and reason; rejected the doctrine of biblical inerrancy; and claimed that the notion of progressive sanctification was a biblical and church doctrine. On May 12, the presbytery voted 44–30 to formally prosecute him for heresy.

Briggs was devastated that his own presbytery turned against him. "I have no confidence whatever that my friends will stand by me," he confided to his closest friend, Union Seminary Hebrew professor Francis Brown. "It is plain to me that my friends blame me for the situation, and I have no confidence in them or in their judgment in the case." He confessed that "the anxiety of the situation gave me a relapse. I had to give up all my examinations and remain quiet at home." Briggs expected the upcoming General Assembly to veto his appointment; more importantly, he doubted that Union's board of directors would resist the General Assembly. "I do not see how I can ever feel at home in the Presbytery again, even if I should win the battle next winter," he told Brown.[70]

From his "enemies" in the presbytery, toned down to "opponents" in a second draft, Briggs demanded to know the precise charges against him; shortly before the 1891 General Assembly convened in Detroit, he got a knowing version of the charges from Union's board of directors, who pressed him to answer eight accusations. Briggs denied that he equated the divine authority of scripture, the church, and reason; he affirmed that he included the conscience and religious feelings in his concept of reason; he affirmed that inspiration secures "an infallible record of God's revelation in respect to both fact and doctrine"; he affirmed that scripture is inerrant in all matters concerning faith and practice; he affirmed that the scriptural miracles were caused by "an extraordinary exercise of divine energy either directly or mediately through holy men"; he denied that he believed in purgatory or the doctrine of a second probation; he affirmed that a person who dies impenitent has no further opportunity of salvation; and he clarified that the concept of the "middle state" referred to the progressive sanctification of already-justified and regenerated souls. With these assurances, the Union board of directors and the Union faculty publicly affirmed their support of Briggs, two days before the General Assembly convened in Detroit.[71]

The General Assembly of 1891 demonstrated the denominational influence of Princeton Seminary. It elected William Henry Green as the church's moderator and Francis Patton as its chair of the standing committee on theological seminaries. Union Seminary historian George Prentiss later recalled that he doubted that 5 percent of the General Assembly commissioners in Detroit could have explained what higher criticism was: "Their one impression seemed to be that it was a frightful doctrinal disease of some kind, and that Dr. Briggs had it in its most malignant form." General Assembly leaders reinforced this impression. With a shrewdly orchestrated show of force, Green pushed the revision issue off the assembly agenda and moved directly to the case against Union and Briggs. Patton pressed hard for a veto of Briggs's appointment, insisting that the General Assembly would lose its right to disapprove any appointment if it failed to take a stand against Briggs. He refused to allow testimony from Union Seminary representatives, provided no official reason for moving against Briggs, and forced a vote of 447–60 against Briggs and Union.[72]

The following month, Union's board of directors voted 20–2 not to accept the General Assembly veto of Briggs's appointment. Young Arthur McGiffert of Lane Theological Seminary offered his "profound and heartfelt congratulations" to Briggs for his "full vindication" by the board and vowed, "Whatever happens I will stand by the liberal party." Union reaffirmed its support of Briggs a few days before he went to trial for heresy on November 4 at the Scotch Presbyterian Church in New York. The New York Presbytery's committee on prosecution was led by two ministers, George W. F. Birch and Joseph J. Lampe, and a prominent attorney and church elder, John J. McCook. Briggs served as his own counsel, took advice from several legal advisors, and parried brilliantly with the presbytery's prosecutors. His superior knowledge of scripture and church law were fully displayed as he criticized the form of the charges and various specifications against him, objected to point after point, cited church doctrine and abstruse points of church law, and showed that the prosecution often read false meanings into his arguments. In a lengthy debate following his defense, Shedd appealed for a guilty verdict. Briggs won his first battle against the charge of heresy, but his supporters, Henry van Dyke and Francis Brown, lost their battle to end the matter in the Presbytery of New York. The committee on prosecution appealed the case straight to the General Assembly of 1892, bypassing the Synod of New York.[73]

The dismissal of his case unleashed a flood of congratulatory letters from acquired liberal admirers, but Briggs's failure to prevent an appeal cut him deeply. "We have been defeated in the Presbytery in a most shameful manner," he told Brown. "The entire delegation from New York Presbytery will sustain the Appeal and oppose the action of the Presbytery in dismissing the case against me. . . . The conservatives have been at work all winter working up their case and securing votes." To Briggs, the conservative leaders were not really conservatives at all, but radical reactionaries. "The prospects of a radical Assembly are certainly brilliant," he groaned.[74]

Increasingly he viewed himself as the press portrayed him—a singularly valuable leader of the liberal cause. Not all of his liberal supporters were admirers; many of his colleagues and students at Union found him arrogant and self-preoccupied; others, like Egbert C. Smyth, worried that Briggs fought with the same partisan cunning as his adversaries. But for the most part, liberals rallied to his cause. His mailbox filled up with laudatory greetings from Washington Gladden, George Foote Moore, Frances Willard, Crawford Toy, Henry Codman Potter, and William Rainey Harper; even Egbert Smyth assured that "my whole heart is enlisted in your cause." In 1891 Lyman Abbott's *Christian Union* lauded Briggs as "one of those men to whom the church of a coming generation will build a prophet's tomb." Abbott editorialized: "A man of the most sensitive nature, with one of the warmest and tenderest of hearts, he is yet a controversialist in the grain; splendid in his courage, sincerity, and devotion to truth. What is true to him fills his eye to the exclusion of everything else."[75]

In the wake of his first heresy trial Briggs took heart from his celebrity, the support of his liberal friends, and the steadfast support of friends who were not liberals, notably Union Seminary president Thomas S. Hastings, who confessed, "My heart yearns over our dear Seminary. We have done our duty and I am not frightened but I do feel anxious." Crucially important among Briggs's nonliberal friends was Philip Schaff, who bolstered him throughout his heresy proceedings and published a widely noted defense of his theology after his vindication by the Presbytery of New York. "In Germany Dr. Briggs would be classed with the conservative and orthodox rather than with radicals and rationalists," Schaff observed, conveniently leaving out the liberal mediationists. "He is, in fact, a Calvinist in everything except the questions of higher criticism, where he adopts the opinions of the school of Ewald and Wellhausen, though not without some modifications, and with a distinct disavowal of rationalism."[76]

Briggs's American conservative opponents keenly understood that he was nothing like them, however, and his attempts to pass as orthodox and his wily judicial maneuvers heightened their fury against him. His claim to believe that inspiration secures an infallible record of God's revelation on matters of fact and doctrine seemed plainly mendacious to Shedd and numerous others, and in April 1892, Briggs offended them further by publishing a collection of essays that vaguely affirmed the inspiration and inerrancy of scripture. By then, Shedd's group was convinced of his bad faith. Shedd believed that Briggs was conspiring to subvert the church.[77]

At the General Assembly of 1892, convened in May in Portland, Oregon, Briggs challenged the legality of the appeal of his case to the General Assembly, noting that his accusers bypassed the Synod of New York. He gained a considerate, though decidedly unsympathetic, hearing this time. After three days of parliamentary debate, he won a victory of sorts when the General Assembly voted 431–87 to return the case to the Presbytery of New York for a full formal trial. An omen of his fate was delivered the next day, however, when the assembly approved a "Here We Stand" manifesto called "the Portland Deliverance." Its crucial section read: "Our Church holds that the inspired Word as it came from God is without error. The assertion of the contrary cannot but shake the confidence of the people in the sacred books." The Presbyterian church officially committed itself to the perfect autographs imagined by Warfield and the Hodges, sternly declaring that disbelievers in them "have no right to use the pulpit or the chair of the professor for the dissemination of their errors."[78]

On October 13, 1892, Union's board of directors rescinded the veto power of the General Assembly over faculty appointments and terminated the compact of 1870, thereby breaking the seminary's formal relation to the denomination, though it pledged undiminished loyalty to the doctrine and government of the Presbyterian church. The following day, the Presbytery of New York presented its list of charges against Briggs. The chief accusors were familiar; their charges were stretched to eight; this time Briggs faced a tougher jury. Thirteen of the fourteen new commissioners were conservatives; four of them were members of the prosecuting committee. Birch and McCook charged Briggs with teaching that reason and the church are fountains of saving and divine authority; that scripture contains errors that may have existed in the scriptural autographs; that many Old Testament predictions were mistaken; that the Pentateuch was not written by Moses, nor the book of Isaiah entirely by Isaiah; that the process of redemption extends to the world to come; and that sanctification is not complete at death.

In four exhausting sessions, Briggs gave another whirling, commanding, didactic, sometimes sarcastic performance, playing to the majority audience that he believed supported him. On the biblical criticism issues, he drew freely upon a pamphlet that he wrote for the presbytery on the status of higher critical scholarship; otherwise, he defended the scriptural basis of his theology and appealed to a host of church fathers, Reformers, and Puritans. Lampe's fundamentalist rebuttal lasted three afternoons; Briggs called him grossly ignorant in response, "as blind as owls and bats to the truth of history and the facts of the world of reality." When votes were finally taken on December 29–30, Briggs was cleared of all charges.[79] That set the stage for the trial he could not win.

Neither side was content with the outcome of the New York Presbytery trial. Briggs wanted to appeal his acquittal to the synod, because the verdict in his favor pointedly refrained from approving his theological positions "or the manner in which they have been expressed and illustrated." Union president Hastings told Briggs to calm down and count his blessings, pleading that it was time for Briggs to be grateful and appreciative, not righteously aggressive. His friends and colleagues had stood by him under immense pressure, even when they disagreed with him. Briggs's opponents knew where they could win a different verdict, however. The legal obstacles to a General Assembly trial had been removed. Taking heart at the New York Presbytery's implied jab at his views and behavior, the committee on prosecution appealed the case to the General Assembly of 1893, which convened at the New York Avenue Presbyterian Church in Washington, D.C. They found a welcome audience in the assembly's leaders, for the General Assembly of that year was dominated by Pennsylvania and Ohio Valley fundamentalists who believed that the church's gentlemanly Princeton leaders had failed to properly dispose of Briggs and his kin.[80]

Briggs fought the motion to entertain the appeal of his case with a barrage of technical arguments, noting that the Synod of New York had been passed over again, but upon losing this debate by a vote of 410–145, he knew what was coming. The church's sanctuary and galleries were packed for all five days of the trial; Henry Preserved Smith sat with Briggs's family in a gallery; Francis Brown sat with Briggs, who bowed his head through much of the mind-numbing argument against him. After the assembly voted to try the case, Briggs decided to resign from the Presbyterian ministry, but was exhorted by Union board members to see the process through. For the last time, he repeated his familiar objections, clarifications, and didactic points of exegesis and history, while his dogged prosecutors—Birch, McCook, and Lampe—stuck to their scripted assumptions and literal meanings. The distinction between scriptural form and substance meant nothing to them; Birch was fond of replying that "the jot and the tittle are as divine as the concepts."[81]

Briggs was accused of teaching heresy concerning the authority of reason and the church, the inerrancy of scripture, the facts of messianic prediction, the authorship of Isaiah and the Pentateuch, the notion of a "middle state" after death, and the doctrine of progressive sanctification. The prosecutors made little attempt to answer Briggs's explanations of what "biblical infallibility" meant to Luther, or why the Mosaic authorship of the Pentateuch was actually not a doctrine of the church. Appealing to the audience they had long waited for, the prosecutors won their case by a vote of 379–116. The beginnings of a broad-church constituency had taken root in the Presbyterian church, but in 1893 it was too small to save Briggs. The following day the General Assembly suspended him from the ministry, repudiated Union Seminary, and reaffirmed the Portland Deliverance. Upon hearing a protest from the floor that the Portland Deliverance set up an imaginary Bible as the test of orthodoxy and thus disparaged the Bible that exists, former moderator William C. Young refined the precise meaning of inerrancy, which was claimed to express the doctrine always taught by Christian orthodoxy. The General Assembly resolved: "That the Bible as we now have it, in its various translations and versions, when freed from all errors and mistakes of translators, copyists, and printers, is the very word of God, and consequently wholly without error."[82]

ECUMENICAL ORTHODOXY
AND ECUMENICAL LIBERALISM

The key to the entire polemical and prosecutorial campaign against Briggs was the prospect of a victorious revision movement. He later reflected: "The Presbyterian Church was deliberately thrown into a panic about the Bible in order to defeat the revision movement and to discredit Union Seminary. I was only an incident in this warfare. Circumstances made me the convenient target on which to concentrate the attack. In all respects this conspiracy was successful. The revision movement was defeated; Union Seminary was discredited; and I was suspended from the ministry of the Presbyterian Church." The inerrancy purge did not end with the campaign against him, however. In 1894 Henry Preserved Smith was condemned at a General Assembly heresy trial by an even larger margin (396–102). This trial focused precisely on the charge that Smith disbelieved in the perfect inerrancy of the biblical autographs. It also struck a devastating blow against Lane Theological Seminary, a formerly New School outpost in the Old School environment of Cincinnati. By then it was hard not to notice the institutional upshot of the Briggs controversy; in slightly more than a year, two of the three formerly New School seminaries were effectively disqualified from exercising theological leadership in the Presbyterian church. Union withdrew from the church; Lane was censured by it; only Auburn Seminary escaped untarnished. Several months before he watched his friend unsuccessfully defend his ordination and seminary position, Briggs began to confide to friends that he was thinking about converting to the Episcopal church.[83]

Some of them tried to dissuade him. Newman Smyth sympathized in 1893 that Briggs had good reason not to wait "to have the next Assembly decapitate you," but he protested that Briggs surely did not belong in the Anglican communion. His own Congregational denomination was more free and freedom-respecting, Smyth urged; moreover, the New Haven Central Association would surely welcome Briggs with open arms: "The working relation is the paramount thing. . . . The Congregational Church may be your next harbor of refuge until these calamities be overpast."[84]

Meanwhile, at Union Seminary the board of directors' vow to keep the institution faithfully Presbyterian was taken very seriously; Union had become formally independent, but it was still thoroughly Presbyterian. Briggs understood that he owed a sizable debt to Union's directors and faculty, though he could be grudging in acknowledging it. Numerous students and colleagues did not regard Briggs highly as a person or teacher; many students found him unapproachable, self-absorbed, and pedagogically impossible, just like his friend, Philip Schaff. William Adams Brown later recalled, more than once, that during the heresy trials "the only place where you could go without hearing the Briggs case discussed was Union Seminary." All things considered, Briggs was fortunate that Union stood by him throughout the controversy and then immediately reaffirmed its commitment to him shortly after his General Assembly conviction.[85]

Briggs was objectively alienated from his own church, yet the life and future of the church catholic meant everything to him, and his consuming passion was church unity. Moreover, he had long made it clear that he regarded the Anglican communion as the key to the future of ecumenism. Liturgically, theologically, and ecclesiastically, he regarded Anglicanism as an open-ended form of orthodox Christianity that mediated between Protestantism and Catholicism. Briggs was deeply committed to church unity among Protestants, between Protestants and Catholics, and between Western and Eastern Christianities. At the outset of *Whither?* he wrote that the Anglican Lambeth Conference's recent proposals for comprehensive church unity pointed in the right direction: "The Church of England is entitled to lead. Let all others follow her lead and advance steadily toward Christian Unity."[86]

This sentiment and his deepening attraction to Anglican theology and polity moved Briggs to join the Episcopal church in 1898; the following year he was ordained a priest. The fact that the Anglican communion welcomed his views on biblical criticism was important to him. From the sixteenth century onward, Anglicanism had affirmed scripture, tradition, and reason as authorities for theology; in the 1860s, Anglican scholars such as John William Colenso, Mark Pattison, and various contributors to the controversial *Essays and Reviews* (1860) grappled seriously with historical criticism and evolution; by the early 1890s, the Church of England had largely made its peace with historical criticism and evolution. But these were not the subjects to which Briggs devoted his later career, for he judged that his heresy trials gave more than sufficient publicity to his opinions on the legitimacy of higher critical methods. They also exhausted his taste for movement advocacy on this topic.[87]

Conceiving his new Anglican home as an ideal base, Briggs gave most of his later career to ecumenical advocacy, calling for closer ties between Catholics and Protestants. He told a Catholic priest that he "consecrated the remainder of my life to the Reunion of Christendom," and in the service of this cause, he proposed to work with Catholic scholars; biblical criticism was a sideline interest by comparison. "I shrink from again entering into a battle for Biblical Criticism," he explained. "There is no need again to make that a burning question. Other greater questions are before us." From the Protestant side, he did what he could to uphold the doctrines of the Virgin Birth and the Immaculate Conception, "the latter doctrine at some cost to myself in the Protestant world."[88]

In 1905 Briggs and Pope Pius X conducted a respectful discussion of Catholic-Protestant relations that boosted Briggs's hopes for the future of ecumenism; later he was keenly disappointed when Pius X condemned modernist currents in French and German Catholicism. "I do not despair, although the present attitude of the Curia towards the so-called Modernists, the best scholars and the men most inclined to Union in the Catholic Church, is certainly discouraging," he reflected. "I had a long talk with the Pope on the matter of

Reunion . . . but he certainly has changed his mind since then under the influence of the reactionaries." Briggs lectured widely on behalf of church unity,
wrote articles and books as an advocate of the ecumenical movement, and
helped create two of the major ecumenical scholarly projects of modern times.[89]
His later biblical scholarship reflected his ecumenical hopes by emphasizing the
unity of the Bible, the ideal of church unity, and the links between scriptural
and ecclesial unity. After his last heresy trial, he returned to his interrupted tril-
ogy on messianic theology, which accented the essential unity of the biblical
message. The second and third volumes of this major project were published in
1894 and 1895. With coeditors S. R. Driver and Alfred Plummer, Briggs
launched the influential *International Critical Commentary* series in 1895; the
following year, he and S. D. Diamond inaugurated the massive *International
Theological Library* series.[90]

For a brief period he had to endure the discomfort of being the only
non-Presbyterian at Union Seminary, knowing that he disappointed various
board members and faculty colleagues by joining the Episcopal church. "It was
a new thing under the sun that an Episcopalian should continue as Professor in
a Presbyterian theological school," he told S. R. Driver. He would have converted several years earlier, he added ruefully, "if it had not been for the supposed interests of Union Seminary." As it was, his conversion took place at a
vulnerable moment for Union, because Union's controversial church historian,
Arthur C. McGiffert, was then impaled in a very Briggs-like situation with the
Presbyterian church.[91]

McGiffert was a promising American protégé of eminent church historian and
Ritschlian theologian Adolf von Harnack. A strong supporter of Briggs, he was
also Henry Preserved Smith's strongest ally at the General Assembly heresy trial
of 1894. In 1898 the Presbytery of Pittsburgh condemned McGiffert's book, *A
History of Christianity in the Apostolic Age,* as a "daring and thorough-going attack
on the New Testament." From McGiffert's perspective, the book was a mainstream Harnackian exercise in historical criticism. To the Pittsburgh Presbytery,
it was a "flagrant and ominous scandal" that attributed various errors to the Bible
and treated scripture "irreverently." A peace-seeking General Assembly took no
action on the Pittsburgh overture, but the following year, ten presbyteries made
overtures against McGiffert, and the General Assembly of 1899 referred the matter to the Presbytery of New York. McGiffert's New York colleagues responded
ambivalently to the accusations against him, condemning parts of the book, such
as McGiffert's claim that Christ did not institute the Lord's Supper, but judging
that a formal heresy trial would do more harm than good. At this point, however,
stated clerk George Birch—of Briggs trial fame—filed heresy charges as a private
prosecutor. Though the New York Presbytery refused to act on his accusation
against McGiffert, Birch appealed to the General Assembly of 1900. McGiffert
knew that he had no chance of being acquitted at a General Assembly trial.[92]

That was the last straw for Briggs, who left the Presbyterian denomination
during the first phase of the McGiffert controversy. To his relief, he did not have

to wait long for non-Presbyterian company on the Union faculty. With the blessing of Union's board of directors, McGiffert resigned from the Presbyterian church and averted a General Assembly verdict of guilt. Following Henry Preserved Smith, who later joined the Union Seminary faculty, McGiffert converted to the Congregational church. Union Seminary was happy to dodge a second heresy conviction; Briggs was happy to lose his singular status as an outsider. "There seems to be no difficulty about his remaining in Seminary as a Congregationalist," Briggs told Francis Brown. "That will help me. My situation has been very difficult indeed. I shall not be able to endure it long unless others than I are non-Presbyterians." Union found itself becoming what it claimed to be, an ecumenical, interdenominational seminary. Four years later, the seminary abolished its policy of requiring board directors and faculty to swear an oath of allegiance to the Westminster Confession.[93]

Briggs spent the last seven years of his teaching career at Union as the Charles Butler Graduate Professor of Theological Encyclopedia and Symbolics. Wearing a title fit for Philip Schaff, he carried on his friend's scholarly concerns and ecumenical dreams, and though Union fell considerably short of his vision of a "theological university," he did become its first graduate professor. In 1897 he watched his daughter, Emilie Grace Briggs, become the seminary's first female graduate. A diligent scholar of biblical languages and an expert on the Christian deaconness movement, she gave much of her life to the production and supervision of her father's work.

Much less agreeably, Briggs also witnessed the seminary's outright liberalization. He appreciated that Arthur McGiffert made his later career at Union ecclesiastically tolerable, but relations between them soured nonetheless. McGiffert was schooled in a later generation of German criticism than Briggs; his idea of an exemplary theological scholar was Harnack, not Isaak Dorner. He took it for granted that the gospel message—which Harnack called the dispensable "husk" of the gospel "kernel"—was not off-limits to historical-critical deconstruction. This generational assumption offended Briggs deeply, for he regarded any deconstruction of the gospel message as a betrayal of Christianity. Briggs insisted that the infancy narratives in Matthew and Luke are historically credible. He chafed at colleagues who did not share his high Christology or his belief in the historical reliability of scriptural narrative.

By the end of his career at Union, he had acquired several such colleagues, a trend that was alarming to him. It made him fear that modern Protestantism had a self-destructive impulse. Near the end of his career, Briggs decided that he couldn't retire without issuing a formal protest to Union's board of directors. He told Francis Brown that he was going to press heresy charges against McGiffert. Fortunately for McGiffert and Union, Brown, who had become the seminary's seventh president in 1908, took his longtime friend aside and noted the absurdity of the situation. Briggs owed his career to older colleagues and board directors who had defended him and stood by him, even after he offended them. Now was he going to end his career by starting a heresy campaign against McGiffert? Briggs backed down and kept his resentment off the record. He could see where liberal Protestantism was going; he wanted to protest that McGiffert had already gone too far; he did protest that historical critics overstepped their bounds whenever they negated Christian dogmas.[94]

His last book, edited by his daughter in 1913, collected his lectures on symbolics. In it, Briggs proposed that there were three main options in theology. The first was the strategy of reaction, which imposed the fossilized dogmatics of the seventeenth century on modern churches at the cost of perpetual theological warfare. The second was the radical strategy, increasingly prominent in Germany, which swept away all creedal statements and constructed syncretistic theologies out of a comparative study of religions, usually in the form of a speculative philosophy. The third way, infinitely better, was the "wholesome Irenic" approach that sought to reunite the various Christian churches "on the basis of the fundamental principles of Historical Christianity." The fundamental principles of faith are explicated in the creeds of the ancient church, he instructed. All "legitimate decendants of Historical Christianity" adhered to the Nicene and Apostles' Creeds. The way forward in genuinely Christian theology was to employ modern critical understanding to interpret the unitive meaning of the church's authoritative creeds. Briggs tried to end where he began, with the claim that legitimate modern criticism always yields the Christ of faith.[95]

LIBERAL THEOLOGY BEYOND CONGREGATIONALISM

The liberalization of Union Theological Seminary was important both in its own right and as an example of a trend. Under the leadership of McGiffert and William Adams Brown, Union Seminary became the flagship institution of a broadly Ritschlian, social-gospel-oriented movement for progressive Christianity. Liberal theology overcame its belated march through the institutions in the 1890s; upon getting through the door at Union and the keystone Congregationalist seminaries—Andover Seminary, Bangor Theological Seminary, and Yale Divinity School—it took barely a decade for McGiffert's generation to build a new theological establishment. At the turn of the century another Congregationalist institution, Oberlin College, became an important player in the liberal theology movement, chiefly through the work of its new president, Henry Churchill King. The Congregationalist tradition was the wellspring of American theological liberalism for most of the nineteenth century, not least in the educational institutions that it gave to the movement.

But it was not Congregationalism that gave the movement its powerhouse academic institutions in the early twentieth century. The transformation of Union Seminary was significant as an example of the liberal theology movement's penetration into denominations beyond its Congregational base, a development vital to the movement's ascendancy at the end of the century. The trend began within the theological orbit of Congregationalism, at Union Seminary, which was led by New School Presbyterians closely linked to the Congregationalist tradition; later it moved out of the Congregationalist orbit.

In 1894 the Chicago Baptists of the American Education Society launched a new university headed by William Rainey Harper, the University of Chicago, that soon played a major role in the development of American theological liberalism. Eighteen years before "Harper's University" sprang to life, Boston University president William F. Warren brought the Northern Methodist Episcopal church into the liberal theology picture by hiring Borden Parker Bowne as the university's first professor of philosophy. Harper was a critically trained biblical scholar who knew, more or less, what he was doing when he hired Shailer Mathews, George Burman Foster, and other theological liberals. A generation earlier, Warren was not thinking about theological liberalism when he hired Bowne; he was looking for a high-powered philosopher who was also a good Methodist. He and Harper got a similar result. In the twentieth century, Boston University and the University of Chicago Divinity School, along with Union Seminary, became the leading institutions of the liberal theology movement.

Only one of them developed into a philosophical school in the precise sense of the term. Union Seminary housed an eclectic range of Ritschlian, social gospel, humanistic, and metaphysical liberalisms before the neo-orthodox reaction of the 1930s. The University of Chicago Divinity School embraced historical criticism and empiricist method, but joined these commitments to a variety of philosophical theories and theological strategies. The exception was Boston University, which built a distinctive theological school on the philosophy of a single founder, Borden Parker Bowne.

METHODISM AND LOTZEAN IDEALISM: THE MAKING OF A PERSONALIST

American Methodist theology was a markedly self-contained tradition before Bowne gave it a new philosophical framework. In the early nineteenth century, English theologians Richard Watson and Thomas Ralston systematized the Wesleyan concepts of the freedom of the will, scripture as a book of salvation, and the simultaneity or close relation between the experiences of justification and sanctification.[96] English and American Methodist theologians in the later nineteenth century built upon Watson's *Theological Institutes* and Ralston's *Elements of Divinity*, usually emphasizing that just as the work of justification is incomplete without regeneration, the Holy Spirit's work of personal regeneration is incomplete without entire sanctification. Methodist theologians in this tradition included William Burt Pope, Amos Binney, Luther Lee, Miner Raymond, and John Miley.[97]

Bowne was at home in the piety of this tradition, but theologically and philosophically, he believed that Methodism needed to be thoroughly rethought. Born in 1847 to Margaret and Joseph Bowne of Leonardville, New Jersey, his family traced its ancestry to the first generation of English Puritans who lived in

Salem, Massachusetts, and later ancestors were leaders in the settlement of New Jersey. The Bownes were deeply pious, morally serious Methodists. Margaret Bowne's piety was a type of Wesleyan sanctificationist mysticism, devoted to the attainment of a sinless state of grace, and her bookshelves contained long rows of the monthly Methodist *Guide to Holiness,* which she studied assiduously. Joseph Bowne, a farmer, local preacher, and justice of the peace, shared his wife's concern with personal sanctification, though not her mysticism; he was personally reticent, but outspoken in his opposition to slavery and alcohol.[98]

Bowne admired his parents greatly and inherited their zeal for righteousness; a brilliant autodidact who eventually taught himself seven languages, he was classified as "privately tutored" upon enrolling at New York University, from which he graduated in 1871 as class valedictorian. During his college years, Bowne wrote his first critical response to the philosophy of Herbert Spencer, which was then gaining prominence in England and America—the first of many critiques of Spencer that he wrote in his long career. Bowne argued that Darwinian evolutionary theory was credible as a scientific description but virtually worthless as a philosophical theory of meaning or causation. Darwin's perceptive empiricism was good science, he allowed, but Spencer's Darwinian system was bad philosophy, mainly because of its crude mechanism in treating mind, not as "the beginning and primal cause of things," but as merely "the final outcome of nature—the highest point to which the whirling atoms climb." Bowne fought the atheistic and Darwinian "apostles of mechanism" for the rest of his life and cautioned two generations of theologians against giving up the personality of God out of Darwinist anxiety.[99]

Though confirmed in his autodidacticism by the time that he graduated from college, he attended lectures in Paris, Halle, and Göttingen between 1873 and 1875, studying under Oxford logician John Cook Wilson at Göttingen and philosopher of religion Hermann Ulrici at Halle. Bowne's graduate training at Göttingen was life-changing by virtue of a third relationship, a formative intellectual and personal friendship with Albrecht Ritschl's favorite philosopher and colleague, Rudolf Hermann Lotze (1817–81). Lotze was a post-Hegelian idealist who shared Ritschl's disregard for the intellectualism of German metaphysical idealism, but not Ritschl's late-career rejection of metaphysics as such. Like Ritschl, though with greater logical rigor, he held out for the primacy of feeling over thought.

Without denying that nature can be explained mechanistically, Lotze blended idealist and personalist motifs and argued that the work of philosophy transcends science. His major work, *Microcosmos,* contended that mechanism is absolutely universal in extent and completely subordinate in significance to consciousness. Lotze's idealistic personalism ascended to the personal cause, character, and telos of reality, theorizing the organic unity of nature in spirit. He urged that philosophy is obliged to explicate the transcendent reality of spirit and solve real-life problems raised by science, ethics, social conflict, and the arts. The empirical sciences are necessarily mechanistic, he reasoned, but mechanistic forms of explanation cannot account for the unity of consciousness. In his teaching, the latter project was fundamental to the ongoing work of philosophy.[100]

Lotze's post-Hegelian variant of metaphysical idealism was strongly personalistic. With significant qualifications, he shared the Berkeleyan belief that, logically speaking, only persons exist. He taught that personality is the ultimate reality and that the existence and teleological agency of a personal deity in history is disclosed to human agents principally through feeling. In young Borden Bowne he found a kindred spirit; on one occasion, when Bowne mentioned to Lotze that a thunderstorm was approaching, Lotze replied with appreciation, "That is nothing [compared] to the storm of questionings you have raised in my mind concerning my own philosophic system." Lotze wanted Bowne to complete a doctorate with him, but Bowne, caring little for degrees, reasoned that he should be able to land an academic position without a doctorate. This conviction was tested for a year after he returned to the United States, as Bowne spent a year writing highly intellectual editorials for *The Independent*—Washington Gladden was a staff colleague—before Boston University invited him to chair its philosophy department in 1876.[101]

Led by William F. Warren, Boston University, then seven years old, had little identity and no prestige, but Warren had a vision of it as an unapologetically Methodist institution with exacting scholastic standards. He perceived that Bowne shared his ambitions for modern Methodism and his loyalty to it. Years later, after his early books made him a prominent religious philosopher, Bowne was courted by Yale president Noah Porter and University of Chicago president William Rainey Harper, but he remained at Methodist Boston University. He was fond of telling his tempters, "Ephraim is wedded to his idols. Let him alone." For thirty-five years he chaired the university's philosophy department; from 1888 to 1910 he also served as dean of the Graduate School of Arts and Sciences. Bowne was a strong proponent of women's suffrage; under his leadership Boston University became the first American institution to award a Ph.D. to a woman. His seventeen books and nearly two hundred articles and reviews laid the theoretical foundation of the Boston personalist school of philosophical and social theology. For over a century, this school taught Boston University seminarians and philosophers to equate Bowne's personalistic blend of epistemological realism and idealism with good progressive Methodism.[102]

CRITICAL IDEALISM BEYOND KANT: BOWNE'S PERSONALISTIC THEISM

For years Bowne puzzled over the name that best described his distinctive metaphysical system. He was a synthetic thinker with strong interests in psychology, physics, evolutionary theory, ethics, and theology but cared most about the religious aspects and implications of philosophy. In his early career he worked out his philosophy of theism, polemicized against mechanistic philosophy, and wrote textbooks on metaphysics, psychology, and ethics. Long after he developed his philosophy of religion and settled on a name for his philosophical system, he acknowledged that both were difficult to categorize. For many years, with caveats, he called his system "objective idealism"; in 1905 he settled on the term "personalism." A year before his death, in 1909, he explained,

> It is hard to classify me with accuracy. I am a theistic idealist, a Personalist, a transcendental empiricist, an idealistic realist, and a realistic idealist; but all these phrases need to be interpreted. They cannot well be made out from the dictionary. Neither can I well be called a disciple of any one. I largely agree with Lotze, but I transcend him. I hold half of Kant's system, but sharply dissent from the rest. There is a strong smack of Berkeley's philosophy, with a complete rejection of his theory of knowledge. I am a *Personalist,* the first of the clan in any thoroughgoing sense.[103]

From Kant he took his theory of knowledge and his ethical conception of the person; from Berkeley he took his immaterialism; from Lotze's personalist idealism he took the idea of his own system.

Bowne's constructive philosophy was based on the Berkeleyan/Lotzean attribution of personality in all that is real. By virtue of its philosophical pluralism and personalism, his version of metaphysical idealism broke from the absolute idealisms of F. H. Bradley, Bernard Bosanquet, William E. Hocking, Josiah Royce, and other contemporary neo-Hegelians. With Lotze and George Berkeley, he conceived personality as essentially self-conscious intelligence and argued that self-consciousness is the necessary presupposition of all thinking and the world of objects. At the same time, his philosophy had an insistently realist dimension; against the epistemology of absolute idealism (and Berkeleyan philosophy), he affirmed the existence of a world of objects exterior to consciousness. "We have no way of creating reality, and we also have no such *apriori* insight into its nature that we can tell in advance what reality must be," he asserted in a major work, *Metaphysics.* His method, which was critical, not deductive or creative, took experience as a whole as its datum, under the rule of the question, "How must we think about reality on the basis of this experience as interpreted by thought?" Against the a priori pure idealism and pantheism of the absolute idealist tradition, Bowne's metaphysical idealism was thus qualified by his assurance that the world of things is real and that divine reality is not to be identified with the world of its creation.[104]

His major works on metaphysics and epistemology developed his distinctive philosophical method, which pursued and substantially modified Kant's critical idealist project of reuniting reason and experience. Like Kant, Bowne emphasized the creative role of reason and the reality of the external world of things; at the same time he judged that Kant's appeal to an unknowable "thing-in-itself" failed to describe or secure the reality of an external world. The key to Bowne's constructive philosophy was the personalist principle that personality is the single reality that cannot be explained by anything else. One cannot account for the reality of consciousness on impersonal grounds, he argued, but everything else can be accounted for by the reality of personality. Moreover, the true relation of God and humanity is not identity or absorption, but interpersonal communion. Human persons are distinct from the divine person while sharing God's purposes. The category of purpose was central to Bowne's personalistic theism. Though he took at least half of Kant's critical idealism into his own system, he rejected the Kantian noumenal thing-in-itself and further insisted, against Kant, that purpose is constitutive in pure reason.

Bowne accepted Kant's basic account of knowledge as an a priori synthetic activity of the mind, as well as Kant's epistemic dualism of subject and object, but did not accept Kant's restriction of pure reason to knowledge of phenomena. He granted that reason has no direct access to reality and that scientific knowledge is necessarily restricted to appearances. Against Kant, however, he insisted that experience yields certain metaphysical clues about reality that deserve to be regarded as genuine knowledge. Though we cannot claim apodictic certainty for metaphysical knowledge, Bowne allowed, it is impoverishing and unwarranted to rule out metaphysical arguments on that account. For example, the cosmological and teleological arguments for the existence of God do not qualify as proofs, as Kant demonstrated, but still have value as powerful arguments. It is unreasonable and disastrous to restrict theoretical reason to science, Bowne argued. Kant found a role for purpose or will in his accounts of practical reason and aesthetic judgment, but not in his account of theoretical reason. Kant's *Critique of Pure Reason* ascribed no role to purpose as a category of knowledge. Bowne's dissent on this point was crucial to his rehabilitation of metaphysical reasoning as a form of knowledge; it also gave his thinking a pragmatic cast that William James appreciated.[105]

Bowne put the matter plainly in his major work on epistemology, *Theory of Thought and Knowledge*. No experience is intelligible apart from the conceptual categories of being, space, time, and causation, he observed. It is through these rules of mind that reason reaches the world of things that appear, through sense perception, of being given to us ready-made. "But these categories alone would keep us among isolated things and events," he cautioned. "Space and time separate rather than unite; and causality, at least in its mechanical form, provides for no system. For the further systematization and unification of our objects a higher category is needed; and this we find in purpose, or, rather, in the elevation of causality to intelligent and volitional causality, with its implication of plan and purpose." There is no knowing without self-conscious intelligence, and intelligence is nothing without purpose. For Bowne, the crucial either/or was always between personal and mechanical worldviews. "The principle we need here can never be found in any impersonal or mechanical conception whatever," he maintained. "The unity and system demanded must be internal, and this true inwardness can be found only in self-determining, self-conscious causality, guiding itself according to plan and purpose."[106]

Bowne did not claim that, as a category of thought, purpose belongs on the same plane as the law of causality. He allowed that the category of purpose does not play much of a role in elementary experience. All objects are in space, all events are in time, and every event has a cause, but comparatively few events seem to require a purpose. When we view things in isolation, as science usually does, it is easy to miss altogether the relation of purpose in life. For Bowne the importance of purpose came into view, not in accounting for prereflective experience, but only in higher forms of thought. Purpose is indispensable to reflection and constitutive of it, he contended; the necessity of purpose is hidden to intuition but revealed to reflection. "Mechanical causality is entangled with unintelligible potentialities which remove all progress from it," Bowne explained. The meaninglessness of mere mechanical causality catches thought in a self-destructive regress. Without meaning, reflective thought has no basis of maintaining itself or attaining systematic completeness: "It is only when thought becomes systematic and aims at completeness that the rational significance of purpose is seen."[107]

Central to Bowne's system was his contention that reason is obliged to make sense of all dimensions of human experience. He lamented the limitations of Kant's service to Christian philosophy; reason has important work to do in the field of science, he acknowledged, but truth-seeking theoretical reason is also obliged to make sense of other dimensions of human experience. Kant, by restricting reason to knowledge of phenomena, excluded the deepest and most certain knowledge that reason possesses, the reflective self's knowledge of itself: "It is possible to look upon things as phenomenal only; but to look upon the self which views these phenomena as itself phenomenal in the same sense is altogether impossible." There are no phenomenal objects of knowledge without a perceiving subject. Without claiming to understand fully the nature and processes of consciousness, Bowne admonished that there is no secure knowledge of anything without a continuous and unified center of mental life and experience.[108]

He gave short shrift to the Kantian thing-in-itself. To Bowne, this conceptual refuge was a poor substitute for the extraphenomenal ground that secure knowledge requires. "Any doctrine of phenomenalism which affirms a series of unknowable noumena behind phenomena is in unstable equilibrium," he contended. On its own terms, Kant's phenomenalism cannot yield any knowledge whatsoever about noumenal realities that transcend phenomena; therefore, Bowne judged, all of Kant's speculation on this theme was philosophically worthless. The thing-in-itself has no content and fails the tests of the categories; it is not in space or time; it is neither one nor many; it is neither cause nor effect; it is neither substance nor attribute. "The thing in itself, or things in themselves, must be brought within the range of thought or must go out of existence," Bowne maintained. "As soon as we remember that these things are affirmed solely for the sake of making experience intelligible to us, the emptiness of this kind of agnosticism immediately appears."[109]

He countered that experience itself, with the personal self as its subject, is the primary fact of knowledge, and anything that reason affirms beyond this fact must be for its explanation. This test excludes the thing-in-itself, to which none of the categories of thought apply. Only a living, personal intelligence can deliver reason from suicidal skepticism, Bowne contended. The Kantian thing-in-itself is a poor solution to the problem of phenomenalism, but some solution is necessary if the reality of truth is to be upheld. In book after book, Bowne exhorted that mechanical causation cannot be the last word about existence because it is self-refuting as a last word. The truth of this word cannot be trusted, since it is a mere outcome of mental events: "A purely logical and contemplative intellect that merely gazed upon the relations of ideas, without choice and initiative and active self-direction, would be absolutely useless in explaining the order of life."[110]

Personalism is a philosophy of the fecundity and invisible personal ground of life; the reflective self is the ground of all knowing and being, Bowne observed, yet this ground is invisible, for no one has ever seen a self. The human body is merely an instrument for expressing and manifesting its inner life. Every self knows itself in immediate experience and knows other selves only through their effects; every self is thus as formless and invisible as God. Moreover, Bowne observed that the meanings by which we live and the motives that move us are all invisible, as are the objects that we call literature, history, and government. The great drama of life has its seat in the invisible world of meanings, passions, and relations of personal wills. Most of what matters in existence is not only out of sight, but unpicturable. If we assign a seat to this "great world of reality," Bowne reflected, we must assign it not to space, but to consciousness, for the mind is neither in space nor time. The world of consciousness is the seat of "the great human drama of individual life and of human history," while space and time are merely forms of organizing our experience.[111]

Bowne cautioned that this does not negate the reality of the world of things, but merely relocates the seat of the world's reality. From the perspective of personalist idealism, he assured, the world remains "as real as ever," but the world is "not to be thought of in phenomenal terms of space and time, but rather in terms of itself, in the incommensurable terms of life and feeling, and love and hate, and aspiration or dejection, and hope and despair." Neither is the reality of the space world negated in personalist idealism: "We simply mean that it is not a self-sufficient something by itself, but is rather a means of expression of the underlying personal life which is the deepest and only substantial fact." Imagination feeds on living and dwells in invisible mystery; within this invisible world, space has a merely symbolical function. With Kant, Bowne affirmed the primacy of free-willed practical reason, but beyond Kant, he affirmed that reason and will are partners in all fields of knowledge and all dimensions of human experience.[112]

Bowne believed that Kant was right to emphasize the constructive action of mind in producing knowledge and the need to secure the objective reality of the external world, but Kant never reconciled the contradictory impulses inherent in his attempt to reunite reason and experience. He successfully mapped the problem of the split between the world of things and the world of finite spirits, but his critical idealism stopped short of solving the problem. Bowne proposed that the problem can be solved only by making the world of things the expression of a thought world that is behind or immanent within being. The mind of God is as necessary for philosophy as it is for theology, and for the same reasons: "Our thought must content itself with recognition. Its last word must be God. As it was in the beginning, is now, and ever shall be, God is that with which all our inquiry must end."[113]

THE THEISTIC POSTULATE:
PERSONALISM AS PHILOSOPHY OF RELIGION

This was the philosophical groundwork of what became the Boston personalist school of theology. Bowne admonished that philosophy is unavoidable for theologians. In war, he analogized, the success of a campaign seldom depends solely upon direct assaults: "It often depends equally, and even more fundamentally, upon seizing and holding certain strategic positions which may command the enemy's communications, or threaten his rear, or make his position untenable." He urged that philosophical problems hold this kind of strategic status for theology. Every theology operates on the basis of certain implicit or explicit philosophical conceptions, and theologians must find and use the best philosophical system available, since working without any philosophical conceptions is not an option. Aware that the way that we think about thinking shapes the way that we think about religion and everything else, Bowne warned that bad modern philosophies were doing immense damage to Christianity: "Some harmless-looking doctrine is put forth in epistemology, and soon there is an agnostic chill in the air that is fatal to the highest spiritual faiths of the soul, or some sensual blight and mildew spread over the fairer growths of our nature. Space and time are made supreme laws of existence, and determinism and materialism and atheism are at the door."[114]

What came to be called "Boston school personalism" was a strategy to beat back the advance of determinism, materialism, and atheism. Bowne did not claim that he could prove that personalistic theism is true; he claimed only that it explained the world more convincingly and fruitfully than any competing hypothesis: "There is an element of faith and volition latent in all our theorizing. Where we cannot prove, we believe. Where we cannot demonstrate, we choose sides. This element of faith cannot be escaped in any field of thought, and without it the mind is helpless and dumb." The latter point applied especially to latter-day Christian scholastics and apologists who took the bait from their scientist critics: "Absurd demands for 'proof' have been met with absurd 'proofs,'" he observed. "The argument has thus been transferred from the field of life and action, where it mainly belongs, to the arid wastes of formal logic." Bowne protested that this was no way to defend modern Christianity, because the basis of religious belief is vital and practical, not syllogistic. Logic has an important regulative function in theology, but the great beliefs of religious faith are expressions not of logic but of life, Bowne insisted: "They depend for their force on the energy of the life that produces them." Though it is not possible to prove the reality of divine existence, the postulate that God exists "cannot be denied without wrecking all our interests."[115]

Personalist theism asserted that life makes sense and bears good fruit only under the faithful supposition that the world exists through a mind analogous to the human mind. On this view, Bowne observed, the world of things and the world of thought are commensurable; thought and being are both founded in the nature of reason. To relinquish the postulate of personal theism is to lose the only possible basis for affirming that being has any thought within it. Without the postulate of personal theism, the world of things simply exists in a mechanical way, "independent of all thought and the negation of all thought," and the very possibility of self-reflexive thought is inconceivable. Lacking the postulate of a divine mind, "there is no way to thought at all, and still less is there any provision for knowledge."[116]

Bowne appreciated that the God postulate is a stumbling block to those who worry about what God might have done before creation. Isn't "God" simply another mystery-X solution to an unsolvable problem, like Kant's thing-in-itself? He acknowledged that if one assumes that time is infinite and that the cosmic process in time might be finite, the problem of God's procreative activity is very serious. On this set of assumptions, the eternal God must have been doing something before the creation of the universe, but at the same time, owing to the potency of number, God must have needed to wait for this pre-creative eternity to have passed before being able to do anything. Bowne judged that this verdict is too bizarre to be true; neither is it solvable by appealing to the impossibility of making an infinite by the summation of finites.

A better solution appeals to the ideality of time. "The denial of any ontological time compels us to limit temporal relations to the cosmic movement, without extending them to the Creator," he reasoned. "In his absolute, self-related existence, God is timeless. Hence he did not create at a certain point of absolute time, but he created, and thus gave the world and time their existence." The world was not created in a particular moment of the eternal flow of God's time, for God has no eternal flow of temporality; thus, creation did not take place in a moment within God's falsely imagined eternal time; rather, creation is the beginning of all things, including time. It followed for Bowne that there is no need to speculate about what God did in the eternity before creation, because no such eternity existed; temporal terms have meaning with reference to the cosmic process, which is relative, but they are meaningless when applied to God, who is absolute: "There was simply the self-existent, self-possessing, timeless God, whose name is I Am, and whose being is without temporal ebb and flow."[117]

Bowne's approach to the relation of nature and the supernatural was a page from Horace Bushnell, though not acknowledged as such. Aside from his book reviews and apologetic writings, he rarely referred to any other thinker, even Lotze. In his view, the question of the relation of nature to supernature remained controversial in modern religion only because conservatives and their mechanistic counterparts habitually filled the air with nonsense on this subject, and Bowne never tired of setting himself against both camps. Religious conservatives disastrously set Christian truth against science, while anti-Christian positivists assumed that there must be a mechanical explanation for everything. "We maintain the fact of a purpose in all things, but reserve the right to criticise any specific interpretation," he declared. "For the full expression of our thought in this matter we have to maintain a supernatural natural; that is, a natural which roots in a divine causality beyond it; and also a natural supernatural, that is, a divine causality which proceeds by orderly methods." All events have natural and supernatural aspects. Against religious conservatives, modern Christianity affirmed that all events are natural in the manner and order of their occurrence, but against secular positivists, it affirmed that all events are supernatural in their causality.[118]

Philosophically, Bowne had respectable company, though he undercut his professional reputation by refusing to write for philosophical journals. His commitment to a pluralistic form of idealism was shared by American philosophers G. H. Howison, G. T. Ladd, and G. H. Palmer, as well as by British philosophers Hastings Rashdall and James Ward. Despite his often acerbic attacks on absolute idealism, his philosophy was also taken seriously by neo-Hegelians such as W. E. Hocking and Josiah Royce. Hocking praised Bowne's "thought-filled and thought-provoking" work and his "consistent dignity," remarking that Bowne's religious philosophy was "throughout the work of a mind of distinction and power. Its effect and also its intrinsic interest are permanent." In Hocking's judgment, there was "no more powerful and convincing chapter in American philosophy" than Bowne's critique of the failures of impersonalism.[119]

G. T. Ladd's distinguished colleague at Harvard, William James, was another admirer; James and Bowne were longtime friends and vigorous rivals. James shook his head at Bowne's self-assuredness, and for years he treated his classes, with feigned incredulity, to quotes from Bowne's work, sometimes with the preface, "Now let's see what God Almighty has to say." At other times he complained that Bowne theorized his doctrine of a substantial self by crawling into a hole and pulling the hole in after him. These were friendly gibes, however, and in their later careers, the relationship between James and Bowne moved beyond friendly rivalry. Upon reading Bowne's *Personalism* in 1908, James enthused that "you and I are now aiming at exactly the same end, though, owing to our different past, from which each retains special verbal habits, we often express ourselves so differently." For all of Bowne's metaphysical rationalism, James perceived that he and Bowne were allies, defending a pragmatist conception of truth, albeit in contrasting philosophical languages.[120]

James noted that he and Bowne shared the same opponent and the same intellectual goal. Their common foe was "the dogmatist-rationalist-abstractionist." Their common goal was "to redeem the concrete personal life which wells up in us from moment to moment, from fastidious (and really preposterous) dialectical contradictions, impossibilities, and vetoes." Bowne's version of this project took the form of a post-Kantian transcendental empiricism, while James pursued a pragmatic radical empiricism. James noted approvingly, however, that Bowne's emphasis on the category of purpose corrected the abstract intellectualism of his philosophical tradition with the real-life concreteness of will. On the things that mattered, they were comrades: "You, starting near the rationalist pole, and boxing the compass, and I traversing the diameter from the empiricist pole, reach practically very similar positions and attitudes. It seems to me that this is full of promise for the future of philosophy."[121]

Bowne's disciples later disagreed about the extent of his philosophical kinship with James. Albert C. Knudson and many others tended to subsume the pragmatic aspect of Bowne's thinking under his rationalism; others such as Edward Ramsdell argued for the priority of Bowne's pragmatism. They agreed, however, that Bowne and James shared the formative concern to reclaim personality from the impersonality of the contingent world described by science. Following Bowne's example, some of the Boston schoolers mined James's *Varieties of Religious Experience* for apologetic material. More deeply than even William James, Bowne's heart was in religion, and his concern about the future of philosophy was bound up with his deeper care for the future of Christianity. He wrote extensively for church publications, usually with a religious-apologetic thrust. All of his work was fueled by his piety, a fact that was often obscured for his opponents and church allies alike by his highly pitched abstractions and his frequently caustic wit.

He displayed his taste for sarcastic polemic in his advocacy of various causes, especially women's suffrage, and in his book reviews. As a youth Bowne luxuriated in Jonathan Swift's *Tale of a Tub*, which gave him a model of the art of intellectual insult. By the time that he began his academic career, he knew the book virtually by heart, and practiced its art. Against a rising tide of fundamentalism, Bowne pleaded that inerrancy advocates should at least have the good taste to keep silent until they "made the Books of Chronicles and the Books of Kings tell accurately the same story." His verdict on the mechanistic atheism of David Friedrich Strauss was similarly tart. Explaining why he could not recommend Strauss's *The Old Faith and the New,* Bowne remarked, "The amount of talent necessary to construct this argument is not remarkably great, but the amount required to believe it borders on the supernatural." Later he reached for a stronger insult, claiming that with Strauss's book "the limits of absurdity have not only been reached but transcended."[122]

BOSTON PERSONALISM AS THEOLOGY

For nearly twenty years Bowne devoted himself to building a philosophical system and to apologetics. He would later lament that his preoccupation with refuting the likes of Herbert Spencer caused him to barely notice the sublime preaching and career of Phillips Brooks at Trinity Church, Boston. In 1895, however, his metaphysical preoccupations were punctured by the outbreak of controversy in the Methodist Episcopal church over the legitimacy of biblical higher criticism. The focal point of this controversy was Bowne's Boston University colleague, Old Testament scholar Hinckley G. Mitchell, whose academic position was jeopardized by attacks from conservatives. Belatedly recognizing that certain bishops were rabidly anti-Mitchell and that, on this account, the "ship was already in the breakers," Bowne spoke out in his colleague's defense. His advocacy saved Mitchell's position—at least, for five years—and heightened Bowne's resolve to take stands on divisive theological issues. An essay on the nature of revelation launched the theological phase of his career; subsequently Bowne wrote discourses on the atonement and the religion of moral and intellectual progress that sealed his status as a liberal theology leader.[123]

He was predisposed to bloodless abstractions and logic-chopping arguments. Bowne's favorite conversation starter was, "Now let us have a word about pure being." When he turned to religious topics, however, his writing was often remarkably direct and evocative; he started a discussion of the revelational status of scripture by noting that the Bible is "a most embarrassing book" if one does not read it from a precisely correct standpoint. Most of the Bible seems to have little to do with the moral and spiritual interests of good, healthy, regenerative, progressive religion, he acknowledged. Most of it is consumed with "obsolete questions" about temple rites, idol worship, the prophetic burdens of Moab and Tyre, "the tiresome purifications of the Mosaic law, the disputes between Pharisees and Sadducees, the eating of things offered to idols." Convinced that if modern people were not to be driven to the conclusion that scripture is worthless, they needed to find a concept of revelation that fruitfully illuminates the whole of scripture, he found this concept in the principle that revelation is to be identified with certain scriptural ideas about God, not with the text of scripture. The Bible is not revelation, but it contains revelation and "consists essentially in certain ways of thinking about God, his character, his purpose in our creation, and his relation to us," he proposed. "It has these great ideas for its contents, and it is to be approached, studied, and understood only in connection with these ideas."[124]

The controlling idea of scripture is that God and human beings are personally related; as long as we hold fast to the biblical view of the divine-human relation, Bowne asserted, it does not matter whether biblical history is always correct, or how many authors wrote the book of Isaiah, or how the Pentateuchal question shakes out in biblical scholarship. What matters in Christianity is not the doctrine of geology taught in Genesis, but its doctrine of creation: "With this view, we can dispense with everything else; and without this view, it matters little what else we have." The biblical concept of the world as personally created and personally related is distinctive and true, he contended. For Bowne, this worldview, the key to Christian teaching, was the answer to fundamentalists and liberal religious syncretists alike.[125]

The comparativist approach to world religions was newly ascendant in 1896; Bowne judged that for the most part, this was a good thing. "I am in full sympathy with the desire to find the non-Christian religions as elevated as possible," he declared. "I have no objection even to parliaments of religions, provided they do not hide the facts behind vague and general phrases, and provided they escape the defiling touch of the advertising harpy." Modern Christians should welcome the advent of a truly comparativist approach to religion, he contended, because any genuinely objective comparison will confirm the superiority of the Christian idea. "The central idea in any religion is its idea of God," he explained. In the Christian religion, every claim for pantheism, polytheism, and idolatry is eviscerated on the first page of holy writ, and this is what a self-affirming modern church should proclaim to the world, Bowne exhorted: "No Osiris, Isis, and Set; no Anu, Hea, and Bel; no Sun, Moon, and Venus; no Moloch, Rimmon, and Ashtoreth, whose worship defiled the nations for ages, but God, the Everlasting Father and Lord. The more we study religious history, the greater the value of the Bible appears."[126]

Against the impression that liberal theology is weak and temporizing, Bowne made a case for confident liberal self-assertiveness. Modern Protestantism is both open and superior, he assured, superior because it is open and God-centered, and open because its superiority and God-centeredness make openness a strength. Christianity can afford to be open-ended because it is based on superior ideas. "There is no good reason why a Christian should not rejoice at finding traces of God's presence and inspiration everywhere among men, especially as his own Bible teaches him that there is a Light which lighteneth every man that cometh into the world," Bowne instructed. "And for both a Christian and a theist it must be clear that the great non-Christian systems have had a place in the divine purpose for men."[127]

On the other hand, religions must be tested by the goodness and beauty of their fruit. By this standard, he averred, no religion comes close to Protestant Christianity: "We may say, for instance, that the early Hindus set out on their way toward God, and that their religious literature is the record of their Godward journey; but when we consider the abominations of the Hindu pantheon and of the popular Hindu religion, we must admit that somehow or other they grievously missed their way. The thwarting, paralyzing, and defiling influences of Hindu society have concentrated and incarnated themselves in the Hindu religion. India is socially, industrially, and politically paralyzed by her religion. Caste is sanctified, the masses are hopeless, the people are divided by all manner of impassable gulfs due to their religion." By comparison, the Protestant West was thriving in prosperity, moral progress, and democratic reform movements. If the Hindu mind could somehow be swept clean of its religious conceptions, Bowne fantasized, and their place taken by Christian ideas, "it would be a blessing great beyond all comparison."[128]

To Bowne, taking modernity seriously meant that non-Christian religions were not to be taken very seriously. In the modern world, he explained, the relationship between Christianity and other religions is not an important issue, because the non-Christian religions have no future worth discussing: "As soon as they come into contact with our Western thought, science, and individualism, it becomes apparent that their day is done." This state of affairs set the context in which Christian theology needed to be revised. "Which religion?" is not a serious question in the modern world, he contended; the serious question is "Christianity or irreligion?" Will the Christian theistic idea prevail in the West, or will it be replaced by mechanistic materialism? Bowne exhorted that everything depended on the answer to this question.[129]

He sought to clear the field of unnecessary Christian commitments—like biblical inerrancy—that impeded the church's appeals to modern minds and hearts. As the foundational principle of theological scholasticism, he judged, the theory of inerrancy was "a piece of closet logic, a verbal intimidation, resulting from considering the subject in an abstract and academic fashion," the idol of "ignorant ark-savers" who had no comprehension of the Bible as literature. The scholastic approach to revelation, a related mistake, claimed literal infallibility for the Bible and then identified revelation with biblical propositions. Bowne protested that this procedure was impossibly backward. "The Church was Christian long before it had the Bible, as the Christian ideas long preceded the completion of the biblical canon," he observed. "The Church is Christian because of the effective presence of these ideas, not because of its doctrine of Scripture."[130]

It followed that the authority of scripture lies in the religious power of its ideas, not in any a priori doctrine of scriptural infallibility. The Bible plainly contains "mythical and unhistorical matter," Bowne noted, but this fact does not prevent scripture from being the special vehicle of God's revelation. Bowne was too deeply rooted in personalist metaphysics to speak the language of Ritschlian historicism, but when he turned to the question of the locus of revelation in the biblical witness, the echoes of Ritschl were strong. "What the Christian thinker should maintain is the divine presence and guidance in the revealing movement as a whole," he asserted. What mattered was never the historicity of any particular narrative, but the revelatory power of the scriptural witness and tradition as a whole that produced the central ideas of Christianity.[131]

The notion that scripture cannot be the vehicle of God's Word if it contains errors was familiar to Bowne in a philosophical form; he noted that it is basically the same argument that philosophical skeptics press against sense knowledge: if our senses deceive us on some occasions, how can we know that they do not always deceive us? In both cases, he urged, the problem is solved through practice, not by abstract theorizing. Through experience we know that the senses sometimes deceive us and often yield valuable knowledge. We gain wisdom about the limitations and usefulness of the senses not by theorizing about them, but by using them. The same pragmatic principle applies to the scriptural witness. The revelation that scripture contains is available only to those who wrestle with the biblical text, he argued; scripture is not actually revelatory to fundamentalists. When regarded as a sourcebook of inerrant propositions, the Bible stands against enlightenment and progress; when studied critically for its commanding ideas, the Bible is a witness to true religion.[132]

Though he projected an air of philosophical and religious confidence, Bowne was not one to minimize the negative. His books contained long lists of Christian problems and failures, and his thorough acquaintance with anti-Christian literature reinforced his predisposition to chastise Christian conservatives. "There has hardly been a step of progress—social, scientific, economic, religious—which has not been resisted as fatal to the claims of the Bible," he admonished. "The humiliating history would be a profitable subject of reflection for any one who is inclined to resist any departure from his view as fatal to the Bible. Texts have been arrayed against astronomy, geology, political economy, philosophy, geography, religious toleration, anti-slavery, mercy to decrepit old women called witches, anatomy, medicine, vaccination, anaesthetics, fanning-mills, lightning-rods, life-insurance, women speaking in church and going to the General Conference. All of these, particularly the last, have been declared, solemnly and with much emotion, to make the Word of God of none effect."[133]

Bowne's understanding of the atonement dispensed with an equal load of unfortunate Christian tradition. With a Bushnellian emphasis on the metaphorical character of biblical language, but with even less regard than Bushnell for traditional atonement theorizing, he held out for a purely moral interpretation of Christ's sacrifice and discarded even the word "atonement." In the historical context of early Christianity, he allowed, it made sense for the Jewish Christian authors of the Gospels and New Testament epistles to speak of Christ as the Lamb of God who takes away the sins of the world and as the redeemer who gave his life as a ransom for many. This pictorial, dramatic, and metaphorical language assumed the religion of altar and temple, as well as the legal practices of the time. With this relative language, against the background of these relative practices, the Gospel writers expressed the fact of Christ's atonement, which was his work of revealing the Father to human beings and bringing them to the Father. But for modern people, Bowne contended, these are not the best ways to express Christ's loving and gracious work. Moreover, while the New Testament deals mainly with the fact of the atonement and not with its theory, classical Christian teaching on this subject is mainly theoretical. Conceding nothing, Bowne asserted that the idea of objective atonement and its legacy in Christian tradition were thoroughly disastrous.[134]

He noted that the New Testament makes use of two figurative notions pertaining to atonement that cannot be reconciled when taken literally as components of a single theory. The first is the notion of substitution, based on the sacrificial system of Hebrew religion; the second is the notion of the imputation of Christ's merit and righteousness to sinners. Bowne read most of the history of Christian atonement theology as a series of misguided attempts to take these figures literally and join them together. The various satisfactionist models of atonement theory all claim that objective atonement is necessary for the forgiveness of sins, he observed, but in truth, these models make forgiveness unnecessary and unreal: "To demand satisfaction, whether by substitution, or otherwise, is to collect the debt or inflict the penalty which in forgiveness is forgiven. But if the debt is paid, or the penalty is exacted, there is nothing to forgive. If, after such satisfaction, payment or penalty is still demanded, we have no forgiveness, but simply a trick whereby the debtor and his surety are defrauded, while the creditor gets paid twice." In this way, he charged, objective atonement theology negates the forgiveness and even the love of God; love is ascribed to Christ, "but the Father is simply satisfied by paying the debt, and has no further claims." Objective atonement theologies picture God as a wrathful, vengeful incarnation of primitive justice, "needing to be propitiated by sacrifice and suffering of some kind." Bowne protested that this picture turns the biblical understanding of atonement on its head: "The love of God to man is made the effect of the atonement, whereas the Scriptures represent the atonement as the effect of the Father's love."[135]

Traditional atonement theologies are about justice, not the grace and redeeming love of God, Bowne objected; even their notion of justice is repugnant, however, for they assume an abstract conception of justice that impugns God's virtue and which exists only in theory: "If justice demands anything, it is the punishment of the sinner himself. Only a mind debauched by theology would ever dream of calling anything justice which contented itself with penalty, no matter who paid it; and only the same type of mind could tolerate a justice which demanded or permitted double payment." According to Bowne, the speculative doctors of objective atonement theology were oppressed by their presuppositions. They assumed that the metaphorical language of scripture must be taken as dogma and interpreted like a statute. The church has paid a heavy price for this misunderstanding, Bowne lamented, sparing no terms of condemnation in rejecting it: it was "odious and abominable" for the church to discuss Christ's atonement "in terms of things and apply them to the relations of moral persons," and "utterly impossible" that any person should take the place of another in his or her moral relations.[136]

Bowne affirmed that modern progressive Christians still believe in the fact of the "great work of grace" that God effected in Christ. He still believed that Christ gave himself for the salvation of the world and that God gave Christ to the world for this purpose. He was still willing to sing "Rock of Ages, cleft for me" and had no desire to purge the New Testament of its sacrificial and substitutionary language. The problem was the church's creedal theory of atonement and the morally repugnant picture of God that it sanctions; instead of picturing God as a ruling monarch anxious for his own claims and laws, Bowne exhorted, the church should speak of God as a divine Father "in the midst of his human family, bearing with his children and seeking by all the discipline of love and law to build them into likeness to and fellowship with himself." The church's theology of reconciliation requires no more substantive content than this. Moreover, Bowne countered, the moral influence view of atonement, charged with being merely sentimental, is in fact, unlike traditional orthodoxy, grounded in moral realism.[137]

The problem of atonement is the problem of how to save sinful creatures from their sin, he observed. If God is to forgive unrighteous people, "some way must be found of making them righteous." Objective atonement theory is no help at all. "To forgive wicked men while they remain wicked would be immoral," Bowne asserted. Objective atonement theology is immoral not only in its concepts, but also in its effects. "The fundamental problem is to find a way whereby the righteous God can make righteous the ungodly; and this cannot be secured by calling or declaring them righteous, but only by a spiritual transformation." Bowne was a good Wesleyan on the theme of sanctification. Against Wesley's rather passive acceptance of substitutionary atonement doctrine, however, Bowne insisted that the objectivist theories of atonement contain merely a single element of truth, that sin must never be treated as a matter of indifference, which they fail to take seriously. The proponents of atonement orthodoxy were right to contend that the consequences of sin cannot be canceled without an atonement, but they failed to grasp that the consequences of sin are not canceled *with* an objective, forensic atonement. In this area, Bowne contended, orthodox atonement theology, like modern humanistic sentimentalism, fails to face up to the fact that consequences are not forgiven.[138]

The basic problem is terribly concrete. No word of forgiveness cancels the destructive consequences of sin. There is such a thing as the cancellation of personal guilt, Bowne allowed, but there is no such thing as forensic cancellation of the concrete consequences of sin. Not even God can remove the destructive results of sin with a word: "The problem is a moral one and must receive a moral solution." The only serious solution to the problem of sin is to save people from their enslavement to sin; human beings must be brought back to God and made righteous. The salvation of Christ is moral. "There is no other salvation which the moral reason will accept," Bowne contended. Though he allowed that theology might transcend the intuitions of conscience, he categorically denied that Christian truth ever contradicts the enlightened conscience. Washington Gladden's test of good doctrine was the right one; any theology that violates enlightened moral reason is false.[139]

Bowne was not an active social gospeler, but his straightforwardly moral account of salvation exemplified the fundamental link between the liberal theology and social gospel movements. "The solution must be sought in accordance with God's fundamental purpose in our human world," he taught, with echoes of *Christian Nurture*: "That purpose is to have a family of spiritual children, made in his image and likeness, who shall know him and love him, and upon whom he may bestow himself in blessing for ever and ever." The aim of Christian regeneration is not to satisfy the demands of formal justice, nor to save people from penalty, but to save them from sinning; the method of Christian regeneration is growth and development. Bowne was a good Methodist and a good Victorian. "There are animal beginnings with moral endings," he assured. That was the hope of a progressive and progressing liberal Christianity.[140]

THEOLOGY AS A VOICE
OF REASON AND PROGRESS

Bowne's penchant for cutting repartee, which offended his enemies and liberal Victorian friends alike, may have stoked the outrage of his chief nemesis, Methodist pastor George A. Cooke, who lodged heresy charges against him. Cooke was slow to perceive that by the turn of the century, Bowne was not only tolerated in the northern Methodist church, but admired. In a heresy trial before the church's New York East Annual Conference of 1904, Cooke alleged that Bowne violated established doctrinal standards and the Methodist Articles of Religion in his writings on the Trinity, miracles, inspiration, atonement, and redemption. To hear the case against him, the conference appointed a distinguished fifteen-person "Select Number" committee chaired by prominent social gospeler Frank Mason North.

Though weighted with some historical importance, Bowne's trial for heresy was not a high-powered affair. His accuser—a member of another Annual Conference—was out of his depth, as were the three prosecutors appointed by the New York East Conference. Bowne faced them on April 7, 1904. He explained that his book on metaphysics had nothing to do with the Trinity, that thoughts are not in the mind spatially any more than the world is in God spatially, that biblical criticism is a legitimate and mostly beneficial academic enterprise, and that he certainly did not believe that belief in the historicity of minor incidents described in the Bible is necessary to be a Christian. His prosecutors parried with him longest on biblical inerrancy and put up less of a fight on atonement.

The latter tack was curious, since Bowne's claim not to be heretically out of step with church teaching was most vulnerable on the atonement. In reply, he skewered the contradictions within and between various atonement doctrines, quoted Methodist theologian John Miley that there were thirteen different theories of atonement, and called for a clearing of the air on the subject. Under Miley's influence, he noted, many Methodists had recently adopted the governmental view, but this theory was merely a revision of the old discredited doctrine of substitution. "I reject anything which needs to be carried forward," Bowne declared. "[The governmental view] was carried forward from the things behind it, but we are compelled to go on."[141]

After sixteen hours of deliberation, the committee voted unanimously that Bowne was innocent on all counts. A sizable faction of the church had already embraced Bowne-style personalism as a new orthodoxy; Bowne, embittered by the experience of having to defend himself against heresy charges, seethed against "reactionaries" for the rest of his life. But his trial, a watershed for American Methodism and American liberal theology, brought an end to heresy trials in the Methodist church and vindicated the doctrinal revisionism of what became the Boston school.[142]

In Bowne's work liberal Protestantism spoke with a strongly self-confident and intellectually sophisticated voice. He celebrated his heresy vindication with a triumphant lecture tour in China and Japan in 1905; the same year, his contempt for reactionaries hardened as Hinkley Mitchell was removed from his teaching position at Boston University. Bowne gave his last years to the cause of religious progress. "The progress of thought is slow, but there is progress nonetheless," he asserted in *The Immanence of God*.[143] Repeatedly he cautioned that religious conservatism is like other kinds of conservatism: inevitable, rooted in human nature, and necessary, but also invariably a roadblock to progress. Institutions are even more constitutively conservative than human beings, he cautioned; when people of mediocre intellect and character gain control of religious institutions, religious progress depends on the courage, imagination, and faith of educated religious visionaries. "When the inferior men are brought to the front, then lower interests become prominent," Bowne explained. "The financial aspects of religion are brought forward and emphasized. The value of place likewise becomes significant, and we tend to have men in prominence who have very little interest in the truth as such, but rather in maintaining the present order, in securing position and the perquisites of religious place."[144]

The cause of religious progress depends mainly on the church's capacity to raise up faithful leaders who are devoted to the truth, he exhorted. Progress in religion, like progress in other fields, requires the flourishing of discussion and criticism. If the Catholic church had had its way near the end of the Middle Ages, Bowne reminded, "modern civilization would never have developed, and humanity would have been ruined." Modern liberal theologians were the beneficiaries of emancipating historical forces that their ancestors bitterly resisted, and resistance was not only a pattern of the past, he cautioned. For the most part, the Christian church was still an intellectually backward institution, which was "nothing less than a calamity to religion, because it begets and continues the notion that religion is essentially a thing of inferior intellect, and that it is afraid to come out into the open field of the world where plain secular daylight shines, and be tested."[145]

Modern Christian thinkers faced a daunting challenge, seeking to defend and improve a religious institution that took little interest in improvement. Instead, the church punished its creative truth-seekers and rewarded its steeple-chasing mediocrities. Bowne implied by example that there was a role for effective insult in this situation. Modern Christian thinkers had to be willing not to be nice; they needed to shame church leaders into recognizing what it means to pursue serious scholarship in the modern world. "Questions of scholarship can be settled only by scholarship," he lectured. "Questions of fact can be settled only by evidence. The very notion of deciding them by authority is absurd. How many papal bulls, or how big an ecclesiastical club, or how large a majority of ignorant votes would be needed to overturn the Copernican astronomy? Ignorance, in high or low places, is entitled to no opinion on these matters. Authority only makes itself ridiculous when it assumes to dictate. Majorities are equally absurd, unless they rest on the facts and the evidence."[146]

The heresy trial of Henry Preserved Smith was a showcase example of what modern theology was up against within its own house. Bowne noted that at Smith's trial, the question of truth was ruled out of order. Precisely the question whether Smith's positions were true according to the evidence was excluded from discussion; the only thing that mattered was whether his positions conformed to a seventeenth-century confession of faith. Bowne noted that the same mentality was displayed at a recent heresy trial that he pointedly refrained from identifying. "The same principle was announced with equal satisfaction, as being something like a revelation from above," he acidly remarked. "But what a pitiable comment on the pretense of high veracity and zeal for the truth!"[147]

It was precisely in Bowne's generation that a Christian thinker with his views could now keep his position, but the liberalization of the church occurred much too slowly for him. Elsewhere he accented the positive. The forgiveness of sins is essential to Christianity, he observed, but merely introductory; good scholarship is important, but not the main thing; forms of worship are important, but instrumental in their significance; even practices of piety are not the thing itself; their significance also is instrumental, consisting in what they help us do. Bowne reflected that the thing itself,

> the central thing, is the recognition of the divine will in all life, and the loyal, loving effort to make that will prevail in all life: first of all in the hidden life of the spirit, and then in family life, in social life, in political life, in trade, in art, in literature, in every field of human interest and activity. Only thus can religion be saved from unwholesome and baneful subjectivities. Only thus can it gain the healthy objectivity needed to keep it sane and sweet. The religious spirit must have all fields for its own; and at the same time we must remember that all that is normal to man and demanded by his life has its place in the divine purpose and its justifying function in the divine training of men. To think otherwise is atheism.[148]

He epitomized the liberal Christian thinker as a defender of an embattled Christendom against both an aggressive culture of atheism and a potent fundamentalist reaction. Theologically, he exemplified the liberal shift from objective atonement-oriented Christologies to the claim that Christianity is based on the incarnation of Christ as "the highest revelation of God." Bowne's philosophy of the person reached its culminating religious expression in the doctrine of the incarnation. To say that God was in Christ is not to claim that an infinite being was compressed into the limits of a human form, he cautioned, nor that "in some picturable way he put on our humanity like an external covering."[149]

Picture thinking is especially hazardous in Christology, Bowne cautioned. We speak of ourselves as being in the body, for example, "but we are not in the body as something that contains us"; embodiment means nothing more than having a type of experience that is physically conditioned. Bowne maintained that this elementary principle of personalist philosophy applies instructively to Christology. To say that God was in Christ is not to proclaim some impossible duality of divine and human natures born of picture thinking. It is to assert, rather, that Christ "became subject to the conditions, laws, and limitations of human life, and thus became in the truest sense of the word a man." This confession of God's assumption of our nature and living of our life in Christ is the heart of Christian faith, Bowne contended. It discloses God's ethical perfection and moral grandeur in God's highest revelation, and contains everything that is distinctively Christian: "A Divine Person working for love's sake a divine work for man's redemption is the centre of the Christian faith and the source of its power. Drop it out of our teaching, and, though the external form and facts may remain unchanged, the life is gone nevertheless." Liberal theology within and beyond the personalist school based its essential claim to continuity with traditional Christianity on that confession.[150]

In his generation only Hocking came close to having similar influence as a Christian philosopher of religion. Few thinkers outside the Boston school shared Bowne's blend of idealist, neo-Kantian, romanticist, and rationalist motifs, much less his Methodist emphasis on sanctification and individual freedom, but virtually all liberal Protestant thinkers of his generation looked to him for intellectual leadership. Though he firmly identified with the Wesleyan tradition, his discussions of personal freedom and will owed more to Kant than Wesley, which made his valorization of autonomy, practical reason, and personality accessible to liberals from other religious traditions. At Union Theological Seminary, George Albert Coe, a friend and philosophical disciple, played a formative theoretical role in the field of religious education. At Oberlin College, liberal social gospel leader Henry Churchill King based his theological system on personalist principles. Washington Gladden also took instruction from Bowne's philosophical and theological writings. "I have followed his brilliant career with the keenest interest; I have found much help in his stimulating thought, and I have greatly enjoyed the freshness and pungency with which that thought is expressed," Gladden reflected. "My belief is that he has done for his generation, and especially for the church to whose fellowship he has lent honor, a most important service."[151]

Bowne was respected and heeded by the youthful liberal generation that inherited the elite seminaries and divinity schools in the early twentieth century. He was a member of the generation that accommodated Christianity to Darwinism, but he kept evolution in its place. Evolution was not his master concept, and he conveyed no Darwinist anxiety that Christianity had to translate its theologies and liturgies into the language of religious evolution. Neither did he counsel, in the manner of other liberals of his generation, that some revision of Schleiermacher romanticism was the only hope of theology. Bowne's personalism was epistemologically dualistic, metaphysically pluralistic, and ethical in orientation. In agreement with an ascending Ritschlian school in theology, he affirmed that only personal beings can be the objects of God's love; in agreement with an ascending social gospel movement, he affirmed that true religion is ethical without remainder, though his ethical standpoint was essentially individualistic. With help from the Ritschlian school, he convinced an ample portion of the social gospel generation that Christianity rightly speaks the language of personalist idealism.

A major figure in his time, Bowne became a towering figure in the Methodist church after his death, though his influence was slightly exaggerated by Albert Knudson, who claimed that Methodism escaped the modernist-fundamentalist battles of the 1920s chiefly because of Bowne's influence. (The eighteenth-century pietist roots of Methodism and the fourfold Wesleyan view of religious authority were stronger factors.) In the classroom Bowne was a dazzling performer, converting students to personalist Christian idealism by the brilliance of his arguments and by the force of his classroom personality; one student later recalled that Bowne's lectures made students feel "as though their heads were expanding to the bursting point."[152]

In both senses of the term he founded a school: Boston personalism exercised an immense influence over twentieth-century Methodism, and it was institutionalized at Boston University. Four generations of Boston personalists embraced Bowne's epistemological dualism, his metaphysical pluralism, and his liberal religious moralism. Though his ethical thinking was emphatically individualistic, his disciples developed a personalist social ethic as well as a systematic theology. Integrative in its approach to theology, philosophy, and the sciences, the Boston school sustained the commitment of its founder to an account of the person as a self-reflexive, purposive, knowledge-constructing, value-seeking moral agent, while setting this account in a wider social-ethical framework.

Bowne's second generation of disciples included theologian Albert C. Knudson, philosopher Edgar S. Brightman, bishop and social Christian leader Francis J. McConnell, and *Personalist* founding editor Ralph T. Flewelling. A third generation included philosophers Peter Bertocci and John Lavely, theologians Harold DeWolf, Georgia Harkness, Paul Deats, and S. Paul Schilling, and social ethicist Walter Muelder. A fourth generation included Martin Luther King Jr.—who studied under Brightman, DeWolf, Muelder, and Schilling at Boston University—and theologian F. Thomas Trotter. An appreciable segment of twentieth-century American theological liberalism is represented by these names. In the course of building and defending a school, Bowne personalism acquired the limitations of every self-contained philosophical system, but for many years after the social gospel went into eclipse, it kept alive one of the few profound and inspiriting schools of progressive American Christianity.[153]

7.
The Victorian Gospel:
Religion and Modernity in Progress

This volume ends on the verge of an eruption. Progressive Christianity was well imagined in the nineteenth century, but only as that century expired did liberal theology become a powerful movement. In the past two chapters we have briefly crossed into the world of a triumphant liberal Protestantism, because the generation that built the liberal theology and social gospel movements lived to see the ascendancy of these movements in a new century. In their old age, Theodore Munger, Washington Gladden, Newman Smyth, Charles A. Briggs, and Borden Parker Bowne witnessed the vindication of their labors. They took pride in the liberalization of keystone Protestant institutions. With the mixed exception of Briggs, they were gratified by the accolades of their successors, and with no exceptions, they celebrated the emergence of new ecumenical institutions that accompanied the liberal theology and social gospel movements. These institutions included the World's Student Christian Federation (an international social Christian fellowship founded in 1895) and the Federal Council of Churches in America (the forerunner of the National Council of Churches).

The founders of the liberal theology movement poured out books and sermons on the movement's behalf to the end of their days. Munger died in 1910, Gladden in 1918, Smyth in 1925, Briggs in 1913, Bowne in 1910; all of them took a broad view of the goal of the ecumenical movement. Though many of their social gospel comrades confined their ecumenical hopes to Protestants, Smyth and Briggs were especially devoted to ecumenical dialogue between Protestants and Catholics, in addition to ecumenical cooperation among the Protestant denominations. In 1908, the year that thirty-three American Protestant denominations founded the Federal Council of Churches, Smyth ventured that the great hope of world ecumenism was the reunion of the Roman Catholic and various Protestant churches. (Eastern Orthodoxy was still out of view.) He urged that theologically modernist currents in British and French Catholicism showed that the hope of a reunified Christendom was not a utopian fantasy; modernism was the vehicle of progress and unity in ecumenical relations. Just as Protestant openness to modern knowledge and experience had begun to remove entrenched ecclesiastical barriers to inter-Protestant ecumenism, so would the modernization of Roman Catholicism promote reunion between the Catholic and Protestant churches.[1]

CATHOLIC MODERNISM
AND PROTESTANT ECUMENISM

The liberal Protestants tried to believe that they would live to see the fulfillment of this dream and looked for signs of modernizing progress in the Catholic church, while the popes of their time condemned modernism as the devil's brew. In the Catholic modernist movements of England, France, and Italy, the American liberal Protestants recognized kindred spirits; in the United States they cheered for the founder of the Paulist order, Isaac Hecker, whose colorful background and many years of mission work among Roman Catholic immigrants to the United States gave him a perspective on American Catholicism that was ahead of its time.

A native of New York, Hecker was a Methodist, an Emersonian transcendentalist, and a Redemptorist priest before he founded the Paulist missionary order. Like his friend Orestes Brownson, his keen interest in the social conditions of working-class people influenced his conversion from transcendentalism to Catholicism. From the early 1860s until his death in 1888, Hecker maintained that Roman Catholicism was at least potentially compatible with modern science, American political democracy, and American-style religious liberty. He argued for the possibility of a genuinely *Catholic* American Catholicism that affirmed the American separation of church and state. Though Hecker's later life was consumed by controversy, his cause became increasingly respectable in the early years of the pontificate of Leo XIII (1878–1903). In 1891, in his encyclical *Rerum Novarum,* Leo XIII endorsed the exercise of wage settlements by free agreement, the legitimacy of trade unions, and the principle of a just wage— and thus signaled to many that the church's teaching magisterium was opening itself to the modern world. Several U.S. Catholic church leaders reasoned that in their context, the implications of the pope's apparent opening to the modern world were favorable to American-style modernization. "Americanism" became a good word for a time in the American Catholic church, attracting the support of such important U.S. church leaders as Archbishop John Ireland and Cardinal James Gibbons—until Leo XIII explicitly condemned Americanism by name in *Testem benevolentiae* (1899). American-style religious freedom was not the wave of the future in the Catholic church, but a condemnable heresy.[2]

For the Americanists and their Protestant sympathizers, the Vatican's about-face on modernity was chilling. Though the pope's anathema did not specifically condemn Hecker and his followers, it fell hard on Hecker's Americanizing friends. Notre Dame chemistry and physics professor and Holy Cross priest John Zahm was forced to repudiate his pro-evolutionist book, *Evolution and Dogma*, in 1899; eleven years later one of Hecker's leading disciples, former Paulist priest William L. Sullivan, denounced Catholicism on account of the Vatican's effective repression of theological modernism. The idea of a modernized Catholicism was assiduously condemned by Leo's successors, Pius IX and Pius X, who defined modernity exhaustively in the course of repudiating it; the particulars included biblical higher criticism, individual interpretation, evolutionary theory, liberal democracy, the separation of church and state, and other beliefs cherished by American liberal Protestants. Pius X, in a 1907 decree *Lamentabili Sane*, condemned sixty-five modernist propositions, including the idea that modern biblical criticism is a legitimate enterprise and the notion that modern Catholicism "can be reconciled with true science only if it is transformed into a non-dogmatic Christianity; that is to say, into a broad and liberal Protestantism." The pontiff's encyclical of the same year, *Pascendi Dominici Gregis*, heightened the Vatican's polemical relation to modernism, arguing that modernist theology was the synthesis of all heresies. Three years later, the Vatican instituted an oath against modernism, to be required of all Catholic clergy and theology professors.[3]

The Protestant keepers of the modernist ecumenical hope insisted that the Vatican did not understand what it was condemning. Despite the anathemas of *Lamentabili Sane*, which certainly indicated a detailed acquaintance of some kind, Smyth insisted that the papal magisterium was profoundly ignorant of modern thought and that the popes and their advisors betrayed this ignorance by supposing that modernism could be crushed by sacred authority. The Vatican was determined "to destroy in the seminaries every trace of Modernism, and in every diocese to repress the publication and to prevent the sale of writings suspected of any taint of it," Smyth observed. But the proposal to defeat modernism by repression merely proved that the Vatican didn't fathom the spiritual power of modern knowledge and democracy. Smyth celebrated that fully modernist currents of Catholic thinking already existed in England and France, though not in the United States. He praised English theologian George Tyrrell and French historical theologian Alfred Loisy as full-fledged comrades in the struggle for an enlightened ecumenical Christianity. He admired their attempts to show that Catholicism and modernity were theologically compatible, even as he worried that their work was scaring the Vatican into overreacting against modernity in general.[4]

Smyth accented the positive. In the writings of Tyrrell and Loisy, he enthused, a strong beginning had been made in the epochal project of reconciling Catholic teaching to modern science and historical consciousness: "They are in the stream, they are afloat on the mighty flood of the world's present thought and life." It was not plausible to him that Catholic seminaries and universities would always teach that the likes of Alfred Loisy were condemnable heretics for working out terms of a Catholic peace with modernity. Like his Anglican friend Charles Briggs, Smyth looked forward to the ecumenism of a modernized Roman Catholic church. He did not doubt that Isaac Hecker would have heirs on religious freedom issues, that American Catholicism would eventually produce its own forms of theological modernism, and that Rome would either reform or self-destruct. If the Vatican were to face up to modernity, he counseled, Protestantism would no longer be necessary. The age of Protestantism would pass into the age of the One Holy Catholic Church: "And if the age of Protestantism which passeth away was with glory, much more that which remaineth is with glory."[5]

The liberal Protestants were assured by their own history that modernity is unifying, progressive, and undefeatable. For decades the modernizing project in American theology had belonged to a Unitarian offshoot of Congregationalism and a handful of Congregationalists. It was only in recent years that modern American Protestantism had become a multidenominational affair. The fact that Congregationalism was the dominant denomination of Puritan New England had made the church's first controversy over liberalism an especially bitter affair. The Unitarian schism cost the Congregationalists nearly a hundred churches in Massachusetts alone, but for decades after the Congregationalists bid good riddance to their liberals—who agreed to call themselves Unitarians—it remained the Congregational church that produced America's theological seers and movement pioneers. Bushnell, Beecher, and the Bushnellians were all Congregationalists, though Beecher and Gladden had New School Presbyterian roots. Put differently, all of America's founding theological liberals came out of the denomination that experienced an early schism over liberalism and then set itself against a second one.

The same factors that engendered Unitarian liberalism continued to make Congregationalism the leading breeder of modernist revision. Congregationalist clergy were comparatively well educated by virtue of their class privileges and their connections to institutions like Harvard, Yale, Bowdoin, and Amherst, and they were members of a denomination that was structurally organized to exercise very little ecclesiastical control. The second factor was as important as the first to liberal theology. The Bushnellians emphasized that Congregationalism had no creeds of its own and nothing like an episcopal figure or structure. Gladden, Munger, and Smyth pressed both points to their advantage. Though closely related to the New School Presbyterian movement, the Bushnellians shuddered at the ecclesiastical power that Presbyterian polity and the Westminster Confession of Faith gave to conservatives in the Presbyterian church. The Bushnellian Congregationalists perceived that in their own denomination, a peaceful evolution into theological progressivism was possible.

This mentality was epitomized in Munger's 1883 manifesto for the New Theology movement. The New Theology was a movement, but not a party, Munger declared. It was effecting a revolution in American religion, but it unfurled no banners and sought no factional victories. The Bushnellians wanted a revolution without victims or executioners, for like the early Unitarian liberals, they hated factional parties and fighting; in their case they also had the benefit of a cautionary example in the Unitarian schism. In 1820, Channing embraced his party's epithet as a badge of honor and set the Unitarian schism into motion. The Bushnellians, determined not to replicate the Unitarian schism, wanted to avoid a factional showdown over liberalism; they also believed that in the age of Darwin factional warfare over orthodoxy was outdated and unneccessary.

The old orthodoxy was discredited, and modern educated people lived in a different world from the world of Francis Turretin and Jonathan Edwards. Moreover, in the Congregational system, the old orthodoxy did not possess the sanction of creed or bishop. The Presbyterians were bound by the Westminster Confession; Lutheranism was defined by the Augsburg Confession; even Anglicanism was at least guided by the Thirty-Nine Articles of Religion (which was not a creed or confession). Congregationalists had nothing like these regulative ecclesiastical controls on correct belief; it had only the loosened authority of scripture and the heritage of a decentralized form of the Reformed tradition to guide them in determining what it meant for them to follow Christ in their time.

The old orthodoxy was to be cast aside, respectfully, not fought over in a factional war for position. Munger and the Bushnellians stood for peaceful evolution in church doctrine, reasoning that Christian teaching needed to evolve continually, just as they had already evolved beyond Bushnell. The New Theology would simply inherit the church's seminaries and pulpits without having to drive out its enemies, rewrite a church creed, or wage factional debates about who was right in the past. The Bushnellians were happy to call their theology "progressive orthodoxy" if that aided the cause of consensual religious progress; mediationism was good theology and good church politics. They believed that a peaceful modernization of the church's teaching and keystone institutions should be possible, at least in their own educated, well-positioned, decentralized denomination, and this is essentially what happened in the Congregational church in the generation that followed Munger's call for a new liberal orthodoxy. The liberal professors at Andover Seminary all kept their jobs, even as they heightened the progressive aspects of progressive orthodoxy; many Congregational congregations remained conservative, but the seminaries and church leadership liberalized. The progressives prevailed, in relative peace, for a generation; Munger died just as American fundamentalists began to assemble an interdenominational backlash movement.

Liberal theology took the path of peaceful evolution in the denomination that gave theological liberalism to America; elsewhere it was a battleground. This explains why the leadership of the liberal theology movement began to shift away from Congregationalism at the turn of the century. That other denominations entered the picture is obviously crucial; equally important, the struggle to liberalize in the other denominations required forms of theological argument and factional strife that had not been necessary in American Congregationalism. Presbyterian, Lutheran, and Reformed church theologians had to contend with the weight of highly defined confessional legacies; Methodists and Episcopalians had to negotiate with episcopal systems of church governance; lacking any other authority, in a tradition that fervently proclaimed the sole and sufficient authority of scripture, the fight over scriptural authority in the Northern Baptist church was especially intense.

The leaders of a succeeding generation of theological liberalism came from the latter churches in the process of waging these arguments. Most of them were ecumenical enough in their liberalism to ascribe a merely secondary significance to historic confessional differences. Congregationalism continued to give creative thinkers to the liberal theology movement, especially through Yale Divinity School and Oberlin Theological Seminary, but theological leadership passed to thinkers from other Reformed traditions, especially the Presbyterian, Northern Baptist, and Evangelical and Reformed churches, as well as the Methodist Episcopal church, where modernization proponents could not rely on peaceful evolution. The mainline traditions that evolved more slowly and with comparatively little fighting—the Episcopal and Lutheran churches—also made comparatively little impact on the development of modern American theology.

The creative theorists of American liberal theology in the first half of the twentieth century belonged mostly to nonliturgical traditions that had to fight off a strong fundamentalist reaction. Every Protestant denomination was a house of authority; in every tradition theological liberalism was therefore intensely controversial. At the end of the nineteenth century, Congregationalism was still the heart of the movement, but by 1925, the movement's three leading institutions were products of other traditions: the University of Chicago (Baptist), Boston University (Methodist), and Union Theological Seminary (historically Presbyterian). In each case, the theologians of progressive religion fought off a fundamentalist backlash while contending that ecclesiastical differences should matter less than they had in the past.

SPIRIT OVER NATURE: LEGACY
OF A THEOLOGICAL CENTURY

From the labors of their nineteenth-century forebears, the theologians of a triumphant liberal Protestantism took for granted the relativization of traditional Protestant dogma. Channing struck the keynote of liberal theology in his late-life reflection that "a respect for the human soul" breathed through all of his preaching and writing. The nineteenth-century liberals refused to accept religious teachings that offended their moral, intellectual, and spiritual sensibilities. They began with the Calvinist doctrines of human nature, atonement, and divine predestination, which for them failed the moral test. The early liberals were eventually defined by their Arianism and anti-Trinitarianism—they accepted the Unitarian label—but their protest was rooted in moral revulsion against the Calvinist picture of God and humanity.[6]

From the beginning, liberal theology was a third way. It was not radical, infidel, agnostic, or atheist, though it was routinely called all of these; liberal theology was both a morally humanist alternative to Protestant orthodoxy and a religious alternative to rationalistic atheism. It shared the humanistic moral impulses of modern rationalism, as the guardians of New England Theology readily perceived, but it defended biblical religion in a manner that accorded with its image of Christ. Channing loved to preach on John 5:19: "He that hath seen me hath seen the Father" (KJV). Liberal theology acquired a mainline Protestant heritage after Horace Bushnell similarly refused to believe things about God that for him brought moral dishonor upon God. The liberal Protestants interpreted the invisible God who dwells in light inaccessible in the light of their understanding of Christ. Throughout the nineteenth century, they had modern biblical scholarship on their side in this project.

Bushnell's most popular work was the tenth chapter of *Nature and the Supernatural,* which was republished as a separate volume titled *The Character of Jesus.* He cautioned that the faithful reader of scripture is not obliged to assume the truth of the Gospel narrative "by which the manner and facts of the life of Jesus are reported to us." That was the matter in question. "We only assume the representations themselves, as being just what they are, and discover their necessary truth, in the transcendent, wondrously self-evident, picture of divine excellence and beauty exhibited in them." Bushnell counseled that the biblical narrative is not very impressive aside from the extraordinary character of its pivotal figure, but the more that we study the figure of Jesus, "a picture shining in its own clear sunlight upon us," the more clearly we are brought into the source and light of all truth: "Jesus, the Divine Word, coming out from God, to be incarnate with us, and be the vehicle of God and salvation to the race."[7]

That was the evangelical core of the liberal gospel. The Word of Christ is not a doctrine or the end of an argument, but a self-authenticating life; it is morally regenerative spiritual power claimed in Christ's spirit. Bushnell accented the outward-moving divine character of Christ: "He grows more great and wise, and sacred, the more he is known—needs, in fact, to be known, to have his perfection seen. And this, we say, is Jesus, the Christ; manifestly not human, not of our world—some being who has burst into it, and is not of it." Moving beyond their mentor, the Bushnellians accented the humanity of Christ; Munger and Gladden lifted Jesus' teaching above any claims about his person. In both cases, however, a self-authenticating moral image conceived as the power of true religion was in control. The true religion is the way of Christ.[8]

Traditional Protestant orthodoxies placed the substitutionary atonement of Christ at the center of Christianity, conceiving Christ's death as a propitiatory sacrifice that vicariously satisfied the retributive demands of divine justice. This doctrine claimed the mind of Bushnell in a way that became simply foreign to his followers; Munger wished that Bushnell had spent his later years puzzling over another subject. The Bushnellians did not share his concern to wring some kind of objectivity out of the vicarious character of Christ's atoning work; before long they dropped even the language of vicarious sacrifice. It was Bushnell who redirected American Protestant thinking on this subject, however. He shared Channing's moral objections to substitutionary atonement doctrine and most of his theological objections to its abstract Trinitarian legalism, but he struggled as a Trinitarian Christian to rethink the meaning of Christ's atoning work. His emphasis on the metaphorical nature of religious language broke the power of orthodox exegesis and, thus, the orthodox claim to scriptural necessity. The scriptural metaphors of the altar are metaphors, he admonished; they are not proof-texts for the legal payment of a penalty to God. How can God pay a debt to God? What sort of God is "satisfied" by the execution of his Son? Orthodoxy made the inner Trinitarian life of God the site of the meaning of Christ's sacrifice; this picture located the problem of sin with God. Bushnell's protest was poignant: "How distracting and painful, how dreadfully appalling is the faith that we have a God, back of the worlds, whose indignations overtop his mercies, and who will not be satisfied, save as he is appeased by some other, who is in a better and milder feeling."[9]

The liberal theologians followed Bushnell in maintaining that sin is a terribly human problem. Penal atonement theory is abstract and unreal, Bowne observed, but sin is terribly concrete; the consequences of sin cannot be negated by an abstract decree, and the meaning of Christ's atonement is moral and vital, like the problem of sin. Bushnell reasoned that love is essentially vicarious; Christ bore our sins in his feeling in the way that a mother lovingly bears all the injuries and sufferings of her children. Bowne agreed that human parental love is the right model for atonement thinking: "Profit and loss have no place here, but only the incommensurable relation of parental and filial love. A father does not value his child for what he can make out of it considered as a financial investment or speculation; he values it as his child. We are struck with horror and filled with indignation when we see the parental relation degraded to the level of pecuniary standards." Liberal theology plainly expressed the same revulsion for penal atonement theory.[10]

This was not merely a sentimental judgment. The liberal theologians, preaching a moral-influence concept of atonement, claimed to take the reality of sin more seriously than prevailing orthodoxies. The problem of sentimentalism was a serious one in modern religion, Bowne acknowledged, but the problem was perpetuated by orthodoxists and liberal humanists, not by progressive

Christianity. A sentimentalist is a person who fails to grasp that consequences cannot be forgiven; this was a defining liberal Christian theme and the heart of the social gospel. "If we wish the thing, we must fulfill the conditions," Bowne explained. "It is God's purpose to have and to bless only a world wherein dwelleth righteousness. However inconvenient we may find it, and however strong our desire for sport may be, the unrighteous must come to grief; and God will never depart from his moral laws to make it otherwise." Orthodoxy fixated on the forensic penalty for sin, while liberal humanism treated sin as mere ignorance. In his later career, Bowne recognized that Unitarian Christianity had already taken the liberal humanist road and that mainline liberal Protestantism was spawning its own currents of optimistic culture religion. In words that could have been spoken by Channing, Parker, Bushnell, Beecher, Gladden, Smyth, or Briggs, he blasted all theologies that failed the test of realism about evil: "So long as any one wishes to be saved not from sin but from the penalty of sin there can be no salvation for him. He knows neither the Scriptures nor the moral reason. True salvation is from sin, not from penalty. It means deliverance from the sinful life and establishment in the life of active righteousness, which is the only possible condition of fellowship with the Holy God."[11]

This was a Methodist theme, to be sure, but it was also a characteristically liberal theme, with or without Bowne's flourishes about sanctification. All of the major nineteenth-century liberal theologians conceived true religion in the way that came to be called Victorian. All of them were deeply concerned to provide an alternative to infidelism; all of them took very seriously the duty of good religion to cultivate civilizing moral virtues; all of them regarded religion as the cultivation of a spiritual self and a good society; all of them conceptualized the fundamental problem of human life in terms of the conflict between spirit and nature. Channing and the Unitarians conceived the spiritual cultivation of a higher self as "self-culture"; Bushnell emphasized the social-organic nurturing of character; Beecher celebrated the individuality and expansive love-character of personality; Bowne developed a religious philosophy of spiritualized personality; the social gospelers insisted that spiritually uplifted personality and a good society are necessary to each other.

The Victorian spiritual dimension of nineteenth-century liberal Protestant theology may seem less remarkable for its commonality, of course, when one considers that all the major liberal theologians were also church-oriented Christians and professional religious leaders. Yet even Cady Stanton, who was neither, took for granted the Victorian view of the self as a battleground between the self's spiritual and carnal impulses. Cady Stanton roared against the gender roles of Victorian morality and she was far from prudish about sensual pleasures—to Susan B. Anthony's annoyance, she especially enjoyed sex, food, rest, recreation, and pretty things—yet she was a match for any Victorian preacher on the theme of the triumph of enlightened spirit over nature. Like Parker, whose blend of Enlightenment rationalism and religious humanism she shared, she prized the rationality of the "immortal, high-born soul" as the "highest light" of human beings. Like Beecher, she valued the rational and spiritual "highest light" in human beings over the emotions and appetites, though not in a way that deprecated the body or living in this world. Like both of them, she sought to alleviate Victorian morality of its oppressive features while pressing hard on the theme that true religion is about the triumph of the "higher self" over its lower impulses.[12]

Liberal theology was committed to this view of true religion and its implicit understanding of sin before Victorianism had a name; it was already amply developed in Channing's preaching. The American liberal founders were half-fledged romanticists, in the cases of Emerson and Beecher, full-fledged, yet their romantic idealism was checked by their strong sense of personal and collective evil. Aside from Emerson, who left the church, all of the major liberal founders preached continually on the ways of sin, especially Channing, Parker, Bushnell, and Beecher. After evolution became a dominant category in liberal Protestant thinking, the Victorian dualism of spirit and nature was reconceptualized by Munger, Gladden, Lyman Abbott, the Andover theologians, and others, but it remained no less persistent in liberal theology. The Darwin-accommodating liberals gave religious meaning to evolution by interpreting divine reality as a creative, personalizing factor in the evolutionary process. Human beings are dually constituted as creatures of nature and children of God, they taught: finite spirits created in the image of the divine Spirit, but also evolutionary products of the lower organic forms of natural existence.

It followed for all nineteenth-century liberal theologians that sin is the residue and expression of the bestial impulses of humankind's animal nature. Liberal Protestantism was persistently Victorian in its diagnosis of the fundamental problem of human life and the role of religion in addressing it. It was deeply earnest in explicating this theme. The liberal Victorians took with great seriousness their duty to solve the crisis of belief of their generation; they believed fervently in immortality, preached the civilizing mission of good religion, and took the threat of infidelism very much to heart. They were eloquent in speaking to the doubts of their audiences, but rarely funny. The chief exception had to defend himself for being humorous; one of the featured accusations at the Beecher trial was that Plymouth Church parishioners often laughed and applauded during the sermons. Beecher's lawyers felt compelled to defend his seriousness and deny that his parishioners ever applauded in church. Almost every Beecher sermon contained the core of the liberal Victorian gospel, with or without the laugh lines: The good news of the gospel is the triumph of spirit over nature as mediated by the example and teaching of Jesus. Under the influence of Jesus, the perfectly God-conscious redeemer, human beings are liberated from the selfish impulses of their animal nature and transformed into persons in right relation with God. To be saved is to experience the fulfillment of one's moral and spiritual personality through the triumph of the indwelling spirit of Christ over nature.

Channing and Beecher found this theme on nearly every page of scripture. The evolutionary Bushnellians emphasized that progress takes place through the gradual emergence of the spiritual in humankind and its growing victory over animal nature. The social gospelers added that to follow Christ in spiritual freedom is to build the kingdom of God. Every nineteenth-century liberal theologian can be quoted on this theme. Bowne cautioned his contemporaries to keep evolution in its place, but he gave typical Victorian expression to the liberal Christian conception of the human problem and its answer. "The method of procedure is that of growth and development," he instructed. "There are animal beginnings with moral endings. Love and law are omnipresent throughout the whole of the work; and judgment is possible only at the end."[13]

This way of conceiving the problem of sin had a fateful trajectory. If progress takes place through the gradual emergence of the spiritual in humanity and its growing victory over animal nature, it follows that the human sense of sin is the consciousness that accompanies humanity's process of growth; the sense of sin is a necessary stage in the evolution of humanity. Explicitly, the liberal theologians taught that animal beginnings gradually give way to moral endings; implicitly, this meant that sin is a stage that can be outgrown. In the nineteenth century, the liberal theologians took the residue of their animal beginnings quite seriously, but by the turn of the century, a new generation of progressives believed that progress was advancing at a very rapid rate. The world was getting better; American power and democracy were expanding; education was expelling the evils of ignorance; religious orthodoxy was dethroned; the kingdom of God was within reach. The rationale for not taking sin realistically was built into liberal rhetoric about it from the beginning. Beecher preached against the wages of sin throughout his career, even after he evoked knowing smirks by doing so; had he preached another twenty years, into the twentieth century, he probably would not have done so.

THE GERMAN CONNECTION
AND THE SCHOOL OF SCHLEIERMACHER

American theological liberalism had barely begun to absorb the Ritschlian historicist turn in recent German theology when the nineteenth century ended. The project of appropriating Albrecht Ritschl and his school to the American scene was taken up in the twentieth century by the generation that followed Smyth, Briggs, and Bowne to Germany. Liberal theologians such as William Adams Brown, Arthur C. McGiffert, George Burman Foster, and Shailer Mathews were part of an American generation that surged to German universities in record numbers. The traffic began with Edward Everett and George Ticknor during the early Unitarian controversy; it continued with Edward Robinson, Harry Boynton Smith, and Charles Hodge; it yielded a liberal movement with the generation of Newman Smyth, Charles C. Briggs, and Borden Parker Bowne; and it defined a liberal theological establishment in the succeeding generation.

On occasion, American academics studied in Germany simply to meet the enemy or take its measure; more often, they sought to acquire the tools of modern historical-critical and theological scholarship. Approximately ten thousand Americans matriculated in German universities between 1830 and 1930, half of them at the University of Berlin. Americans appreciated Berlin's spirit of intellectual freedom and its history. In the wake of Napoleon's dismemberment of Prussia, the university's founders had sought, in King Friedrich III's memorable image, to make up for Prussia's physical loss through intellectual gain. Aspiring American theologians appreciated that one of the university's cofounders and first rectors was Friedrich Schleiermacher. The lure of learning theology at the school of Schleiermacher and Hegel persisted long after their deaths in the early 1830s. To Smith, Smyth, and Briggs, the mediating-school theology of Isaak Dorner carried on the legacy of Schleiermacher at its best; a later generation of American students felt that Berlin historical theologian Adolf von Harnack bore the same relation to the legacy of Albrecht Ritschl.[14]

The traffic of Americans to Germany reached its peak with this later generation, in the 1890s, when approximately 2,000 Americans studied in German universities, more than 1,300 of them at Berlin. To select Berlin usually meant something. Friedrich Paulsen would later observe that the better German universities were devoted to a novel idea, that students were "not to be regarded as merely preparing for future service as state officials, but as young men to be trained in independence of thought and in intellectual and moral freedom by means of an untrammelled study of science." The principle of German higher education was freedom and independence, he explained, not unity and subordination. Certainly that is what a succession of aspiring American theologians sought in Germany throughout the nineteenth century. American liberal theology increasingly tacked in a German direction under their influence, beginning with Joseph Buckminster's early articles on historical criticism and Edward Everett's Harvard lectures, recently cribbed from Göttingen, that awoke an intellectually slumbering Ralph Waldo Emerson. It became a tradition after Edward Robinson and Henry Boynton Smith returned from Berlin to report that a German education was necessary for Christian scholarship and not injurious to faith.[15]

Dorner's mediating theology dominated German theology in the mid-nineteenth century and shaped the thinking of two generations of American liberal academics and liberal forerunners; like all liberal theologies, it posed as a third way. Unlike earlier liberalisms, German mediating theology took root in American Protestantism and played a crucial role in shaping and legitimizing American progressive orthodoxy, but it gained a foothold in American academe too late to have a lengthy American career. In the late 1880s and 1890s, aspiring American theologians learned a different brand of liberal theology at Berlin,

Göttingen, and Marburg, where an ascending Ritschlian school founded in the biblical historicist theology of Albrecht Ritschl had eclipsed the mediationist school of Schleiermacher. The story of American Ritschlianism, however, belongs to another volume and age, the early-twentieth-century age of the liberal eruption.

THEOLOGICAL PROGRESSIVISM IN PROGRESS

The nineteenth-century liberals and liberal forerunners sought to imagine a progressive Christianity. This project was both religious and political; nineteenth-century liberal Protestantism yielded a bountiful sociopolitical harvest. In their lifetimes, however, the nineteenth-century founders did better with the religion than the politics of progressive Christianity. Crucial to their religious reform was the preaching of a Coleridgean understanding of religion and religious language; Emerson and Bushnell were the leading theorists of religion as Spirit-uplifted experience and the leading exemplars of religious speech as imaginative metaphorical expression. More than they realized, their ideas soaked into the consciousness of American churchgoers. Bushnell was condemned in his time for his moral theory of atonement and his emphasis on the metaphorical character of religious language; Emerson judged that even the Unitarian church was hopeless as a home for a (liberally interpreted) Coleridgean approach to religious truth. But Emerson and Bushnell lived to see Coleridge popularized by the most influential cleric of the nineteenth century, Henry Ward Beecher, who was important to modern theology less for what he said than for the fact that he made a spectacular success in saying it.

Liberal theology had to be preached before it could become an academic movement in America. For most of the nineteenth century it was preached with extraordinary inspiring power, if only by a few. By the end of Beecher's life, it was almost prosaic for Munger and Gladden to assert that Christianity is essentially a life, not a doctrine. On this notion the social gospelers built a culturally formative Christian movement. After liberal theology became an academic movement, they constructed a systematic theology. None of the nineteenth-century founders of American theological progressivism aspired to systematic theology, but they did their theological task effectively. Much of the religious content of the progressive religion they imagined was so deeply absorbed into modern theology that it was taken for granted even by later neo-orthodox theologians who bitterly attacked theological liberalism.

Coleridge taught Emerson and Bushnell to read the Bible like any other great work of literature, and the Emersonian and Bushnellian streams of liberal theology played up the imaginative nature of religious truth and the play of metaphor in religious speech. At the end of the nineteenth century, it was not clear how far the mainstream of an ascending liberal theology movement would go in relativizing the historical claims of scriptural narrative. How far was liberal theology to go in demythologizing the biblical picture of God as a partisan, intervening, miracle-making divine agent? In the biblical story, God created the world in six days, the fall of humankind occurred in a real space/time Eden, and the patriarchs received audible commands from God; later, God intervened directly in history to cause the plagues in Egypt, the pillar of fire, the parting of the sea, and the deliverance of the Mosaic law; later, God brought about the conquest and the formation of Israel; still later, the prophets were instructed by God's audible voice.

To the biblical writers and church fathers, there was no ambiguity about what it meant to say that God "acted" or "spoke" in history; the Bible uses these terms univocally, speaking of God in the same ways it speaks of human beings acting and speaking in space and time. But what did nineteenth-century theology mean when it spoke of God "acting" or "speaking" in history? Were all of the miracle stories to be relegated to the sphere of "religious interpretation"? Did the liberal assumption of a causal continuum of space/time experience require theologians to deny the historicity of all scriptural portrayals of God's direct agency in history? Schleiermacher taught modern theology to begin with religious experience and to think of divine reality as the immanent universal "spirit of the whole." Put differently, he taught that God is not an hypostatized transcendent being and that theology must not begin with the authoritative propositions of external religion. Does this mean that liberal theology is obliged to read the entire scriptural testimony to God's saving acts in history as the reflections of Hebrew and Christian religion? What happens to the language of divine action in a modernized theology? Are some scriptural portrayals of divine agency more credible than others? What exactly does faith contribute to the religious understanding of scriptural narrative?

American theology had barely begun to grapple with these questions when the nineteenth century ended. The first systematic theology from an American liberal perspective was published in 1898 by Colgate University theologian William Newton Clarke, a Baptist, who minimized the break between the premodern and modern approaches to Christianity. Clarke's doctrine of God was a carefully balanced personal theism. He emphasized God's immanent presence in nature and consciousness while insisting that God's relation to the world is also personal and transcendent. He ruled out the doctrine of verbal inspiration while assuring that "the divine element in the Scriptures will never be disproved." Inspiration applies to human beings, not to documents, he explained; "inspiration is exaltation, quickening of ability, stimulation of spiritual power; it is uplifting and enlargement of capacity for perception, comprehension, and utterance." Like all liberals, he established the principle that "Christianity is not a book-religion, but a life-religion." Like most liberals of the time, Clarke was vague about how far he would go in stripping scriptural narrative of its divine interventions.[16]

Modern scholarship was in the process of determining the relative historicity of the biblical record, he observed, and the jury was out on the record of the founding of Christianity. Though his own theology made little direct use of historical-critical scholarship, Clarke affirmed the necessity of biblical criticism, arguing that the historical nature of Christianity demands the best historical knowledge that can be attained about it. Because Christianity claims to be founded in history, it is not free to claim exemption from the laws of historical evidence. At the same time, he asserted, because Christianity is founded "in the reality of its facts," modern Christianity has nothing to fear from ongoing critical research: "Christianity is really founded in history, and will stand firm as a living reality, whatever may prove to be the manner in which the record of its founding has been written."[17]

That "whatever" was typical of American liberals near the turn of the century. Briggs was an exception, resisting the leftward drift of his discipline and movement, but tellingly, he expressed this opposition mostly in private. His late-career turn to ecumenical activism allowed him to avoid public disputes with liberal colleagues like Arthur McGiffert. Munger and Bowne exemplified the prevailing trend in theology; while they were careful not to elaborate how much of the biblical witness they were prepared to relinquish as history, the answer implicit in their writings was, as much as necessary. On a host of specific issues, American theological liberalism was still in a formative stage; its essential strategy was to take Schleiermacher's option of beginning with religious experience. If necessary, the American liberals would give up even beliefs that Schleiermacher held dear, such as the apostolic authority of the fourth Gospel, by invoking Schleiermacher's distinctions about what is essential to true religion. For those who were receptive to it, American religion had a compelling early example of this approach to religion in the Christian Unitarianism of Channing; for others, liberal Christianity began with Bushnell. In either case, and for the later liberals of the Ritschlian school, American liberal theology sought to pass modern tests of moral and intellectual credibility by appealing to Schleiermacher's invention, which was the notion of true religion as a field unto itself.

This ambitious intellectual and ecclesiastical project amounted to and required a theological revolution in American churches. The American liberals of the social gospel generations did not believe that it was enough to merely reform theology, however. To most of them, liberal theology and the world-changing ethic of the social gospel belonged together. Some of the liberal theologians were not active social gospelers, and some of the social gospelers had no connection to liberal theology, but most of each movement was intertwined with the other. Together they engendered the first Christian movement in the history of Christianity to imagine the progressive transformation of society. The social gospel was not their project alone; it was also a European and Canadian phenomenon that accompanied the rise of modern socialism. Near the end of his classic work on the history of Christian social teaching, published in 1912, at the high tide of the American social gospel movement, Ernst Troeltsch observed that modern liberal Christianity was distinguished in

Christian history by its assumption of an "entirely new" project that Aquinas or Calvin could not have imagined: the notion that Christianity has a transformative social mission.[18]

In Troeltsch's rendering, eighteen centuries of premodern Christianity had developed only two social philosophies worthy of the name. The first was the feudalistic social philosophy of medieval Catholicism, which was centered on the patriarchal family, the guild, and the hierarchy of social classes. The second was the ascetic social philosophy of the Calvinist and pietist traditions, which endorsed a politically liberal concept of the individual's right to freedom, the notion of work as a vocational calling, a work ethic of vocational diligence, and a strong emphasis on the moral responsibilities of individuals to their families and communities. Troeltsch regarded modern social Christianity as a third possibility. The social gospelers rejected "the glorification of the prevailing bourgeois order," he observed. They perceived that there is such a thing as social salvation, which is inextricably linked to personal salvation. In Troeltsch's words, the social gospelers recognized "that the possibility of a spiritual and ethical development depends entirely upon the substructure of a healthy collective social constitution, and that spiritual factors are very closely connected with physical and economic factors." Modern social Christianity rejected the pietistic withdrawal into private spirituality and evangelism "because it implies an attitude of despair towards the world, and an attempt to quiet the Christian conscience by winning a few souls, many of whom are not of the best."[19]

Troeltsch was too worldly-wise to believe that Christian socialism could succeed in transforming modern society—he judged that the social gospelers were very much overmatched by the "brutal facts" of modern politics and economic development—yet he admired their ethical spirit. Modern social Christianity marked a break from the church's traditional acceptance of class hierarchy and, more recently, the injustices of bourgeois capitalism. "Christian Socialism alone has broken through these theories, and forced men to think out afresh the social ethic of Christianity and its relation to the actual changes in the social order," he observed. "It has laid bare the worm-eaten condition of the previous conventional Christian ethic, which, at its best, offered something for the ethics of the family and the individual, but which, on the other hand, had no message for social ethics save that of acceptance of all existing institutions and conditions, much to the satisfaction of all in authority. Christian Socialism has regained for the Christian ethic its Utopian and revolutionary character."[20]

The latter sentence made little sense applied to more than a handful of people in either Germany or the United States. German Christian socialism was deeply conservative, and there were few revolutionaries to speak of in the American social gospel movement. Troeltsch exaggerated the radicalism of modern social Christianity. Most of the American social gospelers of the late nineteenth and early twentieth centuries were middle class and politically conventional; they were ambivalent about trade unions; they were easy prey for nationalistic appeals; they did not think of blacks or women as possessing intellectual or political agency; and many of them embraced the dominant culture's Anglo-Saxon racial mythology. In these crucial respects they resembled their liberal forerunners. Liberal theology was a product of middle-class anxiety and privilege, it was easily drafted for nationalistic causes, and it gave the sanction of progressive Christian reason to racial and sexual discrimination. Among the founders of American theological liberalism, only Theodore Parker was a movement abolitionist, and even he reflected the pervasive racism of his society.

Parker's abhorrence of slavery was consuming. Unlike Emerson, he could not content himself with occasional protests against the Fugitive Slave Law. Unlike Channing, he kept in mind the difference between the horror of slavery and the unattractiveness of abolitionist self-righteousness; thus he did not allow personal qualms about abolitionists to restrict his participation in the antislavery movement. Unlike Beecher, he was not fazed by the social stigma of abolitionism; unlike Bushnell, he had too much feeling for American blacks as human beings to hope for the withering away of the African American population. Yet Parker took it for granted that American blacks belonged to an inferior foreign race that was unlikely to survive among superior Anglo-Saxons. He expressed plainly racist opinions while devoting his life to the liberation of enslaved Americans. With the same chauvinism as Bushnell, albeit less lyrically, he argued that the Caucasians were the most advanced race in the world, the Teutons were the most advanced among the Caucasians, and among the Teutons, the Anglo-Saxons, "especially that portion of them in the Northern states of America," were "advancing most rapidly in their general progress."[21]

Progress and Anglo-Saxonism were closely linked for most of the American progressivists. Relatively few liberal Christian or social gospel leaders were racists in the precise sense of the term; social gospelers Thomas Dixon Jr. and Alexander McKelway were among the few who believed that race itself had a determinative biological significance that made blacks inferior to whites. But cultural racism captured all but a few Christian progressives on the other end of the social gospel spectrum. The American Christian progressives believed too deeply in the redeemer mission of their nation not to believe that Anglo-Saxons were the leaders and saviors of the world. They further believed that modern evolutionary science was on their side; Darwinism was a secular explanation of the leadership mission of Anglo-Saxon America as a world-civilizing agent. Progressive Christianity was therefore ripe for the siren calls of William McKinley and Theodore Roosevelt to benevolent imperialism; later it embraced the Great War as a democratizing social gospel cause. The social gospel movement was not lacking in figures who vigorously supported racial equality and opposed American imperialism, but principled anti-imperialism was a minority impulse. Most of the movement's leaders played to larger caucuses.

The contest for the mantle of Beecher exposed how far even a respectable mainstream leader of the social gospel movement could move in the direction of the reactionary right. Lyman Abbott's American imperialism was unabashed and militant, of a piece with his fervent Anglo-Saxonism. As Beecher's successor at Plymouth Church and editor of the mass-circulation *Outlook,* Abbott assured a large liberal Christian following that American Anglo-Saxon Protestantism was the hope of the world. He also supported restrictions on black suffrage in the South, arguing in 1903 that in light of the gross inferiority of blacks to whites and the high rates of black illiteracy in the South, the action of the North Carolina state legislature to restrict black suffrage was "highly creditable." If American blacks wanted the franchise, they had to earn it by raising themselves to the status of acculturated citizens.[22]

This argument had a progressive gloss; it was pitched as a case for America to assume responsibility for educating its black population. Abbott played a major role in making Booker T. Washington the national symbol of white and black America's hope for black Americans. Fortunately the truly progressive social gospelers protested that this was no way to advance the cause of black education; Abbott's successor at Plymouth Church, Newell Dwight Hillis, added that neither was it any way to honor the legacy of Henry Ward Beecher. "If the Negro is to be disfranchised then the Declaration of Independence is wrong," Hillis objected. "If universal suffrage is wrong, then the fifteenth amendment to the Constitution must be given up; then Abraham Lincoln was wrong in his speech at Gettysburg and the million soldiers who gave up their lives for liberty spilled their blood in the interests of folly and superstition." Abbott replied that he could cite Beecher to the contrary; he might have replied that more than a few social gospelers and feminist leaders could be cited as well. Beecher had warned that universal suffrage would fail without universal education, Abbott recalled. Now Beecher's opposition to Reconstruction looked prophetic: Reconstruction had been a disaster, American blacks were still uneducated, and they had failed to use the vote effectively. It was time for a change of strategy, he urged; this time blacks would have to win their rights by educating themselves and relying upon the protection of the best Southern men.[23]

That was the nadir of American progressive Christianity. The fact that the social gospelers seriously debated black suffrage in the early twentieth century confutes their image as a radical movement. A decade later, at the height of the movement's idealism and momentum, many social gospel leaders were still conflicted about women's suffrage as well. The social gospelers averted the abyss of reaction on racial justice by endorsing only the education part of Abbott's prescription. Without relinquishing their Anglo-Saxonist ideology, they accented their better impulses, following the example of an inspiring new leader, Rochester Seminary theologian Walter Rauschenbusch. Rauschenbusch expressed the movement's latent idealism with a transformative power that measured up to Troeltsch's praise for the movement as a whole. His prophetic passion lifted the movement to new rhetorical and socioethical heights. His sermons and books imagined a Christianized American century that redeemed the Puritan dream of Christian America in the form of an ecumenical Protestant democratic socialism.

Theologically Rauschenbusch was a left-Ritschlian. In the heyday of the social gospel, left-Ritschlianisms abounded at American divinity schools, and Union Seminary theologian William Adams Brown developed a Ritschlian social gospel theology that emphasized the links between Ritschl and Schleiermacher. Boston University developed a school of semi-Ritschlian personalist theology that kept alive Bowne's progressive legacy for decades. Oberlin theologian Henry Churchill King formulated a more explicitly Ritschlian personalism that carried forward the Congregationalist legacy of Bushnell and Beecher. The newly founded University of Chicago Divinity School began with a commitment to Ritschlian historicism, moved to post-Ritschlian historicism, and then found a new basis for the social gospel in American pragmatism and empiricism.

By the time the phrase "social gospel" acquired currency in the early years of the twentieth century, progressive Christianity was no longer something only to be imagined. The heirs of Channing and Bushnell had free reign to modernize Christianity as they saw fit. They had very ambitious hopes for the liberal gospel and used "modernize," "democratize," and "Christianize" as interchangeable terms. They sought to Christianize America and the world, insisting that the kingdom of God was being built in their mission to complete the process of Christianization in America and convert the world to modernist Christian democracy. Only belatedly did they question whether they had granted too much authority to modern culture in the course of liberating American Christianity from its scriptural and ecclesiastical houses of authority.

Notes

Introduction: The Liberal Idea in American Religion

1. See Francis Turretin, *Institutes of Elenctic Theology*, trans. George Musgrave Giger, ed. James T. Dennison Jr. 3 vols. (1679; reprint, Phillipsburg, N.J.: Presbyterian & Reformed Publishing Co., 1992); *Reformed Dogmatics: J. Wollebius, G. Voetius, F. Turretin*, ed. and trans. John W. Beardslee III (New York: Oxford University Press, 1965); Johann Andreas Quenstedt, *Theologia didactico-polemica* (Wittenberg: Johannes Ludolph Quenstedt and Elerd Schumacher Haeredes [Matthaeus Henckel], 1685); Richard Miller, *Post-Reformation Reformed Dogmatics*, 2 vols. (Grand Rapids: Baker Book House, 1987); Robert D. Preus, *The Theology of Post-Reformation Lutheranism*, 2 vols. (St. Louis: Concordia Publishing House, 1970).

2. See Richard Hooker, *Of the Laws of Ecclesiastical Polity* I, xiv. 1-5 (1593; reprint New York: E. P. Dutton, 1958), 1: 276–82; Paul Elmer More and Frank Leslie Cross, eds., *Anglicanism: The Thought and Practice of the Church of England, Illustrated from the Religious Literature of the Seventeenth Century* (London: SPCK, 1951), 89–96.

3. See Immanuel Kant, *Religion within the Limits of Reason Alone*, trans. Theodore M. Greene and Hoyt H. Hudson (1793; reprint, Chicago: Open Court, 1934); Friedrich Schleiermacher, *On Religion: Addresses in Response to Its Cultured Critics* (1799), trans. Terrence N. Tice (1799; reprint, Richmond: John Knox Press, 1969); Schleiermacher, *The Christian Faith* (1830), ed. H. R. Mackintosh and J. S. Stewart (1928, reprint, Edinburgh: T. & T. Clark, 1968); Johann Gottfried Eichhorn, *Einleitung in das Neue Testament*, 5 vols. (Leipzig: Weidmann, 1804–27); Bernard Orchard and Thomas R. W. Longstaff, eds., *J. J. Griesbach: Synoptic and Text-Critical Studies,* SNTS Monograph Series, no. 34 (Cambridge: Cambridge University Press, 1978); Wilhelm Martin Leberecht de Wette, *A Historico-Critical Introduction to the Canonical Books of the New Testament*, trans. F. Frothingham (Boston: Crosby, Nichols & Co., 1858).

4. See Ferdinand Christian Baur, *Symbolik und Mythologie, oder die Naturreligion des Alterthums,* 2 vols. (Stuttgart: J. B. Metzler, 1824–25); David Friedrich Strauss, *Die christliche Glaubenslehre in ihrer geschichtlichen Entwicklung und im Kampfe mit der modernen Wissenschaft dargestellt,* 2 vols. (Tübingen: C. F. Osiander, 1840, 1841); Isaak August Dorner, *System der christlichen Glaubenslehre,* 2 vols. (Berlin: W. Hertz, 1879, 1881); Albrecht Ritschl, *The Christian Doctrine of Justification and Reconciliation*, ed. H. R. Mackintosh and A. B. Macaulay (1874; reprint, Edinburgh: T. & T. Clark, 1902); Julius Wellhausen, *Prolegomena to the History of Israel* (Edinburgh: A. & C. Black, 1885); Adolf von Harnack, *What Is Christianity?* trans. Thomas Bailey Saunders (1900; reprint Philadelphia: Fortress Press, 1986); Ernst Troeltsch, *Die Absolutheit der Christentums und die Religionsgeschichte* (Tübingen: J. C. B. Mohr [Paul Siebeck], 1912).

5. John Henry Cardinal Newman, *Apologia Pro Vita Sua* (New York: Doubleday & Co., 1956), 205–12; Daniel Day Williams, *God's Grace and Man's Hope* (New York: Harper & Brothers, 1949), 22.

6. Lloyd J. Averill, *American Theology in the Liberal Tradition* (Philadelphia: Westminster Press, 1967), 22–26; Donald E. Miller, "Liberalism," and James Richmond, "Liberal Protestantism," in Alan Richardson and John Bowden, eds., *The Westminster Dictionary of Christian Theology* (Philadelphia: Westminster Press, 1983), 324–25, 325–28. See Miller, *The Case for Liberal Christianity* (San Francisco: Harper & Row, 1981).

7. Text of June 1, 1827, prospectus signed by Lücke, Gieseler, Nitzsch, Ullmann, and Umbreit, reprinted in Jörg Rothermundt, *Personale Synthese. 189 Isaak August Dorners Dogmatische Methode* (Göttingen: Vandenhoeck & Rupprecht, 1968), 12; Carl Immanuel Nitzsch, *System der christlichen Lehre* (Bonn: Adolph Marcus, 1829); Richard Rothe, *Die Anfänge der christlichen Kirche*, 3 vols. (Wittenberg: Zimmerman, 1837); Richard Rothe, *Zur Dogmatik* (Gotha: Perthes, 1863). See Werner Elert, *Der Kampf um das Christentum. Geschichte der Beziehung zwischen dem evangelischen Christentum in Deutschland und dem allgemeinen Denken seit Schleiermacher und Hegel* (Munich: C. H. Beck, 1921); Colin Brown, *Jesus in European Protestant Thought, 1778–1860* (Durham, N.C.: Labyrinth Press, 1985), 254–76; Max Huber, *Jesus als Erlöser in der liberalen Theologie. Vermittlung, Spekulation, Existenzverständnis* (Winterthur: Verlag P. G. Keller, 1956).

8. See Carl Ullmann, *Historisch oder Mythisch? Beiträge zur Beantwortung der gegenwärtigen Lebensfrage der Theologie* (Hamburg: Perthes, 1838); Julius Müller, *Die christliche Lehre der Sünde*, 2 vols. (Stuttgart: A. Heitz, 1839, 1844); August Twesten, *Vorlesungen über die Dogmatik*, 4th ed. (Hamburg: Perthes, 1838); Willibald Beyschlag, *Die Christologie des Neuen Testaments* (Berlin: Rauh, 1866); Dorner, *System der christlichen Glaubenslehre;* Isaak August Dorner, *Entwicklungsgeschichte der Lehre von der Person Christi von den ältesten Zeiten bis auf die neueste*, 2 vols. (Stuttgart: S. G. Liesching, 1956).

9. See Karl Rudolph Hagenbach, *A Text-Book of the History of Doctrines*, trans. H. B. Smith, 2 vols. (New York: Sheldon, 1862); Alexander Schweizer, *Die Glaubenslehre der evangelisch-reformirten Kirche dargestellt und aus den Quellen belegt*, 2 vols. (Zurich: Orell & Füssli, 1844, 1847); Hans Lassen Martensen, *Christian Dogmatics* (Edinburgh: T. & T. Clark, 1898).

10. See Frederick Denison Maurice, *Theological Essays* (1853; reprint, New York: Harper & Brothers, 1957); Maurice, *The Kingdom of Christ*, 2nd ed., 2 vols. (1852; reprint, London: SCM Press, 1958); Auguste Sabatier, *Religions of Authority and the Religion of the Spirit*, trans. Louise Seymour Houghton (New York: McClure, Phillips, & Co., 1904); Jean Réville, *Le Protestantisme liberal, ses origines, sa nature, sa mission* (Paris: Librairie Fischbacher, 1903); Réville, *Les phases successives de l'histoire des religions* (Paris: E. Leroux, 1909); Charles Gore, ed., *Lux Mundi: A Series of Studies in the Religion of the Incarnation* (London: John Murray, 1889); Alfred Loisy, *The Birth of the Christian Religion* and *The Origins of the New Testament*, trans. L. P. Jacks, one-volume ed. (New Hyde Park, N.Y.: University Books, 1962).

11. William R. Hutchison, *The Modernist Impulse in American Protestantism* (Cambridge: Harvard University Press, 1976; reprint, Durham, N.C.: Duke University Press, 1992).

Chapter 1: Unitarian Beginnings

1. See John Locke, *The Reasonableness of Christianity as Delivered in the Scriptures*, ed. George W. Ewing (1695; reprint, Lanham, Md: Regnery Gateway, 1965); Samuel Clarke, *A Demonstration of the Being and Attributes of God* (London: James Knapton, 1705); Joseph Butler, *The Analogy of Religion, Natural and Revealed, to the Constitution and Course of Nature* (London: SPCK 1736; reprint, New York: M. H. Newman & Co., 1851); Conrad Wright, *The Beginnings of Unitarianism in America* (Boston: Starr King Press, 1955; reprint, Hamden, Conn.: Archon Books, 1976); Edward M. Griffin, *Old Brick: Charles Chauncy of Boston, 1705–87* (Minneapolis: University of Minnesota Press, 1980); Edwin S. Gaustad, *The Great Awakening in New England* (New York: Harper & Brothers, 1957); Alan Heimert, *Religion and the American Mind: From the Great Awakening to the Revolution* (Cambridge: Harvard University Press, 1966); David Robinson, *The Unitarians and the Universalists* (Westport, Conn.: Greenwood Press, 1985); James W. Jones, *The Shattered Synthesis: New England Puritanism before the Great Awakening* (New Haven, Conn.: Yale University Press, 1973).

2. Charles Chauncy, *Enthusiasm Described and Caution'd Against: a Sermon preach'd at the Old Brick Meeting-house in Boston* (Boston: J. Draper, 1742), 230–36; quotes on Whitefield and "bitter shriekings" in Chauncy, *Seasonable Thoughts on the State of Religion in New-England, a Treatise in Five Parts* (Boston: Rogers & Fowle, 1743), 35–36, 76–77; excerpts reprinted in David B. Parke, *The Epic of Unitarianism: Original Writings from the History of Liberal Religion* (Boston: Starr King Press, 1957), 51–53; quote on Tennent's preaching in Chauncy, "A Letter from a Gentleman in Boston, to Mr. George Wishart, One of the Ministers of Edinburgh, Concerning the State of Religion in New England," reprinted in *The Clarendon Historical Society's Reprints,* Series I, 1882–84, (1883); and *Issues in American Protestantism: A Documentary History from the Puritans to the Present,* ed. Robert L. Ferm (Garden City, N.J.: Anchor Books, 1969), 83–95. An excerpt from Chauncy's *Seasonable Thoughts on the State of Religion in New England* is also available in *An American Reformation: A Documentary History of Unitarian Christianity,* ed. Sydney E. Ahlstrom, with Jonathan Sinclair Carey (Middletown, Conn.: Wesleyan University Press, 1985; reprint, San Francisco: International Scholars Publications, 1998), 60–66.

3. Charles Chauncy, *Five Dissertations on the Scripture Account of the Fall and Its Consequences* (London: Charles Dilly, 1785), 33, 186–87; Chauncy, *The Mystery hid from Ages and Generations, made manifest by the Gospel-Revelation: or, The Salvation of All Men, The Grand Thing Aimed at in the Scheme of God* (London: Charles Dilly, 1784; reprint, New York: Arno Press, 1969), quote on 364. See Chauncy, *The Benevolence of the Deity, Fairly and Impartially Considered* (Boston: Powars & Willis, 1784); Jones, *The Shattered Synthesis,* 180–81; Wright, *The Beginnings of Unitarianism in America,* 187–99.

4. Jonathan Mayhew, *Seven Sermons Upon the following Subjects: viz. I. The Difference betwixt the Truth and Falsehood, Right and Wrong. II. The natural Abilities of Men for discerning these Differences. III. The Right and Duty of Private Judgment. IV. Objections considered. V. The Love of God. VI. The Love of our Neighbor. VII. The first and great Commandment* (Boston: Rogers & Fowle, 1749; 85–87, 101; excerpts reprinted in Parke, *The Epic of Unitarianism,* 54–55. Closing quote on eternal laws in Mayhew's pamphlet, *Discourse Concerning Unlimited Submission and Non-resistance to the Higher Powers; With some Reflections on the Resistance Made to King Charles I* (Boston: D. Fowle, 1750; reprint, Boston: Hall & Goss, 1818), reprinted in *Pamphlets of the American Revolution, 1750–1776,* ed. Bernard Bailyn (Cambridge: Harvard University Press, 1965), I: 242. For reprinted editions of both *Seven Sermons* and the *Discourse Concerning Unlimited Submission,* together with Mayhew's *The Snare broken, a Thanksgiving-Discourse* (1766), see Mayhew, *Sermons: Seven Sermons; A Discourse, Concerning the Unlimited Submission and Non-Resistance to the Higher Powers; The Snare Broken* (New York: Arno Press, 1969). See Mayhew, *Two Sermons Preached on the Nature, Extent and Perfection of the Divine Goodness* (Boston: D. & J. Kneel, 1763); "Jonathan Mayhew," *A Miscellany of American Christianity,* ed. McMurry S. Richey (Durham, N.C.: Duke University Press, 1963), 317–18; Charles W. Akers, *Called unto Liberty: A Life of Jonathan Mayhew* (Cambridge: Harvard University Press, 1964).

5. Chauncy, *The Mystery hid from Ages and Generations,* vi; Ebenezer Gay, *Natural Religion, as Distinguish'd from Revealed* (Boston: John Draper, 1759), quotes on 6, 34. See Gay, *The Mystery of the Seven Stars in Christ's Right Hand* (Boston: John Draper, 1752); Gay, *A Discourse on the Transcendent Glory of the Gospel* (Boston: D. Henchman, 1728); Robert J. Wilson III, *The Benevolent Deity: Ebenezer Gay and the Rise of Rational Religion in New England, 1696–1787* (Philadelphia: University of Pennsylvania Press, 1983); Earl Morse Wilbur, *A History of Unitarianism in Transylvania, England, and America* (Cambridge: Harvard University Press, 1952), 385–86; Conrad Wright, *The Liberal Christians: Essays on American Unitarian History* (Boston: Beacon Press, 1970), 9–11.

6. See Conrad Wright, "The Election of Henry Ware: Two Contemporary Accounts Edited with Commentary," *Harvard Library Bulletin* 17 (1969): 245–78; Daniel Walker Howe, *The Unitarian Conscience: Harvard Moral Philosophy, 1805–1861* (Cambridge: Harvard University Press, 1970), 4–5.

7. Channing quote in Anna Le Breton, ed., *Correspondence of William Ellery Channing, D.D., and Lucy Aikin (1826–1842),* (Boston: Roberts Brothers, 1874); 224, letter dated August 1834. On Channing's family life, see William Henry Channing, *Memoir of William Ellery Channing, with Extracts from His Correspondence and Manuscripts,* 2 vols. (London: George

Routledge & Company, 1850), 1:1–31; and John White Chadwick, *William Ellery Channing: Minister of Religion* (Boston: Houghton Mifflin, 1903), 12–14.

8. Channing, *Memoir of William Ellery Channing*, 1: 11; see George Gibbs Channing, *Early Recollections of Newport, RI, from the year 1793 to 1811* (Newport, R.I.: A. J. Ward, C. E. Hammett, Jr, 1868; reprinted Salem, Mass.: Higginson Book Co., 1987); Edward Tyrrel Channing, *Lives of William Pinkney, William Ellery and Cotton Mather* (New York: Harper, 1856); Edwards A. Park, "Memoir of Samuel Hopkins," in *The Works of Samuel Hopkins*, ed. Edwards A. Park, 3 vols. (Boston: Doctrinal Tract & Book Society, 1854), 1:83–84.

9. See Samuel Hopkins, *The System of Doctrines, Contained in Divine Revelation. Explained and Defended. Shewing Their Consistence and Connexion with Each Other. To Which Is Added, a Treatise on the Millennium*, 2 vols. (Boston: Thomas & Andrews, 1793), 1:545–46; Hopkins, *A Dialogue Concerning the Slavery of the Africans* (New York: Arno Press, 1969); Park, "Memoir of Samuel Hopkins," 67–84.

10. William Ellery Channing, "Christian Worship: Discourse at the Dedication of the Unitarian Congregational Church, Newport, Rhode Island, July 27, 1836," in *The Works of William E. Channing, D.D.*, 6 vols. (Boston: James Munroe, 1841–43), 4:341–48; reprinted in Channing, *The Works of William E. Channing, D.D.*, revised, one-volume edition (Boston: American Unitarian Association, 1883), 423–26. Hereafter all references to Channing's works will be to the revised one-volume edition unless noted otherwise. See Park, "Memoir of Samuel Hopkins," 28–31; Joseph Haroutunian, *Piety versus Moralism: The Passing of the New England Theology* (New York: Henry Holt, 1932), 61–63.

11. Channing, "Christian Worship," 425.

12. "Unmingled vengeance" quote in Charles T. Brooks, *William Ellery Channing: A Centennial Memory* (Boston: Roberts Brothers, 1880), 105; see William Allen, *Memoir of John Codman, D.D.* (Boston: T. R. Marvin & S. K. Whipple, 1853), 267–68. "Indescribable ruin" quote in William Ellery Channing, *A Sermon Delivered at the Ordination of the Rev. John Codman, to the Pastoral Care of the Second Church of Christ in Dorchester, Dec. 7, 1808* (Boston: Joshua Belcher, 1808), 16.

13. For example, see Herbert W. Schneider, "The Intellectual Background of William Ellery Channing," *Church History* 7 (1938): 4; Robert Leet Patterson, *The Philosophy of William Ellery Channing* (New York: Bookman Associates, 1952), 15–16; David P. Edgell, *William Ellery Channing: An Intellectual Portrait* (Boston: Beacon Press, 1955), 71–83, 97–98. For a critique of this reading, see Wright, *The Liberal Christians*, 22–33.

14. Channing, "Christian Worship," 424.

15. Channing, *Memoir of William Ellery Channing*, 1:24–25; Elizabeth Palmer Peabody, *Reminiscences of Rev. W. Ellery Channing, D.D.* (Boston: Roberts Brothers, 1880), 62–63. See Jack Mendelsohn, *Channing: The Reluctant Radical* (Boston: Little, Brown, 1971), 22–24; Chadwick, *William Ellery Channing*, 23–24.

16. Channing, "Christian Worship," 421–23.

17. William Ellery to William Ellery Channing, July 10, 1794, William Ellery Channing Papers, Massachusetts Historical Society, Boston, Massachusetts; see Channing, *Memoir of William Ellery Channing*, 1:29–31; F. B. Dexter, *Biographical Sketches of the Graduates of Yale College*, 6 vols. (New Haven: Yale University Press, 1913), 4:183–86.

18. Channing, *Memoir of William Ellery Channing*, 1:43.

19. Paine's *Age of Reason* was published in 1794; Watson's reply was published two years later.

20. Channing, *Memoir of William Ellery Channing*, 1:43; William Ellery to William Ellery Channing, April 22, 1795, Channing Papers, Massachusetts Historical Society.

21. See Francis Turretin, *Institutes of Elenctic Theology*, trans. George Musgrave Giger, ed. James T. Dennison, Jr., 3 vols. (Phillipsburg, N.J.: Presbyterian & Reformed Publishing, 1992, 1994, 1997); Stephen Charnock, *The Existence and Attributes of God* (Grand Rapids: Baker Books, 1996).

22. George Whitefield, *George Whitefield's Journals (1737–1741)*, ed. William V. Davis (Gainesville, Fla.: Scholars' Facsimiles and Reprints, 1969), 463; cited in Robinson, *The Unitarians and the Universalists*, 11.

23. Channing, *Memoir of William Ellery Channing*, 1:47–48.

24. See Francis Hutcheson, *A System of Moral Philosophy in three books*, 2 vols. (Glasgow and London: R. & A. Foulis, 1755); 1:174–75; Hutcheson, *An Inquiry into the Original of our Ideas of Beauty and Virtue*, 2d ed. (London: J. Darby and many others, 1726); 1725 edition

reprinted, in part, as *An Inquiry Concerning the Originals of Our Idea of Virtue and Moral Good* in *British Moralists, 1650–1800,* ed. D. D. Raphael, 2 vols. (Oxford: Clarendon Press, 1969), 1:259–321. The third Earl of Shaftesbury (1671–1713), normally referred to simply as Shaftesbury, was an early critic of Locke who emphasized feeling rather than reason as the source of morality. Named Anthony Ashley Cooper, he invented the term "moral sense" doctrine.

25. Channing, *Memoir of William Ellery Channing,* 1:46.

26. Adam Ferguson, *An Essay on the History of Civil Society,* 4th ed. (London: T. Caddel and others, 1773), 87–90, quote on 89; see Ferguson, *Principles of Moral and Political Science* (Edinburgh: A. Strahan & T. Cadell, 1792); Ferguson, *The History of the Progress and Termination of the Roman Empire* (New York: Harper & Brothers, 1859).

27. Thomas Reid, *An Inquiry into the Human Mind, on the principles of Common Sense,* 3d ed. (Dublin: R. Marchbank, 1779); abridged edition reprinted in Reid, *Inquiry and Essays,* ed. Ronald E. Beanblossom and Keith Lehrer (Indianapolis: Hackett Publishing Co., 1983), quote on 118. See Roger L. Emerson, "Science and Moral Philosophy in the Scottish Enlightenment," in *Studies in the Philosophy of the Scottish Enlightenment,* ed. M. A. Stewart (Oxford: Clarendon Press, 1990), 32–38; Mark A. Noll, "Common Sense Traditions and American Evangelical Thought," *American Quarterly* 37 (1985): 216–38; S. A. Grave, *The Scottish Philosophy of Common Sense* (Oxford: Oxford University Press, 1960); Sydney Ahlstrom, "The Scottish Philosophy and American Theology," *Church History* 24: 257–69.

28. Hutcheson, *An Inquiry Concerning the Originals of Our Idea of Virtue and Moral Good,* 299; Richard Price, *A Review of the Principal Questions and Difficulties in Morals,* 2d ed. (London: T. Cadell, 1769), 58–63, 84–94; reprinted as *A Review of the Principal Questions in Morals,* ed. D. D. Raphael (Oxford: Oxford University Press, 1948); see D. O. Thomas, *The Honest Mind: The Thought and Work of Richard Price* (Oxford: Oxford University Press, 1977); Howe, *The Unitarian Conscience,* 46–47.

29. Price, *A Review of the Principal Questions and Difficulties in Morals,* 59–60, 92–96, 375–78; Thomas Reid, "Essay Five: Of Morals," in *Essays on the Intellectual Powers of Man* (1785), reprinted in Reid, *Inquiry and Essays,* 351–68; see Ahlstrom, "The Scottish Philosophy and American Theology," 260–68; Arthur W. Brown, *William Ellery Channing* (New York: Twayne Publishers, 1961), 65–66; David Robinson, "The Legacy of Channing: Culture as a Religious Category in New England Thought," *Harvard Theological Review* 74 (1981): 221–39.

30. Channing, *Memoir of William Ellery Channing,* 1:48; on the Harvard tradition of Scottish Enlightenment-influenced Unitarian moral philosophy, see Howe, *The Unitarian Conscience: Harvard Moral Philosophy, 1805–1861;* and Benjamin Rand, "Philosophical Instruction in Harvard University from 1636 to 1906," *Harvard Graduates' Magazine* 37 (1928): 25–46.

31. Channing, *Memoir of William Ellery Channing,* 1:57. See Le Breton, *Correspondence of William Ellery Channing, D.D. and Lucy Aikin,* 82–83.

32. Channing, *Memoir of William Ellery Channing,* 1:59, 61–62.

33. Ibid., 59–95, quotes on 94.

34. Ibid., 94–95, 97.

35. See Mark A. Noll, *Princeton and the Republic, 1768–1822* (Princeton: Princeton University Press, 1989), 28–58; Theodore Dwight Bozeman, *Protestants in an Age of Science* (Chapel Hill, N.C.: University of North Carolina Press, 1977).

36. Channing, "Remarks on the Character and Writings of Fénelon," reprinted in *The Works of William E. Channing, D.D.,* 559–61; quote in Channing, *Memoir of William Ellery Channing,* 1:109.

37. Channing, "Christian Worship," 423–28.

38. For selections from his early sermons on devotion to God, the divine attributes, spiritual regeneration, the religion of Christ, and similar themes, see Channing, *Memoir of William Ellery Channing,* 1:185–237.

39. Quoted in Wright, *The Liberal Christians,* 127.

40. Channing letters to the Hon. William Ellery, Mar. 1806 and May 1806, reprinted in Channing, *Memoir of William Ellery Channing,* 1:261–63.

41. Channing letter to the Hon. William Ellery, May 1807, reprinted in ibid., 263–264.

42. Channing letter to anonymous correspondent, Feb. 1840, reprinted in ibid., 260.

43. See Channing, "Man's Spiritual Perfection the End of Providence," sermon of 1810, reprinted in ibid., 203–4.

44. Quote from sermon preached on July 23, 1812, reprinted in ibid., 255–56. See also Channing's sermon of Apr. 5, 1810, against French despotism, reprinted in ibid., 248–55; Channing, "Duties of the Citizen in Times of Trial or Danger," 1812, reprinted in Channing, *The Works of William Ellery Channing, D.D.*, 679–88; and Channing, "Remarks on the Life and Character of Napoleon Bonaparte," (1827–28), reprinted in ibid., 522–59.

45. Channing, "Introductory Remarks," 10–11; "War: Discourse Delivered January 25, 1835," 654–64; "Lecture on War," 664–79; all reprinted in *The Works of William Ellery Channing, D.D.*

46. See Joseph Stevens Buckminster, "Notice of Griesbach's Edition of the New-Testament, Now Printing at Cambridge," *Monthly Anthology* 5 (Jan. 1808): 18–21; Buckminster, "Abstract of Interesting Facts Relating to the New Testament," *Monthly Anthology* 5 (Oct. 1808): 544–47, 580–85, 633–40; Buckminster, "Review of Thompson's Septuagint," *Monthly Anthology* 7 (1809): 396–400; Buckminster, "Review of Griesbach's New Testament," 10 (1811): 107–14, 403–21; Buckminster, "On the Accuracy and Fidelity of Griesbach," *General Repository and Review* 1 (1812): 89–101; Johann Jacob Griesbachii, *Novum Testamentum Graece* (Cantabrigiae Nov-Anglorum: Published with sponsorship of the President and Fellows of Harvard University, 1809); See citations and discussion in Jerry Wayne Brown, *The Rise of Biblical Criticism in America, 1800–1870: The New England Scholars* (Middletown, Conn.: Wesleyan University Press, 1969), 10–26.

47. See Joseph Stevens Buckminster, *Sermons, with a Memoir of His Life and Character* (Boston: John Eliot, 1814; 3d ed., Boston: Wells & Lilly, 1821); Buckminster, *Sermons, Now First Published from the Author's Manuscripts* (Boston: Carter & Hendee, 1829); Eliza Buckminster Lee, *Memoirs of Rev. Joseph Buckminster, D.D. and of His Son, Rev. Joseph Stevens Buckminster* (Boston: Ticknor, Reed, & Fields, 1851); Andrews Norton, "Character of Rev. Joseph Stephens Buckminster," *General Repository and Review* 2 (1812): 307–14. On the tributes to Buckminster, see Lawrence Buell, "Joseph Stevens Buckminster: The Making of a New England Saint," *Canadian Review of American Studies* 10 (spring 1979): 1–29; on Buckminster's preaching, see Samuel Kirkland Lathrop, *A History of the Church in Brattle Street, Boston* (Boston: William Crosby & H. P. Nichols, 1851), 171–76; on the auction of his library, see Brown, *The Rise of Biblical Criticism in America, 1800–1870*, 27–29.

48. See Channing's letter to the Rev. Noah Worcester, Jan. 11, 1813; Channing, "Mistakes as to the Nature of Religion," *The Christian Disciple* 2, 10 (1814): 308; Channing, "Humility in the Investigation of Christian Truth," *The Christian Disciple* 1, 1 (1813): 18; all reprinted in Channing, *Memoir of William Ellery Channing*, 269–78.

49. Jeremiah Evarts, "Review of American Unitarianism," *Panoplist and Missionary Magazine* 11 (1815): 251–54, 260–63; reprinted in *Tracts on the Unitarian Controversy* (Boston: Wells & Lilly, 1816); Jedidiah Morse, *Review of American Unitarianism* (Boston: Samuel T. Armstrong, 1816); Thomas Belsham, *American Unitarianism: or, a Brief History of "The Progress and Present State of the Unitarian Churches in America"* (Boston: Nathaniel Willis, 1815); Belsham, *Memoir of the Late Reverend Theophilus Lindsey*, 2d ed. (London: R. Hunter, 1820); Belsham, *Letters upon Arianism and other Topics in Metaphysics and Theology* (London: E. Hemsted, 1808); Belsham, *Uncorrupted Christianity Unpatronised by the Great* (London: Johnson & Company, 1811). See Conrad Wright, "The Controversial Career of Jedidiah Morse," *Harvard Library Bulletin* 31 (1983): 67–84.

50. Evarts, "Review of American Unitarianism," 260–69.

51. See Michael Servetus, *The Two Treatises of Servetus on the Trinity*, trans. Earl Morse Wilbur (Cambridge: Harvard University Press, 1932); Joachim Wach, "Caspar Schwenckfeld," in *Types of Religious Experience* (Chicago: University of Chicago Press, 1951), 135–70; Earl Morse Wilbur, *A History of Unitarianism: Socinianism and its Antecedents* (Cambridge: Harvard University Press, 1945); Wilbur, *A History of Unitarianism in Transylvania, England, and America*, 16–43; Wilbur, *Our Unitarian Heritage: An Introduction to the History of the Unitarian Movement* (Boston: Beacon Press, 1925), 148–80.

52. See Wilbur, *A History of Unitarianism in Transylvania, England, and America,* 185–343; Wilbur, *Our Unitarian Heritage,* 285–388; Parke, *The Epic of Unitarianism,* 29–39, 44–46.

53. See Joseph Priestley, *An History of the Corruptions of Christianity,* 2 vols. (Birmingham: J. Johnson, 1782); Priestley, *The Theological and Miscellaneous Works,* ed. John Towill Rutt, 23 vols. (London: G. Smallfield, 1818; reprint, New York: Kraus Reprint Co., 1972); Wilbur, *A History of Unitarianism in Transylvania, England, and America,* 289–315; Wright, *The Beginnings of Unitarianism in America,* 213–17; Ann D. Holt, *A Life of Joseph Priestley* (London: Oxford University Press, 1931), 145–79.

54. See James Freeman, *Sermons on Particular Occasions,* 3d ed. (Boston: Sewell Phelps, 1812); Henry Wilder Foote, "The Historical Background of the Present King's Chapel," *Journal of the Universalist Historical Society* 8, pt. 2 (1950); Joseph Priestley, *Unitarianism Explained and Defended* (Philadelphia: John Thompson, 1796); Henry Wilder Foote, *The Religion of Thomas Jefferson* (Boston: Beacon Press, 1960), 68–79.

55. Priestley, *An History of the Corruptions of Christianity,* 2:7–9, 28–29, 440–43; reprinted in Priestley, *The Theological and Miscellaneous Works,* 5; see citations and discussion in Parke, *The Epic of Unitarianism,* 47–50; Robinson, *The Unitarians and the Universalists,* 22–23.

56. Quotations from *An History of the Corruptions of Christianity* excerpted in Parke, *The Epic of Unitarianism,* 48–49.

57. William Ellery Channing, *A Letter to the Rev. Samuel C. Thacher, on the Aspersions Contained in a Late Number of the Panoplist, on the Ministers of Boston and the Vicinity,* 3d. ed. (Boston: Wells & Lilly, 1815); extracts reprinted in Channing, *Memoir of William Ellery Channing,* 1:289–301; original text reprinted as "A Letter to the Rev. Samuel C. Thacher," in *William Ellery Channing: Selected Writings,* ed. David Robinson (New York: Paulist Press, 1985), 39–69; quote on 46, 48, 62–63.

58. "A Letter to the Rev. Samuel C. Thacher," 48.

59. Ibid., 48–49.

60. Ibid., 50–51.

61. Ibid., 54–55, 57.

62. Ibid., 56.

63. William Ellery Channing, "The Spirit of Christ," 1817, reprinted in Channing, *Memoir of William Ellery Channing,* 1:363–64; Buckminster quoted in Eliza Buckminster Lee, *Memoirs of Rev. Joseph Buckminster, D.D., and of His Son Rev. Joseph Stevens Buckminster* (Boston: W. Crosby & H. P. Nichols, 1849), 336.

64. William Ellery Channing, "Extracts from Remarks on the Rev. Dr. Worcester's Letter to Mr. Channing," Aug. 1815, reprinted in *Memoir at William Ellery Channing,* 1:307, 309.

65. Ibid., 309–10.

66. William Ellery Channing, "Extracts from Remarks on the Rev. Dr. Worcester's Second Letter to Mr. Channing," Nov. 1815, reprinted in ibid., 310–11.

67. William Ellery Channing, "Unitarian Christianity," in Channing, *The Works of William E. Channing, D.D.,* 367–84. This sermon has been reprinted many times, sometimes in un-authorized versions. It is said to have circulated in the United States more widely in its time than any pamphlet except Tom Paine's *Common Sense.* For other reprints, see Conrad Wright, ed., *Three Prophets of Religious Liberalism: Channing-Emerson-Parker* (Boston: Unitarian Universalist Association, 1961), 47–89; Sydney E. Ahlstrom, ed., *Theology in America: The Major Protestant Voices from Puritanism to Neo-Orthodoxy* (Indianapolis: Bobbs-Merrill Co., 1967), 196–210; Robinson, ed., *William Ellery Channing: Selected Writings,* 70–102.

68. See Herbert B. Adams, *The Life and Writings of Jared Sparks, comprising Selections from his Journals and Correspondence,* 2 vols. (Boston: Houghton, Mifflin, 1893), 1:126–37; Conrad Wright, "Introduction," *Three Prophets of Religious Liberalism,* 9–11.

69. Channing, "Unitarian Christianity," in *The Works of William E. Channing, D.D.,* 367.

70. Joseph Stevens Buckminster, "Review of *A theoretick explanation of the science of sanctity, according to reason, scripture, common sense, and the analogy of things,* by Thomas Fessenden," *Monthly Anthology* 2 (1805): 413; Samuel Clarke, *The Scripture Doctrine of the Trinity, in Three Parts* (London: James Knapton, 1712); Channing, "Extracts from Remarks on the Rev. Dr. Worcester's Second Letter to Mr. Channing," 310; see Clarke, *Sermons on Several Subjects,* 2 vols. (London: John & Paul Knapton, 1738); Clarke, *The Leibniz-Clarke Correspondence* (New York: Barnes & Noble, 1984).

71. See Johann Gottfried Eichhorn, *Einleitung in das Neue Testament*, 2d ed., 3 vols. (Leipzig: Weidmannischen Buchhandlung, 1810–20); Johann Jacob Griesbach, *Vorlesungen über Hermeneutik des Neuen Testaments, mit Anwendung auf die Leidens und Auferstehungsgeschichte Christi*, ed. J. C. S. Steiner (Nuremberg: In der Zeh'schen Buchhandlung, 1815); Johann David Michaelis, *Einleitung in die göttlichen Schriften des Neuen Bundes*, 2 vols. (Göttingen: Jandenhoeck, 1777); Johann Georg Rosenmüller, *Scholia in Novum Testamentum*, 6th ed., 5 vols. (Nuremberg: in officina Felseckeriana, 1815–31).

72. Channing, "Unitarian Christianity," 368.

73. Ibid.

74. Ibid., 368–69.

75. Ibid., 369.

76. Ibid., 371–73.

77. Ibid., 376–77.

78. Ibid., 378–80.

79. Ibid., 382–84.

80. Moses Stuart, *Letters to the Rev. Wm. E. Channing, containing remarks on his Sermon recently Preached and Published at Baltimore*, 3d ed. (Andover, Mass.: Flagg & Gould, 1819); reprinted as "Letters to Dr. Channing on the Trinity" in Moses Stuart, *Miscellanies* (Andover, Mass.: Allen, Morrill, & Wardwell, 1846), 9–13, 29–43, quote on 175–76. Stuart's later edition (10–11) noted his original failure to grasp that Channing "admitted the divine authority of the Old Testament only in a very limited and qualified sense," and that Channing understood the New Testament to *contain* the Word of God.

81. Leonard Woods, *Letters to the Rev. William E. Channing, Containing Remarks on His Sermon, Recently Preached and Published at Baltimore at the Ordination of the Rev. J. Sparks* (Andover, Mass.: Flagg & Gould, 1820), 20–26, quote on 21–22.

82. Andrews Norton, "Review of Moses Stuart's *Letters to the Rev. Wm. E. Channing containing Remarks on his Sermon recently Preached and Published in Baltimore*," *Christian Disciple* 1 (1819): 316–33, 370–431 (reprinted, Boston: Wells & Lilly, 1819); Norton, *A Statement of Reasons for Not Believing the Doctrines of Trinitarians Respecting the Nature of God, and the Person of Christ* (Boston: Wells & Lilly, 1819); excerpts reprinted in *An American Reformation: A Documentary History of Unitarian Christianity*, 67–75, quotes on 68–69; see Norton, *Thoughts on True and False Religion* (Boston: Wells & Lilly, 1820).

83. Henry Ware, "The Nature of Man," in *Letters Addressed to Trinitarians and Calvinists, Occasioned by Dr. Woods' Letters to Unitarians* (Cambridge: Hilliard & Metcalf, 1820), excerpt reprinted in *An American Reformation*, 199–209, quotes on 204. See Ware, *Answer to Dr. Woods' Reply, in a Second Series of Letters Addressed to Trinitarians and Calvinists* (Cambridge: Hilliard & Metcalf, 1822); Ware, *Two Letters on the Genuineness of the verse, 1 John, v. 7, and on the Scriptural Argument for Unitarianism*, 2d ed. (Boston: J. W. Burditt, 1820); Ware, *A Postscript to the Second Series of Letters Addressed to Trinitarians and Calvinists, Occasioned by Dr. Woods' Letters to Unitarians* (Cambridge: Hilliard & Metcalf, 1823); Leonard Woods, *A Reply to Dr. Ware's Letters to Trinitarians and Calvinists* (Andover, Mass.: Flagg & Gould, 1821); Woods, *Remarks on Dr. Ware's Answer* (Andover, Mass.: Flagg & Gould, 1822); Channing, "Objections to Unitarian Christianity Considered," (1819), in *The Works of William E. Channing, D.D.*, 401–8.

84. On the parish/church distinction in New England Congregationalism, see Wilbur, *A History of Unitarianism in Transylvania, England, and America*, 431–32; court decision quoted in Albert E. Dunning, *Congregationalists in America* (New York: J. A. Hill, 1894), 302; cited in John von Rohr, *The Shaping of American Congregationalism, 1620–1957* (Cleveland: Pilgrim Press, 1992), 253; see Conrad Wright, "The Dedham Case Revisited," *The Unitarian Controversy: Essays on American Unitarian History* (Boston: Skinner House Books, 1994), 111–35.

85. "Furniture" quote in Robinson, *The Unitarians and the Universalists*, 37; Lyman Beecher quote in von Rohr, *The Shaping of American Congregationalism*, 253; Beecher Stowe quotes in Lyman Beecher, *The Autobiography of Lyman Beecher*, ed. Barbara M. Cross, 2 vols. (Cambridge: Harvard University Press, 1961), 2:81–82; figures on the Unitarian-Congregational split in Wilbur, *A History of Unitarianism in Transylvania, England, and America*, 432–33. On the formation of the American Unitarian Association, see William C. Gannett, *Ezra Stiles Gannett: Unitarian Minister in Boston, 1824–1871*

(Boston: Roberts Brothers, 1875), 97–104; George Willis Cooke, *Unitarianism in America* (Boston: American Unitarian Association, 1902), 106–36.

86. Ralph Waldo Emerson, "Historic Notes of Life and Letters in New England," reprinted in *The Complete Works of Ralph Waldo Emerson,* ed. Edward Waldo Emerson, 12 vols. (Boston: Houghton Mifflin & Co., 1903–4), 10:323–70, quote on 339–40; excerpt reprinted in *The Transcendentalists: An Anthology,* ed. Perry Miller (Cambridge: Harvard University Press, 1950), 494–502, quote on 500.

87. Theodore Parker, *An Humble Tribute to the Memory of William Ellery Channing, D.D.* (Boston: Charles C. Little & James Brown, 1842), 6.

88. "Address of Rev. Frederic H. Hedge," in *Services in Memory of Rev. William E. Channing, D.D., at the Arlington-Street Church, Boston, on Sunday Evening, October 6, 1867* (Boston: John Wilson & Son, 1867), 27. For discussion of this often-cited tribute, see Robinson, ed., *William Ellery Channing: Selected Writings,* 4–6.

89. Channing, "The Moral Argument Against Calvinism," (1820), in *The Works of William E. Channing, D.D.,* 459–68, quotes on 461, 468. Also reprinted in Robinson, *William Ellery Channing: Selected Writings,* 103–21.

90. William Ellery Channing, "The Evidences of Revealed Religion," (1821), in *The Works of William E. Channing, D.D.,* 220–32, quote on 225; also reprinted in *William Ellery Channing: Selected Writings,* 122–44. See Channing, "Evidences of Christianity," in *The Works of William E. Channing, D.D.,* 188–220; David Hume, *Enquiries Concerning Human Understanding and Concerning the Principles of Morals* (1777), ed. L. A. Selby-Bigge and Ph. H. Nidditch, 3d ed. (Oxford: Clarendon Press, 1975), 109–31.

91. Channing, "Evidences of Christianity," 193.

92. "To sacrifice" quote in William Ellery Channing, "Christianity a Rational Religion," in *The Works of William E. Channing, D.D.,* 233; latter quote in Channing, "Evidences of Christianity," 189–204, quote on 193.

93. Andrews Norton, *The Evidences of the Genuineness of the Gospels* 3 vols. (1, Boston: American Stationers' Company, 1837; 2 and 3, Cambridge: John Owen, 1844), 1:cxxxi–cxxxviii; Bancroft quoted in Orie W. Long, *Literary Pioneers* (Cambridge: Harvard University Press, 1935), 120–21; cited in Brown, *The Rise of Biblical Criticism in America, 1800–1870,* 43.

94. See Norton, *Thoughts on True and False Religion;* Norton, *Internal Evidences of the Genuineness of the Gospels* (Boston: Little, Brown, 1855); Norton, *The Pentateuch and its Relation to the Jewish and Christian Dispensations* (London: Longman, 1863); Ware, *An Inquiry into the Foundations, Evidences, and Truths of Religion* (Cambridge: James Munroe, 1842). On Norton as a person and scholar, see George H. Williams, ed., *The Harvard Divinity School: Its Place in Harvard University and in American Culture* (Boston: Beacon Press, 1954), 43–52; Howe, *The Unitarian Conscience,* 16.

95. See Henry Ware Jr., *On the Formation of the Christian Character, Addressed to Those who are Seeking to Lead a Religious Life* (Cambridge: James Munroe & Co., 1850); Ware Jr., *Hints on Extemporaneous Preaching* (Boston: Cummings, Hilliard, 1824); Ware Jr., *The Nature, Reality and Power of Christian Faith* (Boston: James Munroe & Co., 1837); Ware Jr., *The Works of Henry Ware, Jr.,* 4 vols. (Boston: James Munroe & Co., 1846–47). In December 1828, Emerson sought to assuage Ware's fears by explaining that for him, "our religion is nothing limited or partial, but of universal application." The following year he tried to assure Ware that he wasn't really a heretic. See Emerson's letters to Ware, December 30, 1828, and July 1, 1829, in *The Letters of Ralph Waldo Emerson,* ed. Ralph L. Rusk, 6 vols. (New York: Columbia University Press, 1939), 257, 273. On Ware's relationship with Emerson, see Ralph L. Rusk, *The Life of Ralph Waldo Emerson* (New York: Charles Scribner's Sons, 1949), 138–39; Robert D. Richardson Jr., *Emerson: The Mind on Fire* (Berkeley: University of California Press, 1995), 90–91.

96. Richardson, *Emerson: The Mind on Fire,* 11, 18–22; quote on 21; James Elliot Cabot, *A Memoir of Ralph Waldo Emerson,* 2 vols. (Boston: Houghton Mifflin, 1888), 1:40–42; on William Emerson's Christology, see Phyllis Cole, *Mary Moody Emerson and the Origins of Transcendentalism: A Family History* (New York: Oxford University Press, 1998), 125.

97. See Cole, *Mary Moody Emerson and the Origins of Transcendentalism,* 83–106, 123–24, 174; Mary Moody Emerson, *The Selected Letters of Mary Moody Emerson,* ed. Nancy Craig

Simmons (Athens: University of Georgia Press, 1993), critique of Emerson's "mixture of heathen greatness" in MME's Jan. 8, 1833, letter to Charles Chauncy Emerson, 330–31; Emerson's original version of the "except herself" quip was later elongated, in his journal, to say, "Aunt Mary wished everybody to be a Calvinist except herself; like Dr. Johnson's minister in the Hebrides who wished him to believe in Ossian, but did not himself." Journal GL entry of October/November 1861 in *The Journals and Miscellaneous Notebooks of Ralph Waldo Emerson,* ed. Linda Alladt, David W. Hill and Ruth H. Bennett, 16 vols. (Cambridge: Harvard University Press, 1982), 15:152. The latter reference was to Samuel Johnson. See Richardson, *Emerson: The Mind on Fire,* 20–28; Carlos Baker, *Emerson among the Eccentrics* (New York: Penguin Books, 1996), 17–22.

98. "Acquintance with his own heart" quote in Cole, *Mary Moody Emerson and the Origins of Transcendentalism,* 124, citing statement by Mary Wilder Van Schalkwyck, a close friend of Mary Emerson's. See Paul A. Varg, *Edward Everett: The Intellectual in the Turmoil of Politics* (Selinsgrove, Pa.: Susquehanna University Press, 1992); Paul Revere Frothingham, *Edward Everett, Orator and Statesman* (Boston: Houghton Mifflin Co., 1925); biographical introduction in Miller, ed., *The Transcendentalists,* 19–20; Richardson, *Emerson: The Mind on Fire,* 7.

99. Emerson, "Historic Notes of Life and Letters in New England," 10:330–31; excerpted in *The Transcendentalists,* 496–97; see Richardson, *Emerson: The Mind on Fire,* 13; Miller, ed., *The Transcendentalists,* 19–20. On the early mythical school tradition, see Christian Hartlich and Walter Sachs, *Der Ursprung des Mythosbegriffes in der modernen Bibelwissenschaft* (Tübingen: J. C. B. Mohr, 1952).

100. Wide World XIII entry, Apr. 18, 1824, *The Journals and Miscellaneous Notebooks of Ralph Waldo Emerson,* ed. William H. Gilman, Alfred R. Ferguson, Merrell R. Davis, 2:238–40; Gay Wilson Allen, *Waldo Emerson: A Biography* (New York: Viking Press, 1981), 39–59.

101. Wide World XIII entry, Apr. 18, 1824, *The Journals and Miscellaneous Notebooks of Ralph Waldo Emerson,* 2:238–39.

102. Quoted in Rusk, *The Life of Ralph Waldo Emerson,* 103.

103. Oct. 16, 1823, letter to Mary Moody Emerson, *The Letters of Ralph Waldo Emerson,* 1:138–39; see Channing, "Evidences of Christianity," in *The Works of William E. Channing, D.D.,* 188–220.

104. William Ellery Channing, "Remarks on the Character and Writings of John Milton," in *The Works of William E. Channing, D.D.,* 497–98, 503–9, 513.

105. William Ellery Channing, "Remarks on the Life and Character of Napoleon Bonaparte," in ibid., 522–59, quote on 541.

106. Emerson, "Historic Notes of Life and Letters in New England," 10:339.

107. William Ellery Channing, "Remarks on National Literature," in *The Works of William E. Channing, D.D.,* 124–38, quote on 135.

108. William Ellery Channing, "Likeness to God: Discourse at the Ordination of the Rev. F. A. Farley, Providence, R.I., 1828," in *The Works of William E. Channing, D.D.,* 293.

109. Quoted in Peabody, *Reminiscences of Rev. Wm. Ellery Channing, D.D.,* 365.

110. "God in us," Blotting Book III entry, July 15, 1831, in *The Journals and Miscellaneous Notebooks of Ralph Waldo Emerson,* ed. Wiliam H. Gilman and Alfred R. Ferguson (1963), 3:273; "God must be sought," Journal B entry, *The Journals and Miscellaneous Notebooks of Ralph Waldo Emerson,* Jan. 7, 1835, ed. Merton M. Sealts Jr. (1965), 5:5; "Make your own Bible," Journal B entry, July 21, 1836, ibid., 5:186.

111. Channing, "Likeness to God," 292–93.

112. Ibid., 293–94.

113. Ibid., 294.

114. Ibid., 296.

115. Ibid., 299.

116. William Ellery Channing, "Introductory Remarks," (1841), in *The Works of William E. Channing, D.D.,* 1.

117. See especially Channing, "War: Discourse Before the Congregational Ministers of Massachusetts, Boston, 1816," in ibid, 642–53; "War: Discourse Delivered Jan. 25, 1835," in ibid, 654–64; "Lecture on War," in ibid., 664–79.

118. William Ellery Channing, "Spiritual Freedom: Discourse preached at the Annual Election, May 26, 1830," in ibid., 173.

119. Ibid., 176.

120. Channing, *Memoir of William Ellery Channing*, 2:273, 275.

121. See ibid., 278–82; Brown, *William Ellery Channing*, 45–46.

122. Lydia Maria Child, *An Appeal in Favor of That Class of Americans Called Africans*, 2d ed. (1836; reprint, New York: Arno Press, 1968), 16; see Bruce Mills, *Cultural Reformations: Lydia Maria Child and the Literature of Reform* (Athens, Ga.: University of Georgia Press, 1994), 30–54.

123. Letter quoted in Channing, *Memoir of William Ellery Channing*, 2:283.

124. Samuel May, *Some Recollections of Our Antislavery Conflict* (Boston: Fields, Osgood, 1869), 172–74; reprinted in ibid., 2:284–86.

125. William Ellery Channing, *Slavery*, (1835), reprinted in *The Works of William E. Channing, D.D.*, 688–743, quotes on 691, 695, 703.

126. *Memoirs of John Quincy Adams: Comprising Portions of his Diary from 1795 to 1848*, ed. Charles F. Adams, 12 vols. (Philadelphia: J. B. Lippincott, 1874), 9:266; on Adams's role in overturning the "gag rule" on Congressional antislavery petitions in the 1830s, see William Lee Miller, *Arguing About Slavery: John Quincy Adams and the Great Battle in the United States Congress* (New York: Vintage Books, 1995).

127. Channing, "The Present Age: An Address delivered before the Mercantile Library Company of Philadelphia, May 11, 1841," in Channing, *The Works of William E. Channing, D.D.*, 159–72, quote on 170.

128. Channing to Harriet Martineau, July 28, 1836, reprinted in *Memoir of William Ellery Channing*, 2:304–5; Channing, "The Abolitionists: A Letter to James G. Birney," in *Works of William E. Channing, D.D.*, 743–52, quotes on 744.

129. Channing, "A Letter to the Hon. Henry Clay, On the Annexation of Texas to the United States," in *Works of William E. Channing, D.D.*, 752–81; for other Channing letters pertaining to "the Texas plot," see *Memoir of William Ellery Channing*, 2:305, 312–16; on the Faneuil Hall protest meeting, ibid., 2:319–32.

130. *The Complete Works of Ralph Waldo Emerson*, 10:352; see Channing, "On the Elevation of the Laboring Classes," (1840), and Channing, "The Present Age: An Address delivered before the Mercantile Library Company of Philadelphia, May 11, 1841," in *The Works of William E. Channing, D.D.*, 36–66, 159–72.

131. Brown, *William Ellery Channing*, 48–49, quote on 48; Edgell, *William Ellery Channing*, 43.

132. Channing, "Slavery," 725–37.

133. Ibid., 725, 728.

134. Channing, "The Abolitionists," 747–48; see Henry Mayer, *All on Fire: William Lloyd Garrison and the Abolition of Slavery* (New York: St. Martin's Griffin, 1998), 300–63.

135. Channing, "The Abolitionists," 747.

136. Channing, "Slavery," 732; "The Abolitionists," 748.

137. Channing, "Introductory Remarks," 8–9.

138. Channing, "Self-Culture: An Address Introductory to the Franklin Lectures, delivered at Boston, Sept. 1838," in *The Works of William E. Channing, D.D.*, 12–36, quote on 14.

139. Channing, "The Christian Ministry: Discourse at the Dedication of Divinity Hall, Cambridge, 1826," in ibid., 257–69, quote on 265.

140. Channing, "Introductory Remarks," 6.

141. Channing, "The Christian Ministry," 263, 265; Channing, "Self-Culture," 24; see William W. Fenn, "William Ellery Channing and the Growth of Spiritual Christianity," *Pioneers of Religious Liberty in America* (Boston: American Unitarian Association, 1903), 187–223.

Chapter 2: Subversive Intuitions

1. See Ralph Waldo Emerson letters to William Emerson, May 20, 1824; July 8, 1824; Sept. 12, 1824; Nov. 20, 1824; and notes on William Emerson's letters to RWE, *The Letters of Ralph Waldo Emerson*, ed. Ralph L. Rusk, 6 vols. (New York: Columbia University Press, 1939), 1:141–55; Ralph L. Rusk, *The Life of Ralph Waldo Emerson* (New York: Charles Scribner's Sons, 1949), 105–7.

2. See note 12 in *The Letters of Ralph Waldo Emerson*, 1:160–62; Rusk, *The Life of Ralph Waldo Emerson*, 112–13; Robert D. Richardson, *Emerson: The Mind on Fire* (Berkeley: University of California Press, 1995), 64–65.

3. Mary Moody Emerson to William Emerson, Dec. 11, 1825, *The Selected Letters of Mary Moody Emerson*, ed. Nancy Craig Simmons (Athens, Ga.: University of Georgia Press, 1993), 201–2.

4. Mary Moody Emerson to William Emerson, Mar. 21, 1826, ibid., 205–6.

5. Mary Moody Emerson to Ralph Waldo Emerson, Apr. 27, 1826, ibid., 208–9.

6. Rusk, *The Life of Ralph Waldo Emerson*, 115; "I know that I exist," Emerson to Mary Moody Emerson, June 15, 1826, cited in Richardson, *Emerson: The Mind on Fire*, 69; see Ralph Waldo Emerson letter to Mary Moody Emerson, Sept. 23, 1826, *The Letters of Ralph Waldo Emerson*, 1:174–75; Mary Moody Emerson to Ralph Waldo Emerson, Sept. 27, 1825, *The Selected Letters of Mary Moody Emerson*, 198–99; Mary Moody Emerson to William Emerson, Mar. 21, 1826, ibid., 207; Ralph Waldo Emerson, *The Complete Sermons of Ralph Waldo Emerson*, ed. Albert J. von Frank, Teresa Toulouse, Andrew Delbanco, and Ronald J. Bosco, 3 vols. (Columbia, Mo.: University of Missouri Press, 1989).

7. Emerson, Blotting Book Y, Oct. 9, 1829, *The Journals and Miscellaneous Notebooks of Ralph Waldo Emerson*, ed. William H. Gilman and Alfred R. Ferguson (1963), 3:164; Samuel Taylor Coleridge, *Aids to Reflection* (Burlington, Vt.: Chauncy Goodrich, 1829), quote on 257; reprints include *Aids to Reflection* (London: Bohn Library, 1913; and Port Washington, N.Y.: Kennikat Press, 1971); abridged edition in *Samuel Taylor Coleridge*, ed. H. J. Jackson (Oxford: Oxford University Press, 1985), 666–85.

8. Quotations in *Samuel Taylor Coleridge*, 672–73; see James Marsh, "Preliminary Essay" to Coleridge, *Aids to Reflection*, 8–41; Richardson, *Emerson: The Mind on Fire*, 92–93.

9. "Makes his own religion," Emerson sermon of Feb. 14, 1830, recorded in Blotting Book Y, Feb. 11, 1830, *The Journals and Miscellaneous Notebooks*, 3:179; "elevated conception," Blotting Book Y, Mar. 2, 1830, ibid., 3:182.

10. "God in us," Blotting Book III, July 15, 1831, ibid., 3:273; succeeding quotes from Blotting Book III, July 29, 1831, ibid., 3:279. Emerson used the latter material in his sermon of July 31, 1831.

11. "The simplest person," in Emerson, "The Over-Soul" (1841), reprinted in *The Essays of Ralph Waldo Emerson* (Cambridge: Harvard University Press, 1987), 173; "to demonstrate," Journal Q entry, July 11, 1833, *The Journals and Miscellaneous Notebooks*, ed. Alfred R. Ferguson (1964), 4:77.

12. Journal Q, of Sept. 1, 1833, *The Journals and Miscellaneous Notebooks*, 4:78–79.

13. Journal Q, Sept. 3, 1833, ibid., 4:83–84.

14. "Relation of the soul," Blotting Book PSI, June 20, 1831, ibid., 3:260; "Great religious shows," Blotting Book III, Oct. 27, 1833, ibid., 3:301.

15. Quotes from Journal Q, July 15, 1832, ibid., 4:30–31. For the text of Emerson's resignation letter of Sept. 11, 1832, see *The Letters of Ralph Waldo Emerson*, 1:355–57. In Feb. 1832, Mary Moody Emerson expressed her alarm that Emerson was apparently "at war with that angelic office." By the following summer she was so disheartened by his apparent determination to leave the ministry that she bade him farewell, though only for a time. See Mary Moody Emerson to Ralph Waldo Emerson, Feb. 1832 and July 15, 1832, *The Selected Letters of Mary Moody Emerson*, 313–14, 318. See Rusk, *Ralph Waldo Emerson*, 151–67; Gay Wilson Allen, *Waldo Emerson: A Biography* (New York: Viking Press, 1981), 186–92.

16. See Victor Cousin, *Introduction a l'histoire de la philosophie*, 4th ed. (Paris: Didier et cie., 1861), 166–71; Cousin, *Leçons sur la philosophie de Kant* (Paris: Librairie Philosophique de Ladrange, 1844); Cousin, *Philosophie de Locke*, 4th ed. (Paris: Didier et cie., 1861); Cousin, *Elements of Psychology, Included in a Critical Examination of Locke's Essay on the Human Understanding*, trans. Caleb Sprague Henry, 3d. ed. (New York: Dayton & Saxton, 1842).

17. See Marsh, "Preliminary Essay," 12–52; excerpts reprinted in *The Transcendentalists: An Anthology*, ed. Perry Miller (Cambridge: Harvard University Press, 1950), 34–39, quotes on 38–39. See John J. Duffy, ed., *Coleridge's American Disciples: The Selected Correspondence of James Marsh* (Amherst, Mass.: University of Massachusetts Press, 1973), 75–154; Noah Porter, "Coleridge and His American Disciples," *Bibliotheca Sacra* 4 (1847): 117–71; Peter Carafiol, *Transcendent Reason: James Marsh and the Forms of Romantic Thought* (Gainesville, Fla.: University Presses of Florida, 1982).

18. See Stephen Prickett, *Romanticism and Religion: The Tradition of Coleridge and Wordsworth in the Victorian Church* (Cambridge: Cambridge University Press, 1976); Prickett, *Words and The Word: Language, Poetics, and Biblical Interpretation* (Cambridge: Cambridge University Press, 1986), 132–48; J. D. Boulger, *Coleridge as Religious Thinker* (New Haven, Conn.: Yale University Press, 1961); Fuller quoted in *The Transcendentalists,* 35.

19. Frederic Henry Hedge, "Coleridge," *The Christian Examiner* 14 (Mar. 1833): 109–29; excerpts reprinted in *The Transcendentalists,* 66–72, quotes on 69.

20. Quotes in "Coleridge," *The Christian Examiner,* 121, 124, 125; Hedge's "nature and Intelligence" phrase reversed in last quote, following Richardson, to make Hedge's parallelism clear. See Richardson, *Emerson: The Mind on Fire,* 165–66; J. G. Fichte, *The Science of Knowledge* (1794), ed. and trans. Peter Heath and John Lachs (Cambridge: Cambridge University Press, 1982); F. W. J. Schelling, *System of Transcendental Idealism* (1800), trans. Peter Heath (Charlottesville, Va.: University Press of Virginia, 1978); Schelling, *Ideas for a Philosophy of Nature as Introduction to the Study of This Science* (1797), trans. Errol E. Harris and Peter Heath (Cambridge: Cambridge University Press, 1988).

21. "Leaping Logos," Ralph Waldo Emerson to Edward Bliss Emerson, Dec. 22, 1833, *The Letters of Ralph Waldo Emerson,* 1:401–2; closing quotes in Ralph Waldo Emerson to Edward Bliss Emerson, May 31, 1834, ibid., 1:412–13.

22. Frederic Henry Hedge to Mrs. Caroline Dall, Feb. 1, 1877, reprinted in Stanley M. Vogel, *German Literary Influences on the American Transcendentalists* (New Haven, Conn.: Yale University Press, 1955), 114–16. This letter contains Hedge's account of the membership and mechanics of the Transcendental Club. Andrews Norton, *The Evidences of the Genuineness of the Gospels,* 3 vols. (1, Boston: American Stationers' Company, John B. Russell, 1837; 2 and 3, Cambridge: John Owen, 1844), quote in 1:1; Hedge quoted in Richardson, *Emerson: The Mind on Fire,* 245.

23. See Octavius B. Frothingham, *Transcendentalism in New England: A History* (New York: G. P. Putnam's Sons, 1876; reprint, New York: Harper & Row, 1965), 105–41; Arthur M. Schlesinger Jr., *The Age of Jackson* (Boston: Little, Brown & Co., 1945), 359–60, 380–90; *Margaret Fuller: American Romantic,* ed. Perry Miller (Ithaca, N.Y.: Cornell University Press, 1963); Anne C. Rose, *Transcendentalism as a Social Movement, 1830–1850* (New Haven, Conn.: Yale University Press, 1981); Richardson, *Emerson: The Mind on Fire,* 245–51.

24. George Ripley, "Martineau's Rationale," *The Christian Examiner* 21 (Nov. 1836): 225–54; excerpt reprinted in *The Transcendentalists,* 129–32. See William Henry Furness, *Remarks on the Four Gospels* (Philadelphia: Carey, Lea, & Blanchard, 1836); Orestes A. Brownson, "New Views of Christianity, Society, and the Church," (1836); and George Ripley, "Discourses on the Philosophy of Religion Addressed to Doubters Who Wish to Believe," (1836), in *The Transcendentalists,* 114–23, 132–40.

25. George Ripley, "Schleiermacher as a Theologian," *The Christian Examiner* 20 (Mar. 1836): 1–46; excerpt reprinted in *The Transcendentalists,* 99–102; see Friedrich Schleiermacher, *On Religion: Addresses in Response to its Cultured Critics* (1799), trans. Terrence N. Tice (Richmond, Va.: John Knox Press, 1969), 39–47, 67–176; Schleiermacher, *The Christian Faith* (1830), eds. H. R. Mackintosh and J. S. Stewart (Edinburgh: T. & T. Clark, 1989), 5–83.

26. Ripley, "Martineau's Rationale," 132.

27. Andrews Norton, "Ripley's Martineau," letter to the editor, *The Boston Daily Advertiser* 42:13933 (Nov. 5, 1836); and Ripley, "To Andrews Norton," *The Boston Daily Advertiser* 42:13936 (Nov. 9, 1836); reprinted in *The Transcendentalists,* 159–60, 160–63.

28. Journal C, May 19, 1837, *The Journals and Miscellaneous Notebooks,* ed. Merton M. Sealts Jr., (1965), 5:329.

29. Journal C, Oct. 16, 1837, ibid., 5:398. Noyes served as Hancock Professor of Hebrew and Dexter Professor of Sacred Literature at Harvard 1840–68. See Noyes, *A New Translation of the Hebrew Prophets,* 3 vols. (Boston: James Munroe, 1837); Noyes, *A New Translation of the Book of Psalms* (Boston: James Munroe, 1846); Noyes, "Causes of the Decline of Interest in Critical Theology," *The Christian Examiner* 43 (1847): 325–44.

30. Journal C, Nov. 6, 1837, *The Journals and Miscellaneous Notebooks,* 5:424.

31. Journal C, Dec. 3, 1837, and Mar. 4, 1838, ibid., 5:442, 456.

32. Journal C, May 7, 1838, ibid., 5:324.

33. Journal C, Mar. 18, 1838, ibid., 5:463–64.

34. Mar. 21, 1838 letter of invitation to Emerson reprinted in *The Letters of Ralph Waldo Emerson,* 2:147.

35. See Moncure Daniel Conway, *Autobiography, Memories and Experiences,* 2 vols. (Boston: Houghton Mifflin Co., 1904), 1:169; Robert E. Burkholder, "Emerson, Kneeland, and the Divinity School Address," *American Literature* 58 (Mar. 1986): 1–14; Conrad Wright, *The Liberal Christians: Essays on American Unitarian History* (Boston: Beacon Press, 1970), 56–57; Wright, "Introduction" to *Three Prophets of Religious Liberalism: Channing-Emerson-Parker,* ed. Conrad Wright (Boston: Unitarian Universalist Association, 1961), 26–27; Allen, *Waldo Emerson,* 316.

36. Ralph Waldo Emerson, "The Divinity School Address: Delivered before the Senior Class at the Harvard Divinity School, Cambridge on July 15, 1838," reprinted in *Three Prophets of Religious Liberalism: Channing-Emerson-Parker,* 90–112, quotes on 90–91. This 1849 edition, containing Emerson's minor stylistic corrections but not the later corrections of James Elliot Cabot's 1884 "Riverside Edition" or the further-amended Centenary Edition of 1903, was published by Emerson under the title *Nature; Addresses, and Lectures* (Boston: James Munroe, 1849), 113–46. The 1849 edition is also reprinted in *Theology in America: The Major Protestant Voices from Puritanism to Neo-Orthodoxy,* ed. Sydney E. Ahlstrom (Indianapolis: Bobbs-Merrill Co., 1967), 296–316.

37. Journal B, July 27, 1835, *The Journals and Miscellaneous Notebooks,* 5:71–72.

38. Emerson, "The Divinity School Address," 96–97.

39. Ibid., 97–98.

40. Ibid., 97, 99, 101.

41. Ibid., 102–11, quotes on 105, 107, 108, 111. See Journal C entry of May 18, 1838, *The Journals and Miscellaneous Notebooks,* 5:500–1.

42. Andrews Norton, "The New School in Literature and Religion," *The Boston Daily Advertiser* 43:14475 (Aug. 27, 1838); reprinted in *The Transcendentalists,* 193–96, quotes on 193.

43. *The Transcendentalists,* 194–96.

44. "Emerson's Address," *The Christian Examiner* 25 (November 1838): 266–68; reprinted in *The Transcendentalists,* 196–98, quote on 197. Ware's sermon, "The Personality of the Deity," was preached on Sept. 23, 1838, as the third in a series of five doctrinal sermons. Henry Ware Jr., *The Works of Henry Ware, Jr.,* 4 vols. (Boston: James Munroe, 1846–47), 3:26–27, 39. On the day after Emerson's address, Ware told Emerson in a letter that because his teaching tended "to overthrow the authority and influence of Christianity," he looked "with anxiety and no little sorrow to the course which your mind has been taking." John Ware, *Memoir of the Life of Henry Ware, Jr.* (Boston: James Munroe, 1846), 395. For Emerson's respectful reply, see letter to Henry Ware Jr., July 28, 1838, *The Letters of Ralph Waldo Emerson,* 2:146–50.

45. Mary Moody Emerson to William Emerson, Sept. 30, 1838, *The Selected Letters of Mary Moody Emerson,* 394; remaining quotes collected in editorial notes corresponding to Emerson's 1838 letters in *The Letters of Ralph Waldo Emerson,* 2:148–49.

46. Orestes A. Brownson, "Emerson's Address," *The Boston Quarterly Review* 1 (Oct. 1838): 500–14; James Freeman Clarke and Christopher Pearse Cranch, "R. W. Emerson and the New School," *The Western Messenger* (Nov. 1838); both reprinted in *The Transcendentalists,* 198–200, 200–4, quote on 201. See Robert D. Habich, *Transcendentalism and the Western Messenger: A History of the Magazine and Its Contributors, 1835–1841* (London: Associated University Presses, 1985), 105–10. Theodore Parker's journal entry of July 15, 1838, reprinted in John Weiss, *Life and Correspondence of Theodore Parker,* 2 vols. (New York: D. Appleton & Co., 1864; reprint, Freeport, N.Y.: Books for Libraries Press, 1969), 1:113; letter to George E. Ellis quoted in Octavius Brooks Frothingham, *Theodore Parker, a Biography* (Boston: James R. Osgood & Co., 1874), 106. There are two editions of Parker's collected works: *The Collected Works of Theodore Parker,* ed. Frances P. Cobbe, 14 vols. (London: Trübner & Co., 1863–74); and *The Works of Theodore Parker,* 15 vols., Centenary Edition (Boston: American Unitarian Association, 1907–11). Both sets are riddled with textual inconsistencies and errors, however, and neither edition has adequate footnotes (the Cobbe edition has no footnotes or index at all). Closing quote on Emerson in Parker's late-life memoir, *Theodore Parker's Experience as a Minister* (Boston: Rufus Leighton Jr., 1859),

51; reprinted as "The Letter from Santa Cruz, Called 'Theodore Parker's Experience as a Minister,'" Appendix 2 in Weiss, *Life and Correspondence of Theodore Parker* 2:447–515, quote, 458–59.

47. Journal D, Oct. 19, 1838, *The Journals and Miscellaneous Notebooks,* ed. A. W. Plumstead and Harrison Hayford (1969), 7:110–11.

48. Ralph Waldo Emerson to Henry Ware Jr., Oct. 8, 1838, *The Letters of Ralph Waldo Emerson,* 2:166–67.

49. Andrews Norton, *A Discourse on the Latest Form of Infidelity; Delivered at the Request of the "Association of the Alumni of the Cambridge Theological School," on the 19th of July, 1839. With Notes* (1839), excerpts reprinted in *An American Reformation: A Documentary History of Unitarian Christianity,* ed. Sydney E. Ahlstrom, with Jonathan Sinclair Carey (Middletown, Conn.: Wesleyan University Press, 1985; reprint, San Francisco: International Scholars Publications, 1998); 445–61, quotes on 449, 458. See also reprinted excerpts in *The Transcendentalists,* 210–13.

50. Believing that the Gospel of Matthew must have been written originally in Hebrew, Norton judged that Matthew 1–2 was a later insertion by a Greek translator; see Andrews Norton, *The Evidences of the Genuineness of the Gospels,* 1:21–23; on other spurious passages, see ibid., 1:liii–xc. He believed that the apostolic books of the New Testament were the four Gospels, thirteen epistles of Paul, and the first epistles of John and Peter; see Norton, "On the Author of the Epistle to the Hebrews," *The Christian Examiner* 4 (1827): 495–519, and 6 (1829): 198–225, 330–47; on Moses and true religion, see *The Evidences of the Genuineness of the Gospels* 2:xlvii–xlviii; see discussion in Brown, *The Rise of Biblical Criticism in America, 1800–1870,* 91–93.

51. Orestes A. Brownson, "Norton's Evidence," *The Boston Quarterly Review* 2 (January 1839): 86–113; excerpts reprinted in *The Transcendentalists,* 205–9, quotes on 209. For his autobiographical account of his conversion from agnosticism to Unitarianism, see Orestes A. Brownson, *Charles Elwood: or, the Infidel Converted* (Boston: C. C. Little & J. Brown, 1840); for his account of his later conversion to Roman Catholicism, see Brownson, *The Convert: or, Leaves from My Experience* (New York: E. Dunigan & Brother, 1857). Brownson's key writings during his transcendental period were *New Views of Christianity, Society, and the Church* (Boston: C. C. Little & J. Brown, 1836) and *The Mediatorial Life of Jesus* (Boston: C. C. Little & J. Brown, 1842). For outside accounts of his life and thought, see Arthur M. Schlesinger Jr., *Orestes A. Brownson: A Pilgrim's Progress* (Boston: Little, Brown & Co., 1939); and Hugh Marshall, S.T., *Orestes Brownson and the American Republic* (Washington, D.C.: Catholic University of America Press, 1971).

52. George Ripley, *"The Latest Form of Infidelity Examined"* (1839), pamphlet excerpted in *The Transcendentalists,* 213–20, quotes on 214, 216, 217, 220. See Ripley, *Discourses on the Philosophy of Religion Addressed to Doubters Who Wish to Believe* (Boston: James Munroe, 1836).

53. See Weiss, *Life and Correspondence of Theodore Parker,* 1:2–48; Frothingham, *Theodore Parker: A Biography,* 1–66; Henry Steele Commager, *Theodore Parker* (Boston: Little, Brown & Co., 1936), 3–39; John White Chadwick, *Theodore Parker: Preacher and Reformer* (Boston: Houghton Mifflin Co., 1900), 5–65; Parker, *Theodore Parker's Experience as a Minister,* 36–39, quote on 36. For key examples of his early writings, especially on issues cited, see Theodore Parker, "The Alleged Mistake of the Apostles," *The Scriptural Interpreter* 5 (1835): 161–70; Parker, "How Ought the Bible to be Read?" *The Scriptural Interpreter* 6 (1836): 226–34; Parker, "The Laws of Moses," *The Scriptural Interpreter* 7 (1837): 5–23, 60–80, 103–14, 159–78, 210–27, 258–71. For his early sermons, see Theodore Parker, *West Roxbury Sermons by Theodore Parker, 1837–1838,* ed. Samuel J. Barrows (Boston: Roberts Brothers, 1892).

54. Parker to G. W. Ellis, Jan. 3, 1839; and journal entry of May 1840, both reprinted in Weiss, *Life and Correspondence of Theodore Parker,* 1:118–19, 155.

55. Theodore Parker, "D. F. Strauss's *Das Leben Jesu,*" *The Christian Examiner* 27 (July 1840): 273–316, quotes on 276, 314. See Strauss, *The Life of Jesus Critically Examined,* 4th ed. (1840), trans. George Eliot (Ramsey, N.J.: Sigler Press, 1994). On Parker's early fixation on Strauss's book, see Chadwick, *Theodore Parker: Preacher and Reformer,* 88. In Apr. 1838, Channing mused to Parker—"very archly"—that making Strauss available in English might

be a good job for one of Abner Kneeland's followers; Weiss, *Life and Correspondence of Theodore Parker*, 1:109. See Parker, "The Relation of the Bible to the Soul," *The Western Messenger* 8 (1840–41): 337–40, 388–96.

56. Theodore Parker (Levi Blodgett), *"The Previous Question between Mr. Andrews Norton and His Alumni, Moved and Handled in a Letter to All Those Gentlemen"* (Boston: Weeks, Jordan, & Co., 1840), pamphlet reprinted as an appendix in John Edward Dirks, *The Critical Theology of Theodore Parker* (New York: Columbia University Press, 1948), 137–59, quotes on 137, 139.

57. *The Previous Question,* 140–41.

58. Ibid., 143–44, 151.

59. Ibid., 152–54.

60. Ibid., 158–59.

61. George Ripley, "Letter to the Church in Purchase Street," (Oct. 1, 1840); reprinted in *The Transcendentalists,* 252–53.

62. Ripley, "A Farewell Discourse," (Mar. 28, 1841), reprinted in ibid., 259; see Ripley, *The Claims of the Age on the Work of the Evangelist: A Sermon Preached at the Ordination of Mr. John Sullivan Dwight, as Pastor of the Second Congregational Church in Northampton, May 20, 1840* (Boston: Weeks, Jordan, & Co., 1840); Octavius Brooks Frothingham, *George Ripley* (Boston: Houghton Mifflin, 1882).

63. Journal entry of Dec. 5, 1840, reprinted in *Life and Correspondence of Theodore Parker*, 1:158.

64. Theodore Parker, *The Transient and Permanent in Christianity: Delivered at the Ordination of Rev. Charles C. Shackford in the Hawes Place Church, Boston on May 19, 1841,* pamphlet reprinted in Parker, *Critical and Miscellaneous Writings* (Boston: Horace B. Fuller, 1843); this edition reprinted in *Three Prophets of Religious Liberalism: Channing-Emerson-Parker,* 113–49, quote on 118.

65. Parker, *The Transient and Permanent in Christianity,* 140.

66. Ibid., 125–26.

67. Ibid., 126–27, 130.

68. Ibid., 131.

69. Ibid., 132–33.

70. Theodore Parker to Miss C. W. Healey, Dec. 3, 1841, reprinted in *Life and Correspondence of Theodore Parker,* 1:175.

71. Citation from a statement by John Weiss, reprinted in ibid., 1:173.

72. Lothrop article of July 3, 1841, in *The Christian Register,* cited in editor's introduction, *Three Prophets of Religious Liberalism: Channing-Emerson-Parker,* 39–40.

73. Theodore Parker letter to Dr. Convers Francis, June 24, 1842, reprinted in *Life and Correspondence of Theodore Parker,* 1:183–84.

74. Theodore Parker journal entry of Jan. 23, 1843 reprinted in ibid., 1:188–91.

75. Ibid., 188–93; Parker letter to the Rev. Chandler Robbins, Jan. 27, 1843, reprinted in ibid., 1:193–95; Robbins and Parker letters reprinted in Frothingham, *Theodore Parker: A Biography,* 168–72. The standard account of the episode is in Frothingham's biography, 158–75; see also Commager, *Theodore Parker,* 87–90; Perry Miller, "Theodore Parker: Apostasy within Liberalism," *Harvard Theological Review* 54 (1961), 275–95; William R. Hutchinson, *The Transcendentalist Ministers* (New Haven, Conn.: Yale University Press, 1959), 115–20.

76. *Theodore Parker's Experience as a Minister,* 59; reprinted in *Life and Correspondence of Theodore Parker,* 2:462.

77. Journal entry of May 1840, reprinted in *Life and Correspondence of Theodore Parker,* 1:157.

78. Parker's edition of Wilhelm Martin Leberecht de Wette, *Lehrbuch der historisch-kritischen Einleitung in die kanonischen und apocryphischen Bücher des Alten Testaments,* was published as *A Critical and Historical Introduction to the Canonical Scriptures of the Old Testament from the German of Wilhelm Martin Leberecht De Wette,* 2 vols. (Boston: Charles C. Little & James Brown, 1843; reprint, 1850), quote on 1:4; for discussion of Leviticus, see 2:117–18. In his article "Theodore Parker: Apostasy within Liberalism," 275–95, Perry Miller argued that Parker's de Wette volume was published chiefly as a challenge to the Unitarians. Jerry Wayne Brown aptly notes, however, that Unitarians such as Norton and George R. Noyes were already as prepared as Parker to accept negative criticism of the Old Testament; for discussion of this point and Parker's de Wette volume, see Brown, *The Rise of Biblical Criticism in*

America, 1800–1870, 164–69; and Dirks, *The Critical Theology of Theodore Parker,* 33–40;
on de Wette, see Hans-Joachim Kraus, *Geschichte der historisch-kritischen Erforschung des Alten
Testaments* (Neukirchen Kreis Moers: Buchhandlung des Erziehungsvereins, 1956), 160–75.

79. Journal entry of May 1840, reprinted in *Life and Correspondence of Theodore Parker,* 1:157.

80. On Parker's disappointment at the lack of response to his de Wette volume, see his letter
of Sept. 28, 1845, to de Wette and his letter of Nov. 19, 1858, to George Ripley, both
reprinted in *Life and Correspondence of Theodore Parker,* 1:258–59, 401–3; "Some good
work" quote in Hannah E. Stevenson, "A Biographical Sketch," preface to fourth edition of
Theodore Parker, *A Discourse of Matters Pertaining to Religion* (New York: G. P. Putnam's
Sons, 1877; [first edition, 1842]), liii.

81. See Theodore Parker, *Theism, Atheism, and the Popular Theology* (Boston: Little, Brown &
Co., 1853).

82. *A Discourse of Matters Pertaining to Religion,* 3–5, 7.

83. Friedrich Schleiermacher, *The Christian Faith,* (second German edition, 1830), ed. H. R.
Mackintosh and J. S. Stewart (1928; reprint, Edinburgh: T. & T. Clark, 1968), 16; see
12–14, 31–34.

84. *A Discourse of Matters Pertaining to Religion,* 17.

85. Immanuel Kant, *Critique of Pure Reason* (first German edition, 1781), trans. Norman Kemp
Smith (London: Macmillan, 1933, reprint 1973), 65–91.

86. *Theodore Parker's Experience as a Minister,* 37–38.

87. See René Wellek, "The Minor Transcendentalists and German Philosophy," *The New
England Quarterly* 15 (1942): 652–80; Charles Follen, *The Works of Charles Follen with a
Memoir of His Life,* 5 vols. (Boston: Hilliard, Gray, & Company, 1842).

88. *A Discourse of Matters Pertaining to Religion,* 21–22.

89. Theodore Parker, "Transcendentalism," *The Works of Theodore Parker,* 6:3–8; reprinted in
Theodore Parker: American Transcendentalist, A Critical Essay and a Collection of his Writings
(Metuchen, N.J.: Scarecrow Press, 1973), 49–74; *A Discourse of Matters Pertaining to
Religion,* 19–24; Dirks, *The Critical Theology of Theodore Parker,* 77–82; George F.
Newbrough, "Reason and Understanding in the Works of Theodore Parker," *The South
Atlantic Quarterly* 47 (Jan. 1948): 64–75.

90. *A Discourse of Matters Pertaining to Religion,* 20.

91. Ibid., 22–23.

92. Ibid., 22.

93. Ibid., 20.

94. Parker, "Transcendentalism," 33; see *The Critical Theology of Theodore Parker,* 83–85.

95. *A Discourse of Matters Pertaining to Religion,* 28.

96. For a detailed analysis of this episode and Strauss's argument, see Gary Dorrien, *The Word as
True Myth: Interpreting Modern Theology* (Louisville, Ky.: Westminster John Knox Press,
1997), 31–45.

97. "True criticism" quote was the thesis of Strauss's dogmatics, which was published simultaneously with his fourth-edition *Life of Jesus Critically Examined.* David Friedrich Strauss, *Die
christliche Glaubenslehre in ihrer geschichtlichen Entwicklung und im Kampfe mit der modernen
Wissenschaft dargestellt,* 2 vols. (Tübingen: C. F. Osiander, 1840–41), 1:71.

98. Undated journal entry of 1841, reprinted in *Life and Correspondence of Theodore Parker,*
1:169.

99. *A Discourse of Matters Pertaining to Religion,* 22.

100. Ibid., 227, 232.

101. Ibid., 236–37, quotes on 241, 243.

102. Ibid., 251.

103. Ibid., 267, 260.

104. Ibid., 449, 433–34, 446.

105. Ibid., 440–41.

106. Ibid., 443.

107. Parker letter to "A Friend in Germany," June 5, 1847, reprinted in *Life and Correspondence
of Theodore Parker,* 1:270.

108. Ibid., 270–71.

109. See Theodore Parker, *A Letter to the People of the United States Touching the Matter of Slavery*
(1848), reprinted in *The Works of Theodore Parker,* 11:32–119.

110. Theodore Parker, "Speech at Faneuil Hall, Before the New England Anti-Slavery Convention, May 31, 1848," reprinted in Parker, *Speeches, Addresses, and Occasional Sermons,* 3 vols. (Boston: Horace B. Fuller, 1867), 2:344–59, quotes on 347, 349–50. See Parker, "A Speech at a Meeting of the American Anti-Slavery Society, to Celebrate the Abolition of Slavery by the French Republic, Apr. 6, 1848," ibid., 331–43.

111. Parker, "Speech at Faneuil Hall, Before the New England Anti-Slavery Convention," 349.

112. See Theodore Parker, "A Speech Delivered at the Anti-War Meeting in Faneuil Hall, Feb. 4, 1847"; Parker, "A sermon of the Mexican War, Preached at the Melodeon, on Sunday, June 25, 1848," reprinted in Parker, *Speeches, Addresses, and Occasional Sermons,* 2:113–26, 127–84; David B. Chesebrough, *Theodore Parker: Orator of Superior Ideas* (Westport, Conn.: Greenwood Press, 1999); Garry Wills, *Lincoln at Gettysburg: The Words That Remade America* (New York: Simon & Schuster, 1992), 107; Chadwick, *Theodore Parker: Preacher and Reformer,* 322–23.

113. *The Works of Theodore Parker,* Centenary Edition, 9:219–40, "wrong things" quote on 9:220; ibid., 7:352–71; excerpts reprinted in *Theodore Parker: An Anthology,* ed. Henry Steele Commager (Boston: Beacon Press, 1960), 241–48; Chesebrough, *Theodore Parker: Orator of Superior Ideas,* 48–49.

114. Theodore Parker, "John Brown and the Philosophy of Freedom," letter to Francis Jackson, Nov. 24, 1859, reprinted in ibid., 257–68, quotes on 259.

115. Editor's preface, *A Discourse of Matters Pertaining to Religion,* xiv–xv.

116. Quoted in editor's introduction, *Theodore Parker: An Anthology,* 5.

117. Quoted in Thornton Kirkland Lothrop, *Some Reminiscences of the Life of Samuel Kirkland Lothrop* (Cambridge, Mass.: John Wilson & Son, 1888), 202.

118. For the text of the preamble of the Constitution of the National Convention of Unitarian Churches, see *The Epic of Unitarianism: Original Writings from the History of Liberal Religion,* ed. David B. Parke (Boston: Starr King Press, 1957), 121–22.

119. Octavius Brooks Frothingham, *Recollections and Impressions, 1822–1890* (New York: G. P. Putnam's Sons, 1891), 115–22.

120. See Octavius Brooks Frothingham, *Transcendentalism in New England: A History;* Octavius Brooks Frothingham, *Boston Unitarianism, 1820–1840: A Study of the Life and Work of Nathaniel Langdon Frothingham* (New York: G. P. Putnam's Sons, 1890); Octavius Brooks Frothingham, *Beliefs of the Unbelievers and other discourses* (New York: G. P. Putnam's Sons, 1875).

121. Frothingham, *Recollections and Impressions,* 5, 33–34, 290.

122. Ibid., 54; see Frothingham, *Theodore Parker: A Biography,* 537–82.

123. See *Theodore Parker's Experience as a Minister,* 37–38.

124. Octavius Brooks Frothingham, *The Religion of Humanity* (New York: David G. Francis, 1873), 57–82, 98–109, 254–264; see *Prayers by Theodore Parker,* preface by Louisa M. Alcott (Boston: Roberts Brothers, 1892).

125. Francis E. Abbott, "Fifty Affirmations," reprinted in *The Epic of Unitarianism,* 123–25.

126. See Octavius Brooks Frothingham, *George Ripley;* Frothingham, *A Memoir of William Henry Channing* (Boston: Houghton, Mifflin, & Co., 1886; Frothingham, *Boston Unitarianism, 1820–1840.*

127. Frederic Henry Hedge, "Antisupernaturalism in the Pulpit" (1864), reprinted in *An American Reformation,* 419–31, quotes on 424.

128. Frederic Henry Hedge, *Reason in Religion* (Boston: Walker, Fuller & Co., 1865), 218–19; see Hedge, "Natural Religion," *The Christian Examiner* 52 (Jan. 1852): 117–36.

129. Quoted in Frothingham, *Recollections and Impressions,* 117.

130. Text of "A Humanist Manifesto," drafted by Roy Wood Sellars of the University of Michigan and signed by 34 intellectuals, including Harry Elmer Barnes, Edwin Arthur Burtt, John Dewey, A. Eustace Haydon, and John Herman Randall Jr., reprinted in *The Epic of Unitarianism,* 138–42; see James Eells, "Theodore Parker and the Naturalization of Religion," *Pioneers of Religious Liberty in America* (Boston: American Unitarian Association, 1903), 343–66.

131. Jack Mendelsohn, *Why I Am a Unitarian Universalist* (New York: Thomas Nelson & Sons, 1964), 65.

132. Joseph Henry Allen, *Our Liberal Movement in Theology: Chiefly as Shown in Recollections of the History of Unitarianism in New England* (Boston: Roberts Brothers, 1892; reprint, New York: Arno Press, 1972), 85–86, 90–113, quote on 125.

133. Ibid., 124–125.

134. Ibid., 127.

Chapter 3: Imagination Wording Forth

1. Noah Porter, "Horace Bushnell, A Memorial Sermon Preached in the Chapel of Yale College, Sunday, March 26th, 1876," *New Englander* 36 (January 1877): 152–69; Mary Bushnell Cheney, *Life and Letters of Horace Bushnell* (New York: Harper & Brothers, 1880; reprint, New York: Arno Press, 1969), 3–34. Noah Porter, Yale president and longtime colleague of Bushnell's, reported that Bushnell belonged to an infidel club as a youth; Mary Bushnell Cheney discounted the notion that her father was ever an infidel. Her memoir is invaluable for its extensive collection of letters, all but two of which were later destroyed. The Horace Bushnell Papers at Yale University Library, Divinity Library Special Collections, contains five Bushnell diaries that his daughter drew upon in her book, in addition to manuscript and published copies of Bushnell sermons and discourses. For a stylish, though flawed biography that emphasizes Bushnell's social context and ambitions, see Barbara M. Cross, *Horace Bushnell: Minister to a Changing America* (Chicago: University of Chicago Press, 1958), 1–20; for a more recent, well-researched biography, folksy and admiring, see Robert L. Edwards, *Of Singular Genius, Of Singular Grace: A Biography of Horace Bushnell* (Cleveland: Pilgrim Press, 1992), 1–20.

2. Horace Bushnell to John T. Sewall, undated, reprinted in Cheney, *Life and Letters,* 208.

3. Recollection by Robert McEwan quoted in ibid., 55–56.

4. Horace Bushnell, "The Dissolving of Doubts," 1871 sermon preached at Yale College Chapel, published in Bushnell, *Sermons on Living Subjects* (New York: Scribner, Armstrong & Company, 1872), 166–84; reprinted in Conrad Cherry, ed., *Horace Bushnell: Sermons* (New York: Paulist Press, 1985), 162–73 quotes, 168.

5. Ibid., quotes, 169.

6. See Nathaniel William Taylor, *Essays, Lectures, Etc. Upon Select Topics in Revealed Theology* (New York: Clark, Austin, & Smith, 1859); Sidney Earl Mead, *Nathaniel William Taylor (1786–1858): A Connecticut Liberal* (Chicago: University of Chicago Press, 1942), 95–157, "fifty year" estimate on 145; editor's introduction to "Nathaniel William Taylor: Theologian of New School Protestantism," in *Theology in America: The Major Protestant Voices From Puritanism to Neo-Orthodoxy,* ed. Sydney E. Ahlstrom (Indianapolis: Bobbs-Merrill Co., 1967), 211–13; John Herbert Giltner, *Moses Stuart: The Father of Biblical Science in America* (Atlanta: Scholars Press, 1988); Lyman Beecher, *The Autobiography of Lyman Beecher,* ed. Barbara M. Cross, 2 vols. (Cambridge: Harvard University Press, 1961); Stuart C. Henry, *Unvanquished Puritan: A Portrait of Lyman Beecher* (Grand Rapids: Wm. B. Eerdmans Publishing Co., 1973); Stephen Snyder, *Lyman Beecher and His Children: The Transformation of a Religious Tradition* (Brooklyn: Carlson Publishing, 1991).

7. Nathaniel William Taylor, *Regeneration the Beginning of Holiness in the Human Heart: A Sermon* (New Haven: Nathan Whiting, 1816); Taylor, "Review of Norton's Views of Calvinism," *Christian Spectator* 4 (1822): 299–318; John T. Wayland, *The Theological Department in Yale College, 1822–1858* (New York: Garland Publishing, 1987), 79–83.

8. Nathaniel William Taylor, "Review of Norton's Views of Calvinism," *Christian Spectator* 5 (1823): 196–224, quote on 216; Nathaniel William Taylor, *Concio ad Clerum. A Sermon Delivered in the Chapel of Yale College, 10 September 1828* (New Haven: Hezekiah Howe, 1828); reprinted in *Theology in America,* 213–49, quote on 215; see Taylor, *An Inquiry into the Nature of Sin: As Exhibited in Dr. Dwight's Theology* ([New Haven]: Hezekiah Howe, 1829); editor's introduction, *Horace Bushnell,* ed. H. Shelton Smith (New York: Oxford University Press, 1965), 14–15.

9. See Nathaniel W. Taylor, *Lectures on the Moral Government of God,* 2 vols. (New York: Clark, Austin, & Smith, 1859); Mead, *Nathaniel William Taylor, 1786–1858: A Connecticut Liberal,* 102–20; editor's introduction, *Horace Bushnell,* 15–16; Wayland, *The Theological Department in Yale College, 1822–1858,* 89–105.

10. Samuel Hopkins, *A System of Doctrines, Contained in Divine Revelation. Explained and Defended. Shewing Their Consistence and Connexion with Each Other. To Which Is Added, a Treatise on the Millennium,* 2 vols. (Boston: Thomas & Andrews, 1793), 2:98–129; Jonathan Edwards Jr., *The Necessity of Atonement, and the Consistency Between that and Free Grace, in Forgiveness: Illustrated in Three Sermons* (New Haven, Conn.: Meigs, Bowen, & Dana, 1785); Edwards A. Park, "The Rise of the Edwardean Theory of the Atonement: An Introductory Essay," in *The Atonement: Discourses and Treatises by Edwards, Smalley, Maxcy, Emmons,*

Griffin, Burge, and Weeks, ed. Park (Boston: Congregational Board of Publication, 1859), xi–xxxix; Joseph Haroutunian, *Piety Versus Moralism: The Passing of the New England Theology* (New York: Henry Holt, 1932; reprint, Hamden, Conn.: Archon Books, 1964), 157–76; Caleb Burge, *An Essay on the Scripture Doctrine of Atonement, Showing its Nature, its Necessity, and its Extent, to which is Added, an Appendix Containing Remarks on the Doctrine of Universal Salvation* (Hartford: Peter B. Gleason & Co., 1822); Frank Hugh Foster, *A Genetic History of the New England Theology* (Chicago: University of Chicago Press, 1907; reprint, New York: Russell & Russell, 1963), 107–61.

11. Park, "The Rise of the Edwardean Theory of the Atonement: An Introductory Essay," xi.

12. Burge, *An Essay on the Scripture Doctrine of Atonement,* 33–53, 116–21, 151–65, 241–55; citations and discussion in editor's introduction, *Horace Bushnell,* 19.

13. William Ellery Channing, "The Moral Argument Against Calvinism" (1820), *The Works of William E. Channing, D.D.* (Boston: American Unitarian Association, 1883), 468; judgments against rectoral doctrine in Channing, "Unitarian Christianity: Discourse at the Ordination of the Rev. Jared Sparks; Baltimore, 1819," ibid., 378–79; Burge, *An Essay on the Scripture Doctrine of Atonement,* 264–65.

14. "Relic" in Theodore Davenport Bacon, *Leonard Bacon, a Statesman in the Church* (New Haven, Conn.: Yale University Press, 1933), 318; cited in Mead, *Nathaniel William Taylor, 1786–1858,* 234; Noah Porter, "Dr. Taylor and His Theology," *The Semi-centennial Anniversary of the Divinity School of Yale College, May 15th and 16th, 1872* (New Haven, Conn.: Tuttle, Morehouse, & Taylor, 1872), 98–99; Taylor, *Lectures on the Moral Government of God,* 2:2–3.

15. Taylor, *Lectures on the Moral Government of God,* "structure of the mind" quote on 1:200; "the highest good" quote on 1:153; see Taylor, *Practical Sermons* (New York: Austin & Smith, 1858).

16. Alexis de Tocqueville, *Democracy in America,* trans. Henry Reeve, 2 vols. (New York: J. & H. G. Langley, 1840; reprint, New York: Vintage Books, 1990), 2:10–11; cited in Cross, *Horace Bushnell: Minister to a Changing America,* 15.

17. *Autobiography of Lyman Beecher* 1:252–53; Henry, *Unvanquished Puritan,* 69–83; Timothy Dwight, *Theology, Explained and Defended,* 4 vols. (Middletown, Conn.: Clark & Lyman, 1818), 4:123–44; Lyman Beecher, "The Republican Elements of the Old Testament," *Lectures on Political Atheism* (Boston: John P. Jewett & Co., 1852), 176–90; Timothy Dwight, *A Discourse in Two Parts, Delivered July 23, 1812, on the Public Fast* (New Haven: Howe & Deforest, 1812); citations and discussion in Conrad Cherry, *Nature and Religious Imagination: From Edwards to Bushnell* (Philadelphia: Fortress Press, 1980), 116–17, 127–28.

18. Taylor and Harvey quotes in Mead, *Nathaniel William Taylor,* 223–24; Bennet Tyler, *Letters on the Origin and Progress of the New Haven Theology* (New York: Robert Carter & Ezra Collier, 1837), 4–10. See Foster, *A Genetic History of the New England Theology,* 369–81; George N. Boardman, *The History of New England Theology* (New York: A. D. F. Randolph, 1899), 249–62.

19. Nathaniel William Taylor, *Dr. Taylor's Reply to Dr. Tyler's Examination* (Boston: Peirce & Parker, 1832); Boardman, *The History of New England Theology,* 253; *Autobiography of Lyman Beecher,* 2:160, 173–74, "indiscreet" quote on 158; Bacon and Munger quotes in Mead, *Nathaniel William Taylor,* 160, 164; White quote in Benjamin Wisner Bacon, *Theodore Thornton Munger, New England Minister* (New Haven: Yale University Press, 1913), 56. Munger also called Taylor "a genius in theology" who "makes you *feel* a few important truths *strongly.* He makes you think for yourself" (*Theodore Thornton Munger,* 73–74).

20. Quoted in Mead, *Nathaniel William Taylor,* 161. On Taylor's career and legacy, see Noah Porter, "Introduction" to Taylor, *Lectures on the Moral Government of God,* 1:iii–viii; Roland H. Bainton, *Yale and the Ministry* (New York: Harper & Brothers, 1957), 96–101; Wayland, *The Theological Department in Yale College, 1822–1858,* 84–86.

21. "Movements of the spirit" in Bushnell, "Natural Science and Moral Philosophy," divinity school term paper, MS at Yale Divinity School, cited in editor's introduction, *Horace Bushnell: Selected Writings on Language, Religion, and American Culture,* ed. David L. Smith (Chico, Calif.: Scholars Press, 1984), 8: "If we must have a philosophy, let it be one such as reveals itself in the spontaneous, we may almost say unconscious movements of the spirit. There is no other; and that is religion, Christianity itself." For discussion of Bushnell's thinking during his divinity school years, see Cheney, *Life and Letters,* 62–65.

22. See Cheney, *Life and Letters,* 62–63; Cross, *Horace Bushnell,* 19–20. Cheney quotes a Divinity School professor as recalling that as a student, Bushnell was consistently "t'other side" in theological discussions.

23. See Josiah Willard Gibbs, "Historical and Critical View of Cases in the Indo-German Language," *Quarterly Christian Spectator* 9 (1837): 109–34, 415–34; Gibbs, "On the Biblical Use of the word 'Son,'" *Quarterly Christian Spectator* 6 (March 1834): 156–59; William D. Whitney, *Language and the Study of Language* (New York: Charles Scribner & Co., 1869); see Muriel Rukeyser, *Willard Gibbs* (Garden City, N.Y.: Doubleday, 1942); Bainton, *Yale and the Ministry,* 87–90; Wayland, *The Theological Department in Yale College, 1822–1858,* 106–12.

24. Quoted in Timothy Dwight Jr., *Memories of Yale Life and Men, 1845–1899* (New York: Dodd, Mead, & Co., 1903), 265; frequently cited, as in Mead, *Nathaniel William Taylor,* 159; Brown, *The Rise of Biblical Criticism in America, 1800–1870,* 173; Wayland, *The Theological Department in Yale College, 1822–1858,* 120.

25. Josiah Willard Gibbs, "The Ante-Mosaic Origin of the Sabbath, and Septuple Times in the Pentateuch," *New Englander* 16 (August 1858): 691–95; Gibbs, "Biblical Criticism and Remarks," *American Biblical Repository* 2 (October 1839): 480–85; Gibbs, "Critical Miscellanies," *New Englander* 15 (November 1857): 666–74; Gibbs, "Common Version and Biblical Revision," *New Englander* 17 (May 1859): 489–528.

26. For discussions of this aspect of Bushnell's thinking in the context of American biblical scholarship of his time, see James O. Duke, *Horace Bushnell: On the Vitality of Biblical Language* (Chico, Calif.: Scholars Press, 1984), 6–10; Brown, *Biblical Criticism in America,* 179.

27. Josiah Willard Gibbs Sr., *Philological Studies with English Illustrations* (New Haven, Conn.: Durrie & Peck, 1857), 17–18.

28. Ibid., 15–16; see Gibbs, "Historical and Critical View of Cases in the Indo-German Language," 109–34; editor's introduction, *Horace Bushnell,* 36–37.

29. Gibbs, *Philological Studies with English Illustrations,* 197–98, 225–26.

30. On his divinity school paper, see Cheney, *Life and Letters,* 64–65; Bushnell statements about reading Coleridge quoted by William W. Patton and John T. Sewall in recollections reprinted in ibid., 207–9. These accounts contain some confusion about the period in question. In Patton's report, Bushnell recalled that he first studied Coleridge while he was "in college," but Sewall quotes Bushnell as recalling that his conversion of 1831 occurred "shortly after" his first attempt to understand *Aids to Reflection.* The later date makes greater sense, and coincides with the availability of Marsh's popular American edition.

31. Bushnell to Mary Bushnell, September 7, 1839, reprinted in Cheney, *Life and Letters,* 89–90. Bushnell later confessed that during his early career, "I did not really expect to remain in the ministry long. I thought if I could sometime be called to a professorship of moral philosophy, it would be a more satisfactory and higher field of exertion" (Horace Bushnell, *Twentieth Anniversary,* A Commemorative Discourse, Delivered in the North Church, of Hartford, May 22, 1853 [Hartford: Elihu Geer, 1853], 9).

32. See Horace Bushnell, *An Oration Pronounced Before the Society of Phi Beta Kappa, at New Haven on the Principles of National Greatness, August 15, 1837* (New Haven, Conn.: Herrick & Noyes, 1837), reprinted as "The True Wealth or Weal of Nations," in Bushnell, *Work and Play* (New York: Charles Scribner's Sons, 1903), 76–77; Bushnell, *A Discourse on the Moral Tendencies and Results of Human History, Delivered Before the Society of Alumni in Yale College, Wednesday, August 16, 1843* (New Haven: T. H. Pease, 1843); quotes in Bushnell to Mary Bushnell, September 7, 1839, 90. On Bushnell's relationship to the upper-class establishment of Hartford, see Cross, *Horace Bushnell,* 31–51; on the disestablishment of New England Protestant clergy in the mid-nineteenth century, see Ann Douglas, *The Feminization of American Culture* (New York: Alfred A. Knopf, 1977; reprint, New York: Noonday Press, 1998), 17–43.

33. Horace Bushnell, "Revelation," address delivered to the Porter Rhetorical Society of Andover Seminary, Sept. 3, 1839, MS in Yale Divinity School Library, 1–32; excerpts reprinted in Bushnell, *The Spirit in Man: Sermons and Selections* (New York: Charles Scribner's Sons, 1903), 357–59; and *Horace Bushnell: Selected Writings,* 29–31.

34. Bushnell, "Revelation," in *Horace Bushnell: Selected Writings,* 13, 16–18, 29–32. Bushnell's citations from Psalm 19:1–3 and William Wordsworth, "Intimations of Immortality from Recollections of Early Childhood," paraphrase of lines 113–14; see *Wordsworth: Poetical*

Works, ed. Thomas Hutchinson and Ernest De Selincourt (Oxford: Oxford University Press, 1936), 461.

35. See Jonathan Edwards, *Images or Shadows of Divine Things* (New Haven, Conn.: Yale University Press, 1948); Stephen J. Stein, "Jonathan Edwards and the Rainbow: Biblical Exegesis and Poetic Imagination," *New England Quarterly* 47 (Sept. 1974): 455–57; Mason Lowance, "'Images or Shadows of Divine Things' in the Thought of Jonathan Edwards," *Typology and Early American Literature,* ed. Sacvan Bercovitch (Ann Arbor: University of Michigan Press, 1972), 222–36; Perry Miller, *The New England Mind: The Seventeenth Century* (Cambridge: Harvard University Press, 1939), 207–35; Ralph Waldo Emerson, *Nature* (1836), reprinted in *The Selected Writings of Ralph Waldo Emerson,* ed. Brooks Atkinson (New York: Modern Library, 1950), 3–42, discussion of language in 14–20.

36. Bushnell to Mary Bushnell, September 7, 1839, *Life and Letters,* 90; ministry and church relations discussed in ibid., 92–93; and Theodore T. Munger, *Horace Bushnell: Preacher and Theologian* (Boston: Houghton, Mifflin & Company, 1899), 51–59.

37. Bushnell, *Twentieth Anniversary,* 13–14.

38. Horace Bushnell, *The Crisis of the Church,* Delivered at the North Church, Hartford, Conn. (Hartford: Daniel Burgess, 1835), 9–11, 18–36, quote on 18; Bushnell, "Taste and Fashion," *New Englander* 1 (Apr. 1843): 153–68; Bushnell, "The Natural History of the Yaguey Family," *Hours at Home* 2 (Mar. 1866): 413–18; "Christianizing" theme in Bushnell, "How to Be a Christian in Trade," reprinted in Bushnell, *Sermons on Living Subjects* (New York: Scribner, Armstrong, & Company, 1872), 243–67.

39. Horace Bushnell, *Politics under the Law of God,* A Discourse delivered in the North Congregational Church, Hartford; on the Annual Fast of 1844 (Hartford, Conn.: Edwin Hunt, 1844), 6–18, quote on 10; Letter from "Constans" (Horace Bushnell), "Reply to Dr. Taylor," *Christian Freeman* (Hartford), Dec. 12, 1844; see Bushnell, "American Politics," *American National Preacher* 14 (Dec. 1840): 189–204.

40. Horace Bushnell, *A Discourse on the Slavery Question,* Delivered in the North Church, Hartford, Thursday Evening, Jan. 10, 1839 (Hartford: Case, Tiffany, 1839), 6. For important examples of racially whitewashed Bushnellia, see *Life and Letters,* 78, 80; and Munger, *Horace Bushnell: Preacher and Theologian,* 45, 61. Throughout her memoir, Mary Bushnell Cheney noted her father's antislavery positions while carefully avoiding any reference to his racial views. (She evidently shared these views, however; see her "scale of being" quote on 466–67.) Munger portrayed Bushnell as a virtual abolitionist. The vast Bushnell literature of the social gospel era mostly ignored the race issue, as in the 1902 symposium, *Bushnell Centenary: Minutes of the General Association of Connecticut at the One Hundred and Ninety-Third Annual Meeting Held in Hartford, June 17, 18, 1902* (Hartford: Case, Lockwood, & Brainard Co., 1902), 15–121, and the texts listed in notes 156–58 below. Barbara Cross's handling of this issue was particularly unfortunate. Despite her general focus on Bushnell's social views and context, her 1958 biography gave only one paragraph to his anti-immigration prejudices and a single sentence to his antiblack racism; at the same time, this lone sentence attributed a viciously demeaning racism to Bushnell that he expressly repudiated; see Cross, *Horace Bushnell,* 41; and note 46 below.

41. Bushnell, *A Discourse on the Slavery Question,* 8, 10. See George M. Frederickson, *The Black Image in the White Mind: The Debate on Afro-American Character and Destiny, 1817–1914* (New York: Harper & Row, 1971), 155–56; Thomas F. Gossett, *Race: The History of an Idea in America* (Dallas: Southern Methodist University Press, 1963), 180, 185; Howard A. Barnes, "The Idea that Caused a War: Horace Bushnell *versus* Thomas Jefferson," *Journal of Church and State* 16 (winter 1974): 79–80.

42. Bushnell, *A Discourse on the Slavery Question,* 12, 17. See Charles C. Cole, "Horace Bushnell and the Slavery Question," *New England Quarterly* 23 (Mar. 1950): 19–30; Louis Weeks, "Horace Bushnell on Black America," *Religious Education* 68 (Jan.-Feb. 1973): 28–41; Ralph E. Luker, "Bushnell in Black and White: Evidences of the 'Racism' of Horace Bushnell," *New England Quarterly* 45 (Sept. 1972): 408–16.

43. "Essentially barbarous" in Horace Bushnell, *Barbarism the First Danger,* A Discourse for Home Missions (New York: American Home Mission Society, 1847), 18; reprinted in Bushnell, *Work and Play* (2d ed., New York: Charles Scribner's Sons, 1881); "made a farce" and "moral desolation" in Bushnell, *Politics under the Law of God,* 18; Fugitive Slave Law quote in Bushnell to Cyrus Bartol, May 6, 1851, *Life and Letters,* 248; see also 411,

447–48, 473–74; for discussions of Bushnell's opposition to the Missouri Compromise, the Fugitive Slave Law, and the Mexican War, see Edwards, *Of Singular Genius,* 63–64; Munger, *Horace Bushnell: Preacher and Theologian,* 60–61; and Cross, *Horace Bushnell,* 79–80.

44. "Walled in" in Horace Bushnell, "Respectable Sin," reprinted in Bushnell, *Sermons for the New Life* (New York: Charles Scribner & Co., 1858; rev. ed., 1899), 326–45, quotes on 330; "new and old" in Horace Bushnell, "Christian Comprehensiveness," *New Englander* 6 (1848), reprinted in Bushnell, *Building Eras in Religion* (New York: Charles Scribner's Sons, 1881), 386–459, quote on 421; see Bushnell, "Unconscious Prophecy," *The Spirit in Man: Sermons and Selections* (New York: Charles Scribner's Sons, 1903), 54–55; Irving H. Bartlett, "Bushnell, Cousin, and Comprehensive Christianity," *The Journal of Religion* (1957), 99–104; Robert L. Edwards, "Portrait of a People: Horace Bushnell's Hartford Congregation," in *Studies of the Church in History: Essays Honoring Robert S. Paul,* ed. Horton Davies (Allison Park, Pa.: Pickwick Press, 1983), 151–53; David E. Swift, *Black Prophets of Justice: Activist Clergy before the Civil War* (Baton Rouge, La.: Louisiana State University Press, 1989), 57–59.

45. Quotes in Bushnell, *A Discourse on the Slavery Question,* 12–13; closing demographic prediction in Horace Bushnell, *The Census and Slavery:* A Thanksgiving Discourse delivered in the Chapel at Clifton Springs, N.Y., 29 November 1860 (Hartford: L. E. Hunt, 1860), 4; see Bushnell, *The Northern Iron* (Hartford: E. Hunt & Son, 1854); Swift, *Black Prophets of Justice: Activist Clergy before the Civil War,* 216; Edwards, *Of Singular Genius, Of Singular Grace,* 53–54. For a strong abolitionist critique of Bushnell's race theorizing and antiabolitionism, see Francis Gillette, *A Review of the Rev. Horace Bushnell's Discourse on the Slavery Question Delivered in the North Church, Hartford, January 10, 1839* (Hartford: S. S. Cowles, 1839).

46. Horace Bushnell, *The Moral Uses of Dark Things* (New York: Charles Scribner & Co., 1868), 299–300.

47. Ibid., 300–1; Charles Cole's important article, "Horace Bushnell and the Slavery Question," unfortunately misconstrued Bushnell's position in *The Moral Uses of Dark Things,* 29–30. Ann Douglas's discussion of Bushnell's racism relied entirely on Cole's article and therefore repeated his seriously mistaken claim that Bushnell regarded blacks as "animals" not belonging to the human race; see *The Feminization of American Culture,* 34–35. Barbara Cross similarly claimed that Bushnell regarded blacks as "animals rather than human beings" (*Minister to a Changing America,* 41). These distorted interpretations were corrected by Luker, "Bushnell in Black and White," 408–16, but Luker wrongly failed to acknowledge that many of Bushnell's statements about blacks and other "aliens" were repugnant.

48. Bushnell, *The Moral Uses of Dark Things,* 316–17.

49. Bushnell, *A Discourse on the Slavery Question,* 21; Bushnell, "American Politics," 198–99.

50. Horace Bushnell, *Women's Suffrage: The Reform against Nature* (New York: Charles Scribner & Co., 1869), 51–54.

51. Ibid., 135–36; excerpts reprinted in *Horace Bushnell: Selected Writings on Language, Religion, and American Culture,* 167–73; see Bushnell to (daughter) Mary Bushnell, Oct. 6, 1845, *Life and Letters of Horace Bushnell,* 139–43; Barbara Welter, "The Cult of True Womanhood, 1820–860," *American Quarterly* 18 (1966), 151–74; Nancy F. Cott, *The Bonds of Womanhood: "Woman's Sphere" in New England, 1780–1835* (New Haven, Conn.: Yale University Press, 1977).

52. Horace Bushnell, "The Evangelical Alliance," *New Englander* 5 (Jan. 1847): 102–25; Bushnell, *Barbarism the First Danger,* 5–6, 23–25, "wild race" quote on 6; see Cross, *Horace Bushnell,* 81–82; *Life and Letters,* 107, 138. He could be nearly as rough on Anglicans; see Bushnell, "Review of the Errors of the Times," *New Englander* 2 (Jan. 1844): 143–75.

53. Horace Bushnell, *A Letter to His Holiness, Pope Gregory XVI,* dated Apr. 2, 1846 (London: Ward & Company, 1846); reprinted as "A Letter to the Pope among the Papists," *The Religious Herald* (Hartford), May 9, 1846; reprinted with original title in Bushnell, *Building Eras in Religion* (New York: Charles Scribner's Sons, 1881), 356–85, quotes on 358, 360, 363–64.

54. *Life and Letters,* 171–72; Munger, *Horace Bushnell: Preacher and Theologian,* 61–62.

55. Horace Bushnell, "The Spiritual Economy of Revivals of Religion," *Quarterly Christian Spectator* 10 (Feb. 1838): 131–48. This essay was reprinted in Bushnell's second edition of *Christian Nurture* after the book's first edition was suppressed by the Massachusetts Sabbath-

School Society; see Bushnell, *Views of Christian Nurture, and of Subjects Adjacent Thereto* (Hartford: Edwin Hunt, 1847), 123–46; also reprinted in Bushnell, *Building Eras in Religion*, 150–81. There are four versions of *Christian Nurture*. *Discourses on Christian Nurture* (1847) contained only two discourses; *Views of Christian Nurture, and of Subjects Adjacent Thereto* reprinted the original essays and also included Bushnell's polemical self-defense, "Argument for 'Discourses on Christian Nurture'" (49–121), and four additional articles: "Spiritual Economy of Revivals of Religion," "Growth, Not Conquest, the True Method of Christian Progress" (147–81), "The Organic Unity of the Family" (183–209), and "The Scene of the Pentecost, and a Christian Parish" (211–44). Bushnell's definitive version of the book, expanded and reworked, was published in 1860 under the title *Christian Nurture* (New York: Charles Scribner's Sons, 1860). In 1916, various anti-Semitic remarks were excised from the book's 1860 edition (New York: Charles Scribner's Sons, 1916, reprint 1923); this edition has been reprinted many times. "Grow up a Christian" principle in *Views of Christian Nurture*, 6; *Christian Nuture* (1923), 4–5.

56. For examples of 1830s cult of domesticity literature, see John S. C. Abbott, *The Child at Home, or, The Principles of Filial Duty Familiarly Illustrated* (New York: American Tract-Society, 1833); Abbott, *The Mother at Home, or, The Principles of Maternal Duty Familiarly Illustrated* (3d edition, Boston: Crocker & Brewster, 1833; enlarged edition, New York: Harper & Brothers, 1873); Gardiner Spring, *Hints to Parents: A Sermon on the Religious Education of Children* (New York: Jonathan Leavitt, John T. West, 1833); Lydia H. Sigourney, *Letters to Mothers on Their Various Important Duties and Privileges* (London: T. Tegg, 1839); Johann Heinrich Pestalozzi, *Letters of Pestalozzi on the Education of Infancy. Addressed to Mothers* (Boston: Carter & Hendee, 1830); "beginning to attract" in Bushnell, *Views of Christian Nurture*, 5; *Christian Nurture*, 7.

57. Bushnell, *Views of Christian Nurture*, 5, 8; *Christian Nurture*, 7.

58. Bushnell, *Views of Christian Nurture*, 21–22, 36–37, 183; *Christian Nurture*, 22, 27, 39. Bushnell's early organicism was mainly social, naturalistic, and based fundamentally on the family; see Bushnell, *Views of Christian Nurture*, 183–209; Conrad Cherry, "The Structure of Organic Thinking: Horace Bushnell's Approach to Language, Nature, and Nation," *Journal of the American Academy of Religion* 40 (Mar. 1972): 3–20; John H. Krahn, "Nurture versus Revival: Horace Bushnell on Religious Education," *Religious Education* 70 (July-Aug. 1975): 375–82; Howard A. Barnes, *Horace Bushnell and the Virtuous Republic* (Metuchen, N.J.: The American Theological Library Association and the Scarecrow Press, 1991), 32–43.

59. Bushnell, *Views of Christian Nurture*, 41; latter quotes in *Christian Nurture*, 261, 281. On the centrality of the family in Bushnell's program of nurture, see David S. Steward, "Bushnell's Nurture Process: An Exposition," *Religious Education* 64 (July 1969): 296–302; Garland Knott, "Bushnell Revisited," *Religious Education* 64 (July 1979): 291–95; Wesner Fallaw, "The Role of the Home in Religious Nurture," *Religious Education*, ed. Marvin J. Taylor (New York: Abingdon Press, 1960); David L. Smith, *Symbolism and Growth: The Religious Thought of Horace Bushnell* (Chico, Calif.: Scholars Press, 1981), 76–77.

60. Though her seminal work on this subject oddly ignored *Christian Nurture*, Ann Douglas identified Bushnell as a prominent example of the effeminate, influence-seeking, nineteenth-century cleric, weak in mind and body (she made a partial exception for Bushnell's mind), who specialized in polite speech, performed mostly for women, and depended upon the favor of privileged women for employment and social status. This portrait fit many of its objects better than Bushnell, as some of his defenders insist. Bushnell biographer Robert Edwards protests that Bushnell had "a thoroughly masculine personality." Without denying that the "feminization" thesis applies to many nineteenth-century Protestant clergy, he argues that "such a cultural change never affected" Bushnell, the rugged farm boy who loved vigorous outdoor work, mountain climbing, sailing, and the like. Regardless of how one interprets Bushnell's various illnesses, Edwards and Daniel Walker Howe are correct to protest that he had a vigorously masculine personality in many respects. At the same time, they miss what matters. *Christian Nurture* was a prime example of feminized religious discourse, notwithstanding Bushnell's masculine personal bearing and outdoor enthusiasms. It epitomized the religiosity of cultured mid-century New Englanders, mostly women, who preferred to be socialized into religious awareness by the tender sentiments of polite literature and preaching. See Douglas, *The Feminization of American Culture*, 52–54, 87–89, 127–30, 139–41; Daniel Walker Howe, "The Social Science of Horace Bushnell," *Journal of American History* 70 (Sept. 1983): 305–22; Edwards, *Of Singular Genius, Of Singular Grace*, 3.

61. Bushnell, *Views of Christian Nurture*, 41–42; *Christian Nurture*, 45, 50; see "Alleged Suppression of Dr. Bushnell's Book," *Boston Recorder* 32 (Oct. 7, 1847): 158.

62. Bennet Tyler, *A Letter to Rev. Bushnell which discusses his book "Discourses on Christian Nurture"* (East Windsor Hill, Mass.: Massachusetts Sabbath-School Society, 1847); Tyler, *Letters to the Rev. Horace Bushnell, D.D., Containing Strictures on his Book, Entitled "Views of Christian Nurture and of Subjects Adjacent Thereto"* (Hartford, Conn.: Brown & Parsons, 1848), seven letters, 5–80; editorial, "Review of Horace Bushnell's *Discourses on Christian Nurture,*" *Christian Observatory* 1 (July 1847): 323–30, quote, 323; T. F. C., "The Baptist and Pedobaptist Theories of Church Membership," *Christian Review* 12 (1847): 547, cited in Cross, *Horace Bushnell: Minister to a Changing America*, 71; Charles Hodge, "Bushnell on Christian Nurture," *Biblical Repertory and Princeton Review* 19 (October 1847): 502–39; John Williamson Nevin, "Educational Religion," *Weekly Messenger of the German Reformed Church* 12, New Series; four-part series (June 23, June 30, July 7, July 14, 1847); Noah Porter, "Bushnell on Christian Nurture," *New Englander* 6 (Jan. 1848): 120–47.

63. "Singular outrage" in Bushnell, *Views of Christian Nurture*, 245; Bushnell, *An Argument for "Discourses on Christian Nurture,"* Addressed to the Publishing Committee of the Massachusetts Sabbath-School Society (Hartford, Conn.: E. Hunt, 1847), reprinted in *Views of Christian Nurture*, "new day" quote on 121. The Theological Institute of Connecticut later evolved into Hartford Seminary.

64. Bushnell, *Views of Christian Nurture*, 149–50, 152, 168–69, "this outrage" quote on 245.

65. Bushnell, *Christian Nurture*, 165–89; Munger, *Horace Bushnell: Preacher and Theologian*, 51.

66. Bushnell, *Christian Nurture*, 175–77.

67. Horace Bushnell, *Christian Nurture*, 1860 edition, 203–4.

68. Bushnell, *Christian Nurture*, 177, 180. On the Dutch Boers, see Bushnell, *Barbarism the First Danger*, 23.

69. Bushnell, *Christian Nurture*, 181.

70. Recollection of Mary Bushnell, and Horace Bushnell to C. A. Bartol, July 19, 1847, both in *Life and Letters*, 184, 191; see Cyrus A. Bartol, *Discourses on the Christian Spirit and Life* (Boston: Wm. Crosby & H. P. Nichols, 1850; reprint, New York: Arno Press, 1972).

71. Account of Bushnell's mystical conversion experience in *Life and Letters*, 192.

72. Key examples of his postconversion preaching and lecturing are Bushnell, "Christ the Form of the Soul," sermon preached at North Church, Hartford, in Feb. 1848, published in Horace Bushnell, *The Spirit in Man, Sermons and Selections* (New York: Charles Scribner's Sons, 1903), 39–51; reprinted in Cherry, ed., *Horace Bushnell: Sermons*, 54–61; and Horace Bushnell, "Work and Play," speech delivered before the society of Phi Beta Kappa at Harvard on Aug. 24, 1848, published in Bushnell, *Work and Play* (New York: Charles Scribner, 1864), 9–42. See Sereno E. Dwight, "Memoirs of Jonathan Edwards," *The Works of Jonathan Edwards*, 2 vols. (Carlisle, Pa.: Banner of Truth Trust, 1992), xlvi–xlviii.

73. Bushnell, "Christ the Form of the Soul," 55, 56, 59, 60.

74. "I seemed to pass" quoted in *Life and Letters of Horace Bushnell*, 192; Bartol's comparison of Bushnell to Channing, in Bartol to Mary Bushnell, undated, reprinted in ibid., 186.

75. Horace Bushnell, *God in Christ: Three Discourses, Delivered at New Haven, Cambridge, and Andover, with a Preliminary Dissertation on Language* (Hartford, Conn.: Brown & Parsons, 1849), 97, 116.

76. Theodore Parker, *A Discourse of Matters Pertaining to Religion* (New York: G. P. Putnam's Sons, 1877), 416; Bushnell, *God in Christ*, 30.

77. Bushnell, *God in Christ*, 40–43.

78. Ibid., 43–46, quote on 46.

79. Ibid., 46–47.

80. Ibid., 48–49, 56. On Bushnell's scriptural interpretations, see Duke, *Horace Bushnell on the Vitality of Biblical Language*, 23–87.

81. *God in Christ*, 56–57.

82. Ibid., 69.

83. Ibid., 69–70.

84. Ibid., 74–75.

85. See *Life and Letters*, 209, 499.

86. *God in Christ*, 87, 95, 96.

87. Ibid., 82, 99.

88. Ibid., 101, 106, 163; see 244–49, 343–47.

89. [Chauncy A. Goodrich], "What Does Dr. Bushnell Mean?," *The New York Evangelist* 20 (Mar. 29, 1849): 49–50; Enoch Pond, *Review of Dr. Bushnell's "God in Christ,"* (Bangor, Maine: E. F. Duren, 1849), 4–5, 22; David N. Lord, "Dr. Bushnell's 'Dissertation on Language,'" *Theological and Literary Journal* 2 (July 1849): 61–130, especially 69–76; David N. Lord, "Dr. Bushnell's Discourses," *Theological and Literary Journal* 2 (Oct. 1849): 173–222; Orestes A. Brownson, "Bushnell's Discourses," *Brownson's Quarterly Review* 3 (1849): 497–98.

90. Charles Hodge, "Bushnell's Discourses: Review of *God in Christ*, by Horace Bushnell," *Biblical Repertory and Princeton Review* 21 (Apr. 1849): 259–98, quotes on 264, 266–67, 298; see [J. H. Morison], "Bushnell's Discourses," *Christian Examiner and Religious Miscellany* 46 (Sept. 1849): 453–84; [Morison], "Replies to Horace Bushnell," *Christian Examiner and Religious Miscellany* 47 (Dec. 1849): 238–47; "Review of *God in Christ*," *Christian Observatory* 3 (June 1849): 329–30; "Bushnell's *God in Christ*," *Biblical Repository and Classical Review* 5 (Apr. 1849): 371–72.

91. Charles Hodge, "A Review of Recent Doctrinal and Ecclesiastical Conflicts in Connecticut," *Biblical Repertory and Princeton Review* 25 (Oct. 1853): 598–637; Edwin Pond Parker, *The Hartford Central Association and the Bushnell Controversy* (Hartford, Conn.: Case, Lockwood, & Brainard Co., 1896), 3–29. Bushnell's disillusionment with the church and human progress was expressed esp. in Bushnell, *Spiritual Dislodgements: A Sermon of Reunion,* preached in the North Church, Hartford, Feb. 22, 1857 (Hartford, Conn.: L. E. Hunt, 1857), 1–21.

92. "CC" [Amos S. Chesebrough], "No. 1. Do They Understand Him?" "No. 2. What Is Orthodoxy?" "No. 3. A Divine Person—What?" and seven additional articles reprinted in *Contributions of CC, Now Declared in Full as Criticus Criticorum* (Hartford: Brown & Parsons, 1849), 4–60, "speculations" quote on 11; Chesebrough recollections in Amos S. Chesebrough, "Reminiscences of Controversy," *Bushnell Centenary*, 50, 51, 52.

93. Bushnell to Henry Goodwin, May 26, 1851, *Life and Letters,* 248; Henry M. Goodwin, "Thoughts, Words, and Things," *Bibliotheca Sacra* 6 (May 1849): 271–300.

94. Bushnell conversation with Patton recounted in *Life and Letters,* 207–8; Bushnell to Cyrus Bartol, Nov. 18, 1851, reprinted in ibid., 250–51. For a thorough survey of the debates over Bushnell's theory of language, see Donald A. Crosby, *Horace Bushnell's Theory of Language in the Context of Other Nineteenth Century Philosophies of Language* (The Hague: Mouton, 1975), 229–86.

95. *Remonstrance and Complaint of the Association of Fairfield West to the Hartford Central Association, together with the Reply of the Hartford Central Association* (New York: Benedict, 1850), 15–19, 23–24; see Amos S. Chesebrough, "Reminiscences of the Bushnell Controversy," in *Bushnell Centenary,* 50.

96. Horace Bushnell, *Christ in Theology; Being the Answer of the Author, Before the Hartford Central Association of Ministers, October 1849, for the Doctrines of the Book Entitled "God In Christ"* (Hartford, Conn.: Brown and Parsons, 1851), 15. David L. Smith asserts that Bushnell could not have believed in intuitively known truth of any kind independent of communication, though Bushnell appeared to affirm exactly this as a narrowly limited possibility for consciousness in a precognitive, prediscursive state. See Bushnell, "The Immediate Knowledge of God," *Sermons on Living Subjects* (New York: Charles Scribner's Sons, 1890), 114–28; Smith, *Symbolism and Growth,* 135. Barbara Cross inexplicably claimed that Bushnell discarded his language theory shortly after 1848, though her book cited later writings in which Bushnell assumed and made use of it; see Cross, *Horace Bushnell,* 113.

97. Bushnell, *Christ in Theology,* 15.

98. Ibid., 16.

99. Ibid., "not my design," 16; "I was well aware," 34; "we must have," 64; "If it were possible," 66.

100. Ibid., 90.

101. *Appeal of the Association of Fairfield West, to the Associated Ministers Connected with the General Association of Connecticut* (New York: Printed for the Association of Fairfield West by Baker, Godwin & Co., 1852), 7, 11.

102. "Looked upon" and "this theory" quotes in Bushnell, *God in Christ,* 163, 154; on the anti-Nestorian New England background of this argument, see Foster, *A Genetic History of the New England Theology,* 409–10.

103. Bushnell, *Christ in Theology,* 99–100.

104. Hodge, "Bushnell's Discourses," 277–81; *Remonstrance and Complaint of the Association of Fairfield West, to the Hartford Central Association,* 9–10; *Appeal of the Association of Fairfield West,* 11. The Fairfield West conservatives accused Bushnell of three fundamental heresies: denial of the "tripersonality in the Divine nature," denial that Christ possessed a "reasonable" or human soul, and denial "that the sufferings and death of Christ are truly vicarious."

105. Munger argued that while Bushnell did not adopt Sabellianism as a theory of the mode of divine existence, he was essentially a Sabellian in his focus on the manifestation of God in Christ and his refusal to "go farther into deity than the Logos." Munger, *Horace Bushnell: Preacher and Theologian,* 123–24, 126–28. For similar readings of his position, see Williston Walker, "Dr. Bushnell as a Religious Leader," *Bushnell Centenary,* 27; Frank H. Foster, *The Modern Movement in American Theology: Sketches in the History of American Protestant Thought from the Civil War to the World War* (New York: Fleming H. Revell, 1939), 65.

106. This discussion was based on Schleiermacher's "On the Discrepancy between the Sabellian and Athanasian Method of Representing the Doctrine of the Trinity," translated and published with extensive commentary by Moses Stuart in the *Biblical Repository and Quarterly Review* 5 (Apr. 1835): 265–53, and 6 (July 1835): 1–116. Stuart's edition contained a lengthy orthodox rebuttal of Schleiermacher's interpretation of Trinitarian doctrine. Bushnell pictured Schleiermacher and Stuart as opposite sides of the same coin, since both took normative positions on the nature of the immanent Godhead.

107. Bushnell, *Christ in Theology,* "very tenor," 130; others 120–21.

108. Ibid., "feel obliged," 177; "dramatic show," 137; discussion of the Nicene Council, 177–87. On scholarship, "outspeaking" and his writing of *Christ in Theology,* see Bushnell to Cyrus Bartol, Mar. 10, 1851, in *Life and Letters,* 246–47; and recollection of the Rt. Rev. Thomas M. Clark, ibid., 20.

109. *Christ in Theology,* 172.

110. Ibid., 170, 175.

111. Ibid., 176–77, closing quotes, 186–87.

112. Horace Bushnell, "The Christian Trinity a Practical Truth," *New Englander* 12 (Nov. 1854), 485–509; reprinted in Bushnell, *Building Eras in Religion,* 106–49; quotes 118, 119–20.

113. *Building Eras in Religion,* 122.

114. Ibid., 145, 148. For discussions that, like the present account, interpret Bushnell's later theology as belonging to the tradition of classical Trinitarianism, see Fred Kirchenmann, "Horace Bushnell: Orthodox or Sabellian?" *Church History* 33 (Mar. 1964), 49–59; Bruce M. Stephens, *God's Last Metaphor: The Doctrine of the Trinity in New England Theology* (Chico, Calif.: Scholars Press, 1981), 63–74; *Horace Bushnell,* ed. H. Shelton Smith, 196–98.

115. See *Life and Letters,* 252–54; exchanges of letters between Bushnell and Joel Hawes, Mar. 20, 1854–Apr. 3, 1854, reprinted in ibid., 326–38. Not pertinent to the present discussion, but of historical interest is the fact that Bushnell and Finney shared a cordial friendship.

116. See ibid., 345–405; Edwards, *Of Singular Genius,* 3.

117. Bushnell to Henry M. Goodwin, *Life and Letters,* 420.

118. Horace Bushnell, *Nature and the Supernatural: As Together Constituting the One System of God* (New York: Charles Scribner's Sons, 1907), 320, 18.

119. See Bushnell, "The Christian Trinity a Practical Truth," 126–27; William A. Johnson, *Nature and the Supernatural in the Theology of Horace Bushnell,* Studia Theologica Lundensia, 25 (Lund: Gleerup, 1963), 143–65.

120. Bushnell, *Nature and the Supernatural,* 31; Samuel Taylor Coleridge, *Aids to Reflection* (Burlington, Vt: Chauncy Goodrich, 1829; reprint, Port Washington, N.Y.: Kennikat Press, 1971), 108–10, 236–37. Bushnell appropriated Coleridge's basic distinction between powers and things, but held a more positive view of the human will than Coleridge.

121. Bushnell, *Nature and the Supernatural,* 31–32.

122. Bushnell, "The Christian Trinity a Practical Truth," 127.

123. Bushnell, *Nature and the Supernatural,* 4–5. Bushnell reported that he spent an evening with Parker in June 1843, when they "went over the whole ground of theology together" (*Life and Letters,* 108).

124. *Nature and the Supernatural,* 5–6.

125. Ibid., 9–10.

126. Ibid., 10–11.

127. Ibid., 56–67.

128. Citations from Parker's *A Discourse of Matters Pertaining to Religion* quoted in *Nature and the Supernatural,* 130.

129. *Nature and the Supernatural,* 130–31.

130. Ibid., 173; see Bushnell, *Moral Uses of Dark Things,*

131. *Nature and the Supernatural,* 318–25, quote on 322.

132. Ibid., 336–337, 343.

133. Bushnell, *Christ in Theology,* 100; see *Nature and the Supernatural,* 263–318.

134. Bushnell, *Nature and the Supernatural,* 314–15, 479–80.

135. "Mustard seed" and "luminous" quotes in Bushnell, "Twentieth Anniversary," 8–9; Cyrus Bartol, "Dr. Furness and Dr. Bushnell: A Question of Words and Names," *Christian Examiner* 66 (Jan. 1859): 115, 118–21; Noah Porter, "Nature and the Supernatural," *New Englander* 17 (Feb. 1859): 224–58; John Williamson Nevin, "Notice of *Nature and the Supernatural,* by Horace Bushnell," *Mercersburg Review* (Apr. 1859), reprinted in Theodore Appel, *The Life and Work of John Williamson Nevin* (Philadelphia: Reformed Church Publishing House, 1889; reprint, New York: Arno Press, 1969), 529–50; David N. Lord, "Dr. Bushnell's Nature and the Supernatural," *Theological and Literary Journal* 11 (Jan. 1859): 529–76.

136. Horace Bushnell, *Sermons for the New Life* (New York: Charles Scribner, 1858); Henry M. Goodwin, "Dr. Bushnell's *Sermons for the New Life,*" New Englander 17 (May 1859): 382–99; see Goodwin, "Horace Bushnell," *New Englander* 39 (Dec. 1880): 803–27.

137. Bushnell to Henry Goodwin, *Life and Letters,* 420; Bushnell to Henry Bushnell, Dec. 3, 1858, ibid., 419–20.

138. Retirement comments in ibid., 441, and Bushnell to Mary Bushnell, Apr. 1, 1861, ibid., 450; "slave holding sections" in undesignated letter, Jan. 5, 1861, ibid., 443; remarks on Lincoln in Bushnell to Mary Bushnell, Feb. 26, 1861, and Mar. 7, 1861, ibid., 447–48.

139. Bushnell, *Nature and the Supernatural,* 506–8; "heaven-given thought" quote in Bushnell to Mary Bushnell, Jan. 29, 1861, *Life and Letters,* 445.

140. *Nature and the Supernatural,* 506–7; closing quote in Bushnell letter to a friend, Jan. 1, 1859, cited in *Life and Letters,* 422.

141. Bushnell to Mary Bushnell, Mar. 21, 1861 and Apr. 1, 1861, *Life and Letters,* 448–49.

142. Horace Bushnell, *Popular Government by Divine Right,* Delivered on the day of the National Thanksgiving, Nov. 24, 1864, in the South Church, Hartford (Hartford: L. E. Hunt, 1864); reprinted in Bushnell, *Building Eras in Religion,* 286–318, "horrid rebellion," ibid., 288; "shake off Providence" and "only blood," ibid., 310–11; "low regrets" statement to Cyrus Bartol, quoted in *Life and Letters,* 481; anti-Jeffersonian "bad politics" arguments in Horace Bushnell, *Reverses Needed, A Discourse Delivered on the Sunday after the Disaster of Bull Run, in the North Church, Hartford* (July 28, 1861) (Hartford: L. E. Hunt, 1861), 9–14. See Bushnell, "Our Obligations to the Dead," An oration given at the Commemorative Celebration held in New Haven, on Wednesday of Commencement Week, July 26, 1865, reprinted in *Building Eras in Religion,* 319–55; William A. Clebsch, "Christian Interpretations of the Civil War," *Church History* 30 (June 1961): 212–21.

143. Bushnell to Mary Bushnell, Jan. 29, 1861, *Life and Letters,* 445–46.

144. See Horace Bushnell, *Christ and His Salvation: In Sermons Variously Related Thereto* (New York: Charles Scribner & Co., 1864). On other themes, see Horace Bushnell, *Work and Play; or, Literary Varieties* (New York: Charles Scribner & Co., 1864); Bushnell, *Moral Uses of Dark Things;* Bushnell, *Women's Suffrage;* Bushnell, *Sermons on Living Subjects* (New York: Scribner, Armstrong, & Company, 1872); and Bushnell, *The Spirit in Man.*

145. Quote in Horace Bushnell, *The Vicarious Sacrifice, Grounded in Principles of Universal Obligation* (New York: Charles Scribner & Company, 1866), 33.

146. Ibid., 37.

147. Bushnell, *Christ in Theology,* 226–28.

148. Ibid., 228–29.

149. Ibid., 220. See *Atonement in Modern Religious Thought: A Theological Symposium* [articles from *Christian World,* 1899–1900] (London: James Clarke, 1900); Robert Macintosh, *Historic Theories of Atonement, with Comments* (London: Hodder & Stoughton, 1920).

150. Bushnell, *The Vicarious Sacrifice,* 29.

151. Bushnell, *Christ in Theology*, 233.

152. Ibid., 234–38, quote on 235–36.

153. Frederick Denison Maurice, *The Doctrine of Sacrifice Deduced from the Scriptures: A Series of Sermons* (London: Macmillan & Co., 1854), 194; see Maurice, *The Kingdom of Christ, or, Hints to a Quaker Respecting the Principles, Constitution, and Ordinances of the Catholic Church*, 2 vols., 2d ed. (1842; reprint, London: SCM Press, 1958); Maurice, *Theological Essays*, 1st ed. (1853; reprint, New York: Harper & Brothers, 1957).

154. Bushnell, *The Vicarious Sacrifice*, 73.

155. Ibid., 73; on Bushnell's "romantic anthropomorphism," see Thomas E. Jenkins, *The Character of God: Recovering the Lost Literary Power of American Protestantism* (New York: Oxford University Press, 1997), 125–28.

156. Bushnell, *Nature and the Supernatural*, 504; Bushnell, *The Vicarious Sacrifice*, 155.

157. Bushnell, *The Vicarious Sacrifice*, 213, 214, 215.

158. Ibid., 224–25, 227, 230.

159. Ibid., 341.

160. Horace Bushnell, "Our Gospel a Gift to the Imagination," *Hours at Home* 10 (Dec. 1869): 159–72; republished in Bushnell, *Building Eras in Religion*, 249–85, quotes on 261–63; also reprinted in *Horace Bushnell: Sermons*, ed. Conrad Cherry, 95–117. See Bushnell, *The Vicarious Sacrifice*, 449–523.

161. Horace Bushnell, *Forgiveness and Law, Grounded in Principles Interpreted by Human Analogies* (New York: Scribner, Armstrong, & Co., 1874), 12. This book was later republished as vol. 2 of Bushnell, *The Vicarious Sacrifice, Grounded in Principles Interpreted by Human Analogies*, 2 vols. (New York: Charles Scribner & Co., 1877); Bushnell to Mary Bushnell, Aug. 5, 1872, and Aug. 7, 1870, *Life and Letters*, 516, 526–27.

162. Bushnell, *Forgiveness and Law*, 10–11.

163. Ibid., 11–12, 62.

164. E. C. Towne, "The Vicarious Sacrifice," *Christian Examiner* 80 (Mar. 1866): 276–80; James Freeman Clarke, "Bushnell on Vicarious Sacrifice," *Christian Examiner* 80 (May 1866): 360–77; W. G. T. Shedd, "Bushnell on the Atonement," *American Theological Review* 8 (Jan. 1866): 169; Charles Hodge, "Bushnell on Vicarious Sacrifice," *Princeton Review* 38 (Apr. 1866): 161–94; Noah Porter, "Review of Dr. Bushnell on *The Vicarious Sacrifice*," *New Englander* 25 (Apr. 1866): 228–82; Henry James Sr., "Review of *The Vicarious Sacrifice*," *North American Review* 102 (Apr. 1866): 556–71; see "Review of *The Vicarious Sacrifice*, by Horace Bushnell," *New Englander* 25 (Jan. 1866): 160–62; Edwards Amasa Park, "Review of Horace Bushnell's *The Vicarious Sacrifice*," *Bibliotheca Sacra* 23 (Apr. 1866): 345–50; W. W. Andrews, *Remarks on Dr. Bushnell's "Vicarious Sacrifice"* (Hartford, Conn.: Case, Lockwood, 1866); Review of Bushnell's *Vicarious Sacrifice*, *Methodist Quarterly Review* 48 (July 1866): 350–70.

165. Bushnell to Amos Chesebrough, May 21, 1874, *Life and Letters*, 538–39. Barbara Cross quotes Theodore Munger as recalling that Bushnell isolated himself during this period, fixated "on his absorbing theme," but this was Munger's recollection of Bushnell's 1848 address at Yale on the divinity of Christ, when Munger was a college student. See Cross, *Horace Bushnell*, 136; Munger, *Horace Bushnell: Preacher and Theologian*, 116.

166. Washington Gladden, *Recollections* (Boston: Houghton Mifflin Co., 1909), 165.

167. The installation occurred on June 12, 1867; Gladden mistakenly reversed the sequence of events in his memoir, as shown in Jacob Henry Dorn, *Washington Gladden: Prophet of the Social Gospel* (Columbus, Ohio: Ohio State University Press, 1966), 43–44. Bushnell to Gladden, Nov. 2, 1867, is filed in the Washington Gladden Papers and Church Records, First Congregational Church archives, Columbus, Ohio. Citations in Gladden, *Recollections*, 119, 165–66; Bushnell's installation sermon, "The Gospel of the Face," was reprinted in Bushnell, *Sermons on Living Subjects*, 73–95.

168. Quotes in Gladden, *Recollections*, 165–66; see discussion in Dorn, *Washington Gladden: Prophet of the Social Gospel*, 44.

169. Munger, *Horace Bushnell: Preacher and Theologian*, 244; see John White Chadwick, "Munger's Bushnell," *The Nation* 69 (Oct. 10: 1899), 318; E. M. Chapman, "God's Way with a Soul: A Review of Dr. Munger's Horace Bushnell," *Congregationalist and Christian Mirror* 84 (Sept. 21, 1899): 396–97.

170. See Benjamin Wisner Bacon, *Theodore Thornton Munger, New England Minister* (New Haven, Conn.: Yale University Press, 1913), 201–34; Theodore Munger, *The Freedom of*

Faith (Boston: Houghton, Mifflin, and Co., 1883); Munger, "Horace Bushnell," *Christendom Anno Domini MDCCCCI: A Presentation of Christian Conditions,* ed. William D. Grant, 2 vols. (New York: Chauncy Holt, 1902), 2:120–27; Munger, "Horace Bushnell," *Prophets of the Christian Faith: A Series of Essays* (New York: Macmillan Co., 1896), 169–92; "Horace Bushnell: The Centenary of a Great Alumnus," *Yale Alumni Weekly* (Apr. 9, 1902).

171. Theodore Munger, "The Secret of Horace Bushnell," *Bushnell Centenary,* 35–46, "thought is not moving," quote on 45; reprinted in *Outlook* 71 (Aug. 30, 1902): 1063–68, and Munger, *Essays for the Day* (Boston: Houghton, Mifflin, & Company, 1904), 155–82; Munger, *Horace Bushnell: Preacher and Theologian,* 253, 258, 267; on Bushnell's discussion of the Fall, see *The Vicarious Sacrifice,* 250–51; on the ascendance of Bushnellian theology in the 1880s, see Charles Dole, "Horace Bushnell and His Work for Theology," *New World* 8 (Dec. 1899): 699–714; John C. Learned, "Dr. Bushnell," *Unity* 5 (July-Aug. 1880): 158–59, 177–79; Washington Gladden, "Horace Bushnell and Progressive Orthodoxy," *Pioneers of Religious Liberty in America* (Boston: American Unitarian Association, 1903), 227–63; John Wright Buckham, *Progressive Religious Thought in America: A Survey of the Enlarging Pilgrim Faith* (Boston: Houghton Mifflin Co., 1919), 3–52; George Gordon, *My Education and Religion: An Autobiography* (Boston: Houghton Mifflin, 1925), 214–15.

172. Horace Bushnell, "Science and Religion," *Putnam's Magazine* 1 (Mar. 1868): 265–75. When Darwin's theory is proved, Bushnell warned, "if that must be the fact, we may well enough agree to live without religion" (271); Munger, *Horace Bushnell: Preacher and Theologian,* 343–44.

173. See G. S. Drew, "An American Divine: Horace Bushnell," *Contemporary Review* 35 (Aug. 1879): 815–31; John Dyer, "Dr. Horace Bushnell," *Penn Monthly* 7 (Apr. 1876): 287–97; George Park Fisher, "Horace Bushnell," *International Review* 10 (Jan. 1881), 13–25; Cyrus A. Bartol, "Dr. Horace Bushnell and the Quandaries of Our Theology," *Unitarian Review* 14 (Sept. 1880): 236–48; C. C. Nott, "Dr. Bushnell," *The Nation* 31 (Aug. 9, 1880): 136–37; Walter Allen, "Horace Bushnell," *Atlantic Monthly* 85 (Mar. 1900): 415–25; Lewis O. Brastow, *Representative Modern Preachers* (New York: Hodder & Stoughton, 1904), 143–94; Williston Walker, "Dr. Bushnell as a Religious Leader," *Bushnell Centenary,* 15–34; Edwin Pond Parker, "Horace Bushnell—Christian Prophet," in *Bushnell Centenary,* 86–99; Lyman P. Powell, *Heavenly Heretics* (New York: G. P. Putnam's Sons, 1909), 79–109; Gladden letter to Theodore Munger, reprinted in Munger, *Horace Bushnell: Preacher and Theologian,* 375.

174. *Life and Letters,* 456; Horace Bushnell, "Inspiration by the Holy Spirit," uncompleted treatise begun in Jan. 1875, published in Bushnell, *The Spirit in Man. Sermons and Selections,* 7–33, definition of "inspirableness" and "inbreathes something," 7; excerpts reprinted in *Horace Bushnell: Sermons,* 37–54. For his description of the book, see Bushnell to George Bacon, Feb. 21, 1875, *Life and Letters,* 549.

175. Bushnell to daughter, probably Mary Bushnell, Jan. 5, 1861, reprinted *Life and Letters,* 443–44.

176. See Lyman Abbott, *Henry Ward Beecher* (Boston: Houghton, Mifflin, and Co., 1903), 100–32; Marie Caskey, *Chariot of Fire: Religion and the Beecher Family* (New Haven, Conn.: Yale University Press, 1978), 233–34, 268–74; Paxton Hibben, *Henry Ward Beecher: An American Portrait* (New York: George H. Doran, 1927), 129–30; Edwards, *Of Singular Genius,* 145–48; Clifford E. Clark Jr., *Henry Ward Beecher: Spokesman for a Middle-Class America* (Urbana, Ill: University of Illinois Press, 1978), 81–83.

177. Henry Ward Beecher, "The True Religion," reprinted in Beecher, *Sermons, Preached in Plymouth Church, Brooklyn, New York* (London: Richard D. Dickinson, 1871), 219, 223.

178. Bushnell, "Our Gospel a Gift to the Imagination," 271–72.

179. Ibid., 272, 280.

180. Ibid., 283, 284–85; Francis Turretin, *Institutes of Elenctic Theology,* trans. George Musgrave Giger, ed. James T. Dennison Jr., 3 vols. (1679; reprint, Phillipsburg, N.J.: Presbyterian & Reformed Publishing Co., 1992); John Bunyan, *The Pilgrim's Progress from This World to That Which is to Come,* 6th ed. (London: J. Paramore, 1787; reprint, London: J. F. Shaw and Company, 1910).

Chapter 4: Victorianism in Question

1. Population figures in Harold C. Syrett, *The City of Brooklyn, 1865–1898* (New York: Columbia University Press, 1944), 20; see Stephen M. Griswold, *Sixty Years with Plymouth*

Church (New York: F. H. Revell Co., 1907); Clifford E. Clark Jr., *Henry Ward Beecher: Spokesman for a Middle-Class America* (Urbana, Ill.: University of Illinois Press, 1978), 76–77.

2. Henry Ward Beecher, *New Star Papers, Views and Experience* (New York: Derby & Jackson, 1859), 219; see Herbert Hovenkamp, *Science and Religion in America, 1800–1860* (Philadelphia: University of Pennsylvania Press, 1978), 57–95, 165–86; William G. McLoughlin, *The Meaning of Henry Ward Beecher: An Essay on the Shifting Values of Mid-Victorian America, 1840–1870* (New York: Alfred A. Knopf, 1970), 35–36.

3. William C. Beecher and Samuel Scoville, assisted by Mr. Henry Ward Beecher, *A Biography of Rev. Henry Ward Beecher* (New York: Charles L. Webster & Co., 1888), 98–105, quote on 98; see Lyman Beecher, *A Reformation of Morals Practicable and Indispensable* (Andover, Mass.: Flagg & Gould, 1814); Forrest Wilson, *Crusader in Crinoline: The Life of Harriet Beecher Stowe* (Philadelphia: J. P. Lippincott, 1941); Joan D. Hedrick, *Harriet Beecher Stowe: A Life* (New York: Oxford University Press, 1994); Charles Edward Stowe and Lyman Beecher Stowe, *Harriet Beecher Stowe: The Story of Her Life* (Boston: Houghton Mifflin Co., 1911).

4. Harriet Beecher quoted in Edward Wagenknecht, *Harriet Beecher Stowe: The Known and the Unknown* (New York: Oxford University Press, 1965), 37; Henry Ward Beecher to Harriet Beecher, Apr. 5, 1832, cited in Clark, *Henry Ward Beecher,* 19; Beecher and Scoville, *A Biography of Rev. Henry Ward Beecher,* 123–35; Lyman Beecher, *The Autobiography of Lyman Beecher,* ed. Barbara M. Cross, 2 vols. (Cambridge: Harvard University Press, 1961), 2:167–206, 240–53; Lyman Beecher, *A Plea for the West* (Cincinnati: Truman & Smith, 1835); Wilson, *Crusader in Crinoline,* 147.

5. Lyman Beecher, *The Autobiography of Lyman Beecher,* 2:240–49, trustee quotes, 245, 246; Milton Rugoff, *The Beechers: An American Family in the Nineteenth Century* (New York: Harper & Row, 1981), 146–51; Robert Meredith, *The Politics of the Universe: Edward Beecher, Abolition, and Orthodoxy* (Nashville: Vanderbilt University Press, 1968), 85–86; J. Earl Thompson Jr., "Lyman Beecher's Long Road to Conservative Abolitionism," *Church History* 49 (Mar. 1973): 89–109; Gilbert H. Barnes, *The Anti-Slavery Impulse, 1830–1844* (New York: D. Appleton-Century, 1933), 74–75; Clark, *Henry Ward Beecher,* 22–23; Hedrick, *Harriet Beecher Stowe: A Life,* 102–3; James H. Fairchild, *Oberlin: The Colony and the College, 1833–1883* (Oberlin, Ohio: E. J. Goodrich, 1883), 50–66; Robert S. Fletcher, *A History of Oberlin College,* 2 vols. (Oberlin, Ohio: Oberlin College, 1943), 1:150–66.

6. Beecher and Scoville, *A Biography of Rev. Henry Ward Beecher,* 136–56; Rugoff, *The Beechers,* 165; Clark, *Henry Ward Beecher,* 24, 29–31; Lyman Abbott, *Henry Ward Beecher* (Boston: Houghton, Mifflin & Co., 1903), 46; see Lewis Tappan, *The Life of Arthur Tappan* (New York: Hurd & Houghton, 1870), 232–33.

7. Lyman Beecher, *The Autobiography of Lyman Beecher,* 2:81–82, 252; Theodore Bacon, *Leonard Bacon, A Statesman of the Church* (New Haven, Conn.: Yale University Press, 1931), 117–43; Clark, *Henry Ward Beecher,* 22; George Marsden, *The Evangelical Mind and the New School Experience* (New Haven, Conn.: Yale University Press, 1970).

8. Lyman Beecher, *The Autobiography of Lyman Beecher,* 2:265–71; Lyman Beecher, *Views in Theology* (Cincinnati: Truman & Smith, 1836); Lyman Beecher Stowe, *Saints, Sinners, and Beechers* (Indianapolis: Bobbs-Merrill Co., 1934), 336–40; Clark, *Henry Ward Beecher,* 35–36; Paxton Hibben, *Henry Ward Beecher: An American Portrait* (New York: George H. Doran Co., 1927), 70–71.

9. Citation from Beecher's 1888 address to London ministers quoted in Abbott, *Henry Ward Beecher,* 1–2.

10. Beecher and Scoville, *A Biography of Rev. Henry Ward Beecher,* 160–67; Clark, *Henry Ward Beecher,* 43–44.

11. Jane Shaffer Elsmere, *Henry Ward Beecher: The Indiana Years, 1837–1847* (Indianapolis: Indiana Historical Society, 1973), 8–75; John H. Thomas, *An Historical Sketch of the Presbyterian Church of Lawrenceburgh, Indiana* (Lawrenceburgh, Ind.: Sam Chapman, 1887), 8; Beecher and Scoville, *A Biography of Rev. Henry Ward Beecher,* 173–80; Mrs. Henry Ward Beecher, "Mr. Beecher as I Knew Him," *Ladies Home Journal* (Nov. 1891): 8–9.

12. Elsmere, *Henry Ward Beecher: The Indiana Years,* 76–86; see Hillis, "The Ruling Ideas of Henry Ward Beecher's Sermons," in Lyman Abbott, et al., *Henry Ward Beecher as His Friends Saw Him* (Boston: Pilgrim Press, 1904), 11–12.

13. Henry Ward Beecher, *Seven Lectures to Young Men on Various Important Subjects* (Indianapolis: Thomas B. Cutler, 1844), 156, 157.

14. Ibid., 133–34, 193.

15. Columns of *Indiana State Journal,* Jan. 28, 1846; Feb. 4, 1846; and Mar. 4, 1846, cited in Hibben, *Henry Ward Beecher,* 118–19; Beecher sermons of May 1846, Beecher Family Papers, Yale University, cited in Clark, *Henry Ward Beecher,* 66–68.

16. See Alfred G. Riddle, "Discovery of Henry Ward Beecher," *Magazine of Western History* 5 (Apr. 1887): 854–57; Elsmere, *Henry Ward Beecher: The Indiana Years,* 203–20.

17. "Everyone has" quote in Elsmere, *Henry Ward Beecher: The Indiana Years,* 90; Samuel Merrill to David Merrill, Nov. 14, 1840, ibid., 120; Eunice Beecher, "Mr. Beecher as I Knew Him," 11.

18. John L. Ketcham to David Merrill, Aug. 12, 1847, quoted in Elsmere, *Henry Ward Beecher: The Indiana Years,* 294; Eunice Beecher to Harriet Beecher Stowe, Dec. 27, 1846; and Eunice Beecher to Henry Ward Beecher, Mar. 3, 1847, quoted in Clark, *Henry Ward Beecher,* 64, 70; Mrs. Henry Ward Beecher, *From Dawn to Daylight, or, The Simple Story of a Western Home* (New York: Hurst & Co., 1900).

19. Records of the Second Presbyterian Church of Indianapolis, 83–84, quoted in Elsmere, *Henry Ward Beecher: The Indiana Years,* 292; Samuel Merrill to David Merrill, Sept. 5, 1847; and John L. Ketcham to David Merrill, Sept. 29, 1847, both quoted in ibid., 296, 297; see Joseph Howard Jr., *The Life of Henry Ward Beecher* (Toronto: J. S. Robertson, 1887), 131–32.

20. Beecher sermon, Oct. 11, 1847, and second parishioner quotation from John Raymond Howard, *Remembrance of Things Past: A Familiar Chronicle of Kinfolk and Friends Worth while* (New York: Thomas Y. Crowell Co., 1925), 48, both cited in Clark, *Henry Ward Beecher,* 77, 78; first parishioner quote in Constance Mayfield Rourke, *Trumpets of Jubilee: Henry Ward Beecher, Harriet Beecher Stowe, Lyman Beecher, Horace Greeley, P. T. Barnum* (New York: Harcourt, Brace & Co., 1927), 165; see Abbott, *Henry Ward Beecher,* 72–76.

21. Henry Ward Beecher to Harriet Beecher Stowe, undated, quoted in Clark, *Henry Ward Beecher,* 79; John Henry Barrrows, *Henry Ward Beecher: The Shakespeare of the Pulpit* (New York: Funk & Wagnalls Co., 1893), 108–14; Abbott, *Henry Ward Beecher,* 72–88.

22. Beecher, *Seven Lectures to Young Men on Various Important Subjects,* 116; Henry Ward Beecher to Harriet Beecher Stowe, undated letter, quoted in Clark, *Henry Ward Beecher,* 80.

23. Henry Ward Beecher to J. H. Raymond, Aug. 30, 1848, quoted in Clark, *Henry Ward Beecher,* 82.

24. Henry Ward Beecher to Thomas K. Beecher, Nov. 1848; and Beecher letter to unknown correspondent, Nov. 29, 1851, both quoted in ibid., 82, 85.

25. "Last week" quote in Abbott, *Henry Ward Beecher,* 394; "zig-zag" in Beecher and Scoville, *A Biography of Rev. Henry Ward Beecher,* 659; "fine feelings" in Henry Ward Beecher to Rev. Charles Jones, Oct. 22, 1852, quoted in Clark, *Henry Ward Beecher,* 83.

26. Beecher and Scoville, *A Biography of Rev. Henry Ward Beecher,* 223–24; Abbott, *Henry Ward Beecher,* 77–78; Rourke, *Trumpets of Jubilee,* 164–66, quote on 165.

27. Rourke, *Trumpets of Jubilee,* 168–69; Beecher quoted in Barrows, *Henry Ward Beecher, The Shakespeare of the Pulpit,* 119.

28. Charles Beecher to Harriet Beecher Stowe, May 1, 1848, quoted in Clark, *Henry Ward Beecher,* 88; see Hedrick, *Harriet Beecher Stowe: A Life,* 122–201; Thomas F. Gossett, *Uncle Tom's Cabin and American Culture* (Dallas: Southern Methodist University Press, 1985), 48–63, 87–99.

29. Editorial, "The Edmondson Sisters," *The Independent* 1 (Dec. 21, 1848): 1; *The Life of Harriet Beecher Stowe, Compiled from Her Letters and Journals,* ed. Charles Edward Stowe (Boston: Houghton, Mifflin & Co., 1891), 178–80; Beecher and Scoville, *A Biography of Rev. Henry Ward Beecher,* 292–94, quote on 293; Barrows, *Henry Ward Beecher,* 117–18; Harriet Beecher Stowe, *The Edmondson Family and the Capture of the Schooner Pearl* (Cincinnati: American Reform Tract and Book Society, 1856).

30. "Unreportable" quote, editorial comment, "Lecture by Henry Ward Beecher on 'Character,'" *The Independent* 3 (Jan. 16, 1851): 9; Frank Luther Mott, *A History of American Magazines, 1741–1905,* 4 vols. (Cambridge: Harvard University Press, 1938-1957), 3:457–72; Louis Filler, "Liberalism, Anti-Slavery, and the Founders of *The Independent,*" *New England Quarterly* 27 (Sept. 1954): 294–95.

31. Henry Ward Beecher, "The Fugitive Slave Bill at Its Work," *The Independent* 2 (Oct. 3, 1850): 162; Harriet Beecher Stowe to Henry Ward Beecher, undated letters quoted in Clark, *Henry Ward Beecher,* 94–95; Henry Ward Beecher, "Law and Conscience," *The Independent* 2 (Nov. 7, 1850): 1; see editorial, "How to Oppose the Fugitive Slave Law," *The Independent* 2 (Oct. 24, 1850): 174; Mott, *A History of American Magazines, 1741–1905,* 2:370; Clark, *Henry Ward Beecher,* 90–91.

32. "Have the plague" quote, Henry Ward Beecher, "Wendell Phillips," in Beecher, *Lectures and Orations by Henry Ward Beecher,* ed. Newell Dwight Hillis (New York: Fleming H. Revell Co., 1913), 216; Henry Ward Beecher, "American Slavery," *The Independent* 3 (May 13, 1851): 1; Clark, *Henry Ward Beecher,* 96; Harriet Beecher Stowe, *Uncle Tom's Cabin; or, Life Among the Lowly* (Boston: John P. Jewett & Co., 1852); closing Beecher quote in Barrows, *Henry Ward Beecher,* 166–67; see George Frederickson, *The Black Image in the White Mind: The Debate on Afro-American Character and Destiny, 1817–1914* (Middletown, Conn.: Wesleyan University Press, 1987); Leon Litwack, *North of Slavery, the Negro in the Free States, 1790–1860* (Chicago: University of Chicago Press, 1961).

33. Henry Ward Beecher, "Silence Must Be Nationalized," *The Independent* 6 (June 12, 1856): 1; Beecher and Scoville, *A Biography of Rev. Henry Ward Beecher,* 300–5; Clark, *Henry Ward Beecher,* 120–25; Abbott, *Henry Ward Beecher,* 199–222. In another work, Beecher's close ally and successor, Lyman Abbott, treated his leave of absence more evasively. In 1856, he wrote, Plymouth Church, "at the request of a number of eminent clergymen and others, voted him leave of absence to traverse the country in behalf of the cause of liberty, then felt to be in peril." In this case, the "cause of liberty" was a polite expression for political campaigning. Lyman Abbott and S. B. Halliday, *Henry Ward Beecher: A Sketch of His Career* (Hartford, Conn.: American Publishing Co., 1887), 47.

34. Henry Ward Beecher, "The Nation's Duty to Slavery," Oct. 30, 1859, reprinted in Beecher, *Freedom and War: Discourses on Topics Suggested by the Times* (Boston: Ticknor & Fields, 1863), 1–27, quotes on 6–7; Beecher, "Against a Compromise of Principle," reprinted in Beecher, *Freedom and War,* 28–56, quotes on 39.

35. Beecher, "Against a Compromise of Principle," 33, 40–41.

36. Henry Ward Beecher, "The Battle Set in Array," Apr. 14, 1861, reprinted in Beecher, *Freedom and War,* 84–110, quotes on 94, 95, 97, 103.

37. Ibid., 104; Henry Ward Beecher, "The National Flag," reprinted in Beecher, *Freedom and War,* 111–29, quotes on 120, 121; Hibben, *Henry Ward Beecher,* 182–83.

38. Henry Ward Beecher, "Modes and Duties of Emancipation," Nov. 26, 1861, reprinted in Beecher, *Freedom and War,* 174–99, "this conflict" quote on 188; Henry Ward Beecher, "The Country's Need," *The Independent* 14 (July 10, 1862): "gist" quote on 1; Henry Ward Beecher, "The Contrast," *The Independent* 14 (Sept. 11: 1862), 1; Thomas K. Beecher to Henry Ward Beecher, Aug. 10, 1862, and Harriet Beecher Stowe to Henry Ward Beecher, Nov. 2, 1862, cited in Clark, *Henry Ward Beecher,* 154, 155; Henry Ward Beecher, "National Injustice and Penalty," reprinted in Beecher, *Freedom and War,* 311–40, closing quotes, ibid., 335, 337.

39. "I toss to you," Theodore Tilton to Henry Ward Beecher, September 18, 1863, Beecher Family Papers, Yale University Library; "My Dear Bishop" was Tilton's usual salutation to Beecher in their written correspondence, for which he occasionally substituted "My Best of Friends," e.g., Tilton to Beecher, Aug. 9, 1863; Tilton to Beecher, Sept. 24, 1863, Beecher Family Papers; "I loved" quote from Tilton's cross-examination statement preceding the Beecher trial of 1875, reprinted in Charles F. Marshall, *The True History of the Beecher Scandal* (Philadelphia: National Publishing Co., 1874), 113. Hibben, *Henry Ward Beecher,* 167, 184–85; Clark, *Henry Ward Beecher,* 152–53; Barbara Goldsmith, *Other Powers: The Age of Suffrage, Spiritualism, and the Scandalous Victoria Woodhull* (New York: HarperCollins, 1998), 75; Richard Wightman Fox, *Trials of Intimacy: Love and Loss in the Beecher-Tilton Scandal* (Chicago: University of Chicago Press, 1999), 54, 374–75. Beecher's trial testimony discussed his kissing habits in some detail. On April 7, 1875, the *New York Graphic* responded editorially that Beecher apparently "kissed pretty nearly everybody, whether male or female, with whom he had any intercourse. The public will begin to ask whether the alleged seduction of Mrs. Tilton, or the confessed kissing of Theodore's mouth, was the more unbecoming a Christian minister" (quoted in Fox, *Trials of Intimacy,* 374–75).

40. "Golden" silence, Theodore Tilton to Henry Ward Beecher, Aug. 7, 1863, Beecher Family Papers; "a friend of mine," and "in New York" quotes in Tilton to Beecher, Aug. 7, 1863, sec-

ond letter of Aug. 7; "far stronger," Tilton to Beecher, Sept. 24, 1863; Tilton to Beecher, June 17, 1863; "the old man," "most popular," and Lincoln quotes in Tilton to Beecher, Sept. 18, 1863, Beecher Family Papers; Harriet Beecher Stowe, "Getting Ready for a Gale," *The Independent* 13 (Apr. 25, 1861), 1; Stowe, "To Our Readers," *The Independent* 13 (Dec. 5, 1861), Stowe, "Lazarus at the Gate," *The Independent* 14 (Aug. 7, 1862): 1.

41. *American Rebellion: Report of the Speeches of Henry Ward Beecher Delivered at Public Meetings in Manchester, Glasgow, Edinburgh, Liverpool, and London* (Manchester: Union and Emancipation Society, 1864), quotes on 55, 96, 149.

42. Henry Ward Beecher to Theodore Tilton, Oct. 18, 1863, reprinted in *Beecher-Tilton Investigation: The Scandal of the Age* (Philadelphia: Barclay & Co., 1874), 61–63; "Mr. Beecher's Own Account of the Speeches in England," in Henry Ward Beecher, *Patriotic Addresses in America and England, from 1850 to 1885, on Slavery and the Civil War, and the Development of Civil Liberty in the United States* (Boston: Pilgrim Press, 1887), 640–51; Oliver Wendell Holmes, "Our Minister Plenipotentiary," *The Atlantic Monthly* (January 1864), reprinted in Abbott and Halliday, *Henry Ward Beecher: A Sketch of His Career,* 404–11, quote on 409; Clark, *Henry Ward Beecher,* 158; Abbott, *Henry Ward Beecher,* 262; Barrows, *Henry Ward Beecher,* 330–44; E. D. Adams, *Great Britain and the American Civil War,* 2 vols. (New York: Russell & Russell, 1924), 2:184.

43. "My love for you," Theodore Tilton to Henry Ward Beecher, Aug. 7, 1863 (first letter), Beecher Family Papers; *Theodore Tilton vs. Henry Ward Beecher, City Court of Brooklyn, Verbatim Report by the Official Stenographer,* 3 vols. (New York: McDivitt, Campbell & Co., Law Publishers, 1875), 2: 737; Henry Bowen to Theodore Tilton, June 16, 1863, published in *The Brooklyn Eagle,* Jan. 21, 1875, cited in Goldsmith, *Other Powers,* 76.

44. "Wish to oblige" quoted in J. G. Randall and Richard N. Current, *Lincoln the President: Last Full Measure* (Urbana, Ill.: University of Illinois Press, 1955), 155; "wish to oblige" and Henry Ward Beecher to Robert Bonner, Feb. 8, 1864, cited in Clark, *Henry Ward Beecher,* 159, 161; Henry Ward Beecher, "Address at the Raising of the Union Flag over Fort Sumter, April 14, 1865," in Beecher, *Patriotic Addresses,* 676–97, quotes on 688, 689; Goldsmith, *Other Powers,* 93; William S. McFeely, *Yankee Stepfather: General O. O. Howard and the Freedmen* (New York: W. W. Norton & Co., 1968), 58–62.

45. Theodore Tilton to Henry Ward Beecher, Nov. 30, 1865, quoted in Beecher and Scoville, *A Biography of Rev. Henry Ward Beecher,* 489; Robert Bonner to Henry Ward Beecher, Apr. 22, 1865, quoted in Clark, *Henry Ward Beecher,* 170; Abbott, *Henry Ward Beecher,* 265–87; see Eric Foner, *Reconstruction: America's Unfinished Revolution, 1863–1877* (New York: Harper & Row, 1988), 1–34; John Hope Franklin, *Reconstruction after the Civil War* (Chicago: University of Chicago Press, 1994), 14–52.

46. Abraham Lincoln, "Fourth Lincoln-Douglas Debate, Charlestown, Illinois" (Sept. 18, 1858), in Abraham Lincoln, *Speeches and Writings, 1832–1858* (New York: Library of America, 1989), 636; see Rugoff, *The Beechers,* 395; Goldsmith, *Other Powers,* 119; Hibben, *Henry Ward Beecher,* 200–1; Abbott, *Henry Ward Beecher,* 266–87. Lincoln never found a satisfactory Latin American colony, though he seriously considered a province in Panama for a time; he opposed Liberia on account of climate and cost. See Thomas F. Gossett, *Race: The History of an Idea in America* (New York: Schocken Books, 1977), 254–55.

47. Editorial, "A Great Political Sermon," *The New York Times* (Oct. 24, 1865); [Tilton editorial], *The Independent* (Oct. 27, 1865), quotes and discussion in Goldsmith, *Other Powers,* 99.

48. Henry Ward Beecher, "Letter to the Convention," Aug. 30, 1866, reprinted in Beecher, *Patriotic Addresses,* 736–41, quotes on 740, 741; see Beecher, "Letter to a Parishioner," Sept. 8, 1866, ibid., 742–49.

49. Editorial, *The Independent* 18 (Sept. 6, 1866): 1; Harriet Beecher Stowe to Eunice Beecher, Sept. 23, 1866, quoted in Clark, 176; Abbott, *Henry Ward Beecher,* 282–87; Goldsmith, *Other Powers,* 119.

50. "No army," Henry Ward Beecher, "Letter to a Parishioner," Sept. 8, 1866, reprinted in Beecher, *Patriotic Addresses,* 742–49, quote on 742–43; "Not be seduced," Henry Ward Beecher sermon, Oct. 8, 1865, reprinted in *The Independent* 17 (Oct. 2, 1865): quoted in Hibben, *Henry Ward Beecher,* 196; Harriet Beecher Stowe to Henry Ward Beecher, Oct. 8, 1866, quoted in Clark, *Henry Ward Beecher,* 177; Beecher and Scoville, *A Biography of Rev. Henry Ward Beecher,* 464–78.

51. Robert Bonner to Henry Ward Beecher, Jan. 25, 1865, quoted in Clark, *Henry Ward Beecher,* 169; Beecher to Bonner, reprinted as preface to Henry Ward Beecher, *Norwood, or, Village*

Life in New England (reprint, New York: Charles Scribner & Co., 1887); cited in McLoughlin, *The Meaning of Henry Ward Beecher,* 63.

52. Henry Ward Beecher, *Norwood, or, Village Life in New England* (New York: Charles Scribner & Co., 1868), 21.

53. Ibid., 56–57, 58–59.

54. Ibid., 58, 60.

55. Ibid., 263–64.

56. Henry Ward Beecher, "The True Religion," published in Beecher, *Sermons, Preached in Plymouth Church, Brooklyn, New York* (London: Richard D. Dickinson, 1871), 205–35, quotes on 207, 211–12.

57. Ibid., 224, 233.

58. Henry Ward Beecher, "The Ideal of Christian Experience," in *Sermons, Preached in Plymouth Church, Brooklyn, New York,* 236–63, quotes on 249, 250.

59. Henry Ward Beecher, "Beauty," in *Sermons, Preached in Plymouth Church, Brooklyn, New York,* 119–43, quotes on 137, 138; see Henry Ward Beecher, *Plain and Pleasant Talk about Fruits, Flowers, and Farming* (New York: Derby & Jackson, 1859; rev. ed., New York: J. B. Ford, 1874).

60. Henry Ward Beecher, "Follow Thou Me," *Sermons, Preached in Plymouth Church, Brooklyn, New York,* 415–33, quotes on 431, 432.

61. Henry Ward Beecher, *Yale Lectures on Preaching,* 3 vols. (New York: J. B. Ford & Co., 1872, 1873, 1874; three volumes in one edition, Boston: Pilgrim Press, n.d.), 182.

62. Ibid., 183, 187, 189, 194. Beecher testimonials often made a considerable point of his physical strength. For example, Brooklyn Methodist pastor J. O. Peck wrote of him, "The foundation of all he is, and all he has done is his physical system. . . . Mr. Beecher has one of the best animal organizations in this generation. He has those qualities of fineness, elasticity, susceptibility, vigor, nerve, and endurance—I beg pardon, but in one word—*thoroughbred*" (J. O Peck, "Analyses of His Power, and Reminiscences," in Abbott and Halliday, *Henry Ward Beecher: A Sketch of His Career,* 325–33); quotes on 327, 328.

63. Beecher, *Yale Lectures on Preaching,* 182; Henry Ward Beecher, "The Science of Right Living," Beecher, *Sermons in Plymouth Church, Brooklyn* (New York: Fords, Howard & Hulbert, 1882), 329–49, quotes on 330, 334.

64. Beecher, "The Science of Right Living," 338, 344.

65. Henry Ward Beecher, "Night and Darkness," *Sermons, Preached in Plymouth Church, Brooklyn, New York,* 160–82, quotes on 170–71, 173, 174, 178.

66. Mott, *A History of American Magazines,* 3: 446; Clark, *Henry Ward Beecher,* 207–8; Henry Ward Beecher, "Soul-Power," *Sermons in Plymouth Church, Brooklyn,* 381–400, quote on 390.

67. See Henry Ward Beecher, "Woman's Influence in Politics," *The Independent* 12 (Feb. 16, 1860): 1; Henry Ward Beecher, *Universal Suffrage, and Complete Equality in Citizenship* (Boston: Geo. C. Rand & Avery, 1865).

68. Elisabeth Griffith, *In Her Own Right: The Life of Elizabeth Cady Stanton* (New York: Oxford University Press, 1984), 3–5; Lois W. Banner, *Elizabeth Cady Stanton: A Radical for Woman's Rights* (Boston: Little, Brown & Co., 1980), 1–2.

69. Elizabeth Cady Stanton, *Eighty Years and More: Reminiscences, 1815–1897* (New York: T. Fisher Unwin, 1898; reprint, New York: Schocken Books, 1971), 4, 20–21; another reprint of this book is vol. 1 of *Elizabeth Cady Stanton as Revealed in Her Letters, Diary and Reminiscences,* ed. Theodore Stanton and Harriot Stanton Blatch, 2 vols. (New York: Harper & Brothers, 1922).

70. *Eighty Years and More,* 1–50; quote in Theodore Tilton, "Mrs. Elizabeth Cady Stanton," *Eminent Women of the Age,* ed. Theodore Tilton (Hartford, Conn.: S. M. Betts, 1868), 334, cited in Griffith, *In Her Own Right,* 11. Stanton's mother, Margaret Cady, was remembered more affectionately by her grandchildren, and some of her father's colleagues found him taciturn and cunning; see Griffith, *In Her Own Right,* 8–10, 12; Banner, *Elizabeth Cady Stanton,* 4–5, 7.

71. Stanton, *Eighty Years and More,* 25.

72. Griffith, *In Her Own Right,* 17; Alma Lutz, *Created Equal: A Biography of Elizabeth Cady Stanton, 1815–1902* (New York: John Day Co., 1940), 10.

73. Stanton, *Eighty Years and More,* 41, 42.

74. Ibid., 42–43, 44.

75. Ibid., 51–70; see Charles A. Hammond, *Gerrit Smith: The Story of a Noble Man's Life* (Geneva, N.Y.: W. F. Humphrey, 1900); Ralph V. Harlow, *Gerret Smith: Philanthropist and Reformer* (New York: Holt, Rinehart & Winston, 1939); Banner, *Elizabeth Cady Stanton,* 16–18. Smith was one of the six men who helped buy weapons for John Brown's attack on Harper's Ferry in 1859; the others were Samuel G. Howe, Theodore W. Higginson, Theodore Parker, Franklin Sanborn, and George Stearns. See Otto J. Scott, *The Secret Six: John Brown and the Abolitionist Movement* (New York: New York Times Books, 1979).

76. Stanton, *Eighty Years and More,* 58.

77. Ibid., 58–59, 60.

78. Griffith, *In Her Own Right,* 30–31, "giddy whirl" quote, 28; Stanton, *Eighty Years and More,* 71; Lutz, *Created Equal,* 20–23.

79. Stanton, *Eighty Years and More,* 79–85, quote on 81; Griffith, *In Her Own Right,* 36–37; Elizabeth Cady Stanton, "The World's Anti-Slavery Convention, London, June 12, 1840," *History of Woman Suffrage,* ed. Elizabeth Cady Stanton, Susan B. Anthony, Matilda Joslyn Gage, et al., 6 vols. (New York: Fowler & Wells, 1881–86; reprint, New York: Source Book Press, 1970), 50–62.

80. Orelia Cromwell, *Lucretia Mott,* 2d ed. (New York: Russell & Russell, 1971), "thoroughly imbued" quote, 125; Elizabeth Cady Stanton, "Lucretia Mott," *History of Woman Suffrage,* 1: 407–40, "ready to be translated," 420; see Griffith, *In Her Own Right,* 38–39; Margaret Hope Bacon, *Valiant Friend: The Life of Lucretia Mott* (New York: Walker, 1980).

81. Cady Stanton, "Lucretia Mott," 420–21; Cady Stanton, "The World's Anti-Slavery Convention," "great need" quote, 61.

82. Elizabeth Cady Stanton to John Greenleaf Whittier, Nov. 28, 1843, in *Elizabeth Cady Stanton as Revealed in Her Letters, Diary and Reminiscences,* 2:11; Elizabeth Cady Stanton to Elizabeth Neall Gay, Feb. 3, 1846, cited in Griffith, *In Her Own Right,* 45.

83. Stanton, *Eighty Years and More,* 145–48, quotes on 147.

84. Ibid., 148; see Muriam Gurko, *The Ladies of Seneca Falls: The Birth of the Woman's Rights Movement* (New York: Macmillan Co., 1974); Lutz, *Created Equal,* 44–54.

85. "Declaration of Sentiments [and Resolutions]," *History of Woman Suffrage,* 1: 70–73.

86. Editorials reprinted in *History of Woman Suffrage,* 1:802–5; Elizabeth Cady Stanton, "New York," *History of Woman Suffrage,* 1:63–69, quotes on 68; see "Mrs. Stanton's Reply," ibid., 1:806.

87. See Griffith, *In Her Own Right,* 62–85; Banner, *Elizabeth Cady Stanton,* 58–68; Ida Husted Harper, *The Life and Work of Susan B. Anthony,* 2 vols. (Indianapolis: Bowen-Merrill, 1899); Katharine Anthony, *Susan B. Anthony: Her Personal History and Her Era* (Garden City, N.Y.: Doubleday & Co., 1954).

88. Stanton, *Eighty Years and More,* 187–89; Elizabeth Cady Stanton to Susan B. Anthony, Sept. 10, 1855, *Elizabeth Cady Stanton as Revealed in Her Letters, Diary and Reminiscences,* 2:59–60. For citations and discussion, see Griffith, *In Her Own Right,* 82, 84. Cady Stanton's daughter, Harriot Stanton Blatch, further testified, "From the time Mrs. Stanton first began her public work she had one long serious battle with her father" (Blatch, *A Sketch of the Life of Elizabeth Cady Stanton* [n.p., 1915], cited in Griffith, *In Her Own Right,* 246, n. 62).

89. Elizabeth Cady Stanton to Susan B. Anthony, Apr. 10, 1859, in *The Selected Papers of Elizabeth Cady Stanton and Susan B. Anthony,* ed. Ann D. Gordon (New Brunswick, N.J.: Rutgers University Press, 1997), 1:387; see Lutz, *Created Equal,* 105–6.

90. Elizabeth Cady Stanton, "Tenth National Woman's Rights Convention," in *The Selected Papers of Elizabeth Cady Stanton and Susan B. Anthony,* 1:418–30, quotes on 1:426–27, Anthony's defense on 1:428.

91. Quotations from the *New York Daily Tribune,* May 30, 1860; the New York *Evening Post,* May 23, 1860; the *New York Herald,* May 16, 1860, and the *New York Observer,* May 17, 1860, all cited in *Selected Papers of Elizabeth Cady Stanton and Susan B. Anthony,* 1:431.

92. Elizabeth Cady Stanton to William H. Seward, Sept. 19, 1861, *Elizabeth Cady Stanton as Revealed in Her Letters, Diary and Reminiscences,* 2:88–89.

93. Elizabeth Cady Stanton to Martha C. Wright, Dec. 20, 1865; and Elizabeth Cady Stanton to Wendell Phillips, Dec. 26, 1865, both in *Elizabeth Cady Stanton As Revealed in Her Letters, Diary and Reminiscences,* 2:108–9, 109–11.

94. Eleanor Flexner, *Century of Struggle: The Woman's Rights Movement in the United States,* rev. ed. (Cambridge: Harvard University Press, 1975), 145–47; Goldsmith, *Other Powers,* 112–13.

95. Henry Ward Beecher, *Woman's Duty to Vote: Speech by Henry Ward Beecher, at the Eleventh National Woman's Rights Convention* (New York: American Equal Rights Association, 1867), quotes on 1, 6; see Henry Ward Beecher, "Woman's Influence in Politics"; Beecher, *Universal Suffrage, and Complete Equality in Citizenship.* The icy tension between Tilton and Beecher was further displayed to the audience immediately after Beecher's lecture, when they "humorously" needled each other over Beecher's "gift" of a New Testament to Tilton, which Tilton announced was actually "the property of a lady." For the text of Beecher's speech and his interchanges with Tilton, see Stanton, Anthony, Gage, eds., *History of Woman Suffrage,* 2:155–67.

96. Beecher, *Woman's Duty to Vote,* 7.

97. Ibid., 8–9, 10.

98. Ibid., 15, 16, 17–18.

99. Ibid., 23, 24.

100. Flexner, *Century of Struggle,* 145–54; Sara M. Evans, *Born for Liberty: A History of Women in America* (New York: Free Press, 1997), 122–23.

101. "Low down" and "to stand aside," quoted in Goldsmith, *Other Powers,* 137, 134; Flexner, *Century of Struggle,* 152–53; *The Elizabeth Cady Stanton-Susan B. Anthony Reader: Correspondence, Writings, Speeches,* ed. Ellen Carol DuBois (Boston: Northeastern University Press, 1981), 119; Alice Stone Blackwell, *Lucy Stone, Pioneer of Woman's Rights* (Boston: Alice Stone Blackwell Committee, 1930), 206–13, William Lloyd Garrison to Susan B. Anthony, Jan. 4, 1868, reprinted on 211–12; Lutz, *Created Equal,* 145–56.

102. Andrew Sinclair, *The Better Half: The Emancipation of the American Woman* (New York: Harper & Row, 1965), Barton quote on 189; Flexner, *Century of Struggle,* 150–51.

103. "The May Anniversaries in New York and Brooklyn," *History of Woman Suffrage,* 2:378–82.

104. Ibid., Cady Stanton's speech, 348–55, quotes, 353, 354. Ernestine L. Rose and Anna E. Dickinson were feminist leaders.

105. Ibid., 353, 354, 355.

106. Ibid., 382.

107. Ibid., 382–83.

108. Evans, *Born for Liberty,* 123–24; Flexner, *Century of Struggle,* 153–57. "My continuous wrath," Elizabeth Cady Stanton to Susan B. Anthony and Matilda Joslyn G. Gage, June 25, 1873, quoted in Griffith, *In Her Own Right,* 155; "the male element" quote in Cady Stanton, "National Conventions—1869," *History of Woman Suffrage,* 2:351; see Blackwell, *Lucy Stone: Pioneer of Woman's Rights,* 222–31.

109. Beecher quoted in Katharine Anthony, *Susan B. Anthony: Her Personal History and Her Era,* 239.

110. Elizabeth Cady Stanton to Susan B. Anthony, May 30, 1870, in *Elizabeth Cady Stanton as Revealed in Her Letters, Diary and Reminiscences,* 2:126–27; Goldsmith, *Other Powers,* 217–18; Anthony, *Susan B. Anthony,* 239; Mari Jo Buhle and Paul Buhle, eds., *The Concise History of Woman Suffrage: Selections from the Classic Work of Stanton, Anthony, Gage and Harper,* 2 vols. (Urbana, Ill.: University of Illinois Press, 1978), 2:427.

111. "Getting a divorce," Elizabeth Cady Stanton to Susan B. Anthony, June 27, 1870, in *Elizabeth Cady Stanton as Revealed in Her Letters, Diary and Reminiscences,* 2:127; see Evans, *Born for Liberty,* 123–24; Flexner, *Century of Struggle,* 153–57; Griffith, *In Her Own Right,* 148–52; Ellen Carol DuBois, *Feminism and Suffrage: The Emergence of an Independent Women's Movement in America, 1848–1869* (Cambridge: Belknap Press, 1975); Elizabeth Cady Stanton to Isabella Beecher Hooker, Apr. 12, 1871, in *Elizabeth Cady Stanton as Revealed in Her Letters, Diary and Reminiscences,* 2:131–32; Johanna Johnston, *Mrs. Satan: The Incredible Saga of Victoria C. Woodhull* (New York: G. P. Putnam, 1967).

112. Beecher, *Yale Lectures on Preaching,* quote on 255.

113. See Hibben, *Henry Ward Beecher,* 200; Goldsmith, *Other Powers,* 219–21; Henry Ward Beecher, *The Life of Jesus, the Christ* (New York: J. B. Ford & Co., 1871).

114. "Mr. Beecher as a Social Force," *Scribner's Monthly* 4 (Oct. 1872): 754; quoted in Clark, *Henry Ward Beecher,* 197.

115. Victoria Woodhull, "Victoria C. Woodhull's Complete and Detailed Version of the Beecher-Tilton Affair," [1872], (Washington, D.C.: J. Bradley Adams, 1876), reprinted in *The Victoria Woodhull Reader*, ed. Madeleine B. Stern (Weston, Mass.: M. & S. Press, 1974), 4–8; Cady Stanton interview published in "Beecher's Trial," *Chicago Tribune* (July 28, 1874), 1; *Official Report of the Trial of Henry Ward Beecher*, with notes and references by Austin Abbott, 2 vols. (New York: George W. Smith & Co., 1875), 2:134–35; *The Great Brooklyn Romance: All the Documents in the Famous Beecher-Tilton Case, Unabridged* (New York: J. H. Paxon, 1874), sec. 1, 2, 3, 12, 13, n.p.; Marshall, *The True History of the Brooklyn Scandal*, 194; see Hibben, *Henry Ward Beecher*, 238–39; Goldsmith, *Other Powers*, 223–24.

116. Elizabeth Cady Stanton to Isabella Beecher Hooker, Nov. 3, 1873, Letters and Papers, Isabella Beecher Hooker Project, cited in Goldsmith, *Other Powers*, 358. Theodore Tilton to "My Complaining Friend," Dec. 27, 1972, in Marshall, *The True History of the Brooklyn Scandal*, 540–41; "Mrs. Tilton's Cross-Examination," in Marshall, ibid., 208; "love babe" letter, Elizabeth Tilton to "Friend and Sister" [probably Laura Curtis Bullard], Jan. 13, 1871, in Marshall, ibid., 318; Woodhull, "Victoria C. Woodhull's Complete and Detailed Version of the Beecher-Tilton Affair," 11-13; Fox, *Trials of Intimacy*, 401. Elizabeth Tilton told the Plymouth Church Investigating Committee that on many occasions at home, Tilton railed "that he did not know whom his children belonged to" (Marshall, *The True History of the Brooklyn Scandal*, 207–8). Much of the early Beecher literature defends Beecher's innocence on all or most counts. For examples, see Beecher and Scoville, *A Biography of Rev. Henry Ward Beecher*, 488–536; Abbott, *Henry Ward Beecher*, 288–99; Barrow, *Henry Ward Beecher*, 380–98; Thomas W. Knox, *Life and Work of Henry Ward Beecher* (Philadelphia: International Publishing Company). For a more recent defense of Beecher's innocence that reads the evidence itself as "ambiguous," see Edward Wagenknecht, *Ambassadors for Christ: Seven American Preachers* (New York: Oxford University Press, 1972), 72, 249–54. In *Trials of Intimacy*, Richard Wightman Fox emphasizes that all the evidence we possess is pervaded by self-interested fictionalizing. Because Woodhull, Beecher, and the Tiltons were all prodigious "truth-decorators," he cautions, we cannot know for certain whether Beecher and Elizabeth Tilton were lovers. Most of the literature that assumes Beecher's guilt adopts Theodore Tilton's narrative frame and claims. A bemused example of this genre is Robert Shaplen's *Free Love and Heavenly Sinners: The Story of the Great Henry Ward Beecher Scandal* (New York: Alfred A. Knopf, 1954). Some recent interpretations try to convict Beecher with Tilton's testimony without granting much credibility to Tilton, however. Anita Waller's *Reverend Beecher and Mrs. Tilton* (Amherst, Mass.: University of Massachusetts Press, 1982), tends to credit Tilton's story against Beecher without accepting Tilton's story about himself. In a crowded field, Barbara Goldsmith's *Other Powers* is distinguished chiefly by her privileging of Woodhull's version of the story and her belief in Woodhull's extrasensory powers. Goldsmith accepts most of Woodhull's account as literal fact, which exempts her from having to rely on Tilton, whom she also skewers. While judging that Goldsmith's "belief in Woodhull's real powers" enables her to cast new light on the subject, Fox strongly criticizes Goldsmith for fictionalizing the evidence with one-sided portraits and unsubstantiated rumors.

117. Woodhull, "Victoria C. Woodhull's Complete and Detailed Version of the Beecher-Tilton Affair," 1–22; "Beecher's Trial," *Chicago Tribune* (July 28, 1874, and Aug. 2, 1874), 1, 1; Fox, *Trials of Intimacy*, 162–66; *The Great Brooklyn Romance*, sec. 2, 3, 4, n.p.; Hibben, *Henry Ward Beecher*, 239–41; Marshall, *The True History of the Brooklyn Scandal*, 194–95, 527–31; Goldsmith, *Other Powers*, 224–25, 229.

118. *Theodore Tilton vs. Henry Ward Beecher*, 2:717; Marshall, *The True History of the Brooklyn Scandal*, 207–8, 259–62; Theodore Tilton to Henry Ward Beecher, Dec. 26, 1870, Marshall, ibid., 312; Elizabeth Tilton to Theodore Tilton and Mrs. Morse, Nov. 1870, in Marshall, ibid., 535–37; J. E. P. Doyle, compiler, *The Romance of Plymouth Church. Plymouth Church and Its Pastor, or Henry Ward Beecher and His Accusers* (Hartford, Conn.: Park Publishing Co., 1874), 527–28; Goldsmith, *Other Powers*, 235; Abbott, *Henry Ward Beecher*, 290–92. Elizabeth Tilton told her "friend and sister" that her miscarriage was caused by her emotional turmoil: "Anxiety day and night brought on my miscarriage: a disappointment I have never before known—a *love babe* it promised, you know. I have had sorrow almost beyond human capacity." Elizabeth Tilton to "Friend and Sister," Jan. 13, 1871, Marshall, *The True History of the Brooklyn Scandal*, 349–50.

119. *Theodore Tilton vs. Henry Ward Beecher*, 2:716, 3:412–19; *The Great Brooklyn Romance*, sec. 12, 13, 41, 46; Beecher and Scoville, *A Biography of Rev. Henry Ward Beecher*, 501-4; J. E. P. Doyle, compiler, *The Romance of Plymouth Church. Plymouth Church and Its Pastor, or Henry Ward Beecher and His Accusers* (Hartford, Conn.: Park Publishing Co., 1874), 527–28; Marshall, *The True History of the Brooklyn Scandal*, 259–62; Goldsmith, *Other Powers*, 237–39; Hibben, *Henry Ward Beecher*, 240–45.

120. *Official Report of the Trial of Henry Ward Beecher*, 2:137–38; *Theodore Tilton vs. Henry Ward Beecher*, 1:171–73, 186–89; *The Great Brooklyn Romance*, sec. 12, 13, 41, "fell like a thunderbolt," 41; *Theodore Tilton vs. Henry Ward Beecher*, 1: Marshall, *The True History of the Brooklyn Scandal*, 195–96, 317; Goldsmith, *Other Powers*, 242–45; Shaplen, *Free Love and Heavenly Sinners*, 92–93; Hibben, *Henry Ward Beecher*, 246–57. Elizabeth Tilton's recantation letter read: "Wearied with importunity and weakened by sickness I gave a letter inculpating my friend Henry Ward Beecher under assurances that that would remove all difficulties between me and my husband. That letter I now revoke. I was persuaded to it—almost forced—when I was in a weakened state of mind. I regret it, and recall all its statements" (Marshall, *The True History of the Brooklyn Scandal*, 317).

121. *Official Report of the Trial of Henry Ward Beecher*, 2:144–45; *Theodore Tilton vs. Henry Ward Beecher*, 1:247–57; *The Great Brooklyn Romance*, sec. 23; Hibben, *Henry Ward Beecher*, 261–63, 271–72.

122. "Make her a friend," Theodore Tilton to a "Friend in the West," Dec. 31, 1872, in Marshall, *The True History of the Brooklyn Scandal*, quote on 373–74; Theodore Tilton, *The Golden Age Tracts—No. 3. Victoria C. Woodhall. A Biographical Sketch* (New York: Golden Age, 1871), quote on 32; excerpts reprinted in *The Great Brooklyn Romance*, sec. 27; *Theodore Tilton vs. Henry Ward Beecher*, 1:415; Helen Lefkowitz Horowitz, "Victoria Woodhull, Anthony Comstock, and Conflict over Sex in the United States in the 1870s," *Journal of American History* 87 (Sept. 2000): 403–34.

123. *The Great Brooklyn Romance*, sec. 28, 29; Woodhull, "Victoria C. Woodhull's Complete and Detailed Version of the Beecher-Tilton Affair," 16; Doyle, *The Romance of Plymouth Church*, 215, 216; Goldsmith, *Other Powers*, 286–88, 291; *Official Report of the Trial of Henry Ward Beecher*, 2:164–71. Woodhull claimed that Beecher's private carriage "could have been seen waiting before our door every afternoon for many months, to take us riding to Central Park." Quoted in Doyle, ed., *The Romance of Plymouth Church*, 216. See Shaplen, *Free Love and Heavenly Sinners*, 145–47; Fox, *Intimate Trials*, 152–54; Emanie Sachs, *The Terrible Siren: Victoria Woodhull (1838–1927)* (New York: Harper & Brothers, 1928), 96–97. Goldsmith remarks of Woodhull's "in my arms" quote, "Perhaps it was said by a Victoria possessed by the spirits, who was another woman altogether." Goldsmith, *Other Powers*, 290.

124. "Make her such" quote, Theodore Tilton to a "Friend in the West," Dec. 27, 1872; "ragged edge" letter, Henry Ward Beecher to Frank Moulton, Feb. 5, 1872, Marshall, *The True History of the Brooklyn Scandal*, 275–77; see Henry Ward Beecher to Frank Moulton, Apr. 2, 1872, *The Great Brooklyn Romance*, sec. 38; Marshall, *The True History of the Brooklyn Scandal*, 361, 373–74; Goldsmith, *Other Powers*, 312; and Hibben, *Henry Ward Beecher*, 273.

125. Woodhull, "Victoria C. Woodhull's Complete and Detailed Version of the Beecher-Tilton Affair;" published originally in *Woodhull & Claflin's Weekly* (Nov. 2, 1872); reprinted with related documents in *The Great Brooklyn Romance*, sec. 28, 29.

126. *Official Report of the Trial of Henry Ward Beecher*, 2:184; Marshall, *The True History of the Brooklyn Scandal*, 40–42; Elizabeth Tilton to Theodore Tilton, Dec. 28, 1872, in Marshall, ibid., 540–41; Edward H. G. Clark, *The Thunderbolt* (New York, Albany, Troy; May 1873); see Hibben, *Henry Ward Beecher*, 298–99; Fox, *Intimate Trials*, 159–60; Goldsmith, *Other Powers*, 376–77.

127. *The Great Brooklyn Romance*, sec. 1, 11, 13, 15, 30; "dog and a knave," Apr. 2, 1873, sec. 31; *Theodore Tilton vs. Henry Ward Beecher*, 2:672–75; *Official Report of the Trial of Henry Ward Beecher*, 2:727–76, Beecher and Emma Moulton quotes on 730, and *Theodore Tilton vs. Henry Ward Beecher*, 1:725; see Doyle, *The Romance of Plymouth Church*, 114–42; Marshall, *The True Story of the Brooklyn Scandal*, 40–63; Henry Ward Beecher to Frank Moulton, June 1, 1873, in Marshall, ibid., 280–82.

128. *The Great Brooklyn Romance*, sec. 31, 32, 41, 51, 52, 53, Elizabeth Tilton quotes in 32, Beecher quotes in 41; Marshall, *The True History of the Brooklyn Scandal*, 196–98.

129. Ibid., sec. 41, 4, 47; "When Beecher falls," Elizabeth Cady Stanton to Susan B. Anthony, July 30, 1874, *Elizabeth Cady Stanton as Revealed in Her Letters, Diary and Reminiscences,* 2:146; see Marshall, *The True History of the Brooklyn Scandal,* 188–89, 286–307, 273, 387; Goldsmith, *Other Powers,* 389–91, 395, 398–99, 402; Shaplen, *Free Love and Heavenly Sinners,* 187.

130. *Theodore Tilton vs. Henry Ward Beecher,* 3:806–17; Marshall, *The True History of the Brooklyn Scandal,* 256–71, 478–79, 565. Near the beginning of his cross-examination, Porter asked Moulton, "Did you lie for him?" Moulton affirmed that he did. Porter's laugh-line response was, "We have your word." *Theodore Tilton vs. Henry Ward Beecher,* 1:145. The Tilton-Tilton letters were published in the Aug. 13, 1874 issue of the *Chicago Tribune;* the best collection of them is in Fox, *Trials of Intimacy,* 251–91. Eunice Beecher took heart before the trial that her husband's eyes "are at last opened, and he sees both Tilton and Moulton in their naked depravity and baseness." Eunice Beecher to Harriet Beecher Scoville, Aug. 9, 1874, Beecher Family Papers, Box 35, Yale University Library Manuscripts and Archives; see E. L. Godkin, "Some Plain Truths about the Scandal," *The Nation* (June 3, 1875), 372–73; Godkin, "Tilton Against Beecher," *The Nation* (July 8, 1875), 22–23; Fox, *Trials of Intimacy,* 309–10.

131. *Theodore Tilton vs. Henry Ward Beecher,* 3:704–1018, Elizabeth Tilton statement, 3:323; "Last Statement," *Chicago Tribune* (Feb. 17, 1875), 1; Fox, *Trials of Intimacy,* 98.

132. "Resolved to smite" quote in *Harper's Weekly,* June 5, 1875, cited in Clark, *Henry Ward Beecher,* 224; "Mrs. Tilton Pleads Guilty," *The New York Times* (Apr. 16, 1878), 1; "Mrs. Tilton's Confession," *New York Times* (Apr. 19, 1878), 5; Beach closing statement, *Theodore Tilton vs. Henry Ward Beecher,* 3:813–1018, orthodoxy arguments, 996–1010.

133. Moulton public letter, Aug. 21, 1874, in *The Great Brooklyn Romance,* sec. 45; "kite" quote in Stanton and Blatch, eds., *Elizabeth Cady Stanton as Revealed in Her Letters, Diary and Reminiscences,* 2:180. See Beecher and Scoville, *A Biography of Rev. Henry Ward Beecher,* 488–536; Abbott, *Henry Ward Beecher,* 288–99; and Barrow, *Henry Ward Beecher,* 380–98.

134. 'Pursued" quote in Beecher and Scoville, *A Life of Rev. Henry Ward Beecher,* 553; and Barrows, *Henry Ward Beecher,* 399. Barrows was one of the admiring observers who remarked on the diminishment of Beecher's effective religious influence; see 391. "Old cheery smiles," Eunice Beecher to Harriet Scoville, Jan. 16, 1876, cited in Clark, *Henry Ward Beecher,* 228; on Beecher's reaction to Elizabeth Tilton's confession and Bowen's testimony, see Shaplen, *Free Love and Heavenly Sinners,* 262–64, 266–67; "for so many years" quote in Beecher and Scoville, *A Biography of Rev. Henry Ward Beecher,* 546. On Beecher's sexualized "spiritual engineering," see Richard Wightman Fox, "The Culture of Liberal Protestant Progressivism, 1875–1925," *Journal of Interdisciplinary History* 23 (winter 1993): 639–60, and Fox, *Trials of Intimacy.*

135. Henry Ward Beecher, "Patriotism Above Party," in Beecher, *Lectures and Orations,* ed. Newell Dwight Hillis (New York: Fleming H. Revell Co., 1913), 284–311, quote on 311.

136. Shaplen, *Free Love and Heavenly Sinners,* 264–68, 271–72; Goldsmith, *Other Powers,* 438; Fox, *Trials of Intimacy,* 29–36; Hibben, *Henry Ward Beecher,* 331; Tilton testimony, *Theodore Tilton vs. Henry Ward Beecher,* 1:629.

137. Asa Gray, *Darwiniana* (New York: Appleton, 1876), 70, 357; Charles Hodge, *What Is Darwinism?* (New York: Scribner, Armstrong, 1874), 173, 177; Frank Hugh Foster, *The Modern Movement in American Theology: Sketches in the History of American Protestant Thought from the Civil War to the World War* (New York: Fleming H. Revell Co., 1939), 38–58.

138. See Herbert Spencer, *First Principles* (New York: D. Appleton & Co., 1864); John Fiske, *Outlines of Cosmic Philosophy,* 2 vols. (Boston: Houghton, Mifflin & Co., 1874); Fiske, *Darwinism and Other Essays* (Boston: Houghton, Mifflin & Co., 1884).

139. Henry Ward Beecher, "The Herbert Spencer Dinner," in Beecher, *Lectures and Orations,* 312–24, quotes on 314, 315, 318, 322–23.

140. Henry Ward Beecher, *Evolution and Religion* (New York: Fords, Howard & Hulbert, 1885), 128, 3.

141. Ibid., 4.

142. Ibid., 53; see 139.

143. Ibid., 70.

144. Ibid., 140.

145. Henry Ward Beecher, "William Ellery Channing," in Beecher, *Lectures and Orations,* 157–82, quotes on 159–60, 161–62.

146. See Catherine Beecher, *Woman's Suffrage and Woman's Profession* (Hartford, Conn.: Brown & Cross, 1871); Catherine Beecher, *Letters on the Difficulties of Religion* (Hartford, Conn.: Belknap & Hammersley, 1836); Catherine Beecher, *A Treatise on Domestic Economy* (Boston: Source Book Press, 1841); Hedrick, *Harriet Beecher Stowe,* 353–79, "love roost" quote, Harriet Beecher Stowe to Mrs. Mary Claflin, Aug. 22, 1874, in ibid., 377.

147. Elizabeth Cady Stanton to Martha C. Wright, Mar. 21, 1871, in *Elizabeth Cady Stanton as Revealed in Her Letters, Diary and Reminiscences,* 2:130–31; Griffith, *In Her Own Right,* 163–64.

148. "I was born and reared a Quaker, and am one still," Anthony affirmed. At the same time she insisted that "today all sectarian creeds and all political policies sink into utter insignificance compared with the essence of religion and the fundamental principle of government—equal rights." To her, social justice activism and true piety were the same thing: "I pray every second of my life; not on my knees, but with my work. My prayer is to lift woman to equality with man. Work and worship are one with me. I can not imagine a God of the universe made happy by my getting down on my knees and calling him 'great'" (quoted in Ida Husted Harper, *The Life and Work of Susan B. Anthony,* 3 vols. [Indianapolis: Hollenbeck Press, 1898–1908], 2:793, 2:859). For an example of a biography that presents Anthony as thoroughly secular, see Kathleen Barry, *Susan B. Anthony: A Biography* (New York: New York University Press, 1988); for a reading that highlights Anthony's religious background and beliefs, see Mary D. Pellauer, *Toward a Tradition of Feminist Theology: The Religious Social Thought of Elizabeth Cady Stanton, Susan B. Anthony, and Anna Howard Shaw* (Brooklyn: Carlson Publishing, 1991), 153–217.

149. Elizabeth Cady Stanton to Elizabeth Smith Miller, Mar. 26, 1879, in *Elizabeth Cady Stanton as Revealed in Her Letters, Diary and Reminiscences,* 2:159–60; Lucy Stone to Elizabeth Cady Stanton, Aug. 30, 1876, cited in Griffith, *In Her Own Right,* 180.

150. "Over thirty years" quote in Elizabeth Cady Stanton to Isabella Beecher Hooker, May 10, 1880, in *Elizabeth Cady Stanton as Revealed in Her Letters, Diary, and Reminiscences,* 2:169; "I have no time" in Elizabeth Cady Stanton to Susan B. Anthony, May 30, 1870, ibid., 2:126; "become conservative" in Elizabeth Cady Stanton to Susan B. Anthony, Jan. 10, 1880, ibid., 2:165; "get more radical," Elizabeth Cady Stanton, diary entry of Jan. 9, 1889, 2:254.

151. "Take your position" in Elizabeth Cady Stanton to Susan B. Anthony, Jan. 10, 1880, *Elizabeth Cady Stanton as Revealed in Her Letters, Diary and Reminiscences,* 2:163–164.

152. Elizabeth Cady Stanton, "The Solitude of Self," *History of Woman Suffrage,* 4:189–91.

153. Quote in Lutz, *Created Equal,* 313; see Elizabeth Cady Stanton, *The Bible and Church Degrade Woman* (Chicago: H. L. Green, 1894); Pellauer, *Toward a Tradition of Feminist Theology,* 105–52.

154. Elizabeth Cady Stanton, Jan. 31, 1889, diary entry, in *Elizabeth Cady Stanton as Revealed in Her Letters, Diary and Reminiscences,* 255; "Miss Anthony has one idea," Elizabeth Cady Stanton to Clara Colby, undated, 1896, quoted in Lutz, *Created Equal,* 296, and Griffith, *In Her Own Right,* 194.

155. Elizabeth Cady Stanton, diary entry of Aug. 31, 1886, *Elizabeth Cady Stanton as Revealed in Her Letters, Diary and Reminiscences,* 2:233; Dorothy C. Bass, "Women's Studies and Biblical Studies, An Historical Perspective," *Journal for the Study of the Old Testament* 22 (1982): 3–72, on the Society for Biblical Literature and Anna Ely Rhoads, 7–9; Lutz, *Created Equal,* 295–98.

156. See *Productions of Mrs. Maria W. Stewart* (Boston: "published by friends of freedom and virtue," 1835; reprinted in Schomburg Library of Nineteenth-Century Black Woman Writers, *Spiritual Narratives* [New York: Oxford University Press, 1988]); Sarah Moore Grimké, *Letters on the Equality of the Sexes and the Condition of Woman* (Boston: Isaac Knapp), 1838; Elisabeth Schüssler Fiorenza, "Transforming the Legacy of *The Woman's Bible,*" in *Searching the Scriptures,* Vol. 1: *A Feminist Introduction,* ed. Elisabeth Schüssler Fiorenza (New York: Crossroad, 1995), 1–24.

157. See Anna Julia Cooper, *A Voice from the South,* ed. Mary Helen Washington; Schomburg Library of Nineteenth-Century Black Women Writers (New York: Oxford University Press, 1988); Karen Baker-Fletcher, "Anna Julia Cooper and Sojourner Truth: Two Nineteenth-Century Black Feminist Interpreters of Scripture," in *Searching the Scriptures,* 41–51.

158. Elizabeth Cady Stanton, et al., *The Woman's Bible, Part 1, Comments on Genesis, Exodus, Leviticus, Numbers and Deuteronomy* (New York: European Publishing Company, 1895); *The Woman's Bible, Part 2, Comments on the Old and New Testaments from Joshua to Revelation* (New York: European Publishing Co., 1898); (reprint, parts 1 and 2, New York: Arno Press, 1972), 1:7.

159. *The Woman's Bible* 1:7–8; 2:8.

160. Ibid., 1:10, 12.

161. Ibid., 1:13–14, 18, 21, 126.

162. Ibid., 1:120; 2:26; see John William Colenso, *The Pentateuch and the Book of Joshua Critically Examined* (2d ed. London: Longman, Green, Longman, Roberts & Green, 1862).

163. *The Woman's Bible*, 2:113.

164. Ibid., 2:164–65, 184.

165. Citations in Lutz, *Created Equal*, 303, 304–5.

166. "Interpret and twist" quoted in Lutz, *Anthony*, 280; and Griffith, *In Her Own Right*, 213; Anna Howard Shaw, with Elizabeth Jordon, *The Story of a Pioneer* (New York: Harper Brothers, 1915), 192. Shaw reported that Anthony introduced her to audiences as "orthodox of the orthodox" and told her: "I am glad that you are a Methodist, for now they cannot claim that we are not orthodox." See Wilmer Albert Linkugel, "The Speeches of Anna Howard Shaw, Collected and Edited with Introduction and Notes." Ph.D. dissertation, University of Wisconsin, 1960; Carolyn A. Haynes, *Divine Destiny: Gender and Race in Nineteenth-Century Protestantism* (Jackson, Miss.: University of Mississippi Press, 1998), 47–76; Carolyn De Swarte Gifford, "Politicizing the Sacred Texts: Elizabeth Cady Stanton and *The Woman's Bible*," in *Searching the Scriptures*, 52–63.

Chapter 5: Progessivism Ascending

1. In 1880, the chair of theology at Yale was held by Samuel Harris; at Andover, by Edwards A. Park; at Union, by William G. T. Shedd; at Princeton, by A. A. Hodge; at Chicago, by George N. Boardman; at Oberlin, by James Harris Fairchild. See Frank Hugh Foster, *A Genetic History of the New England Theology* (Chicago: University of Chicago Press, 1907; reprint, New York: Russell & Russell, 1963); George N. Boardman, *The History of New England Theology* (New York: A. D. F. Randolph, 1899); Joseph Haroutunian, *Piety Versus Moralism: The Passing of the New England Theology* (New York: Henry Holt, 1932; reprint, Hamden, Conn.: Archon Books, 1964).

2. Benjamin Wisner Bacon, *Theodore Thornton Munger, New England Minister* (New Haven, Conn.: Yale University Press, 1913), 7–29; "Theodore T. Munger," *National Cyclopaedia of American Biography* (New York: James T. White & Co., 1898), 1:533.

3. Bacon, *Theodore Thornton Munger*, 30–59, quote on 46.

4. Munger to John Willcocks Noble, Dec. 14, 1852; and Munger to Elisha Mulford, Dec. 26, 1856, ibid., 68, 72–74. John Willcocks Noble later became Secretary of the Interior under President Harrison and father of American forest conservation; Elisha Mulford became an Episcopal priest and Munger's closest personal friend.

5. Ibid., 99–100, 105–12, quote on 99.

6. Horace Bushnell, *Nature and the Supernatural: As Together Constituting the One System of God* (New York: Scribner, 1858; reprint, New York: Charles Scribner's Sons, 1907), 18, 31–32; *Theodore Thornton Munger, New England Minister*, 116–18; Theodore T. Munger, *Horace Bushnell: Preacher and Theologian* (Boston: Houghton, Mifflin & Company, 1899), 209–33.

7. *Life and Letters of Frederick W. Robertson, M.A.*, ed. Stopford A. Brooke, 2 vols. (London: Smith, Elder & Company, 1866; Boston: Tickner & Fields, 1866). Robertson respected the Oxford Tractarians; he read John Henry Newman's sermons "with profit and delight to the day of his death," but rejected their dogmatism; see ibid., 1:122–24. Munger remarks at the fiftieth anniversary commemoration of his ordination, 1906, in New Haven, quoted in *Theodore Thornton Munger*, 118–19. On Robertson's influence on Munger-generation liberals, see William J. Tucker, *My Generation: An Autobiographical Interpretation* (Boston: Houghton, Mifflin and Co., 1919), 58–62.

8. *Life and Letters of Frederick W. Robertson*, 2:160–61, cited from Robertson's sermon, "The Glory of the Virgin Mother." Brooke remarks that "the whole of his controversial teaching was founded" on the first principle and that the formula of the second principle "eliminated

the positive truth with which he confronted the errors he exposed." In context, Robertson's principles were explicated as a way of dealing with the Roman Catholic doctrine of the Adoration of the Virgin. On Robertson's career, see Lewis O. Brastow, *Representative Modern Preachers* (New York: Hodder & Stoughton, 1904), 50–97.

9. Munger to Elisha Mulford, Dec. 1859, reprinted in *Theodore Thornton Munger,* 122–24.

10. *Theodore Thornton Munger,* quotes, 101, 141, 128.

11. Washington Gladden, *Recollections* (Boston: Houghton Mifflin Co., 1909), 1–12, quote on 11–12.

12. Ibid., 31–37, quote on 34.

13. Ibid., 46–47.

14. Congregationalist losses may have exceeded one thousand congregations, with the heaviest losses occurring in Ohio and western New York. One Congregational leader bitterly lamented, "They have milked our Congregational cows, but have made nothing but Presbyterian butter and cheese." Eminent Congregational historian Williston Walker judged, to the contrary, that Congregationalism was victimized chiefly by its own structural handicaps and lack of religious vigor. See Williston Walker, *The Creeds and Platforms of Congregationalism* (Boston: Pilgrim Press, 1960), 532–33, "milked," 533; Walker, *A History of the Congregational Churches in the United States* (New York: Christian Literature Company, 1894), 370–71; John von Rohr, *The Shaping of American Congregationalism, 1620–1957* (Cleveland: Pilgrim Press, 1992), 262–65.

15. Gladden, *Recollections,* 62–64, quote on 63–64; Walker, *A History of the Congregational Churches in the United States,* 371; Jacob Henry Dorn, *Washington Gladden: Prophet of the Social Gospel* (Columbus, Ohio: Ohio State University Press, 1967), 12–13.

16. Theodore Clarke Smith, *The Life and Letters of James Abram Garfield,* 2 vols. (New Haven, Conn.: Yale University Press, 1925), 1:79; quoted in Dorn, *Washington Gladden,* 17; Gladden, *Recollections,* 67–84, Hopkins quote on 72.

17. Washington Gladden, *Fifty Years in the Ministry* (Columbus, Ohio: Lawrence Press Co., 1910), 2–3, 6–11; Gladden, *Recollections,* 85–89, quote on 88.

18. Gladden, *Recollections,* 89–91, 114, quote on 90; see Dorn, *Washington Gladden,* 31–32; Henry Ward Beecher, "Against a Compromise of Principle" (1860), reprinted in Beecher, *Freedom and War: Discourses on Topics Suggested by the Times* (Boston: Ticknor & Fields, 1863), 28–56.

19. Gladden, *Recollections,* 114–16, 121–23, quote on 115.

20. Ibid., 119–20.

21. Washington Gladden, "Horace Bushnell and Progressive Orthodoxy," *Pioneers of Religious Liberty in America* (Boston: American Unitarian Association, 1903), 256, 260.

22. Washington Gladden, *Amusements: Their Uses and Their Abuses* (North Adams, Mass.: James T. Robinson & Company, 1866); Gladden, *Plain Thoughts on the Art of Living* (Boston: Ticknor & Fields, 1868), 140–47; Gladden, *From the Hub to the Hudson: With Sketches of Nature, History, and Industry in North-Western Massachusetts* (Boston: New England News Co., 1869), 28–41.

23. Gladden, *Amusements: Their Uses and Their Abuses,* 5–11; Gladden, *Plain Thoughts on the Art of Living,* 169–86; Dorn, *Washington Gladden,* 46–47; John W. Buckham, *Progressive Religious Thought in America: A Survey of the Enlarging Pilgrim Faith* (Boston: Houghton Mifflin Co., 1919), 250. Buckham noted that "Oh, Master, let me walk with thee" is a heretic's hymn—"a 'heretic of yesterday' and a saint of to-day."

24. Gladden, *Recollections,* 173–75, 182–83, quote on 183; Dorn, *Washington Gladden,* 54.

25. Frank Luther Mott, *A History of American Magazines, 1741–1905,* 4 vols. (Cambridge: Harvard University Press, 1938–57), 3:457–72; Gladden, *Recollections,* 185–91, quote on 190; Dorn, *Washington Gladden,* 55.

26. Gladden, *Recollections,* 192–222, quote on 221; Dorn, *Washington Gladden,* 57; "three R's" quote in editorial, *Independent* 23 (Apr. 6, 1871): 6, cited in Dorn, 55.

27. Washington Gladden, "Immoral Theology," *The Independent* 25 (July 3, 1873), 848; see Gladden, *Recollections,* 223–25.

28. See Gladden editorials in *The Independent* 25 (Aug. 7, 1873): 992; 25 (Aug. 28, 1873): 1076; 25 (Sept. 4, 1873): 1105; discussion in Gladden, *Recollections,* 225–27; Dorn, *Washington Gladden,* 143; William R. Hutchison, *The Modernist Impulse in American Protestantism* (Durham, N.C.: Duke University Press, 1992), 58–59.

29. David Swing, *Truths for Today, Spoken in the Past Winter* (Chicago: Jansen, McClurg & Company, 1874); Swing, *David Swing's Sermons* (Chicago: W. B. Keen, Cooke, & Co., 1874); Joseph Fort Newton, *David Swing: Poet-Preacher* (Chicago: Unity Publishing Co., 1909), 56–57; Gladden, *Recollections*, 226.

30. "Temporary Inspiration" argument in David Swing, "Old Testament Inspiration" (1882), reprinted in *David Swing's Sermons*, 94–99; remaining references in Swing, *Truths for Today, Spoken in the Past Winter*, quotes on 121, 139, 64; see David Swing, *Truths for Today, Second Series* (Chicago: Jansen, McClurg & Co., 1876), 277–94.

31. *The Trial of the Rev. David Swing, before the Presbytery of Chicago*, ed. David S. Johnson, Francis L. Patton, George C. Noyes (Chicago: Jansen, McClurg & Co., 1874), 67–133, 173–86, quotes on 67, 79, 83, 186; see Newton, *David Swing: Poet-Preacher*, 97–98; Hutchison, *The Modernist Impulse in American Protestantism*, 58–65; Lefferts A. Loetscher, *The Broadening Church: A Study of Theological Issues in the Presbyterian Church since 1869* (Philadelphia: University of Pennsylvania Press, 1957), 13–14.

32. *The Trial of the Rev. David Swing*, Mathews quotes, 249–50; Swazey quote, 220; Forsyth quote, 234; Beecher remarks, 275–76; Patterson remarks, 187–204; Swing remarks, 144–45, "dark theology" quote on 19.

33. [Washington Gladden], "Come-outers and Stay-inners," *The Independent* 23 (June 22, 1871): 6; see *The Independent* 26 (Mar. 5, 1874): 16; *The Independent* 26 (May 14, 1874): 16–17.

34. Washington Gladden, "A Good Fight Declined," *The Independent* 26 (May 28, 1874): 16.

35. *Theodore Thornton Munger, New England Minister*, 156–204, quote on 160.

36. Gladden letter to Lyman Abbott, Nov. 3, 1874, quoted in Dorn, *Washington Gladden*, 59; Gladden, *Recollections*, 239–40.

37. Washington Gladden, *Being a Christian: What It Means and How to Begin* (Boston: Congregational Publishing Society, 1876), quote on 61–62; Gladden, *The Christian Way: Whither It Leads and How to Go On* (New York: Dodd, Mead & Co., 1877), quotes on 10, 88.

38. See Washington Gladden, "To Bolt or Not to Bolt," *Scribner's Monthly* 20 (Oct. 1880): 906–13; Gladden, "Superfluous Praying," *Sunday Afternoon* 2 (Aug. 1878): 137–42; Gladden, "How to Use the Bible," *Sunday Afternoon* 2 (Nov. 1878): 451–56; Gladden, et al., *Constitution and By-Laws of the Union Relief Association, also Report on Organization* (Springfield, Mass.: Atwood & Noyes, 1877); Gladden, *The Lord's Prayer. Seven Homilies* (Boston: Houghton, Mifflin & Co., 1880); *Theodore Thornton Munger, New England Minister*, 203–11, 215–16. Gladden's lectures on labor/capital issues from this period were published as *Working People and Their Employers* (New York: Funk & Wagnalls Co., 1894).

39. Dorn, *Washington Gladden*, 148–51; Gladden, *Recollections*, 262–64.

40. Munger to Gladden, Jan. 30, 1878, cited in Dorn, *Washington Gladden*, 152–53; *Theodore Thornton Munger, New England Minister*, 224–34, Porter citation on 233.

41. Roswell Smith to Gladden, Oct. 2, 1882, Ohio State Historical Society, Gladden Papers; Gladden, *Recollections*, 283.

42. Theodore T. Munger, *On the Threshold*, 19th ed. (Boston: Houghton, Mifflin & Co., 1887; 1st ed., 1880); Munger recollection and "garner his wheat" story both cited in *Theodore Thornton Munger, New England Minister*, 237, 252–53.

43. Newman Smyth, *Recollections and Reflections* (New York: Charles Scribner's Sons, 1926), 9–11, 24–25, 37–38, quote on 25.

44. Ibid., quotes on 40, 43, 79.

45. Buckham, *Progressive Religious Thought in America*, 186–89; Newman Smyth, *Recollections and Reflections*, 76–87, quote on 87.

46. Friedrich Schleiermacher, *Brief Outline on the Study of Theology*, trans. Terrence N. Tice (Atlanta: John Knox Press, 1966); Friedrich Aug. Gottreu Tholuck, "Theological Encyclopedia and Methodology," *Bibliotheca Sacra* 1 (1844): 565–66, 194–95; see Edward Farley, *Theologia: The Fragmentation and Unity of Theological Education* (Philadelphia: Fortress Press, 1983), 49–95; W. Clark Gilpin, *A Preface to Theology* (Chicago: University of Chicago Press, 1996), 53–63.

47. Smyth, *Recollections and Reflections*, 88–94, quote on 89.

48. Newman Smyth, *The Religious Feeling: A Study for Faith* (New York: Scribner, Armstrong, & Co., 1877), v–vii, 15–19, 29–52, quotes on 17, 34–35.

49. Ibid., 64–65, 80–83, quotes on 65, 82; see John Stuart Mill, *An Examination of Sir William Hamilton's Philosophy and of the Principal Philosophical Questions Discussed in His Writings.* (London: Longman, 1865).

50. Smyth, *The Religious Feeling,* 162–63; Newman Smyth, *Old Faiths in New Light* (New York: Charles Scribner's Sons, 1879; reprint, London: Charles Higham & T. Fisher Unwin, 1882), quote on 3.

51. Smyth, *Old Faiths in New Light,* 27, 56.

52. Ibid., 32.

53. Newman Smyth, *Orthodox Theology of To-Day* (New York: Charles Scribner's Sons, 1881; reprint, London: Ward, Lock, & Co., 1882), 8–9.

54. Ibid., 36–39, 41–54, quotes on 37.

55. Ibid., 55–70, quote on 64.

56. Ibid., 80–89, quotes on 80, 82.

57. See A Society of Clergymen, "Thoughts on the State of Theological Science and Education in Our Country," *Bibliotheca Sacra* 1 (1844): 736–49, 757–63; William Warren Sweet, "The Rise of Theological Schools in America," *Church History* 6 (1937): 271–72; Egbert C. Smyth, *The Value of the Study of Church History in Ministerial Education* (Andover, Mass.: Warren P. Draper, 1874); Daniel Day Williams, *The Andover Liberals: A Study in American Theology* (New York: King's Crown Press, 1941), 26–27.

58. See John P. Gulliver, *Christianity and Science* (Andover, Mass.: Trustees of Andover Seminary, 1880); William Jewett Tucker, *My Generation: An Autobiographical Interpretation* (Boston: Houghton, Mifflin & Co., 1919), 125–28; Williams, *The Andover Liberals,* 27–29; Frank Hugh Foster, *The Modern Movement in American Theology: Sketches in the History of American Protestant Thought from the Civil War to the World War* (New York: Fleming H. Revell Co., 1939), 24–36.

59. See Levi L. Paine, *A Critical History of the Evolution of Trinitarianism and its Outcome in the New Christology* (New York: Houghton Mifflin Co., 1900); Paine, *The Ethnic Trinities and their Relations to the Christian Trinity: A Chapter in the Comparative History of Religions* (Boston: Houghton Mifflin Co., 1901); Egbert C. Smyth and others, "Christianity and Its Modern Competitors," *Andover Review* 6 (Nov.–Dec. 1886): 510–14, 642–58; "Christianity and Its Modern Competitors," *Andover Review* 7 (Jan. 1887): 64–77, 295–308, 391–405; F. H. Johnson, "Mechanical Evolution," *Andover Review* 1 (Jan. 1884): 631–49; Borden Parker Bowne, "The Natural History of Atheism," *Andover Review* 10 (July–Dec. 1888): 169–82. *The Andover Review, a Religious and Theological Monthly,* had a nine-year run, from 1884 to 1893. On the heresy proceedings, see *The Andover Trial, Professor Smyth's Argument with the Statements of Professors Tucker, Harris, Hincks, and Churchill* (Boston: Houghton Mifflin & Co., 1887); and *The Andover Defence* (Boston: Cupples, Upham & Co., 1887).

60. *Progressive Orthodoxy: A Contribution to the Christian Interpretation of Christian Doctrines,* ed. Egbert C. Smyth, William J. Tucker, J. W. Churchill, George Harris, Edward Y. Hincks (Boston: Houghton Mifflin & Co., 1885), quotes on 9, 12–13, 106; see Williams, *The Andover Liberals,* 31–83; Tucker, *My Generation,* 185–221; Buckham, *Progressive Religious Thought in America,* 194–214.

61. Munger, "The New Theology," in Munger, *The Freedom of Faith* (Boston: Houghton, Mifflin & Co., 1883), 6–9.

62. Theodore T. Munger, "On the Reception of New Truth," in Munger, *The Freedom of Faith,* 50–53; and Munger, "The New Theology," ibid., 10, 12–13.

63. Munger, "The New Theology," ibid., 15.

64. Munger, "On the Reception of New Truth," ibid., 65; Munger, "The New Theology," ibid., 18–19.

65. Munger, "The New Theology," ibid., 28–30, 32–33.

66. Munger, "On the Reception of New Truth," ibid., 60.

67. Munger, "The New Theology," ibid., 6, 43.

68. Theodore T. Munger, "God Our Shield," in *The Freedom of Faith,* 78–79.

69. Theodore T. Munger, "Immortality and Science," in *The Freedom of Faith,* 218, 226, 228–29; Munger, "The Resurrection from the Dead," ibid., 297–313.

70. See reviews of *The Freedom of Faith,* John E. Todd, *Bibliotheca Sacra* 43 (Apr. 1886): 335–56; A. A. Hodge, *Presbyterian Review* 4 (Oct. 1883): 874–76; Queen Victoria's remarks to her

chaplain, Bishop Boyd Carpenter, cited in *Theodore Thornton Munger*, 258. The Smyth book that she read was *The Orthodox Theology of To-Day.* "Dominated" quote in preface to Theodore T. Munger, *The Appeal to Life*, 8th ed. (Boston: Houghton, Mifflin & Co., 1894; 1st ed. 1887), v.

71. Munger, *The Appeal to Life*, v; Munger, "The Witness from Experience," in *The Appeal to Life*, 2; all sermon titles from this book.

72. Newman Smyth, *Old Faiths in New Light*, 129–66; Munger, *The Appeal to Life*, 214.

73. Munger, "Evolution and the Faith," in *The Appeal to Life*, 215–16.

74. Ibid., 216–17.

75. Ibid., 217.

76. Henry Ward Beecher, *Evolution and Religion;* Smyth, *Old Faiths in New Light;* John Fiske, *The Idea of God as Affected by Modern Knowledge* (Boston: Houghton, Mifflin & Co., 1885); *The Appeal to Life*, 219.

77. Munger, "Evolution and the Faith," 220–21.

78. Ibid., 225–26, 230, 234; see Munger's sermon, "Man the Final Form in Creation," in *The Appeal to Life*, 283–306.

79. Theodore T. Munger, *Character through Inspiration, And Other Papers* (New York: Thos. Whittaker, 1897), 12–13; Newman Smyth, *The Place of Death in Evolution* (New York: Charles Scribner's Sons, 1897); Newman Smyth, *Through Science to Faith* (New York: Charles Scribner's Sons, 1902), quotes on vii, 47, 272.

80. Theodore T. Munger, "The Interplay of Christianity and Literature," in Munger, *Essays for the Day* (Boston: Houghton, Mifflin & Co., 1904), 55–101, quote, 98; see Munger, "Truth through and by Life," in *The Freedom of Faith*, 51–58.

81. Theodore T. Munger, "Horace Bushnell," in *Prophets of the Christian Faith: A Series of Essays* (New York: Macmillan Co., 1896), 169–92; Munger, "Horace Bushnell: The Centenary of a Great Alumnus," *Yale Alumni Weekly* (Apr. 9, 1902); Munger, "The Secret of Horace Bushnell," in *Bushnell Centenary: Minutes of the General Association of Connecticut at the One Hundred and Ninety-Third Annual Meeting Held in Hartford, June 17, 18, 1902* (Hartford, Conn.: Case, Lockwood & Brainard Co., 1902), 35–46.

82. Munger letter to Horace E. Scudder, 1888, cited in *Theodore Thornton Munger*, 304.

83. Munger, "God Our Shield," in *The Freedom of Faith*, 80–81; Theodore T. Munger, *Horace Bushnell, Preacher and Theologian* (Boston: Houghton, Mifflin & Co., 1899), 413–14.

84. Recollections by George L. Walker and George A. Gordon reprinted in *Theodore Thornton Munger*, 372–75 (Walker), and 377–98 (Gordon); see George A. Gordon, *My Education and Religion: An Autobiography* (Boston: Houghton Mifflin Co., 1925), 315–18.

85. Gladden, *Recollections*, 284–90; see Alfred E. Lee, *History of the City of Columbus: Capital of Ohio*, 2 vols. (New York: Munsell & Co., 1892), 1:830–36; Daniel Day Williams, *The Andover Liberals* (New York: Octagon Books, 1970); William Jewett Tucker, *My Generation: An Autobiographical Interpretation* (Boston: Houghton Mifflin Co., 1919), 101–247.

86. See Gaius Glenn Atkins, "Washington Gladden—And After," *Religion in Life: A Christian Quarterly* 5 (winter 1936): 599–600; Dorn, *Washington Gladden*, 71–75; Wilbur A. Siebert, "A Reminiscence," *First Church News: The Gladden Centennial* 6 (Feb. 1936): 10; Washington Gladden, *The Christian Pastor and the Working Church* (Edinburgh: T. & T. Clark, 1898), 50–51; Gladden, *Recollections*, 98; Peter Clark Macfarlane, "Washington Gladden, The First Citizen of Columbus," *Colliers* 49 (June 29, 1912): 20–24; Charles Reynolds Brown, *They Were Giants* (New York: Macmillan Co., 1935), 211–40. Gladden's wife, Jennie, was actively involved in church and community affairs, serving for many years as president of the Women's Missionary Society of First Church Congregational. After a prolonged illness, she died during the period that Gladden wrote his autobiography, an experience that undoubtedly heightened his strong sense of privacy.

87. Quotes in Gladden, *Recollections*, 291, 292; see Dorn, *Washington Gladden*, 208–9; John L. Shover, "Washington Gladden and the Labor Question," *Ohio Historical Quarterly* 68 (Oct. 1959): 337.

88. Washington Gladden, "The Wage-Workers and the Churches," in Gladden, *Applied Christianity: Moral Aspects of Social Questions* (Boston: Houghton, Mifflin & Co., 1889), 173.

89. Washington Gladden, "Is It Peace Or War?" in Gladden, *Applied Christianity*, 102–45, quotes on 131, 141, 145.

90. Washington Gladden, "Christianity and Wealth," in Gladden, *Applied Christianity*, 8–32; see Gladden, *Recollections*, 300–4.

91. Three systems argument in Gladden, *Working People and Their Employers*, 44–45; "industrial system" quote in Gladden, "Christianity and Wealth," 32–33.

92. Gladden, "Christianity and Wealth," 34–35. See Richard T. Ely, ed., *A History of Cooperation in America* (Baltimore: Johns Hopkins University Press, 1888); Nicholas Paine Gilman, *Profit Sharing between Employer and Employee: A Study in the Evolution of the Wages System* (London: Macmillan Co., 1890); Gladden's thinking on profit sharing was strongly influenced by Sedley Taylor, *Profit-Sharing between Labor and Capital, Six Essays* (New York: Humboldt Publishing Co., 1886).

93. Washington Gladden, "The Strength and Weakness of Socialism," in Gladden, *Applied Christianity*, 53–101, quotes on 98, 100.

94. Washington Gladden, *Tools and the Man: Property and Industry under the Christian Law* (Boston: Houghton, Mifflin & Co., 1893), quotes on 214, 124; discussion of cooperative ownership, 190–203.

95. Ibid., 130, 271.

96. Ibid., 264–65; closing quote in Washington Gladden, *Christianity and Socialism* (New York: Eaton & Mains, 1905), 141.

97. Gladden, *Christianity and Socialism*, 102–38, right to property statement on 92; Washington Gladden, *Social Facts and Forces* (New York: G. P. Putnam's Sons, 1897), 80–86; Gladden, *Recollections*, 308–9; Gladden, *Tools and the Man*, 294–302, quotes on 299, 300.

98. Washington Gladden, *The Labor Question* (Boston: Pilgrim Press, 1911), 3–55, 98–110, quote on 55; Gladden, *Recollections*, 306–8; Gladden, *Social Facts and Forces*, 81–82; unidentified "vindictive opposition" quote in *Recollections*, 305; see John L. Shover, "Washington Gladden and the Labor Question," *Ohio Historical Quarterly* 68 (Oct. 1959): 344–45.

99. Gladden, *Tools and the Man*, 1–2.

100. Ibid., 3–4, 6; see Washington Gladden, *Social Salvation* (Boston: Houghton, Mifflin & Co., 1902), 1–31; Gladden, "Where Is the Kingdom of God?" in Gladden, *Burning Questions of the Life That Now Is, and of That Which is to Come* (London: James Clarke & Co., 1890), 223–48; Gladden, *The Church and the* Kingdom (New York: Fleming H. Revell Co., 1894); Gladden, *The Lord's Prayer*, 59–81.

101. Gladden, *Tools and the Man*, 18–19.

102. See J. N. Darby, *The Collected Writings of J. N. Darby*, ed. William Kelly, Doctrinal No. 1 35 vols. (reprint, Sunbury, Pa.: Believers Bookshelf, 1971), 3:1–43; C. Norman Kraus, *Dispensationalism in America: Its Rise and Development* (Richmond: John Knox Press, 1958); Ruth A. Doan, *The Miller Heresy, Millennialism, and American Culture* (Philadelphia: Temple University Press, 1987); Gary Dorrien, *The Remaking of Evangelical Theology* (Louisville, Ky.: Westminster John Knox Press, 1998), 28–32.

103. Gladden, *Tools and the Man*, "dismal and dreadful spectacle" quote, 23; Gladden, *Social Salvation*, "no political responsibilities" quote, 21.

104. Charles H. Hopkins, *The Rise of the Social Gospel in American Protestantism, 1865–1915* (New Haven, Conn.: Yale University Press, 1940), 113–17, 175–76, 194–95, 260; Henry F. May, *Protestant Churches and Industrial America* (New York: Harper & Brothers, 1949), 254; Dorn, *Washington Gladden*, 200–1; Josiah Strong, *Our Country* (New York: Baker & Taylor Co., 1885), 138–39; Richard T. Ely, *Ground under Our Feet: An Autobiography* (New York: Macmillan Co., 1938), 140–43.

105. Washington Gladden, *Present Day Theology* (Columbus, Ohio: McClelland & Co., 1913); Gladden, *Seven Puzzling Bible Books: A Supplement to "Who Wrote the Bible?"* (Boston: Houghton, Mifflin & Co., 1897); Gladden, *Who Wrote the Bible?: A Book for the People* (Boston: Houghton, Mifflin & Co., 1891), "fields of destructive criticism," 276; Patton quoted in *First Church News, The Gladden Centennial*, 6–7; see Gladden, *Social Salvation*, 12–31; Gladden, *Ruling Ideas of the Present Age* (Boston: Houghton, Mifflin & Co., 1895), 3–16, 165–87.

106. Richard Hofstadter, *Social Darwinism in American Thought*, rev. ed. (Boston: Beacon Press, 1955), 31–50, quote on 33; Herbert Spencer, *First Principles* (New York: D. Appleton & Co., 1864); Spencer, *The Man Versus the State*, ed. Truxton Beale (New York: Mitchell Kennerley, 1916); Spencer, *The Principles of Sociology*, 3 vols. (New York: D. Appleton & Co.,

1876–97); Spencer, *The Principles of Ethics,* 2 vols. (New York: D. Appleton & Co., 1895–98); William Graham Sumner, *The Challenge of Facts and Other Essays* (New Haven, Conn.: Yale University Press, 1914); Sumner, *Essays of William Graham Sumner,* ed. Albert G. Keller and Maurice R. Davie, 2 vols. (New Haven, Conn.: Yale University Press, 1934).

107. Henry Drummond, *Natural Law in the Spiritual World* (Chicago: Donohue Brothers, 1881); Drummond, *The Ascent of Man* (New York: James Pott & Co., 1895); Peter Kropotkin, *Mutual Aid: A Factor in Evolution* (London: McClure, Phillips, 1902); American Economic Association statement of principles quoted in Ely, *Ground under Our Feet: An Autobiography,* 140; Ely's trade union statement in Richard T. Ely, *The Labor Movement in America* (New York: Macmillan Co., 1905), 138; "tool in the hands" in Ely, "The Past and Present of Political Economy," in *Johns Hopkins University Studies in Historical and Political Science* (Baltimore: Johns Hopkins University Press, 1884), 202; Washington Gladden, "Why I Am Thankful," *The Congregationalist* 82 (Nov. 18, 1897): 734–35; Gladden, *The Church and the Kingdom,* 46–67; Dorn, *Washington Gladden: Prophet of the Social Gospel,* 191–92; Hofstadter, *Social Darwinism in American Thought,* 108–9.

108. John Fiske, "Evolution and Religion," in Fiske, *Excursions of an Evolutionist* (Boston: Houghton, Mifflin & Co., 1891), 294–305, "mighty rhythmic" quote, 302; "continuous adjustment" quote and evolution of the eye description in Fiske, *Through Nature to God* (Boston: Houghton, Mifflin & Co., 1899), 178, 184; Washington Gladden, "Has Evolution Abolished God?" in Gladden, *Burning Questions of the Life that Now Is, and of That Which Is to Come,* 3–33; Washington Gladden, *How Much Is Left of the Old Doctrines?* (Boston: Houghton, Mifflin & Co., 1899), 1–45; Charles Darwin, *The Origin of Species* (London: J. Murray, 1859); Darwin, *The Descent of Man and Selection in Relation to Sex,* 1st ed. (London: J. Murray, 1871).

109. Fiske, *Through Nature to God,* 131–94, quotes on 190–91; see John Fiske, *The Destiny of Man Viewed in the Light of His Origin* (Boston: Houghton, Mifflin & Co., 1884), 108–19; Fiske, *A Century of Science and Other Essays* (Boston: Houghton, Mifflin & Co., 1899); Fiske, *Outlines of Cosmic Philosophy,* 2 vols. (Boston: Houghton, Mifflin & Co., 1874).

110. John Fiske, "Darwinism Verified," in Fiske, *Darwinism and Other Essays* (Boston: Houghton, Mifflin & Co., 1884), 1–31, quote on 7; Gladden, *What Is Left of the Old Doctrines?* "veritable evangel" and "greatest fact" quotes on 19, 23; Gladden, "Has Evolution Abolished God?" closing quote on 28; see Fiske, "In Memoriam: Charles Darwin," in Fiske, *Excursions of an Evolutionist,* 337–69; Fiske, *The Idea of God as Affected by Modern Knowledge,* 135–57. Among Fiske's sizable corpus of writings, the key works, for Gladden, were *The Destiny of Man Viewed in the Light of His Origin, The Idea of God as Affected by Modern Knowledge,* and especially, *Through Nature to God.*

111. Washington Gladden, *Where Does the Sky Begin?* (Boston: Houghton, Mifflin & Co., 1904), 50–51; Gladden, *How Much Is Left of the Old Doctrines?* 24–25; Lyman Abbott, *The Theology of an Evolutionist* (Boston: Houghton Mifflin Co., 1897), vi, 176–77.

112. Abbott, *The Theology of an Evolutionist,* 178–84, quote on 179; see Lyman Abbott, *Reminiscences* (Boston: Houghton Mifflin Co., 1923), 456–466. Abbott outlined the preoccupation with evolution that fixated his generation in its prime; the theological evolutionist barely mentioned evolution in his late-life spiritual autobiography: Abbott, *What Christianity Means to Me: A Spiritual Autobiography* (New York: Macmillan Co., 1921), 153–56.

113. John Fiske, *American Political Ideas* (New York: Harper & Brothers, 1885); Fiske, *Civil Government in the United States* (Boston: Houghton, Mifflin & Co., 1890).

114. Fiske, "Manifest Destiny," originally delivered to the Royal Institute of Great Britain, 1880, reprinted in Fiske, "Manifest Destiny," *Harper's Magazine* 70 (Mar. 1885): 578–90; and Fiske, *American Political Ideas,* 101–52, quotes on 131, 140–41.

115. Fiske, *American Political Ideas,* 146, 148.

116. Josiah Strong, *Our Country, Its Possible Future and Its Present Crisis* (New York: American Home Missionary Society, 1886; rev. ed., New York: Baker & Taylor, 1891; reprint, Cambridge: Harvard University Press, 1963, ed. Jurgen Herbst), x–xi; Horace Bushnell, *Barbarism the First Danger: A Discourse for Home Missions* (New York: American Home Missionary Society, 1847); Edward T. Root, "Josiah Strong: A Modern Prophet of the Kingdom of God," *New Church Review* 29 (June 1922): 47–54; Shailer Mathews, "The

Development of Social Christianity in America," *Journal of Religion* 7 (July 1927): 376–86; Hofstadter, *Social Darwinism in American Thought*, 177–78.

117. Strong, *Our Country*, 210–11, see Harvard edition, 41–58.

118. Ibid., 200–2, 205.

119. Ibid., 206, 208, see 195–99.

120. Ibid., 209, 210, 212; Darwin, *The Descent of Man and Selection in Relation to Sex*, rev. 2d ed. (New York: D. Appleton & Co., 1888), 142.

121. Darwin, *The Descent of Man and Selection in Relation to Sex*, 1st ed. (1871), 154; Horace Bushnell, *Christian Nurture* (New York: Charles Scribner's Sons, 1861), 213; Strong, *Our Country*, 213–15.

122. Hopkins, *The Rise of the Social Gospel in American Protestantism, 1865–1915*, 113–16; *The Christian Union* 32 (Dec. 17, 1885): 6–8; May, *Protestant Churches and Industrial America*, 194; Hofstadter, *Social Darwinism in American Thought*, 178.

123. On early social gospel sociology, see Evangelical Alliance for the U.S.A., *Christianity Practically Applied: The Discussions of the International Christian Conference held in Chicago, Oct. 8–14, 1893*, 2 vols. (New York: Baker & Taylor Co., 1894); Aaron I. Abell, *The Urban Impact on American Protestantism, 1850–1900* (Cambridge: Harvard University Press, 1943), 224–45; James Dombrowski, *The Early Days of Christian Socialism in America* (New York: Columbia University Press, 1936), 60–73; William Jewett Tucker, *My Generation: An Autobiographical Interpretation* (Boston: Houghton, Mifflin Co., 1919), 169–77; May, *Protestant Churches and Industrial America*, 194–95; Josiah Strong, *The New Era, or, The Coming Kingdom* (New York: Baker & Taylor Co., 1893), 296–341, "no church taking" quote on 321.

124. Strong, *The New Era*, 17–40, 41–53, 54–80, 178–202, quotes on 77, 80.

125. Washington Gladden, "The Issues of the War," *The Outlook* 59 (July 16, 1898): 673–75; Gladden sermon on England and America standing together, "The Future of the Aristocracy," preached on Oct. 11, 1891, Gladden Papers; discussion of Gladden's views of Anglo-American solidarity and the Spanish-American War in Dorn, *Washington Gladden*, 402–12; quote on Cubans cited by Dorn from Gladden sermon reprinted in the *Ohio State Journal*, Jan. 5, 1897.

126. Josiah Strong, *Expansion, under New World-Conditions* (New York: Baker & Taylor Co., 1900), 280–81; editorial, *The Outlook* 70 (July 29, 1899): 699; on clerical anti-imperialism during this period, see Winthrop S. Hudson, "Protestant Clergy Debate the Nation's Vocation, 1898–1899," *Church History* 42 (1973): 110–18; Robert T. Handy, *A Christian America: Protestant Hopes and Historical Realities*, 2d ed. (New York: Oxford University Press, 1984), 243.

127. Lyman Abbott, *The Rights of Man: A Study in Twentieth Century Problems* (Boston: Houghton, Mifflin & Co., 1901), 274.

128. "Morally unthinkable" and "degraded races" in Washington Gladden, "The Signing of the Treaty," sermon, Dec. 18, 1898, Gladden Papers; Gladden, "The Problem of the Philippines," sermon, Sept. 3, 1899, Gladden Papers; Gladden, "The People of the Philippines," sermon, Sept. 10, 1899, Gladden Papers; Gladden, "The Chinese Mind," sermon, Sept. 9, 1900, Gladden Papers; Gladden, "Good News from the Wide World," sermon, Sept. 22, 1901; Gladden Papers; "Good News from the Wide World," sermon, Dec. 27, 1908, Gladden Papers; Dorn, *Washington Gladden*, 412–15.

129. In 1893, ex-President Rutherford B. Hayes interviewed Gladden and informed him that the Ohio State University board of trustees, of which Hayes was president, had selected Gladden to be the university's next president. The state legislature was controlled by anti-Catholics, however, who blocked Gladden's appointment. See *Diary and Letters of Rutherford Birchard Hayes: Nineteenth President of the United States*, 5 vols. (Columbus, Ohio: Ohio State Archaeological and Historical Society, 1922–26), 5:81, 94; Gladden, *Recollections*, 414–15; Dorn, *Washington Gladden*, 118–19.

130. "No unnatural fusion" and "perfect equality" quotes in Washington Gladden, *The Negro's Southern Neighbors and His Northern Friends* (New York: Congregational Rooms, [1903]); Gladden, "Sociological Aspects of A.M.A. Work," *The Congregationalist* 81 (Oct. 29, 1896): 646–49; Gladden, "The Negro Crisis: Is the Separation of the Two Races to Become Necessary?" *American Magazine* 63 (Jan., 1907), 296–301; Gladden, *Recollections*, 366–76; citations and discussion in Dorn, *Washington Gladden, Prophet of the Social Gospel*, 293–302;

see Ralph E. Luker, *The Social Gospel in Black and White: American Racial Reform, 1885–1912* (Chapel Hill, N.C.: University of North Carolina Press, 1991), 211–16.

131. Luker, *The Social Gospel in Black and White*, 193–230; see Ronald C. White Jr., *Liberty and Justice for All: Racial Reform and the Social Gospel (1877–1925)* (New York: Harper & Row, 1990); David M. Reimers, *White Protestantism and the Negro* (New York: Oxford University Press, 1965).

132. Editorial, "Two Typical Leaders," *The Outlook* 74 (May 23, 1903): 214–16; W. E. B. DuBois, *The Souls of Black Folk* (Chicago: A. C. McClurg & Co., 1903), 53–54; citations and discussion in Luker, *The Social Gospel in Black and White*, 214–16, 230; see Booker T. Washington, *Up from Slavery* (New York: A. L. Burt Co., 1901).

133. Washington Gladden, "Some Impressions Gained during a Visit to the Southern United States," sermon, May 31, 1903, Gladden Papers; "Even These Least," sermon, Jan. 9, 1916, Gladden Papers; "no reason" and "moral universe" quotes in Gladden, *Recollections*, 375–76; see Luker *The Social Gospel in Black and White*, 215–16.

134. Gladden, *Recollections*, 419, 431.

135. Washington Gladden, *The Great War—Six Sermons* (Columbus, Ohio: McClelland & Co., 1915), corrupt rulers argument, 8–9; Gladden, *Is War a Moral Necessity? Sermon Preached before First Congregational Church of Detroit, Apr. 18, 1915* (Detroit: Printed by Friends, 1915), 6–15; Gladden, "What War Must Bring," *War and Peace* (Columbus, Ohio: First Congregational Church, 1914), 30–31; Gladden, "Universal Righteousness," sermon, Mar. 29, 1915, Gladden Papers; Gladden, "Nations Are Members One of Another," sermon, Apr. 11, 1915, Gladden Papers; Gladden, "Does Human Nature Change?", sermon, May 30, 1915, Gladden Papers; Gladden, "Christ's Light in the World," sermon, Dec. 26, 1915, Gladden Papers; Gladden, "Getting Ready for War," sermon, Jan. [?] 1916, Gladden Papers; Charles S. Macfarland, *Pioneers for Peace through Religion: Based on the Records of the Church Peace Union (Founded by Andrew Carnegie), 1914–1945* (New York: Fleming H. Revell Co., 1946), 46; Dorn, *Washington Gladden*, 417–23; Richard D. Knudten, *The Systematic Thought of Washington Gladden* (New York: Humanities Press, 1968), 175–85.

136. Washington Gladden, "A Communication: A Pacifist's Apology," *The New Republic* 5 (Nov. 20, 1915): 75–76; caveat against absolute pacifism in Gladden, *The Great War—Six Sermons*, 14; "new machinery" quote in Gladden, "A Plea for Pacifism," *The Nation*, Supplement to vol. 103 (Columbus, Ohio: Champlin Press, 1916), 7.

137. Woodrow Wilson, "An Annual Message on the State of the Union," Dec. 7, 1915, in *The Papers of Woodrow Wilson*, ed. Arthur S. Link, 69 vols. (Princeton, N.J.: Princeton University Press, 1980), 35:293–310; Wilson, "An Address to the Federal Council of Churches," Dec. 10, 1915, in ibid., 35:329–36, quotes on 329, 330, 332; Washington Gladden to Woodrow Wilson, Dec. 11, 1915, in ibid., 35:344–45; Woodrow Wilson to Washington Gladden, Dec. 14, 1915, in ibid., 35:353.

138. "Just now it appears," Gladden sermon, "Christ's Light in the World," Dec. 26, 1915, Gladden Papers; "What is going," Gladden sermon, "Getting Ready for War."

139. Washington Gladden, *The Forks of the Road* (New York: Macmillan Co., 1916), 31–32, 98, 106–7.

140. Gladden, "A Plea for Pacifism," 7.

141. Gladden, *The Forks of the Road*, 137–38.

142. Woodrow Wilson, "An Appeal for a Statement of War Aims," Dec. 18, 1916, in *The Papers of Woodrow Wilson*, 40:273–76; Wilson, "An Address to the Senate," Jan. 22, 1917, in ibid., 40:533–39, quotes on 536.

143. See Thomas J. Knock, *To End All Wars: Woodrow Wilson and the Quest for a New World Order* (Princeton, N.J.: Princeton University Press, 1992), 108–22; Ronald Schaffer, *America in the Great War: The Rise of the Welfare State* (New York: Oxford University Press, 1991), xiv–xvii; Henry F. May, *The End of American Innocence: A Study of the First Years of Our Own Time, 1912–1917* (New York: Alfred A. Knopf, 1959), 355–86.

144. "Darkest cloud" and "All the great people," Gladden sermon, 'High Lights of Mercy," Feb. 11, 1917, Gladden Papers.

145. Woodrow Wilson, "An Address to a Joint Session of Congress," Apr. 2, 1917, in *The Papers of Woodrow Wilson*, 41:519–27, quote on 525; Lyman Abbott, *The Twentieth Century Crusade* (New York: Macmillan Co., 1918), 62; Shailer Mathews, *Patriotism and Religion*

(New York: Macmillan Co., 1918), 4; Ray H. Abrams, *Preachers Present Arms* (New York: Round Table Press, 1933), 54–55.

146. Washington Gladden, "America at War," sermon, Apr. 29, 1917, Gladden Papers.
147. Wilson, "An Address to a Joint Session of Congress," 41:525; Gladden, "America at War."
148. Washington Gladden, "The Nation Is at School," July 1, 1917; Gladden, "Religion after the War," Sept. 2, 1917; Gladden, "Industry after the War," Sept. 12, 1917; Gladden, "Education after the War," Sept. 19, 1917; Gladden, "The High Calling of America," Sept. 23, 1917; Gladden, "The Family after the War," Sept. 26, 1917; Gladden, "The Good Fight," Nov. 4, 1917; Gladden, "The Crying Need for Religion," Nov. 24, 1917; Gladden, "Wilson's Message to the Belligerants," [?] 1917; Gladden, "Where Are We?" 1917, Gladden Papers.
149. "All that is needed" in Washington Gladden, "Loyalty," reprinted in Gladden, *The Interpreter* (Boston: Pilgrim Press, 1918), 81–96, quote on 96; "this war" in Gladden, "America at War."
150. Washington Gladden, "What Is Progress?" sermon, Mar. 14, 1915, Gladden Papers.
151. Washington Gladden, "A New Heart for the Nation," in Gladden, *The Interpreter,* 131–47, quotes on 145.

Chapter 6: Enter the Academics

1. The chief source of information on Briggs' life is the Charles A. Briggs Collection at Burke Library, Union Theological Seminary. It consists of approximately sixty boxes of materials, a few scrapbooks, and twelve ledger books of transcribed correspondence. The letters were copied by hand by Briggs' daughter, Emilie Grace Briggs. Other important biographical sources include Arthur Cushman McGiffert, "Charles Augustus Briggs," *Dictionary of American Biography* (New York: Charles Scribner's Sons, 1958), 2:40–41; Max Gray Rogers, "Charles Augustus Briggs: Heresy at Union," in *American Religious Heretics: Formal and Informal Trials,* ed. George H. Shriver (Nashville: Abingdon Press, 1966), 89–90; Mark Stephen Massa, S.J., *Charles Augustus Briggs and the Crisis of Historical Criticism* (Minneapolis: Fortress Press, 1990), 25–28; Emilie Grace Briggs, "A Sketch of Dr. Charles Augustus Briggs," *The Alumni Bulletin,* University of Virginia 5 (Feb. 1899): 92–100.
2. Alonson Briggs to Charles A. Briggs, Dec. 7, 1858, Ledger Book 3, Briggs Collection, Burke Library, Union Theological Seminary, New York.
3. Marvin Briggs to Charles A. Briggs, Apr. 15, 1857, Ledger Book 3; Marvin Briggs to Charles A. Briggs, Oct. 9, 1858, Ledger Book 3; Marvin Briggs to Charles A. Briggs, Oct. 19, 1858, Ledger Book 3; "on your own account," Marvin Briggs to Charles A. Briggs, Dec. 9, 1858, Ledger Book 3.
4. "The Christian is," Marvin Briggs to Charles A. Briggs, Nov. 30, 1858, Ledger Book 3; Marvin Briggs to Charles A. Briggs, Jan. 30, 1859, Ledger Book 3; "the lecture abounded," Marvin Briggs to Charles A. Briggs, Mar. 1, 1859, Ledger Book 3.
5. Robert T. Handy, *A History of Union Theological Seminary in New York* (New York: Columbia University Press, 1987), 1–18, quote from article 6 of Union's founding constitution, 9.
6. Elizabeth L. Smith, ed., *Henry Boynton Smith, His Life and Work* (New York: A. C. Armstrong & Son, 1881), 12–16; Lewis F. Stearns, *Henry Boynton Smith* (Boston: Houghton, Mifflin & Co., 1892), 31–35; Marvin R. Vincent, "Professor Henry Boynton Smith," *The Presbyterian Quarterly and Princeton Review* 6 (1877): 277–78; William Stoever, "Henry Boynton Smith and the German Theology of History," *Union Seminary Quarterly Review* 24 (1968): 69–89; George L. Prentiss, *The Union Theological Seminary: The First Fifty Years* (New York: Anson D. F. Randolph, 1889), 254–66; George Marsden, *The Evangelical Mind and the New School Experience* (New Haven, Conn.: Yale University Press, 1970).
7. Henry Boynton Smith, *The Inspiration of the Holy Scriptures* (New York: John A. Gray, 1855; Cincinnati: Herald & Presbyter, 1891), 5–8, 19–20.
8. Henry Boynton Smith, "The Idea of Christian Theology as a System," *Faith and Philosophy, Discourses and Essays by Henry B. Smith, D.D., LL.D.,* ed. George L. Prentiss (New York: Scribner, Armstrong & Co., 1877), 6; Henry B. Smith and Roswell Hitchcock, *The Life, Writings, and Character of Edward Robinson, D.D., LL.D.* (New York: Anson D. F. Randolph, 1863), 5–15; Richard A. Miller, "Henry Boynton Smith: Christocentric Theologian," *Journal of Presbyterian History* 61 (winter 1983): 429–44.

9. Julius A. Bewer, "Edward Robinson as a Biblical Scholar," *The Journal of Biblical Literature* 58 (1939): 356–63; William F. Albright, "Edward Robinson," *Dictionary of American Biography* (New York: Charles Scribner's Sons, 1936), 16:39–40.

10. Edward Robinson, *Biblical Researches in Palestine*, 3 vols., 11th ed. (Boston: Crocker & Brewster, 1874); see Robinson, "Theological Education in Germany," *The Biblical Repository* 1 (1831): 1–51, 201–26, 409–51; Robinson, *The Bible and its Literature* (New York: Office of the *American Biblical Repository*, 1841); Robinson, "Genuineness of Isaiah, Chap. XL-LXVI, from Hengstenberg's *Christologie des Alten Testaments*," *The Biblical Repository*, 1 (1831): 700–733; Friedrich Heinrich Wilhelm Gesenius, *A Hebrew and English Lexicon of the Old Testament, Including the Biblical Chaldee: Translated from the Latin of William Gesenius by Edward Robinson* (Boston: Crocker & Brewster; New York: Leavitt, Lord, & Co., 1833). F. M. Abel, "Edward Robinson and the Identification of Biblical Sites," *The Journal of Biblical Literature* 58 (1939): 365–72; Jerry Wayne Brown, *The Rise of Biblical Criticism in America, 1800–1870:* The New England Scholars (Middletown, Conn: Wesleyan University Press, 1969), 111–24.

11. See David Schaff, *The Life of Philip Schaff* (New York: Charles Scribner's Sons, 1897); Philip Schaff, *The Principle of Protestantism as Related to the Present State of the Church* (Chambersburg, Pa.: Publication Office of the German Reformed Church, 1845); James Hastings Nichols, *Romanticism in American Theology: Nevin and Schaff at Mercersburg* (Chicago: University of Chicago Press, 1961); George H. Shriver, "Philip Schaff: Heresy at Mercersburg," in *American Religious Heretics: Formal and Informal Trials*, 18–20.

12. Charles Augustus Briggs, *The Authority of Holy Scripture: An Inaugural Address*, 4th ed. (New York: Charles Scribner's Sons, 1893; 1st ed., 1891), quote on 93; see Charles Augustus Briggs, *The Higher Criticism of the Hexateuch* (New York: Charles Scribner's Sons, 1892), 62; H. B. Smith, "Dorner's History of the Doctrine of the Person of Christ," *Bibliotheca Sacra* 6 (1849): 175–77; Ernst Hengstenberg, *The Christology of the Old Testament*, trans. Theodore Meyer and James Martin 4 vols. 2d ed. (Edinburgh: T. & T. Clark, 1865).

13. "New light" statements," Charles A. Briggs to Marvin Briggs, Jan. 8, 1867, Ledger 1, Briggs Collection; "incarnation of doctrine," Briggs to Marvin Briggs, Mar. 1868, Ledger 1; "much nearer" and "I am better," Briggs to Sarah Briggs, Jan. 14, 1867, Ledger 3.

14. Charles A. Briggs to Henry Boynton Smith, May 6, 1868, Ledger 3; see I. A. Dorner, *A System of Christian Doctrine*, trans. Alfred Cave and J. S. Banks 4 vols. (Edinburgh: T. &. T. Clark, 1888–96); Dorner, *Divine Immutability: A Critical Reconsideration*, trans. Robert R. Williams and Claude Welch (Minneapolis: Fortress Press, 1994); Jurgen Herbst, *The German Historical School in American Scholarship* (Ithaca, N.Y.: Cornell University Press, 1965).

15. Charles A. Briggs to Marvin Briggs, Mar. 1868, Ledger 1.

16. Charles A. Briggs to Henry Boynton Smith, Nov. 25, 1868, Ledger 3.

17. "Orthodoxy or heterodoxy" quote in Henry Boynton Smith, *Faith and Philosophy, Discourses and Essays by Henry B. Smith, D.D., LL.D.*, 284.

18. Briggs to Henry B. Smith, May 6, 1868, Ledger 3; see Lewis G. Vander Velde, *The Presbyterian Churches and the Federal Union, 1861–1869* (Cambridge: Harvard University Press, 1932).

19. Charles A. Briggs, Inaugural Sermon, "Blessed are they which are persecuted for righteousness sake," Apr. 23, 1871, Ledger 4.

20. Karl Moll, *The Psalms, Lange's Commentary on Holy Scripture*, trans. Charles A. Briggs, John Forsyth, James B. Hammond, and J. Frederick McCurdy, 9 vols. (New York: Scribner, Armstrong & Co., 1872); quotation in Massa, *Charles Augustus Briggs and the Crisis of Historical Criticism*, 44.

21. Charles Augustus Briggs, *Biblical Study: Its Principles, Methods, and History*, 2d ed. (New York: Charles Scribner's Sons, 1885; 1st ed., 1883), 210, 212–13.

22. Charles Augustus Briggs, *Exegetical Theology, especially in the Old Testament* (New York: Rogers & Sherwood, 1876), 15.

23. See J. N. Darby, *The Collected Writings of J. N. Darby*, ed. William Kelly, Doctrinal No. 1, 35 vols. (reprint, Sunbury, Pa.: Believers Bookshelf, 1971); C. I. Scofield, *Rightly Dividing the Word of Truth* (Westwood, N.J.: Revell, 1896); Nathaniel West, *The Thousand Year Reign of Christ* (1899; reprint, Grand Rapids: Kregel Publications, 1993); William E. Blackstone, *Jesus Is Coming* (New York: Revell, 1908).

24. Charles A. Briggs, "The Anti-Nicene Church and Premillenarianism," *New York Evangelist,* Jan. 2, 1879, 6; see Briggs, "Shall the Premillennialist Be Tolerated?," *New York Evangelist,* Sept. 12, 1878, 1; Briggs, "Various Forms of Premillenarianism," Nov. 28, 1878, 2; Briggs, "Reformation Testimonies Against the Premillenarians," Dec. 5, 1878, 2; quote in Massa, *Charles Augustus Briggs and the Crisis of Historical Criticism,* 48. See Benjamin B. Warfield, *Studies in Perfectionism* (Philadelphia: Presbyterian & Reformed Publishing Co., 1958); Warfield, review of *What the Bible Teaches: A Thorough and Comprehensive Study of What the Bible Has to Say concerning the Great Doctrines of Which It Treats,* by Reuben A. Torry, *Presbyterian and Reformed Review* 39 (July 1898): 562–64.

25. "The right and the interest," A. A. Hodge to William Adams, Jan. 4, 1879, Ledger 5; "I have not the gifts," A. A. Hodge to William Adams, Feb. 19, 1879, Ledger 5; see George L. Prentiss, *The Union Theological Seminary in the City of New York: Its Design and Another Decade of Its History* (Asbury Park, N.J.: M., W. & C. Pennypacker, 1899), 328–29. On Briggs's ecumenism, see Richard L. Christensen, *The Ecumenical Orthodoxy of Charles Augustus Briggs (1841–1913)* (Lewiston, N.Y.: Edwin Mellen Press, 1995); and Donald G. Dawe, *The Ecumenical Vision of Charles Augustus Briggs* (Surrey, United Kingdom: Ecumenical Society of the Blessed Virgin Mary, 1985).

26. A. A. Hodge, *Outlines of Theology* (ca. 1860; reprint, Edinburgh: Banner of Truth Trust, 1991), 66. See Francis Turretin, *Institutes of Elenctic Theology,* trans. George Musgrave Giger, ed. James T. Dennison Jr., 3 vols. (1679; reprint, Phillipsburg, NJ: Presbyterian & Reformed Publishing Co., 1992); Charles Hodge, *Systematic Theology,* 3 vols. (ca. 1872, reprint, Grand Rapids: Wm. B. Eerdmans Publishing Co., 1993).

27. A. A. Hodge and Benjamin B. Warfield, "Inspiration," *Presbyterian Review* 2 (Apr. 1881): 225–60, Hodge quote on 238; Warfield quote on 245; reprinted in A. A. Hodge and Benjamin B. Warfield, *Inspiration* (Grand Rapids: Baker Book House, 1979); see Benjamin B. Warfield, "Inspiration," in *The International Standard Bible Encyclopedia,* ed. James Orr (Chicago: Howard-Severance Co., 1915), 3:1473–83; Warfield, *The Inspiration and Authority of the Bible* (1948; reprint, Philadelphia: Presbyterian & Reformed Publishing Co., 1964).

28. William Robertson Smith, "The Question of Prophecy in the Critical Schools of the Continent," in *Lectures and Essays of William Robertson Smith,* ed. John S. Black and George Chrystal (London: A. & C. Black, 1912), 163–343, quotes on 164–65; Warner M. Bailey, "William Robertson Smith and American Biblical Studies," *Journal of Presbyterian History* 51 (1973): 285–308; see William Robertson Smith, "Christianity and the Supernatural," in *Lectures and Essays of William Robertson Smith,* 123–24; citation in Massa, *Charles Augustus Briggs and the Crisis of Historical Criticism,* 20; Willis B. Glover, *Evangelical Nonconformists and Higher Criticism in the Nineteenth Century* (London: Independent Press, 1954), 110–11; Ronald Nelson, "Higher Criticism and the Westminster Confession: The Case of William Robertson Smith," *Christian Scholar's Review* 8 (1978): 199–216; T. K. Cheyne, *The Founders of Old Testament Criticism* (New York: Charles Scribner's Sons, 1893). The charges against Smith were not sustained, and he did not lose his ordination, but he was dismissed from his teaching position in 1881.

29. Charles A. Briggs, "Critical Theories of the Sacred Scriptures in Relation to Their Inspiration," *Presbyterian Review* 2 (July 1881): 550–79.

30. Ibid., 551–54, quote on 554; William Robertson Smith, "The Question of Prophecy in the Critical Schools of the Continent," 163–203. On Princeton Theology and its relation to the Reformationist and scholastic traditions, see Gary Dorrien, *The Remaking of Evangelical Theology* (Louisville, Ky.: Westminster John Knox Press, 1998), 17–28.

31. Briggs, "Critical Theories of the Sacred Scriptures in Relation to Their Inspiration," 573, 579, 552, 551.

32. "Pretty strong historical lever," Newman Smyth to Charles A. Briggs, Sept. 16, 1881, Ledger 6; Briggs, "Critical Theories of the Sacred Scriptures in Relation to Their Inspiration," 558.

33. Willis J. Beecher to Charles A. Briggs, Aug. 20, 1882, Ledger 5; Henry Preserved Smith, "The Critical Theories of Julius Wellhausen," *Presbyterian Review* 3 (Apr. 1882): 357–88, quote on 386; Samuel Ives Curtiss, "Delitzsch on the Origin and Composition of the Pentateuch," *Presbyterian Review* 3 (July 1882): 553–88, reference on 573–74; Willis J. Beecher, "The Logical Methods of Prof. Kuenen," *Presbyterian Review* 3 (Oct. 1882): 701–31.

34. "It is significant" in Briggs, "Critical Theories of the Sacred Scriptures in Relation to Their Inspiration," 557; Charles A. Briggs, "A Critical Study of the History of the Higher Criticism with Special Reference to the Pentateuch," *Presbyterian Review* 4 (Jan. 1883): 69–130, discussion on 70–83; see Preserved Smith, "The Critical Theories of Julius Wellhausen," 374.

35. "Much less sanguine," Henry Preserved Smith to Charles A. Briggs, June 18, 1882, Ledger 6; "with the Princeton men," Preserved Smith to Briggs, July 10, 1882, Ledger 6.

36. Briggs, *Biblical Study: Its Principles, Methods and History,* viii.

37. Ibid., 140–43.

38. Ibid., ix.

39. The Westminster Confession of Faith (1647), par. 6.005, *The Book of Confessions* (Louisville, Ky: Office of the General Assembly, Presbyterian Church [U.S.A.], 1991); Rutherford quoted in Jack B. Rogers and Donald K. McKim, *The Authority and Interpretation of the Bible: An Historical Approach* (San Francisco: Harper & Row, 1979), 206. The Westminster Assembly of Divines was called by the English Parliament from 1643 to 1649 for advice on religious reform. It consisted of seven Englishmen and four Scots.

40. Briggs, *Biblical Study: Its Principles, Methods and History,* 160–61.

41. Ibid., 161; Henry Boynton Smith, *The Inspiration of the Holy Scriptures* (New York: John A. Gray, 1855), 27.

42. Briggs, *Biblical Study: Its Principles, Methods, and History,* 162.

43. Most of Wellhausen's work on the Hebrew Bible appeared between 1870 and 1885. His monumental *Geschichte Israels* was published in 1878 as the first volume of a projected two-volume work. Instead of publishing a second volume, however, Wellhausen wrote several other works and then published a revised, renamed volume titled *Prolegomena zur Geschichte Israels.* An English edition of this epochal work was published two years later: Wellhausen, *Prolegomena to the History of Israel,* trans. J. S. Black and Allan Menzies, preface by W. Robertson Smith (Edinburgh: A. & C. Black, 1885; reprint, Atlanta: Scholars Press, 1994). Briggs subsequently lauded Dillmann, Hengstenberg's successor at Berlin, as Germany's premier contemporary scripture scholar; see Briggs, *The Authority of Holy Scripture,* 93. On early German criticism on the Hebrew Bible, see Hans-Joachim Kraus, *Geschichte der historisch-kritischen Erforschung des Alten Testaments,* 4th ed. (Neukirchen-Vluyn: Neukirchener Verlag, 1988); C. Houtman, *Inleiding in de Pentateuch: Een beschrijving van de geschiedenis van het onderzoek naar het ontstaan en de compositie van de eerste vijf boeken van het Oude Testament met een terugblik en een evaluatie* (Kampen: J. H. Kok, 1980). On Wellhausen's anti-Judaism, see Rolf Rendtorff, "Die jüdische Bibel und ihre antijüdische Auslegung," *Auschwitz—Krise der christlichen Theologie: Eine Vortragsreihe,* ed. Rolf Rendtorff and Ekkehard Stegemann (Munich: Christian Kaiser, 1980), 99–116; Lou H. Silberman, "Wellhausen and Judaism," *Semeia* 25 (1982): 75–82.

44. Briggs, *Biblical Study: Its Principles, Methods, and History,* 162–63.

45. Francis L. Patton, "The Dogmatic Aspect of Pentateuchal Criticism," *Presbyterian Review* 4 (Apr. 1883): 341–410, quote on 344; see William Henry Green, "Professor W. Robertson Smith on the Pentateuch," *Presbyterian Review* 3 (January 1882): 108–56. For Briggs's dispute with Green, see Charles A. Briggs, "The Revised English Version of the Old Testament," *Presbyterian Review* 6 (July 1885): 507–8; Briggs, "Dr. Green's Defense of the Revised Version," *The New York Evangelist* 56 (July 30, 1885): n.p.; William Henry Green, "The Critics of the Revised Version of the Old Testament," *Presbyterian Review* 7 (Apr. 1886): 304–54.

46. See Lefferts A. Loetscher, *The Broadening Church: A Study of Theological Issues in the Presbyterian Church since 1869* (Philadelphia: University of Pennsylvania Press, 1954), 39–47; *Minutes of the General Assembly of the Presbyterian Church in the U.S.A.* (Philadelphia: McCalla & Co., 1888), 79.

47. Charles A. Briggs, "The General Assembly of the Presbyterian Church in the United States of America," *Presbyterian Review* 10 (Oct. 1889): 467; Charles A. Briggs, *American Presbyterianism: Its Origin and Early History* (New York: Charles Scribner's Sons, 1885).

48. Briggs, "The Origin of the Phrase, 'In necessariis unitas, in non necessariis libertas, in utrisque caritas,'" *The Presbyterian Review* 8 (July 1887): 496–99; "Premature" and "three parties" quotes in Prentiss, *The Union Theological Seminary in the City of New York: Its Design and Another Decade of Its History,* 330; "more comprehensive" quote in Briggs, "The Westminster Standards: III. Methods of Relief," *The Independent* 41 (Aug. 1, 1889): 979.

49. Charles A. Briggs, "Subscription and Revision," *The Christian Union* 40 (Dec. 12, 1869): 764.

50. Charles Augustus Briggs, *Whither? A Theological Question for the Times* (ca. 1889, 3d ed., New York: Charles Scribner's Sons, 1890), viii–ix. Mark Massa's generally excellent study of Briggs does not distinguish between those who wanted to change the Westminster Standards and those who advocated a new consensus creed. His discussion of the revision controversy is flawed on that account; Briggs may have been "jubilant over Nassau Presbytery's overture," but he struggled for months to determine his strategy toward it, and he never supported the movement to revise the Westminster Standards. See Massa, *Charles Augustus Briggs and the Crisis of Historical Criticism*, 77–78.

51. Briggs, *Whither? A Theological Question for the Times*, ix–x.

52. Ibid., 72–73.

53. Ibid., 7–9, 274–75.

54. Ibid., 91–140, quotes on 137.

55. Ibid., 146–49, quote on 148.

56. Ibid., 154–57, quotes on 156.

57. Ibid., 276–85, quotes on 278, 285.

58. W. W. Moore, "Review of *Whither?*" *Presbyterian Quarterly* 4 (1890): 124–32; James McCosh, *Whither? O Whither? Tell Me Where* (New York: Charles Scribner's Sons, 1889); see George Harris, "Review of *Whither?*" *Andover Review* 12 (1889): 552–55; G. Frederick Wright, "Dr. Briggs's *Whither?*" *Bibliotheca Sacra* 47 (1890): 136–53; W. G. T. Shedd, *The Proposed Revision of the Westminster Standards* (New York: Charles Scribner's Sons, 1890).

59. Benjamin B. Warfield, "The Meaning of Revision," *Presbyterian Journal* (Nov. 14, 1889): 60–61; T. W. M. Paxton to Charles A. Briggs, June 5, 1889, Ledger 7; Briggs to Paxton, June 7, 1889, Ledger 7; Benjamin B. Warfield to Briggs, Aug. 16, 1889, Ledger 7; Briggs to Francis Patton, Sept. 22, 1889, Ledger 7; Francis Brown to Briggs, Oct. 4, 1889, Ledger 7. On the reaction to *Whither?* and the termination of *Presbyterian Review*, see Massa, *Charles Augustus Briggs and the Crisis of Historical Criticism*, 80–82; Christensen, *The Ecumenical Orthodoxy of Charles Augustus Briggs*, 92–94; Rogers, "Charles Augustus Briggs: Heresy at Union," 93–95.

60. Charles A. Briggs, "Revision of the Westminster Confession," *The Andover Review* 13 (Jan. 1890): 45–68, quotes on 45, 48.

61. W. G. T. Shedd, *The Proposed Revision of the Westminster Standards* (New York: Charles Scribner's Sons, 1890); Charles A. Briggs, "The Advance Towards Revision," *How Shall We Revise the Westminster Confession of Faith?* ed. Charles A. Briggs (New York: Charles Scribner's Sons, 1890), 1–33; *Minutes of the General Assembly of the Presbyterian Church in the U.S.A.* (Philadelphia: McCalla & Co., 1890), 122–23; see Massa, *Charles Augustus Briggs and the Crisis of Historical Criticism*, 82–83; Christensen, *The Ecumenical Orthodoxy of Charles Augustus Briggs*, 95–96; Rogers, "Charles Augustus Briggs: Heresy at Union," 96–97.

62. Prentiss, *The Union Theological Seminary, Its Design and Another Decade of Its History*, 332; Rogers, "Charles Augustus Briggs: Heresy at Union," 97–98.

63. Briggs, *The Authority of Holy Scripture: An Inaugural Address*, quotes on 33, 35, 37, 26–27.

64. Ibid., 27, 62–63, 54, 41. Briggs interpeted Matt. 5:48, John 17:17, Rom. 8:29–30, and 1 John 3:2 as teaching a doctrine of a post death middle state of conscious higher life "in the communion of Christ and the multitude of the departed of all ages."

65. See Francis R. Beattie, "The Inauguration of Dr. Charles A. Briggs at Union Seminary, New York," *Presbyterian Quarterly* 5 (1891): 270–83; "The Anvil Chorus on Professor Briggs," *New York Evangelist* (Feb. 9, 1891); "A Very Important Question," *New York Sun* (Feb. 12, 1891); "Religious Breastworks," *The Independent* (Feb. 19, 1891), 1–2; "Briggsdoxy," *Mail and Express* (July 11, 1891); Massa, *Charles Augustus Briggs and the Crisis of Historical Criticism*, 90; Christensen, *The Ecumenical Orthodoxy of Charles Augustus Briggs*, 98; Gaius Glenn Atkins, *Religion in Our Times* (New York: Round Table Press, 1932), 96–98.

66. Charles A. Briggs, "The Theological Crisis," *North American Review* 153 (July 1891): 99–114, quotes on 101, 103; cited in Massa, *Charles Augustus Briggs and the Crisis of Historical Criticism*, 91; Briggs, appendix to *The Authority of Holy Scripture*, 85–90, quote on 86.

67. See Cushing Strout, "Faith and History: The Mind of William G. T. Shedd," *Journal of the History of Ideas* 15 (Jan. 1954): 153–62; W. G. T. Shedd, *Discourses and Essays* (Andover, Mass.: W. F. Draper, 1859); Shedd, *Dogmatic Theology*, 2 vols. (New York: Charles Scribner's

Sons, 1888); William Adams Brown, *A Teacher and His Times: A Story of Two Worlds* (New York: Charles Scribner's Sons, 1940), 76–77. Brown identified William Pierson Merrill as the most persistent of his classmates in questioning whether "classical election" offered a moral brief for infanticide.

68. Briggs, appendix to *The Authority of Holy Scripture,* 94–95.

69. Ibid., 92–93.

70. Charles A. Briggs to Francis Brown, May 15, 1891, Ledger 8.

71. Charles A. Briggs to S. D. Alexander, stated clerk of the presbytery, May 21, 1891, Ledger 8; Rogers, "Charles Augustus Briggs: Heresy at Union," 101–2; see Prentiss, *The Union Theological Seminary, Its Design and Another Decade of Its History,* 544. The Union faculty had seven members at the time of the first Briggs trial: Briggs, Francis Brown, (President) Thomas S. Hastings, George L. Prentiss, Philip Schaff, W. G. T. Shedd, and Marvin R. Vincent. All of them supported Briggs (Brown conveyed his support from Oxford) except Shedd, who had entered emeritus status the year before but was still teaching because no successor was in place. See Handy, *A History of Union Theological Seminary in New York,* 76.

72. Prentiss, *The Union Theological Seminary, Its Design and Another Decade of Its History,* 94–110, quote on 94; *Minutes of the General Assembly of the Presbyterian Church in the United States of America* (Philadelphia: McCalla & Sons, 1891), 23–26; Loetscher, *The Broadening Church,* 53–55; Handy, *A History of Union Theological Seminary in New York,* 76–77.

73. See *The Presbyterian Church in the United States of America against the Reverend Charles A. Briggs: The Report of the Committee of Prosecution with the Charges and Specifications Submitted to the New York Presbytery, October 5, 1891* (New York: John C. Rankin, 1891); George W. F. Birch to Charles A. Briggs, Mar. 19, 1892, Ledger 8; Briggs to Birch, Mar. 22, 1892, Ledger 8; Henry van Dyke to Briggs, Apr. 13, 1892, Ledger 8; Prentiss, *The Union Theological Seminary, Its Design and Another Decade of Its History,* 110–24; Rogers, "Charles Augustus Briggs: Heresy at Union," 105–7; Handy, *A History of Union Theological Seminary in New York,* 77–79; Loetscher, *The Broadening Church,* 55–57; Henry van Dyke was then pastor of the Brick Presbyterian Church in New York City; later he went on to an outstanding literary career.

74. Charles A. Briggs to Francis Brown, Apr. 12, 1892, Ledger 8.

75. Egbert C. Smyth to Charles A. Briggs, May 21, 1891, Ledger 8; editorial, "Progressive Religious Leaders. The Presbyterian Church," *The Christian Union* (Dec. 19, 1889), cited in Christensen, *The Ecumenical Orthodoxy of Charles Augustus Briggs,* 88.

76. Thomas S. Hastings to Charles A. Briggs, May 28, 1891, Ledger 8; Hastings to William Allen Butler, June 29, 1891, Ledger 8; "my heart yearns," Hastings to Butler, June 14, 1891, Ledger 8; Philip Schaff, "Other Heresy Trials and the Briggs Case," *The Forum* 12 (Jan. 1892): 626.

77. Charles A. Briggs, *The Bible, the Church, and the Reason* (New York: Charles Scribner's Sons, 1892); see W. G. T. Shedd, "The Work before the Next General Assembly," *The Presbyterian* (May 11, 1893), 36; Massa, *Charles Augustus Briggs and the Crisis of Historical Criticism,* 100–1.

78. Original text of the Portland Deliverance published in *The Tribune Monthly* 4 (May 1892), "Tenth Day," 90; cited in Rogers, "Charles Augustus Briggs: Heresy at Union," 110–11; Handy, *A History of Union Theological Seminary in New York,* 81.

79. *The Defense of Professor Briggs before the Presbytery of New York, December 13, 14, 15, and 19, 1892* (New York: Charles Scribner's Sons, 1893), quote on 189; Briggs, *The Higher Criticism of the Hexateuch* (ca. 1892, 3d ed., New York: Charles Scribner's Sons, 1897) was the published version of his Presbytery primer, "Who Wrote the Bible?"; Rogers, "Charles Augustus Briggs: Heresy at Union," 112–19; Handy, *A History of Union Theological Seminary of New York,* 83–85.

80. Hastings quoted in Rogers, "Charles Augustus Briggs: Heresy at Union," 120; see *The Case Against Professor Briggs,* 3 parts (New York: Charles Scribner's Sons, 1892); Prentiss, *The Union Theological Seminary, Its Design and Another Decade of Its History,* 264–80; Handy, *A History of Union Theological Seminary in New York,* 82–83.

81. *The Presbyterian Church in the United States of America against the Rev. Charles A. Briggs, D.D., Argument of Rev. George W. F. Birch, D.D.* (New York: John C. Rankin, 1892), quote on 41 (made in 1892 New York Presbytery trial); see John J. McCook, *The Appeal in the*

Briggs Heresy Case before the General Assembly of the Presbyterian Church (New York: John C. Rankin, 1893).

82. *Minutes of the General Assembly of the Presbyterian Church in the United States of America, 1893, 105th Annual Meeting* (Philadelphia: McCalla & Co., 1893), 169; resolution also cited in "Inspiration of the Scriptures," *The Tribune Monthly* (June 1, 1893), 114; McCook, *The Appeal in the Briggs Heresy Case before the General Assembly of the Presbyterian Church;* Rogers, "Charles Augustus Briggs: Heresy at Union," 122–37; Handy, *A History of Union Theological Seminary in New York,* 86–89.

83. Quoted in Prentiss, *The Union Theological Seminary, Its Design and Another Decade of Its History,* 333; see John Llewelyn Evans, *Biblical Scholarship and Inspiration,* 3d ed., (Cincinnati: Robert Clarke, 1892), contains two papers by Preserved Smith; Loetscher, *The Broadening Church,* 63–68.

84. Newman Smyth to Charles A. Briggs, Dec. 5, 1893, Ledger 9.

85. William Adams Brown, "A Century in Retrospect," *Union Theological Seminary: One Hundredth Anniversary, New York, May 16–19, 1936,* cited in Handy, *A History of Union Theological Seminary in New York,* 90; on student and faculty views of Briggs and Schaff, see Handy, ibid., 90–91; Brown, *A Teacher and His Times: A Story of Two Worlds,* 77–78.

86. Briggs, *Whither? A Theological Question for the Times,* xi; see Briggs, "The Lambeth Conference of Bishops of the Anglican Communion," *Presbyterian Review* 9 (Oct. 1888), 657–59.

87. See *Essays and Reviews,* 2d ed. (London: John W. Parker, 1860); John William Colenso, *The Pentateuch and the Book of Joshua Critically Examined,* 2d ed. (London: Longman, Green, 1862); *Lux Mundi: A Series of Studies in the Religion of the Incarnation,* ed. Charles Gore (London: John Murray, 1889).

88. Charles A. Briggs to Dom. Laurentius Janssens, Feb. 19, 1907, Ledger 10.

89. Quotes, Charles A. Briggs to F. Meagher, Feb. 18, 1908, Ledger 12; see Charles A. Briggs, *Church Unity: Studies of its Most Important Problems* (New York: Charles Scribner's Sons, 1909); Briggs, "Ecclesiastical Jurisdiction in its Relation to Church Unity," *The New World* 6 (1897): 117–43; Briggs and Baron von Hügel, *The Papal Commission and the Pentateuch* (London: Longmans, Green & Co., 1906); Briggs, "Christian Irenics," 2 parts, *The Churchman* (Mar. 16, 1901; Mar. 30, 1901); Briggs, "The One Flock of Christ," *Reformed Quarterly Review* 18 (1896): 304–15; Briggs, "The Present Crisis in the Church of England and Its Bearings on Church Unity," *North American Review* 170 (1900): 87–98; Briggs, "The Biblical Doctrine of the Church," *The American Journal of Theology* 4 (1900): 1–22.

90. Charles A. Briggs, *The Messiah of the Gospels* (New York: Charles Scribner's Sons, 1894); Briggs, *The Messiah of the Apostles* (New York: Charles Scribner's Sons, 1895); Briggs, S. R. Driver, and Alfred Plummer, eds., *International Critical Commentary* (New York: Charles Scribner's Sons, 1895ff.); Briggs and S. D. F. Salmond, eds., *The International Theological Library* (New York: Charles Scribner's Sons, 1896).

91. Briggs to S. R. Driver, Aug. 9, 1898, Ledger 9.

92. Text of Pittsburgh Presbytery statement in Henry Sloane Coffin, *A Half Century of Union Theological Seminary, 1896–1945* (New York: Charles Scribner's Sons, 1954), 35–36; Arthur C. McGiffert to Charles A. Briggs, Dec. 28, 1892, Ledger 8; see Arthur C. McGiffert, *A History of Christianity in the Apostolic Age* (New York: Charles Scribner's Sons, 1897); Loetscher, *The Broadening Church,* 71–74.

93. Briggs to Francis Brown, Mar. 16, 1900, Ledger 10; Handy, *A History of Union Theological Seminary in New York,* 113–14.

94. Coffin, *A Half Century of Union Theological Seminary, 1896–1945,* 39-40; Handy, *A History of Union Theological Seminary in New York,* 97, 131–32.

95. Charles Augustus Briggs, *The Fundamental Christian Faith: The Origin, History, and Interpretation of the Apostles' and Nicene Creeds* (New York: Charles Scribner's Sons, 1913), vii–viii; see Philip Schaff, *The Creeds of Christendom,* 3 vols. (New York: Harper & Brothers, 1877).

96. See Richard Watson, *Theological Institutes: Or, a View of the Evidences, Doctrines, Morals, and Institutions of Christianity,* ed. J. M'Clintock, 2 vols. 1825; 3d ed. (New York: Carlton and Porter, 1850); Thomas Ralston, *Elements of Divinity; Or, A Concise and Comprehensive View of Bible Theology; Comprising the Doctrines, Evidences, Morals and Institutions of Christianity,* ed. T. O. Summers (1847; 3d ed., Nashville: A. H. Redford, 1871).

97. See William Burt Pope, *Compendium of Christian Theology; Being Analytical Outlines of a Course of Theological Study, Biblical, Dogmatic, Historical,* 3 vols. (New York: Phillips & Hunt, 1880); Amos Binney, *Binney's Theological Compend, Improved; Containing a Synopsis of the Evidences, Doctrines, Morals, and Institutions of Christianity* (New York: Eaton & Mains, 1874); Luther Lee, *Elements of Theology; Or, An Exposition of the Divine Origin, Doctrines, Morals, and Institutions of Christianity,* 2d ed. (Syracuse, N.Y.: S. Lee, 1859); Miner Raymond, *Systematic Theology,* 3 vols. (New York: Nelson & Phillips, 1877); John Miley, *Systematic Theology,* 2 vols. (New York: Hunt & Eaton, 1893).

98. Francis John McConnell, *Borden Parker Bowne: His Life and Philosophy* (New York: Abingdon Press, 1929), 9–15, 23–28.

99. Borden Parker Bowne, *The Philosophy of Herbert Spencer* (New York: Nelson & Phillips, 1874), quotes on 12; see Kate M. Bowne, "An Intimate Portrait of Bowne," *The Personalist* 2 (1921), 5–15; Bowne, "Herbert Spencer's Laws of the Unknowable," *The New Englander* 31 (Jan. 1872): 86–110; Bowne, "Herbert Spencer's Laws of the Unknowable," *The New Englander* 32 (Jan. 1873), 1–34; Bowne, "The Philosophy of Herbert Spencer," *Methodist Review* 56 (Jan. 1874): 510–14.

100. See Hermann Lotze, *Microcosmos: An Essay Concerning Man and His Relation to the World,* trans. Elizabeth Hamilton and Emily E. C. Jones, 2 vols. (Edinburgh: T. & T. Clark, 1888); Lotze, *Grundzüge der Religionsphilosophie* (Leipzig: G. Hirzel, 1884); Lotze, *Metaphysik* (Leipzig: F. Meiner, 1912); Lotze, *Logik* (Leipzig: Weidmann'sche Buchhandlung, 1843); Lotze, *Grundzüge der Ästhetik* (Leipzig: S. Hirzel, 1884); Borden Parker Bowne, "Ulrici's Logic," *The New Englander* 33 (July 1874): 458–92; Bowne, "Prof. Ulrici's *Gott und die Natur,*" *The New Englander* 33 (Oct. 1874): 623–54; Hermann Ulrici, "Review of Bowne's *Philosophy of Herbert Spencer,*" *Zeitschrift für Philosophie und philosophische Kritik* 66 (1875): 160–64.

101. "Storm" anecdote quoted in McConnell, *Borden Parker Bowne,* 37; see Borden Parker Bowne, "Philosophy in Germany," *The Independent* 32 (Jan. 22, 1874): 4–5; Bowne, "Faith and Morals," *The Independent* 26 (May 14, 1874): 3; Bowne, "The Materialistic Gust," *The Independent* 26 (July 30, 1874): 2–3; Bowne [unsigned], "Immortality or Pessimism," *The Independent* 27 (Jan. 7, 1875): 10–11; Bowne [unsigned], "Of Materialism," *The Independent* 27 (May 6, 1875): 14–15; Bowne [unsigned], "Professor Tyndall on Materialism," *The Independent* 27 (Dec. 23, 1875): 14–15; Gilbert H. Jones, *Lotze und Bowne: Eine Vergleichung ihrer philosophischen Arbeit* (Weida: Thomas & Hubert, 1909).

102. "Ephraim" quote in McConnell, *Borden Parker Bowne,* 91. McConnell studied under Bowne from 1894 to 1899 and was a longtime friend and associate of Bowne's. He was elected a bishop of the Methodist Episcopal Church in 1912. See William H. Barnhardt, *The Influence of B. P. Bowne upon the Theological Thought in the Methodist Church* (Chicago: University of Chicago, 1928); Albert C. Knudson, "Bowne in American Theological Education," *The Personalist* 28 (summer 1947): 247–56. The last four of Bowne's books were published posthumously.

103. Bowne letter to Mrs. K. M. Bowne, May 31, 1909, reprinted in Bowne, "An Intimate Portrait of Bowne," in *The Personalist,* 10; see Borden Parker Bowne, *Metaphysics: A Study in First Principles* (New York: Harper & Brothers, 1882); Bowne, *Introduction to Psychological Theory* (New York: Harper & Brothers, 1886); Bowne, *Principles of Ethics* (New York: Harper & Brothers, 1892); Francis J. McConnell, "Bowne and Personalism," *Personalism in Theology: A Symposium in Honor of Albert Cornelius Knudson,* ed. Edgar Sheffield Brightman (Boston: Boston University Press, 1943), 21–39.

104. Bowne's *Metaphysics: A Study in First Principles* was republished in a retitled and substantially revised edition in 1898: Borden Parker Bowne, *Metaphysics* (New York: Harper & Brothers, 1898), 4–9, quotes on 5; Bowne, *Philosophy of Theism* (New York: Harper & Brothers, 1887; thoroughly revised and expanded edition, *Theism,* New York: American Book Co. 1902), 15–24. See Bowne, "The World-Ground as Intelligent," *Chautauqua Assembly Herald* 7 (Aug. 12, 1882): 4–5; Bowne, "The Logic of Religious Belief," *Methodist Review* 66 (Oct. 1884): 642–65; Bowne, "Realistic Philosophy," *Zion's Herald* 64 (Apr. 20, 1887): 121.

105. Bowne, *Theism,* 44–65; Bowne, *Metaphysics,* 111–20; Borden Parker Bowne, *Theory of Thought and Knowledge* (New York: Harper & Brothers, 1897), 35–69; see Peter A. Bertocci, "Borden Parker Bowne and His Personalistic Theistic Idealism," in *The Boston Personalist*

Tradition in Philosophy, Social Ethics, and Theology, ed. Paul Deats and Carol Robb (Macon, Ga: Mercer University Press, 1986), 55–79; John H. Lavely, "Personalism's Debt to Kant," in *The Boston Personalist Tradition,* 23–37; W. E. Hocking, "The Metaphysics of Borden P. Bowne," *Methodist Review* 105 (May 1922), 371–74.

106. Bowne, *Theory of Thought and Knowledge,* 104–5.

107. Ibid., 106–14, quotes, 108.

108. Borden Parker Bowne, *Personalism* (Boston: Houghton, Mifflin & Co., 1908), 88; see Bowne, *Theory of Thought and Knowledge,* 302–16.

109. Bowne, *Personalism,* 89–90.

110. Ibid., 257; see Borden Parker Bowne, "Logic and Life," *British and Foreign Evangelical Review* 36 (Oct. 1887): 723–40; Bowne, "Notes on Philosophy—IV. Problem of Knowledge," *The Independent* 42 (June 12, 1890): 871–72; Bowne, "Notes on Philosophy— VI. Skepticism," *The Independent* 42 (July 10, 1890): 952–53; Bowne, "The Recession of Mechanism," *The Independent* 55 (Jan. 20: 1903): 245–48; Bowne, "Spencer's Nescience," *The Independent* 56 (Jan. 14, 1904): 67–81; Bowne, "The Passing of Mechanical Naturalism," *Homiletic Review* 51 (Jan. 1906): 16–20.

111. Bowne, *Personalism,* 268–77, quote on 274.

112. Ibid., 274–75; see Bowne, *Metaphysics,* 263–71; Bertocci, "Borden Parker Bowne and His Personalistic Theistic Idealism," 67–68.

113. Bowne, *Metaphysics,* 115–20, quote on 119; Bowne, *Theism,* 144–45.

114. Bowne, *Personalism,* vii–ix.

115. Bowne, *Theism,* iv.

116. Ibid., 132–33.

117. Ibid., 224–25.

118. Ibid., 242–44, quote on 243.

119. Hocking, "The Metaphysics of Borden P. Bowne," 373–74.

120. McConnell, *Borden Parker Bowne,* 76–78; "hole" image quoted in Francis J. McConnell, "Bowne and Personalism," in *Personalism in Theology: A Symposium in Honor of Albert Cornelius Knudson,* ed. Edgar S. Brightman (Boston: Boston University Press, 1943), 24.

121. William James to Bowne, Aug. 17, 1908, Appendix A in *Representative Essays of Borden Parker Bowne,* ed. Warren E. Steinkraus (Utica, N.Y.: Meridian Publishing Co., 1980), 189–90; McConnell, *Borden Parker Bowne,* also reprints James's letters to Bowne, 274–80.

122. Albert C. Knudson, *The Philosophy of Personalism: A Study in the Metaphysics of Religion* (New York: Abingdon Press, 1927); Edward T. Ramsdell, "The Religious Pragmatism of Borden Parker Bowne (1847–1910)" *The Personalist* 15 (October 1934): 305–14. Borden Parker Bowne, "The Inerrancy of the Scriptures," *Zion's Herald* 76 (Jan. 5, 1898): 7–8; Bowne, "'The Old Faith and The New,' by D. F. Strauss, A Review," *Methodist Review* 56 (Apr. 1874): 268–96; see McConnell, *Borden Parker Bowne,* 31. An adapted version of Bowne's article on inerrancy is incorporated in Bowne, *The Christian Revelation* (Cincinnati: Curts & Jennings, 1898), 50–58. See William James, *The Varieties of Religious Experience* (New York: Longmans, Green & Co., 1902).

123. McConnell, *Borden Parker Bowne,* 180–82. McConnell explained that it was not Bowne's direct influence over the bishops that saved Mitchell's position, but his influence over church leaders who did have standing with the bishops. Mitchell was removed from his position at Boston University in 1905, while Bowne was lecturing in China and Japan.

124. "Pure being" quote from McConnell, *Borden Parker Bowne,* 93. Parts of Bowne's essay on revelation were originally published as articles in *Zion's Herald.* See Bowne, "The Christian Revelation," *Zion's Herald* 74 (June 10, 1896); and Bowne, "The Inerrancy of the Scriptures." Bowne published the essay in book form as *The Christian Revelation* (see note 29), and later republished it as the opening chapter of Bowne, *Studies in Christianity* (Boston: Houghton Mifflin Co., 1909), 1–83, quotes on 4. All citations of "The Christian Revelation" from the latter text.

125. Bowne, "The Christian Revelation," 6–7.

126. Ibid., 10, 12, 15.

127. Ibid., 15.

128. Ibid., 15–16.

129. Ibid., 19.

130. Ibid., 40–41.

131. Ibid., 44.
132. Ibid., 37-38.
133. Ibid., 71.
134. Borden Parker Bowne, "The Atonement: I," *Zion's Herald* 77 (July 26, 1899): 942–43; Bowne, "The Atonement: II," *Zion's Herald* 77 (Aug. 9, 1899): 1006–7; Bowne, "The Atonement: III," *Zion's Herald* 77 (Aug. 16, 1899): 1038–39; Bowne, "The Atonement: IV," *Zion's Herald* 77 (Aug. 23, 1899), 1072–73; articles collected and republished as Bowne, *The Atonement* (Cincinnati: Jennings & Pye, 1900); reprinted as second half of chapter 2, "The Incarnation and the Atonement," in Bowne, *Studies in Christianity,* 85–193. All of the following citations are from the latter text.
135. Bowne, "The Incarnation and the Atonement," 126–27, 129.
136. Ibid., 132–33, 138.
137. Ibid., 139, 144.
138. Ibid., 148, 154–55.
139. Ibid, 159–60, 163, 167.
140. Ibid., 159, 166.
141. Bowne testimony published in Elliott, "The Orthodoxy of Bowne," 399–413; reprinted in McConnell, *Borden Parker Bowne,* 189–201; see Smith, "Borden Parker Bowne: Heresy at Boston," 157–76; Miley, *Systematic Theology,* 2:155–94.
142. See "The Acquittal of Professor Bowne," *The Christian Advocate* 89 (April 14, 1904): 571; George Elliott, "The Orthodoxy of Bowne," *The Methodist Review* 38 (May-June 1922): 399–413; Harmon L. Smith, "Borden Parker Bowne: Heresy at Boston," in *American Religious Heretics: Formal and Informal Trials* (Nashville: Abingdon Press, 1966), 148-187; F. Thomas Trotter, "Methodism's Last Heresy Trial," *The Christian Advocate* 4 (Mar. 31, 1960): 9–10; George A. Cooke, *The Present and Future of Methodism: An Examination of the Teachings of Prof. Borden P. Bowne* (Boston: Cushman Press, n.d.). The official trial transcript, 240 pages in length, was either lost or stolen.
143. Borden Parker Bowne, *The Immanence of God* (Boston: Houghton, Mifflin & Co., 1905), 1.
144. Bowne, "The Church and the Truth," *Studies in Christianity,* 364, 366.
145. Ibid., 368, 371–72.
146. Ibid., 382.
147. Ibid., 391–92.
148. Bowne, *The Immanence of God,* 146.
149. Bowne, "The Incarnation and the Atonement," 89–91.
150. Ibid., 93, 103.
151. Washington Gladden, "Introduction" to Charles Bertram Pyle, *The Philosophy of Borden Parker Bowne and its Application to the Religious Problem* (Columbus, Ohio: S. F. Harriman, 1919), 3.
152. Albert C. Knudson, *The Philosophy of Personalism: A Study in the Metaphysics of Religion* (New York: Abingdon Press, 1927), 253; Elmer A. Leslie, "Albert Cornelius Knudson, the Man," in Brightman, ed., *Personalism in Theology,* quote on 7.
153. See Paul Deats, "Introduction to Boston Personalism," in *The Boston Personalist Tradition,* 1–13; Bowne, *The Principles of Ethics;* Bowne, *Introduction to Psychological Theory;* F. Thomas Trotter, "Boston Personalism's Contributions to Faith and Learning," in *The Boston Personalist Tradition,* 15–22.

Chapter 7: The Victorian Gospel

1. Newman Smyth, *Passing Protestantism and Coming Catholicism* (New York: Charles Scribner's Sons, 1908), 40–131; see Charles C. Briggs, *Church Unity: Studies of Its Most Important Problems* (New York: Charles Scribner's Sons, 1909); Samuel McCrea Cavert, *The American Churches in the Ecumenical Movement, 1900–1968* (New York: Association Press, 1968); Henry J. Pratt, *The Liberalization of American Protestantism: A Case Study in Complex Organizations* (Detroit: Wayne State University Press, 1972).
2. See Joseph McSorley, *Isaac Hecker and His Friends* (New York: Paulist Press, 1972); David J. O'Brien, *Isaac Hecker: An American Catholic* (Mahwah, N.J.: Paulist Press, 1992); Walter Elliott, *The Life of Father Hecker* (New York: Columbus Press, 1891); Vincent F. Holden, *The Yankee Paul: Isaac Thomas Hecker* (Milwaukee: Bruce Publishing Co., 1958); Scott Appleby,

"Church and Age Unite!": The Modernist Impulse in American Catholicism (Notre Dame, Ind.: University of Notre Dame Press, 1991); Gerald P. Fogarty, *The Vatican and the Americanist Crisis: Denis J. O'Connell, American Agent in Rome, 1885–1903* (Rome: University Gregoriana, 1974; Thomas Timothy McAvoy, *The Americanist Heresy in Roman Catholicism, 1895–1900* (Notre Dame, Ind.: University of Notre Dame Press, 1963).

3. John A. Zahm, *Evolution and Dogma* (reprint, New York: Arno Press, 1978); William L. Sullivan, *Letters to His Holiness, Pope Pius X* (Chicago: Open Court Publishing Co., 1910); Pope Pius X, *Lamentabili Sane,* July 3, 1907; Pius X, *Pascendi Dominici Gregis,* Sept. 8, 1907, in *The Papal Encyclicals,* ed. Anne Fremantle (New York: New American Library, 1963), 202–7, 197–201.

4. Smyth, *Passing Protestantism and Coming Catholicism,* 99; see Alfred F. Loisy, *The Gospel and the Church,* trans. Christopher Home (New York: Charles Scribner's Sons, 1903); Loisy, *The Birth of the Christian Religion* and *The Origins of the New Testament,* single-volume edition, trans. L. P. Jacks (New Hyde Park, N.Y.: University Books, 1962); George Tyrrell, *Tradition and the Critical Spirit: Catholic Modernist Writings,* ed. James C. Livingston (Minneapolis: Fortress Press, 1991; Maurice Blondel, *L'Action: Essai d'une critique de la vie et d' une science de la pratique* (Paris: Alcan, 1893).

5. Smyth, *Passing Protestantism and Coming Catholicism,* 70, 209; see T. M. Schoof, *A Survey of Catholic Theology, 1800–1970,* trans. N. D. Smith (Paramus, N.J.: Paulist Newman Press, 1970), 14–156.

6. William E. Channing, *The Works of William E. Channing* (Boston: American Unitarian Association, 1893), 1.

7. Horace Bushnell, *The Character of Jesus: Forbidding His Possible Classification with Men* (reprint, 1884; New York: Charles Scribner's Sons, 1860), 10, 11–12.

8. Ibid., 127.

9. Horace Bushnell, *The Vicarious Sacrifice, Grounded in Principles of Universal Obligation* (New York: Charles Scribner & Co., 1866), 72.

10. Borden Parker Bowne, *Studies in Christianity* (Boston: Houghton Mifflin Co., 1909), 105–93, quote on 178; Bushnell, *The Vicarious Sacrifice,* 46.

11. Ibid., 155, 157.

12. See Elizabeth Cady Stanton, "Woman's Pet Virtue," in *The Revolution* (Sept. 16, 1869), 168–69; Cady Stanton, *The Bible and Church Degrade Woman* (Chicago: H. L. Green, 1894); Cady Stanton, "The Solitude of Self," *History of Woman Suffrage,* ed. Elizabeth Cady Stanton, Susan B. Anthony, Matilda Joslyn Gage, et all., 6 vols. (New York: Fowler & Wells, 1881–86; reprint, New York: Source Book Press, 1970), 4:189–191; Mary D. Pellauer, *Toward a Tradition of Feminist Theology: The Religious Social Thought of Elizabeth Cady Stanton, Susan B. Anthony, and Anna Howard Shaw* (Brooklyn: Carlson Publishing, 1991), 107–9.

13. Bowne, *Studies in Christianity,* 159.

14. Charles F. Thwing, *The American and the German University* (New York: Macmillan Co., 1928); Friedrich Paulsen, *German Universities* (New York: Charles Scribner's Sons, 1906), 51–52; Donald M. Love, *Henry Churchill King of Oberlin* (New Haven, Conn.: Yale University Press, 1956), 68–69; *Friedrich Schleiermacher: Pioneer of Modern Theology,* ed. Keith Clements (Minneapolis: Fortress Press, 1991), 15–34, Wilhelm III quote on 29.

15. Paulsen, *German Universities,* 52.

16. William Newton Clarke, *An Outline of Christian Theology* (15th ed., 1906; New York: Charles Scribner's Sons, 1898), 21, 41.

17. Ibid., 38–39; see Emily A. Clark, ed., *William Newton Clarke: A Biography* (New York: Charles Scribner's Sons, 1916).

18. Ernst Troeltsch, *The Social Teaching of the Christian Churches,* trans. Olive Wyon, 2 vols. (1st German ed., 1912; 1st English ed., New York: Macmillan Co., 1931; reprint, Louisville, Ky.: Westminster/John Knox Press, 1992), 2:1011.

19. Ibid., 2:1011–12, quotes on 727.

20. Ibid., 2:727–28.

21. *The Collected Works of Theodore Parker,* ed. Francis Power Cobbe, 14 vols. (London: Trubner & Co, 1864), 6:244.

22. Lyman Abbott, "The Race Question: Points of Agreement," *Outlook* 73 (Apr. 25, 1903): 939; see Abbott, "Impressions of the Conference," in *Proceedings of the Conference for Education in the South: The Sixth Session. Richmond, Va., April 22d to 24th, and at the*

University of Virginia, April 25th (Richmond: n.p., 1903), 224–27; cited in Ralph E. Luker, *The Social Gospel in Black and White:* American Racial Reform, 1885–1912 (Chapel Hill N.C.: University of North Carolina Press, 1991), 206.

23. Dwight Newell Hillis, "Parkhurst, Abbott and Hillis," *The Independent* 55 (May 21, 1903): 1227; Lyman Abbott, "Mr. Beecher on Reconstruction," *Outlook* 74 (May 30, 1903): 280–81; cited in Luker, *The Social Gospel in Black and White,* 211; see Abbott, *Henry Ward Beecher* (Boston: Houghton, Mifflin & Co., 1903), 264–87.

Index